CREATIVE
CRAFTS
ENCYCLOPEDIA

CREATIVE CRAFTS
ENCYCLOPEDIA

CHARTWELL
BOOKS. INC.

Advisory Editors   Angela Jeffs (chief)
Wendy Martensson, Patsy North

Publishing Staff   Project Editor: Lydia Segrave
Editors: Judith Scott, Rosemary Canter, Anne Bosman
Art Editor: Andrew Lawson
Picture Editor: Polly Friedhoff
Production: John Sanders, Elizabeth Digby-Firth
Managing Editor: Giles Lewis

Design and   Designer: Edward Gould
Photography   Photographers: Peter Pugh-Cook, Graham Murrell,
Sandra Lousada, Eric Howard
Stylist: Ann Moore

First published in Great Britain in 1977 by
Equinox (Oxford) Ltd

This 1987 edition
Published by

CHARTWELL BOOKS, INC.
A Division of
BOOK SALES, INC.
110 Enterprise Avenue
Secaucus, New Jersey 07094

© Equinox (Oxford) 1977

This book was planned and produced by
Equinox (Oxford) Ltd., Oxford

ISBN 1-55521-153-4

Printed in Hong Kong

Introduction

Most of the crafts that are still being worked today had their origin in practical need. Basketwork, for example, provided light but strong containers hundreds of years before plastic was thought of; needlecraft was born when prehistoric man roughly stitched fur pelts together to protect himself from the cold. The history of crafts reflects this concern for fashioning articles of use with one's hands. It may come as a surprise to the inexperienced craft worker to discover in these pages that these articles often took a beautiful and sometimes artistic form, for the embellishment of simple utensils naturally follows the pride and satisfaction experienced in transforming basic materials into complete and practical objects.

It is this personal involvement and satisfaction provided by handicrafts that ensures their continuing popularity in an otherwise automated world. The increasing amount of leisure time made available by labor-saving devices has had the paradoxical effect of encouraging a return to the handiwork that was part of the daily routine of our ancestors. We probably now get more pleasure than them in the pride of using or giving something we ourselves have made, something unique since even two people working from the same pattern will not produce the same result. There is also the extra pleasure to be derived from the knowledge that you have made something for a fraction of the cost of its mass-produced equivalent.

As the interest in crafts grows, so does the need for clear and comprehensive guides on the subject. In *Creative Crafts* we have endeavored to introduce in one volume most of the crafts and their techniques. Whether you want to amuse your children with inexpensive attractive toys, or wish to advance your knowledge of woodwork by learning about marquetry, you will find it clearly explained. After introducing a craft and depicting its historical development, our team of specialist writers introduce you, by way of simple step-by-step drawings and photographs, to the first design to make. Then with further techniques explained in the same way, they lead you on to more advanced projects. Complete beginners need not be daunted by the more complicated techniques described in the later stages of some of the crafts. Provided you start at the beginning you will be clearly and quickly led to understanding many of the terms and techniques used by professional craftsmen.

For those who have already mastered the skills of one craft, the many color illustrations of projects — all specially commissioned for this book — will lead the adventurous to attempt new skills in other crafts, besides providing opportunities for producing articles specifically designed to reflect their own particular utility and beauty.

Contents

ABCDEFGHIKLMNOPQRSTVWXY   IANE ROTOCKE 15

ALICE LEE WAS BORNE THE 23 OF NOVEMBER
6 TWESDAY IN THE AFTER NOONE 1596

Embroidery

Throughout history, embroidery has been one of the most intricately worked and colorful forms of decorative needlework. But only in a very few instances do very early records exist giving details of stitches and patterns in general use throughout the centuries.

An account in the Book of Exodus, however, does tell us that even in those early times, Aaron's robe was lavishly embellished with "pomegranates of blue and of purple and of scarlet round the hem thereof; and bells of gold between them round about." Remains of delicate embroideries have been found during excavations into ancient Egyptian burial sites; and a number of early Oriental pieces are also preserved. The world-famous Bayeux Tapestry provides not only a contemporary reportage of the Battle of Hastings but also an authentic picture of the nature of 11th-century European embroidery. Similarly, the decorative needlework of Mary Queen of Scots is both intrinsicially magnificent and also a pointer to later developments in stitchery. Yet perhaps the most informative of all historic embroideries are the early samplers, providing as they do accurate and detailed records of techniques that date from the 1500s.

The sampler itself is basically a repertory of various stitches and designs, usually embroidered onto loose-weave linen. The term is derived from the Old French word *essamplaire* meaning pattern or model. Originally, the sampler served mainly as a form of stitchery notebook, listing selections of techniques first learned and then practiced in repeated horizontal rows. Only later did the sampler become something of an art form with scope for more original work.

Fascinating stitches like roco, Hungarian, Florentine and Algerian Eye worked in silver and silver-gilt all featured fairly early in the sampler's history, when the linen used

Left: An extensive assortment of stitches is displayed in Jane Bostocke's sampler of 1598 — one of the earliest to survive.

Center: Hannah Taylor from Newport, Rhode Island, made this sampler in 1774, depicting her home and family in an intricate combination of cross stitch, satin stitch and crewel work.

was characteristically long and narrow in shape — often between six and twelve inches wide and up to five times as long. The sampler only became squarer and more pictorial around the mid-18th century. But, strangely, one of the very oldest examples now displayed in the impressive collection at the Victoria and Albert Museum, London, is almost square. Worked in 1598 by Jane Bostocke, it displays groupings of satin, chain, ladder, buttonhole, arrowhead and cross stitch among others, in metal thread and silk, with pearl and bead decoration. These very first samplers date from an era when ornamental dress was at the very height of fashion in Europe. Clearly, the skilled and professional needlewoman had to keep details of her dress designs not only for personal use, but also as patterns to be followed by both staff and future generations. During the 18th and 19th centuries in Europe and America, it became common practice for young girls to make at least one such sampler while still in school. Embroidery was an all-important part of the female school curriculum at the time: and so the sampler was soon to become not just a souvenir of childhood — possibly a small girl's first exercise in stitchery — but also a pattern memorandum.

Over the years, pastoral designs or birds, flowers and trees commonly featured on the sampler; but on some occasions, rather less fanciful subjects — aspects of the American Revolution, for example — were selected for embroidery. What almost all samplers have in common from the late 17th century onwards, however, is that the maker's name and either her age or the date are usually stitched quite prominently into the total design. Alphabetical and numerical themes were particularly popular, and a great number of samplers were certainly quite stylized. But some do show considerable creativity — map samplers, family trees and the perpetual almanac as worked by Elizabeth Knowels in 1787, for example. The wealth of stitches to be found displayed on these historic samplers is truly remarkable. Feather, ermine, chessboard, honeycomb filling, Cretan, Pekinese, twisted chain, wheat ear and sheaf are all featured. But equally intriguing are the pious verses and scriptural extracts often additionally selected for embroidery and surrounded by highly decorative borders. In the 19th century, Harriot Tullet, at only seven years of age, lent a highly moral tone to her sampler of cross and satin stitch worked in silk on wool, with the following lines:

> If oddly spent, no art or care
> time's blessing can restore.
> And God requires a strict account
> for every misspent hour.
> Short is our longest day of life
> and soon its prospect ends.
> Yet on that day's uncertain date,
> eternity depends.

Not all small girls were quite so diligent, however. One is even quoted as having stitched on her sampler the following inscription, no doubt with tongue in cheek. "Patsy Polk did this and she hated every stitch she did in it. She loves to read much more."

The antique hand-stitched sampler is now a costly collector's item. But there is no reason why this essentially practical art form should not be revived. Skillful use of color will give added dimension.

Ever since stitching with needle and yarn ceased to be purely utilitarian, embroidery has been a source of pleasure for those

A collection of embroidery frames and silks.

Basic materials

The materials available for embroidery are as varied as the techniques themselves. For any project, consider the overall effect desired and choose a fabric, yarn and needle which will help you to achieve this end.

Fabrics. It is possible to use almost any fabric for free embroidery, from the finest silk to the coarsest linen or canvas. Counted thread embroidery, however, requires an even weave fabric for regular stitches.

Yarns. Most embroidery yarns are suitable for free and counted thread work. Stranded embroidery floss (embroidery silk) is useful, as it has 6 loosely twisted strands which can be separated for finer work. Other suitable yarns include pearl cotton No. 8 and coton à broder for fine to medium fabrics and pearl cotton No. 5 for heavier fabrics. Woolen yarns can also be very effective. There are also some beautiful metallic threads available in silver and gold colors.

Needles, scissors and thimble. For free embroidery on fine to medium fabrics, use crewel needles and for heavy fabric, chenille needles. For counted thread embroidery you will need round-tipped tapestry needles. Sharp, pointed scissors and a well-fitting thimble are essential.

Frames. A frame keeps the fabric flat and taut. For small pieces, use a round screw ring, which consists of two rings, one fitting closely inside the other. Stretch the fabric over the inner ring with the threads straight, then screw the outer ring to the correct diameter and press it down over the top. For larger pieces use a square or rectangular frame.

Both types of frame are available on a floor stand, which allows you to keep both hands free for stitching. Keep one hand below the frame, the other above, and stitch with an upright motion.

Free embroidery

Free-style embroidery involves stitching a design which has been transferred onto fabric. From the wealth of possible stitches, choose those that will best convey the appropriate textures and shapes. This technique allows great scope for experiment and does not require careful counting as with counted thread embroidery.

who appreciate creative design and skilled workmanship. Certain techniques have enjoyed great revivals of popularity at different times, only to fall out of favor, and embroiderers today may have neither the time nor the inclination to attempt the minute stitches of our more leisured ancestors. Much of the satisfaction of embroidery comes from adapting age-old stitches and patterns, and once you have mastered the basic techniques, you can allow your imagination to take over.

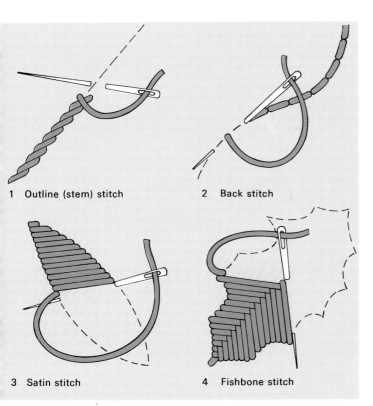

1 Outline (stem) stitch

2 Back stitch

3 Satin stitch

4 Fishbone stitch

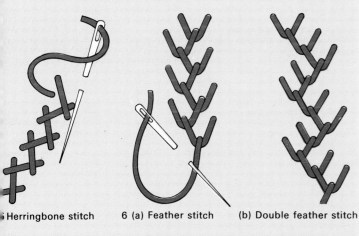

5 Herringbone stitch

6 (a) Feather stitch

(b) Double feather stitch

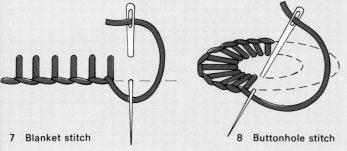

7 Blanket stitch

8 Buttonhole stitch

Marking designs on the fabric

Designs for free embroidery may be applied to the surface of the fabric in several different ways.

Specially prepared transfers. These have a design already printed on them that is transferred to fabric by pressing with an iron. Place the transfer face down on the fabric and press with a warm iron, being careful not to smudge the design. Test the heat of the iron on the fabric first with the scrap lettering from the transfer. Transfers can usually be re-used several times.

Tracing designs

Original designs or designs from books and magazines can be traced in their actual size and marked on the fabric in a number of ways. Secure the tracing to the fabric with tape or weights so that you do not smudge the design.

Dressmaker's carbon paper. Use this special paper in a light color on dark fabric and vice versa. Place the carbon paper face down on the fabric with the tracing on top and go over the lines of the design with a sharp pencil.

Pricking and pouncing. Trace the design onto firm tracing paper. Then, using a needle, prick through the paper along the lines of the design at close intervals. Position the tracing on the fabric and rub either powdered charcoal or chalk (depending on the fabric color) through the holes with a felt pad or soft cloth. Remove the tracing paper, blow off any excess powder and join the dots with watercolor paint and a fine brush.

Tracing through the fabric. With fine, transparent fabrics such as organdy, place the tracing underneath and draw directly onto the fabric with a soft pencil or use watercolor paint.

Basting outline. Use this method for coarse or textured fabrics, which will not take a transfer. Trace the design onto fine tracing paper and baste it onto the fabric. Go over the lines of the design with small running stitches, then tear away the paper.

Enlarging a design from a graph pattern. Designs are sometimes shown reduced in size on a grid in which each small square represents a larger one. The scale will be indicated by a key — for example, each square

= 2.5cm (1in). To enlarge the design, draw a square measuring 2.5 × 2.5cm (1 × 1in) for each square in the grid onto a large sheet of paper. Then draw the design onto the new large grid so that the lines cross the squares in the same places as on the small grid. It will help to make tiny marks in these places and join them up.

Free embroidery stitches

Here is a selection of stitches to use in free-style embroidery, grouped under the "family" of stitches to which they belong.

Outline stitches

Outline (stem) stitch (fig.1). This is worked from left to right with small regular stitches. Each slightly slanted stitch emerges to the right of the previous one.

Back stitch (fig.2). Bring the thread through, take a small stitch back along the design and bring the needle up slightly in front of the thread for the next stitch.

Flat stitches

Satin stitch (fig.3). This is used to fill in a small area such as a leaf shape, with straight stitches worked from edge to edge. Do not make the stitches too long.

Fishbone stitch (fig.4). This stitch is also used for filling in small shapes. Bring the needle through at one end of the area to be filled in and make a small straight stitch along the center line. Bring the needle up at the edge of the shape and make a sloping stitch across the center line at the base of the first stitch. Make a third stitch from the opposite edge to overlap the second stitch at the center line and continue working alternately from each side.

Crossed stitches

Herringbone stitch (fig.5). Make a line of alternately sloping stitches, taking a small stitch back to the left after each one.

Looped and chained stitches

Feather stitch (fig.6a and b). Make a looped stitch alternately to the left and right (a), holding the thread down with the thumb until it is secured. For double feather stitch (b), take two stitches to the left and right alternately.

Blanket stitch (fig.7). Bring the needle out

11

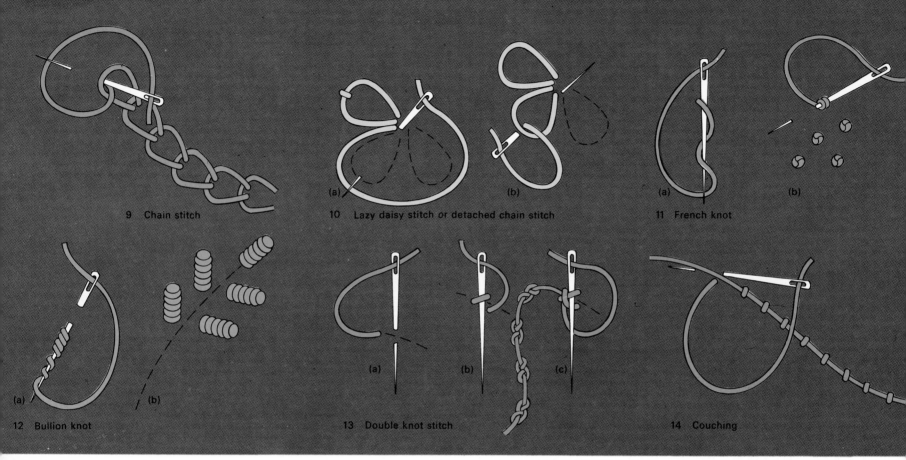

9   Chain stitch

10   Lazy daisy stitch or detached chain stitch

11   French knot

12   Bullion knot (a) (b)

13   Double knot stitch (a) (b) (c)

14   Couching

on the line of the design. Then make a straight vertical stitch, looping the thread beneath the needle. Pull up firmly.
Buttonhole stitch (fig.8). This is done in the same way as blanket stitch but with the stitches closer together.
Chain stitch (fig.9). Bring the needle out and loop the thread around it, holding the thread down. Re-insert the needle and take a stitch forward, catching the loop.
Lazy daisy stitch or detached chain stitch (fig.10a and b). This is similar to chain stitch, but each loop is separate (a) and fastened by a small stitch at the outer edge (b).

Knotted stitches

French knot (fig.11a and b). Bring the thread out and wind it twice around the needle (a). Holding the thread securely, re-insert the needle and pull the thread through (b).

Bullion knot (fig.12a and b). Make a back stitch, bringing the needle tip out where the thread last emerged. Wind the thread several times around the needle tip (a) and hold firmly. Pull the needle through still holding the thread firmly. Re-insert the needle and pull the thread through until the coiled knot lies flat (b).
Double knot stitch (fig.13a, b and c). Bring the needle up and take a small stitch across the line of the design (a). Pass the needle downward under this stitch, without taking it through the fabric (b). Pass the needle under the first stitch again, keeping the thread below the needle (c). Pull the thread firmly to form a knot. Continue working in this way, spacing the knots evenly and close together to create a beaded effect.

Couched stitches

Couching (fig.14). Lay one thread on the fabric surface and stitch over it at intervals with another thread.

The largest stitch sampler of them all
Practice your newly mastered collection of basic stitches on a rug or blanket, old or new, and throw the resulting giant-sized sampler over a bed or couch.
You will need:
large blanket □ assortment of brightly colored yarns □ large-eyed needle.
Embroidering the blanket. If the edges of the blanket have frayed, turn them under twice and baste before stitching with large, regularly spaced blanket stitches. Draw out the design with chalk first or alternatively work free style, allowing the design to develop as you stitch. The stitches used on the blanket in the photograph include cross stitch, feather, chain, outline (stem), satin stitch and French knots.

Flowers for summer

This attractive summer smock is embroidered in bright colors for maximum impact. All the basic stitches from the previous pages are incorporated into the design, so the smock is ideal as a first project for a beginner. You can easily change the mood by using more subtle colors for the embroidery.

You will need:
commercial paper pattern for smock with round neck ☐ cotton fabric ☐ stranded embroidery floss (embroidery cotton) in blue, black, white, bright green, dark green, red ☐ embroidery frame ☐ dressmakers' carbon paper ☐ tracing paper.

Positioning the design. The embroidery should be stitched before the smock is sewn. Pin the yoke pattern piece to the fabric and baste around the outline. Mark the center front with basting stitches. Cut around the shape roughly, overcasting the raw edges to prevent fraying. Trace the design and transfer centrally onto the fabric. The design can be extended for a wider yoke by lengthening the stems or adding extra leaves.

Stitching the embroidery. Stretch the fabric on an embroidery frame and work the design following the stitch key on the tracing pattern. Place the colors as shown in the photograph, using 2 strands of stranded cotton.

Finishing. When the embroidery is complete, press from the wrong side. Trim the bodice to the correct shape and sew the smock together.

Long and short stitch

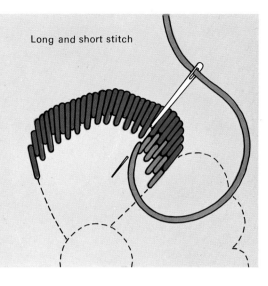

This fills in a shape too large for satin stitch. In the first row work alternate long and short stitches along the outline. The stitches in the next row are staggered for a smooth effect.

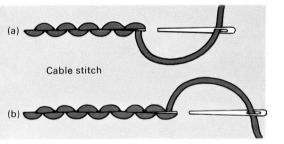

(a)

Cable stitch

(b)

(a) Make a stitch along line of design, bring needle out halfway along with thread below. (b) Repeat for next stitch, but with thread above.

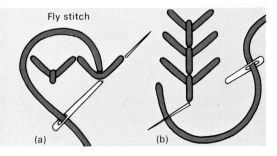

Fly stitch

(a)   (b)

Bring thread out at top left, hold down with left thumb; insert needle to the right. Secure thread with small stitch at center. Work across (a) or down (b).

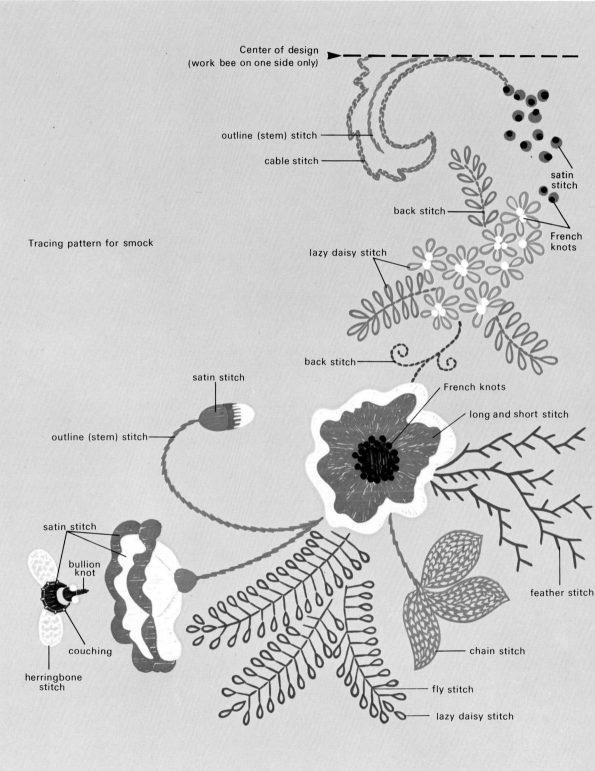

Center of design
(work bee on one side only)

outline (stem) stitch

cable stitch

satin stitch

back stitch

French knots

lazy daisy stitch

Tracing pattern for smock

back stitch

satin stitch

French knots

outline (stem) stitch

long and short stitch

satin stitch

bullion knot

couching

herringbone stitch

feather stitch

chain stitch

fly stitch

lazy daisy stitch

15

Materials and stitches

Crewel embroidery conjures up images of rich, free-flowing designs, often incorporating flowers, leaves and fruit. Its distinguishing characteristic is the worsted woolen yarn used, and the word "crewel" is believed to have been derived from the Anglo-Saxon *cleow* (later *clew* and *crule*) meaning "a ball of thread."

Crewel work was especially popular during the 17th century in England and the 18th century in America, although far earlier examples still exist, notably the 11th-century Bayeux Tapestry. An important influence on the development of crewel work was the growth of trade with the Orient during the 17th century, when needlewomen were inspired by the beautiful Indian and Chinese embroideries. The "tree of life" designs that became a traditional feature of crewel work were introduced to England from India during this time. In both England and America, bed curtains, covers and cushions were the most common items chosen for this form of decoration.

Crewel embroidery can still be applied successfully to such items as well as to pictures and wall hangings.

Basic materials
Fabrics. Even weave linen or linen twill are the traditional fabrics for crewel work, but any firmly woven cloth is suitable, such as heavy cotton, with threads that can be separated by the needle.

Yarns. Choose the yarn to suit the fabric and to achieve the texture required. Crewel yarn itself is quite fine, but several strands · can be used together for bolder stitches on fine to medium fabrics. Tapestry yarn can also be used to similar effect. For coarse fabrics, use rug or knitting yarn.

Needles. Use a crewel or chenille needle that will make an opening in the fabric just large enough for the thread to pass through without breaking the fabric weave. Tapestry needles are useful for stitches woven on the surface of the fabric.

Stitches
Most of the stitches used in embroidery are suitable for crewel work and it is very satisfying to develop the skill of choosing the right stitches for different motifs. An embroidery frame, though not necessary for all stitches, is essential for some, such as couching.

Jacobean couching or trellis (fig.1). Crewel work is sometimes known as Jacobean work and this filling stitch is traditionally used for the centers of flowers or for shapes where an open "lattice" effect is required. Take long, evenly spaced stitches across the space horizontally and vertically or diagonally and secure with one stitch (shown) or a cross stitch at each intersection.

An early 18th-century example of English crewel work is seen in this detail from a bedhanging.

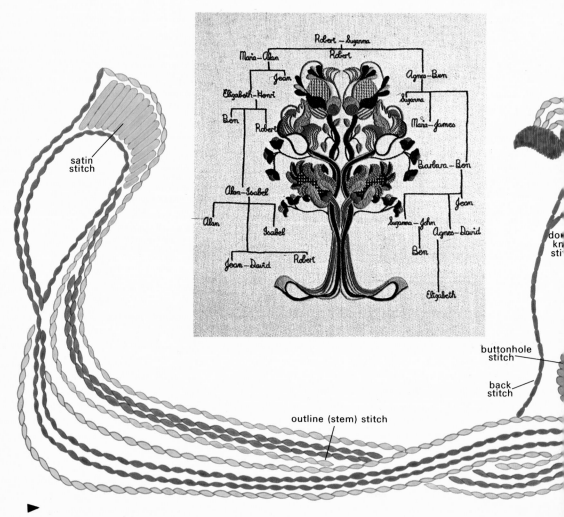

satin stitch

outline (stem) stitch

buttonhole stitch

back stitch

▶ 2 Tracing pattern for family tree

An embroidered family tree is a piece of work to keep and treasure. Plan the name chart so that you can add to it if necessary. A selection of decorative stitches has been used and the tree can also be treated as a crewel work sampler.

You will need:

crewel or Persian yarn in the following quantities and colors: 2 skeins each of blue, pale green, leaf green and olive green; 1 skein each of amber gold, magenta and pink □ 2 skeins of brown stranded embroidery floss (embroidery cotton) □ 0.75m (¾yd) medium-weight beige embroidery fabric, 90cm (36in) wide □ No. 18 chenille needle □ No.6 and No.5 crewel needles □ tracing paper □ dressmaker's carbon paper □ piece of plywood 61 × 53cm (24 × 21in) for mounting.

Transferring the design. The tracing pattern (fig.2), gives the left-hand side of the family tree design. Trace the design and transfer to the fabric with dressmaker's carbon paper, repeating in reverse for the right-hand side.

Note: to find the center of the fabric, fold in half both ways and crease lightly. The center of the pattern should coincide with the lengthwise fold on the fabric.

Stitching the embroidery. Follow the stitch key on the tracing pattern to work the family tree in crewel or Persian yarn, using a No. 18 chenille needle. Use brown stranded embroidery floss for the name chart, working the connecting lines in outline stitch with 6 strands and a No. 5 crewel needle and the names in back stitch with 4 strands and a No. 6 crewel needle.

Mounting. Stretch the completed work over the plywood backing and frame it. Or hang it from a dowel at the top with another at the bottom to weigh it down.

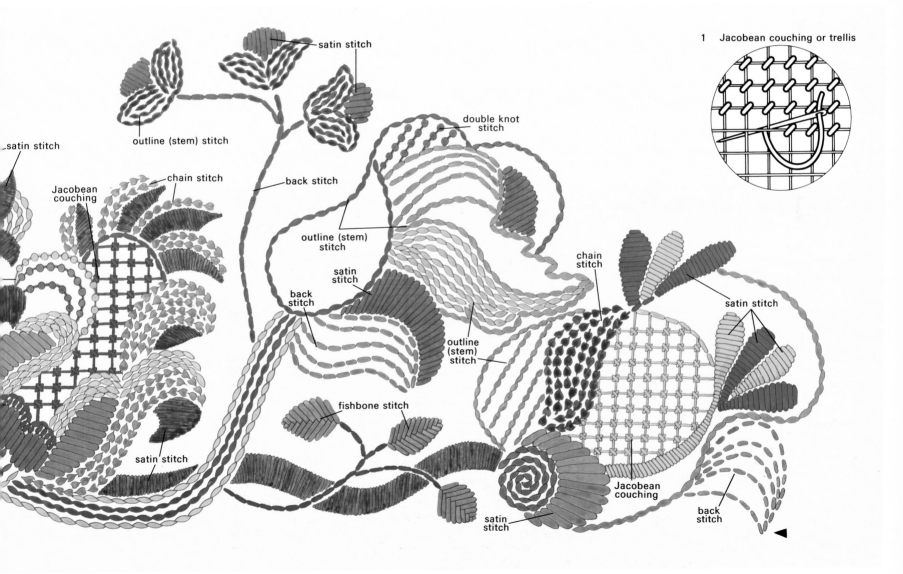

1 Jacobean couching or trellis

satin stitch

outline (stem) stitch

satin stitch

chain stitch

back stitch

double knot stitch

outline (stem) stitch

Jacobean couching

satin stitch

back stitch

satin stitch

outline (stem) stitch

chain stitch

satin stitch

fishbone stitch

satin stitch

Jacobean couching

back stitch

satin stitch

Counted thread embroidery can be divided into several techniques, each with its own distinctive characteristics. The main groups are cross stitch, Spanish blackwork, Assisi work, Hardanger, drawn thread and drawn fabric embroidery. Each technique uses certain basic stitches, in some cases introducing extra ones to add variety to a design. Satin stitch can be used in both free embroidery and in counted thread embroidery, whereas other stitches lend themselves more to either one or the other.

Cross stitch

This is one of the oldest and most universal embroidery stitches. The easiest way to work cross stitch is on an even weave fabric, counting over an equal number of threads down and across. Work a row of diagonal stitches in one direction. Then stitch back the other way, completing the crosses as shown in fig.1. It is important that the upper stitches always lie in the same direction, as a mistake will show up clearly.

Traditional cross stitch mat

The design of this mat is adapted from the motif on an old English sampler and measures 40.5×27.5cm ($16 \times 10\frac{3}{4}$in).
You will need:
0.5m ($\frac{1}{2}$yd) even weave linen, 27 threads to 2.5cm (1in) □ stranded embroidery floss (embroidery cotton) in dark green, mid-green and gray-green.
Stitching the embroidery. Cut a piece of fabric to measure about 44.5×32cm ($17\frac{3}{4} \times 12\frac{1}{2}$in). Mark the center horizontally and vertically with basting stitches. The chart (fig.2) shows a quarter of the design. Stitch this section first in the upper left-hand corner of the mat, beginning centrally. Stitch the upper right-hand corner as a mirror image. Turn the mat and stitch the lower half in the same way. Both cross stitch and chevron lines of half cross stitch (ie sloping in opposite directions) have been used as indicated on the chart. They are done over 2 threads of fabric each way. Use 2 strands of floss throughout.
Finishing. Press the embroidery from the wrong side. Turn under a 1cm ($\frac{3}{8}$in) hem twice, mitering the corners. Work a border of 2 rows of half cross stitch. Give the mat a final press on the wrong side.

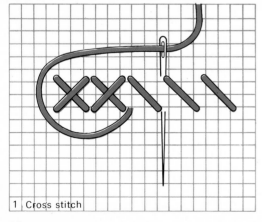

1 Cross stitch

Counted thread embroidery, as the name implies, is worked by counting the threads of the background fabric which must have an even weave. The stitches are made over an exact number of threads to produce the design; unlike free embroidery, no tracing or transfer is required as the pattern can be reproduced on a chart. Linen is especially suitable as a background fabric and is available in a variety of weaves which are graded according to the number of threads per cm (in). A needle with a rounded tip should always be used to avoid damaging the threads.

2 Chart for cross stitch mat

Assisi embroidery has its origins in the beautiful Italian town of the same name that is the renowned birthplace of Saint Francis. Many examples of decorated ecclesiastical garments of the 13th and 14th centuries are still carefully preserved in local churches there. Assisi work is also traditionally a peasant craft and used to decorate items of clothing and for furnishings. The original stylized designs are still used but gradually embroiderers have found inspiration in other sources, such as decoratively carved wood, wrought iron and mosaics. Assisi work is typified by fantastic animal and bird motifs, often set in elaborate geometric borders, and this style continues to flourish today.

Basic materials and techniques
Assisi work is a counted thread technique and therefore requires a firm even weave fabric such as linen.

Assissi during the time of St Francis—an engraving from *Collis Paradisi Amœnitates* (1704). "Collis Inferni" (Hell Hill) was the name attributed to the rock outside the main city because that was where all criminals were executed; but on the death of St Francis, Pope Gregory IX decreed that the name should be changed to Paradise Hill in memory of the saint.

The most suitable yarns to use are stranded embroidery floss (embroidery cotton), coton à broder, matte (soft) embroidery cotton and pearl cotton. The traditional colors are blue or rust with black outlines.
Outline. Work the design outline and any lines inside the basic motifs in double running (Holbein) stitch (see diagrams on page 21). Curves can be indicated by working stepped or diagonal stitches.
Background. Fill in the background with horizontal lines of cross stitch, leaving the motifs showing through in the unworked fabric. Do not carry the yarn over to fill in

19

Border in blue and white

any small spaces, but finish these separately; the work should look as neat on the back as on the front. If the outline runs diagonally at any point, fill in with a half cross stitch.

Border in blue and white

The border on this white tablecloth, with its bird and flower motifs outlined in black on a blue background, illustrates perfectly the traditional features of Assisi work. The cloth measures 128cm (50$\frac{1}{2}$in) square and the border is 61cm (24in) square.

You will need:
1.5m (1$\frac{1}{2}$yd) white even weave fabric, 137cm (54in) wide, 25 threads to 2.5cm (1in) □ 3 balls No.8 pearl cotton in blue and 1 ball in black □ No.24 tapestry needle.

Preparing the fabric. Turn under an even hem all around the fabric, sewing with slip stitch or with a decorative hem stitch and mitering the corners.

Using the chart. The chart (fig.1) gives the design for half of one side, the corner and the beginning of the second side and shows the outline to be made in double running stitch, with the blue cross stitch background area filled in. Each square represents one stitch. Stitch the second half of each side as a mirror image of the first half.

Stitching the design. Find the center of the cloth by counting the threads or by folding it in four. From this center point, count down 270 threads. This marks the point where you should start working the design as indicated on the chart. Using black thread, stitch the design outline in double running stitch worked over 3 threads to complete the first half of the first side, including the bottom left-hand corner. Diagonal stitches are made by counting 3 threads up or down and 3 across.

Note: work any detail inside the design, such as the flower petals, as you follow the outline.

Work the second half of the first side as a mirror image, then continue from each corner to complete the square.

When the design outline is complete, fill in the blue background with cross stitch made over 3 threads.

Press the work face down on a padded surface with a warm iron.

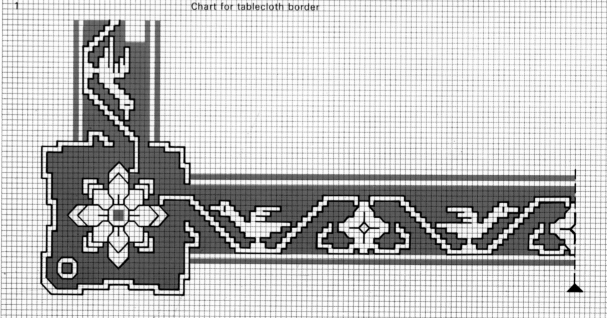

1 Chart for tablecloth border

A fine example of Spanish blackwork is seen here in the 16th-century portrait of Mary Cornwallis. Praise should perhaps be shared equally between the needlewoman who created such a magnificent display of stitches and the artist, George Gower, whose task it was so faithfully to record them.

Basic Spanish blackwork stitches
Running stitch (fig.1). Make stitches of equal length, passing the needle under and over the fabric.

Holbein or double running stitch (fig.2). Work running stitch around the design from right to left. Return left to right filling in spaces.

Whipped back stitch (fig.3). Work back stitch around the design, then whip over each stitch without entering the fabric.

Coral stitch (fig.4). Work from right to left. Bring the thread through and hold down with the left thumb. Make a small stitch at right angles to the thread, going under then over. Pull tight.

Spanish blackwork, a form of embroidery worked in black thread on a white background, is probably of Moorish origin. It was very popular in England during the 16th century due mainly to the influence of Katharine of Aragon, the Spanish wife of Henry VIII. The Elizabethans and Tudors used blackwork to decorate the elaborate collars, sleeves and cuffs of their costumes and their designs have been recorded in many of the court paintings of the day, including several by Hans Holbein the Younger. In fact, one of the basic stitches in blackwork, double running stitch, is also called Holbein stitch. It produces the same pattern on the front and back of the fabric which was ideal for ruffles at the neck and wrists where both sides were visible. Traditionally, blackwork was always worked as black on white with the occasional addition of metallic threads, to create intricate-looking lacy patterns. Modern examples of blackwork have introduced other colors into both the thread and the background fabric, such as brown thread on cream fabric, but the most dramatic effect is still achieved by working different stitches in black on white to produce areas of contrasting tone values.

Basic materials. Spanish blackwork is a counted thread technique and should be worked on an even weave fabric such as linen. The weave can range from as many as 39 threads to 2.5cm (1in) to as few as 13, producing a variety of effects.
To find a suitable yarn bear in mind the thickness of the fabric and choose a yarn which corresponds. However, this can be varied if a definite pattern of fine yarn against a heavier one is desired. Stranded embroidery floss (embroidery cotton), pearl cotton, sewing thread and metallic threads are all suitable for Spanish blackwork.

Basic stitches. The filling stitches which create the lacy patterns in blackwork are variations of straight stitches such as running stitch, back stitch, cross stitch and double running or Holbein stitch. By experimenting, it is possible to build up numerous patterns from one basic motif. The filling stitches can be outlined with a variety of stitches — for example, outline, coral, back or whipped back stitch and couching.

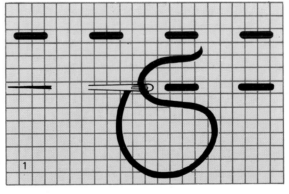

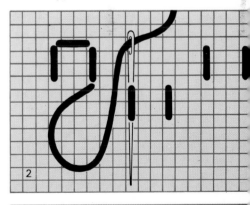

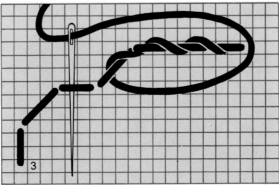

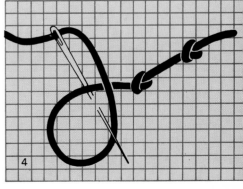

Embroidery
Spanish blackwork

Chessboard

Here's a clever idea to show off the beautiful designs which can be embroidered in blackwork. The chessboard has eight basic patterns which are repeated with slight variations to illustrate just how versatile this form of embroidery is. The finished board measures approximately 42 × 43cm (16½ × 17in).

You will need:

4 skeins black stranded embroidery floss (embroidery cotton) □ 0.75m (¾yd) of 70cm (27in) wide even weave linen, 19 threads to 2.5cm (1in) □ embroidery frame □ 1.5cm (½in) plywood and glass cut to size for mounting □ picture clips

Making the embroidery. Part of each of the 8 basic designs on the chessboard is given on the chart, where each square represents 1 thread of linen. One or both of the center points is also indicated. Each blackwork square is 36 threads across by 36 threads down, except for square 1 which is 36 across and 35 down. (Remember to allow for this extra thread when working the squares below and to either side.)

The order of working the squares is given on the diagram of the chessboard. When the first 8 are finished, they are repeated in reverse order as shown, with slight variations to the basic patterns. This is an opportunity to improvise, but the 8 patterns can be repeated exactly if you wish. The other half of the board is repeated in reverse order.

The stitches used are cross stitch, back stitch, running stitch and double running stitch. Stitch over the number of threads shown on the chart using 2 strands of embroidery floss. It is advisable to use an embroidery frame to stretch the linen. The border is worked in plait stitch over 4 threads across and 3 down. Work the corners in satin stitch to make them neat. The finished embroidery measures approximately 40.5 × 39cm (16 × 15½in) from border to border.

Right: **Plait stitch.** Work the first stitch across four threads and three stitches vertically from bottom left to top right. Bring the needle out three threads below and work back diagonally across two threads and bring the needle out directly below. Repeat to form a plait. Work one row for the border, filling in each corner with a star of satin stitch.

Far right: A detail from the chessboard.

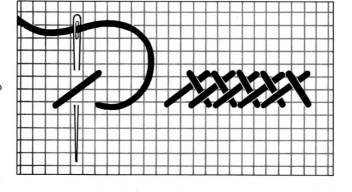

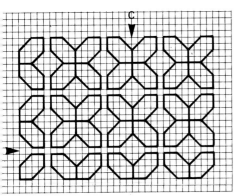

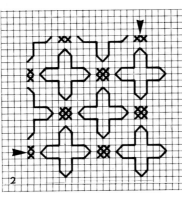

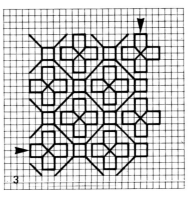

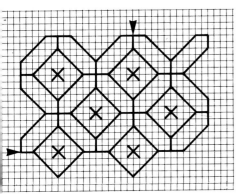

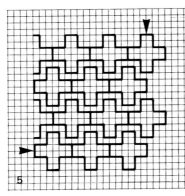

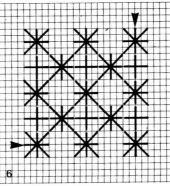

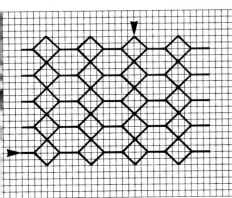

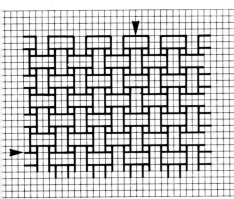

Mounting the chessboard. Trim the linen leaving a 7.5cm (3in) border of unstitched fabric all around. Stretch the linen over the plywood, lacing it closely across the back with strong thread.

Place the glass on top and hold in position with picture clips. A good backing fabric may be sewn onto the bottom of the board to finish it off neatly.

Top: Here are the eight basic stitch patterns for the chessboard, shown as 1–8 on the key below, and improvised upon for the remaining 16 squares in the center section. The stitches used are cross stitch, running stitch and double running stitch as appropriate.

Bottom center: The key to the chessboard.

	1		2		3		4
5		6		7		8	
	4a		3a		2a		1a
8		7a		6a		5a	
	5a		6a		7a		8
1a		2a		3a		4a	
	8		7		6		5
4		3		2		1	

Traditional hardanger embroidery from Norway.

Hardanger embroidery comes from the area around the Hardanger fjord in Western Norway and is still popular in Scandinavia as a decoration on household linen and clothes. Although traditionally worked in white on white, modern designs often use both colored fabric and yarn. Embroidery of this type has very ancient origins and is possibly developed from old Persian and Asian embroideries worked with colored silks on transparent gauze.

Basic materials
As Hardanger embroidery is a drawn thread technique, it must be done on an even weave fabric such as fine linen or a special Hardanger cloth. Suitable yarns are stranded embroidery floss (embroidery cotton) or pearl cotton in varying thicknesses. Two different thicknesses of yarn are required for each piece of work – a thick yarn for the satin stitch blocks and a finer one for the

woven bars and the fillings. You will also need tapestry needles and very sharp, pointed scissors.

Working methods
For Hardanger embroidery, first stitch the surrounds for the spaces, then the bars and finally the filling stitches. For extra decorative effects, such as horizontal or diagonal lines, use four-sided stitch (see page 27).

Satin stitch blocks (fig.1a and b). Satin stitch is used for creating blocks which form the surround for the cut-out spaces. Make the stitches first (a), using an embroidery frame and counting the threads accurately. Cut the threads carefully very close to the stitches and draw out each horizontal thread, then each vertical one (b).

Note: always work all blocks of satin stitch

on a piece of work before cutting any of the threads.

Bars
These are formed by drawing out certain threads and pulling the remaining threads together with a series of stitches.

Woven bars (fig.2). Withdraw an even number of threads and weave under and over through the remaining threads.

Overcasting (fig.3). Withdraw the required number of threads, and pass the needle under and over the remaining threads to form the bar.

Filling stitches
These stitches, as the name suggests, are used for creating a decorative filling once the satin stitch blocks and bars have been worked.

Loop stitch filling (fig.4). Bring the needle

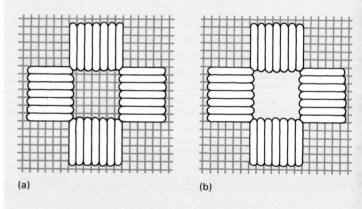

1 Satin stitch blocks

(a)   (b)

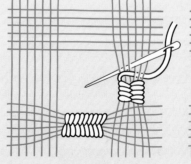

2 Woven bars   3 Overcasting

up through the top of a satin stitch block, then pass the thread once around the woven bars, working around each side of the cut-out square.

Spider's web filling (fig.5). Bring the needle up in one corner between the blocks of satin stitch, then take the thread diagonally across to the opposite corner. Pass the thread vertically or horizontally under the satin stitch block, bring the needle up in the third corner and take the thread over to form the second diagonal. Work a twisted bar over the first diagonal thread by passing the needle under and over. Work in the same way for the other diagonal thread until you reach the center, then stitch twice around the spokes at the center. Finish the twisted bar over the second half of the diagonal.

Ribbed wheel (fig.6). Work satin stitch blocks to form a square over 18 threads on

each side. Then cut and withdraw six threads each way, skip six threads and withdraw six more. Form horizontal and vertical bars across the center by overcasting the remaining threads. Work four twisted bars diagonally, one from each corner to the center, then fill in the central "wheel" by working back stitch under and over the twisted and overcast bars. Continue around until the wheel is the required size.

Finishing

Hardanger work should be finished with a plain or hemstitched hem. Alternatively work buttonhole stitch around the edge of the fabric and trim close to the line of stitching.

Butterfly

Butterflies make interesting motifs and lend themselves well to Hardanger embroidery. Here a motif is stitched on a window shade so that the light will show up the design. The finished butterfly is approximately 18cm (7in) wide and 10cm (4in) deep. It could be repeated several times if preferred, and would also adapt well for cushions, bedspreads or other household linens.

You will need:
2 balls No. 5 white pearl cotton □ 1 ball No. 8 white pearl cotton □ even weave embroidery fabric, 29 threads to 2.5cm (1in) □ No. 20 and No. 24 tapestry needles □ window shade kit.

Preparing the fabric. Mark the center of the fabric lengthwise with a line of basting stitches. Decide on the position for the motif, bearing in mind its relationship to the window sill and the window frame when the shade is pulled down. Mark accordingly with tailor's chalk.

Making the embroidery. The chart (fig.7) shows one half of the butterfly motif, the center of which is marked with an arrow. This should correspond with the line of basting stitches. The diagram also shows the arrangement and placement of the stitches on the threads of the fabric. Blank areas indicate where threads should be withdrawn. Work the given half of the design then work the second half in reverse.

Finishing the shade. Press the embroidery on the wrong side and make the shade by attaching it to the rollers from the kit.

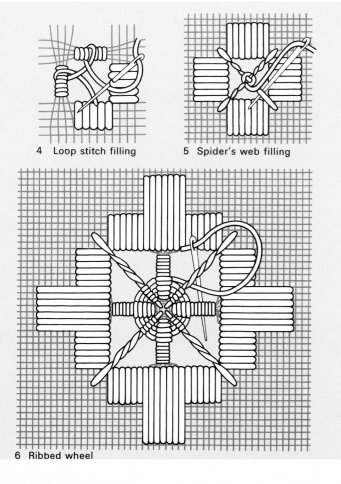

4 Loop stitch filling

5 Spider's web filling

6 Ribbed wheel

7 Chart for butterfly blind

Embroidery
Drawn thread and drawn fabric work

Drawn thread work is a fascinating variation of counted thread embroidery, and has been practiced for thousands of years. It is traditionally used for decorative borders on household linen such as pillow cases, tablecloths, napkins and placemats, but can also be applied very successfully to garments if these are made of a suitable fabric.

Basically, the technique involves cutting and withdrawing threads from even weave fabric, then decorating the remaining threads, edges and corners with various stitches.

Stranded embroidery floss (embroidery cotton) is the best thread for this embroidery and the number of strands used will depend on the thickness of the threads of the fabric. A coarse fabric, for example, will require three, four or five strands, while a fine cotton needs only one or two strands of floss. Use a tapestry needle to avoid splitting the threads of the fabric.

Drawn thread techniques
Withdrawing the threads (fig.1). Place the fabric on a flat surface, with the grain straight so that you can measure accurately where the drawn thread bands are to be positioned. Snip the required number of threads at the center of the band and pull them out gradually toward the edges with the point of a needle.

Weaving the corners (fig.2). Where two bands of drawn threads meet at right angles, a space is formed at the corner. Weave the ends of the drawn threads under and over the threads of the fabric as shown, then make the edges neat with close buttonhole stitch.

Drawn thread embroidery stitches
Hemstitch (fig.3). This can be used to edge a band of drawn threads or to sew up a hem in a decorative way. It can be done over varying numbers of threads depending on the effect you wish to achieve. The diagram (fig.3) shows the stitch worked over two threads down and two across. Draw out the number of threads required. Bring out the yarn two threads below the space and pass it behind the two loose threads to the left. Take it around the same two threads again and pass the needle

through the fabric two threads down and to the left. Repeat for the next stitch.

If you are sewing up a hem, baste it up to the edge of the space, then work hemstitch through all the layers of fabric.

Ladder hemstitch (fig.4) Here hemstitch is worked along both edges of the drawn thread space to create a decorative ladder effect.

Zigzag hemstitch (fig.5). Work the first row as for simple hemstitch over groups containing an even number of loose threads. In the second row, stitch over half the threads from one group together with half from the next group so as to divide and stagger the threads in each group.

Interlaced hemstitch (fig.6a and b). Work ladder hemstitch along both edges as previously described, then secure one end of a long thread in a central position at the right-hand side of the drawn thread band. Take the needle over two groups of threads and bring it up between them (a), then twist the two groups by bringing the needle up between them again in the opposite direction (b).

Corner stitches
Fill in the corner spaces with loop stitch filling or spider's web filling as described on page 25.

Drawn fabric embroidery
In drawn fabric embroidery the threads of fabric are not removed as for drawn thread work but are pulled firmly together by various embroidery stitches. This forms an openwork pattern on the fabric which is in fact much stronger than its rather fragile appearance suggests. Drawn fabric embroidery probably has its origins in Greece, and was a traditional peasant craft in many parts of Europe during the 17th and 18th centuries.

Drawn fabric embroidery stitches
For clarity, the threads of the fabric in the stitch diagrams are not shown pulled together. When embroidering, however, pull the yarn firmly at each stitch. The following three stitches can either be used as borders or as filling stitches for all-over patterns. The last stitch (punch stitch) is a filling stitch only.

An example of Danish drawn thread work. Dated 1758, threads have been withdrawn from cotton fabric and the remaining threads have been embroidered with silk and linen. The bottom corner motifs are embroidered in chain stitch, the date and name in cross stitch.

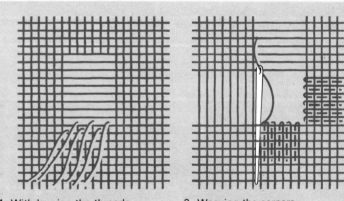

1 Withdrawing the threads

2 Weaving the corners

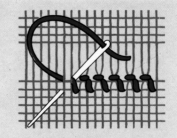

3 Hemstitch

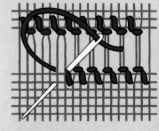

4 Ladder hemstitch

**Embroidery
Drawn thread and
drawn fabric work**

Drawn into fashion

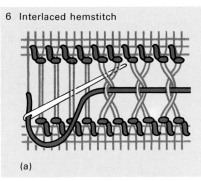

5 Zigzag hemstitch

6 Interlaced hemstitch

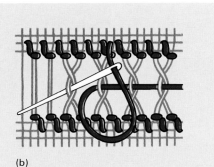

(a)

(b)

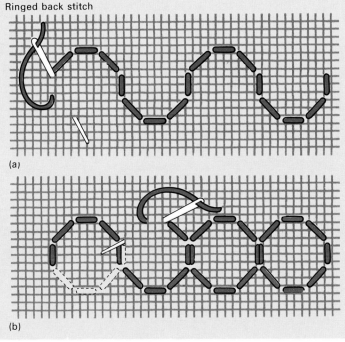

7 Ringed back stitch

(a)

(b)

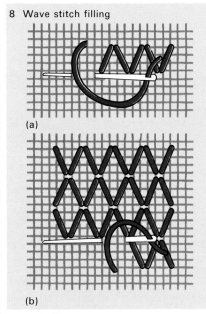

8 Wave stitch filling

(a)

(b)

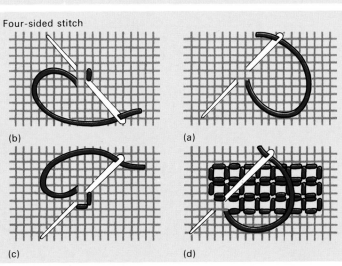

9 Four-sided stitch

(b)

(a)

(c)

(d)

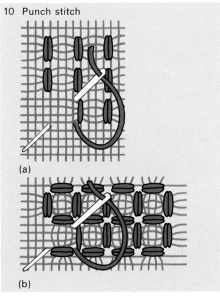

10 Punch stitch

(a)

(b)

Ringed back stitch (fig.7a and b). This stitch is worked from right to left. Bring the needle up through the fabric and work back stitch to form semicircles (a). Turn the fabric around and work back stitch as before to complete the rings (b).

Wave stitch filling (fig.8a and b). Bring the needle up through the fabric and make a diagonal stitch up over four threads and two along to the right. Pass the thread under four threads to the left, then make a second diagonal stitch back to the starting place to form a V shape. Pass the thread under four threads to the left and repeat the procedure along the row (a). Turn the fabric around to complete the diamonds in the same way (b).

Four-sided stitch (fig.9a-d). Bring the needle back up through the fabric and make the first stitch as shown (a). Make the second stitch by inserting the needle at the starting place and taking it up diagonally (b). Make the third stitch as shown (c), then repeat each step to continue the row of squares. Turn the fabric around and work a second row of squares from right to left (d).

Punch stitch (fig.10a and b). Make two straight stitches over the same four threads, then take the needle diagonally under and along four threads (a). Continue along the row in the same way. Turn the fabric and make a second row from right to left. Turn the fabric sideways and work two more rows to form the squares (b).

Drawn into fashion

This pure wool overblouse is an excellent example of how both drawn thread and drawn fabric embroidery can be combined for decorative effect on a garment. The following instructions are for the sleeve border only but the pattern could be repeated elsewhere. Use any basic blouse pattern that will show off the embroidery.

You will need:
stranded embroidery floss (embroidery cotton) in the following quantities and colors: 5 skeins of terra cotta; 3 skeins of cream; 2 skeins of salmon pink □ medium-weight woolen fabric, approximately 15 threads to 2.5cm (1in) □ commercial blouse pattern □ No. 24 and No. 20 tapestry needles.

Embroidery
Drawn thread and drawn fabric work

Drawn into fashion

Preparing the fabric: All the embroidery must be done before the garment is made, so allow extra fabric for the sleeves. Mark out with basting stitches and cut out with larger seam allowances than usual. Cut out all other pieces using the pattern and following the cutting layouts in the usual way.

Following the chart. The chart (fig.11) shows the different bands of stitches used in the border in the order in which they occur on the sleeve. Work through each band once, then repeat in reverse order to complete the top half of the border. The arrows indicate the center of the repeat section to be worked around the width of the sleeve.

Stitching the embroidery

The design is made of 6 bands of drawn thread or drawn fabric embroidery. Use a No. 24 tapestry needle when 1, 2 or 4 strands of floss are stated and No. 20 when 6 strands are to be used. Finish off the end of each row neatly so that there will be no additional bulk in the sleeve seam when it is stitched.

First band. Withdraw 6 threads and work ladder hemstitch over 2 threads in cream, using 2 strands of floss. Finish by stitching the interlacing in terra cotta, using 2 strands of floss.

Second band. Work blocks of satin stitch, in salmon pink, using 6 strands of floss.

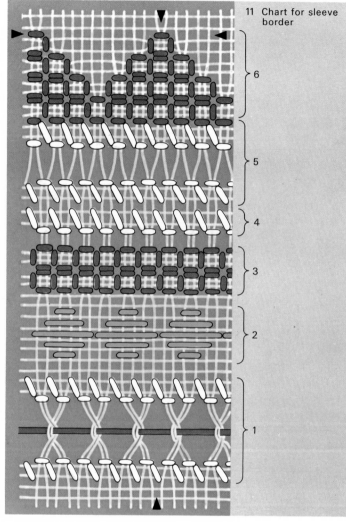

11 Chart for sleeve border

Third band. Work 2 rows of four-sided stitch over 2 threads in terra cotta, using 4 strands of floss.

Fourth band. Withdraw 2 threads and work hemstitch over 2 threads in cream, using 2 strands of floss.

Fifth band. Withdraw 4 threads and work zigzag hemstitch over groups of 2 threads in cream, using 2 strands of floss.

Sixth band. Work four-sided stitch over 2 threads in terra cotta, using 1 strand of floss.

Work each band in reverse order to complete the top half of the border.

Make the garment in the usual way, then trim seam allowance on the sleeves if necessary.

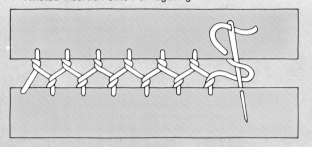

1 Twisted insertion stitch or fagoting

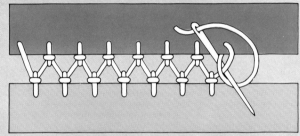

2 Knotted insertion stitch

3 Tailor's buttonhole insertion stitch

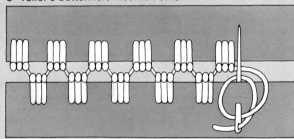

4 Italian buttonhole insertion stitch

(a)   (b)   (c)

The purpose of insertion stitches is to join together two edges of fabric, either curved or straight, in a decorative way. Some insertion stitches are stronger than others and should be selected according to the type and purpose of the fabric used. The space between the two edges of fabric will vary with different stitches — some need more space than others. Always baste the two edges of fabric onto paper or sturdy backing material to prevent the work from puckering. Most embroidery threads are suitable for working insertions.

Insertion stitches

Twisted insertion stitch or fagoting

(fig.1). This is one of the simplest and most quickly worked insertion stitches. Bring the needle up at the edge of the bottom piece of fabric and take the thread up diagonally through the top piece of fabric. Take the thread down and a little to the right, passing the needle under and over the thread as shown.

Knotted insertion stitch. (fig.2). This stitch gives a strong firm finish. Bring the needle up close to the edge of the top piece of fabric and make a single buttonhole stitch above and a little to the right. Make a second buttonhole stitch over the first, picking up both threads as shown. Repeat on the bottom piece of fabric and continue working on alternate edges in the same way.

Tailor's buttonhole insertion stitch (fig.3). Work regular groups of buttonhole stitch alternately on both edges of the fabric. The effect of the stitch will vary according to the amount of space left between each group.

Italian buttonhole insertion stitch (fig.4a,b and c). This stitch requires a space between the two edges of fabric of at least 1cm ($\frac{3}{8}$in). Bring the needle through on the top piece of fabric and make a horizontal bar across to the bottom piece. Work five buttonhole stitches over this bar from left to right. Take the thread through the top piece of fabric 0.5cm ($\frac{1}{4}$in) beyond the first stitch and across diagonally to the bottom piece. Make three buttonhole stitches from left to right (a). Take the thread through on the top piece of fabric 0.5cm ($\frac{1}{4}$in) lower down, then work three buttonhole stitches from the center out towards the left, over the double thread of the diagonal bar (b). Take the thread through the bottom piece and make three buttonhole stitches from the center out towards the right over the double thread (c). Continue in this way to complete the whole row.

The illustration below shows how insertion stitches can be used in dressmaking for extra decorative effects.

Seventeenth-century English cut and drawn thread work with needlepoint stitches.

Cut work, with its delicate open appearance, is often regarded as being a type of lace. But cut work, unlike needlepoint lace or bobbin (pillow) lace, is worked on a background fabric, usually linen, and is therefore more correctly described as a form of embroidery.

Punto tagliato – the original name for cut work – was first developed in Italy during the 14th century and flourished for the next 300 years, especially in Venice. The influence of Venetian cut work and laces was widespread and early in the 17th century Cardinal Richelieu, who was chief minister to King Louis XIII of France, brought in skilled laceworkers from Venice to establish new centers and workshops. From that time, cut work was generally known as Richelieu embroidery.

Other forms of cut work, such as Renaissance remained popular and though varying in intricacy, it still follows the same basic technique of joining motifs with buttonhole bars and then cutting away the background fabric.

Fabrics and yarns

Closely woven fine fabrics, such as linen or good quality cotton, are required for cut work. Coton à broder is well-suited to this work; alternatively stranded embroidery floss (embroidery cotton) can be substituted, using two or three strands depending on the thickness of the fabric. Traditionally, cut work is worked in white on white or in natural colors, but, as with other modern embroidery, color can be introduced.

Basic techniques

Preparation. Transfer the design to the fabric with the grain running straight. For simple cut work outline the motifs with a double line of small running stitches on the right side of the fabric. Where the cut spaces are larger these need to be strengthened with buttonhole bars. All bars should be worked first. The foundation of the bar and the running stitch outline are both worked in one journey. Start the outer line of the running stitches at any point of the design and continue until the position of the first bar. Take the thread across and pick up a tiny stitch and take the thread opposite once more and then work the bar back with buttonhole stitch, over the loose threads as shown in fig.1, without taking up any of the material underneath.

Making the embroidery. When the foundation is complete, edge the motifs in very close neat buttonhole stitch over the running threads. To make the edges stand out more, lay two or three strands of floss between the running stitches and buttonhole stitch over these.

Picots (fig.2a and b). These can be added to the bar for extra decoration. Secure one of the buttonhole loops with a pin and take the needle behind this loop and through the next one (a). Pull the thread firmly and continue working buttonhole stitch (b). Other surface stitches, such as outline (stem) stitch and French knots, can also be introduced to embellish the work.

Cutting the fabric. With sharp, pointed scissors, cut away the fabric carefully, keeping close to the buttonhole stitch edges and taking care not to snip into the bars or knots. Press on the wrong side over a padded surface. The cut work is now complete (fig.3).

Baby's best bonnet

This delightful bonnet, with its border of flowers and scalloped edge, will be treasured long after the baby has grown out of it. The design is simple cut work elaborated with small buttonhole bars and the finished bonnet is 35.5cm (14in) long and 14cm (5½in) wide.

You will need:
piece of fine linen, 46 × 23cm (18 × 9in)
□ 1 skein of white coton à broder or No. 8 pearl cotton □ 0.5m (½yd) medium thickness piping cord □ 1m (1yd) narrow ribbon for ties □ tracing paper.

Making the bonnet. Mark out a rectangle on the fabric measuring 35.5 × 14cm (14 × 5½in), plus a seam allowance of 2.5cm (1in) all around (fig.4).

Trim the fabric to a manageable size, but do not cut it out exactly until all the embroidery is complete. Trace the design from the tracing pattern (fig.5), repeating for the right-hand half. Center the design and with the scalloped edge 2.5cm (1in) down from the top of the fabric, transfer the design to the fabric, using dressmaker's carbon

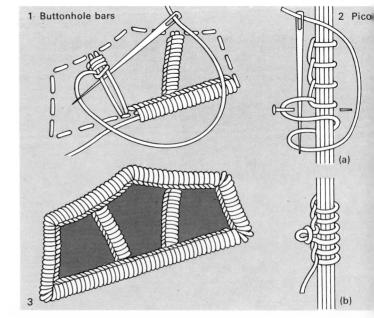

1 Buttonhole bars
2 Pico
(a)
3
(b)

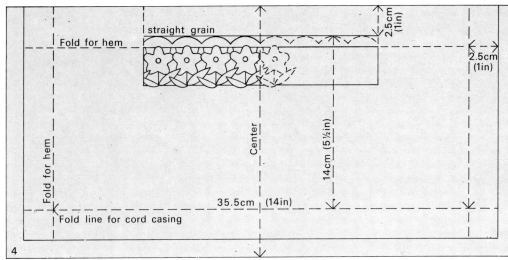

paper, making sure that the design runs accurately along the grain.

Making the embroidery. Work the bars and around the edges of each flower petal and leaf first. Stitch the scalloped edge, cut away the background spaces and then the fabric from the scallops, snipping in vertically at the beginning point of the first scallop and the end point of the last one. Cut out the rectangle to size allowing for seams as previously described. Trim the seam allowance at the sides and front edges of the bonnet and make narrow hems. Make the back edge of the bonnet neat and make a line of outline stitch on the right side to outline the hems.

Press the bonnet on the wrong side under a damp cloth. Fold the back edge over the piping cord and make a casing with small running stitches sewn close to the cord (fig.6). Catch one end of the cord firmly to the wrong side of the casing and draw up the other end to gather up the back of the bonnet to measure 23cm (9in). Catch this end of the cord firmly as before and trim.

Stitch both corded ends together to form the back of the bonnet. Make ribbon ties and sew in position at the sides.

Shi-sha embroidery
Embroidery has always been popular in the Indo-Pakistan subcontinent and is believed to have been practiced during the ancient Indus Valley civilization which flourished between 2500 and 1500 BC.

Though India and Pakistan are known for many different forms of embroidery, the one style that is considered to be unique is the mirror embroidery known as "Shishakari" or "Shi-sha", which originated many centuries ago in the arid plateaux of Sind and Baluchistan in Pakistan. Traditional costumes of both these regions are embroidered with beautiful designs, and those of the Sind are particularly bold

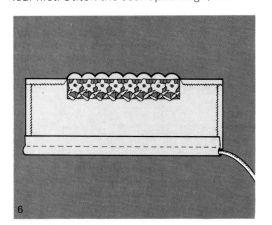

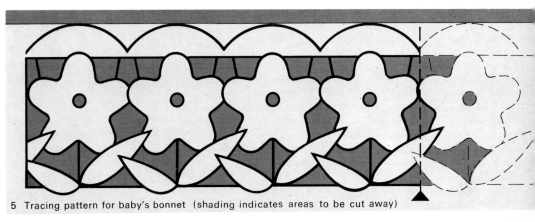

5 Tracing pattern for baby's bonnet (shading indicates areas to be cut away)

**Basic techniques
Embroidered
cushion**

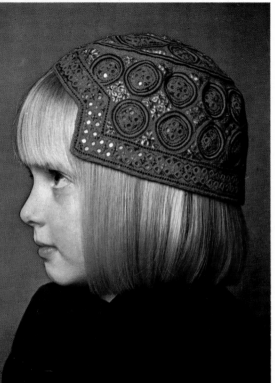

A child's cap decorated with shi-sha embroidery.

both in color and design. Women's dresses usually have a wide panel in front and sleeves that are decorated with tiny mirrors sewn in place with different stitches in silk thread. The intricacy and amount of embroidery done on a garment usually depends on the occasion for which it is being made, though most dresses have at least some embroidery on them.

At present, the traditional designs and colors are being modified in the East to suit the present trend towards Western fashions, just as the West begins increasingly to turn to the East for ethnic inspiration.

Basic techniques

For shi-sha embroidery a small mirror (shi-sha), paillette or large flat sequin is held in place by a criss-cross pattern of threads and then a stitch similar to herringbone is worked over the shi-sha and the thread to form a circular shape around them. Various stitches such as lazy daisy, herringbone, chain, outline (stem) and buttonhole stitch can be worked around the shi-sha to form

different designs. Shi-sha can be washed and does not need any special care.

Securing the shi-sha. Place the mirror in position on the fabric and using two strands of embroidery floss (embroidery cotton) bring the needle up through the fabric on the left-hand side. Make a stitch above the mirror as shown in fig.1a. Make a second stitch on the right-hand side (fig.1b) and a third below the mirror (fig.1c), then complete the criss-cross pattern as shown in fig.1d.

Begin the second criss-cross pattern by bringing the needle up above the mirror and making a diagonal stitch under the bottom left-hand corner (fig.2a). Make a second stitch under the bottom right-hand corner (fig.2b) and a third under the top right-

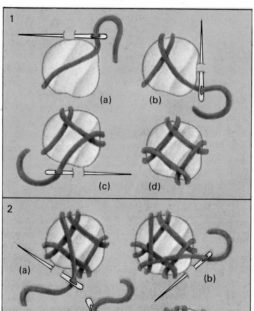

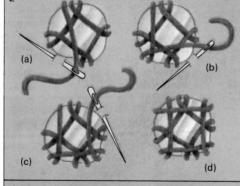

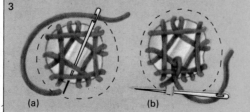

hand corner (fig.2c), then complete the pattern as shown in fig.2d.

Bring the needle up through the fabric and pass it under two threads as shown in fig.3a. Make a stitch as shown in fig.3b, then continue working around in a circle, passing the needle under two threads each time until complete.

Shi-sha embroidered cushion

Add a touch of mirrored luxury to your bedroom or living room with an embroidered shi-sha cushion made of cotton, with a border and backing of rich velvet. The cushion measures approximately 69cm (27in) in diameter and the embroidery section 36cm (14in) in diameter.

You will need:

0.5m (½yd) red cotton fabric □ 1m (1yd) red panne velvet □ stranded embroidery floss (embroidery cotton) in yellow, lilac, pink, light green, dark green and maroon □ 21 shi-sha mirrors, paillettes or flat sequins 2cm (¾in) in diameter □ 15 shi-sha mirrors, paillettes or flat sequins 1.5cm (½in) in diameter □ piece of unbleached muslin (calico) and stuffing or circular cushion pad, approximately 61cm (24in) in diameter □ 30.5cm (12in) zipper.

Making the design. Mark a circle on the red cotton fabric measuring 36cm (14in) in diameter and work around it with running

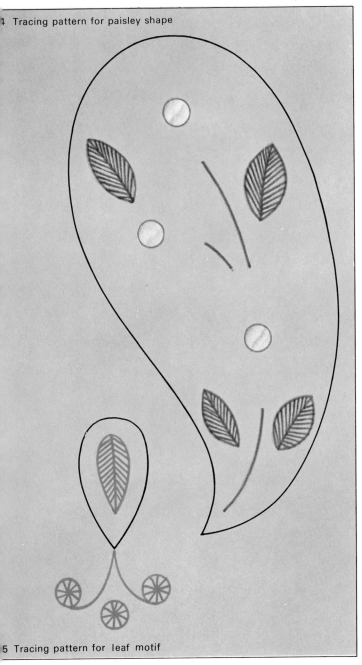

4 Tracing pattern for paisley shape

5 Tracing pattern for leaf motif

stitches. Position one of the larger shi-sha mirrors exactly in the center and secure it as previously described, using 2 strands of yellow floss.

Trace the paisley shape (fig.4) and transfer the tracing around the central shi-sha 5 times at equal distances.

Note: the small circles on the tracing pattern indicate the position of the shi-shas. Trace the leaf motif (fig.5) and transfer the tracing 5 times — once between each paisley shape.

Position the remaining shi-shas, using the smaller size for inside the paisley pattern and the rest for around the central shi-sha and the leaf motifs. Secure each shi-sha, using 2 strands of yellow floss for the smaller size and 2 strands for maroon floss for the others.

Embroidering the paisley shapes. Work around the outline of each paisley shape in outline (stem) stitch, using 3 strands of lilac for the outer row and 3 strands of pink floss for the inner row.

Make the leaves in satin stitch and the stems in outline stitch, using 3 strands of dark green floss. Work around each shi-sha in herringbone stitch, using 2 strands of yellow floss.

Embroidering the leaf motifs. Make the outer row in herringbone stitch, the inner row in outline stitch and the 2 outer circles in buttonhole stitch, using 3 strands of maroon floss. Work the middle circle in buttonhole stitch, using 3 strands of yellow and the inner leaf in satin stitch, using 3 strands of light green floss.

Embroidering the shi-shas. Finish the embroidery by stitching around the remaining shi-shas in herringbone stitch, using 2 strands of light green floss.

Making the cushion. Cut a circle of panne velvet to measure 65cm (25½in) in diameter. This will be the back of the cushion. For the front, cut 2 strips of velvet each measuring 100 × 17cm (39 × 6½in) and with right sides together, stitch the short ends together to form a circle. Run gathering stitches around one long side, then gather until this edge is the same size as the circumference of the embroidered circle of cotton.

With right sides together, baste and stitch the gathered velvet edge to the outer edge of the embroidered section. Cut an opening across the center of the back piece of the cushion and sew the zip in position. Pin and tack the top and bottom of the cushion together, stitch around the edge and turn right side out. Insert the cushion pad (ready made or made from muslin stuffed with kapok).

Metal thread embroidery

Metal thread embroidery, with its sumptuous use of gold and silver threads, has a long history dating back to biblical times. The best-known early English example is the remnant of the *Stole and maniple of St. Cuthbert*, worked in silks and silver-gilt thread on silk taffeta. These vestments were made for Frithestan, Bishop of Winchester and presented to him in around 909 by Queen Æfflæd.

Gifts of this kind were commonly made to the Church by royal patrons and a great deal of exceptionally fine embroidery for ecclesiastical use was produced, mainly by professional craftsmen, between the middle of the 13th and the middle of the 14th centuries. This period of *opus anglicanum* (English work) is always regarded as the golden age of English embroidery.

England's influence on other countries such as France, Belgium and Spain was considerable. In the East, India, China and Japan also developed their own techniques and styles. Much of the Chinese work, for example, makes use of silk threads covered with gold and silver paper, rather than actual metal threads.

From the 15th century onwards, metal thread techniques began to be used in Europe by amateur embroiderers for the decoration of domestic furnishings such as bedhangings, pillow covers and cushions. Silver, gold and silk threads and fine damask and linen were all costly materials, however, and available only to the wealthy. Written documents record that metal thread embroidery was an absorbing pastime engaged in by several queens of England, including Katharine of Aragon, Katharine Parr, Elizabeth I and by Mary Queen of Scots, all of whom were undoubtedly expert needlewomen.

Metal threads are still expensive to buy today unfortunately, but the modern embroiderer is fortunate in having a selection of silver and gold substitutes to choose from. Many of these can be combined effectively with real metal threads to produce designs not only for garments and furnishings, but also for collages and wallhangings.

The main purpose of gold and silver work is to produce an interesting light-reflecting

Basic equipment and materials

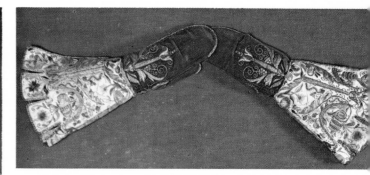

Above: Elizabethan velvet and satin mittens embroidered with silks, silver gilt and silver thread in long and short and satin stitches and couched work.

Left: Japanese 19th-century *fukusa* — a cloth used for covering ceremonial gifts — in gold thread and colored silks.

ing, No.10 for stitching purls (lengths of gold wire) and a No.18 chenille needle for finishing.

Cutting board. Make a cutting board from a piece of strong cardboard 10cm (4in) square and cover it with felt. Use this when cutting purls into the required lengths.

Beeswax. Always draw embroidery threads over a block of beeswax before use to prevent them from knotting and being damaged by friction with metal threads.

Tools. Metal thread embroidery does not require any special tools, but you should handle purls with tweezers and cut them with straight-bladed nail scissors. A stiletto or pointed tool such as an awl is necessary for pushing threads through to the back of the fabric.

Materials

Fabrics. Almost any kind of background fabric is suitable, with the exception of some cheaper dress materials, which tend to split when worked on.

A backing of cotton, unbleached muslin (calico) or similar natural fiber is also needed because of the heavy nature of metal thread work. A padded foundation, for instance, must be supported by a backing, otherwise the work is likely to pucker. The threads are finished off by securing them to the backing.

Threads. Gold and silver threads are available in different qualities, the best being pure gold or silver wound around silk.

surface, which contrasts with a matt background material or complements a silk one. The effect can be further enhanced by the use of traditional embroidery silks and cottons in combination with metal threads.

Basic equipment

Frame. A square or circular frame measuring approximately 23cm (9in) across is necessary for holding and slightly stretching the fabric while it is being worked. Use a small clamp to attach the frame to a working surface so that both hands are left free to manipulate the threads.

Needles. Use a No.5 crewel needle for strong thread, No.8 or No.10 for couch-

Others contain a proportion of real gold or silver. Synthetic threads are usually brighter and should be used for contrast.

To prevent damage to these threads, wind them around a roll of felt and wrap in tissue paper when not in use.

Purls. Purls are available in various forms and consist of gold wire drawn out very finely or coiled together like a minute spring. Rough purl has a checkered finish, smooth purl a bright finish, and check purl has a sparkling checkered finish. Pearl purl is a heavier wire and should be very slightly drawn out before use so that the sewing thread can be slipped between the coils.

Braids. Narrow gold and silver braids provide added textural interest to a piece of work and can be obtained in a wide range of twisted and braided forms.

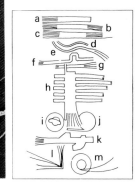

a) Couching over looped gold thread
b) Couching over looped gold thread with "brick" effect
c) Alternative method of couching over looped gold thread
d) Stretched pearl purl
e) Twisted cord stitched diagonally
f) Flat braid
g) Braid stitched down center
h) Couching over string
i) 1st and 2nd layers of felt for padding
j) Gold leather over felt padding, embellished with pearl purl and smooth and check purl
k) Couching over cardboard
l) Corner
m) Circle worked from outside in towards center

Basic techniques

Preparing the fabric. Stretch the backing and baste the background fabric to it, marking the center of each beforehand. Keep all sides parallel with the grain on the backing and baste with straight long and short stitches. Stitch through both layers as one, then stretch onto or in the frame, parallel with the edges and as taut as possible.

Cutting purl. Purl is pliable and can be cut to different lengths as required. It can be cut to make very small individual "seeds" or stretched out and couched directly onto the background fabric. Use lengths of about 1cm ($\frac{3}{8}$in) to lie over padded shapes or curved areas. Use nail scissors to cut purl: place the purl on the cutting board and make a sharp quick cut, keeping the scissor blades at right angles to the thread.

Couching (fig.1). To couch down passing thread or any other simple thread use a No.8 crewel needle and waxed sewing thread. Start with a knot on the wrong side and make a double back stitch, leaving the needle on the top surface of the work. Hold the passing thread in position and leaving approximately 2.5cm (1in) free at the end, take two stitches over two strands of metal thread and at right angles to it. Continue with stitches approximately 0.5cm ($\frac{1}{4}$in) apart ensuring that the threads are pulled firmly. Couch the first row with the needle at a "V" angle, passing under the double metal thread on either side.

When working subsequent rows, bring the needle up under the previous row and angle back under the one being stitched so that each double thread is pulled up with no gaps between the rows. To finish off, take a double back stitch under the metal thread and bring the sewing thread to the right side about 0.5cm ($\frac{1}{4}$in) from the end of the line and snip off close to the embroidery. Leave 2.5cm (1in) loose metal thread. This will be taken to the wrong side on completion of the embroidery and will cover the finishing stitches.

Alternative method of couching (fig.2). Complete one row as before, then turn one of the double metal threads back on itself for the next row. Lay a third thread across the work, then work the couching over the second and third threads, spacing the

stitches to produce a "brick" effect.

Couching purl and braids. Most purls can be couched in the usual way: knot the sewing thread, then make a double back stitch, pick up purl and take the needle down. Stitch down pearl purl with a small, slightly angled stitch between its twists as often as required. All cord-like threads should be stitched with a slanting back stitch going down the middle. Couch flat braids in the normal way and stitch more complex braids by taking small back stitches down the center and leaving a small gap between stitches.

Laidwork. This is a form of couching done over laid threads, and produces a rich geometric pattern. Work the threads horizontally and vertically to form a grid of squares and use a contrasting thread or color to work over the intersecting points.

Couching over string. Use thick firm string and secure it in position with back stitches at close intervals on either side. Twist the string while working to make it firmer. Start and finish with two double stitches at either end, passing the needle through the middle of the string (fig.3). Finish off by

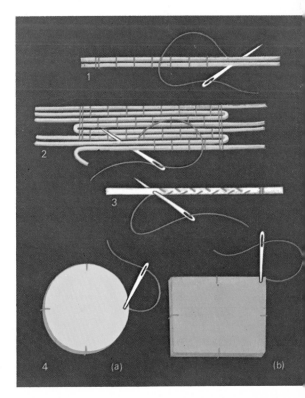

An extravagance of gold work

lifting the ends of the string and cutting them close to the double stitches. Couch down the metal threads over the string, passing them over one or two strings as preferred. Create a basketweave effect by couching the metal threads between alternate rows of string. When couching over string, always start in the middle and work towards each side, keeping the metal threads close together so that all the string is covered.

Couching over cardboard. Cut a piece of thin cardboard not wider than 2cm (¾in) and baste it in position using large stitches and working from the outside in. Take the metal thread over the cardboard and couch close to the edges to produce a raised area.

Padding (fig.4a and b). Place a small piece of felt in position and stitch in place, catching in four places at equal intervals first (a), then filling in with small stitches all around the edge. If the piece is rectangular, continue by catching at each corner (b) and then filling in. Place a second piece of felt of the same shape but slightly larger over the first piece and stitch in the same way. Add a third layer if preferred. Apply a top layer of kid or suede and stitch as before.

Corners (fig.5a and b). Couch along a straight row, then make a double back stitch underneath, 0.5cm (¼in) from the corner. At the corner, couch the outer of the two threads in position by bending the metal threads around the needle (a) and making a stitch from the inside towards the outside. Couch the inner thread in the same way (b) and make the next straight couching stitch 0.5cm (¼in) from the corner.

Circles and shapes (fig.6). Mark the shape required with basting stitches, then work around the shape from the outside inward towards the center, making corners as described if necessary.

Finishing. Take the loose ends of couched threads through to the wrong side of the work when all the embroidery is completed or if working over a large area, after a particular section has been done. Insert a No.18 chenille needle in the position where the metal thread is to finish, thread the needle with the loose end and pull sharply through to the wrong side of the work. If the thread or braid is too thick for the needle, push through to the back with a stiletto.

An extravagance of gold work

The design for the jewelry box lid incorporates flower and leaf motifs and is worked in different shades of gold and turquoise. Gold thread has been combined with synthetic metallic (Lurex®) and crochet threads and leather, sequins and beads. The embroidery measures approximately 15cm (6in) square for a wooden box lid of the same size.

You will need:

even weave upholstery fabric, 20cm (8in) square ☐ square of backing fabric to fit the frame ☐ gold threads and purl ☐ smooth threads of a suitable color for couching ☐ synthetic metallic thread (Lurex®) and crochet threads ☐ piece of gold leather, 5 · 2.5cm (2 · 1in) ☐ felt for padding ☐ small gold beads and sequins ☐ wooden box approximately 15cm (6in) square and 7cm (2¾in) deep ☐ twisted cord or 3 skeins stranded embroidery floss (embroidery cotton) for edging ☐ quilt batting (wadding). 15cm (6in) square ☐ cardboard, 15cm (6in)

square ☐ felt to cover sides and base of the box ☐ fabric adhesive ☐ tracing paper ☐ embroidery frame.

Embroidering the design. Before beginning the embroidery, baste the background fabric to the backing fabric as described previously and stretch it onto the frame. The basic outline for the design is given in fig.7 in which 1 square equals 1cm (⅜in). Draw the design onto tracing paper and then baste through the design onto the background fabric, using gold colored sewing thread.

The key will give you some idea of the different materials and techniques used for

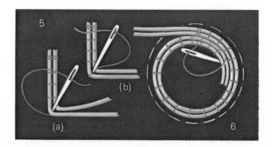

a) Laidwork in turquoise thread couched with metallic thread   b) Couching over cardboard in gold thread, metallic thread and yellow thread   c) Metallic thread, thick gold cord, braid and gold thread couched with yellow thread   d) Laidwork in yellow and turquoise thread and metallic thread couched with yellow thread   e) Laidwork in turquoise thread couched with yellow thread and embellished with beads   f) Laidwork in yellow thread couched with metallic thread   g) Couched rows of contrasting gold thread, pearl purl, braid and metallic thread   h) Basketweave of gold thread, metallic thread and yellow thread couched over 5 rows of string   i) Padded gold leather embellished with pearl purl, smooth purl and check purl   j) Metallic threads embellished with gold sequins and beads   k) Laidwork in gold thread and yellow thread couched with metallic thread   l) Filling of gold thread.

the embroidery as shown in the photograph, though you may prefer to work out your own design and colors instead.

Note: take some of the threads through to the wrong side as you work rather than leaving them all to the end.

Finishing the box. Glue the batting to the piece of cardboard. Place the embroidery on top and secure by glueing onto the underside of the cardboard, mitering the corners. Glue to the lid. Cut the felt slightly larger all around than the required finished size and glue the pieces to the sides and base of the box. Trim the felt when the glue is dry.

Stitch the twisted cord in 2 rows around the lid or make a cord from stranded embroidery floss. Undo each skein, double it, double again and twist, then double once more.

Machine Embroidery

One of the first sewing machines to be produced was invented in 1830 by Barthélemey Thimmonier in France and by 1841, eighty of these wooden machines were in use. A lock stitch machine was designed by Walter Hunt of New York in 1832 but not developed until 1846 when Elias Howe of Massachusetts patented a machine that incorporated the basic features of Hunt's original design.

During the second half of the 20th century, sewing machines have become much more versatile and sophisticated, ranging from straight stitch and zigzag machines to fully automatic and electronic models. Most are manufactured in lightweight metal and are controlled by pressure on a foot pedal. Speeds can vary — some machines being capable of working at up to 1,000 stitches per minute.

The automatic machine has a bobbin winder, which can wind during sewing, a needle threader and an automatic buttonholer. Most automatic machines produce a variety of stitches from straight and zigzag stitch to decorative embroidery stitches, selected by simple push-button control or by the insertion of a stitch selector disk. Other stitches include blind hem stitch, overedge stitch, overlock stitch and different elastic stitches for use with modern stretch fabrics.

All zigzag machines will take a twin needle to make pin tucks, shadow stitching and two rows of any automatic pattern at a time. A variety of feet can be used for, among other things, piping, buttonholing, appliqué, cording and stitching over thick threads. It is possible to cover large areas when using a standard or darning foot, as the fabric can be guided and left as it is. If using a hoop, on the other hand, this has to be moved according to the area to be covered. Machine embroidery is especially suitable for decorating articles that are durable and washable, for example, household items and of course clothing of all kinds.

Fabrics

Any background fabric can be used, from heavy upholstery fabric to organdy or net. Fine fabrics should be backed with tissue paper, which can be removed later, or fine

backing material, which can be left in place.

Just as the appearance of a stitch varies when the tension is altered, so when the fabric is changed, the stitch will alter its character. It is always easier to machine embroider onto heavy fabrics with heavy thread, or onto lightweight fabrics with lightweight thread, but it is possible to combine them for special effects.

Threads

Threads vary and can be used in many ways to achieve different decorative effects.

Normal threads. Cotton machine thread and various synthetic sewing threads usually used for dressmaking are all suitable for machine embroidery. Thicker sewing thread (buttonhole twist) and pearl cotton No.8 can also be used. Generally, the thicker the thread, the looser the tension should be.

Thick threads. Use a normal thread through the needle and thicker threads through the bobbin, threaded in the normal way under the spring, which should be loosened slightly. When using thick threads underneath, work with the fabric the wrong side up so that these threads emerge on the right side. Suitable thick threads are pearl cotton No.5, matte soft embroidery cotton, coton à broder, crochet threads and medium weight knitting yarn. Tightly twisted knitting yarn (crêpe) is particularly good to use because the needle will not split it easily. If the thread is too thick to be threaded in the normal way, put it through the hole at the end of the spring.

Stitches

Straight stitch and zigzag stitch form the basis for a number of different and interesting effects in machine embroidery.

Straight stitch. Use an ordinary foot to work straight lines of straight stitch and a darning foot for curved or irregular lines. Combine thick and thin threads to create a more interesting pattern of lines. Use this stitch for quilting, stitching on ribbons and braids and to produce tucks in the fabric. For a textured effect work straight stitch in a grid formation or make use of reverse gear to move the needle backwards for

neath. If preferred, however, a two-colored effect can be achieved by using a contrasting color in the bobbin and working with the wrong side of the fabric facing up. Set the appropriate tension for thicker threads. Various effects can be created by altering the width and density of the stitch while working: it is only possible to alter one or other at a time, as one hand must be left free to start the machine and guide the fabric.

Use close zigzag or satin stitch for appliqué work, a wide open zigzag for couching down very thick wool and knobbly threads, which cannot be used in the machine and a narrow open zigzag for stitching on velvet ribbon. Zigzag stitching can be made to twist and turn in a very free original way, with an appearance that is less rigid than normal, if a darning foot is used.

Use close or overlapping groups of zigzag lines for a more textured effect in open or closed satin stitch. A "dotted" texture can be obtained by reversing back a few stit-

ches, continuing forward a little further and then reversing again so that a solid dot of stitching appears now and then.

Free embroidery
Use a hoop measuring 20cm (8in) in diameter. A machine embroidery hoop, which is shallower than a hand embroidery hoop, is best to use and will slide under the needle more easily. Bind the inner ring of the hoop with material, then stretch the fabric to be embroidered across the frame until it is as taut as possible. Smooth cotton fabrics are best to work on when beginning to experiment with free embroidery. Remove the foot from the machine – the hoop will now support the fabric – and engage the presser bar behind the needle at the back of the machine in order to operate the top tension. If there is no top tension the thread will loop up and jam the machine.

Warning: never strain the machine by trying to sew when it has jammed as this will damage the motor. If the machine does jam, ease the needle up by hand, pull the work out, cut the tangled threads, rethread the bobbin and start again.

Use a standard-sized ordinary needle and machine embroidery thread for initial experiments. Thread the needle and hold the thread taut in the left hand and bring the wheel forward in a counterclockwise direction so that the needle passes through the fabric and back. The lower thread should then appear looped around the upper thread. Pull this through to the surface and hold both threads in the left hand to start sewing. It will now be possible to move the hoop in all directions and these movements, fast or slow, will affect the stitch length. (The stitch length selector is ineffective when there is no foot on the machine.) You will need to practice to coordinate the direction and speed of movement and thus control the length and openness of the stitches.

When the top thread is tightened and the bottom thread loosened, loops will be pulled up through the fabric. The looser the thread underneath, the more exaggerated the stitch. When moving from area to area within the hoop cut the top thread only in order to restart. The bottom thread does not have to be cut.

a) Whip stitch (thicker thread) worked with darning foot upside down
b) Straight and reverse stitching for a "dotted" texture
c) Velvet ribbon appliquéd with small zigzag stitches
d) Open zigzag stitching (thicker thread and sewing thread) worked with an ordinary foot
e) Automatic patterns
f) Fabric appliquéd with close zigzag stitching
g) Closely stitched lines of whip stitch in sewing thread worked in a hoop
h) Close zigzag for satin stitch effect
i) Straight stitch worked backwards and forwards in thicker thread and sewing thread with an ordinary foot
j) Variations of whip stitch worked in a hoop
k) Satin stitch
l) Zigzag stitching to couch thick woolen yarn
m) Exaggerated whip stitch worked in loops and spirals for a buttonhole effect

lines of stitching on top of each other.
Zigzag stitch. When using ordinary threads for zigzag stitch, the top tension should be looser than the bottom to give a smooth top surface. It does not matter what color is used in the bobbin as this will stay under-

Design

These bright and bold designs can be used in many kinds of needlework, for example needlepoint, embroidery, patchwork and appliqué.

Combine these images in different ways or adapt one to make an original design.

Smocking

A 19th-century wedding smock from Shropshire, England. The bodice is smocked in bands of rope, cable or basket and chevron patterns; the stitches used to embroider the collar include feather, chain and French knots.

The smock has recently been revived as a fashion garment, often worn with jeans, and probably most popular because of its practicality and comfort. Smocking is a type of embroidery in which the stitches are gathered up on the bodice or yoke or at the wrists or neck of a garment to produce a honeycomb effect. The technique is often used on traditional peasant costumes, especially in Eastern Europe.

The word "smock" comes from an Anglo-Saxon term meaning "shirt" or "shift," and early smocks were indeed a form of chemise; during the Middle Ages they were worn chiefly by women. Later the style was taken over by male farmworkers for whom the smock was essentially a practical overgarment, worn to protect clothing, and with ample room for movement. Some smocks fastened up at the front like a jacket, while others could be worn back to front without any difference in appearance. Often there were several rows of smocking at the yoke and on the sleeves, and many were squarely cut and very wide at the shoulders.

During the 17th century, the rural regions of England adopted various colors and styles of smock as their own. For example, workers employed near London tended to favor cream or white. Green, meanwhile, was popular in Essex and Cambridgeshire, while blue became a general uniform in Nottingham and Leicester. Other counties took gray or black as their own particular shade. The smarter smock, worn on special occasions, was usually white with white stitching.

By the 19th century, the embroidery stitches had become quite elaborate and intricate. Workers such as milkmen, cowhands and shepherds often wore smocks with readily recognizable embroidery so that their occupation could be told at a glance and sometimes a trade emblem would be incorporated into the smocking as a distinguishing design.

Feather stitch, chain stitch, stem and satin stitch were all used to decorate the traditional rural smock. But the Industrial Revolution, with its prospect of mass production and therefore cheaper clothing, signaled the decline of the smock as a popular mode of dress.

Smocking is ideal for many modern garments as the embroidery holding the gathers in place gives elasticity and freedom of movement. It can be used on blouses, dresses and lingerie, and of course for all kinds of children's wear.

Fabrics and thread

Plain or printed silk, cotton, cheesecloth, linen, fine wool or velvet and lightweight synthetic fibers are the most suitable fabrics for smocking. Textured fabrics will not gather well and should be avoided. Traditionally, linen thread was used to smock linen, silk thread for silk and so on, but these are now hard to obtain. Instead, use pearl cotton No.5 for heavier fabrics and No.8 for finer cloths. Six-stranded embroidery floss (embroidery cotton) is also suitable, using varying numbers of strands, but it is more difficult to keep several strands even than a single thread, especially over a long length. Do not use wool as it breaks too easily.

A 19th-century engraving showing a typical country smock of the period.

Smocking methods and patterns

Smocking methods

It is always a good idea to try out the stitches first on a sample piece of fabric. This helps you to practice the stitches, plan the color scheme, check the weight of the thread and see how the material gathers. When a checked or dotted cloth is gathered, it forms bands of color, which makes a helpful guideline to work along and also creates a contrast in width and color to the smocking. Try to vary the type of stitches you use and alternate bands of straight stitching with those that form diamond or wave patterns. A blank line between the bands of smocking is often very effective. Color is a matter of personal choice, but white smocking or one strong contrasting color used for all the smocking on a plain dark fabric can look very striking. On patterned fabric it is a good idea to pick up certain colors in the pattern, though too many showy colors tend to look garish and detract from the overall design.

The width of material required for smocking is usually about three times the finished width. So a yoke of 28cm (11in) for example, will need 84cm (33in) for the gathering. For thicker fabrics the ratio is approximately $2\frac{1}{2}$ to 1 and for very fine materials about $3\frac{1}{2}$ to 1.

Preparing the garment. First cut out the garment, allowing the extra width for the smocked parts as described above. All smocking should be worked before the garment is made, except where the gathering makes it difficult to hem afterwards.

Marking the dots. Accuracy of preparation is essential as the little pleats formed by the gathering threads when drawn up, need to be uniform, otherwise the work will have an uneven finish. The dots must be marked out in evenly spaced rows on the *back* of the fabric. Printed transfers of smocking dots (available from most needlework shops or department stores) can be used for plain or printed fabrics. The spacing between dots should be about 1.5cm ($\frac{1}{2}$in) for thicker fabrics, 1cm ($\frac{3}{8}$in) or 0.5cm ($\frac{1}{4}$in) for finer ones. Trim the transfer sheet to the width and depth of the area to be smocked, ensuring that there are an even number of horizontal rows.

Press the fabric, then place the transfer in position, not too near the seams or edges; make sure that the dots run along the straight grain of the cloth. Iron over the transfer with a warm iron. (A cool iron should be used on synthetic fabrics.) Remove the transfer. It does not matter if the dots show through on the right side. Evenly checked, dotted or striped materials do not necessarily need a transfer as their pattern can be used as a guide for the gathering stitches. Mark the dots on the reverse side of the fabric with a pencil.

Gathering the material. Using strong cotton thread, work along the row of dots, picking up a small portion of material at each dot. A separate thread is used for each row and should be long enough to complete the row. Make a secure knot at the beginning, and at the end of each row and leave the thread lying loose until all rows are completed (fig.1). Pull up the rows in pairs and adjust the gathers on the right side to slightly less than the required finished width.

Once it has been finished, the smocked section will stretch about 4–5cm ($1\frac{1}{2}$–2in). Tie the long ends firmly in pairs, close to the last gathering fold (fig.2). The material is now ready ready to be smocked on the right side.

Smocking. Most stitches are worked from left to right and the gathering threads should be used as a guide to keep the stitches straight. Do not smock too close to the edge of the material or seams. Start each row with a knot and work with a length of thread that is long enough to complete the whole row. Finish off each row by knotting the thread in the last pleat on the wrong side. The smocking stitches should be pulled up as evenly as possible, but not too tightly. When all the smocking is complete, press the work gently under a damp cloth. Do not flatten the work. Then remove the gathering threads and finish the garment.

Traditional smocking patterns

Only three patterns were used on traditional smocks: rope, cable or basket, and diamond or chevron (not to be confused with chevron stitch). All three are worked in outline (stem) stitch.

Rope pattern (fig.3a and b). This pattern is one of the easiest to do. Bring the needle up through the first tube on the left. Then pick up a small piece of material on each following tube across the work, keeping the thread above the needle and inserting the needle at an angle (a). The greater the angle, the shorter the stitch. Draw the thread fairly tight. A second row can be made in the same way, but with the thread below the needle (b). These two rows placed close together create a mock chain effect.

Cable or basket pattern (fig.4a and b). This is made in the same way as the rope pattern, but the needle is inserted horizontally

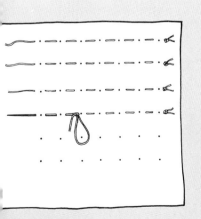
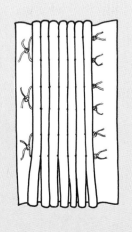

1 Gathering the material   2 Pulling up the gathers

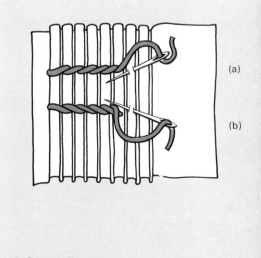

3 Rope pattern

Other patterns and stitches
Three pretty sundresses

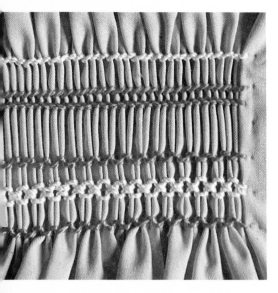

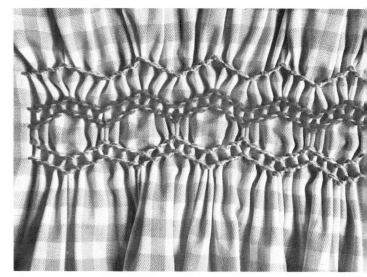

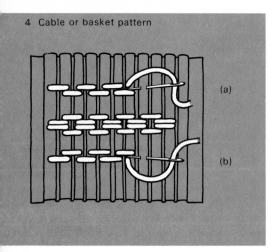

4 Cable or basket pattern

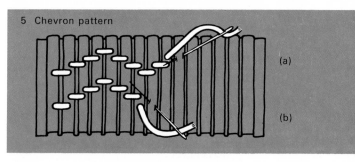

5 Chevron pattern

same time. Start by passing the thread through the first pleat, level with a gathering thread, on the left-hand side of the work. Pick up a small piece of material from the second and first pleats (a). Make another stitch in the same way just above this, then insert the needle at (b) to pass down through the back of the pleat to the next gathering thread below. Repeat the stitches over the second and third pleat and then insert the needle to begin at (c). If three joining stitches are found to be too thick, two may be worked instead.

Alternative method of honeycombing (fig.7). This is done with the thread passing from stitch to stitch on the surface of the fabric. Bring up the needle in the second pleat on the right-hand side of the work. Make a stitch as shown at (a). Insert the needle in the second pleat at the gathering thread of the row above (b). Make a stitch over the third and second pleats, bringing the needle out again in the third pleat. Insert the needle in the third pleat on the row below to begin again at (c).

Chevron stitch (fig.8a and b). This stitch is done from left to right and alternately up and down in groups of two pleats. The thread is kept above the needle in the top stitch (a) and below the needle in the bottom stitch (b). The alternate pleats that have not been joined can be done in the same way in a contrasting color.

Single feather stitch (fig.9a and b). Working from right to left, bring the needle through above the center line of the design, then make a small stitch through the pleat below, to the left, below the center line, catching the thread under the point of the needle. Continue making a series of stitches above (a) and below (b) the center line, inserting the needle at an angle. Single feather stitch and chevron stitch are both useful for building up different patterns or combinations.

Three pretty sundresses
These three little sundresses, for children aged two, four and six, show how smocking can be used for a really pretty effect. The design on each dress is a combination of the basic stitches and patterns described previously and shown in the samples.

and the stitches are made with the thread alternately above (a) and below (b) the needle.

Chevron pattern (fig.5a and b). The stitches for this pattern are made with the thread above the needle in the descending group (a) and below the needle in the ascending group (b). Worked from left to right, the groups of stitches form waves or diamonds.

Other smocking patterns and stitches
Honeycomb or seed stitch (fig.6). This is a term often used synonymously with smocking. The pattern gives great elasticity and is worked to complete two rows at the

Three pretty sundresses

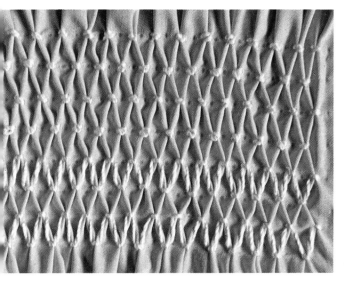

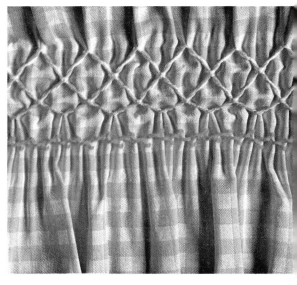

Making the dresses. The 2 smaller dresses can be cut out and made with the selvages running either horizontally or vertically. The largest dress should be made with the selvages running horizontally. Do not bother to hem the top edge if this is the selvage.

Note: all measurements are approximate and are intended only as a rough guide. Measure the width across the front of the chest of the child and then cut a rectangle of material measuring 3 times this measurement plus 4cm (1½in) on either side for each underarm section, which will not be smocked. (The largest dress will need a 5cm (2in) underarm allowance on each side.) So the rectangle for the smallest dress, for example, will be $23 \times 3 + 8$cm $(9 \times 3 + 3$in$) = 77$cm (30in) wide, and 33cm (13in) long plus hem allowance. Taking the measurement for the width across the back of the child, follow the same procedure for the back of the dress.

The depth of smocking is variable and the back of the garment can be smocked to match the front or shirred. Shirring is a form of gathering and can be done on a sewing machine with elastic thread wound onto the bobbin and ordinary sewing thread on the top of the machine. To prepare the area for smocking, press the material and position the gathering dots, which should be equal to 3 times the front chest or back measurements (fig.10). If necessary, hem the top of the dress.

Prepare the gathers and smock the dress as described previously. When the smocking is complete, press and then sew the 2 halves of the dress together with side seams. Hem to the required length. Make 2 narrow shoulder straps and sew them to the inside top of the dress.

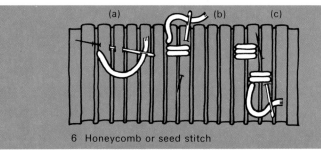

6 Honeycomb or seed stitch

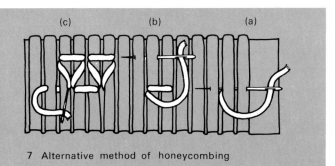

7 Alternative method of honeycombing

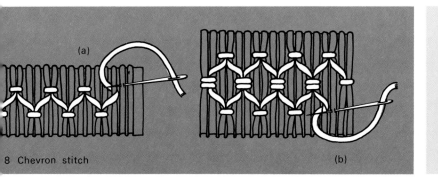

8 Chevron stitch

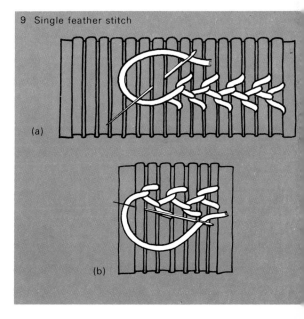

9 Single feather stitch

Size chart

	2	4	6
Years	2	4	6
Chest	53cm (21in)	58cm (23in)	61cm (24in)
Final length from underarm to hem	33cm (13in)	38cm (15in)	48cm (19in)
Depth of smocking	5cm (2in)	10cm (4in)	12.5cm (5in)
Chest front	23cm (9in)	25cm (10in)	28cm (11in)
Fabric width 90cm (36in)	1m (1yd)	1.14m (1¼yd)	1.14m (1¼yd)
Fabric width 102cm (40in)	1m (1yd)	1m (1yd)	1.14m (1¼yd)

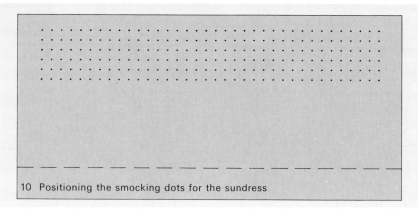

10 Positioning the smocking dots for the sundress

If you have enjoyed making garments following the traditional smocking patterns and stitches, you will want to continue to experiment with slightly different methods. This sample of abstract smocking shows how you can adapt the basic techniques in an original and colorful way. Although the sample shown here is only 7.5cm (3in) square, the design can be repeated over a large area as many times as necessary. It would look particularly effective on the yoke of a dress.

You will need:
black background cotton fabric □ stranded embroidery floss (embroidery cotton) in several bright colors □ smocking transfer sheet with dots at 0.5cm ($\frac{1}{4}$in) intervals □ white carbon paper □ basting thread □ No.6 crewel needle.

Making the smocking. Remember to allow 3 times the required finished width of fabric. Black fabric is difficult to mark successfully so it is advisable to transfer the dots from the transfer to the fabric with white carbon paper. Lay the fabric right side uppermost on a hard surface and place the carbon paper over it right side downwards. Place the transfer on top with the first dot in each row to the selvage. Mark each dot carefully, using a pencil.

Using basting thread, start each row of gathers with a separate thread, beginning at the right-hand side with a knotted end. Start and finish each row two or three dots in from the edge. When all the basting is done, draw up the gathers and tie each pair of threads together. The gathering must not be too tight or the stitches will be difficult to work.

The guide (fig.11) is for the basic lines stitched in red. It is a good idea to do these in the same color first and then work outwards in the selection of colors.

The sample is made throughout in outline (stem) stitch, using 3 strands of embroidery floss. Work from left to right, keeping the thread below the needle.

If you are creating your own design for abstract smocking, make a drawing with the proposed colors filled in, and keep it beside you for reference.

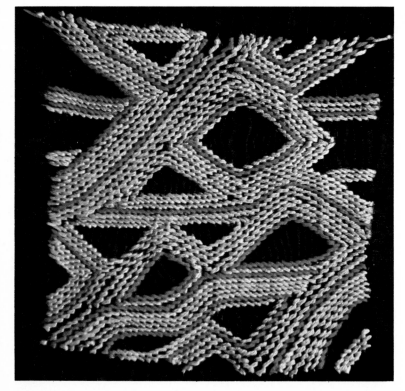

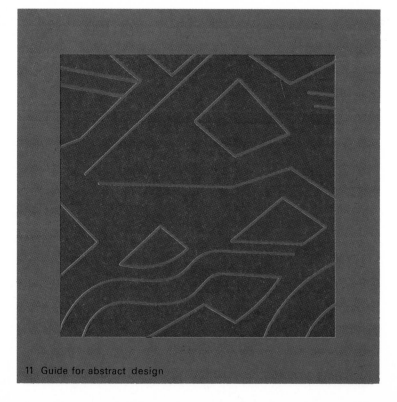

11 Guide for abstract design

Natural dyes

A wonderful array of subtle and soft colors obtained by using natural dyestuffs.

The ancient craft of using natural dyes is being revived as weavers, knitters and needleworkers rediscover the subtle soft colors that only natural dyes can give to yarns and fabrics.

Extracting natural dyes
To obtain full color intensity, pick flower heads, leaves, twigs and stems when the plant is young and vigorous; gather roots in the fall, lichens in winter, resinous barks in spring and berries at their ripest. Collect the dyestuffs in a paper bag or porous sack so that they can breathe and remain fresh. A proportion of 0.5kg (1lb) dyestuff to about 13 liters (3 gallons) of water is the amount of dye solution needed to dye 0.5kg (1lb) of dry weight yarn.

Soaking. Leaves and woody materials require soaking in water to facilitate color extraction. Cut roots, twigs or bark into strips of approximately 5cm (2in) in length. Put them in a large pan containing about 13 liters (3 gallons) of water and leave to soak for 24 hours. Leaves need soaking for 12 hours. Fruits, berries and flower heads do not require soaking.

Simmering. The amount of time needed to draw out the dye varies with each plant. Woody materials take up to 6 hours of simmering while some berries may only need a few minutes before the dye yield is complete. Stir the solution from time to time. Crush fruits and berries against the side of the pan with a wooden spoon. When the color in the dyebath ceases to deepen, the process of extracting dye is complete. Strain off the dye liquid through a piece of cheesecloth (muslin) and store, ready for use.

Mordants
Most dyestuff needs the addition of certain chemicals or *mordants*, to ensure color absorption and permanency. The recipes for mordants vary depending on the color you want and whether you dye linen and cotton, or wool. The most commonly used mordants are alum, tin, chrome and iron. Mordanting is usually done prior to the dyeing process, although the iron mordant can be added directly to the dyebath. Keep all mordants out of reach of children. The quantity for each ingredient given here is in proportion to about 13 liters (3 gallons) of water—which is added during the mordanting process. It is important to use the exact quantity of chemicals as an excess will damage the yarn.

Alum (potassium aluminum sulphate). Alum adds brightness and fixes the color of natural dyes. For dyeing wool use 113g (4oz) alum with 28g (1oz) tartaric acid, and for dyeing linen, use 113g (4oz) alum with 28g (1oz) washing soda.

Tin (stannous chloride). Tin enhances colors, especially reds and yellows. For dyeing wool use 14g ($\frac{1}{2}$oz) tin, with 28g (1oz) tartaric acid. For dyeing linen measure out 2 teaspoons of tin.

Chrome (potassium dichromate). Chrome gives a browny tint to the color. This chemical is extremely sensitive to light and, for maximum performance, must be kept in a sealed container. For dyeing wool use 14g ($\frac{1}{2}$oz) chrome with 28g (1oz) tartaric acid. For dyeing linen, measure out one tablespoon chrome (slightly more if you want a deep tone).

Iron (ferrous sulphate or copperas). Iron darkens the color intensity and can be added directly to the dyebath. For dyeing all yarns use 28g (1oz) tartaric acid with 28g (1oz) iron.

Preparation before mordanting
Yarn must be free from any grease or dirt which will hinder absorption both in the mordanting and dyeing process. It is advisable that beginners use natural unbleached wool, as it needs a less complicated single stage mordanting process, rather than the tougher more resilient fibers. Wind the wool loosely into skeins. It will then be easier to handle during the following stages and will ensure that the mordant and dye can filter through evenly. To prevent it from unraveling, secure it in one or two places with a thread tied loosely around the skein. Then wash the wool in warm water and mild soap and rinse thoroughly in warm water. To prepare linen and cotton yarn, boil with soap and washing soda for one hour. Rinse thoroughly.

Mordanting wool
Choose a mordant and weigh the ingredients. Dissolve them in a small amount of hot water. Pour this solution into a pan containing 13 liters (3 gallons) of water. Place the wet wool in the pan. Make sure that the wool is completely immersed and that there is ample room for free circulation of the solution. Bring the water slowly to simmering point. This will take about 45 minutes. Allow the wool to simmer for another 45 minutes, stirring once or twice. More absorbent finer wools only need about 25 minutes additional simmering time. Leave the wool in the solution until it is cool enough to be handled. Then remove it, squeeze it out gently and wrap it in a cloth. Leave it for 24 hours in order to allow the mordant to mature in the wool. Yarn that is mordanted with chrome must be kept away from light.

Mordanting linen and cotton
Choose a mordant recipe and measure out the ingredients. Place the wet yarn in a solution of the mordant and about 13 liters (3 gallons) of water and let it simmer for one hour. Allow the yarn to cool naturally and leave it for 24 hours in the solution. Remove it and rinse thoroughly but keep the mordant solution for use later. Dissolve 28g (1oz) of tannic acid and add it to a second pan containing 13 liters (3 gallons)

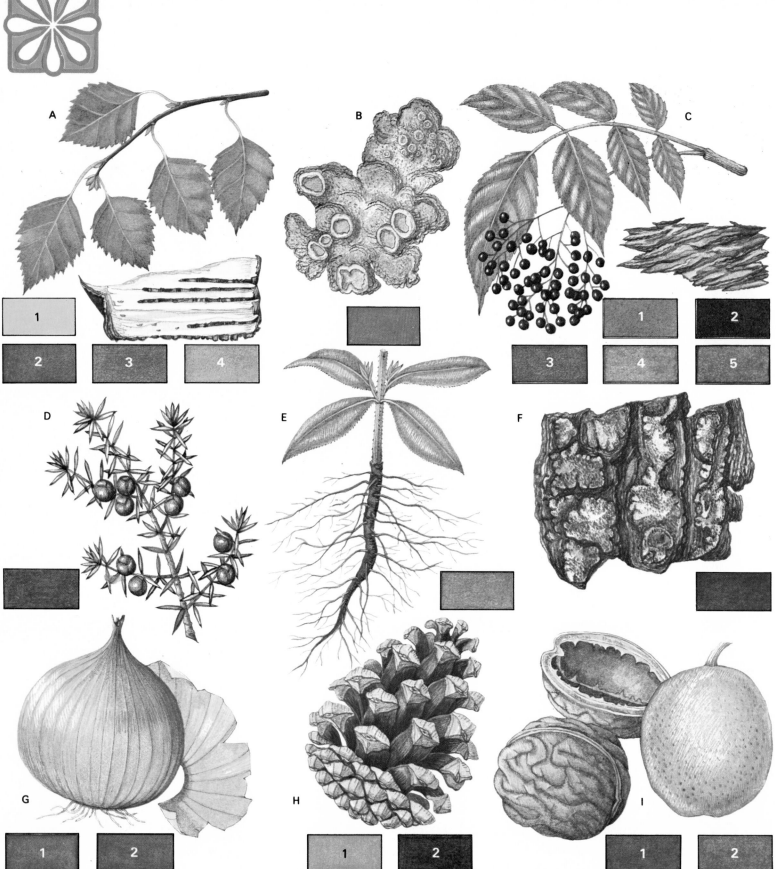

Key to natural dyes:

A = Birch
1 = leaves with alum mordant
2 = bark
3 = bark with iron mordant
4 = bark with alum mordant

B = Lichen (*Lecanora tartarea*)

C = Elder
1 = leaves with alum mordant
2 = bark with iron mordant
3 = berries
4 = berries with alum mordant and salt
5 = berries with alum mordant

D = Juniper

E = Madder (*Rubia peregrina*)

F = Oak

G = Onion skins
1 = with alum
2 = with tin mordant

H = Pine cones
1 = with alum
2 = with iron added

I = Walnut
1 = shrub and husks
2 = with alum mordant

Guide to Dyestuffs and their Colors

Dyestuff	Mordant	Color	Dyestuff	Mordant	Color	Dyestuff	Mordant	Color
Apple tree bark	alum chrome tin	lemon yellow rust bright yellow	Cranberry	alum tin	pink red gold	Grapes	alum	violet
Blackberry berries	alum with salt alum	blueish gray purple brown	Dandelion heads roots whole plant	alum no mordant no mordant	pale yellow purple magenta	St John's Wort flowers	tin	red
green shoots	iron (copperas)	black				Maple tree bark	alum iron	olive purple
Blueberry	alum	blue to purple	Dock leaves and stems	alum chrome	bright yellow bronze green	Marigold flower	alum	yellow to gold
Broom flowers and stems	alum chrome	yellow gold	Fennel	alum chrome	yellow gold	Nettle leaves and stems	alum	green yellow
Buttercups	alum	yellow	Fern buds	alum chrome	yellow green olive green	Rhubarb leaves	alum	strong yellow
Camomile heads	alum	buff				Rose hips	alum	dull rose
Carrot tops	alum tin	pale green yellow bright yellow	Golden rod blossoms	alum	lemon yellow	Saffron flowers	alum	yellow
						Spinach leaves	alum	green yellow

of water. Immerse the wet yarn and leave to simmer for one hour. Let it cool naturally and leave it in the solution for 24 hours before rinsing. Then put the yarn back into the first solution and let it soak for 12 hours. Remove and rinse thoroughly.

Dyeing
The dyeing process is the same for all yarns. Dissolve a cupful of sea salt in a small amount of boiling water and add this to the dyebath (the pan containing the dye solution). Heat the dyebath gently. When the solution is warm, add the wet yarn, making sure there is room for the circulation of the solution. Slowly bring to sim-

mering point. Stir with a stick which has not been used in a dyebath of a different color. Do not stir too often as this can cause the fibers to become matted. Leave to simmer for 40 minutes or until the desired color is achieved. The yarn will always appear several shades deeper when wet. Allow the yarn to cool naturally before rinsing in warm water. Squeeze out excess moisture and hang to dry in a warm place away from sunlight.

Creating unusual effects in dyeing
Cram the bath with yarn so that there is no

room for the circulation of the solution. The result will be a variety of tones. Alternatively, top dyeing—a process of re-wetting and dyeing the yarn in a second dyebath which is a different color from the first—produces unusual shades as well as remedying unsatisfactory colors. Only top dye with mordanted yarn as substantive dyes (dyes which do not require mordanting) tend to run. Top mordanting produces unpredictable but interesting results: re-wet the yarn and immerse it in another mordanting recipe after the completion of the dyeing process.

Quilting

The word "quilt" is believed to be derived from the Latin *culita* or *culitra*, meaning a sack or cushion filled with wool or hair, and a quilt was probably originally used as a blanket-like covering. But this very practical form of needlework has certainly long been used for clothing and other purposes throughout the world, particularly in the East. The British Museum in London houses a carved ivory figure, dating from about 3400 BC, wearing an elegant quilted coat or cloak; and in the Institute of Archaeology, Leningrad there is a prized piece of carpet dating from the 1st century BC which appears to have been quilted with a pattern of spiral and scroll shapes within a geometric border.

However, as with many needlecrafts, only a few of the earliest examples have survived in reasonable condition. One of these is a Sicilian quilt dating from around 1400. Originally made as a magnificent pair, the quilt depicts scenes from the legend of Tristram. Part of the quilt is now in the Victoria and Albert Museum in London and the other is at the Bargello in Florence. We know from household inventories that quilting gained general popularity in Europe during the Middle Ages. Quilted garments became fashionable, and useful —

soldiers often wore quilted gambesons (military tunics), with or without an additional protective covering of chain mail. The outer fabric was usually made from woven cloth, canvas, linen or leather, while the fabrics used for furnishings included sarcenet (a silk-like material), velvets and satins. Wool, and later cotton, was used for the stuffing.

As trading with the East increased, so did the supply of decorative materials. During the 17th century, elaborately quilted garments became popular; quilted pillow covers and cupboard linings also made their appearance in the home. Fashionable ladies wore quilted farthingales, and by the 18th century, skirts were cut so as to reveal a quilted petticoat beneath. Clothiers who supplied ready-quilted fabrics enjoyed a flourishing trade.

From Europe, quilting traveled to North America and then moved west with the early settlers. By the 19th century its popularity was such that Quilting Bees — gatherings at which several women met regularly to help each other with the work — were busy and productive concerns as well as being important social events. The arrival of the sewing machine in the mid-19th century enabled manufacturers

Above: An 18th-century portrait of Nelly O'Brien in a quilted skirt, painted by Sir Joshua Reynolds.

Left: A detail from one of the oldest quilts to have survived. From Sicily and dating from about 1400, it portrays scenes from the life of Tristram.

to produce quilted items more rapidly and profitably but inevitably the designs became less imaginative than the earlier handstitched examples. Today, with the sophisticated attachments that are available for sewing machines, more artistic designs can be achieved; yet as with nearly all needlecrafts, handstitching still produces a more individual and effective result.

Types of quilting
The art of quilting basically involves stitch-

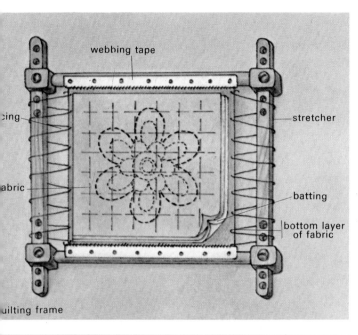

webbing tape

stretcher

cing

abric

batting

bottom layer of fabric

quilting frame

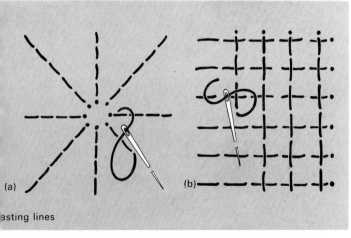

(a)

(b)

asting lines

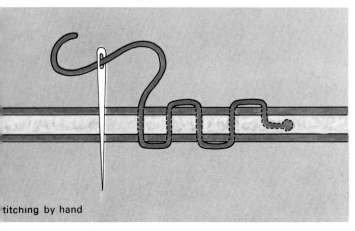

titching by hand

ing together two or more layers of fabric to form a decorative design on the top surface, either to create warmth and softness or simply to add interest. There are four main types of quilting, each with its own characteristics.

Padded or "English" quilting. This is perhaps the best known form of quilting where the entire surface is padded. Two layers of fabric and one of padding are required.

Stuffed or "Trapunto" quilting. Here the design is stitched first, then certain areas are stuffed with padding from behind to make them stand out.

Corded or "Italian" quilting. Only two layers of fabric are used here. The raised design is made by inserting rug yarn, quilting yarn or cord between double lines of stitching.

Flat quilting. Two layers of fabric are held together by an all-over design of decorative stitching, but no padding is inserted. This type of quilting gives body and extra warmth to a fabric without adding bulk.

Materials and preparation

Fabrics. Smooth, closely woven natural fabrics such as cotton, fine linen, silk and satin are most suitable for quilting. The backing fabric can be the same or alternatively, use a loosely woven muslin or other fabric, depending on the article and the type of quilting. The choice of filling depends on the thickness of padding required. One or two layers of cotton batting (wadding) may be used for lightweight but warm garments, while synthetic batting is ideal for all kinds of projects, from clothes to coverlets.

Using a frame (fig.1). Small pieces can be quilted by hand or in a round frame, but larger padded items are more successfully quilted on a rectangular frame which has two bars with webbing attached and two bars as stretchers. Stitch the bottom layer of fabric firmly to the webbing tapes and stretch taut. Lace the sides to the stretchers with heavy thread. Place the batting and top fabric smoothly over it and baste all three layers together as described below. Frames are usually available with tapes of up to 76cm (30in) long. For bed quilts you can improvise a larger frame; alternatively,

make a large piece of quilting in sections and join them together later.

Basting (fig.2a and b). Firm basting is very important in quilting to hold the layers together accurately during stitching; otherwise, the fabric will move and produce a wrinkled effect. Before basting, iron the fabrics thoroughly as creases cannot be removed later. On small pieces, baste in lines radiating out from the center (a); on larger pieces, in horizontal and vertical lines to form a grid (b).

Marking designs

Designs are marked onto the fabric in several different ways.

Needle marking. This is suitable if you are using cardboard templates to build up the design. With a blunt-tipped rug needle, draw around the templates so that an indented line appears. Hold the needle almost parallel to the fabric so that it does not tear it. Mark the design section by section as you work. Tailor's chalk can be used instead of a needle.

Perforating. Trace the design onto tracing paper and place this over the fabric. Using a tracing wheel, a hard sharp pencil or a darning needle, perforate the fabric through the tracing paper.

Dressmaker's carbon paper. This produces solid lines, so it is not suitable if the design is in running stitch as the lines will show through.

Stitching

Stitching by hand. Small, even running stitches are traditionally used for padded quilts and must be done with an upright motion to pierce all three layers correctly (fig.3). With one hand above the work and the other below, pass the needle up and down from one to the other. Back and chain stitch may also be used as a variation.

Stitching by machine. For most simple quilting designs, a medium-length straight or zigzag stitch and a slightly loose tension are suitable. For padded quilting, ease the pressure on the foot and stitch alternate lines in opposite directions to prevent the fabric from shifting. Intricate designs on a machine require a free running stitch with the foot removed, the feed teeth lowered and the work stretched on a frame.

Quilting

Soft and warm

and percale on top as shown in fig.1. Continue to work lines of basting stitches down and across the layers to form a grid as shown in fig.2b.

Stitching the design. Sewing through all the layers (fig.3), make the design in running stitch throughout by hand. Follow the marked lines neatly and precisely, and when necessary fasten off any ends on the back of the work.

Making up the quilt. Cut out a percale backing for the quilt to the size of the completed cover, plus seam allowances of 1.5cm ($\frac{1}{2}$in) all around. Remove the work from the frame. Place the quilting and backing, right sides together and stitch around 3 sides. Turn to right side. Turn in the seam allowances on the fourth side and slip stitch to close.

Soft and warm

This traditionally quilted crib coverlet will keep a baby snug and warm through the coldest winter. The design incorporates straight and curved lines that result in squares, triangles, hearts and other interesting shapes, all of which are easy to stitch. The coverlet measures 74cm (29in) long by 49cm (19in) wide.

You will need:

9 skeins of stranded embroidery floss (embroidery cotton) in pale yellow (2 strands only are used to stitch the design) □ 0.75m (¾yd) cream percale, lawn or similar lightweight cotton fabric, 90cm (36in) wide □ batting medium-weight polyester (wadding)

□ fine muslin for mounting the quilt.

Making the quilt. A quarter of the design is shown on the graph (fig.4) in which 1 square represents 4cm (1½in); the broken lines indicate the center. Draw the design to full size, reversing the design for each corner. Iron the top fabric. Note the direction of the grain and then transfer the design, using dressmaker's carbon paper. Allowing a border of 1cm (⅜in) around the design, plus a seam allowance of 1.5cm (½in), cut out the coverlet to size. Place the percale on top of the batting and then mark the center of the design with basting stitches, lengthwise and widthwise. Stretch the muslin on a frame, then place the batting

4 Graph for quilt   1sq = 4cm (1½in)

Trapunto quilted dove

well, then cut 2 pieces of percale and 1 piece of muslin to size, with seam allowances of 2.5cm (1in) on all edges. Lay one piece of percale aside for the backing. Transfer the design onto the second piece of percale, using the dressmaker's carbon paper method. Then, matching the edges exactly, baste the percale to the muslin around all edges.

Using 1 strand of dark gray embroidery floss sew neat back stitches through both layers of fabric and work along the marked lines of the design. Make all the threads neat on the wrong side of the design. Turn the work over so that the muslin is on top. Draw the threads gently apart and stuff each grape shape with small pieces of batting, using a fine knitting needle. When the stuffing is even and complete, pull the strands of muslin back in place and overcast any gaps that may have appeared. Stuff the leaves and the dove in the same

Trapunto quilted dove

Trapunto quilting lends itself particularly well to pictorial use because of its interesting three-dimensional effect. As an introduction to the technique, make this dove with a bunch of grapes; later you can create your own designs. The finished picture measures approximately 33 × 44cm (13 × 17¼in).

You will need:

1m (1yd) gray percale or lawn, 90cm (36in) wide ☐ 0.5m (½yd) fine muslin, 90cm (36in) wide ☐ 1 skein dark gray stranded embroidery floss (embroidery cotton) ☐ sewing thread to match fabric ☐ small pearl (optional) ☐ 0.5m (½yd) batting (wadding) 90cm (36in) wide ☐ quilting yarn ☐ piece of cardboard, 33 × 44cm (13 × 17¼in) ☐ fine knitting needle ☐ tracing paper ☐ dressmaker's carbon paper ☐ large-eyed blunt needle.

Quilting the picture. Draw the design from the graph (fig.5) in which 1 square equals 4cm (1½in). Press the muslin and percale

5 Graph for dove picture   1sq = 4cm (1½in)

Quilted jacket

the backing fabric 5cm (2in) in from the outside edges of the picture.

Italian quilting

Italian quilting is a purely decorative technique and is not intended to provide additional warmth. The basic technique is to sew together two pieces of fabric – the outer fabric and an inner muslin lining – with decorative stitching in a raised design. This raised effect is achieved by stitching parallel lines about 0.5cm ($\frac{1}{4}$in) apart, through which lengths of quilting yarn are pulled after stitching is complete. Curved designs are obviously the most suitable as maneuvering around corners can be difficult.

Quilted jacket

The minimum of dressmaking skill is needed to make this attractive jacket which has cap sleeves, and simple ties for a front fastening. The flower design, stitched on the front of the jacket, is very suitable for this quilting technique.

You will need:
1m (1yd) outer fabric, 90cm (36in) wide □ 1m (1yd) inner lining fabric, 90cm (36in) wide □ 0.5m ($\frac{1}{2}$yd) fine muslin for backing □ matching thread □ quilting yarn or thick knitting yarn of fine cord □ large tapestry needle □ dressmaker's carbon paper.

Cutting out the pattern. Draw the pattern for the jacket from the graph (fig.6) in which 1 square equals 8cm (3in). A 1.5cm ($\frac{1}{2}$in) seam allowance is included. The pattern itself consists of 1 back, 2 front pieces and 2 cap sleeves. Cut these out in both the outer and lining fabric. Cut 2 strips of outer fabric measuring 36cm (14in) long by 2.5cm (1in) wide for the front ties.

Tracing the design. Cut 2 pieces of muslin slightly larger than the size of the flower motif (fig.7). Trace the design onto 2 pieces of muslin with dressmaker's carbon paper, making the second side in reverse. Baste the traced muslin onto the 2 fronts, wrong sides together.

Stitching the motif. Set your machine for a medium-length stitch, then sew along the parallel lines. Alternatively, if you have a machine with a double needle, you can do the stitching even more easily. If you are

sewing by hand, use a small neat running stitch.

Thread a large tapestry needle with the quilting yarn, pierce the channel made between the 2 rows of stitching from the muslin side, then run the needle and yarn along the channel as far as possible. Come up, make a small loop (fig.8), then continue as before until all the channels are filled. Make sure you do not pull the wool too tightly through the channels or it will cause puckering on the right side.

Making up the garment. Place the fabric and the lining for the cap sleeves together, right sides together. Stitch along the marked seam line of the cap sleeve edge, leaving the armhole edge unstitched. Turn to the right side, press and top stitch close to the edge.

Fold the strips for the ties in half lengthwise, right sides together; then stitch one short end and along the side. Turn to the right side, press and top stitch all around. Stitch the shoulder seams on the outer fabric, then press open the seam allowances. Position the cap sleeves around the armhole and stitch in place. Stitch the shoulder seams of the lining in the same way, then place the lining and garment together, right sides together and stitch around the neck edge. Turn to the right side and press the neckline edge carefully. Turn in the seam allowance around the armhole on the lining, then sew by hand to the garment. Press carefully. Stitch the side seams of the lining and outer fabric separately, working as far as the slit opening marking on the side seams. Press open the seam allowances. Then turn the jacket inside out so that the right sides are together. Stitch the 2 layers of fabric together from the neck edge, down the front (inserting the ties into the seam lines at the marked points), around the curves, the slit openings, around the back and continue, finishing at the outer back edge. Leave an opening of about 7.5cm (3in) in one side of the lining so that you can turn the jacket to the right side. Turn the whole garment through the opening, then sew this up by hand neatly from the inside of the garment. Press the outer edge all the way around, then top stitch 0.5cm ($\frac{1}{4}$in) from the edge for a neat finish.

way. The border around the design and the stalks can be stuffed using a blunt needle and quilting yarn using the Italian technique. Stitch a small pearl in place for the eye if desired.

Making the picture. Press the unstuffed areas of the picture carefully. Stretch the quilting over the cardboard and then back it with the second piece of gray percale. Keeping the cardboard in position, sew the 2 pieces of percale together with neat hemming stitches.

To make loops for hanging the picture, cut a strip of percale measuring 30.5cm (12in) long by 7.5cm (3in). Fold it in half lengthwise, then stitch down the center 1cm ($\frac{3}{8}$in) from the raw edges. Press the seam allowances open down the center of the strip. Cut the strip in half. Turn in the ends of each loop and slip stitch them together. Fold each loop in half, then sew to

8 Bring out the needle through the muslin at intervals to pull the yarn through the channels; re-insert the needle into the same hole

7 Tracing pattern for flower motif

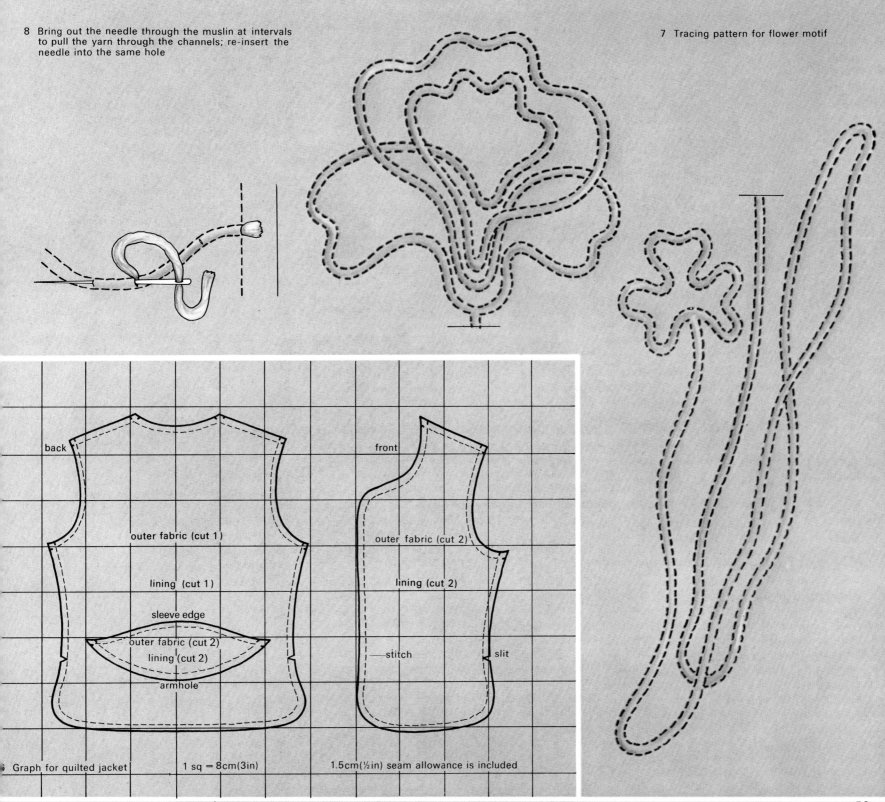

back

outer fabric (cut 1)

lining (cut 1)

sleeve edge

outer fabric (cut 2)

lining (cut 2)

armhole

front

outer fabric (cut 2)

lining (cut 2)

stitch   slit

Graph for quilted jacket   1 sq = 8cm(3in)   1.5cm(½in) seam allowance is included

Needlepoint

Detail from a late 16th-century Spanish needlepoint wall hanging intriguingly entitled "Galceran de Pinos disembarks at Salona near Tarragona and stops the sending of the ransom." The hanging is stitched in silk, wool and metal thread on canvas.

Throughout history, elaborately embroidered garments or furnishings have been popular as a reflection of the wearer's or owner's wealth and social status. From contemporary written accounts historians know that embroidery probably flourished as an art form in Ancient Egypt and other early advanced civilizations. Needlepoint is certainly a form of embroidery, but in many ways it is a craft in its own right.

Unlike other forms of embroidery, needlepoint is generally done as a design or picture to cover the entire background canvas. Embroidery is usually associated with materials like silk and cotton, but from medieval times, wool and other relatively thicker threads have also been used in needlepoint. True tapestry work is wholly hand-woven, without a background

fabric as a basis for the design.

Examples of needlepoint dating from the Middle Ages still exist and the craft thrived throughout this period in most of Western Europe. In Britain its development continued into the Elizabethan era, and many museums now house magnificent bookbindings, purses, cushions, table covers and hangings, all in needlepoint, displaying a variety of colors and a variety of fascinating designs.

Many early needlepoint themes were taken from nature and flowers, trees, animals and birds were frequently featured.

Biblical characters and stories, myths and legends were also adapted into narrative illustration. There was, however, very little respect for the laws of perspective and many of the designs remaining today are quite surprising for this reason. Originality in design was also somewhat restricted, and certain pictorial themes and patterns were widely copied.

It was during the 16th century that a particularly fascinating form of needlepoint, known as "Turkey work," was first done. It was most commonly used for cushion covers and involved the pulling of two strands through the canvas. These were then knotted and cut short, giving a pile-like appearance, similar to that of a rug or carpet.

The oriental influence became widespread as the trade routes to the East opened up during the 17th century. Oriental designs soon became popular as both floral and pastoral needlepoint themes.

In the course of the 18th century there was little real development in needlepoint technique, although Bargello or Florentine stitchery (also known as Hungarian Point) continued to flourish. The early 19th century, however, marked a turning point in needlepoint history: in the very first decade, a bookseller from Berlin first published a needlepoint design marked out on squared paper. Not long afterwards, another German publisher printed numerous similar designs. The project proved successful and thousands of patterns were produced in this way within just a few years. Thereafter there was throughout Europe a rage for needlepoint. Numerous items of furnishings for both household and ecclesiastical use — pincushions, hassocks, kneelers, screens and cushions — were worked with these original patterns. European settlers introduced the craft to North America, but the canvases were generally much smaller than those that had been embroidered in medieval times.

Needlepoint remains highly popular as a craft and the possibilities for originality in design, color and texture are never-ending. Today, needlepoint designs can be followed on a ready-stenciled canvas, by means of a chart or by tracing on the canvas with waterproof ink. The effects

Basic materials and techniques

Late 16th-century English purse and pincushion embroidered with colored silks and silver thread onto canvas in tent stitch.

that can be achieved range from the most delicate pictorial designs to the boldest and brightest geometric patterns. The firm fabric created by needlepoint may be put to many uses, including wall hangings, cushions, bags, belts, chair seats and even clothing.

So, whether you are a traditionalist at heart or whether you prefer to put established techniques to new adventurous uses, you will find great scope for your ideas.

Basic materials and techniques

Canvas. There are two basic types of canvas available, classified according to whether they are double or single canvas, and how many threads or holes there are per 2.5cm (1in). Penelope canvas or double thread canvas, is woven in pairs of threads. Stitches can be worked over the threads as pairs or the two threads can be separated. Mono canvas or single thread canvas, is woven as single threads and is

the more common type used. The thread count varies from the very fine of about 24 threads to 2.5cm (1in) to the much coarser with as few as 3 threads to 2.5cm (1in).

Yarns. The yarns suitable for needlepoint are varied and must be chosen to suit the specific project. A yarn should be thick enough to cover the canvas completely, but not too thick to pass easily through the holes. Tapestry yarn is suitable for fine to medium canvas and stranded embroidery floss (embroidery cotton), embroidery yarns, or crewel wool pass more easily through the holes of very fine canvas. Rug wool is necessary to cover a coarser canvas. To prevent woolen yarn from fraying, it is best to keep the length in the needle shorter than 45cm (18in).

Needles. A tapestry needle with a blunt point should be used; choose a size which holds the yarn easily and passes through

A selection of frames, yarns and canvas suitable for needlepoint.

the canvas without distorting it.

Preparing the canvas for stitching. Cut out the canvas at least 5–7.5cm (2–3in) wider all around than the size of the design, to allow for the final blocking and mounting processes. Bind the raw edges with masking tape to prevent fraying.

The canvas can be mounted in a square or rectangular frame to prevent it from losing its shape during stitching. Frames are available in different widths, with or without a floor stand. They consist of two rollers with tape attached and two side laths, which stretch them apart.

Framing the canvas. First, cut the canvas to size, turn under 1.5cm ($\frac{1}{2}$in) at the raw edges at the top and bottom and sew centrally to the roller tapes. Wind any surplus canvas onto the rollers, then adjust their position until the canvas is taut. Finally, lace the selvages (or raw edges bound with tape) at the sides to the laths with fine string.

Beginning to stitch. When working on a

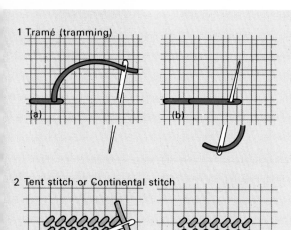

1 Tramé (tramming) (a) (b)

2 Tent stitch or Continental stitch (a) (b) (c) (d)

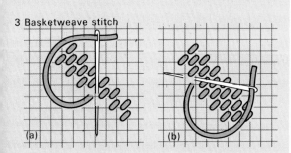

3 Basketweave stitch (a) (b)

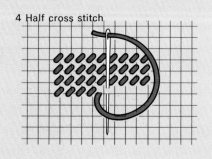

4 Half cross stitch

frame, stitches are made in two movements, with one hand on top of the canvas passing the needle down, the other hand underneath passing the needle up again. Without a frame, the stitches can be worked in one movement as shown in the diagrams. Be sure to keep an even tension. At the beginning of a thread, leave a tail of surplus yarn at the back of the work and stitch over it to avoid making a knot. At the end, run the yarn under a few stitches, and then cut it off.

Needlepoint stitches

Tramé (tramming). These long staggered horizontal stitches (fig.1a and b) may be worked over the canvas before other stitching to "pad" the work or to help cover the canvas threads.

Tent stitch or Continental stitch (fig.2a–d). This is the most extensively used needlepoint stitch. When worked on mono canvas it is also known as *petit point*, and on Penelope canvas as *gros point*. If done in horizontal rows (a and b) it tends to stretch the canvas out of shape and the stitches on the reverse side are long diagonal ones. When done on Penelope canvas over a tramé thread (c) the stitches slope more at the back of the work (d).

Basketweave stitch (fig.3a and b). This stitch, worked in diagonal rows, creates small interlocking stitches like woven fabric on the back of the work. This distorts the canvas minimally.

Half cross stitch (fig.4). This is suitable for thick yarns as the stitches on the reverse side are vertical and not so bulky.

Blocking the finished canvas

When your work is complete, it should be blocked to restiffen it and stretched into shape if necessary before making the final item. Snip into the selvages at 5–7.5cm (2–3in) intervals, but do *not* trim the canvas or remove the taped edges yet. To start, you will need a wooden board or piece of hardboard slightly larger than the piece of canvas. Cover the board with aluminum foil or brown wrapping paper cut to the same size as the finished canvas. This prevents the wood from staining the work. Place the canvas face down over the foil or paper and keep in place using rustproof

tacks (drawing pins) positioned at intervals of about 0.5cm ($\frac{1}{4}$in) and stretching the canvas evenly to the correct shape. The canvas threads should run at right angles. Saturate the canvas with warm water, using a clean sponge. Dab with paper towels to remove excess water and allow to dry for 24 hours. When the work is completely dry, remove the tacks. Trim the excess canvas to the margins allowed for in your project.

Patches and badges

If you have never done any needlepoint before it is advisable to begin with something fairly small so that it will be finished quickly and you have something to show for very little effort and experience.

Patches and badges

Here are three small motifs that can be made up into patches or badges and then sewn onto pockets, jeans or jackets for a bright touch of individuality.

All patches are worked in tent stitch on mono canvas and each square on the charts represents one stitch.

A different type of yarn and canvas has been chosen for each project to enable you to gain experience working with various materials. The small house would be suitable for children's clothes, the sunset for adult casual wear and the art nouveau flower for a more sophisticated decorative effect.

Sunset strip

The sunset patch is worked on medium-gauge canvas with heavy pearl cotton. The base of the finished semicircle is 11.5cm ($4\frac{1}{2}$in) long.

You will need:
14cm ($5\frac{1}{2}$in) square of mono canvas, 14 holes to 2.5cm (1in) ☐ 1 skein of No. 5 pearl cotton in each of the following colors: blue, red, orange, yellow and brown ☐

square of black backing fabric the same size as the canvas ☐ piece of clean blotting paper.

Making the patch. Following the chart (fig.5), make the sun in red, with rays of yellow and orange. The border is stitched in blue and the bird, which can be positioned on the left-hand or right-hand side, is brown.

When the patch is complete, lay it face upwards on damp blotting paper and pin into shape. Press and leave to dry. Trim the excess canvas to within 5 threads of the embroidery and press the turnings to the wrong side, mitering the corners.

Cut out a piece of backing fabric to the same size and shape as the patch, allowing narrow turnings all around. Press the turnings to the wrong side and slipstitch the backing to the patch.

Simple yet sophisticated

The art nouveau patch is worked on fine canvas in stranded embroidery floss (embroidery cotton). The patch measures 7 × 8.5cm ($2\frac{3}{4}$ × $3\frac{1}{4}$in).

You will need:
11.5cm ($4\frac{1}{2}$in) square of mono canvas, 18 holes to 2.5cm (1in) ☐ 1 skein of stranded embroidery floss (embroidery cotton) in black, white, green and 2 shades of beige ☐ square of black backing fabric the same size as the canvas ☐ piece of clean blotting paper.

Making the patch. The patch is stitched using 6 strands of embroidery floss. Follow the chart (fig.6) for each stitch color. When the patch is complete, press and trim and attach the backing as for the previous patch.

Home sweet home

The cottage patch is worked on coarse canvas in tapestry yarn. It is the quickest of all three to work and measures 7.5cm (3in) square.

You will need:
10cm (4in) square of mono canvas, 10 holes to 2.5cm (1in) ☐ 1 skein of tapestry yarn in each of the following shades: white, green, red, light blue, dark blue, light brown and dark brown ☐ square of black

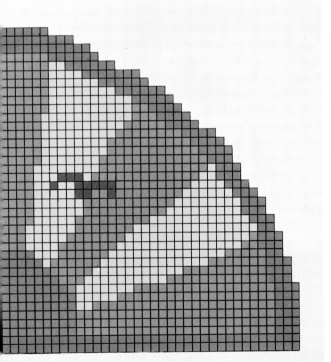

Chart for the sunset patch

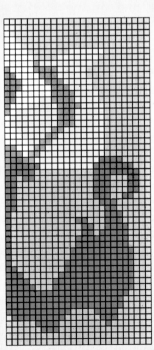

6 Chart for the art nouveau flower patch

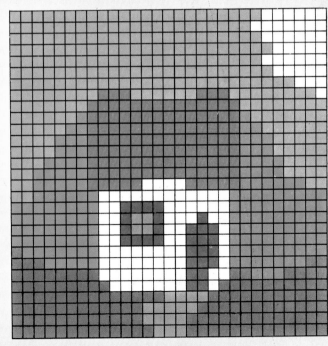

7 Chart for the cottage patch

Shades of the Orient

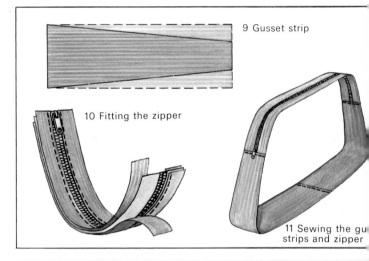

9 Gusset strip

10 Fitting the zipper

11 Sewing the gusset strips and zipper

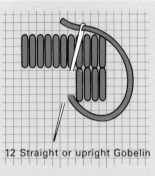

12 Straight or upright Gobelin

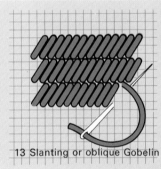

13 Slanting or oblique Gobelin

14 Encroaching Gobelin

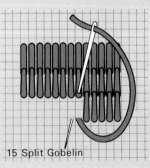

15 Split Gobelin

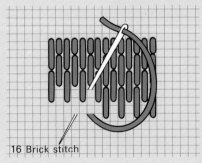

16 Brick stitch

skeins dark blue, 3 skeins rust, 2 skeins red and green, 1 skein yellow, white and light blue □ frame with 70cm (28in) tapes (optional) □ 1m (1yd) corduroy, 115cm (45in) wide □ 1.40m (1⅓yd) interfacing fabric, 80cm (32in) wide □ a wide 70cm (28in) zipper □ 1.15m (1¼yd) lining fabric 90cm (36in) wide □ a piece of cardboard measuring 53.5 × 15cm (21½ × 6in) □ fabric glue.

Stitching the canvas. Cut the canvas to measure 70cm × 58.5cm (28 × 23½in), tape raw edges and mark the center. Stretch the canvas on the frame if using one. The chart (fig.8) gives just over one quarter of the design, with the center indicated by arrows. The other three quarters are repeated as mirror images. Each square on the chart represents 1 stitch. Work from the center outwards in tent stitch, following the chart. Stitch the 2 corner motifs at the bottom only.

Finishing the bag. When the work is complete, block the canvas if necessary. Trim the excess canvas around the edge to 1.5cm (½in) and overcast to prevent fraying. Cut out the back in corduroy to the same dimensions. Cut 2 strips of corduroy 63.5 × 18cm (25 × 7in) for the gusset and taper these to measure 7.5cm (3in) at the top (fig.9). Cut 2 strips 73.5 × 6.5cm (29½ × 2½in) for inserting the zipper. Cut the strips of interfacing and lining to match all these pieces. Cut 2 strips of corduroy 73.5 × 10cm (29½ × 4in) for handles and 2 strips of interfacing 73.5 × 4cm (29½ × 1½in) to fit inside them. Glue the interfacing to the back of the corduroy pieces and the canvas. When stitching the pieces together, allow 1.5cm (½in) for seams. Insert the zipper between the 2 narrow corduroy strips, with the 2 lining strips on the reverse side (fig.10). Stitch the 2 gusset strips and the zipper strip together to form a continuous band (fig.11). Stitch the gusset band around the front and back sections of the bag, with right sides together. Catch in part of the final needlepoint row in the stitching, taking in slightly more at the corners. Trim and clip the fabric at the corners. Turn the bag right side out.

Fold the handle strips in half lengthwise, placing the interfacing in the fold. Turn in all raw edges and topstitch all around.

backing fabric the same size as the canvas □ piece of clean blotting paper.
Making the patch. Following the chart (fig.7), stitch the patch. When it is complete, press and trim and attach the backing as for the previous patch.

Shades of the Orient

This roomy carpet bag, embroidered with a beautiful oriental motif, demonstrates how needlepoint can be put to practical use. It is done in tent stitch on Penelope canvas to produce a firm fabric which will stand up to a lot of wear. The bag measures approximately 53.5 × 43cm (21½ × 17in).

You will need:
0.65m (⅔yd) Penelope canvas, 70cm (28in) wide, 7 holes to 2.5cm (1in) □ 25g (1oz) skeins of rug or thick knitting wool in the following quantities and colors: 4

Decorative stitches

Stitch to the bag 10cm (4in) from the top and 14cm (5½in) from the side.
Insert the cardboard at the bottom. Stitch the lining sides and gusset together in the same way as the bag. Fit inside the bag, turn under the raw edges and slipstitch around the edge.

Decorative stitches
Tent stitch tends to be overused and isolated as the only needlepoint stitch, although there are many others, such as the Gobelin stitches shown here, that can add a new dimension to a design and are fun to do. Practice them in a sampler which you can keep as a special library of stitches to refer to later when you want a particular effect for a new design.
There are several versions of Gobelin stitch, which is a very old stitch, originally used in imitation of tapestry. It takes its name from the Gobelin family who established a tapestry works in Paris in the 16th century. These stitches are done in rows across the canvas and vary in height depending on how many threads they are stitched over. They are done quickly and therefore make good background stitches.

Embroidery in Gobelin stitch is a quick and effective way of creating an attractive needlepoint picture.

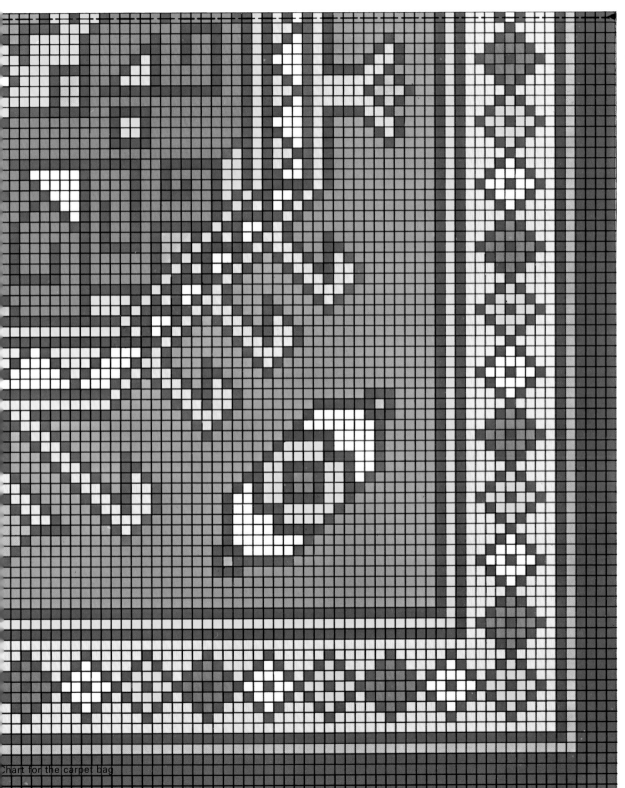

Chart for the carpet bag

Straight or upright Gobelin (fig.12). This forms straight ridges across the work and may be worked over the tramé stitches if necessary.

Slanting or oblique Gobelin (fig.13). This gives the appearance of sloping ridges. Work with an even tension.

Encroaching Gobelin (fig.14). With this stitch, each row overlaps the previous one by one thread of canvas. Use different colored yarns for a shaded effect.

Split Gobelin (fig.15). This is similar to encroaching Gobelin except that each new stitch actually splits the stitch in every previous row. The effect is rather like a knitted fabric.

Brick stitch (fig.16). Although similar to straight Gobelin, this produces a textured effect because of the staggered stitches. This must be worked over an even number of threads, to ensure the correct balance between stitches.

Bargello (Florentine)

Bargello, Florentine, Hungarian Point and Flame stitch are all names given to one of the most attractive and popular forms of needlework.

The earliest examples date from the 13th century and legend tells that Elizabeth of Hungary devised the method of embroidery to be worked by peasants during a time when wool was scarce. Certainly it is one of the quickest and most economical ways of covering a large area, as the long stitches on the front of the work require only a short connecting stitch on the back.

Another story tells of how a Hungarian princess married into the Medici family and impressed the ladies of the Florentine court with her magnificently embroidered trousseau.

Florence was certainly the most important center for this style of needlework and one of the names adopted was taken from the Bargello — a building in the city that served as a prison in the 14th century, and now established as a national museum of art.

By the 17th century, however, Bargello needlepoint was a flourishing art throughout Europe. Some of the best surviving examples were produced during this period, including the bedhangings at Parham Park, Sussex, England, made in wool and

silk during the reign of Charles I and a set of chairs now in the Bargello.

Bargello designs

Foundation. Every Bargello design depends on an accurately worked foundation. In some patterns like Romanesque, the embroidery is filled in above and below a horizontal row of stitches. In patterns like Pomegranate and Lattice, each section or motif is filled in after an outline of stitching in one color has been worked over the

A spectacular example of Bargello needlepoint is seen in these bed hangings from the Great Chamber of Parham Park in Sussex, one of England's finest country houses. By tradition the bedhead and coverlet were embroidered by Mary Queen of Scots.

whole area of canvas.

To begin working any Bargello design, first mark the center of the canvas vertically and horizontally with a line of basting stitches. Start working the foundation from the vertical center of the canvas. It will be easier to count the threads of the canvas

accurately if you make two movements of the needle, in and out, for each stitch in the foundation. When the foundation is complete fill in the rest of the colors one by one. An embroidery frame is not necessary as the vertical stitches do not distort the canvas diagonally.

Design and color. The basis of Bargello work is a row of straight stitches usually covering four or six threads of the canvas. In the simplest patterns, each row of stitches is staggered, moving two threads up or down, to create a zigzag or flame effect. An illusion of curves can be created, as in the Romanesque and Pomegranate designs, by using blocks of satin stitch and varying the number of stitches in each block as the row moves up and down. Lattice, diamond and basketweave designs, where the outline of the design is worked diagonally across the canvas instead of horizontally, are more complex developments of the basic zigzag design. The variety of colors that can be incorporated into a simple Bargello design is perhaps the greatest attraction of the work. Some designs call for as many as 12 colors, others as few as four. A soft shading of

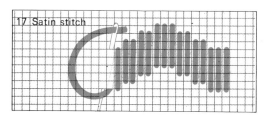

17 Satin stitch

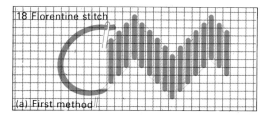

18 Florentine stitch

(a) First method

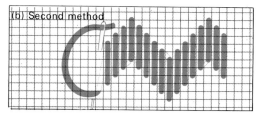

(b) Second method

tones from dark to light is characteristic of Bargello, with the shading vividly enhanced by a contrasting color. There should always be at least two shades of one color included in each pattern.

Canvas. Bargello is best worked on mono canvas. A fairly fine mesh canvas with 16 or 18 threads to 2.5cm (1in) is ideal for tapestry yarn or one strand of Persian wool.

Stitches

All Bargello designs are developed from two simple basic stitches — satin stitch and Florentine or flame stitch. The diagrams show the stitches over six threads of canvas, although the number can vary. Dotted lines show the angle of the stitch on the reverse side of the canvas.

Satin stitch (fig.17). This is repeated over the same number of threads in a straight row. The number of stitches in each block can be varied and stepped up or down to create the illusion of a curve.

Florentine stitch (fig.18a and b). Interlocking rows of this stitch create the fluid change of color that makes Bargello so attractive. There are two ways of doing it. The first method (a) is a more economical use of yarn. A small slanting stitch on the back of the work is all that is needed to connect the long stitches on the front. The second method (b) uses more yarn on the back of the work. Although the finished effect of both methods is exactly the same, the second method creates a tougher fabric and is more suitable for items like chair seats which will get a lot of hard wear.

Desk diary cover and penholder

Two different designs in toning colors make a quick and easy Bargello project. The quantities given are to fit a desk diary 15 × 21.5cm (6 × 8½in) and a penholder 29.5 × 10cm (11½ × 4in) but the em-

Needlepoint
Bargello (Florentine)

Bargello designs

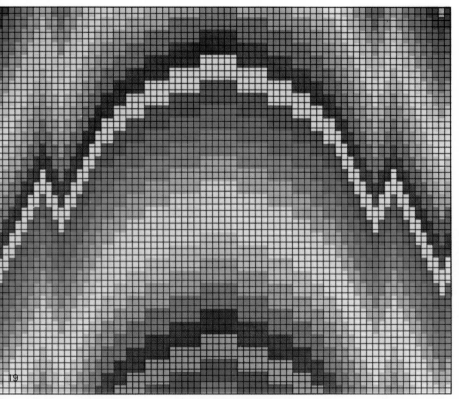

19

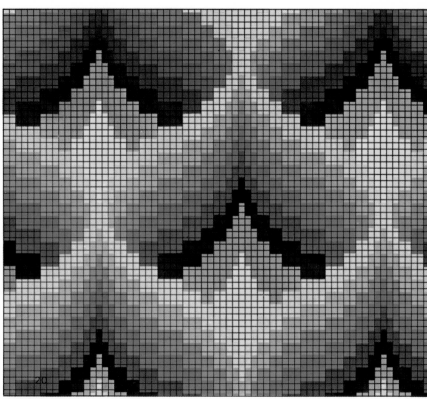

20

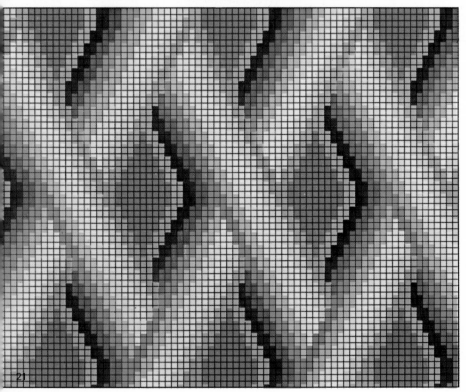

21

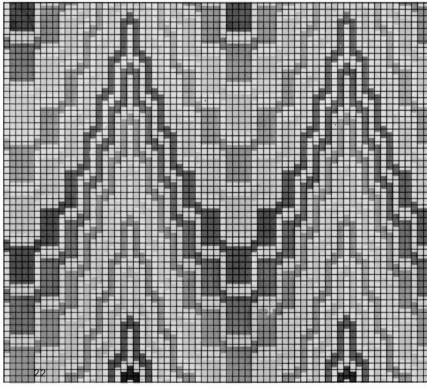

22

The illustration opposite shows four Bargello designs. *Top left:* Romanesque design. *Top right:* Pomegranate design. *Bottom left:* Lattice motif. *Bottom right:* Fountain brocade motif.

broidery can easily be adapted to any size. Both are done in satin stitch for blocks of stitches and Florentine (first method) for the rest.

You will need:

1 skein of tapestry yarn in each of the following colors: 5 shades of blue, 5 shades of gray and 1 shade of yellow, orange and black □ 25cm ($\frac{1}{4}$yd) mono canvas, 18 holes to 2.5cm (1in), 90cm (36in) wide □ tapestry needle □ 25cm ($\frac{1}{4}$yd) blue felt, 90cm (36in) wide □ 1.40m (54in) fine blue cord □ sewing needle □ sewing thread to match felt □ desk diary □ tin can.

Preparing the canvas. Tape or hem the raw edges of canvas. Measure the size of the front of the diary and the height and circumference of the tin can and transfer these measurements to the canvas, outlining the areas to be embroidered with basting stitches. Leave at least 2.5cm (1in) of unworked canvas all around each piece. Mark the center of each piece vertically and horizontally with basting stitches.

Romanesque design for the penholder.

Following the design as shown in fig.19, first work the foundation row in yellow. To center the colors, begin 20 threads up from the intersection of basting stitches and work the 6 satin stitches at the peak of the design, 3 on each side of the vertical center of the canvas. Continue with the foundation row to the right-hand edge of the canvas then begin again at the center and work out to the left-hand edge. Fill in the rest of the colors above and below, making a whole row across the canvas in one color before moving to the next. Start each row at the center and work outwards as for the foundation row. This pattern is done in 12 colors over 4 threads and back 2.

Making the penholder. The completed embroidery should be blocked. Trim the canvas to within 6 threads of the embroidery and clip the corners. With right sides together, stitch the 2 short sides of canvas together close to the embroidery. Turn under the raw edges of the canvas at top and bottom and stitch them down,

folding the canvas over so that no raw edges show. Cut a strip of felt to the exact size of the finished embroidery plus a small seam allowance on the short sides. Sew the 2 short sides together and slip the felt inside the embroidery, wrong sides together. Slipstitch the canvas to the felt around the top and bottom. Sew decorative cord around the top and bottom to trim and slip the completed cover over the tin can.

Pomegranate design for the diary cover.

Following the design as shown in fig.20, work the foundation in the palest blue. To center one pomegranate motif in the middle of the canvas, begin by making the single stitch at the peak of the motif, 22 threads up from the intersection of basting stitches. Continue doing the rows of pale blue to complete the foundation. Fill in the center of each motif. This design is made in 8 colors over 4 threads and back 2.

Finishing the diary cover. Trim the canvas and turn under and stitch the raw edges in the same way as for the penholder. Cut a piece of felt 1.5cm ($\frac{1}{2}$in) higher than the diary and long enough to wrap around it, including a generous flap for the inside back and front covers. Sew the flaps to the covers at the top and bottom with a 0.5cm ($\frac{1}{4}$in) seam allowance. Turn right side out and fold under and slipstitch the excess felt around the spine. Pin the embroidery in position on the front cover, sew in place and sew cord around to trim.

Additional Florentine motifs

Lattice and fountain brocade are two traditional Florentine motifs that can be used on a variety of projects for a really stunning effect.

Lattice motif (fig.21). This intricate motif requires a lot of care in working the foundation. Begin by making a central red diamond in the middle of the canvas over the intersecting basting threads. Make a few stitches surrounding the diamond to establish the sequence of each color. Then stitch diagonally outwards from the center in one color to lay the foundation over the whole of the canvas. The design is done over four threads and back two, and uses nine colors.

Fountain brocade motif (fig. 22). This impressive motif is worked over six threads

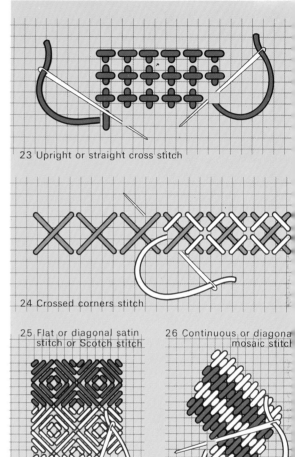

23 Upright or straight cross stitch

24 Crossed corners stitch

25 Flat or diagonal satin stitch or Scotch stitch

26 Continuous or diagonal mosaic stitch

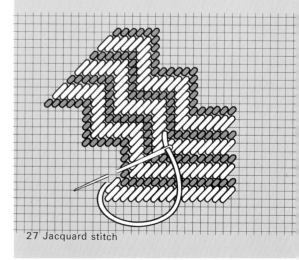

27 Jacquard stitch

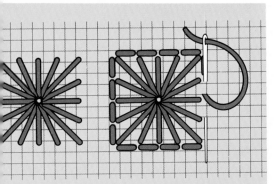

28 Eyelet or eye stitch

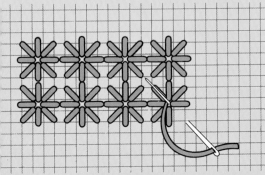

29 Algerian eye or star stitch

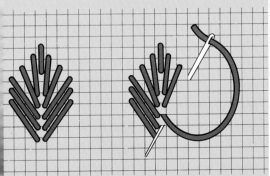

30 Leaf stitch

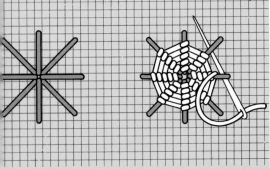

31 Whipped or ribbed spider stitch

and back one and over two threads and back one. A row of yellow alternates with every other color, breaking up the shading sequence. Using yellow for the foundation, begin by making the four short stitches at the lowest part of the design on either side of the vertical center of the canvas.

Additional needlepoint stitches
One of the pleasures of needlepoint is that a variety of textures can be achieved by using different stitches, a selection of which are shown here.

Upright or straight cross stitch (fig.23). This has a knobby texture and can be stitched in two colors for a dotted effect.

Crossed corners stitch (fig.24). This is a traditional stitch, also known as rice stitch or William and Mary stitch; it can look very pretty done in two colors — one for the cross and the other for the tying stitches.

Flat or diagonal satin stitch or Scotch stitch (fig.25). This is done diagonally in units of five stitches to create squares.

Continuous or diagonal mosaic stitch (fig.26). This useful stitch creates a pattern of stripes with serrated edges.

Jacquard stitch (fig.27). This stitch produces a diagonal stepped effect. The rows are done alternately over two threads diagonally and over one thread diagonally.

Eyelet or eye stitch (fig.28). This stitch has 16 spokes radiating from a central hole.

Algerian eye or star stitch (fig.29). This is a variation of eyelet stitch but with only eight spokes. Both are worked from the outside to the center.

Leaf stitch (fig.30). If done in several colors, this stitch can be particularly attractive. It requires careful counting: each stitch starts at the edge and goes into the center.

Whipped or ribbed spider stitch (fig.31). This is done over other needlepoint stitches to produce a raised rosette effect. Stitch spokes first to cover six to eight canvas threads each way, then weave the yarn around them from the center outward, without passing the needle through the canvas, until the "spider" is padded out.

Geometric picture
This brilliantly colored geometric picture incorporates 11 different needlepoint stitches and is cleverly shaded for maximum impact. It measures 34 × 36.5cm (13⅜ ×

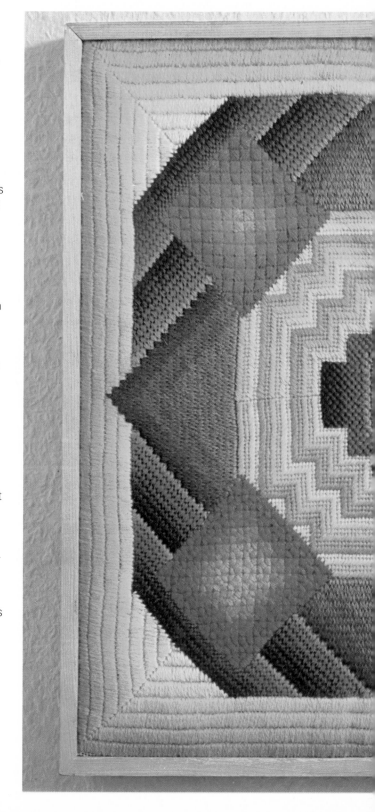

Geometric picture

$14\frac{3}{8}$in) before framing.

You will need:
mono canvas 45cm (18in) square, 14 holes to 2.5cm (1in) □ pink, orange-red, yellow and blue crewel wool in shades ranging from light to dark in the following quantities. Pink: 3 skeins of the lightest shade, 1 skein each of 4 other shades; orange-red: 1 skein each of the 2 lightest shades, 2 skeins each of 3 darker shades; yellow: 2 skeins each of the 2 lightest shades, 3 skeins each of 4 darker shades; blue: 2 skeins each of 7 other shades □ tapestry needle □ tracing paper □ piece of hardboard 34×36.5cm ($13\frac{3}{8} \times 14\frac{3}{8}$in) for the backing.

Preparing to work. One quarter of the design (fig.32) is given as a tracing pattern, so draw up the picture to full size. The center diamond shape given is done in leaf stitch; note that the top left diamond shape of the design is in flat stitch; the bottom left in crossed corners stitch; and the bottom right in eyelet stitch. All these diamonds are worked in orange-red.

When you have drawn the complete picture, go over the lines in a dark color, then place the canvas over the top. The heavy lines will show through and you can trace them onto the canvas with a waterproof felt tip pen. This will give you an approximate outline to work with, although the actual design should be counted out exactly as you work each section. Make sure that you mark the horizontal, vertical and diagonal center lines.

Stitching the design. From the center of the canvas, using the lightest blue shade, count 10 threads along one of the horizontal or vertical center lines. Then make an upright cross stitch on the center line, adding 5 more stitches on either side of this at right angles to the center line. Repeat on the other 3 horizontal or vertical center lines to give a square of 11 stitches each way. Then making the outside of the square, stitch 2 rows of the second shade and 2 more rows of the third shade. Return to the center line on the outer edge of the square. Make 4 stitches on either side of the center line in the first row in the fourth shade. On the second row, make 1 stitch on the center line and 3 stitches on either side of that. Working outwards, repeat the first

and second rows as described for 5 more rows, changing shade every 2 rows until the darkest shade is reached. This first part of the design is very important as it dictates the position of every other stitch in the design. Return to the center square and make the 4 whipped spider stitches over 6 threads in the darkest shade of pink, with tent stitch as the background in the lightest shade of pink.

Finish the inner and outer edges of the upright cross stitch area with half stitches to give a clean edge.

Next work the Jacquard stitch area to follow the outlines of the upright cross stitch shape. The area is divided into quarters by the horizontal and vertical center lines. Stitch the top right-hand quarter first, then the other quarters, changing the stitch direction at the center lines. Do 6 rows, starting with the palest yellow shade and changing to the next shade for each row. Do 6 more rows in the same way.

The 4 diamond shapes are now made in orange-red using flat stitch, eyelet stitch done over 8 threads, crossed corners stitch and leaf stitch. The first 3 are started by counting over 12 threads along the diagonal lines from the edge of the Jacquard stitch; this is the center point of the diamond. Make 4 complete stitches around the center point. Work outwards in complete stitches around the first stitch, changing the shade as you move outwards. The eye stitches are outlined with back stitch. Leaf stitch is started by counting along 12 threads at right angles to the diagonal line at the edge of the Jacquard stitch. This will give you the bottom point of the diamond from which to work upwards with leaf stitch. Continuous mosaic stitch is used to fill in around the leaf patterns. Once these 4 squares are finished, the Jacquard stitch is done over another 4 rows (shades), to complete the center section of the design. Split Gobelin is the next stitch. This is started by counting 38 threads outwards along the center line to find the farthest point of the triangle. Using the darkest shade of pink, make 1 stitch on the center line, move down 1 row and work 2 stitches either side of it. Continue to move the 2 stitches outwards on each row to form a stepped line until the diamond shapes are

Needlepoint

Geometric picture

reached. Then return to the center line and repeat on either side of the center line until all the shades are used, filling in the final space with the lightest shade.

Continuous mosaic is the next stitch to be done. Start on the diagonal lines marked on the canvas. Count out along these lines 4 threads from the diamond shape. Make a stitch over threads 5 and 6 in the darkest shade of blue, then make 27 stitches each way at right-angles to the diagonal lines, finishing with 1 extra tent stitch to give a clean line. Then work back towards the split Gobelin section, changing the shade every row.

Finally edge the whole design with straight Gobelin stitch, done over 4 threads.

With the fourth shade in the yellow range, work from the split Gobelin stitch triangles along the edge of the continuous mosaic stitch until the diagonal lines marked on the canvas are reached. Then turn the corner and continue up to the split Gobelin triangle on the next side.

Blocking the canvas. Block the canvas to stretch it as described previously. Trim the edges of the canvas to 2.5cm (1in). If you do not want to frame the picture simply place it over the hardboard backing and glue the unworked canvas borders to the back.

Framing the picture

The following instructions are for framing the picture as shown in the photograph on the preceding page.

You will need:
Wood for frame: 2 × 16mm ($\frac{5}{8}$in) strips, 3.25 × 35.5cm (1$\frac{1}{4}$ × 14in) □ 2 × 16mm ($\frac{5}{8}$in) strips, 3.25 × 38cm (1$\frac{1}{4}$ × 15in)□ Wood for backing: 2 × 19mm ($\frac{3}{4}$in) strips, 4.5 × 27.5cm (1$\frac{3}{4}$ × 10$\frac{3}{4}$in) □ 2 × 19mm ($\frac{3}{4}$in) strips, 4.5 × 34cm (1$\frac{3}{4}$ × 13$\frac{3}{8}$in) □ hammer and nails □ glue.

Making the frame. Take the 4 strips of wood for backing and position them along the edges of the hardboard backing. Glue them in place. Having blocked the canvas, stretch it over the hardboard and glue the unworked canvas borders to the edges of the wood.

Miter the corners of the frame wood and then nail the pieces over the canvas edges around the picture.

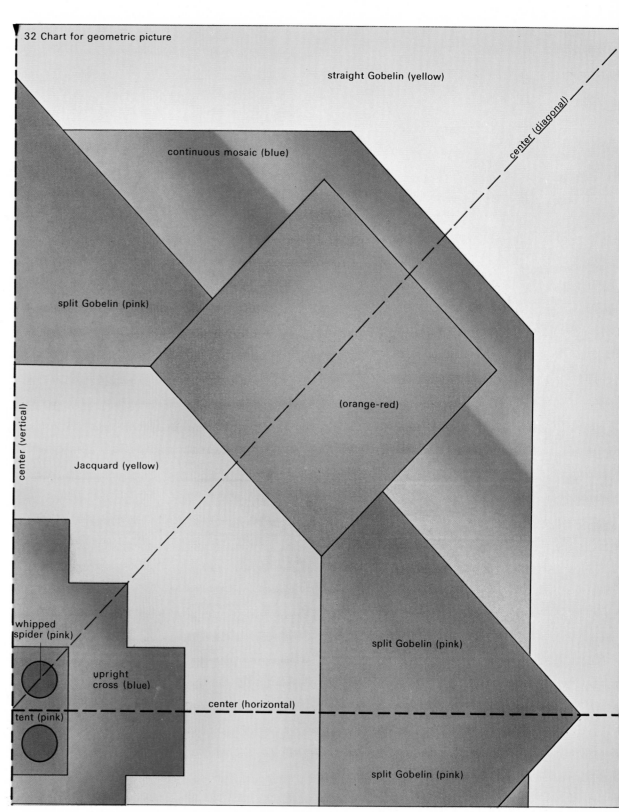

32 Chart for geometric picture

straight Gobelin (yellow)

center (diagonal)

continuous mosaic (blue)

split Gobelin (pink)

(orange-red)

center (vertical)

Jacquard (yellow)

whipped spider (pink)

upright cross (blue)

tent (pink)

center (horizontal)

split Gobelin (pink)

split Gobelin (pink)

A 16th-century wool and silk Persian medallion carpet from Tabriz, Iran. The central gold star medallion, set on an indigo field of scrolling stems and blossoms, represents the sun and at its center are four lotus blossoms in a pool symbolizing the source of rain.

The early history of carpets and rugs is one of the most difficult to document accurately, largely because few examples remain, even in fragment form; floor coverings made from plaited reeds and rushes have certainly been in existence for thousands of years — at least since 5000 BC. Knotted pile carpets originated in Central and Western Asia. The characteristic feature of this type of carpet is the knotting and securing of short strands of material to a foundation weave, so forming the "pile" these pile strands are wound around the foundation warp threads and are then locked in position by the horizontal weft threads.

The oldest known carpet to have been discovered was excavated in 1949 from an open icebound royal tomb in the Altai Mountains of Southern Siberia. This carpet measures approximately 2m (6ft) square and is preserved almost in its entirety. It has a central checkerboard design with an outer border of warriors on horseback and an inner frieze of grazing elk. Probably of Persian origin, the carpet is worked in the Turkish or Ghiordes knot and dates from between the 5th and 3rd century BC. The carpet is now on display at the Hermitage Museum in Leningrad.

The terms carpet and rug are virtually interchangeable nowadays, the latter usually referring to a partial floor covering whereas carpets often stretch from wall to wall and may be tacked down to the floor. Formerly however, carpets often served an aesthetic as well as practical function and were used as royal canopies, blankets, wall hangings and as tent curtains, and they were often offered as gifts to visiting dignitaries. They were also used as saddle covers and storage bags.

Natural vegetable dyes were used for coloring the yarn, and included indigo, madder, turmeric, cassia and saffron; cochineal, made from the kermes insect (*Coccus ilicis*) was used to produce the glowing red often associated with Oriental carpets. Synthetic dyes were not developed until the late 19th century and although they quickly became popular when the mass-production of carpets began, they soon lost their initial brilliance compared with the far more durable and pleasing natural dyes.

A pair of 19th-century pillar rugs. The rug on the right bears a Mongol inscription and the one on the left a Chinese inscription. Traditional cosmological symbols — earth and water (bottom) and clouds (top) — are worked into the main dragon design, and the whole theme forms an uninterrupted pattern when wrapped around the pillar as shown here.

Sheep's wool was generally used, and in some areas camel and goat hair. Some of the more luxurious carpets were made from silk, and the legendary "Spring carpet" of Khosrau is largely woven from silk, studded with emeralds and rare gems and decorated with gold and silver.

There are three main types of carpet motif — geometric, stylized, and illustrative or naturalistic — from which stem an infinite number of variations. It is thought that many of the motifs may have originated from those used in early basket weaving. Symbolism played an important part in the motif designs, many of which represent fertility, life eternal and resurrection. During the Middle Ages, the Persian Medallion carpet, distinguished by the large central medallion connected to pendants, became unrivaled in

Rugmaking

its beauty. One of the finest is now in the Victoria and Albert Museum, London. Woven from wool and silk, it was probably made at Tabriz, Iran, during the mid-16th century. The central gold star medallion represents the sun and is on a rich indigo field filled with an intricate design of stems and blossoms.

The Turkish rugs of this period followed either their own traditional patterns or were influenced by Persian design. Dominated by a rich red ground color, they were very handsome indeed. The Turks produced a plentiful supply of prayer rugs and these were often known as Transylvanian rugs because so many were found in 17th-century Transylvanian churches.

Caucasian rugs have been woven since the earliest times. Again, Persian court rugs often served as models for designs, yet the Caucasians adapted the various familiar motifs into a special style of their own and usually worked a coarse dense weave with bold yet harmonious patterns and colors.

The art of Persian rug weaving traveled to India by way of the Mogul emperors in the 16th and 17th centuries. They commissioned some of the finest silken rugs made with thousands of tiny knots.

Chinese carpets are recognizable from their contoured appearance. Pillar rugs, too, were particular to China: they were designed so that when they were wrapped around a pillar the design along each edge fitted together to form a continuous coiling pattern.

In Europe, the knotted carpet took its cue from the East, although Christian emblems and coats of arms were featured in the motifs and overall designs. However, as the export of Oriental carpets developed — and the demand had a detrimental effect on their quality — European carpet weavers began to imitate the designs of the East and their knotting technique became known as "Turkey work". As carpet production increased in the 18th century and carpets as furnishings became no longer a rich man's prerogative, factories were set up, several of them in England. Two of the most famous — Axminster (Devon) and the Wilton Royal Carpet Factory (Wiltshire) — continued into the 19th century when they merged into one company which still manufactures carpets today.

In France, a soap factory was converted into a carpet factory in the 17th century

Repairing Persian carpets is a skilled art that requires patience and a thorough knowledge of the different rugmaking techniques.

and the "Savonnerie" label was highly sought after. Louis XIV considerably increased productivity with his massive orders for Versailles and the firm, which amalgamated in 1826 with the Gobelin factory is still in production today.

In North America, rugs made by the early settlers were often knitted, crocheted and braided. Colorful hooked rugs developed during the 18th century, and in the late 19th century a factory was established in Milwaukee to weave knotted carpets in the traditional European style. Before the introduction of sheep in the 16th century, Native American Indians had made their flat-woven rugs mainly from cotton and other natural fibers, often with bold abstract patterns incorporating stripes and zigzags.

Scandinavia has used carpet techniques dating from the times of the Vikings. These dotted rugs often had pile on both sides and were known as Rya rugs; the word is an adaptation of the Finnish *ryijy* meaning "shaggy".

The revived interest in rugmaking stems not only from the rise in prices of readymade

A colorful oasis scene is portrayed in this traditional Egyptian woven rug.

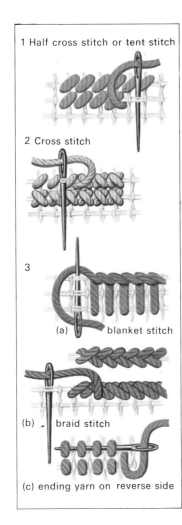

1 Half cross stitch or tent stitch

2 Cross stitch

3

(a) blanket stitch

(b) braid stitch

(c) ending yarn on reverse side

rugs but also from the relaxing nature of the craft which is increasingly recognized and valued.

Rugs can be as inexpensive or expensive as you choose them to be, and the basic techniques are simple enough to learn quickly and easily. As in weaving – and some of the techniques, particularly in the case of rag rugs, are closely allied to weaving – the interest lies in the relationship between the yarns, colors, texture and design of an individual rug; the visual impact can sometimes be so striking that it is no surprise that many handworked rugs end up displayed proudly on a wall rather than underfoot.

Stitched rugs
A stitched rug is made of embroidery stit-

ches that produce a flat surface. You can create different textures by using a variety of stitches. The most commonly used of these are half cross stitch and cross stitch (see figs. 1 and 2).

Materials
Yarn. You will need four- or six-ply rug yarn, or you can use several strands of crewel, Persian or tapestry wool.
Needles. Choose a thick blunt tapestry or rug needle.
Canvas. The canvas should have five holes to each 2.5cm (1 in.).

Technique
When you are designing your own rug, it is a good idea to work it out carefully first on graph paper with the same number of

squares per centimeter (inch) as your canvas has holes. Use felt tip pens to color the graph paper squares to indicate the different wool colors. When you are planning a rug it is always a good idea to try out samples on a small piece of canvas first. Experiment by using new stitches, alone or combined with other stitches. Before you begin to work the main design, turn under approximately 4cm (1½in) for the hem and work one of the edging stitches shown in fig. 3a and b.
To finish neatly, follow fig. 3c.

Floral rug
This beautiful floral rug uses 12 different colors for a subtle effect. If you want to simplify it further you can make the centers of the flower all one color. It would look especially pretty in a bedroom or as.a wall hanging. The finished rug measures 122 × 137cm (48 × 54in).

You will need:
1.75m (1⅞yd) rug canvas, 122cm (48in) wide, with 5 holes per 2.5cm (1in) □ 4-ply rug yarn in the following colors and quantities: rust 425g (15oz); gold 250g (9oz); orange 225g (8oz); yellow 200g (7oz); pink 200g (7oz); mustard 200g (7oz); magenta 175g (6oz); olive green 50g (2oz); sage green 25g (1oz); blue 25g (1oz); pale green 25g (1oz); beige 25g (1oz) □ large tapestry needle.

Making the rug. Begin by turning back approximately 5cm (2in) of canvas at each end and work an edging of braid stitch. Following the design given on the chart (fig.4), work half cross stitch throughout. When the rug is complete, press on the reverse side with a steam iron or under a damp cloth. You can leave the ends plain or you can finish the rug with fringe, using one of the following techniques.

Fringes
Fringe can be bought ready to sew onto finished rugs, and this is especially useful in the case of rag rugs where the edges are often uneven. Making your own fringe, however, is an enjoyable extension of rugmaking and is just as simple. If you are working on a canvas foundation, leave a row of holes at both ends to accommodate the fringe. Use cotton cord, string, or a yarn to

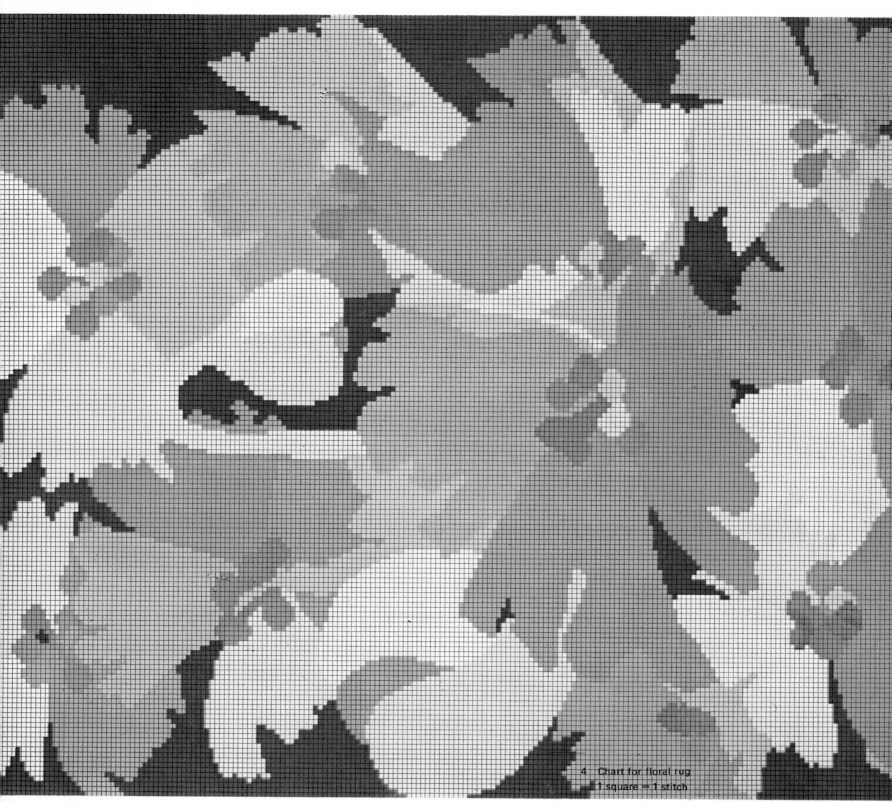

4 Chart for floral rug
1 square = 1 stitch

Backings
Short pile
hooked rugs

match one of the colors in your design. Before you begin, decide on the type of fringe you want: it can be long or short; the knots can be set close together or they can be spaced wide apart. If you want a complicated knotted or braided fringe, you should allow at least double the length of the finished fringe. Begin by making the basic fringe knot shown in fig.5a, using a crochet or latch hook. Fold the strand in half and pull through the canvas holes as shown. Slip the ends through the loop and pull tight to form a knot. Continue along the canvas edge, spacing the knots evenly. When you have completed both edges, trim the fringe evenly. To make the fringe shown in (b), use longer strands of yarn

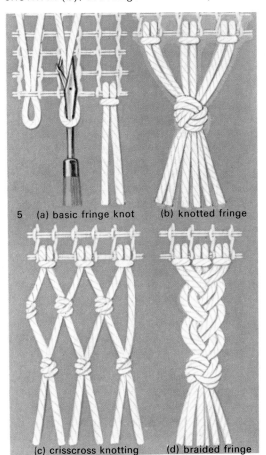

5 (a) basic fringe knot   (b) knotted fringe

(c) crisscross knotting   (d) braided fringe

6   Latch hook

7 Knotting technique

(a)   (b)   (c)   (d)   (e)

and tie a knot halfway down and trim to finish. To work the criss-cross knotted fringe (c), divide each group into two and knot the adjacent halves together. Continue to divide the strands to form a series of criss-crossing groups. To make a braided fringe (d), make three adjacent knots and then braid the lengths together, and secure with a knot and trim to finish.

Backings
Lining a rug is optional, but it does help to lessen wear and gives more body to a finished rug. Use heavy burlap (hessian), denim or canvas. You can also use a latex coated mesh which is applied to the back of a rug to prevent it from sliding around on the floor. As a general rule, pin any backing to the reverse side of the finished work to within approximately 2cm ($\frac{3}{4}$in) of the edge and then sew by hand as neatly and unobtrusively as possible.

Short pile hooked rugs
These rugs are made by hooking short even lengths of yarn onto a rug canvas to create a dense hardwearing pile.

Materials
Yarn. Traditionally wool is used, but there are mixtures of wool and synthetic fibers available. Pre-cut yarn, which eliminates the need to measure and cut yarn, is ideal for making hooked rugs. Rug yarn is also available in hanks or skeins and these are very useful for edging and fringing.
Canvas. This comes in various widths, ranging from approximately 30cm (12in)

to 120cm (48in). The most commonly used canvas has 10 holes to every 7.5cm (3in), but some have as few as four holes to 2.5cm (1in). When you are estimating the amount you will need, remember to allow an extra 15cm (6in) for turnings at both ends.
Equipment. The only tool you need is a latch hook (fig.6). This tool is like a large crochet hook with a hinged latch at the end near the hook that closes when you make a knot.

Technique
For short pile rugs you make one simple knot over and over again in every hole on every row of the canvas. Try to work in one direction only to get an even pile. To practice the knot, gather together the things you need. Lay the canvas onto a table or flat surface with your latch hook to one side with the cut rug yarn. Fold back roughly 5cm (2in) of the canvas with the cut edge on top and the holes corresponding with those underneath.
To make the knot, follow the sequence of diagrams given (fig.7a–e). Double the yarn around the shaft (a), insert the hook under a horizontal canvas thread and push it up through the hole above until the open latchet clears the thread (b). Bring the yarn up, around and under the eye of the hook (c). Pull the hook back through the loop to close the latch (d) and pull the ends of the yarn to tighten the knot (e). This is the basic knot. It is very simple and with a little practice you will be able to do it quickly and automatically.

Geometric rug
Rya rugs

Geometric rug

The pattern for this brightly colored hooked rug is designed in such a way that the squares are interchangeable: you can make it in large or small circles only, or a mixture of the two as illustrated. Its bold and original colors lend themselves well to a modern room setting.

The finished rug measures 90 × 120cm (36 × 48in), with each motif being about 30cm (12in) square. You can, of course, adapt the rug to suit the particular dimensions of your room by making more or fewer of the individual squares.

You will need: 1.15m (1¼yd) rug canvas, 120cm (48in) wide □ ready-cut wool packs with 240 lengths per pack: 5 packs scarlet; 36 packs turquoise; 27 packs purple; 24 packs yellow; 23 packs green □ latch hook □ backing for the finished rug (optional).

Making the rug. The design consists of 2 squares, each in a 2-color variation, and these are worked alternately. Follow the charts (fig.8a and b) where 1 square represents 1 knot. When the rug is complete, turn in the edges and ends, and back it if desired. Alternatively, sew on rugbinding to cover the raw edges.

Rya or shaggy pile rugs

Rya rugs originated in Finland where they were used as coverings on boats, sleds and beds; the long shaggy pile acted as a protection against the bitter cold during the long winter months. Traditional ryas were made by knotting the wool pile onto a warp at intervals, with a woven section in between; the pile was often knotted on both sides to provide extra warmth. Today, a similar effect is achieved by knotting rya rug wool onto ordinary rug canvas. The special look of rya rugs is the way in which the different yarn colors are graded through to varying intensities. To create this impression, use three strands of wool for each knot, mixing different shades together; this, combined with uneven lengths of yarn, gives a unique luminous quality.

Materials

Yarn. Twisted two-ply rya rug wool is generally available in skeins or in pre-cut packs. The skeins cover about 7.5cm (3in)

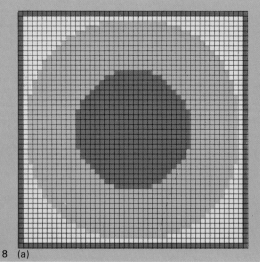
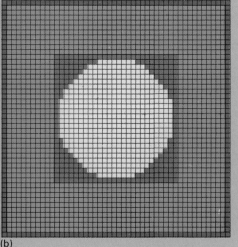

8 (a) (b)

Rya cushion

Technique

The usual way to hook a rya is to work the rows of knots on alternate rows of canvas holes. The knot is made by using the same method as for the short pile rugs. When you start a rya rug, work the first two or three rows over the folded layer of canvas and allow 7.5cm (3in) at each end for turnings. Work the knots to the last hole of the selvage. You can finish the edges as previously described or leave them plain as the long pile will cover them.

Rya cushion

Here is a rich and colorful floor cushion which when finished measures 61cm (24in) square.

You will need:
71cm (28in) rya rug canvas 61cm (24in) wide, with 10 holes per 7.5cm (3in) □ latch hook □ pre-cut packs of rya wool (each containing approximately 168 strands) in the following colors and quantities: 6 packs red; 5 packs scarlet; 11 packs plum; 18 packs purple; 18 packs blue; 1 pack pink; 2 packs magenta □ burlap (hessian) or similar strong fabric for backing 64cm (25in) square □ cushion pad to finished size.

Making the cushion. Follow the chart (fig.9) and accompanying color key. All the knots should have their ends hanging downwards and you must work from one

9 Key to Rya chart showing no. of strands per knot

= purple 3 strands
= blue 3 strands
= purple 1 strand + plum 2 strands
= plum 1 strand + red 2 strands
= plum 1 strand + blue 2 strands
= magenta 1 strand + purple 2 strands
= scarlet 3 strands
= scarlet 1 strand + pink 2 strands

of canvas. If you cut your own lengths, do not worry too much about keeping them even as a rough appearance adds to the effect.
Canvas. This usually has 10 holes to every 7.5cm (3in).
Equipment. You will need a latch hook as for short pile rugs.

Hooked rag rugs
Braided rag rugs

end in one direction only. To start the cushion, turn back 5cm (2in) of one cut end of the canvas. Begin working the basic knot, hooking through the double thickness with the folded edge on top. When you have reached the last 10cm (4in) of the canvas, turn back the last 5cm (2in), with the folded edge on top again, and work the last row through the double layer.

Finishing the cushion. Turn in the edges of the backing material and lay the cushion face downwards onto it. Push the shaggy ends underneath and pin the knotted canvas to the fabric. Leave the selvage open to insert the cushion pad. Stitch the backing to the canvas securely and then turn to the right side. Fold in the selvage, insert the cushion pad and stitch up the opening to close.

Note: do not brush the rya tufts when your cushion needs cleaning; simply shake it vigorously out of doors.

Hooked rag rugs

For many years rag rugs have been a good way of making use of odd scraps of fabric. They are very hardwearing and can be very attractive if a color scheme is followed.

Materials
Fabrics. Any fabrics can be used, but preferably they should be non-fraying.
Canvas. Any rug canvas is suitable, but one with 10 holes per 7.5cm (3in) is easiest to work with.
Equipment. Latch hook.

Technique

Cut strips of cloth roughly 10cm (4in) long and 2cm ($\frac{3}{4}$in) wide. Knot these strips onto the canvas with the latch hook, using the same method as for the previous hooked rugs. Hook every other row as it will be too tightly packed if you knot each row. Plan your rug so that it contains one or two main colors and then use up odd scraps to fill in the design.
Finish off your rug by stitching the ends down to make them neat.

Braided rag rugs

Braided rag rugs are another inexpensive and traditional way of covering floors, and they have the additional advantage of

needing no canvas or other foundation to work on. They are also an excellent way of clearing out a rag bag full of fabric lengths and remnants left over from other craft projects.

Materials. All you need are old or new pieces of fabric, a piece of string, a safety pin and a sewing needle and heavy duty thread.

Technique

Cut the fabrics into long strips. The made-up braids should be of a similar weight, so cut wide strips of thin fabrics and thin strips of thick ones.

To begin, fasten three strips of fabric to the piece of string with a safety pin (see fig.10). Tie the string to the back of a chair or any other stable piece of furniture and begin to braid, keeping the lengths taut as you do so. When you have finished the first braid — and it is best not to have them too long as they tend to become unmanageable — sew or knot on three new lengths and continue; the knots can be concealed when you finally make the rug. Continue in this way until you have a long length of braiding. To see what your eventual rug is going to look like, you can begin to sew it

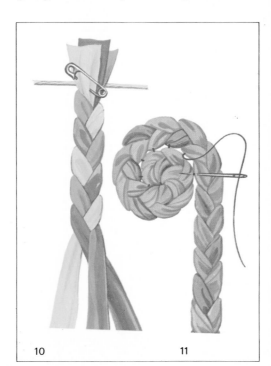

10   11

Crocheted rag rugs

up as you go along. Start by threading a needle with heavy duty thread. Sew the end of the braid into itself and start to make a coil as shown in fig.11. Continue until the braid is used up. You can make several circles and then sew them together, or you can make one large circular rug.

To finish, stitch down all the ends hanging out with heavy duty thread, then sew on a ready made fringe or leave plain.

To make the rug even more substantial, back it with a hardwearing washable backing fabric, such as unbleached muslin (calico) or canvas. When you stitch on the backing, take it to within 1.5cm ($\frac{1}{2}$in) of the edge of the finished rug.

Braided rugs may have a bump in the middle when they are finished. To remove this, press with a damp cloth and a hot iron.

Crocheted rag rugs

Rag strips can be crocheted into runners or circular rugs. The result is a very hardwearing and practical floor covering that can be washed and used for years.

Materials

Fabrics. Any leftover fabrics will do — jersey is particularly suitable as it slips easily through a crochet hook. Tear or cut approximately 2cm ($\frac{3}{4}$in) wide strips along the grain. Knot the lengths together and wind into balls.

Equipment. You will need a large crochet hook.

Technique

Decide whether you want a circular rug or a traditional striped runner. Use a dyed old sheet or curtain fabric to provide a regular color in between the bands of different rag colors.

Abbreviations used: ch, chain; sc, single crochet (dc, double crochet).

To begin, make 85 chains (or more or less depending on the size of rug you wish to make).

1st row. 1 dc in 2nd ch from hook. 1 dc in each ch to end.

2nd row. 1 ch dc in each dc to end.

Repeat the 2nd row throughout.

Finish the ends of the rug with a short string or yarn fringe.

Spinning

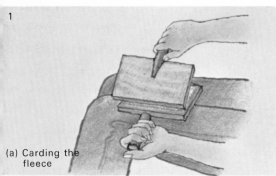

(a) Carding the fleece

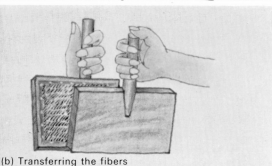

(b) Transferring the fibers

Spinning raw wool is still a popular skill, in spite of the wide availability of commercial yarns. The many different breeds of sheep provide the spinner with a whole range of fleeces that can vary enormously in color and texture.

Carding

Whether you are going to spin with a spindle or a spinning wheel you will need to card the wool first. Take two or three locks of fleece and gently pull them apart; this process is known as "teasing." Discard any soiled or matted wool, and lay the locks of fleece on the left-hand carder. Rest the back of your left hand on your knee and hold the carder, teeth upwards, with the handle pointing away from you. Draw the right-hand carder, teeth downwards, over the left-hand carder lightly but firmly three times (fig.1a). Take care not to let the fringe of fibers at the edge of the carder fold back over the teeth or the fleece will become matted. After three movements of the right-hand carder, the fleece will become transferred to it from the left-hand carder. To transfer it back, hold both carders with handles upwards, bring the base of the right-hand carder to the top of the left one, and push downwards (fig.1b).

Continue carding and transferring until the fibers lie parallel on the carder without folds or bumps.
To free the fleece from the carder, use the transfer movement, but with a sharp movement to gather the wool together at the bottom of one carder. Place the carded fleece on the back of the carder and then roll it lightly with the hands to make it smooth. This roll of fibers is called a "rolag."

Spinning with a spindle

Take a piece of spun yarn about one meter (one yard) long. Wind it around the spindle as shown in fig.2a. Draw out a wisp of fibers 12.5cm (5in) long from the end of a rolag, and overlap them with the end of the yarn. Hold the beginning of the rolag and the end of the yarn between the thumb and first finger of your left hand, with the rolag falling over the back of your hand (b). Twist the spindle sharply to the right with your right hand.
When the 12.5cm (5in) overlap is united by twisting the spindle as described, hold the wool at the top of the newly made yarn with your right hand, and draw more fibers out of the rolag with your left. The twist will then run into these fibers, so making new thread.

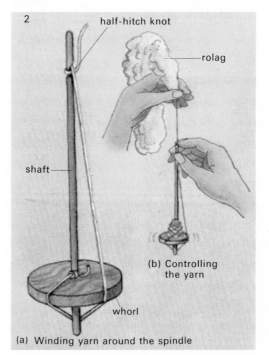

(a) Winding yarn around the spindle

(b) Controlling the yarn

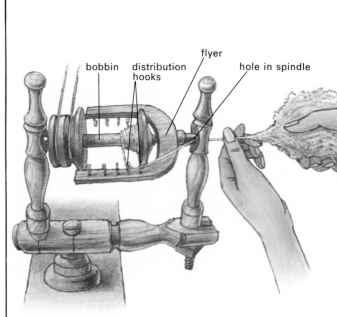

3 A spinning wheel in use, new fibers being drawn out from the rol

When the spindle reaches the ground, untie the half-hitch knot and wind up the new thread on the spindle above the whorl before continuing.
Note: always keep the spindle turning clockwise and do not let the twist run into the rolag.

Spinning with a spinning wheel

The art of this type of spinning is to keep the wheel turning at a regular speed. Begin by practicing treadling. Start the wheel clockwise with your hand and treadle as smoothly and slowly as possible without reversing or stopping. When you can do this smoothly, thread in a length of spun yarn as shown in fig.3. Take a rolag in your left hand, drawing out a wisp 12.5cm (5in) long, and overlap it with the end of the yarn. As the wheel revolves it will twist the two together. Continue treadling, controlling the spin with one hand, and drawing out new fibers from the rolag with the other (fig.3). Aim to pull out the fibers from the rolag evenly, so that the yarn has a smooth appearance.
To start a new rolag, lay a wisp from it over the last wisp of the previous rolag. At the same time transfer the thread onto the next distribution hook on the flyer.

Weaving

Weaving is one of the most ancient and fundamental crafts, which developed independently in many different parts of the world. About 3000 BC the Chinese discovered—and kept closely guarded—the secrets of breeding silkworms. By the beginning of the Christian era, raw silk was being exported to Rome. It was fabulously expensive, literally worth its weight in gold. In the 6th century the Emperor Justinian set up a silk monopoly within the confines of his palace in Constantinople. He wanted to destroy the Persian trade in silk, which he did not succeed in doing, but he did manage to persuade two Persian monks

Left: The ladies in this 15th century royal manuscript are involved in the stages of preparing cloth; spinning, carding and weaving.

Below: A modern wall hanging woven from different textured yarns, and strung with beads to create a fascinatingly varied effect.

Below left: Detail of a cock from a silk twill hanging, dating from 6th century Persia.

who had lived in China to return there and smuggle out some silkworms inside hollow bamboo canes. The few silkworms they brought back were the beginning of all the varieties stocked in Europe until the 19th century.

Silk weaving flourished in Europe from the 6th century, being established in France and elsewhere by the Romans. France rapidly became known for her fine tapestries and embroideries. In 1480 King Louis XI introduced the manufacture of silk at Tours in France, importing weavers from Italy. Lyons was also established as a weaving center, and became known for its production of the finest silk fabrics in Europe. During the 17th-century Wars of Religion in France many silk weavers and tapestry makers fled the country, mainly to Flanders and England. Both these countries already had a wide reputation for their beautiful cloth.

In the East End of London the area known as Spitalfields became the chief center for woven silk damasks and brocades. At the

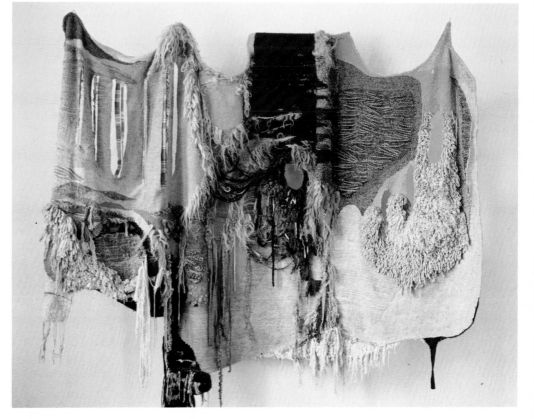

height of the boom in silk production in the late 18th century, 50,000 people were employed. They worked on looms operated in their own homes from materials supplied by a master weaver. But in England, as elsewhere later on, outworkers lost their jobs in thousands as industrial machinery and mass-production techniques were introduced.

Weaving is the interlacing of threads at right angles to form a fabric. Fabric is composed of threads running down the cloth which are called warp ends or threads, and horizontal threads, known as woof or weft threads. One row of weft is called a pick. To interlace these threads, the warp ends are put on a loom in such a way as to hold them at tension. Openings are formed between two layers of warp ends, through which the weft thread can be passed. This opening is known as a shed.

Looms

The most important piece of equipment

you will need is a loom. These vary from very simple models, which can easily be made at home, to the large floor looms used by professional craftsmen.

Frame looms (fig.1). These consist simply of a rectangular frame and you can improvise a good frame loom from a plain picture frame. As the warp ends have to be under high tension, the frame must be quite strong, particularly if you are thinking of weaving a rug or a heavy tapestry. Frame looms are slow to manipulate, but can produce complicated fabrics.

Table looms (fig.2). Table looms are operated by the use of shafts, which are frames holding the warp ends. These are threaded through wire eyes on the shafts, and the shafts worked from levers at the side of the loom. By pressing on a lever a shaft is lifted, thus raising the warp ends threaded on that shaft and forming the shed. Table looms are available in various widths, having between 2–16 shafts.

Floor looms. These are the fastest of all to

use. The shed is formed by pressing foot controlled treadles, leaving the hands free to manipulate the weft. The number of shafts varies from 2–16, though some floor looms have 24 shafts. However, as floor looms are expensive and take up a lot of space, they are not recommended for beginners.

Equipment for looms

Shed stick. This is a smooth flat piece of wood used with a frame loom (see fig.1). When turned on its side in the warp it makes a shed by raising a set of alternate warp ends. To make a shed stick take a piece of wood 2.5 × 0.5cm (1 × $\frac{1}{4}$in) and the same length as the width of the frame loom, and drill a hole 3mm ($\frac{1}{8}$in) in diameter, 2.5cm (1in) from each end.

Beater (fig.3). This is a heavy metal fork, used with frame looms. After each weft pick, use a beater to make sure the weft threads are tightly packed together. This is called beating down the weft threads.

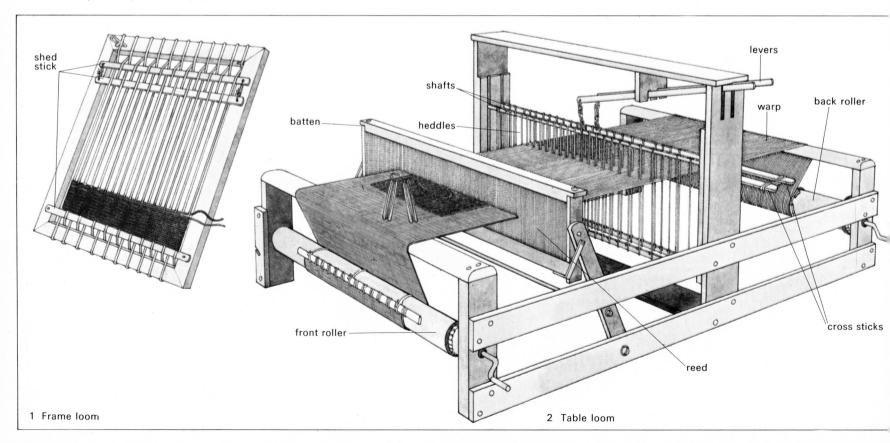

1 Frame loom

2 Table loom

Raddle (fig.4). A raddle looks like a large comb with a removable top. It is used with a table loom for transferring the warp onto the back roller or warp beam. The teeth of the raddle are at regular intervals and the threads are spread in groups between the teeth to equal the number of ends per cm (in). Raddles can be bought from craft stores or can be made at home. Take a piece of wood 2.5 × 4cm (1 × 1$\frac{1}{2}$in) and the same length as the width of the loom, and another piece measuring 4 × 2.5 × 2.5cm (1$\frac{1}{2}$ × 1 × 1in). Nail them together as shown. Hammer in some flat-headed 3cm (1$\frac{1}{4}$in) nails, at 0.5cm ($\frac{1}{4}$in) intervals. Use a long piece of string as a cap. This will be wound around the nails after the warp has been put on the back roller.

Reed. The reed is a metal structure used with all looms (see fig.2). It consists of a series of wires strung between two slats of wood, and is the width of the loom. It has spaces equal to the number of warp threads per cm (in). These spaces are called dents. A reed size 8 therefore has 8 dents per 2.5cm (1in), size 10 has 10 dents per 2.5cm (1in) and so on. The reed is used to beat down the weft.

Threading hook and fish hook (fig.5a and b). The threads are passed through the reed with the aid of a threading hook or fish hook. A threading hook has a notch at one end to pull the threads through the dents, and is used with fairly coarse yarns. Fish hooks are used with finer yarns.

Shuttles

These carry the weft threads across the warp.

Stick shuttle (fig.6). This is the simplest kind of shuttle, and is usually used with a frame loom. It can be handmade out of wood or very heavy cardboard. Take a piece of wood or cardboard measuring 2.5 × 0.5cm (1 × $\frac{1}{4}$in) and slightly longer than the width of the loom. Cut slots at each end 2.5cm (1in) deep and 0.5cm ($\frac{1}{4}$in) wide as shown in fig.6.

Boat shuttle (fig.7). This is made of wood and used on table and floor looms. Some boat shuttles have rollers on the bottom to carry them through the shed faster. In the center is a metal pin which holds the bobbin. This is removed, the yarn wound around it and then replaced. The end of the yarn is threaded through a hole in the side of the shuttle.

The butterfly (fig.8a and b). Instead of using a shuttle you can wind the yarn around your thumb and little finger in a figure eight (a), and then make a bundle (b). This is very flexible and easy to use. Butterflies can always be used on frame looms. They are also used with table and other looms where a pattern is made using several colors.

Yarns. Almost any kind of yarn can be used, from natural fibers such as cotton, linen, wool and silk, to synthetic fibers and even package twine. The yarn used for the warp should be strong, as it is under high tension. Special warp yarns can be obtained.

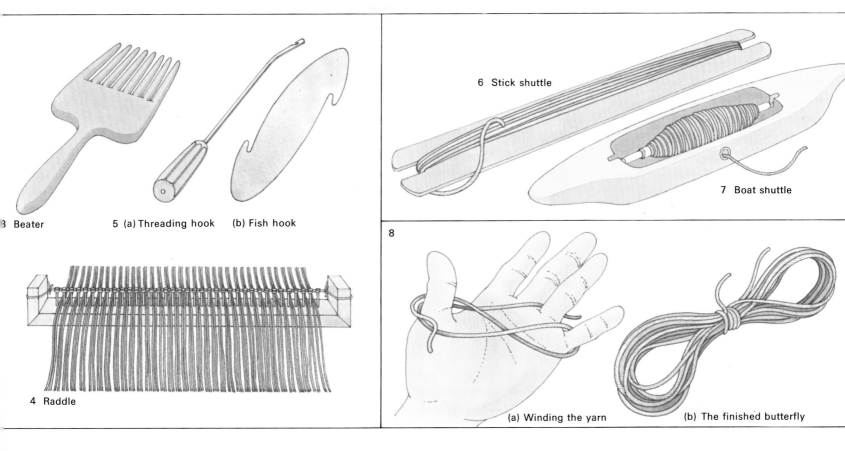

3 Beater   5 (a) Threading hook   (b) Fish hook

6 Stick shuttle

7 Boat shuttle

4 Raddle

8

(a) Winding the yarn   (b) The finished butterfly

Weaving

Warping Patterns

Before weaving, you must calculate the number of warp threads needed and their arrangement on the loom in equal lengths of the same tension. Getting the threads in the right arrangement is known as warping. The density of a fabric is determined by the number of warp ends per cm (in). This is called the "sett" of the cloth. The number of ends in the warp can be easily calculated by using the following formula: for imperial measurements, multiply the number of warp ends per inch × width of cloth = total number of ends in warp. For metric calculations, multiply the number of warp ends per 2.5cm × width of cloth, then divide by 2.5.

There are several methods of warping.

Direct warping (fig.9a and b). On a frame loom you can warp directly onto the frame. Knot the yarn firmly to one end of the frame and wind the yarn around the frame in a continuous figure eight (a). At the center of the frame the warp threads will cross each other in alternate sequence. This cross (b) is an essential feature of all warping. It is formed in different ways for different looms, but is always necessary. It keeps the threads in the correct sequence and prevents them from becoming twisted.

Warping with a board. Boards can be made quite easily. Take a flat piece of 25mm (1in) wood measuring 51 × 102cm (20 × 40in). Drill six holes in it as shown in fig.10, each big enough to take a piece of dowel 18cm (7in) long and 2.5cm (1in) in diameter.

Using the board. Make a loop in the yarn 5–7.5cm (2–3in) long and place this over peg A. Pass the yarn around the pegs as shown in fig.10, forming the cross between pegs B and C. Repeat this until the required number of ends in the warp is complete. A board this size will give a warp about 2.25m (2½yd) long.

To keep count of the warp ends tie a colored string around every 10 or 20 ends. When you have completed the warp, tie strong loops of string around the cross at B and C, and at the two end pegs A and F (fig.11). When winding a very long warp tie ends of string at intervals along it to keep it neat. Then transfer the warp onto the loom. Take it off from peg A first, and wind it around your hand leaving about

30.5cm (12in) free at the other end.

Warping with a tree (mill). A warping tree (mill) is an upright box frame which spins on a central pivot. The pegs can be moved to change the length of the warp and the position of the cross. They are powered by hand or by motor, and are essential for making very long warps.

Patterns

Patterns are formed in weaving by varying the interlacing of warp and weft threads. Paper patterns are called drafts and are marked on graph paper. The squares represent the appearance of the cloth right side up. When a square of the paper is blocked in, the weft goes under the warp. If the square is blank the weft goes over the warp. There are three basic weaving patterns.

Plain weave (fig.12). This is also called "tabby" and is identical to darning, being an over one, under one interlacing of threads. The pattern thus repeats over two warp ends. A variation of plain weave is tapestry weave. In this there are more weft picks than warp ends per cm (in). The weft slides down over the warp and completely covers it. Tapestry weave may be done as two over, two under up to four or five over and under.

Twill weave (fig.13). This forms a simple diagonal effect, repeating over four warp ends. The diagonal twill line can run either to the left or to the right.

Satin weave (fig.14a and b). This has a very smooth surface; either the warp or the weft is hidden. Satin is most successfully worked over eight ends, though it can repeat over five. Warp satin (a) has a raised effect as most of the warp comes to the surface of the cloth and is held in place by the occasional weft thread. Weft satin (b) reverses the process and most of the weft is held on the surface by the occasional warp end.

Beginning and ending weaving

To adjust the tension of your weaving, always weave about 5cm (2in) of waste yarn before beginning the pattern. This will give a good straight edge from which to begin the pattern. When you have finished weaving, weave approximately the same amount of waste yarn before cutting the weaving off the loom.

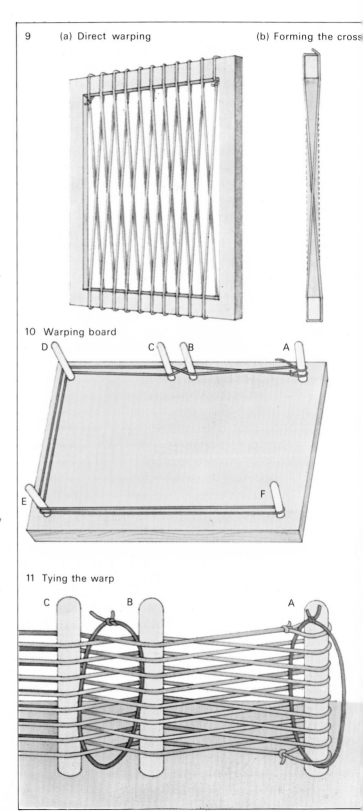

9 (a) Direct warping   (b) Forming the cross

10 Warping board

11 Tying the warp

A country style purse

12 Plain weave

13 Twill weave

14 (a) Eight end warp satin

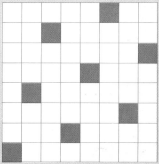

(b) Eight end weft satin

A country style purse

Woven in subtle oatmeal colors with bright contrasting stripes, this purse makes an ideal first project. The fabric measures 42 × 25cm (16½ × 10in) and is then folded in three to make the purse. It is made on a frame loom and incorporates plain weave and tapestry weave.

You will need:

1 frame loom at least 38 × 56cm (15 × 22in) ☐ 1 beater ☐ 3 shed sticks at least 38cm (15in) long ☐ 1 stick shuttle or butterfly ☐ 50 lengths of strong thread, each 20cm (8in) long for leashes ☐ piece of cardboard 42 × 25cm (16½ × 10in) for pattern ☐ piece of lining fabric approximately 28 × 44.5cm (11 × 17½in) ☐ 1 button 2cm (¾in) in diameter ☐ 350g (12oz) 4-ply white rug wool or very strong knitting yarn for warp ☐ 125g (4oz) each of 2-ply knitting yarn in the following colors: black, brown, yellow and white ☐ scraps of: 2-ply knitting yarn in 4 shades of green; 4 shades of pink; gold thread yarn; white bouclé knitting yarn; 4-ply purple knitting yarn.

Weaving

A country style purse

Warping (fig.15a–g). The sett of the cloth is 10 warp ends to 2.5cm (1in). The width is 25cm (10in). Total number of warp ends is therefore $10 \times 10 = 100$. Mark 25cm (10in) in centimeters (inches) in the center of the frame, top and bottom, so that the two sets of marks are precisely opposite each other (a). Knot one end of the yarn to the frame. Wind the warp yarn around the frame in a continuous figure eight, so that the warp threads cross each other in the center of the frame. Wind the yarn around the frame 100 times, keeping the threads at an even tension. Knot the last end to the frame.

Insert a shed stick into the lower part of the cross and push to the top of the frame (b). Make sure the warp threads are evenly spaced along the top of the frame, between the marks, 10 warp ends per 2.5cm (1in). Remove the stick, and insert it in the top half of the cross. Pull the cross down to the bottom of the frame, and space the warp ends evenly along the 25cm (10in), as at the top. Secure the stick to the base of the frame with 2 strings (c). There will now be no cross in the warp threads, so one must be made.

Insert 2 shed sticks about 12.5cm (5in) above the tied stick. Pass one stick over and under alternate warp ends. Pass the other stick over and under the opposite ends (d). When sticks are used to hold cross threads in place they are called cross rods or sticks. Hold them in place by tying them together at the ends with string (e). Push them both to the top of the frame. Tie threads to the warp ends that go over the bottom cross stick (f). These threads are called leashes, and will lift every other warp end to make the second shed. When all 50 warp threads have been tied, tie the leashes in groups of 5. When all the leashes have been tied, remove the lower cross stick. Tie the leashes in their bunches onto the spare stick (g).

Forming the sheds for weaving (fig.16a and b). For the first shed, pull the string leashes (a). For the second shed, turn the top cross stick on its side (b).

Making the pattern. Make a full-size chart on cardboard, marking the proportions of weft color threads as in fig.17. Hold the chart against the cloth as you weave to

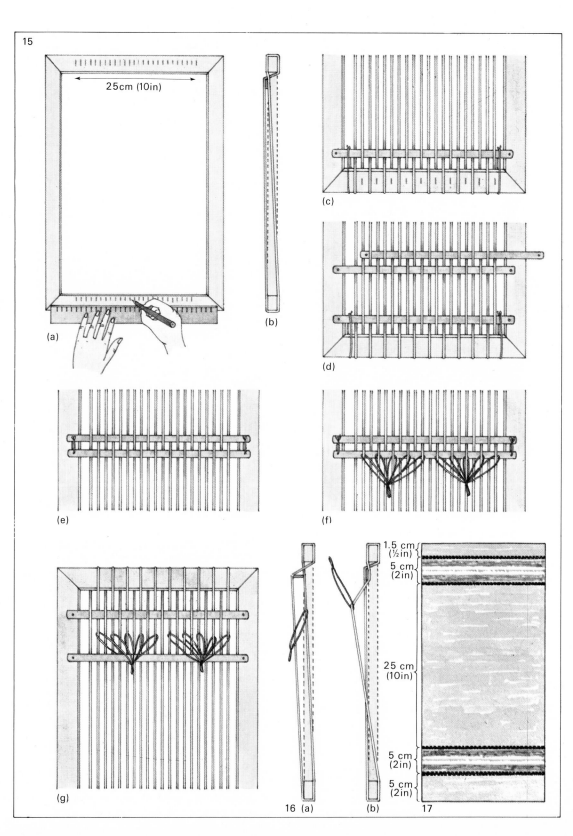

keep the colors and number of rows correct.

The stripe is woven in tapestry weave. As the cross stick and leashes are set for plain weave, they cannot be used. Instead, manipulate the weft by hand, over two warp ends and under two. The next row alternates this.

Weaving the fabric
Weave: 5cm (2in) plain weave, using black, brown, yellow and white yarn as 1 yarn.

Weave: 4 picks of tapestry weave in purple yarn, beating down firmly after each pick with the beater.

Weave: 4 picks of tapestry weave using 4 shades of pink yarn as 1 yarn.

Weave: 4 picks of tapestry weave using 4 shades of green yarn as 1 yarn.

Weave: 4 picks of plain weave with the white bouclé yarn.

Weave: 4 picks of tapestry weave with gold thread.

Then reverse this process, working 4 picks of white bouclé, 4 picks of green tapestry weave etc, until the stripe is complete.

Weave: 25cm (10in) plain weave, using

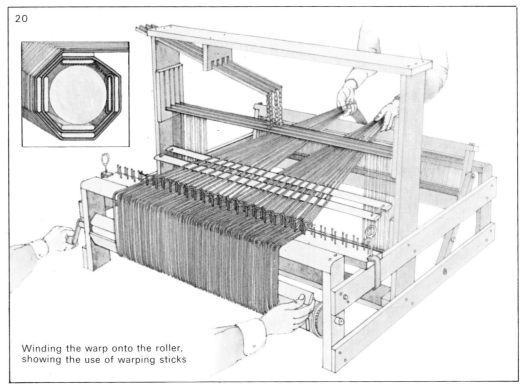

20

Winding the warp onto the roller, showing the use of warping sticks

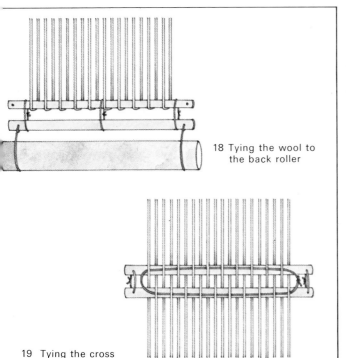

18 Tying the wool to the back roller

19 Tying the cross

black, brown, yellow and white yarn as 1 yarn.

Weave: Colored stripe as before in tapestry weave.

Weave: 2.5cm (1in) plain weave using black, brown, yellow and white yarn as 1 yarn.

Making the purse. Cut the weaving off the frame. Press the material with a steam iron, or over a damp cloth. Lay it face up on a table in front of you. Fold the bottom edge up and over, then fold the top edge until the stripe on the top corresponds with the stripe on the bottom. Sew the edges of the bottom half together on the wrong side. Line with lining fabric. Turn the purse right side out. Braid several strands of purple wool together and sew them in the middle of the flap to make a loop. Sew on the button.

Using a table loom
Table looms speed up the process of weaving, but require some preparation for transferring the ready wound warp onto the back roller of the loom. The process is known as "dressing the loom."

Dressing the loom. The warp is threaded onto the roller with a raddle. Place the warp at the front of the loom. Put a shed stick through the end loop of the warp (where it was on the warping board at F), pull it through the center of the shafts and tie it to the roller on the back of the loom (fig.18). Place the raddle across the loom in front of the back roller and pull the warp over the raddle until you reach the cross. Place a shed stick in each of the two crosses and tie them together with string (fig.19). Find the center of the raddle. Place half the warp threads on one side of this center point, the rest the other side. Take the threads in the same order as they are in the cross and place them between the teeth of the raddle. For example, if you have 32 threads per 10cm (8 threads per in), and four nails per cm (in) you must place two warp ends in each space to give 32 ends per 10cm (8 ends per in).

When the warp has been spaced, check that it has been spread to the correct width. Place the cap onto the raddle. The warp is now ready to be wound onto the back roller of the loom.

Weaving

Using a table loom

Winding the warp onto the roller (fig.20). With a table loom it is easier for two people to wind the warp on, one to turn the roller and hold the loom steady, the other to hold the warp under tension and check that the ends pass through the raddle easily. As you roll on, the tension must be even across the width of the warp. Wind the warp in small sections, making sure there are no slack ends and that there are no snags in the yarn going through the raddle.

Place sticks as shown between the layers of warp as you wind it onto the roller. (Strong paper can be used instead of sticks.) This makes a smooth base for the thread and helps keep the tension even. Wind the warp on until there is just enough thread to reach the front beam. Then unwind the cap of the raddle, take off the threads and remove the raddle. Cut the end loop of the warp where it was at A, so that you can pull through individual ends for threading.

Planning the threading order. This is called

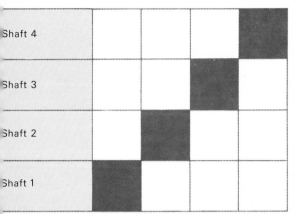

Shaft 4				
Shaft 3				
Shaft 2				
Shaft 1				

21 Drafting the threading order

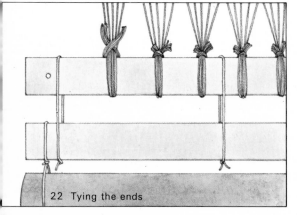

22 Tying the ends

drafting, and entails making a pattern for threading the warp ends through the heddles on the shaft. Heddles are lengths of metal with a central eye through which the warp ends are passed. They are attached to the shafts, and raised or lowered to form different sheds. For instance, for plain weave on four shafts, the first thread will be passed through a heddle on shaft 1 the second through a heddle on shaft 2. The third thread will go through a heddle on shaft 3 and so on. (fig.21).

Denting the reed. After threading the heddles, dent the reed as follows.

Find the center of the reed, pick up the central thread and enter it through the reed. Working from left to right, pull one warp thread at a time through each dent. It is very important to take the warp threads in the same sequence as the order on the shafts. Thread the yarn through the reed with a threading hook or fish hook. When all the ends have been dented, tie the warp onto the roller on the front of the loom.

Tying the ends. Straighten a group of warp ends by running your fingers through the threads, making sure there are no slack ends at the back of the loom. Tie the ends over the stick attached to the roller as shown in fig.22.

Woven cushion cover

When all the ends have been tied to the stick, make sure the tension is even over the width of the cloth. Do not remove the cross sticks. Check the threading and denting for mistakes, by lifting the shafts required for the weave.

Rolling on the warp. When you want to roll the warp on, release the ratchet on the back roller, wind on with the front, then let the ratchet go to secure the back roller again.

Woven cushion cover

This cushion cover measures 38 × 55cm (15 × 22in) and is woven on a table loom in six vivid colors in an interlocking series of triangles, diamonds and irregular shapes.

You will need:

1 table loom 60cm (24in) wide with 2 or more shafts □ 1 raddle □ 1 warping board □ 3 shed sticks □ 1 reed size 8 □ 1 threading hook or fish hook □ strong sewing thread □ sticks or strong paper for winding the warp onto the back roller □ piece of cardboard 38 × 55cm (15 × 22in) for pattern □ 2kg (4lb) each of 8/4 cotton carpet warp □ 125g (4oz) each of 4-ply knitting yarn in each of the following colors: purple, mulberry and red □ 100g (3oz) 4-ply knitting yarn in both orange and yellow

□ 25g (1oz) 4-ply white knitting yarn □ piece of backing fabric 46 × 61cm (18 × 24in) □ 38cm (15in) zipper.

Warping. The sett of the cloth is 8 ends to 2.5cm (1in). The width of the cloth is 38cm (15in). Total number of warp ends is 8 × 15 = 120. The length of the warp is 113cm (44½in).

Wind on the warp as previously described, until there are 120 threads on the board. Then dress the loom, spacing the ends through the raddle with 2 ends in each dent, 8 per 2.5cm (1in).

Drafting the warp. The total number of warp ends = 120. Number of shafts = 4. Therefore 120 ÷ 4 = 30 heddles on each shaft. Take the 30 centrally situated heddles on each shaft and push them to the center. Separate the 1st warp end as it appears in the cross and pull it through a heddle on shaft 1. Pull the 2nd end through the 2nd heddle on shaft 1. The 3rd end goes through a heddle on shaft 2, the 4th end through a separate heddle on shaft 2. Pull the next 2 warp ends through separate heddles on shaft 3, the following 2 through heddles on shaft 4. Then begin again on shaft 1 and repeat until all the warp ends are threaded (fig.23).

Sleying (denting) the reed. Find the center of the reed. Measure 19cm (7½in) to the left of the center and begin threading the warp threads one at a time through each dent. Work from left to right as previously described.

Checking the threading. Tie the ends onto the roller. Check the threading and denting for mistakes by lifting the shafts required for the weave. The levers on the left are the odd numbers, the levers on the right, the even. Check the shed by pressing both levers on the left for the first shed, then both levers on the right for the second. In each shed there should be 2 warp threads up and 2 down across the width of the cloth.

Drawing the design. Draw the design onto cardboard from the graph (fig.24) in which 1 square = 2.5cm (1in). Wind butterflies of the 6 colors. Press the levers on the left for the first shed and insert the wool in the shed, bringing each color out in front at the end of each stripe (fig.25). Release the levers on the right for the 2nd shed. Make the points by moving each pick across 2 warp threads. Carry on pressing first the left levers then the right. Continue to the end of the pattern and weave 5cm (2in) of waste

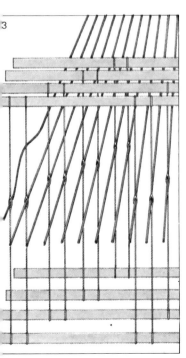

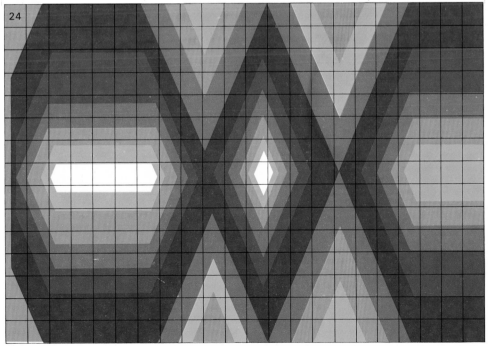

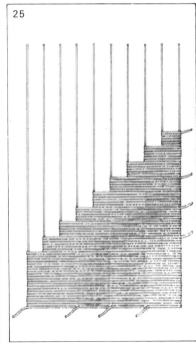

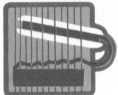

Weaving

Sampler scarf

yarn before cutting off the weaving. The vertical stripes of color will not be interlocked until the point begins to shape. Sew these up with strong thread before making the cushion cover. Sew the tapestry weaving to the backing fabric and insert a zipper at one end.

Sampler scarf
Squares of 32 differing patterns go to make up this attractive man's scarf. It is woven in 3-ply wool on a 4 shaft table loom, and will give you the opportunity to practice a wide range of effects.

You will need:
1 table loom 60cm (24in) wide with 4 shafts □ 1 raddle □ 1 warping board □ 3 shed sticks □ warping sticks or strong paper □ 1 reed size 8 □ 1 threading hook or fish hook □ 125g (4oz) strong 3-ply white yarn for the warp □ 50g (1oz) each of 3-ply wool in the following colors: maroon, dark brown, camel and blue.
Warping. The warp is 178cm (70in) long,

with 16 ends to 2.5cm (1in) and 27.5cm (11in) wide. The warp is made up of the following order of ends: 40 white, 4 blue, 40 white, 4 blue, 40 white, 4 blue, 44 white.
Wind the warp onto the back roller of the loom as previously described. Thread the warp through the heddles on the shafts from left to right in the following order:
Shafts: 1, 2, 3, 4, 3, 2. Do this 7 times, threading 42 ends.
Shafts: 1, 2, 3, 4. Do this 11 times, threading 44 ends.
Shafts: 1, 4, 3, 2, 1, 2, 3, 4. Do this 5 times, threading 40 ends.
Shafts: 2, 1, 2, 3, 2, 3, 4, 1, 2, 3, 2, 1, 4, 3, 2, 3, 2, 1, 2, 1, 4, 1, 4, 1, 4, 1, 2, 1, 2, 3, 2, 3, 4, 1, 2, 3, 2, 1, 4, 3, 2, 3, 2, 1, 2, 1, 4, 1, 4, 1. This threads 50 ends.
Thread 2 warp ends at a time through a size 8 reed. Tie the warp onto the front roller. As the warp ends are used for fringe, do not weave waste yarn at the beginning and end of the work.
Note: each pattern measures approximately 6.5cm (2¾in).
Weave: 10 picks of plain weave in maroon, lifting shafts 1–3, 2–4 alternately.
Pattern 1: still using the maroon yarn, lift the shafts in pairs in the following order: 1–2, 1–4, 3–4, 2–3, 3–4, 1–4. Repeat 12 times.
Weave: 4 picks of plain weave in blue yarn.
Pattern 2: using dark brown yarn, lift the shafts in pairs in the following order: 1–2, 1–4, 3–4, 2–3. Repeat 19 times.
Weave: 4 picks of plain weave in blue yarn.
Pattern 3: using camel yarn, lift the shaft in pairs in the following order: 1–2, 2–4, 3–4, 1–4. Repeat 16 times.
Weave: 4 picks of plain weave in blue yarn.
Pattern 4: using maroon yarn, lift the shafts in pairs in the following order: 2–3, 1–2, 3–4, 1–2, 2–3. Repeat this 13 times.
Weave: 4 picks of plain weave in blue yarn.
Pattern 5: using dark brown yarn lift the shafts in pairs in the following order: 1–2, 2–3, 3–4, 4–1, 3–4, 2–3. Insert 2 picks in the same shed for each lift. Repeat 7 times.
Weave: 4 picks of plain weave in blue yarn.
Pattern 6: using camel yarn, lift the shafts in pairs in the following order: 1–2, 1–4, 3–4, 2–3. Repeat this 7 times, then reverse the lifting 7 times.

Weave: 4 picks of plain weave in blue yarn.
Pattern 7: using maroon yarn lift the shafts in pairs in the following order: 1–4, 1–2, 2–3, 3–4, 1–4, 1–2, 2–3, 3–4, 3–2, 2–1, 2–3, 3–4, 4–1, 1–2, 2–3, 3–4, 4–1, 1–2, 4–1, 3–4. Repeat this 3½ times.
Weave: 4 picks of plain weave in blue yarn.
Pattern 8: weave 3 picks of plain weave in white yarn. Using dark brown yarn, lift the shafts in pairs in the following order: 3–2, 1–4, 3–2. Insert 3 picks in the same shed for each lift. Weave 3 picks of plain weave in white yarn. Repeat this 5 times.
Weave: 4 picks of plain weave in blue yarn. Then repeat the order of patterns in reverse from 7–1, in the same colors, finishing with 10 picks of plain weave in maroon.
Finishing the scarf. Take the scarf off the loom. Cut the warp end 10cm (4in) from the edge of the scarf. Knot every 4 ends close to the end off the scarf to make a fringe.

Upholstery

Upholstery is the addition of padding, springs and textile covering to furniture. The relatively high cost of textiles restricted its use until the second half of the 17th century when the seats and backs of the heavily carved chairs were often covered in Turkey work—an imitation of Turkish carpets—which was fastened to the frame with brass-headed nails. Padding, however, was meager until the end of the 17th century when the armchair with projecting wings and short cabriole legs made its appearance in England and America. The padding was made from curled horsehair, dried hay or grass or sometimes feathers, and was often covered with needlework. With the development of furniture generally during the 18th century, upholstery became an established craft. Paddings were still the same but coverings became more luxurious and were made from damasks, brocades, velvets and silks.

A major development came around 1828 with the introduction of springs. Deep buttoned upholstery was introduced as a means of keeping the springs from moving and of holding the padding in position. Upholstery became heavier with a wider range of covering materials, leather being particularly popular.

Despite the introduction in the 1920s of foam rubber, which is now widely used as an inexpensive and easy substitute for horsehair and grass stuffings, the restoration of upholstery on older furniture is still done using the traditional methods.

Materials and equipment

The materials used in traditional upholstery are the same for small items as for large—they simply vary in the amount required. They are described here in the order they are generally used.

Webbing. This forms the foundation of all upholstery, from simple drop-in seats on dining chairs to large chesterfield sofas. It is a strong woven jute material, usually 5cm (2in) wide, which is stretched tightly in interwoven bands placed approximately 5cm (2in) apart across the frame. Because the webbing takes the main strain of the upholstery, use the best quality available for seats that are likely to receive hard wear. Less expensive webbing may be used for the backs of chairs and on seats that are used less often.

Springs. These are placed on top of the webbing on the seats of some dining chairs and on the seats, backs and arms of many easy chairs and sofas. Springs are made from metal and shaped into a coil and, as their name suggests, they make the upholstery springy and comfortable. They vary in height from 12.5cm (5in) for dining chairs to 25cm (10in) for sofas. A heavy gauge spring (made from thick metal) should be used for chairs intended for heavy wear.

Burlap (hessian). This is a strongly woven fabric made from jute. It should be attached to the frame over the springs, or over the webbing on unsprung seats, as the foundation for the padding. Black burlap or cambric is used for tacking underneath the furniture to hide the rough edges and prevent dust in the stuffing from falling to the floor.

Padding. The material that gives the most comfort is still traditional horsehair. It is sterilized and specially treated to make it curly and springy and, although it is usually mixed with other animal hair, it is unfortunately more expensive than other stuffing materials. The other main padding material used is Southern moss or Algerian fiber, a grasslike material which is cheaper but is less durable than good-quality hair. On larger dining chairs, easy chairs and sofas, the padding is applied in two layers, the first layer of which may be fiber and the second layer horsehair. However, because hair is the easier material for an amateur to use, it is worth the extra expense of using it for both layers.

Coarse muslin (scrim). The two layers of padding are separated by a layer of coarse muslin or other lightweight fabric with a loose open weave such as loosely woven burlap.

Muslin (calico). Unbleached muslin or any type of similar cotton fabric is placed over the second layer of padding to hold it in place.

Cotton wadding or felt. This is placed over the muslin to prevent the hair from working through the muslin and main cover.

Main cover fabric. Choose a fabric specifically designed for upholstery as this will give the best wear. Ideally it should also be

A Queen Anne wing armchair with square section feet and upholstered in tent and cross stitch wool embroidery, dated c. 1720.

of a color that does not show the dirt too quickly, or be of a fiber that can be sponged or dry-cleaned in position. Synthetic velvets are ideal for upholstery as they are usually strong and spongeable.

Tacks. Most of the materials described are attached to the frame with tacks of various sizes (nails should never be used). Upholstery tacks with large flat heads—1.5cm ($\frac{1}{2}$in) long are used for the webbing, and 1cm ($\frac{3}{8}$in) long for the burlap and coarse muslin. Fine tacks—which have smaller heads and thinner shanks—1cm ($\frac{3}{8}$in) long

Equipment and basic techniques

are used to attach the muslin and main cover.

Twine. One of the most important aspects of traditional upholstery is the stitching that holds the springs and stuffing in position. This is all done with flax twine. Spring twine (laid cord), which is much thicker, is used to tie springs together.

Tools

Webbing stretcher (fig.1a). This is used to do what the name implies—to stretch the bands of webbing tautly across the seat. It is possible to substitute a block of wood but if you are intending to do a lot of upholstery, it is worth buying the correct tool.

Tack hammer (fig.1b). This has a small head and, ideally, a claw end. A fine carpenter's hammer may be used on furniture where there is no risk of damaging exposed woodwork or carvings.

Ripping chisel (fig.1c) and **mallet** (fig.1d). These tools are used for removing old upholstery. A ripping chisel has a blunt head and is similar to a screwdriver. An old *blunt* wood chisel may be used instead.

Regulator (fig.1e). This thin metal tool is about 20cm (8in) long with a sharp point at one end and a flat blunt section at the other. It is essential for many processes in upholstery and there is no ideal substitute.

Needles (fig.1f). A curved needle, about 12.5cm (5in) long, is used for stitching on the springs and making loops (bridle ties) to hold the stuffing on the burlap, and a double-pointed straight needle, about 20cm (8in) long, for stitching a roll in which the stuffing is enclosed to form a firm edge around seats and on some backs. You will also need a tape measure, upholsterer's shears, pliers, a utility knife and some chalk.

Quantities of materials

Webbing. Measure the length each strip will span and allow an extra 5cm (2in) for turning over. Add 15cm (6in) to the total to allow for fitting.

Burlap (hessian). Choose a quality 284–340g (10–12oz) per 90cm (36in) square, and allow enough to cover the frame with 2.5cm (1in) spare all around for turning over.

Padding. For an average-sized dining chair with a drop-in seat allow about 450g (1lb) of horsehair. For dining chairs with over-stuffed (stuff-over) seats—where the padding is built up to about 7.5cm (3in) above the frame—allow about 1350g (3lb) of horsehair.

Coarse muslin, muslin, wadding and main cover. Allow enough to cover the frame with 15cm (6in) to spare all around to accommodate the depth of padding. Allow extra on overstuffed seats where the fabric is attached to the underside.

Basic techniques

Removing old upholstery. To lift off the tacks holding on each layer of the old upholstery, hold the ripping chisel parallel to the length of the frame and place the tip under the head of the tack. Tap the handle of the chisel firmly with the mallet until the tack is loosened (fig.2). Repeat for all the tacks around the frame, then lift them out with the claw end of the hammer.

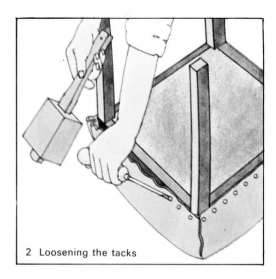

2 Loosening the tacks

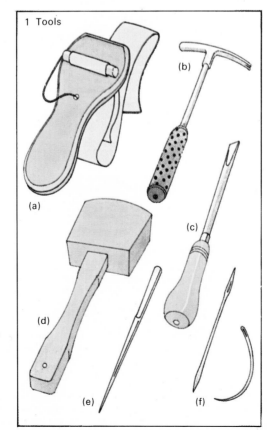

1 Tools

Note: always drive the chisel along the grain of the wood and away from the exposed woodwork to prevent the possibility of splitting it. It is important to remove all tacks from the frame to make room for fixing the new ones.

If the old fabric is held on with staples, prize these up with the point of a regulator and pull out with pliers or use a staple remover. After removing the old cover fabrics, examine the padding. If it is horsehair, which resembles very coarse human hair, it is usually worth washing it for re-use. You can throw away anything else. If necessary, cut through any stitching holding on the padding.

When the frame is completely stripped, examine it carefully, make any necessary repairs to the joints, and apply the appropriate fluid if it has woodworm. If the old tacks have left a lot of holes, fill these in with plastic wood. You should also check that the frame has a chamfered edge between the top and side faces. If necessary, make an edge of about 0.5cm ($\frac{1}{4}$in) with a file.

Tacking and stretching. The webbing is fixed to the upper side of the frame if the seat is unsprung or to the underside if it is sprung.

Place the seat with the appropriate side facing up. Measure the length of each side and mark the center in pencil. Then mark the center line along the length of the rail on each side.

Basic techniques and stitches

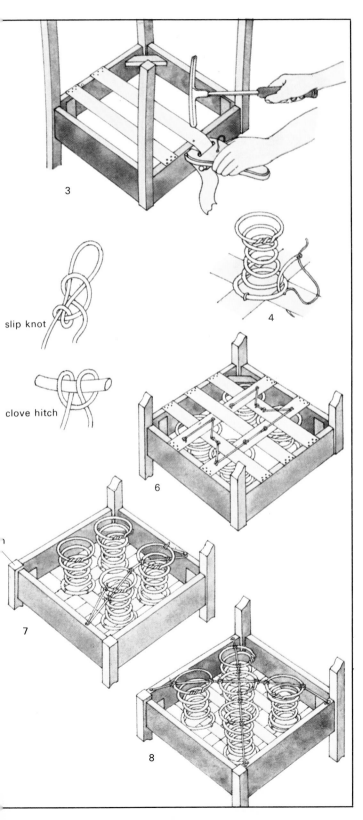

slip knot

clove hitch

Stand in front of the chair so that the back rail is farthest from you. Using the webbing straight from the roll, fold over the end for about 2.5cm (1in) and place the fold, with the turning face upwards, onto the center of the back rail so that the fold is just over the lengthwise center line. Place one tack in each corner, just inside the fold, and a third one in the middle and hammer down so that the heads of the tacks are flush. Place two more tacks to form a "W" shape and hammer down. Insert the webbing into the stretcher as shown in fig.3, adjust the length of the webbing to fit the span of the frame and turn the handle towards you. Press the stretcher against the front edge of the frame above any exposed woodwork to give leverage and pull the webbing taut to the center front. Secure with three tacks through a single thickness, positioning them in a row through the lengthwise center line. Cut the webbing 2.5cm (1in) from the tacks, fold back the excess and secure with two more tacks.

Attach the remaining strips from back to front on the frame in the same way, leaving gaps of about 5cm (2in) between them. On frames where the back is narrower than the front, you may have to leave less than this at the back and more at the front. Determine the position of each strip and adjust the angle of the back fold accordingly so that it lies flat. For the cross strips weave the webbing in and out of the lengthwise strips before attaching as above.

Stitching springs to webbing. Arrange the springs on the junction of the webbing strands in straight rows. Thread the curved needle with a good length of spring twine and insert the needle through the webbing from underneath to come up beside a spring. Pass the needle over the bottom coil of the spring and insert it through the webbing (fig.4). Tie the end of the twine to the main length with a slip knot (fig.5a, shown with the clove hitch fig.5b). Keeping the needle under the webbing, move to the opposite end of the spring, bring up the needle and make a second stitch. Tie the twine underneath the webbing as shown in fig.6 and then make a third stitch to form a "V" shape. Without cutting the twine, move on to the next spring and repeat the procedure. Continue around for the re-

maining springs and tie the twine securely to finish off. This method is also used to stitch the springs to the burlap which covers them.

Tying down springs. This process keeps the springs in shape and prevents them from moving around inside the seat. Attach a 1.5cm ($\frac{1}{2}$in) upholstery tack to the center of the frame in line with each row of springs as shown in fig.7. Tie the springs with clove hitches, winding the twine around the tack before hammering the tack in completely. Fig.8 shows how springs are tied diagonally for a chair with five springs.

Attaching the burlap. Mark the center of each edge and place onto the frame over the springs (or over the webbing on an unsprung seat) so that the center points match on each edge. Secure with a temporary tack (hammered halfway down) at each point. Fold up the back edge so that the fold is 1.5cm ($\frac{1}{2}$in) from the outside edge of the frame and tack down at 4cm ($1\frac{1}{2}$in) intervals to within 5cm (2in) of the corners. Pull the burlap taut to the front, keeping the grain straight, and tack in the same way but through the single thickness only. Tack up to the sides of the horns (the small raised sections) at the corners. Repeat along the sides of the frame.

To miter the corners at the back uprights, fold back the fabric diagonally so that the fold touches the upright. Cut in from the point up to the fold and pull the fabric around to each side of the upright. Trim off the excess triangle at each side and fold over the turnings. Tack down. At the front corners lift the burlap onto the horns and tack. Fold over the turnings along the front and sides and tack, placing the tacks in between those below. Fig.9a shows the burlap in position with the springs stitched in place.

Basic stitches

Bridle ties for stuffing. These stitches are used to hold in the stuffing. Thread the curved needle with a good length of twine and work the stitches into the burlap as shown in fig.9b. The stitches should be loose enough for you to insert your index and middle finger.

For the second stuffing work the stitches in a similar way onto the coarse muslin

Upholstery

Drop-in seats

(scrim) but make them slightly tighter.
Panel stitching. This holds the coarse muslin in place on the chair while the edges are being formed and also encloses the stuffing in the middle of the frame. Using twine and a double-pointed needle, insert the needle into the coarse muslin about 12.5cm (5in) in from the edge and pull through underneath until the eye emerges from the burlap. Push the eye back through the burlap at a slight angle about 1cm ($\frac{3}{8}$in) from where it emerged, to come out on top about 2.5cm (1in) from where it went in. Tie the end of twine to the main length with a slip knot, make a large stitch on top and insert the needle again. Push back in a similar way to the top, make another stitch and repeat around the chair (fig.10a and b).

Blind stitching. This process, together with top stitching, forms the first stuffing into a firm roll around the edge of the frame. They are both worked around the frame in a series of small counterclockwise motions. Blind stitching pulls the stuffing toward the edge of the chair.

Thread the double-pointed needle with twine and insert the needle into the coarse muslin just above the tacks on the chamfered edge and about 2.5cm (1in) from the corner. Slant the needle back to the corner at a 45° angle and incline it at the same angle in the middle of the stuffing. It should emerge on the top of the coarse muslin about 1.5cm ($\frac{1}{2}$in) nearer the corner and about 10cm (4in) in from the edge. Pull the needle through until you can see the eye. Do not withdraw it but twist it down at an angle back into the stuffing, eye first, towards the corner so that it emerges just above the tacks. Tie the end of twine to the main length with a slip knot and pull firmly to the right. Insert the needle again 4cm (1$\frac{1}{2}$in) along the edge at an angle as before. Twist the needle back to emerge just past the first stitch. When the needle is half out, wind the twine which is hanging in a loop below it around the needle twice (fig.11). Pull the needle through the twists and tighten the stitch with one hand at the same time pulling the edge of the stuffing down with the other. Remove your hand and pull the twine firmly to the right (it helps to wind it around your hand, or

around the handle of a hammer) so that the stitch sinks into the side of the stuffing. Continue stitching in this way up to the horn. Insert the needle and twist it to emerge on the other side of the horn. Continue like this around the whole seat. Finish off securely with a knot.

Top stitching (fig.12). This process forms the first stuffing into a firm, sausage-shaped roll round the edge of the seat. Starting at the left-hand corner again, press your fingers into the top of the stuffing and your thumb into the side so that they form a sausage shape from the stuffing. Insert the needle into the stuffing, level with your thumb, and bring it out straight on top, level with your fingers. Pull through completely, leaving a tail of twine on the side about 5cm (2in) long.

Make a back stitch on top about 2.5cm (1in) long and insert the needle into the stuffing to come out on the side level with your thumb. Pull out and tie the tail of twine to the main length with a slip knot. Make a second stitch 2.5cm (1in) further along the side in a similar way but twist the twine around the needle before pulling it out on the side of the stuffing and then tighten it as for blind stitching. Work completely around the seat, making the roll firm and even.

Drop-in seats

The removable drop-in seat of a dining chair is the easiest item to reupholster because it does not involve the elaborate blind and top stitching required on larger pieces of furniture. It does, however, use many of the other basic techniques.

You will need:
webbing ☐ burlap (hessian) ☐ horsehair ☐ muslin (calico) ☐ wadding ☐ main cover fabric ☐ upholstery tacks ☐ curved needle ☐ regulator ☐ tack hammer ☐ webbing stretcher ☐ ripping chisel ☐ mallet.

Stripping the old upholstery. Strip off the old upholstery as described earlier. Make a mark on the upper side of the seat frame so that you can identify it later.

Note: if you are using a thick fabric or a piece of needlepoint to replace a thinner cover, you may have to plane a small amount from the side faces (ie the vertical

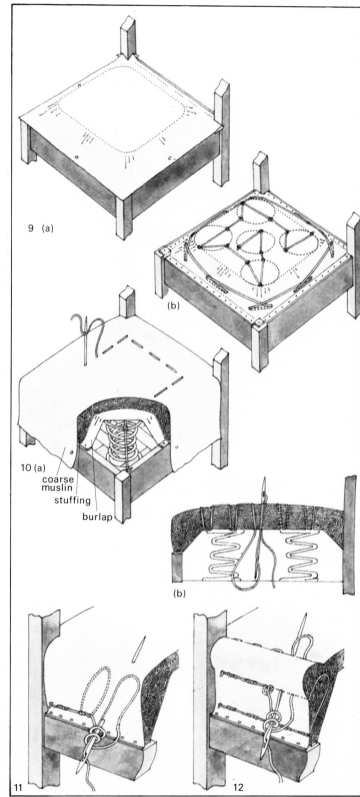

9 (a)

(b)

10 (a)

coarse muslin

stuffing

burlap

(b)

11

12

Overstuffed dining chair

Drop-in seat

in the middle to make a dome shape.

Muslin (calico). Place the muslin centrally over the stuffing and secure to the side faces with a temporary tack in the center of each edge.

Tilt the seat so that it is resting on its front edge and tack the muslin to the underside of the frame along the back edge, using 1cm ($\frac{3}{8}$in) fine tacks placed 2.5cm (1in) apart and 1.5cm ($\frac{1}{2}$in) from the edge. Tilt the seat again so that it is resting on its back edge and smooth the muslin over the stuffing toward the front edge so that it is taut. Temporary-tack to the underside of the frame. Repeat along the side edges, keeping the grain of the fabric straight. Finish the corners by pulling the muslin firmly over the corners of the frame and tacking to the underside. Do not worry about the slight fullness which may form between the tacks at the corners. Examine the shape of the padding critically and adjust if necessary by poking the point of the regulator through the muslin to hook the stuffing in position. When you are satisfied, hammer the tacks in.

Wadding. Cut a piece of wadding to fit over the stuffing and place it on with the backing side face up. Cut out a square at each corner so that the wadding lies flat.

Main cover. Place this over the wadding centrally and start attaching as for the muslin. Finish the corners in a square pleat (fig.13).

Bottoming. Attach the black cambric or burlap on the underside of the chair, turning under the raw edges so that the folds are 0.5cm ($\frac{1}{4}$in) from the edge of the frame. Tack or staple in position.

Replace the finished seat on the chair.

Overstuffed (stuff-over) dining chair

The materials and equipment are the same as those for the drop-in seat. Strip the old upholstery, apply the webbing, any springs and burlap as previously described. Work bridle ties into the burlap.

The stuffing. Tease out handfuls of horsehair and insert the bridle ties so that the stuffing is about 4cm ($1\frac{1}{2}$in) high all around the edge of the seat. Place the remaining stuffing in the middle of the seat so that it forms a dome shape. Place the coarse muslin centrally over the stuffing

Overstuffed chair

and temporary-tack in the middle of each edge to the side faces of the frame. Make the panel stitching in the middle of the seat. Starting on the front edge, remove the temporary tack. Lift up the coarse muslin, even out the stuffing along the edge and add more if necessary, to make a firm roll, 4cm ($1\frac{1}{2}$in) high, which just protrudes beyond the edge of the frame. Pay particular attention to the front corners. Tuck the coarse muslin under the stuffing so that

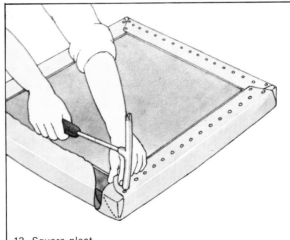

13 Square pleat

sides) of the frame to accommodate the extra thickness.

The new upholstery. Place the seat frame right side up on your work surface. Replace the webbing following the old arrangement. Cut off each strip of webbing leaving 2.5cm (1in) for turning over. Attach the burlap as described previously, turn back the edges with those of the webbing and tack down together.

The stuffing. Work bridle ties into the burlap around the edge of the seat. Tease out handfuls of horsehair and place them under the ties so that the edge of the seat is evenly and well covered. Add more stuffing

Tufting (deep-buttoning)

it is smooth but not tight and fix the folded edge of the coarse muslin to the chamfered edge of the frame with 1cm ($\frac{3}{8}$in) upholstery tacks. Repeat along the sides and then the back of the frame. At the front corners, pinch the coarse muslin into a pleat. At the back uprights, miter the coarse muslin as for the burlap and tack down neatly. To check evenness of the stuffing, kneel down and look at it from each side—it should be the same height all around. Tilt the seat back and look from underneath—it should just protrude evenly all around.

Work the blind stitching and top stitching as previously described. Stitch bridle ties into the coarse muslin and add a top stuffing, following the instructions as given for stuffing a drop-in seat.

Muslin (calico). Place the muslin centrally over the top stuffing and attach with temporary tacks in the middle of each edge on the side face of the frame if the chair has exposed woodwork, or on the underside if the finished cover is attached there. Smooth the muslin over the stuffing and add more tacks along the back edge to within 4cm (1$\frac{1}{2}$in) of the uprights. Smooth the muslin over the stuffing toward the front of the chair, keeping the grain straight, and add more temporary tacks to within 4cm (1$\frac{1}{2}$in) of the corners. Repeat along the sides. Miter the corners at the uprights as shown in fig.14, pulling the muslin down and folding under the edges to touch the uprights. Make the fullness at the front into a square or inverted pleat (fig.15a and b), whichever is appropriate for the shape of the frame. When smooth, hammer the tacks in.

Main cover. Place wadding over the muslin and then apply the main cover as for the muslin. If the chair has exposed woodwork, place the tacks just above the rabbetted (rebated) edge. When the cover is smooth, hammer the tacks in and add more in between until they are almost touching. Trim off the excess fabric close to the tacks.

Braid. If the chair has exposed woodwork cover the raw edges of fabric with braid or gimp in a color to match the fabric. Starting at the left-hand corner, fold under the end of the braid and tack down. Fold the braid over the tack, apply some clear-drying

adhesive onto the back of the braid and press onto the chair so that it is straight and covers the raw edge of the fabric and the tacks. Glue on the braid all around, fold under the end carefully and neatly and glue down.

Bottoming. If the cover is attached underneath the chair, apply black cambric or burlap as for drop-in seats.

Tufting furniture (deep buttoning)

Tufted furniture in which the cover fabric is pulled down deep into the padding and held by buttons, can be done onto backs and seats, and the method for both is very similar. The instructions below are for a dining chair with an unsprung seat, but they can be adapted for other furniture.

Tufted seat. Complete the upholstery as for a plain overstuffed seat up to the bridle ties for the second stuffing. Before adding the stuffing, make a paper template of the seat and draw out the buttoning pattern on this. Start by drawing a center line across the template from back to front. Draw a line across about 10cm (4in) from the front edge and at similar intervals toward the back of the seat. Draw lengthwise lines at the same intervals from the center line. Mark on the positions of the buttons to form diamonds, leaving a clear space of about 10cm (4in) around the seat edge. Transfer these markings to the coarse muslin on the seat with chalk and cut a small hole through the coarse muslin in each button position. Push your finger into the hole through the first stuffing until you can feel the burlap. Cover the required number of 1.5cm ($\frac{1}{2}$in) button molds with cover fabric.

Add the second stuffing and make holes through it with your finger at each button position.

Cut out a piece of muslin to cover the seat, plus 20cm (8in) all around. Mark the muslin with a grid like that on the coarse muslin but make the lines 4cm (1$\frac{1}{2}$in) further apart to allow for the depth of the stuffing.

Place the muslin over the stuffing and align the center button positions. Press the muslin into the hole. Thread a needle with a length of twine and pass it through the muslin and stuffing and bring it out underneath, leaving a long tail of twine on top. Remove the needle from the underside and thread the tail on top. Make a small stitch through the muslin (the buttons are not used for this stage, of course) and pass through the stuffing to the underside. Tie the ends of twine in a slip knot and tighten the knot around a tiny roll of spare burlap to prevent the knot from pulling back through the stuffing. Repeat this process for the remaining button positions of the center diamond, making the fullness that forms between them into a neat diagonal pleat. The fabric should be smooth and taut between the button positions. If necessary, add a little more stuffing by poking it through with a regulator.

When all the button positions are established, make the fullness at the edges of the seat into neat straight pleats along the grain and tack down.

Main cover. Place cotton wadding or felt over the muslin and cut holes in it at each button position. Mark the wrong side of the cover fabric as for the muslin and start the buttoning in the same way, this time threading a button onto the needle before completing each stitch.

Tack down the edges and finish with braid or gimp.

Opposite: A tufted (deep-buttoned) Chesterfield.

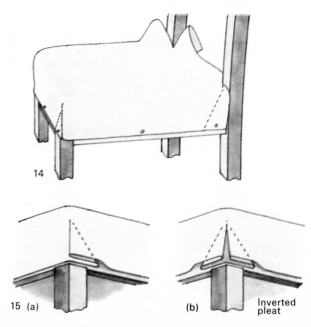

14

15 (a)　　　　(b)　　Inverted pleat

Lampshades

Glass lampshades are still popular—this one is decorated with a handpainted design.

Making lampshades is an absorbing and artistic craft, due to the variety of fabrics available and the different ways of fitting them onto frames.

Choosing materials

First of all, choose the type of lampshade you wish to make by considering the room for which it is intended. You can make either a lampshade that blends subtly with the rest of your interior decoration, or else, by using vibrant contrasting colors, one which serves as a focal point. When choosing colors bear in mind that reds and yellows give a warmer light than blues and greens, and that a white lining reflects the light well. Then, consider the function of the lamp: if it is for reading purposes a direct light is necessary, so select a fairly wide frame and a fabric that does not diffuse the light too much. Also, be sure that the shape of the frame balances well with the base to give a harmonious overall effect. Finally, the type of fabric you choose will depend also on whether you intend to make a soft or a hard shade.

Fabrics for soft shades. A soft shade is made by binding the frame with tape and sewing the fabric onto it. Select a fabric with "stretching" qualities so that it will fit tightly over the frame. The best fabrics to use for the outer cover are crepe-backed satin and silk shantung. Crepe-backed satin is the most suitable for linings as it is

easy to work with and reflects the light well because of its shiny surface. Use silk (jap silk) for small shades only as it tends to tear if used on large surfaces. Avoid using heavy upholstery or furnishing fabrics since they are difficult to work with. Most nylon fabrics are unsuitable for the same reason and are also inflammable. Many cotton fabrics and eyelet embroidery (broderie anglaise) are suitable for making Tiffany-style lampshades. Use colored lining under white eyelet embroidery (broderie anglaise) or lace to create a delicate shade for use in a bedroom or bathroom. The advantage of a soft lampshade is that it can be washed easily. Use warm water and a light detergent, and dry as quickly as possible to avoid rusting.

Fabrics for hard shades. The materials and techniques involved in making hard lampshades are different from those used for soft shades. Hard shades are quicker to make but do not last as long. However, they can be cleaned by rubbing with a soft brush; do *not* wash in water if the fabric is bonded onto paper. The fabrics used for making hard lampshades include covered lampshade cardboard, which is a material bonded to cardboard; and a stiff paper (parbond) with an adhesive on one side to allow you to iron on your own choice of fabric and so match lampshades to curtains and other furnishings. Most upholstery and furnishing cottons are suitable to use with this material. A heavy textured cotton fabric is a suitable fabric to use if you intend to decorate the shade with exterior motifs and objects such as leaves and dried flowers, which can be glued or sewn on.

Frames. Frames for both soft and hard shades are made with various fittings (fig. 1a–c). Choose a firm frame, preferably made from sturdy wire. Old frames are certainly worth using again, provided the wire is in good condition, and that it has enough struts to support the fabric you have chosen. Clean the frame by rubbing with wire wool and then paint with quick-drying enamel to help prevent rusting when you wash the shade. Leave for a few days to dry thoroughly.

Trimmings. These play an important part in the finished effect of the lampshade. As well as adding decoration to the shade,

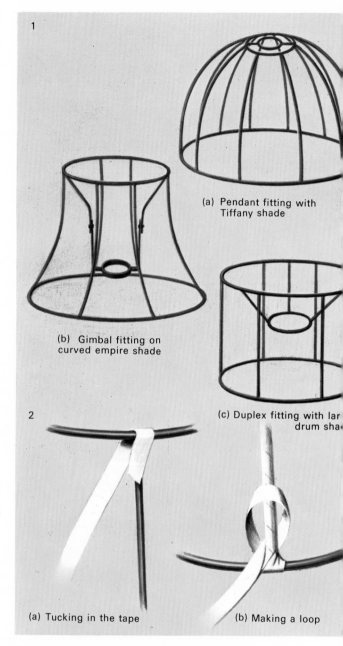

1

(a) Pendant fitting with Tiffany shade

(b) Gimbal fitting on curved empire shade

(c) Duplex fitting with lar drum sha

2

(a) Tucking in the tape

(b) Making a loop

trimmings often serve to cover up seams and stitches. There are many attractive trimmings available but you can also make your own using macramé, beadwork, crochet or tatting. Always choose a trimming that complements the texture and style of the shade.

Tapes. Use a 1.5cm ($\frac{1}{2}$in) wide binding tape to bind the struts and rings of the lampshade frame. You can also use bias

Taping the frame
Three
lampshades

lampshade by tucking in the tape (fig.2a). Bind the strut until the bottom is reached. Pass the tape once around the bottom ring, take it to the left, make a loop and pass it to the right, in a figure eight (fig.2b). Then make a knot and cut off the surplus tape at the ring. Continue in this way with each strut. Then tape the bottom and top rings, making a figure eight twist around the joins of the struts. When binding a ring for a hard shade, secure the tape in place with a piece of adhesive tape. Then finish with a few overcasting stitches on the outside of the ring to secure the tape.

Three lampshades
Here is a selection of lampshades to make —a traditional hard shade, a classical soft shade and a highly decorative modern shade. The sizes given can be modified using the same techniques.

Straight-sided drum lampshade
You will need:
20cm (8in) oval drum shade frame □ 25 × 90cm (10 × 36in) covered lampshade cardboard □ 25 × 90cm (10 × 36in) sturdy brown paper for pattern □ 1.25m ($1\frac{1}{4}$yd) narrow velvet ribbon or similar trimming □ 5m (5yd) binding tape □ 16 clothes pins (clothes pegs) □ ruler □ fabric adhesive □ needle and thread.
Making the shade. Tape the frame as previously described. Find the width of fabric you need by measuring the length of a strut, in this case 18cm (7in), and the length by measuring the circumference of the taped frame, in this case 57cm ($22\frac{1}{2}$in). Add 1.5cm ($\frac{1}{2}$in) to the length to allow for a seam. Before cutting out the lampshade fabric, cut a pattern in sturdy paper and try it on the frame. Use clothes pins (pegs) to keep it in place around the top and cut off the surplus from the bottom. Cut out the fabric, using the paper pattern. Then attach it to the rings, holding it in place with clothes pins (pegs). Blanket stitch the fabric to the frame, working from left to right as in fig.3. When you have sewn up to the join, mark a line with a ruler and trim the fabric to 0.5cm ($\frac{1}{4}$in) to allow for a seam. Carefully overlap the seam and glue firmly with fabric adhesive.
Adding the trimmings. Attach the trimming

binding which is available in a variety of colors, especially if it is necessary to match the struts to the lining, as for example, on a Tiffany-style lampshade where the struts will show.
Other equipment. You will not require any specialist tools for making lampshades. You will need a sharp pair of scissors, matching silk thread, steel dressmaking pins, a good fabric adhesive and needles. The best needles for sewing hard frames are "betweens" needles, which are stiff and short.

Taping the frame
This is an important process in making the lampshade and should be done with care. If the tape is at all slack the whole binding may work loose so that the fabric which is stitched to the tape will also be loose-fitting. To work out the amount of binding you will need, measure twice the length of each strut and twice the circumference of the top and bottom rings. Bind each strut separately and then bind the rings.
Cut a length of tape twice the length of the strut. Start taping at the top of the

Curved empire shade
Tiffany lampshade

with fabric adhesive, being careful to cover the blanket stitching at top and bottom. Turn the ends of the trimming in by 0.5cm (¼in) and butt them together, ie place them end to end without overlapping, and sew together neatly.

Curved empire shade
You will need:
25cm (10in) curved empire frame □ 0.5m (½yd) fabric, 90cm (36in) wide for the cover □ 0.5m (½yd) fabric, 90cm (36in) wide for the lining □ 1m (1yd) lampshade tassel fringe □ 0.5m (½yd) matching braid □ 7m (7yd) binding tape □ needle and thread.

Making the shade. Tape the frame as previously described. Place the frame on its side. Fold the fabric in half along the direction of the grain and with right sides together. Place the fabric on top of half of the frame. Insert a pin at the top and the bottom of the side struts (fig.4). Stretch the fabric gently outwards until it fits closely to the frame. Pin the fabric to the binding of the top and bottom rings. Do not stretch the fabric too much as this will prevent it from molding onto the form of the frame. Mark along the side struts AB and CD with a soft pencil, taking the line 1.5cm

(½in) beyond the top and bottom rings (fig.5): this is the sewing line. Then draw a guideline at right angles, 1.5cm (½in) beyond the top and bottom rings and place a few pins in the fabric to hold both pieces together (fig.6). Take out the rest of the pins and machine stitch down the sewing line of AB and CD. Press flat and trim the seams to 0.5cm (¼in).

Prepare the lining in the same way. As the lining is inserted inside the frame, machine stitch just inside the pencil line. Slip the lampshade cover over the frame with the right sides of the fabric on the outside, and adjust the cover so that the side seams are over the side struts. Match the penciled guidelines to the top and bottom rings, and pin into place. Pin around the top and bottom rings, inserting pins every 2.5cm (1in) and adjust the fabric alternately at the top and bottom until all fullness has been removed.

Overcast the cover to top and bottom rings using matching thread double. Keep the stitching towards the outer edge of the rings and sew from right to left. Then trim the fabric close to the stitches.

Insert the lining by placing it inside the shade, matching the horizontal guidelines to top and bottom rings. Trim the fabric to

fit around the gimbal. Adjust the fabric at both rings until the lining is sufficiently tight (fig.7). Then make the gimbal neat by cutting a strip of fabric on the bias, 2.5cm (1in) wide. Fold the strip into three and press with an iron. Insert under the gimbal fitting and pin onto the top ring (fig.8). Trim ends, then sew in position, keeping the stitches on the outside of the ring.

Adding the trimmings. Turn in one end of braid by 1.5cm (½in) and, starting at one of the side struts, sew around the top of the frame as shown in fig.9. To join the 2 ends of braid together, turn in the loose end by 1.5cm (½in) and butt together at the side strut. If necessary, slipstitch the braid over the join. Sew the tassel fringe to the bottom of the frame in the same way.

Tiffany lampshade
You will need:
Tiffany lampshade frame approximately 25cm (10in) across the base □ 0.75m (¾yd) fabric, 90cm (36in) wide for the cover □ 0.75m (¾yd) fabric, 90cm (36in) wide for the lining □ 1m (1yd) lampshade fringe □ 10m (10yd) binding tape □ fabric adhesive.

Making the shade. Tape the frame as previously described. Both the cover and

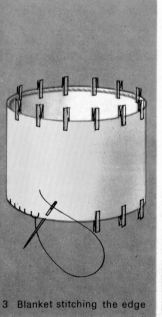

3 Blanket stitching the edge

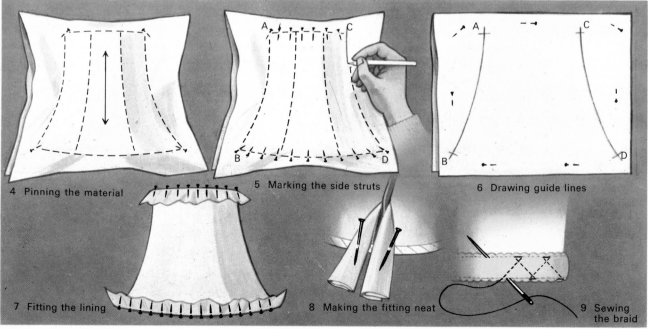

4 Pinning the material
5 Marking the side struts
6 Drawing guide lines
7 Fitting the lining
8 Making the fitting neat
9 Sewing the braid

Tiffany lampshade

lining fabrics are cut on the bias. Cut the lining fabric to form a square so that the width measures the same as the length. Fold the square diagonally and cut, then fold and cut each triangular piece again to give 4 triangles of equal size. Pin 1 piece of lining fabric in position over a quarter of the frame as shown in fig.10. Adjust the pinning by easing and stretching the fabric where necessary to obtain a neat fit. Overcast into position using double thread. Trim surplus fabric close to the stitching. Cover the other three quarters of the frame in the same way, pinning over previous stitching on the struts where necessary. Trim close to the stitching each time. When the lining is completed, cut, pin and stitch the top cover in the same way, pinning and stitching onto the same struts as those used for the lining. Cut 4 strips of fabric on the bias, 2.5cm (1in) wide and the length of the struts plus 2.5cm (1in). Turn in each length to make a strip 1.5cm (½in) wide. Spread fabric adhesive evenly over each strip, then glue in place over the stitching on the struts.

Adding the trimmings. To trim the top ring, cut a strip of fabric on the bias, 2.5cm (1in) wide and the same length as the circumference of the top ring plus 1.5cm (½in). Turn in the length to make a strip 1.5cm (½in) wide, fold under each end and glue in position. Attach the tassel fringe as described for the empire shade.

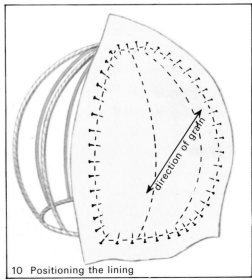

10 Positioning the lining

Beadwork

Beadwork design from a jacket used to decorate an image of *Eshu*, a figure regarded by the Yoruba tribe of West Africa as a messenger of the gods.

Beads have been worn since the earliest times either as ornaments or for their magical properties. In Arab countries today, single blue talismanic beads are attached to animals, children, brides and even cars to ward off the evil eye. The earliest beads were probably plant seeds, but from around 30,000 BC necklaces of sea shells and small fossils have been found. In Egyptian times beads made of turquoise, amber, quartz and ivory were used to make decorative jewelry, often in the shapes of baboons, locusts, hippopotami and birds' heads. Millions of small beads were used to cover mummies. Minoan and Mycenaean civilizations developed gold beads, using them to make lilies and lotuses in their decorations.

Since the Middle Ages, beads have been used on a wide scale for trade and barter: explorers found them valuable as gifts to primitive peoples. The Spanish conquistadores made good use of them,

and until quite recently some primitive tribes in Brazil wore Venetian glass beads which date back to the Renaissance. Beadwork as an extension of embroidery has been practiced in Europe for many hundreds of years. During the Middle Ages, beads were used for the finest decorations on ecclesiastical and ceremonial robes. Exquisitely beaded Bible covers and even beadwork ikons were made. By the Elizabethan period beads were much used as a decoration on fashionable dresses, purses and other small objects. Seed pearls, beads and gilt thread were a popular combination. Beadwork reached a peak of popularity in Victorian times, when elegant dresses with lavishly beaded bodices held pride of place in every society lady's wardrobe. In the 1920s beaded fringing was all the rage. Today much fashion beadwork is inspired by original native American Indian designs.

Materials and equipment

Looms. Metal and wooden looms are obtainable through some bead suppliers and handicraft shops. You can, however, easily construct your own wooden loom and instructions are given on the next page. Plastic looms can be bought for children. They are not as durable as the other two types of loom but are easy to obtain from toy shops and large department stores.

Beads. There are several categories of beads, determined by size, material, finish and shape. Glass beads can be bought in translucent and opaque varieties, sometimes with metal or pearlized finishes. The shapes include round and smooth, round and faceted, cylindrical and smooth, cylindrical and faceted, and also drop shapes in smooth and faceted finishes. The smooth, round opaque bead is called a seed or rocaille bead, the translucent cylindrical bead a bugle. Plastic beads are obtainable in as many varieties as glass beads. Their major advantage is that they are lighter in weight than glass. Wooden beads are obtainable in a variety of shapes, but they are not produced in such small sizes as glass and plastic beads. Paper beads, polished stones, shell, bamboo and seed pods can also be used. Beads are sold both by weight and by number.

Beads in a leaf design decorate this 19th-century hanging pincushion.

Needles and thread. Unless the beads that you are working with have large holes you will need special beading needles. These are long and very fine and are sold in packs of assorted sizes. Button thread or spun nylon thread (not the monofilament variety) should be used for articles which have to take a lot of wear and tear or weight. Otherwise ordinary sewing thread can be used.

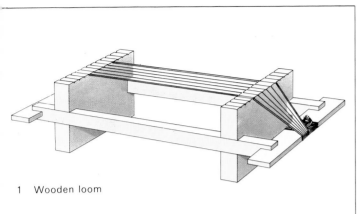

1 Wooden loom

2 Cardboard box loom

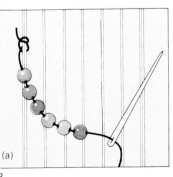

(a)

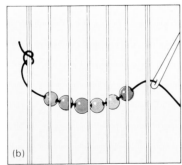

(b)

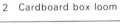

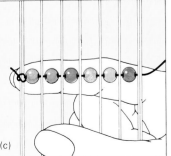

(c)

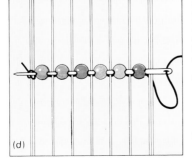

(d)

Making your own bead loom

You can make a wooden loom (fig.1) from plywood or an old wooden box. Cut grooves along the top edge of the loom. These grooves should be spaced at 2mm ($\frac{1}{12}$in) intervals and should be deep enough to hold threads. The only other mechanism needed is a strut on which the threads are tied. If you want to weave long lengths this strut will hold the finished length of bead weaving. It is usual to have a strut at the other end of the loom to hold the unwoven lengths. These struts are movable but the rest of the loom is rigid and immovable.

If you want to make a simpler loom, a cardboard box loom is inexpensive and easy to make: it is also useful for trying out quick ideas, but will not take the strain of really long lengths of work. To make the loom (fig.2), cut V-shaped grooves into each short side of a cardboard box. The grooves hold the threads and should be equally spaced.

Threading a bead loom

To calculate how much thread you will require, first measure the length the finished object will be, the measurement of a choker for your neck or a bracelet for your wrist. Add at least 30cm (12in) to this measurement. To calculate how many threads you will need across the width of your finished object, take up several beads on a beading needle and count how many will be required to make the desired width of the object. To this number add one. The outer threads should be doubled as in fig. 3a, to strengthen them. This is particularly advisable when making belts, bracelets and chokers.

If you are using a wooden loom, thread it as shown in fig.1, tying the threads firmly to the end struts. Thread the cardboard box loom as shown in fig.2. Make sure the threads are taut, as loose threads are difficult to weave. Never use knots to join weft threading, as they ruin the tension and get caught in the beads.

Beadweaving

Knot the loose end of a long thread to one of the double outer threads on the loom (fig.3a). Leave a 7.5cm (3in) length free for finishing purposes. Count the number of spaces there are between threads. You will need as many beads as there are spaces. Pass the threaded beads under the stretched threads (fig.3b). Then, with your finger under the stretched threads, push a bead into each space (fig.3c). Holding the beads in this position, tighten the bead thread to take up any slack. Pass the beading needle back through the center of each bead (fig.3d). Make sure that the needle passes over the stretched threads. The beads are now held in position by two threads, one passing on top and the other underneath the stretched threads.

Sewing in old threads. Ugly lengths of thread at the beginning and end of the work should be threaded onto a beading needle and passed through the beads. Trim off any short ends with scissors.

Joining in new threads. Work the stages shown in fig.3a–d. Using a new length of beading thread, repeat stage 3d. In this row there will be three threads passing through the beads instead of two. Continue working the four stages and repeat the joining process as necessary. When you remove your work from the loom, trim back any excess joining threads with scissors.

Working a design from a chart. Most designs are worked from graphs. Here is an easy one (fig.4) to try out your skill. **Row 1:** thread up 1 bead in color A, 4 beads in color B, and 1 bead in color A. **Row 2:** thread up 1 bead in color B, 1 in color A, 2 in color B, 1 in color A, and 1 in color B. **Row 3:** thread up 2 beads in color B, 2 in color A and 2 in color B. **Row 4:** as row 3. **Row 5:** as row 2. **Row 6:** as row 1. This completes 1 repeat of the design To continue the pattern go back to row 1 and repeat the stages.

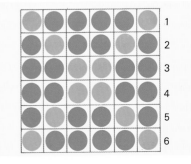

4

Choker with geometric design
Bracelet with traditional design

Choker with geometric design

This choker has been designed as an easy way to practice beadweaving. The finished choker measures 33cm (13in).

You will need:

14g ($\frac{1}{2}$oz) seed (rocaille) beads in each of the following colors: white, red, green and yellow □ beading needles □ 1 spool of white button thread □ beading loom □ pliers □ scissors □ 3cm ($1\frac{1}{4}$in) self-adhering nylon strip (Velcro), 1.5cm ($\frac{1}{2}$in) wide for fastening.

Making the choker. Cut 12 lengths of thread measuring 61cm (24in). Put these lengths on your loom using double threads at each outer edge. The chart (fig.5) shows one repeat of the design and measures just under 4cm ($1\frac{1}{2}$in). Nine repeats measure 33cm (13in). When the beading is as long as is required, remove it from the loom.

Attaching the fastening. With the wrong side of the beading facing you, attach nylon strips as shown in fig.6a and b. The fastening will be invisible (fig.6c).

Bracelet with traditional design

This pattern is based on a native American Indian design and color scheme. The bracelet measures approximately 16.5 × 3cm ($6\frac{1}{2} \times 1\frac{1}{4}$in).

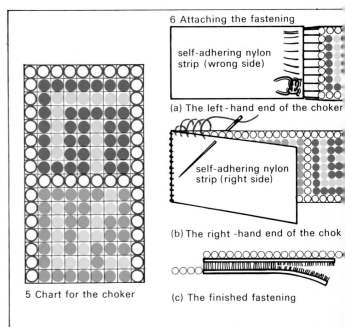

5 Chart for the choker

6 Attaching the fastening

self-adhering nylon strip (wrong side)

(a) The left-hand end of the choker

self-adhering nylon strip (right side)

(b) The right-hand end of the chok

(c) The finished fastening

Glittering belt
Bead mosaic

You will need:

14g (½oz) seed (rocaille) beads in each of the following colors: turquoise, red, blue, black and white □ beading needles □ 1 spool of white button thread □ beading loom □ pliers □ scissors □ 3cm (1¼in) of self-adhering nylon strip (Velcro) 1.5cm (½in) wide for fastening.

Making the bracelet. Cut 18 lengths of thread measuring 53.5cm (21in). The bracelet is formed by working 2 repeats of the graph pattern (fig.7). Each repeat measures approximately 8.5cm (3½in). The bracelet is made up of 2 repeats of the pattern. Put the 18 lengths of thread on your loom making doubled threads at each outer edge, and work the pattern as shown on the graph.

The fastening is the same as for the choker, but fasten nylon strips to the width, rather than to the length of the bracelet.

Glittering belt

The belt is a slightly more advanced project. Designed in delicate pastel shades, it would make an attractive accessory to a summer dress. It is made to fit a 66cm (26in) waist.

You will need:

56g (2oz) white seed (rocaille) beads □

1,000 transparent turquoise beads □ 1,000 transparent pink beads □ 1,000 transparent blue beads □ beading needles □ 1 spool of white button thread □ beading loom □ pliers □ scissors □ fabric glue □ buckle with a link type fastening.

Making the belt. Cut 17 lengths of thread each measuring 1m (1yd). Fit these lengths onto the loom using a double thread on each outer stage. The chart (fig.8) shows one repeat of the design. In each row there are 14 beads arranged in different orders which eventually form the design. Each repeat of the pattern measures slightly over 9cm (3½in).

Fastening the beading to belt buckle (fig.9). Remove the work from the loom. Lay the wrong sides of the 2 halves of the buckle facing you, and knot the threads as shown in fig.9.

To prevent any unraveling, put a small spot of fabric glue on each knot and, when dry, cut off any long ends. Thread the other end of the belt in the same way.

Bead mosaic

This bead picture measures approximately 14.5 × 16.5cm (5¾ × 6½in).

You will need:

28g (1oz) seed (rocaille) beads in both

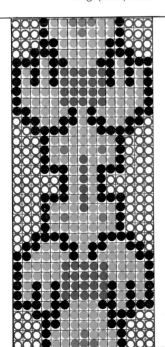

7 Chart for the bracelet

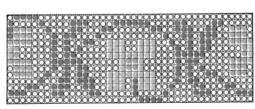

8 Chart for the belt

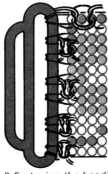

9 Fastening the beading to the belt buckle

Beadwork

Bead threading
Sophisticated evening bag

light blue and dark blue ☐ 2,000 tiny black jet beads ☐ 1,000 tiny beads in each of the following colors: bronze, gold and silver ☐ beading needles ☐ 1 spool of black button thread ☐ beading loom ☐ picture frame approximately 21 × 23.5cm ($8\frac{1}{4}$ × $9\frac{1}{4}$in) ☐ thick cardboard to fit inside a picture frame ☐ 1m (1yd) black velvet ribbon, 4cm ($1\frac{1}{2}$in) wide.

Making the bead picture. Cut 77 lengths of thread each measuring 50.5cm (20in). Fasten the threads to the loom or box and use doubled threads at both outer edges. Fig.10 shows the chart for the bead picture. Follow the design in the same way as for the jewelry and the belt. If your loom is too narrow to take the full width of the picture, it can be woven in 2 halves, split at the mid-vertical line. Join the 2 halves together by working backwards and forwards through the beads at the edge of the mid-line join (fig.11). When the thread is pulled tight the join becomes invisible.

Mounting the picture. Cut out a piece of thick cardboard to the same measurements as the inner dimensions of the picture frame. Draw out the position for the picture onto the cardboard in pencil. Along the top and bottom edges use a pin to pierce an equally spaced number of holes to coincide with the number of threads (ie 75) in the picture. Remove the beading from the loom and place it in position on the cardboard. Pass each length of thread individually through the appropriate pierced hole. When you have completed one edge, turn the cardboard over and knot the threads in bunches to prevent any movement. Work the opposite edge in the same way. When both top and bottom edges are anchored, thread a separate length and catch stitch the sides of the beading to the cardboard at 1.5cm ($\frac{1}{2}$in) intervals. Place the velvet ribbon along all 4 sides of the picture and miter at each corner. Catch stitch the velvet ribbon down to the cardboard backing. Place the picture into the frame.

Bead threading

Bead threading can easily be used in an elementary way to create simple jewelry, fringes and beaded curtains. Used in a more complex way, bead threading can be made into beaded fabrics, to create

10 Chart for the bead picture

11 Joining two pieces of beading invisibly

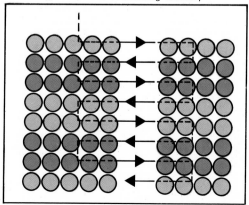

complete garments or to make accessories such as bags.

Sophisticated evening bag

This sparkling bag is the perfect accessory for evening clothes.

You will need :
320 10mm ($\frac{3}{8}$in) round faceted black plastic beads ☐ 88 14mm ($\frac{5}{8}$in) cylindrical faceted black plastic beads ☐ 1 spool of black button thread ☐ piece of black velvet or satin 24 × 23cm ($9\frac{1}{2}$ × 9in) ☐ piece of thick interfacing, canvas or medium-weight cardboard 23 × 21cm (9 × $8\frac{1}{4}$in) ☐ piece of black lining 24 × 23cm ($9\frac{1}{2}$ × 9in)

Sophisticated evening bag
Bead fringing

Row 1 (fig.13a). Keeping close to the edge of the fabric base on the side measuring 23cm (9in), begin threading the beads as shown in fig.13a (1 round bead, 2 cylindrical beads, 3 round beads, 2 cylindrical beads and 1 round bead). Sew each bead individually onto the base, with a space in between measuring the same as a round bead. This first row holds one edge of beading to the base fabric.

Row 2 (fig.13b). Pass the thread through the top edge of your base fabric and thread up a round bead. Then take the thread back through the last bead in the previous row; thread up a round bead; work through the next bead on the last row; thread up another round bead; work through the next bead on the last row; thread up another round bead. Continue in this way, alternating a new round bead between each bead on the previous row. At the end of this second row pass the thread through to the back of the work.

Row 3 (fig.13c). Pass the thread through to the front of the work catching it on the base fabric underneath. Work back through the last bead on the previous row. Thread up a new round bead. Repeat the alternating pattern as described in the previous row, but remember to insert the

cylindrical beads to correspond with the same positions in the first row. Continue by repeating rows 2 and 3 until 42 rows have been worked. Work row 43 as normal and then sew it down to the edge of the base fabric in the same way as row 1. The finished bead fabric should be sewn firmly at all 4 edges to the base.

Finishing the bag. Stitch ribbon binding along both 23cm (9in) edges of the bag. Fold this over the attaching bar at the base of each handle, and stitch it firmly to the bag, with neat stitches. Cut 2 pieces of black ribbon 14cm ($5\frac{1}{2}$in) for the gussets. Taper the ribbon at one end, and with the tapered end at the fold of the bag, overcast invisibly down each side. Fold over 2.5cm (1in) of ribbon at the other end to make a neat finish.

Bead fringing

Be selective when buying beads for bead fringing. If they are too fine and heavy you will constantly be repairing broken threads; use larger and lighter beads. It is easier to make the fringe first and then attach it in place. When making fringes, take care not to jam the beads tightly together. Allow a little slackness in the threads or the fringe will not hang correctly.

□ 1m (1yd) black velvet or satin ribbon, 4cm ($1\frac{1}{2}$in) wide □ pair of plastic bag handles to fit the 21cm ($8\frac{1}{4}$in) width of the beading.

Making the bag. Fig.12 shows the complete pattern to make a section of bead mosaic measuring 23 × 21cm (9 × $8\frac{1}{4}$in). The red line on the diagram marks the fold line at the base of the bag. Baste the piece of black velvet or satin onto the interfacing, canvas or cardboard by overlapping the top fabric around the edges of the stiffening fabric. The beads are threaded along the longer side of the fabric, from bottom to top and back again.

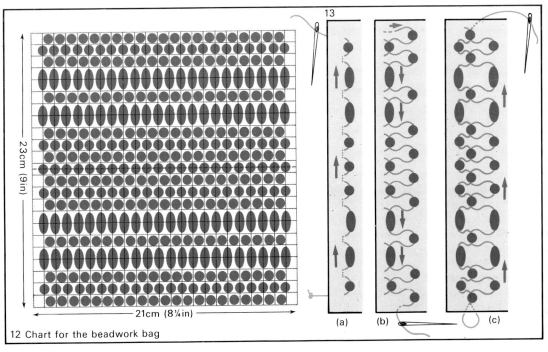

12 Chart for the beadwork bag

(a) (b) (c)

23cm (9in)

21cm ($8\frac{1}{4}$in)

13

Three beaded fringes

Three beaded fringes

Here are three simple but very different types of beaded fringe. The first is based on an Art Deco design. The second, in black jet, is designed to give a sophisticated touch to a simple garment. The daisy chain fringe would look good on a child's dress or as a piece of fun jewelry.

Art Deco fringe

You will need:

seed (rocaille) beads in the following colors: white, black, brown, yellow and orange □ beading needles □ 1 spool each of black and white button thread □ velvet ribbon for attaching beads.

Note: when the majority of beads are black, use black thread, and when they are white use white thread.

Making the fringe. Fasten a length of white thread through the edge of the velvet ribbon.

Row 1. Thread up 4 black beads and 8 white beads. Push the beads up to meet the velvet ribbon, and pass the needle back up through 7 of the white beads and the 4 black beads. The last bead at the bottom of the fringe is only threaded once; it stops the other beads from becoming unthreaded (fig.14).

Row 2. Thread up 5 black beads and 8 white beads. Repeat the process shown in fig.14. Follow the bead design from fig.15.

Jet fringe

You will need:

black seed (rocaille) beads □ black faceted drop beads □ beading needles □ 1 spool of black button thread □ velvet ribbon for attaching beads.

Making the fringe (fig.16). Pass the thread through the edge of the velvet ribbon.

Row 1. Pick up 32 seed beads, 1 drop bead and 4 seed beads. Pass back up the threaded beads at the 5th bead before the drop bead. Work back up 15 beads, then thread up 9 more seed beads, pass through the 5th bead from the beginning, pick up 4 more seed beads. Pass the needle through the edge of the velvet ribbon approximately 0.5cm ($\frac{1}{4}$in) away from where you started. Tighten the thread but leave enough slack for the beads to hang without being jammed against each other. Bring the thread out 2mm ($\frac{1}{12}$in) away from the point where you entered the ribbon.

Row 2. Thread up 9 seed beads, pass through the 10th bead from the beginning on the previous row, thread up 23 seed beads, 1 drop bead and 4 seed beads. Repeat the pattern as in row 1. Continue working rows in this way until you have worked the required length of bead fringe.

Daisy chain fringe

You will need:

seed (rocaille) beads in each of the following colors: green, orange and yellow □ beading needles □ 1 spool of green button thread □ velvet ribbon for attaching the beads.

Making the fringe (fig.17). Pass the thread through the edge of the velvet ribbon. Pick up 4 green beads and 8 yellow beads. Push these beads up to meet the velvet ribbon. Bring the needle to pass around and through the 1st yellow bead for the second

14 Preventing the beads from unthreading

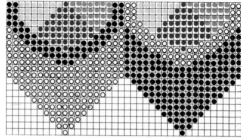

15 Chart for the Art Deco fringe

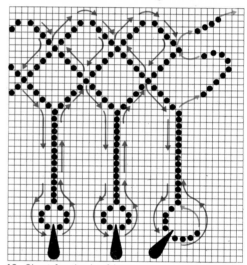

16 Chart for the jet fringe

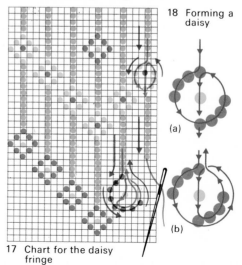

17 Chart for the daisy fringe

18 Forming a daisy

(a)

(b)

Beautiful beading, Tiffany style

time. Pick up 1 orange bead, then pass your needle through the 5th yellow bead. Tighten your thread to form a daisy (fig.18a). Take the needle back to pass through the 1st orange bead for a second time. Pick up 1 yellow bead. Pass the needle back through the 5th, 6th, 7th and 8th orange beads for a second time. Tighten to form a second daisy. Pass the needle back up the row of green beads through the 1st daisy and up the remaining green beads (fig.18b). Work through the edge of the velvet ribbon in the same position as you began. The 1st row of the daisy fringe is now completed. To create the chevron effect vary the number of green beads that are threaded at the beginning of each row. Follow the pattern in fig.17.

Beautiful beading, Tiffany style

This pattern was designed to imitate the style of a Tiffany lampshade in a simple way, to give an expensive look to an inexpensive lampshade. The beaded band is worked on a loom, and the fringe is worked in the same way as for the Art Deco fringe.

You will need:

3,000 turquoise glass bugles □ 1,000 black glass bugles □ 1,000 lime green glass bugles □ 4,000 dark green glass bugles □ 56g (2oz) black seed (rocaille) beads □ beading needles □ 2 spools of black button thread □ beading loom □ lampshade approximately 30.5cm (12in) in diameter □ 1 sheet of thin cardboard 18 × 101cm (7 × 40in) □ 1.5m (1½yd) velvet ribbon (optional).

Making the beading. Using your bead-weaving loom, first make a beaded band which is 6 beads in width and long enough to encircle the base of the lampshade. The band will measure approximately 1.5cm (½in) wide by 1m (1yd) long. Cut 9 lengths of the thread each measuring 1.4m (50in). Complete the whole band in black seed beads. If you do not want to use a bead-weaving band, substitute velvet ribbon as a base for the fringe.

Draw the basic design (fig.19) in which 1 square equals 2.5cm (1in) onto the cardboard. Baste the beadweaving band to the top edge of the card, keeping the lower edge of the beading in line with the top of

the cardboard. Make a line of fine basting stitches around the scalloped lower edge of the design. Fig.20 shows the number of beads and bugles required to work 1 repeat of the design. Note that the design is outlined with black beads. To make the complete fringe, work 12 repeats. Thread up and pass the needle down the 6 beads on the beadweaving band, then pick up 8 green bugles, 2 black beads, 23 turquoise bugles and 1 black bead. Pass the needle through the row of basting stitches around the scallop. Work back up the rows of beads omitting the last black bead threaded (see fig.14). When you reach the beadweaving band work back up 2 beads on the band, across and down the neighboring 2 beads ready to start the next row of the fringe. Continue working the fringe as shown in fig.20. When the fringe is complete sew it with fine stitches to the edge of the lampshade. Make the bead-weaving band neat by passing all the end threads through the edge of the lampshade and knotting them at the back. Join the 2 edges of the beadweaving band as shown in fig.11.

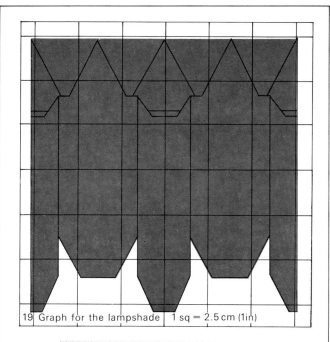

19 Graph for the lampshade   1 sq = 2.5cm (1in)

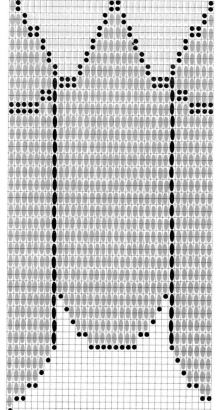

20 Chart for the lampshade

Shellcraft

Shells are the protective covering of the invertebrate animals known as mollusks and come in a variety of shapes, sizes and colors. They have been valued for their exquisite beauty throughout the ages, and used for many ornamental purposes. Archaeologists have discovered shell necklaces over 30,000 years old and gold headdresses encrusted with shells worn by Sumerian queens which are 5,000 years old. The Aztec and Inca peoples incorporated shells and mother-of-pearl (the interior of shells such as oysters and mussels) into elaborate ornaments and jewelry. Some existing tribes still decorate their boats with cowries and adorn them-

An extravagance of stones and shells combine on this church at Vauxbelets, Guernsey, in the Channel Islands, to form a baroque mosaic.

selves with pierced and threaded shells. The art of cameo cutting, which generally uses the pinkish brown interiors of the bull mouth helmet shell was first introduced by the ancient Babylonians and Phoenicians. Cameo cutting enjoyed great popularity with the Victorians who used shells and mother-of-pearl in very lavish designs—such as shells wired to form sprays of flowers and displayed under glass domes.

Mollusks are divided into several different categories according to the shape of their

Selection of shells. From the top row, left to right: Arctic clam, European cowries on each side of a Pacific cowrie, surf clam, star limpet, violet sea snail, top shell, prickly cockle, common cockle, common limpet, common top shells, Queen scallop, olive cowries, flat periwinkles, razor shell, coat-of-mail shell, tusk shell, spindle shell, native oyster, Mediterranean oyster.

shells. The largest class are the gastropods or snails, which are found in the sea and on rocks. They are characterized by a single shell which is often domed or spirally coiled. Gastropods include limpets, top shells, cowries, whelks and periwinkles. Oysters, clams, scallops and cockles are known as bivalves, and live in the sea and

sand. They consist of two shells or valves, hinged together. Tusk shells are slender, tube-shaped shells found in shallow water and sand. Finally, there are the coat-of-mail shells which resemble beetles and are found on rocks.

Collecting shells

Much of the pleasure of shellcraft is in collecting the shells, although the more exotic kinds can be bought, singly or in specially prepared packages, in specialist shops. Your collection should include: ordinary regularly shaped shells, such as bivalves for backgrounds; strong smooth-surfaced species, such as moon snails, to use in jewelry; and some unusual shells, such as star limpets (gastropods), to act as focal points.

Many species of mollusks are in danger of extinction due to pollution, trawling, the dumping of oil from tankers, and from disturbances of the ocean floor caused by oil drilling and mining operations. To help minimize this danger, collect empty shells in preference to those with living animals inside. You will find almost as many empty shells as living ones, and unusual effects can be created with shells that have been eroded by the sea, or, as with the snail species, with only the center spiral remaining. Also, avoid disturbing the habitat of mollusks when looking for suitable shells in such places as shallow pools, on rocks and under stones. Replace stones or rocks to their original place as some fauna depend on them for protection. The best time to collect seashells is when the tide is at its lowest. (Always remember to check the tides before setting out.)

Cleaning shells

Wash empty shells in warm water and, if necessary, scrub with a nail brush. Leave the shells to dry. Then store them in shallow boxes according to their species. Label the various species to help identify them at the later stage of selecting the shells for specific designs.

Making a shell picture

Shells can be glued to backgrounds such as plywood, hardboard, cork and cardboard.

A variety of species make up this bowl of shells embedded in cement and these exotic necklaces.

Preparing a fabric-covered mount. If you do not want to use a plain mount, cover a piece of plywood or hardboard with felt or a closely woven fabric to make a colored textured background for your shell design. Cut the fabric 5cm (2in) larger all around than the board all around. Place the mount on the wrong side of the fabric. Sew the opposite edges of the fabric together with strong thread and keep the fabric taut. Repeat the process for the other two edges and miter the corners. As you sew, join in new lengths of thread with knots. The framing should be completed and picture screws inserted at the back before starting work on the design since some shells are fragile and will break if pressure is applied.

Making the design. Work on a small area of the surface at a time and fix the shells in place with strong adhesive (preferably an epoxy resin), applied with a toothpick.

Embedding shells in cement

Shells can be used to decorate many things, such as lamp bases, bowls and ornaments, using an embedding technique. To embed shells in cement, it is best to start with something small, like an unglazed dish. You will need a small package of cement suitable for indoor use. Plan the design and select the shells before mixing the cement. Mix a sufficient quantity of cement with water to make a smooth, thick paste. Add water-based paint to the cement mixture if desired. Coat the dish with an even layer about 0.5cm ($\frac{1}{4}$in) thick. Place the shells carefully in position, using tweezers if necessary.

Murals. With a little experience, the same technique can be used on both interior and exterior walls, using the appropriate cement (either for indoor or outdoor use). Work on a small area at a time and use lightweight shells such as cockles and razor shells.

Shell jewelry
Pierced and threaded jewelry

Shell jewelry

Turning shells into pieces of jewelry is simple using easy techniques and mounts supplied by specialist craft stores.

Flat mounts. Use flat mounts for rings, clip earrings, brooches and bracelets. Choose strong shells with level bases. Put a little adhesive on the base of the shells (or single shell) and the mount. Stick together and leave to dry upright in a pot filled with salt or sand to a depth of 2.5cm (1in) to hold it in place. Embedding part of the jewelry in salt and placing it within a pot serves to keep it in position while the glue is drying.

Claw mounts. Claw mounts for rings are only suitable for use with single shells.

Shells threaded together in a functional and attractive way as in this curtain and hanging basket.

Work the claws gently outwards with a pair of small long-nosed pliers. Then, put a little adhesive between the shell and the mount, and bend the claws back into position over the shell.

Bell caps. Bell caps are small pronged mounts used for mounting shells to make drop earrings and pendants. Shape the prongs to fit the tops of suitable shells such as olive shells before adding adhesive.

Jump rings. Use jump rings to connect shells mounted on bell caps, to chains and earring mounts. Open and close jump rings with pliers.

Pierced and threaded jewelry

Certain small gastropods like pearly trochus shells can have holes drilled near their openings and be threaded to form necklaces. Place each shell on a wood surface, aperture facing up, and drill a hole in each, using the finest drill bit on (preferably) an electric drill. Alternatively, tap a very fine skewer with a hammer until a hole is pierced. Then cut some strong thread to the required length. Knot it, and string the shells on to it within about 5cm (2in) of the end. Knot both ends together. This technique of piercing and threading shells can also be adapted for making mobiles and decorating hanging baskets.

Macramé

The history of macramé is somewhat obscure for, although primitive man must undoubtedly have had an early need to tie things together and from that probably progressed to more complex weaving and decorative knotting, macramé in its more stylized form as we know it today almost certainly originated in the Middle East. The actual word is thought to originate from the Turkish *maqrama* meaning towel, on which the weaver frequently fastened off his threads with patterned fringes. It was the Turks who brought the craft to Spain and from there it spread throughout Europe where it was taught in the convents. It is said to have been introduced to England by Mary, wife of William of Orange, and quickly became popular with the women of the court.

Macramé had also long been a leisure-time occupation of sailors, already used to tying knots in their work, and their travels around the world undoubtedly helped to spread the knowledge of the craft.

In Victorian England, the technique found favor as one of the statutory "accomplishments" of gentlewomen and it was used for the heavy and ornate decorations with which fashionable Victorians filled their homes. With the less elaborate fashions of the 1920s and 1930s, macramé declined in popularity until the recent revival of interest in crafts of all kinds has drawn attention to it again.

Materials and equipment

The tools required are few, the most important of these being a pair of hands. Fabrics are formed in patterns by knotting together threads which can be of almost any thickness or texture. The only limitations are that the yarns must withstand the tension of tightening the knots and that the texture should be reasonably smooth simply for the sake of the worker's hands. Experiment with twine, fine string and jute.

During progress, the work should be pinned to a firm surface such as a piece of sturdy cardboard covered with a sheet of paper which, although rigid, will also take pins easily. T-pins or glass-headed pins are the most suitable to use. Scissors and a tape-measure are usually the only other things required.

Beginning to work

Although macramé knotting looks complicated, it is really very simple and only needs practice until you feel at home with the knots.

To begin, use a medium thickness of ordinary string and work several rows of each new knot until it feels familiar and comfortable. Cut a length of about 25cm (10in) and tie a knot at each end. Pin the length horizontally across the board so that it is stretched taut with a pin through each knot (fig.1). This is called a mounting or holding cord and forms a base on which to start a piece of work. Sometimes it is removed later. Next cut several lengths of string. Their exact measurement is unimportant for a beginner's practice piece. They should, however, all be the same length, say about 61cm (24in) each so that there is not too much surplus to cope with while the techniques are still unfamiliar. When working on an actual project they should each be about eight times the required length of the finished article. Fold one length in half to form a double cord. Hold the looped end in front of the holding cord, fold it over the top of the holding cord and then down the back of it so that the loop is below the cord. Tuck the two loose ends through the loop and tighten the knot around the holding cord (fig.2). This is called a lark's head knot (setting on knot). Continue in the same way with each cord working along the holding cord.

Basic knots

Horizontal knotting (fig.3a). It is usual to secure the lark's head knots with a row of horizontal knotting, and in learning this particular stage, the half hitch basic knot of all macramé will also be learned.

Each knot is worked over an anchor cord known as the leader or knot bearer. This can be a separate cord placed on the board over the knotting cords and pinned at the left-hand side in the same way as the holding cord or by using the knotting cord at the outer edge. The leader is held taut by the right hand horizontally across the knotting cords close under the holding cord. Working from left to right, take the first knotting cord and wrap it counterclockwise around the leader from front to back twice,

Sailors have always been adept at knotting and creating different rope patterns. This illustration comes from *The Book of Kells*, one of the finest examples of Western illuminated manuscripts dating from the early Middle Ages.

each time coming to the front of the work to the left of itself. The second time around locks the knot.

Continue along the leader, knotting each cord in turn. Horizontal knotting or double half hitches can also be worked from right to left, the leader coming from the right and the knot being reversed (fig.3b). It is very often used within a design and is not only a locking device reserved for the beginning and ending of the work.

Diagonal knotting (fig.4). This is worked in exactly the same way as horizontal double half hitches but the leader is held taut across the knotting cords in a diagonal direction, either to the right or the left, but always downwards.

Square (flat) knots (fig.5a, b and c). These are used frequently in macramé and provided the thread is not too silky, also make a good locking device on the threads.

Macramé

Basic knots

The knot is made with a core of one, two and sometimes more threads and single or multiple outer knotting cords are knotted around them. It is easiest for the beginner to practice with four cords, two as the core or filler threads with one knotting cord on either side. Keep the two filler cords taut by winding them around the third finger of the left hand or by securing them to the board farther down.

Curve the left-hand cord into a loop, passing the end behind the filler cords and over the front of the right-hand working cord. Next take the right-hand cord over the filler cords and into the loop from the front. Pull the ends sideways until the knot closes around the filler cords in the position required. This is the first stage of a square knot (sometimes called a flat knot).

Form the right-hand thread into a loop and pass the end behind the filler cords and in front of the left-hand cord, then take the left-hand cord over the filler cords and into the loop. When this second stage of the knot is drawn tight the completed square knot will lock.

Spirals or sennits (fig.6). These are formed by making only one stage of the square knot, either the first or the second, over and over again. Whichever is chosen will determine the direction in which the spiral will twist.

Overhand knot (fig. 7). This can be done using any number of cords but usually with a minimum of two. However many cords are being used, they are all held together and knotted as one. Form a loop with the ends going behind themselves and then passing through the loop from front to back. Pull the knot tight, positioning it with the help of a pin to prevent it from locking until it is in the correct place. If several cords have been used it is best to pull each one tight individually. The loop can be formed to the right or the left but it looks better if consistency is maintained throughout one piece of work.

Vertical knotting (fig.8). This again is simply a variation on horizontal and diagonal double half hitches. The filler cords are vertical and the knots are formed by either one of the adjacent knotting cords or by a newly introduced cord.

Take the knotting cord behind the leader around the front and behind again, emerging at the front of the work between the leader and itself. Pass it around the leader once more, coming to the front of the work as before to lock the knot. The vertical double half hitches can either continue down the same leader or pass onto the next vertical cord. It can be done from right to left or left to right.

Knotted chain (fig.9). This is made by working simple knots around a filler cord, first one to the right, then one to the left so that the filler cord and the knotting cord constantly change places.

Single knotted chain is worked using two threads. Hold the left-hand thread taut vertically, pass the right-hand thread over it, around the back and through to the front of the work between itself and the left-hand thread. Next hold the right-hand thread taut and pass the left-hand thread over the front of it, around the back and out at the front of the work between the two threads. These two movements combine to make one knotted chain.

A double knotted chain is made in the same way but using four threads in two groups of two.

Finishing. Once these basic knots have been practiced on a sampler, fasten off with one or two rows of horizontal knotting. The work can then be removed from the knotting board.

Now that these knots have become familiar, experiment with combining them to form patterns. Most macramé knots can be worked singly or repeated several times both across the work and down it. It is in this way that designs emerge and because of this, macramé is one of the few crafts where you can easily originate designs of your own.

For the beginner

Here are two quick and easy belts to make, one with its own matching bracelet. The white belt with green beads should be made to measure 56cm (22in) to 63.5cm (25in) long, depending on your waist measurement, by 4cm (1½in) wide. The green and red belt measures 61cm (24in) long, excluding fringes and knots, by 4cm (1½in) wide. The bracelet is the same width and is 20cm (8in) long.

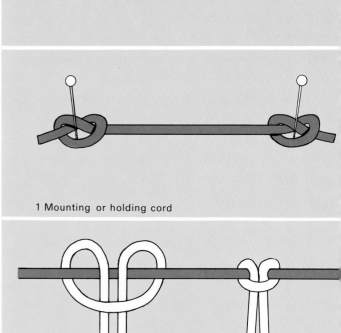

1 Mounting or holding cord

2 Lark's head (setting on) knot

3a Horizontal double half hitches to the right

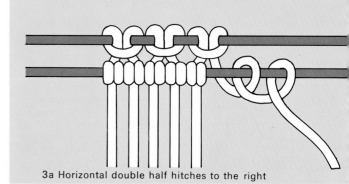

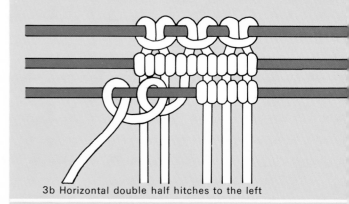

3b Horizontal double half hitches to the left

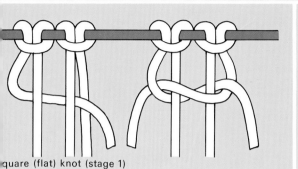

Square (flat) knot (stage 1)

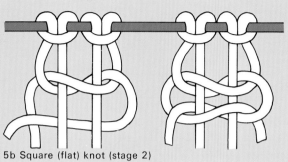

5b Square (flat) knot (stage 2)

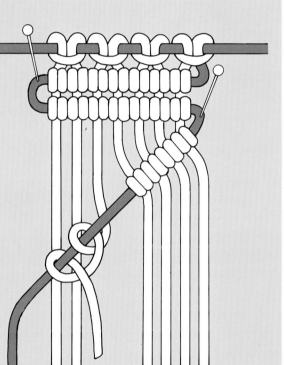

4 Diagonal knotting

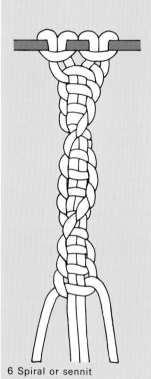

6 Spiral or sennit

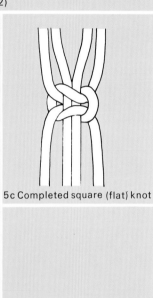

5c Completed square (flat) knot

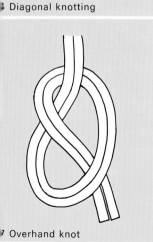

7 Overhand knot

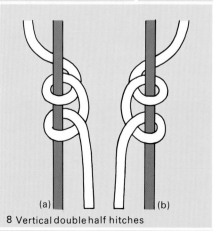

(a)   (b)

8 Vertical double half hitches

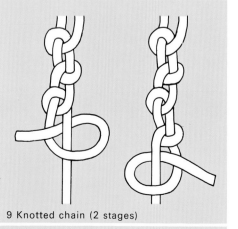

9 Knotted chain (2 stages)

Macramé

Natural string belt

Natural string belt

This belt is knotted in a pattern repeat of 7.5cm (3in) which can be repeated the number of times necessary to make the correct length of belt.

You will need:

34m (37½yd) medium cotton seine twine □ 32 or 36 polished wooden beads 16 × 8mm (⅝ × ⅜in) □ buckle □ 12 rubber bands □ clear drying glue.

Mounting the cords (setting on). Cut 4 lengths to measure 548.5cm (216in) each. Double and mount onto the bar of the buckle with lark's head knots. Cut 2 lengths each 610cm (240in). Fold 1 length so that one end measures 396cm (156in) and the other 214cm (84in) and mount onto the left-hand end of the buckle bar with the longer cord on the outer edge. Fold the remaining length in the same way and mount onto the bar so that the longer cord is at the right-hand outer edge of the bar. Thread seven or eight wooden beads (depending on how many pattern repeats will be required) onto each of the 2nd, 5th, 8th and 11th cords. Make a figure eight hank with each of the cords, winding from the end nearest the work and secure each one with a rubber band. Let out the twine as required.

Knotting the pattern. Using the right-hand end cord as leader, make 1 row of horizontal double half hitches from right to left. *Counting from the left, use cord 1 as leader and knot double half hitches diagonally to the right over the next 5 cords. Using the last cord as leader, knot double half hitches diagonally to the left over the next 11 cords. Using cord 7 as leader, knot double half hitches diagonally to the right over the next 5 cords.

Using the right-hand end cord as leader, make 2 rows of horizontal double half hitches.

Divide the cords into 4 groups of 3. On each group make a square knot, place a bead on each filler cord; make a second square knot to secure. Using cord 1 as leader, make 2 rows of horizontal double half hitches.

Repeat from *7 or 8 times, according to the length of belt required.

Divide the cords into 2 groups of 6 cords each. Knot double half hitches diagonally

Macramé

Green twine bracelet and belt

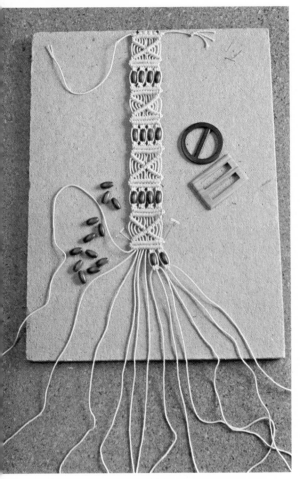

Making the bracelet

Mounting the cords (setting on). Cut 5 lengths of twine each measuring 213cm (84in). Double one of these, make a simple knot at the fold as shown in fig.10 and use as a holding cord. Double the remaining 4 lengths and mount on the holding cord as shown in fig.11, placing 2 on either side of the bead.

Knotting the pattern. *Using the 2 center cords as leaders, knot double half hitches diagonally to left and right, over each of the 4 cords. Repeat twice more to make 3 rows of diagonal double half hitches in all. Counting from the left, use the first 4 cords to make a square knot. Pass the 2 filler cords through a round bead and make another square knot. Pass the next 2 cords through a large oval bead. Knot the last 4 threads as given for the first 4. Using the first and last cords as leaders, knot double half hitches diagonally into the center over each of the 4 cords. Repeat twice more to make 3 rows of double half hitches in all.** Counting from the left, use the first 4 cords to make a square knot. Pass the next 2

cords through a round bead. Using the last 4 cords, make a square knot.*** Repeat from * to *** once more, then from * to ** once.

Using the center 4 cords as filler cords, with 1 working cord on each side, make 2 square knots. Take these 6 cords together as one and make an overhand knot. Pull tightly on each cord in turn, cut ends 7.5cm (3in) from the knot and tease out to form a tassel.

Make an overhand knot on each of the remaining 4 cords close to the work, cut ends and secure with a dab of glue.

Fasten the bracelet by slipping the knot through the space between the triple rows of double half hitches at the opposite end.

Making the belt

The belt will fit waist sizes from 55 to 71cm (22 to 28in). It is made in 2 sections from a ring at the center back.

Mounting the cords (setting on). Cut 5 lengths, each measuring 335cm (132in). Double each length and mount onto the ring with lark's head knots.

Knotting the pattern. Work as given for the

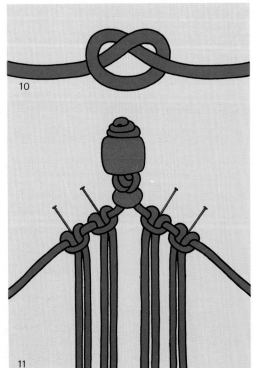

into the center with each group for several rows to form a point.

Divide the cords into 6 groups of 2 cords each. Take each pair of cords together as one and make up an overhand knot. Cut the cords closely under each knot and secure with a dab of glue.

Green twine bracelet and belt

These attractive accessories will add interest to a plain dress.

You will need:

Bracelet: 11m (12yd) cotton twine □ 3 oval polished wooden beads 25 × 14mm (1 × ½in) □ 9 small round wooden beads □ clear drying glue.

Belt: 33m (36yd) cotton twine □ metal ring 2.5cm (1in) in diameter □ 8 oval polished wooden beads 25 × 14mm (1 × ½in) □ 24 small round wooden beads.

bracelet, repeating from * to *** 3 times, then * to ** once.

Pass the 2 center cords through a round bead. Using the 2 cords together as one, make an overhand knot close to the bead. Using all 10 cords together as one, make an overhand knot 5cm (2in) from the bead. Trim ends to 30.5cm (12in).

Make the second half of the belt in the same way. Tie the belt in the front by slipping the knot at one end through the cords above the knot at the opposite end.

For your window . . .

Here is an original and attractive window shade. Made in jute yarn, the design allows the light to filter through. The open motif in the center can be hung with a large shell, a bead or some other interesting object. The shade measures 75cm (29½in) wide by 91cm (36in) deep, including the fringe. Work the shade on a soft board and pin in place as the work progresses. Start from the bamboo or dowel at the top. Instructions are given for the top half, including the whole of the central diamond; the rest of the work is completed to match.

You will need:

1m (1yd) length of dowel or bamboo ☐ about 1kg (2lb) three-strand jute.

Mounting the cords (setting on). Secure the bamboo or dowel across the top of the board with T-pins. Cut 74 lengths of jute 4.8m (16ft) long. Double the cords and mount onto the bamboo with lark's head knots. Cut another piece 1m (1yd) long, and using it as an attached leader, knot 1 row of horizontal double half hitches across all threads.

Knotting the pattern. The background is made of square knots done over groups of 4 cords. As you work you will find that on the alternate rows of square knots the 2 cords at the beginning and end are loose so make these neat by working 3 or 4 rows of vertical double half hitches on the inner cord with the outer one. This will use up a lot of the outer cord, so change the cords over halfway through the work.

Work 3 rows of alternate square knots.

First row of diagonal double half hitches. Using the 2 center cords as leaders, as shown in fig.12, make diagonal double half hitches to left and right over 2 cords on

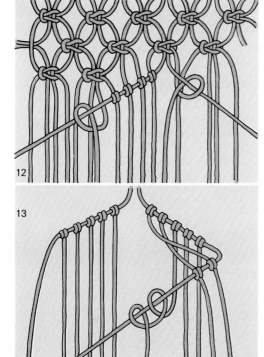

12

13

each side. Continue to work the alternate rows of square knots, and in each row, make diagonal double half hitches knotting the center threads over 2 more cords, pushing the loops together for a firm line. After 30 rows of square knots, when there are 16 cords left on each side, make the horizontal double half hitches and continue outwards over 11 cords. Turn the leaders around a pin, and make horizontal double half hitches back into the center over the same 11 cords, leaving about 2.5cm (1in) space from the previous row of double half hitches. Leave these leaders aside, and return to work the second row of diagonal double half hitches from the center.

Second row of diagonal double half hitches. Take the 2 center cords, measure 5cm (2in) down, make an overhand knot over the 2 together and pin the knot to the board. Using these 2 cords as leaders, make diagonal double half hitches to left and right over 58 cords each side, keeping a distance of 5cm (2in) from the previous row of double half hitches, diminishing to 4cm (1½in). Leave these leaders hanging and return to center.

Third row of diagonal double half hitches. Take 2 center cords, measure 8cm (3⅛in) down, work an overhand knot over the 2 together, pin knot to board. Using these 2 cords as leaders, make diagonal double half hitches to left and right over 51 cords each side. Leave leaders hanging and return to center.

Spirals. Take 4 center cords, make 11 half square knots by bringing the first cord over the center 2 first, so that the bar turns twice to the right. Using the next 9 groups of 4 cords, make 9 similar spirals. Work another 9 spirals to the left of the central top (only this time work the half square knot by bringing the last cord over the center 2 first, so that the bars spiral to the left).

Central diamond. Pin the top central spiral to the board, divide into 2 cords, make diagonal double half hitches to the left and right (each pair used as 1 leader) over 36 cords each side. Turn each pair of cords around a T-pin and knot double half hitches back into the center, knotting the cords on from the center outwards to make an open diamond, as shown in fig.13. Complete the lower half of the shade in the

Front panel for a dress or smock

same way as the upper half, bringing the hanging leaders of the diamond shape back into the center in turn, and making 3 more spirals to fit the points at each side.

When the central motif is complete, work 3 rows of alternate square knots, and then proceed to make the decorative finishing points at the bottom of the shade.

Pointed bottom edge and fringe. Taking the central 36 cords, use the 2 outer ones as leaders for the diagonal double half hitches. Knot double half hitches into the center over 2 cords, work 1 row of square knots, knot double half hitches into the center over 2 cords, make another row of square knots, and continue until there is 1 square knot left in the middle of the point. Complete the point by knotting double half hitches into the center, then make an overhand knot over the 4 leader cords. Make the other 4 points over 28 cords in the same way. Make a knot over the 4 threads at the apex of each point.

Trim the fringe to the required length. Sew in the ends of attached leader in the very first row.

Fine macramé

Originally, macramé was often knotted so finely that it resembled lace. Today, coarser cords are used generally, but here is an idea to trim a very special dress or smock. You will need a lot of time and patience, but the results speak for themselves. The techniques are all basic with the exception of the introduction of blackberry knots as part of the design. The front panel measures 23×9cm ($9 \times 3\frac{1}{2}$in).

You will need:
120g ($4\frac{1}{2}$oz) mercerized crochet cotton □ crewel needle.

Front panel

Mounting the cords. Cut 40 lengths each 183cm (72in) and 5 lengths each 18cm (7in). Tie a knot at each end of a short length and pin it to the knotting board as a holding cord. Double each of the long lengths and mount onto the holding cord with lark's head knots, making 80 working cords.

Making the pattern. Lay one of the short lengths across the work as leader and make 1 row of horizontal double half hitches. Re-

peat with a second short length.

Row 3. Divide the work into 20 groups of 40 cords each and work 1 square knot on each group.

Row 4. Leaving 2 outer cords at each end, divide the work into 19 groups of 4 cords each. On each group make 4 square knots, using the crewel needle to take the filler cords from the front to the back of the work above the first square knot. Bring the cord down behind the work and make 1 square knot to secure as shown in fig.14. This is known as a blackberry knot.

Rows 5–7. As given for row 3.

Row 8. Leaving the 2 outer cords at each end, divide the work into 19 groups of 4 cords each. On groups 5, 10 and 15 work a blackberry knot; on each of the remaining groups work 1 square knot.

Row 9. Work 1 square knot under each square knot worked on the previous row and omit groups with a blackberry knot.

Row 10. As row 9.

Row 11. Divide work into 20 groups of 4 cords each and work across from the left placing 1 knot on each group as follows: 2 square knots, 1 blackberry knot, *4 square knots, 1 blackberry knot, repeat from * twice more, 2 square knots.

Row 12. One square knot on first 4 cords and also on last 4.

Row 13. As row 12.

Row 14. Leaving the 2 outer cords at each end, divide the work into 19 groups of 4 cords each. Work 1 square knot on each group.

Row 15. As row 3.

Row 16. Leaving the 2 outer cords at each end, divide the work into 19 groups of 4 cords each. On the first and every alternate group, work a spiral of 10 half square knots.

Row 17. Divide the work into 20 groups of 4 cords each and place 1 knot on each group as follows: *2 square knots, 1 blackberry knot, repeat from *, ending with 2 square knots.

Row 18. As row 16.

Row 19. As row 3.

Row 20. As row 14.

Rows 21–3. As row 3.

Rows 24–6. As row 14.

Rows 27–9. As row 3.

Row 30. As row 14.

Row 31. Using cord 8 as leader, make diagonal double half hitches to the left over the next 7 cords. Knot the next 4 groups of 8 cords in the same way. Using cord 41 as leader, make diagonal double half hitches to the right over the next 7 cords. Knot the following 4 groups of 8 cords in the same way. Using the center 4 cords, make a blackberry knot.

Row 32. Leaving the 2 outer cords at each end, divide the work into 19 groups of 4 cords each and make 1 knot on each group as follows: (1 square knot, 1 blackberry knot) 9 times, 1 square knot. Using the center 4 cords, make a blackberry knot, keeping the spacing the same as the one above it.

Row 33. Using cord 1 as leader, make diagonal double half hitches to the right over the next 7 cords. Work the next 4 groups of 8 cords in the same way. Using cord 48 as leader, make diagonal double half hitches to the left over the next 7 cords. Work the following 4 groups of 8 cords in the same way.

Row 34. As row 14.

Rows 35–7. As row 3.

Rows 38–40. As row 14.

Rows 41–3. As row 3.

Row 44. As row 14.

Row 45. Skip cord 1 and using cords 2 and 3, work the first stage only of vertical double half hitches 9 times (this will twist), *skip 2 cords, work another vertical double half hitch, repeat from * to end, skipping last cord.

Row 46. As row 14.

Row 47. As row 3.

Row 48. As row 14.

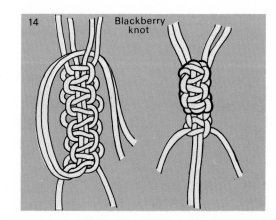

14   Blackberry knot

Row 49. As row 45.
Row 50. As row 14.
Rows 51–3. As row 3.
Rows 54–6. As row 14.
Rows 57–9. As row 3.
Row 60. Leaving the outer 2 cords at each end, divide the work into 19 groups of 4 cords each and work 1 knot on each group as follows: *1 blackberry knot, spiral of 6 half square knots, repeat from * 8 times more, 1 blackberry knot.
Row 61. Using cords 1, 2, 5 and 6, work 1 square knot to make a cross under the blackberry knot of previous row. Take cords 3 and 4 over cords 5 and 6 and make 1 square knot with cords 3, 4, 7 and 8. Work across the panel in this way, crossing cords under each blackberry knot.
Row 62. One blackberry knot under each of the 9 spirals of row 60.
Row 63. Knot a spiral of 6 half square knots under each blackberry knot of row 62.
Row 64. Using cords 1, 2, 5 and 6, work 1 square knot as in row 61 and 1 square knot using cords, 3, 4, 7 and 8. Work across the panel, crossing cords on either side of blackberry knots.
Row 65. Leaving the outer 2 cords at each end, divide work into 19 groups of 4 cords each. Using cords 3, 4, 5 and 6, work a blackberry knot. Repeat on the 9 following alternate groups.
Rows 66–8. As row 3.
Rows 69–71. As row 14.
Rows 72–4. As row 3.
Row 75. Skip 2 cords, (make 1 square knot on next 4 cords) 3 times, *skip 4 cords, (work 1 square knot on next 4 cords) 3 times, repeat from * 3 times more, skip last 2 cords.
Row 76. Skip 4 cords, (work 1 square knot on next 4 cords) twice, *skip 8 cords, (work 1 square knot on next 4 cords) twice, repeat from * 3 times more, skip last 4 cords.
Row 77. Skip 6 cords, work 1 square knot on next 4 cords, *skip 12 cords, work 1 square knot on next 4 cords, repeat from * 3 times more, skip last 6 cords.
Row 78. Work first stage only of vertical double half hitches 4 times with cords 8 and 9, 24 and 25, 40 and 41, 56 and 57, 72 and 73.
Row 79. As row 77.

Row 80. As row 76.
Row 81. As row 75.
Rows 82–4. As row 3.
Rows 85–7. As row 14.
Rows 88–90. As row 3.
Row 91. As row 14.
Row 92. Skip 4 cords, *1 square knot, 1 blackberry knot, 1 square knot, skip 2 cords, 1 spiral of 22 half square knots, skip 2 cords, repeat from * twice more, 1 square knot, 1 blackberry knot, 1 square knot, skip 4 cords.

Row 93. Skip 4 cords, *3 square knots, skip 2 cords, spiral and 2 cords, repeat from * twice more, 3 square knots, skip last 4 cords.
Row 94. As row 93.
Row 95. Skip 2 cords, *1 square knot, 2 blackberry knots, 1 square knot, skip spiral, repeat from * twice more, 1 square knot, 2 blackberry knots, 1 square knot, skip last 2 cords.
Row 96. Skip 2 cords, *4 square knots, skip spiral, repeat from * twice more, 4 square

knots, skip last 2 cords.

Row 97. As row 96.

Row 98. Skip 4 cords, *1 square knot, 1 blackberry knot, 1 square knot, skip 2 cords, spiral and 2 cords, repeat from * twice more, 1 square knot, 1 blackberry knot, 1 square knot, skip last 4 cords.

Rows 99 and 100. As row 93.

Row 101. As row 95.

Rows 102 and 103. As row 96.

Row 104. Two square knots, *1 blackberry knot, 4 square knots, repeat from * twice more, 1 blackberry knot, 2 square knots.

Rows 105 and 106. As row 3.

Rows 107–9. As row 14.

Rows 110–12. As row 3.

Row 113. Skip first 2 cords, 19 blackberry knots, skip last 2 cords.

Rows 114 and 115. Using remaining separate leaders, work 2 rows of horizontal double half hitches.

Completing the panel. Cut off long threads and sew ends to back of work. Stitch the panel in place.

Cavandoli work

This form of macramé is named for the Countess Valentina Cavandoli who originated it as a craft for the orphans in her care at the Casa del Sole in Turin at the end of the 19th century. The children made bookmarks and small items, the sale of which contributed to the upkeep of the orphanage.

The main characteristics of the work are the geometric design, the tightly knotted texture and the colored picot edges. In fine threads it is suitable for belts, watch bands, braids and bookmarks; and in heavier threads for rugs, cushions, chair seats, bags and stool covers.

Materials. Cords should be strong and smooth as they need to lie flat and withstand the tensions of working. A fairly soft cord is advisable as the knotting forms a stiff fabric.

Color. Traditionally two colors only are used, one for the background and one for the pattern. A strong contrast in color or tone is most effective.

Design. Cavandoli designs are worked out on graph paper, in a similar way to cross stitch designs. Each square represents a cord, the blank squares show the horizontal

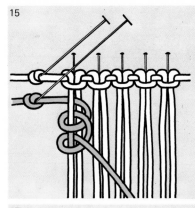

15 Make a knot at one end of the pattern cord and pin to side of work. Pass pattern cord *under* first cord and make a vertical double half hitch on it. The knot is in two movements, both looping clockwise.

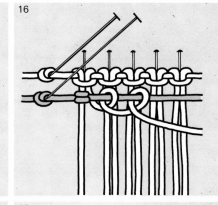

16 Using pattern cord as leader, make a row of horizontal double half hitches from left to right.

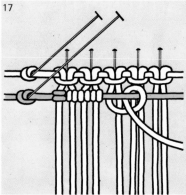

17 The top row of double half hitches goes across the work to secure lark's head knots.

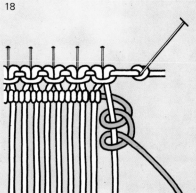

18 At the end of the row make a vertical double half hitch on the last cord in the same way as on the first

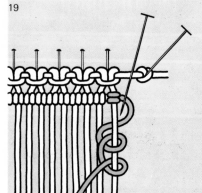

19 Loop the pattern cord around a pin to form a picot. Bring it back *under* the last cord and make another knot under the previous one. Note that when working from right to left the cord loops counterclockwise.

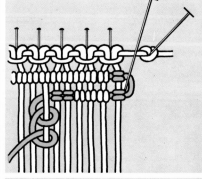

20 Insert vertical double half hitches where color is required. On the graph paper each dot represents one vertical double half hitch.

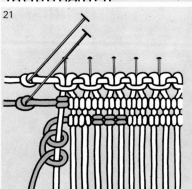

21 When the first cord is reached again, make a vertical double half hitch on it with the pattern cord, looping counterclockwise as last cord.

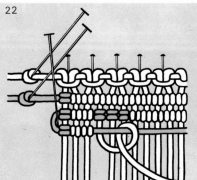

22 Loop cord around pin to form a picot, pass *under* first cord again and make another vertical double half hitch, looping cord clockwise as in fig.15.

The accompanying eight diagrams (figs. 15—22) explain the method.

Child's Cavandoli rug

Here is a delightful bedside rug for a small child. Made in rug yarn, the resulting fabric is firm and hard-wearing. Make the houses and trees from the chart given (fig. 24a) or, alternatively, knot your child's name into the rug from the alphabet also shown as a chart (fig. 24b). The rug measures 37cm (14½in) wide by 89cm (35in) long, including the fringe.

You will need:
550g (19½oz) rug yarn in hanks in main shade, A, yellow □ 250g (9oz) in hanks in contrast, B, orange □ large crochet hook.

Mounting the cords. Cut a length of 51cm (20in) yarn in A for a holding cord. Make a knot at each end and pin to the top of the knotting board.

Mount the lengths by doubling and inserting the loop behind the holding cord as shown in fig.23 instead of over the top. Mount 35 lengths of A in the following sequence, working from left to right:

1. 487.5cm (192in), folded 106.5cm (42in) and 381cm (150in), placed with the shorter cord first.
2. 762cm (300in) doubled.
3. 762cm (300in) doubled.
4. 670.5cm (264in) doubled.
5. 518cm (204in), folded 305cm (120in) and 213cm (84in).
6. 518cm (204in), folded 213cm (84in) and 305cm (120in).
7. 670.5cm (264in) doubled.
8. 731.5cm (288in) doubled.
9. 731.5cm (288in) doubled.

knots and the dots the vertical knots.

All the mounted cords are in the main background color. The pattern color is introduced as a separate ball of cord at the side of the work and is used as a leader for the horizontal double half hitches, the pattern being formed by the working of vertical double half hitches in the pattern color on the background cords.

Technique. Lay the graph paper pattern next to the knotting board. Fix a holding cord on the board, cut and mount the background cords with lark's head knots. The length of these should be 8 times the length of the finished article (or 4 times when doubled). The length of the ball of pattern color will vary with the extent of the colored pattern. Start with a few meters (yards) wound into a hank, secured with a rubber band and add more cord as required at either side. Sew the ends into the back when the piece is complete.

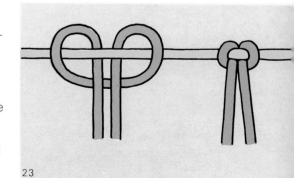
23

(a)

24 Charts for Cavandoli rug

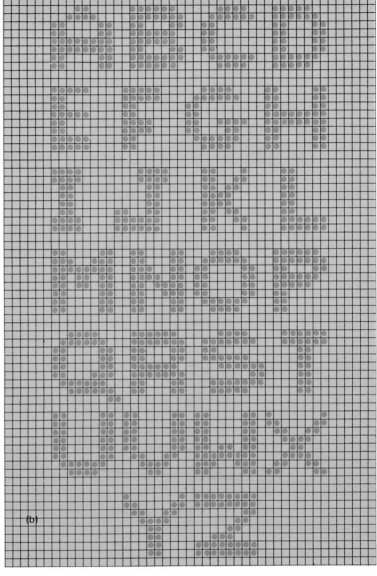

(b)

10. 609.5cm (240in), folded 366cm (144in) and 243.5cm (96in).
11. 487.5cm (192in) doubled.
12. 487.5cm (192in) doubled.
13. 548.5cm (216in) doubled.
14. 548.5cm (216in) doubled.
15. 457cm (180in) doubled.
16. 457cm (180in) doubled.
17. 548.5cm (216in) doubled.
18. 487.5cm (192in) doubled.
Continue to cut and mount cords following these in reverse order, from 17 to 1. Where the lengths are folded unevenly, reverse the figures (in No. 10 for example, fold the length 243.5cm (96in) and 366cm (144in)).

Cut several meters (yards) of B, make a knot at one end and pin to the left of the work, wind up the yarn and secure with a rubber band, letting it out as required.

Making the pattern. Follow the chart for half the pattern. Allow 1 row of horizontal double half hitches and work the second half in reverse.

Making the fringe. When the pattern is completed, make an overhand knot on each pair of cords, close to the last row of double half hitches. Trim 9cm (3½in) from the

knots. Tease out the ends. Turn the work so that the holding cord is at the foot of the knotting board. Cut 35 lengths each 30.5cm (12in) of A from remaining hank and remnants from other trimmed fringe. Using the crochet hook, pull each length through the rug just above the holding cord and between each mounted cord. Double it and make an overhand knot to secure. Trim 9cm (3½in) from the knots. Tease out ends.

Completing the rug. Sew the ends of the holding cord to the back of the work. Sew down the ends where new lengths of B have been introduced.

118

Crochet

and increasing popularity of this form of lacemaking.

In the 16th century crochet became known as "nun's work," as nuns made altar cloths and other items for Church use. By around 1785 the center of the craft was Cork in Ireland and many thousands of women there were involved in a thriving industry. The crochet work they produced was based on patterns derived from original Italian, Greek and French lace designs. The "traditional" Irish rose pattern was in fact taken from Venetian lace. It was during the 19th century that crochet came into its own for both personal and household use. The Sisters of the Ursuline Convent in Ireland taught Irish crochet lacemaking to children, a subject that spread to become part of the curriculum in most convents in the country.

Crochet has become very popular because it is so quick and easy to do. It is a very adaptable craft; lengths of crochet work can be used with other materials, or it can be made into a fabric in its own right. Besides making complete clothes and household items you can make borders and edgings for things such as tablecloths and window shades.

Materials and equipment

There is as wide a selection of yarns for this work as there are things to make from it. All knitting yarns are suitable for crochet designs; you can experiment with the coarsest of yarns or string to make rugs and bags, or make gossamer fabrics from fine yarns for curtains and shawls. You can even create the fine lacy fabrics our grandmothers made from fine cotton thread using a miniature hook.

The only tool you will need is a crochet hook. These are generally made from a lightweight coated metal or plastic, rounded at one end with a hook at the other similar to a shepherd's crook. They are all of a similar length because, unlike knitting, there will rarely be more than one loop on the hook. The size of hook is directly related to the quality of yarn being used. Fine, small hooks are suitable for thin cottons, rayons and baby yarns, and large thick hooks should be used with heavier yarns and string.

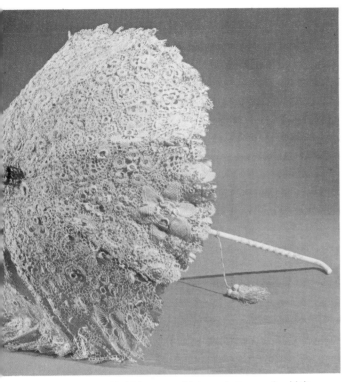

A mid-19th century Irish crochet parasol, which makes delicate use of floral motifs on a lacy background.

Amongst the world's legends is a charming story which relates how thousands of years ago a snow white serpent, the king of the reptiles, was roaming the land. On his travels he met a woman called Eve, who invited him to come and live with her. At first he declined; but after much cajoling on the part of Eve, he agreed, on condition that she should either knit or crochet a pattern on his back to make him more attractive. Eve duly did this, creating a beautiful design for him: the pattern to be found on all pythons today. The truth about the origins of crochet is very obscure, largely because pattern designs and instructions were usually handed down by word of mouth, leaving few written details. However, it is generally thought that crochet has much the same sort of history as knitting, being developed in the East and spreading to the Mediterranean area. The word "crochet" is of French origin, from the verb *crocher* meaning "to hook," and certainly the French did play a part in the development

Crochet hook sizes

American	Old British	ISR* (mm)
(wool)	(wool)	
K	3	7.00
J	4	6.00
I	6	5.00
G	7	4.50
F	8	4.00
E	9	3.50
C	10	3.00
(cotton)	(cotton)	
1	0	2.50
4	1½	2.00
6	2½	1.75
7	3½	1.50
11	5½	1.00
13	6½	0.75
14	7	0.60

ISR is the International Size Range of crochet hooks, the metric sizing.

As many different manufacturers have their own system of sizes for crochet hooks, you may have some difficulty in finding exact equivalents in some cases. Always try out a small crochet sample to check the gauge before starting on any piece of work.

Gauge

Gauge is the number of stitches and rows to a given measurement using a particular yarn and hook size. If you are working from a pattern it is essential to obtain the gauge stated, as all the designer's calculations have been based on this. Before starting a pattern you should always check your gauge by working a test sample, using the yarn and hook sizes stated in the pattern. Crochet a sample approximately 10cm (4in) square. Put the sample on a flat surface and measure out 10cm (4in) with pins both lengthwise and widthwise. Count the number of stitches and rows very carefully. If there are too few stitches and rows your gauge is too loose, and you should make it tighter by changing to a smaller hook. If there are too many stitches, your gauge is too tight and you should change to a larger hook.

Basic techniques and stitches

Making a chain (fig.1a–f). The basis for all crochet stitches is a length of chain formed from a single loop on the hook. First make a slip loop with the yarn and place it on the hook (a and b). Hold the hook in the right hand (c). Hold the yarn in the left hand (d). Winding the yarn around your little finger is very important as this helps to control the yarn and keep the gauge even. Wind the yarn once around the hook and pull the yarn through the slip loop (e). You have one loop remaining on the hook which is not counted as a stitch. Continue making a length of chain (f).

Turning chains. When working in rows in crochet it is necessary to work a number of chains at the beginning of each row. These form the first stitch and correspond in depth to the stitches you will be working. These chains bring the hook up to the correct height for that particular row and are called "turning chains." It is important to turn the work around and then crochet the turning chains, otherwise the chains will become twisted.

Single crochet (fig.2a–d). This is the crochet stitch with the smallest depth. Begin by making the number of chain stitches required plus one extra to act as a turning chain. To work the first row insert the hook from front to back into the third stitch from the hook and wind the yarn around the hook (a). Draw the yarn through the chain stitch, so making two loops on the hook (b). Wind the yarn around the hook again and draw it through both loops on the hook (c). One single crochet has now been worked, with the two missed chain stitches counting as the first single crochet. Work a single crochet into each stitch to the end of the row. The last single crochet should be worked under the turning chain of the previous row. When working into the previous row, insert the hook under the top two loops of the stitch below (d).

Half double (fig.3a, b and c). This is a useful stitch which is halfway in depth between a single crochet and its more common counterpart, a double. Work a number of chain stitches plus one extra as a turning chain. For the first row, wind the yarn around the hook and insert it from front to back into the third chain from the

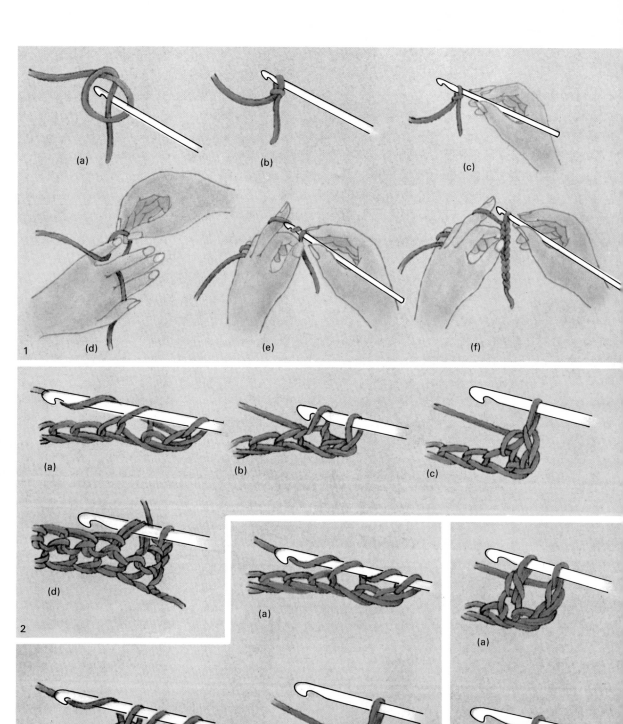

A camisole-style top

hook. Wind the yarn around the hook again (a) and draw it through the chain stitch so making three loops on the hook. Wind the yarn around the hook again (b) and draw it through all three loops on the hook. Then complete the half double (c). When beginning a new row of half doubles, work two extra chains to count as the first stitch.

Double (fig.4a and b). This is perhaps the most common of crochet stitches. Most stitch patterns are based on some form of the double. Make a number of chain stitches plus two extra. To work the first row, wind the yarn around the hook and insert the hook from front to back into the fourth chain from the hook. Wind the yarn around the hook again as shown for a half double (fig.3a). Draw a loop through the chain stitch, so making three loops on the hook. Wind the yarn around the hook again as shown for a half double in fig.3b. Draw the yarn through the first two loops on the hook. There will now be two loops remaining on the hook (fig.4a). Wind the yarn around the hook once more and draw it through the two remaining loops. You can see the completed stitch in fig.4b. Each new row of doubles will require three turning chains to bring the work up to the correct height for the next stitch. Remember, turn the work, then make turning chains.

Slip stitch. This crochet stitch has no depth. This makes it useful for shaping a garment where you want to miss the first few stitches without breaking off the yarn, eg for shaping an armhole. You can work a slip stitch into each stitch that you want to miss by inserting the hook into the stitch and winding the yarn around the hook. Draw the yarn through both the stitch and the loop already on the hook at the same time. You will be left with just one working loop on the hook.

Crochet Abbreviations

alt = alternate	dc = double crochet	patt = pattern	sp(s) = space(s)
beg = begin(ning)	dec = decrease	rem = remain(ing)	ss = slip stitch
ch = chain	foll = follow(ing)	rep = repeat	tog = together
cont = continue or continuing	hdc = half double	rs = right side	ws = wrong side
	inc = increase	sc = single crochet	yoh = yarn over hook

A camisole-style top

This stunning summer top is very simple to make, being worked in one piece. It uses two of the basic stitches already learned and involves the minimum of shaping. Leave it plain or decorate it with ribbons threaded through the stitches.

Sizes: to fit 81[86:91]cm (32[34:36]in) bust. Length to shoulder, 47[48.5:49.5]cm (18½[19:19½]in). The figures in square

Versatile edgings
Rounds and
granny squares

brackets refer to the 86cm (34in) and 91cm (36in) sizes respectively.
Note: hook sizes given are ISR. Consult the table on page 119 for equivalent sizes.
Gauge: 21 sts and 17 rows to 10cm (4in) over patt worked on 3.00mm crochet hook.
You will need:
total of 200[250:275]g (8[9:10]oz) crochet cotton □ 3.00mm crochet hook □ 20 small buttons □ 1.5m (1½yd) narrow ribbon (optional).
Back and fronts. Using 3.00mm hook make 132[142:152]ch and beg at waist. Commence patt and shape sides. **1st row:** (rs) into 4th ch from hook work 1dc, 1dc into each ch to end. Turn. 130[140:150]sts.
2nd row: (inc row) 1ch to count as 1st sc. Skip 1st st, 1sc into each of next 31[33:35] sts, 2sc into each of next 2sts, 1sc into each of next 62[68:74]sts, 2sc into each of next 2sts, 1sc into each of next 31[33:35]sts, 1sc into 3rd of 3ch. Turn. 134[144:154]sts.
3rd row: 3ch to count as 1st dc, 1dc into each st, ending with 1dc into turning ch. Turn. **4th row:** 1ch, 1sc into each st, ending with 1sc into 3rd of 3ch. Turn. **5th row:** (inc row) 3ch, 1dc into each of next 32[34:36]sts, 2dc into each of next 2sts, 1dc into each of next 64[70:76]sts, 2dc into each of next 2sts, 1dc into each of next 32[34:36]sts, 1dc into turning ch. Turn. 138[148:158]sts. Cont in this way, working alt rows of sc and dc and inc 4sts on every foll 3rd row until there are 170[180:190]sts. Patt 10 more rows without shaping, ending with a rs row. Fasten off.
Waist frill. Using 3.00mm hook and with ws of work facing, rejoin yarn to first st of starting ch and work along ws of waist edge as foll: *1 dc into next st, 2dc into next st, rep from * to end. Turn 195[210:215]sts Patt 11 more rows without shaping, ending with a rs row.
Fasten off.
Straps (make 2). Using 3.00mm hook make 96[102:108]ch. **1st row:** (rs) into 4th ch from hook work 1dc, 1dc into each ch to end. Turn. 94[100:106]sts. **2nd row:** 1ch, 1sc into each st, ending with 1sc into 3rd of 3ch. **3rd row:** 3ch, 1dc into each st, ending with last sc into turning ch. Turn. Rep last 2 rows twice more. Fasten off.

Finishing the work. Press under a damp cloth with a warm iron.
Edging. Using 3.00mm hook and with rs of work facing, rejoin yarn to center of lower back edge and work in crab st (ie work in dc from left to right instead of from right to left) all around outer edge, working into each st along lower and top edges and approximately 2sts into each dc row end and 1st into each sc row and down center fronts. Work a similar edging along length of straps. Sew straps in position. Sew on buttons at each dc row end and use 1st sp between sts in row end on opposite front as a buttonhole. Thread ribbon through first 2dc rows above waist.

Versatile edgings
Here are two pretty edgings that will enable you to practice your newfound skill.
1st Crochet edging. Make a chain with multiples of 3 +2 stitches. **1st row:** into 3rd ch from hook work 1sc, 1sc into each ch to end. Turn. **2nd row:** 3ch, skip next 2sc, 1sc into next sc, *2ch, skip next 2sc, 1sc into next sc, rep from * to end. Turn. **3rd row:** into each 2ch sp work 1sc, 1hdc, 1dc, 1hdc and 1sc. Fasten off.
2nd Crochet edging. This pattern is worked from one of the narrow ends back and forth across the depth. Make 5ch for narrow end. **1st row:** into 5th ch from hook work (3hdc, 3ch, 3hdc) (called a shell), turn. **2nd row:** 3ch, work a shell into 3ch loop of previous shell, turn. **3rd row:** 3ch, work a shell into previous shell, turn. **4th row:** 5ch, work a shell into previous shell, turn. **5th row:** 3ch, work a shell into previous shell, 2ch, into next 5ch loop work (1hdc, 2ch) 5 times and 1hdc, 1sc into next 3ch loop, turn, 3ch, 2hdc into first 2ch loop, into each of next four 2ch loops work (1ss, 3ch, 2hdc), 1sc

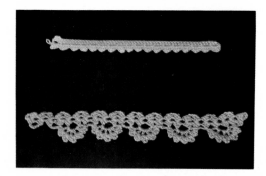

into next loop, 3ch, work a shell into next shell, turn. **6th row:** 3ch, work a shell into previous shell, turn. **7th row:** 5ch, work a shell into previous shell, turn. Rep 5th–7th rows inclusive for the required length. Fasten off.

Working in rounds
Up to this point you have been working your crochet in rows, turning the fabric at the end of each row. Another way of working is in rounds so that the right side of the work is always facing you and there is no need to turn it. Using this method you can make both square and circular shapes. These shapes, or motifs as they are known individually, can be sewn together and used in a variety of ways.

Granny squares
These colorful motifs are ideal for practicing your crochet work and are very economical to make. Use up scraps of yarn, as long as they are all of a similar thickness, by working each round of the square in a different color. Make lots of squares in the same size and join them together for clothes and bedspreads, or crochet an ever-expanding square to form one side of a pillow cover or bag. In this design each round of the square is in a different color.
Making a granny square. Make 6ch. Join these into a circle by working a ss into the 1st ch. **1st round:** 3ch to count as 1st dc, work 2dc into the center of the circle, 2ch, *3dc into the circle, 2ch, rep from * twice

Crocheted edgings can be used to decorate and enhance a whole range of clothes and furnishings - here are a few ideas

Crochet

Rainbow jacket
Rose-patterned shawl

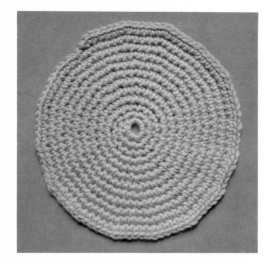

more. Join work into a round by working a ss into 3rd of first 3ch. Break off yarn and fasten off. **2nd round**: join next color to any 2ch sp with a ss, 3ch, 2dc into same sp, *1ch, into next 2ch sp work (3dc, 2ch, 3dc) to form corner, rep from * twice more, 1ch, 3dc into first sp worked into, 2ch. Join by working a ss into 3rd of first 3ch. Break off yarn and fasten off. **3rd round**: join next color to any 2ch sp with a ss, 3ch, 2dc into same sp, *1ch, 3dc into next 1ch, sp, 1ch, into next 2ch sp work (3dc, 2ch, 3dc) to form corner, rep from * twice more, 1ch, 3dc into next 1ch sp, 1ch, 3dc into first sp worked into, 2ch. Join by working a ss into 3rd of first 3ch. Break off yarn and fasten off. **4th round**: join next color to any 2ch sp, 3ch, 2dc into same sp, *(1ch, 3dc into next 1ch sp) twice, 1ch, into next 2ch sp work (3dc, 2ch, 3dc), rep from * twice more, (1ch, 3dc into next 1ch sp) twice, 1ch, 3dc into first sp worked into, 2ch. Join by working a ss into 3rd of first 3ch. Continue in this way for as many rounds as you want. When you have finished, weave in the ends of yarn where the colors have been joined.

Finishing the work. You can join the motifs by sewing them together or crocheting them together with slip stitches. To do this, place the right sides of the motifs together matching the edges, insert the hook through both thicknesses, put the yarn around the hook and draw a loop through the motifs and the stitch on the hook at the same time.

Circular motifs

With these motifs, just keep on working in continuous rounds until the circle is the required size whether it be for a place mat or a rug. Choose any stitch you like and work entirely in that, or try alternating rounds of different stitches such as double and single crochet. The secret of success is to keep the motif flat and the following instructions show you the formula for doing this.

Making a circular motif. Make 6ch. Join these into a circle by working a ss into the 1st ch. **1st round**: 1ch to count as 1st sc, work 7sc into center of the circle. Do not join the stitches, but cont in rounds, working the 1st st of the next round into the 1st ch. **2nd round**: 2sc into each sc to end. 16sc. **3rd round**: 1sc into each sc to end. **4th round**: as 2nd. 32sc. **5th round**: 1sc into each sc to end. **6th round**: *1sc into next sc, 2sc into next sc, rep from * to end. 48sc. **7th round**: 1sc into each sc to end. **8th round**: *1sc into each of next 2sc, 2sc into next sc, rep from * to end. 64 sc. **9th round**: 1sc into each sc to end. **10th round**: * 1sc into each of next 3sc, 2sc into next sc, rep from * to end. 80sc. Continue in this way, working one more stitch between increases and increasing 16 stitches in all on every following alternate round until the motif is the required size.

A rainbow jacket

This child's jacket consists of a series of granny squares sewn together, and edged in a bright contrasting color. You can make the jacket any size or length by varying the size of hook, the thickness of yarn and the number of motifs. Make each square a different color.

Making the jacket. Each motif consists of 3 rounds worked in double knitting yarn with a 3.50mm hook, and measures 7cm (2¾in) square. Sew them together neatly as in fig.5. Sew the shoulder seams together. Taking a bright contrasting color, edge the jacket in 1 round of single crochet. Finish around the armhole edges in the same way.

Making the fastenings. Join yarn at the top of the first right-hand square. Make a chain approximately 30cm (12in) long. Turn. Work the next row in slip stitch. Fasten off. Make a similar chain at the bottom of the

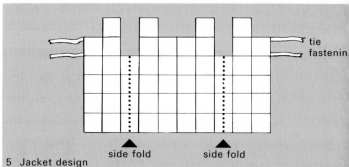

5 Jacket design

granny square. Crochet 2 more to match on the opposite side. Two circular motifs can easily be crocheted or sewn together to make a purse or bag.

Rose-patterned shawl

An unusual combination of raised rose and patterned motifs in subtle colors makes this shawl a challenge for beginners and a

Rose-patterned shawl

6 Rose-patterned shawl

Legend:
- ○ 1st motif
- □ 2nd motif

delight for the experts.

Size: 169cm (66½in) across top edge and 89cm (35in) from center of top edge to lower edge, excluding fringe.

Note: hook sizes given are ISR. Consult the table on page 119 for equivalent sizes.

Tension: each motif worked on 3.50mm hook measures 9cm (3½in) square.

You will need:
Total of 250g (9oz) double knitting yarn in main color, A □ 275g (10oz) of contrasting B □ 3.00mm crochet hook.

First motif. Using 3.50mm hook and A, make 5ch. Join with a ss into 1st ch to form a circle. **1st round:** *into circle work (1 htr, 1tr, 1htr) to form petal, rep from * 3 times more. **2nd round:** *2ch, at back of work ss into base of 2nd htr of next petal, rep from * 3 times more. **3rd round:** *into next 2ch loop work (4tr, 1ss), rep from * 3 times more. Draw B through loop on hook, tighten and fasten off A. **4th round:** *3ch, at back of work ss into base of ss in previous round, rep from * 3 times more.

5th round: *into next 3ch loop work (8dc, 1ss), rep from * 3 times more. **6th round:** as 4th. **7th round:** *into next 3ch loop work (10dc, 1ss), rep from * 3 times more. Draw A through loop on hook, tighten and fasten off B. **8th round:** 3ch to count as 1st dc, 2dc into ss at base of ch, *1ch, between 5th and 6th dc of next petal work (3dc, 2ch, 3dc) to form corner, 1ch, 3dc into next ss between petals, rep from * twice more, 1ch, work a corner between 5th and 6th dc of next petal, 1ch. Join with a ss into 3rd of first 3ch. Fasten off. **9th round:** join B to any 2ch corner sp, 3ch, 2dc into same sp, (1ch, 3dc into next 1ch sp) twice, 1ch, into next corner sp work (3dc, 2ch, 3dc), rep from * twice more (1ch, 3dc into next 1ch sp) twice, 1ch, 3dc into first sp worked into, 2ch. Join with a ss into 3rd of first 3ch. Fasten off.

Make 54 more motifs in the same way.
Second motif. Using 3.50mm hook and and A, make 8ch. Join with a ss into 1st ch to form a circle. **1st round:** 3ch, [(yoh, inser hook into circle, yoh, draw a loop through, yoh and draw through first 2 loops) twice, yoh and draw through all 3 loops. 5ch *(yoh, insert hook into circle, yoh, draw a loop through, yoh and draw through first 2 loops) 3 times, yoh and draw through all 4 loops)] the pattern in square brackets is called 1 cluster. 2ch, work 1 cluster into circle, 5ch, rep from * twice more, work 1 cluster into circle, 2ch. Join with a ss into 3rd of first 3ch. Fasten off. **2nd round:** join B to next 5ch sp, 3ch, (yoh, insert hook into sp, yoh, draw a loop through, yoh and

draw through first 2 loops) twice, yoh and draw through all 3 loops, 2ch, 1 cluster into same sp, *1ch, 3dc into next 2ch sp, 1ch, into next 5ch sp work (1 cluster, 2ch, 1 cluster), rep from * twice more, 1ch, 3dc into next 2ch sp, 1ch. Join with a ss into 3rd of first 3ch. Fasten off. **3rd round:** join A to next 2ch sp, 3ch, (yoh, insert hook into sp, yoh, draw a loop through, yoh and draw through first 2 loops) twice, yoh and draw through all 3 loops, 2ch, 1 cluster into same sp, *1ch, 2dc into next 1ch sp, 1dc into each of next 3dc, 2dc into next 1ch sp, 1ch, into next 2ch sp work (1 cluster, 2ch, 1 cluster), rep from * twice more, 1ch, 2dc into next 1ch sp, 1dc into each of next 3dc, 2dc into next 1ch sp, 1ch. Join with a ss into 3rd of first 3ch. Fasten off.
Make 44 more motifs in the same way.
Finishing the work. Sew in all ends. Press under a dry cloth with a cool iron. Join motifs as shown in fig.6. Press again.
Fringe Cut A and B into 40cm (16in) and 54cm (21in) lengths. Taking 2 strands of both colors together each time, knot around 2 sides of shawl at positions indicated in fig. 6. Trim fringe to an equal length.

Bluebirds

Bluebirds

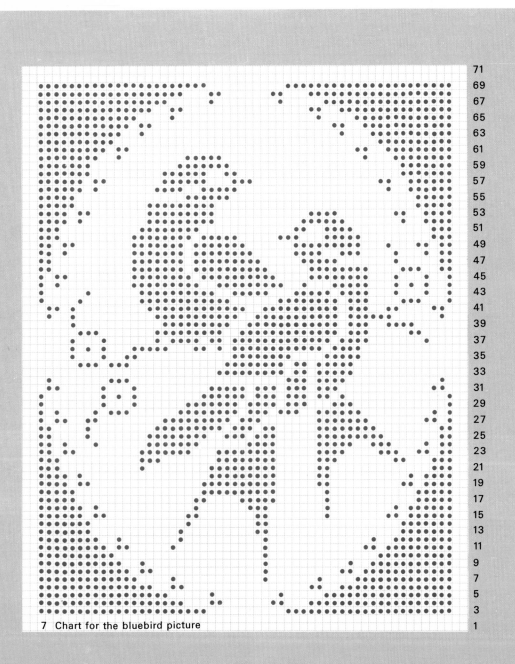

7 Chart for the bluebird picture

71
69
67
65
63
61
59
57
55
53
51
49
47
45
43
41
39
37
35
33
31
29
27
25
23
21
19
17
15
13
11
9
7
5
3
1

Bluebirds

Filet crochet employs the same techniques and stitches, but is worked with very fine cotton and hooks. It lends itself well to creating pictures and openwork designs such as this delightful panel showing two love birds. For the best effect hang it against the light in an attractive old frame, Scandinavian style. The panel measures 24×29.5cm ($9\frac{1}{2} \times 11\frac{1}{2}$in).

Note: Hook sizes given are ISR. Consult the table on page 119 for equivalent sizes.

Gauge: 6 sps and 6 rows to 2.5cm (1in) worked on 1.00mm hook.

You will need:
20g (1oz) crochet cotton ☐ 1.00mm crochet hook ☐ picture frame.

Note: The chart represents a filet crochet grid of blocks and spaces. Spaces are formed by working doubles with 2 chain between them and blocks are spaces which have been filled in with 2 doubles. Remember that when you are beginning a row with a space, you should make 5 turning chains to count as the first double and 2 chain between doubles.

Crocheting the bluebird panel. Using 1.00mm hook make 179ch. **1st row:** into 8th ch from hook work 1dc (2ch, skip 2ch, 1dc into next ch) 57 times. Turn. 58 sps. **2nd row:** 5ch, skip 1st dc, 1dc into next dc, *2ch, 1 dc into next dc, rep from * ending with last dc into 5th of 7ch. Turn. **3rd row:** 5ch, skip 1st dc, 1dc into next dc, 2ch, 1dc into next dc, (2dc into next sp, 1dc into next dc) 22 times, (2ch, 1dc into next dc) 10 times, (2 dc into next sp, 1dc into next dc) 22 times, 2ch 1dc into next dc, 2ch, 1dc into 3rd of 5ch. Turn. **4th row:** 5ch, skip 1st dc, 1dc into next dc, 2ch, 1dc into each of next 58dc, (2ch, skip 2dc, 1dc into next dc) 3 times, (2dc into next sp, 1dc into next dc) twice, (2ch, 1dc into next dc) 6 times, (2dc into next sp, 1dc into next dc) twice, (2ch, skip 2dc, 1dc into next dc) 3 times, 1dc into each of next 57dc, 2ch, 1dc into next dc, 2ch, 1dc into 3rd of 5ch. Turn. Cont in this way, working from fig.7 till 71 rows have been completed. Fasten off.

Completing the work. Dampen and pin out to measurements. Tack into an old frame or lace it into a larger frame for a slightly different effect.

Scents of Summer

Fresh country smells and the fragrance and warmth of summer can be captured throughout the year by preserving the scents of flowers and herbs in sachets, potpourris, pomanders and herb pillows.

Harvesting

Pick the flowers and herbs when they are just opening; if they are past their peak they will have lost much of their perfume. The early morning, when the dew has just dried and the sun is not too hot, is the best time. Pick seeds when they are partially dried and almost ready to fall.

Drying

For maximum fragrance, flowers and herbs must be dried quickly. Spread them on a flat surface somewhere warm, dry and draft-free. A darkened room or cupboard is ideal since bright sunlight could brown the petals and leaves. Leave to dry until they are crisp. Depending on the plant, this could be a couple of days to two weeks. Turn the mixture over daily.

To dry woody herbs, grasses or seedheads, tie the bunch together and invert a paper bag over the heads. Hang the bunch upside down in a warm dry place.

Rose potpourri

Potpourri is a sweet smelling medley of flower petals, leaves, herbs and essential oils.

You will need:
1 liter (2 pints) rose petals □ 0.5 liter (1 pint) rose geranium leaves □ 0.5 liter (1 pint) lavender □ 0.25 liter ($\frac{1}{2}$ pint) rosemary □ 2 tablespoons each of all-spice, ground cloves and cinnamon □ 3 tablespoons each of powdered orrisroot and gum benzoin □ few drops of essential oil of roses.

Making the potpourri. Mix the rose oil with the dried petals, leaves and spices. Then mix in the orrisroot and gum benzoin which will fix the perfume, making it last longer. Place the mixture in an airtight jar and leave for 4 weeks before use. Stir it once or twice weekly.

Other suitable flowers include: geranium, camomile, violet, jonquil, lilac, honey-suckle, lily-of-the-valley, carnation, nasturtium and white jasmin. Other leaves and herbs to use are sage, tarragon, thyme, mint, bay, lemon verbena, sweet cicely and coriander.

Orange and clove pomander

A pomander made from an orange (or lemon), and spiked with cloves, smells deliciously fresh and will retain its fragrance for months.

You will need:
large orange or lemon □ 55g (2oz) whole cloves □ 2 teaspoons powdered orrisroot □ 2 teaspoons ground cloves □ 1m (1yd) narrow ribbon, 0.5cm ($\frac{1}{4}$in) wide □ 2 strips of tape 30cm (12in) long and the same width as the ribbon.

Making the pomander. Tie a piece of tape around the orange. Then tie the second piece of tape at right angles to the first. Stud the uncovered quarters of fruit with cloves. Push the cloves in as far as the heads or they will drop out. Place them close together so that the skin of the orange is completely covered. Put the fruit somewhere warm to dry thoroughly. Drying can take up to a month; it is essential to dry the fruit completely or the pomander will mold.

When the fruit is dry, remove the tape. Mix together the orrisroot and ground cloves. Roll the pomander in the mixture until evenly coated and leave to stand un-disturbed for a week. The orrisroot will act as a fixative for the scent. Tie the ribbon around the fruit where the tape was orig-inally. Pin the ribbon into place using pins and sequins to form a decorative pattern.

Herb pillows

The sweet fragrance of country-fresh herbs is said by some to provide a cure against insomnia. Choose herbs with somnific qualities, such as woodruff, sage, lemon verbena, angelica and borage.

Making the pillow. Make a small rectan-gular inner cover from muslin, approx-imately 30×15cm (12×6in). Fill this with a variety of the herbs already listed, mixed with lavender, mint, rosemary or mock orange flowers. Cover this pillow with a thin cotton case and slip it into your pillow case or just next to your pillow.

Knitting

Knitted fabric tends to deteriorate with great age, though one of the earliest pieces to have survived was discovered on a Syrian site and dates from the 3rd century AD. For earlier forms of knitting, historians have to rely on written accounts or art forms such as sculpture. Many ancient Egyptian, Greek and Persian statues and reliefs, for example, depict figures wearing garments that have the textured appearance of a knitted fabric.

The Bible also hints that certain knitting techniques were known and practiced. It is thought that Joseph's "coat of many colors" might have been knitted and also the Crucifixion robe that Jesus Christ wore: "The coat was without seam, woven from the top throughout." This could not be divided, so the Roman soldiers cast lots for it. By the Middle Ages, knitting was a well established craft throughout Europe, the techniques having been introduced from North Africa by Arab traders. A network of Knitting Guilds was established in France, Britain and other countries and young men served lengthy apprenticeships before they were considered sufficiently skilled to take the title of Master Knitter.

By the middle of the 16th century the Channel Island of Jersey had a thriving handknitting industry, exporting hosiery to France and England. Queen Elizabeth I of England herself wore handknitted stockings or "Jersey hose" and was so anxious to protect the industry that in 1589 she refused a patent to William Lee, who had designed the first knitting machine.

It was inevitable, of course, that knitting machines should eventually force the decline of the handknitting industry. This had already happened in Europe by the middle of the 18th century, although many regions still produced handknitted articles for their own use. The fishermen of the Aran Isles, which lie off the west coast of Ireland and Fair Isle and Shetland situated to the north of the Scottish mainland, continued to wear woolen sweaters knitted to the old traditional patterns.

Modern knitting patterns still draw inspiration from many of these older designs and the specialist collections in the world's major museums often prove to be the best hunting ground for ideas worthy of revival.

Knitting is an unusual craft in that it combines the two skills of making a fabric and shaping it at the same time. With an appreciation of the use of different yarns and a basic knowledge of the stitches and techniques involved, you will soon be ready to pick up your needles and begin.

Yarns

There has never been a wider range of yarns on the market than is available today. From this selection you can choose anything from pure wool, wool and synthetic mixtures to totally synthetic; from very fine to chunky weights and from ultra-smooth to knobbly textures. These all help to make knitting a fascinating and useful pastime. Any spun thread, whether it is a natural fiber, such as wool or cotton, or synthetic like nylon, is described as "yarn." Natural fibers are often combined with synthetic ones, as in a wool and nylon mixture, to make an extra hard-wearing yarn without adding any more bulk.

A single spun thread is known as "ply," but this term does not necessarily indicate the thickness of that thread. A thread is not used singly, but is twisted together with other threads to produce yarns of a particular thickness.

The majority of handknitting yarns, either natural, synthetic or blended, have ply classification, ranging from two ply, which is fine and suitable for baby clothes, through three ply and four ply to double knitting. Double knitting yarns are usually made from four single spun threads to produce yarns which are about twice as thick as four ply, and these, being very thick and warm, are ideal for heavier or outdoor garments.

Specialty yarns, such as crêpe, tweed, bouclé, mohair and many others, make it possible to produce high-quality garments with a variety of textured effects.

Needles

For ordinary flat knitting, worked backwards and forwards in rows, you need a pair of needles. These are usually made of lightweight coated metal or plastic. Each needle is pointed at one end and has a knob at the other to prevent the stitches from slipping off.

Jacob, recumbent in his dream of angels descending and ascending the ladder to Heaven, and below him Adam and Eve flanked by a lion and unicorn. This handknitted carpet comes from Alsace and is dated 1781.

Needles are made in many different sizes and are classified according to diameter. The table opposite gives the main American, British and Continental knitting needle sizes.

Needles are also made in a variety of different lengths and obviously the more stitches required for a piece of work, the longer the needles should be. It will be more difficult to use long needles if you are working with just a few stitches.

Always try to use the recommended needles and yarns as stated in the pattern you are using. There is no point, for example, in using thick needles with a fine baby yarn, as the fabric produced will be ragged, uneven and full of holes.

Knitting Needle Sizes		
American	Old British	Continental (mm.)
0	13	2.00
1	12	2.50
2	11	2.75
3	10	3.00
4	9	3.50
5	8	4.00
6	7	4.50
7	6	5.00
8	5	5.50
9	4	6.00
10	3	6.50
10½	2	7.00
11	1	8.00
13	0	9.00
15	00	10.00

An impressive tribal costume knitted in sisal is worn by a warrior from Zaire.

Tension

Correct gauge is the key to all successful knitting and although vital for the finished article it is something that is often overlooked. Gauge is a matter of producing the correct number of stitches and rows to a given measurement, using the yarn and needles stated.

A designer will have based all measurements for a garment on a test swatch made before beginning to work anything out. You will not produce a garment that fits properly and is the right size unless you achieve the same gauge as stated on the pattern. It is important to knit your own gauge swatch, using the recommended yarn and needle size. Count the number of stitches and rows knitted over a square of 10cm (4in) and check this against the gauge stated on the pattern. Even if the difference is minimal, remember that this could add up to as much as 5cm (2in) over a larger area such as the front of a sweater. Should you have too few stitches, then you are knitting too loosely. Knit another sample on smaller needles. Too many stitches means that the work will be too tight. Try a sample piece again on larger needles. Correct stitch gauge is more important than row gauge. A pattern will give a certain number of stitches to be cast on to produce a calculated width measurement. Rows, however, are often worked to a given measurement such as 7.5cm (3in) and it makes no difference whether you have 25 or 28 rows in that space. This is *not* to say that row gauge can be overlooked entirely the correct gauge overall is important for a perfect finish.

Finishing off

Pressing. Good knitting can be spoiled if the work is not pressed properly before making into the finished garment. Follow the yarn manufacturer's or pattern's instructions for pressing and general treatment of the yarn. Some yarns require no pressing at all and many textured stitch patterns lose their character if they are over-pressed.

In general, it is safe to assume that pure wool or cotton fibers should be pressed under a damp cloth with a warm iron. Synthetic fibers usually require a cool iron and a dry cloth. Do not move the iron continuously across the cloth as you would do normally when ironing. Place a clean cloth over the knitted piece then bring the iron down on top of the cloth and lift it up again before moving on to the next area. Avoid any ribbed or garter stitch edges : pressing these will tend to damage their elasticity.

Blocking. By pinning the knitted pieces to the ironing pad you can check that they will be the correct size after pressing. Place the knitting right side down on the ironing pad and check that the stitches and rows run in straight lines. Do not stretch or pull the fabric out of shape. Pin around the edges using rustproof pins and press as described earlier.

Seams. Use a needle with a blunt end and an eye large enough to take the same yarn as was used for the knitting. Some yarns, such as mohair, are not suitable for sewing, in which case use a fine plain yarn in a matching color.

Use a flat seam for ribbing, such as waistbands and cuffs, which require neat flat edges. With right sides together, hold the work in one hand and sew the seam by passing the needle backwards and forwards through matching edge stitches. Most other sections of knitting require a normal back stitch seam, which is worked about one stitch in from the edge with right sides of the work together. Check the other side of the seam as you work to be sure that you are following a straight line.

When the garment is finished, press all seams to give your work a professional finish.

Casting on

Before you can begin to knit the first row you will need to start by casting on the required number of stitches.

There are several methods of casting on, and the one shown here (fig.1a—e) is often used because it produces a strong flexible border, which looks just as effective on either side of the work.

First make a loop as shown (a), leaving a short end of yarn about 7.5cm (3in). Put this loop on the left-hand needle and tighten slightly (b). Take the other needle in your right hand. Insert the right-hand needle into the slip loop from front to back.

Basic stitches

Guiding the yarn with the index finger of your right hand, wind it under and over the point of the right-hand needle (c), so making a new loop. Draw this loop through the first loop (d). Transfer the new loop to the left-hand needle.

Insert the right-hand needle from front to back between the two loops on the left-hand needle as shown (e). Take the yarn under and over the point of the right-hand needle as before and draw a new loop through. Transfer the new loop to the left-hand needle.

Insert the right-hand needle between the last two loops on the left-hand needle and continue to work in the same way until you have cast on the necessary number of stitches.

Basic stitches

Nearly every form of stitch pattern is produced by working knit (also known as "plain") or purl stitches, or a combination of both. The simplest fabric you can achieve after mastering the basic skills is garter stitch, in which each stitch in every row is knitted.

Garter stitch (fig.2a,b and c). Begin by holding the needle with the cast-on stitches in your left hand and the other needle in your right hand. Insert the right-hand needle from front to back into the first stitch on the left-hand needle. With the yarn at the back of the work, guide it with the index finger of your right hand to pass under and over the right-hand needle (a). Draw a new loop through the stitch on the left-hand needle as shown (b). The new stitch remains on the right-hand needle, while the stitch just worked into is allowed to fall from the left-hand needle (c). Work all the stitches on the left-hand needle in the same way until they have been transferred to the right-hand needle, then switch the needle containing the stitches to the left hand before beginning the next row.

Purling (fig.3a,b and c). To purl a stitch, start by holding the needle with the stitches in your left hand and the other needle with your right hand. Insert the right-hand needle into the first stitch on the left-hand needle from back to front. Keeping the yarn at the front of the work, wind it over the top

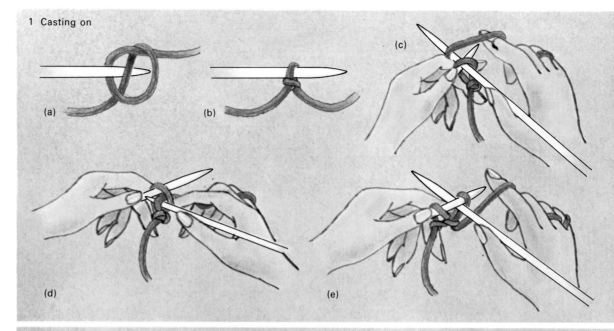

1 Casting on

(a)   (b)   (c)

(d)   (e)

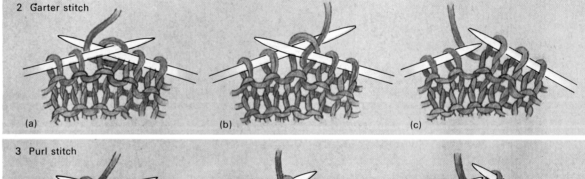

2 Garter stitch

(a)   (b)   (c)

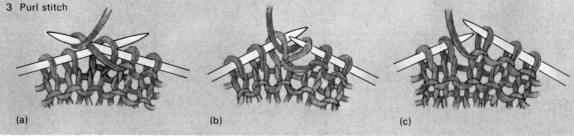

3 Purl stitch

(a)   (b)   (c)

and around the point of the right-hand needle (a).

Draw a new loop through the stitch on the left-hand needle as shown (b). The new stitch remains on the right-hand needle while the stitch just worked is allowed to fall from the left-hand needle (c). Continue in this way until all the stitches have been transferred to the right-hand needle. To work the next row, change the needles around so that the free one is in

your right hand and the one containing the stitches is in your left hand.

Combinations of knit and purl stitches

Knitted stitches are often used in conjunction with purled stitches to create different stitch patterns and textures. The two most common stitch patterns using both knitted and purled stitches are stocking stitch and ribbing.

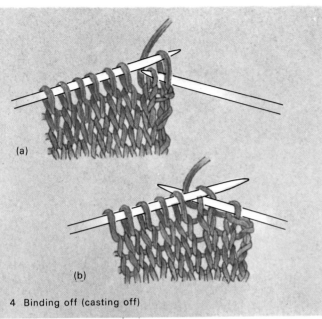

(a)

(b)

4 Binding off (casting off)

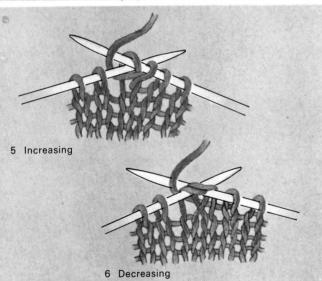

5 Increasing

6 Decreasing

Stocking stitch. This is formed by alternately knitting and purling rows – the knitted side is the right side of the work – and produces an all-purpose, smooth fabric.

Ribbing. This is a way of producing a piece of knitting with a certain amount of elasticity. Single rib is made by knitting and purling alternate stitches in the first row. On subsequent rows all stitches that were knitted in the previous row are purled and all those that were purled are knitted. This fabric is reversible and is useful at all points of a garment where a close fit is required, such as waistbands, neckbands and cuffs.

Casting off

Once you have finished a piece of knitting, or at a given point of shaping, you will need to bind off the stitches (fig.4a and b) so that they do not unravel.

With the needles and yarn in the usual working position, knit the first two stitches so that they are transferred to the right-hand needle. Use the left-hand needle point to lift the first knitted stitch over the second one as shown (a). One stitch is now left on the right-hand needle. Knit the next stitch on the left-hand needle (b) and cast it off as described above. Continue casting off until the last stitch remains on the right-hand needle. Secure this by breaking off the yarn, drawing the cut end through the extended loop of the stitch, and pulling firmly. If working a purl row, you can cast off by purling the stitches instead of knitting them and lifting the first stitch over the second and so on as described. To cast off in rib, knit and purl as required, lifting each stitch over in the same way as before.

Shaping

In order to give shape to a piece of knitting, stitches are increased or decreased as required.

Increasing. There are various methods of increasing stitches, but the one most often used is to knit (or purl) twice into the same stitch so making two stitches out of one. To increase a stitch, knit the next stitch on the left-hand needle in the usual way so forming a loop on the right-hand needle, but do not allow the stitch to fall from the left-hand needle. Insert the right-hand needle from front to back into the back of the same loop on the left-hand needle (fig.5). Knit this loop in the usual way so making two loops on the right-hand needle and allowing the stitch just worked to fall from the left-hand needle.

You can increase stitches at any given point in a row depending on the type of shaping required; instructions for shaping will always be given in the knitting pattern.

For most garments, stitches are usually increased at the beginning or end of a row, or at both ends.

Decreasing. This is done by working two stitches together. Insert the right-hand needle from front to back through the second and then the first stitch on the left-hand needle (fig.6). Knit the two stitches together in the usual way.

Abbreviations used

alt	*alternate*	patt	*pattern*
beg	*begin(ning)*	rem	*remain(ing)*
cont	*continue or*	rep	*repeat*
	continuing	rs	*right side*
dec	*decrease*	st(s)	*stitch(es)*
foll	*follow(ing)*	st st	*stockinette*
g st	*garter stitch*		*stitch (1 row knit,*
	(every row knit)		*1 row purl)*
inc	*increase*	tog	*together*
K	*knit*	ws	*wrong side*
P	*purl*		

Knitted rug of many colors

This brightly colored rug is made in stocking stitch with borders of garter stitch and measures 122×213.5cm (48×84in). Made on large needles with thick wool, it could also be used as a blanket or hung on a wall for decoration.

Note: the needle sizes given are metric Continental sizes. Consult the table on page 129 for equivalent sizes.

Gauge: 11 sts and 18 rows to 10cm (4in) over st st on 3.50mm needles.

You will need:
total of 2800g (90oz) rug wool in 4 colors for main section □ 1800g (64oz) rug wool in 1 color for border □ pair of 3.50mm needles.

Main section. Cast on 35 sts. Beg with a K row and cont in st st introducing new colors as preferred and varying the depth of the colored stripes. Always work an even number of rows in any one color, starting each new color with a K row. When changing colors, leave an end of yarn about 12.5cm (5in) long at the end of the row in the old color and a similar length at the beginning of the row for the new color. (These ends will have to be woven in to make the edges neat later.) Cont working

Knitted rug of many colors
Wrap-around jacket

Easy to knit – easy to wear

Garter stitch and silky mohair make a luxurious fabric for this wrap-around jacket.
Sizes: to fit 81[86:91]cm (32[34:36]in) bust. Length to shoulder, 58.5cm (23in). The figures in square brackets refer to the 86cm (34in) and 91cm (36in) sizes respectively.
Note: the needle sizes given are metric (Continental) sizes. Consult the table on page 129 for equivalent sizes.
Gauge: 21 sts and 48 rows to 10cm (4in) over g st on 6.00mm needles.
You will need:
total of 200[200:250]g (8[8:9]oz) mohair yarn □ pair of 6.00mm needles □ pair 7mm needles □ stitch holder □ 4 hooks and eyes.
Right front. Using 7mm needles cast on 79[81:83] sts. **1st row:** (rs) K1, *P1, K1, rep from * to end. **2nd row:** P1, *K1, P1, rep from * to end. Rep these 2 rows until work measures 7.5cm (3in) from beg, ending with a 2nd row. **Next row:** rib 11 and leave these sts on a holder. Change to 6.00 mm needles and K the rem 68[70:72] sts.
Cont throughout in g st, dec 1 st at beg (front edge) of 2nd and every foll 4th row until 61[63:65] sts rem. Cont to dec at front edge only on every foll 5th row until 38[40:42] sts rem, then on every foll 14th[12th:10th] row until 32[33:34] sts rem. Cont without shaping until work measures 58.5cm (23in) from beg, ending at side edge. **Shape shoulder: bind off at beg of next and every foll alt row 5 sts twice, 5[5:6] sts once, 5[6:6] sts once and 6 sts twice.
Left front. Using 7.00mm needles cast on 69[71:73] sts. Work 7.5cm (3in) rib as given for right front, ending with a 2nd row and dec 1 st in center of last row so that 68[70:72] sts rem. Change to 6.00mm needles. Work as given for right front from ** to end.
Back. Using 7.00mm needles cast on 91[95:99] sts. Work 7.5cm (3in) rib as given for right front, ending with a 2nd row. Change to 6.00mm needles. Cont in g st until work measures same as fronts to shoulders, ending with a ws row. **Shape shoulders:** cast off at beg of next and every row 5 sts 4 times, 5[5:6] sts twice, 5[6:6] sts twice and 6 sts 4 times. Cast off rem 27[29:31] sts.

until the piece measures 183cm (72in) from beg and cast off.
Work 2 more strips in the same way varying the colors of the stripes.
Making the main section. Weave in loose ends of yarn on the ws of the work. Press each strip under a damp cloth with a warm iron. Join the strips together lengthwise with a flat seam to form the main section of the rug.
Top and bottom borders. Cast on 19 sts and cont in g st until the piece measures the same length as the short edge of the main section. Cast off and sew in position with a flat seam.
Rep for the border for the other short edge of the main section.
Side borders. Cast on 19 sts and cont in g st until the piece measures the same length as the long edge of the main section. Cast off and sew in position with a flat seam.
Rep for the border for the other long edge of the main section.
Press all seams.

Armbands. Join shoulder seams with a back stitch seam. Mark a point on front and back side edges with a pin, 20cm (8in) down from each shoulder. Using 7.00mm needles and with rs of work facing you, beg at marked point and pick up and K 64 sts to shoulder, 1 st from shoulder seam and 64 sts from shoulder to other marked point (129 sts). Beg with a 2nd row, work 5cm (2in) rib as given for right front. Cast off loosely in rib

Front border. Using 7.00mm needles and

with ws of work facing you, rejoin yarn to inside edge of sts on holder and rib to end. Cont in rib until border, slightly stretched, fits up right front edge, around the back neck and down left front edge to cast-on edge. Cast off.

Ties. Using 7.00mm needles cast on 9 sts. Cont in rib as given for right front until tie measures 61cm (24in) from beg. Cast off. Rep for second tie.

Finishing the garment. Do *not* press. Join side and armband seams using a back stitch seam for g st sections and a flat seam for ribbing. Sew front border in position with a flat seam. Sew on ties, one inside top of right front waistband edge and the other approximately 12.5cm (5in) in from border edge on left front waistband. Sew 3 hooks onto the waistband on the inside of the right front – one close to the corner below the tie, a second even with this and about 10cm (4in) from the border and a third about 5cm (2in) above the second. Sew the eyes onto the left front waistband to correspond. Position the fourth hook and eye on the front border at the wrap-around point.

Knitting in rounds

Knitting in rounds is done with a set of four straight needles or one circular needle. Also known as circular knitting, this form of knitting is ideal for socks, gloves, hats and even sweaters where a minimum of seaming is desirable.

Although the basic stitch patterns are the same as for ordinary knitting, the techniques used are slightly different. This is because each row or round must be knitted from the right side of the work instead of alternately from the wrong and right sides. Stocking stitch, for example, is made by knitting every round, while garter stitch is produced by knitting one round then purling one round alternately. For single ribbing you must knit the knitted stitches and purl the purled stitches in each round.

Basic equipment

Unlike ordinary knitting needles, the straight needles used for circular knitting are pointed at *both* ends.

You may, however, prefer to use a circular needle, which consists of two short point-

ed needles, connected by a length of nylon wire. Circular needles are available in varying lengths but they should not be used for a small number of stitches as there should be a sufficient minimum to fit easily all around the needles and wire.

Casting on with four needles

Cast on in the usual way, using two needles from the set. Transfer an equal number of stitches to the second and third needles as shown in fig.7.

Before knitting the first round make sure that the stitches are not twisted, then insert the fourth needle into the first stitch as shown in fig.8 and pull the yarn tightly around the needle so that there will be no gap in the work.

It is useful to tie a loop of colored thread around one needle to mark the beginning of a round. To keep track of your place, slip the marker loop from one needle to the next at the beginning of each new round.

Casting on with a circular needle

Cast on in the usual way, allowing the stit-

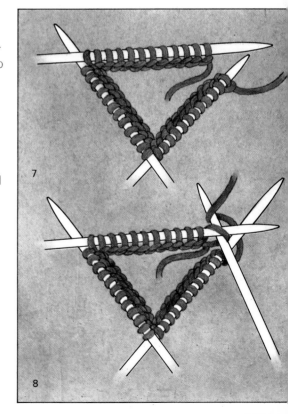

7

8

Knitting
Knitting in rounds

Sweater and socks

ches to spill over onto the nylon wire when the left-hand needle is full. Use a marker loop as previously described. To knit the first round, check that the cast-on stitches are not twisted, then pull the yarn tightly across to the first stitch and continue knitting around to the end of the cast-on stitches.

Fisherman style sweater
Following the traditional knitting of fishermen, this sweater is made on a circular needle and requires absolutely no shaping. A chunky tweed yarn and easy stitch patterns combine to form an interesting textured fabric.

Sizes: to fit 81–86[91–97]cm (32–34 [36–38]in) bust. Length to shoulder, 61cm (24in). Sleeve seam, 38cm (15in). The figures in square brackets refer to the 91–97cm (36–38in) size only.

Note: the needle sizes given are metric (Continental) sizes. Consult the table on page 129 for equivalent sizes.

Gauge: 15 sts and 20 rows to 10 cm (4in) over st st on 3.50mm needles.

You will need:
750[800]g (27[29]oz) chunky knitting yarn □ 3.50 circular knitting needle, 61cm (24in) long □ pair of 3.50mm needles □ spare 3.50mm needle.

Back and front: Using 3.50mm circular needle cast on 144[152] sts and work 7.5cm (3in) in rounds of g st (alt rounds of K and P). Cont in rounds of st st (K each round) until work measures 20cm (8in) from beg. **Next round:** *K1, P1, rep from * to end. **Next round:** *P1, K1, rep from * to end. Rep last 2 rounds until work measures 25cm (10in) from beg. **Next round:** *K4, P4, rep from * to end. Rep last round 3 times more. **Next round:** *P4, K4, rep from * to end. Rep last round 3 times more. **Next round:** *K3, P1, rep from * to end. **Next round:** *P1, K3, rep from * to end. **Next round:** K1, *P1, K3, rep from * to last 3 sts, P1, K2. **Next round:** K2, *P1, K3, rep from * to last 2 sts, P1, K1. Rep last 4 rounds until work measures 35.5cm (14in) from beg. **Next round:** *K1, P1, rep from * to end. **Next round:** *P1, K1, rep from * to end. Rep last 2 rounds until work measures 40.5cm (16in) from beg. **Divide for armholes:** using the pair of 3.50mm needles, K72[76], turn and leave rem sts on

spare needle. Cont on main group of sts for front. Beg with a P row, cont in st st until work measures 53.5cm (21in) from beg, ending with a P row. Work 7.5cm (3in) of g st. Cast off.

Return to sts on spare needle. With rs of work facing and using the pair of 3.50mm needles, rejoin yarn to next st and K to end. Complete to match front.

Sleeves. Using the pair of 3.50mm needles, cast on 64 sts and work 15cm (6in) g st. Beg with a K row, cont in st st until work measures 25cm (10in) from beg, ending with a P row. **Next row:** *K1, P1, rep from * to end. **Next row:** *P1, K1, rep from * to end. Rep last 2 rows until work measures 30.5cm (12in) from beg. **Next row:** *K4, P4, rep from * to end. Rep last row 3 times more. **Next row:** *P4, K4, rep from * to end. Rep last row 3 times more. **Next row:** *K3, P1, rep from * to end. **Next row:** *P1, K3, rep from * to end. **Next row:** K1, *P1, K3, rep from * to last 3 sts, P1, K2. **Next row:** K2, *P1, K3, rep from * to last 2 sts, P1, K1. Rep last 4 rows until work measures 40.5cm (16in) from beg, ending with a ws row. **Next row:** *K1, P1, rep from * to end. **Next row:** *P1, K1, rep from * to end. Rep last 2 rows until work measures 45.5cm (18in) from beg, ending with a ws row. Cast off.

Finishing the garment. Press under a damp cloth with a warm iron. Join sleeve seams with a flat seam, sewing on rs for 7.5cm (3in) of the g st section at beg of sleeve. (This section should then be turned back to form a cuff.) Join shoulder seams with a flat seam for 16.5cm (6½in) from each armhole edge. Sew in sleeves with the seam in the underarm position and sewing the bound-off sts around armhole.

Circular socks
These really warm socks will team up perfectly with the fisherman's sweater and are very easy to knit on four needles. Worked in stripes of contrasting colors and patterns, the socks will fit feet of all sizes.

Size: around top of sock, 26cm (10¼in). Length to toe (with top not turned down), 66cm (26in). Adjust length if required by adding to or subtracting from measurements given in the pattern.

Note: the needle sizes given are metric

(Continental) sizes. Consult the table on page 129 for equivalent sizes.

Gauge: 22 sts and 28 rows to 10cm (4in) over st st on 5.50mm.

You will need:
75g (3oz) double knitting yarn in main color □ 100g (4oz) of first contrast color □ 50g (2oz) of second contrast color □ set of 4 5.50mm needles, pointed at both ends

Socks. Using set of 4 5.50mm needles and main color, cast on 50 sts and transfer 16 to each of first 2 needles and 18 to 3rd needle. Mark beg of round with a loop of colored thread. **1st round:** *K1, P1, rep from * to end. Rep last round for single ribbing until work measures 12.5cm (5in) from beg.

Commence patt: join in first contrast color. Work 7.5cm (3in) in st st (K each round) and stripe sequence of 2 rows each of first, second and main color. Break off main and first contrast color. Using second contrast color only, cont in g st (alt rounds of K and P) until work measures 28cm (11in) from beg. Break off second contrast color and join in first contrast color. Work 2.5cm (1in) st st using first contrast color, then break off yarn and work another 2.5cm (1in) st st using main color. Break off and join in second contrast color. **Next round:** *K1, P1, rep from * to end. **Next round:** *P1, K1, rep from * to end. Rep these 2 rounds for 7.5cm (3in). Break off yarn and join in main color. Work 2.5cm (1in) st st, then break off yarn and work another 2.5cm (1in) st st using second contrast color. Join in main color and cont in st st and stripe sequence of 2 rows each of main, first and second color for 7.5cm (3in). Break off main and second color. Using first contrast color cont in g st until work measures 59.5cm (23½in) from beg. Break off second contrast color and join in main color. **Shape toe: 1st round:** *K8, K2 tog, rep from * to end. Work 2 rounds st st without shaping. **Next round:** *K7, K2 tog, rep from * to end. Work 2 rounds st st without shaping. Cont in this way, working 1 st less between decreases on next and every foll 3rd row until 25 sts rem, then on every foll alt row until 10 sts rem. **Next round:** *K2 tog, rep from * to end. Break off yarn, thread through rem sts, draw up and fasten off securely.

Tatting

Tatting was an occupation for gentlewomen in the 18th century. This portrait of the Duchess of Albemarle was painted by Sir Joshua Reynolds (1723–1792).

Just where and when tatting first began remains very much a mystery; certainly this form of knotting technique is known by various different names throughout the world. In the East, it is quite simply and literally *makouk* or "shuttle." The Italians, however, are far more poetic in their terminology and refer to tatting either as *occhi* meaning "eyes" or *chicchierimo*, a word possibly derived from the Italian verb *chiacchierare*, "to gossip." Indeed, the resulting lace-like work does often appear eye-shaped and possibly the women did traditionally gossip while they tatted. To the French, meanwhile, it is *frivolité*—a delightful reflection of the widespread popular enjoyment this craft has long provided. But for the English term "tatting," there seems to be no known derivation.

Tatting was widely practiced in the courts of 18th-century Europe and many of the charming and decorative shuttles dating from that period are now valuable museum pieces. One, for example, is of fine wrought steel in the form of flowers; others are known to have been made from mother-of-pearl or rock-crystal set with precious stones; while some are gold, and others are rather elaborately enameled.

However, although many beautiful antique shuttles survive today, very few examples of actual tatting remain as illustrations of the delicate art. But we do know that tatting was used to decorate clothing and sometimes even to form complete curtains. Designs were once restricted to the working of simple straight lines but today, with a tatting revival, numerous effects are possible through the use of larger shuttles and various threads, such as mercerised cotton, linen and silk. In their choice of terminology for the technique of tatting, the French certainly seem to have been aware of the creative possibilities of the craft!

Materials and equipment

You will need a tatting shuttle (sometimes two tatting shuttles), thread with a firm twist to it and a small hook for joining (this is sometimes supplied with the shuttle but a fine crochet hook will do).

Preparing the shuttle. Secure the thread to the center of the shuttle and then wind it around and around until the shuttle is full. The thread should not extend beyond the shuttle edges as this will prevent it from running smoothly.

Hold the shuttle in your right hand, gradually letting out the thread as required (fig.1). Form the knots with the left hand.

Basic stitches

Half stitch (figs.2,3 and 4). Release an end of about 51cm (20in) from the shuttle. Hold the end of it with the left hand between the thumb and index finger. Take the thread over the back of the remaining three fingers and back under them to between the thumb and index finger again, thus forming a ring (fig.2). Spread the fingers out to enlarge the ring.

Throw the thread from the shuttle into a loose loop over the top of the left hand and pass the shuttle from underneath, up through the ring and loop from right to left (fig.3).

The next movement is very important because if it is not made correctly the work will lock and the stitches will not run as freely as they should. Lower the middle finger of the left hand to loosen the ring. Tug the shuttle to the right so that the loop is transferred from being formed by the shuttle thread to being formed by the ring thread around the shuttle thread (fig.4). Eventually the knack of this will become instinctive but it is where beginners most often make mistakes.

Raise the middle finger of the left hand to tighten the stitch, sliding it along the shuttle thread until it is in position. Hold it in place with the thumb and index finger of the left hand.

Josephine knot (fig.5). This is formed by making several half stitches, slipping the ring off the left hand and pulling the shuttle thread so that the stitches form a ring. The size of the Josephine knot depends on how many half stitches are worked.

Double stitch (figs.6 and 7). There are two stages to this knot—the first being the half stitch already given. The second is, in fact, the same movement worked in the opposite direction which locks with the first.

With the right hand, pass the shuttle through the loop on the left hand downward from left to right. Tug the shuttle thread as before to transfer the stitch from the shuttle thread to the ring thread, then draw this stitch up against the first half stitch to lock.

Rings. Make several double stitches. Remove the ring from the left hand and draw up as for a Josephine knot.

An ornate gold and enamel shuttle made by J. J. Barrière of Paris in 1769.

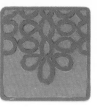

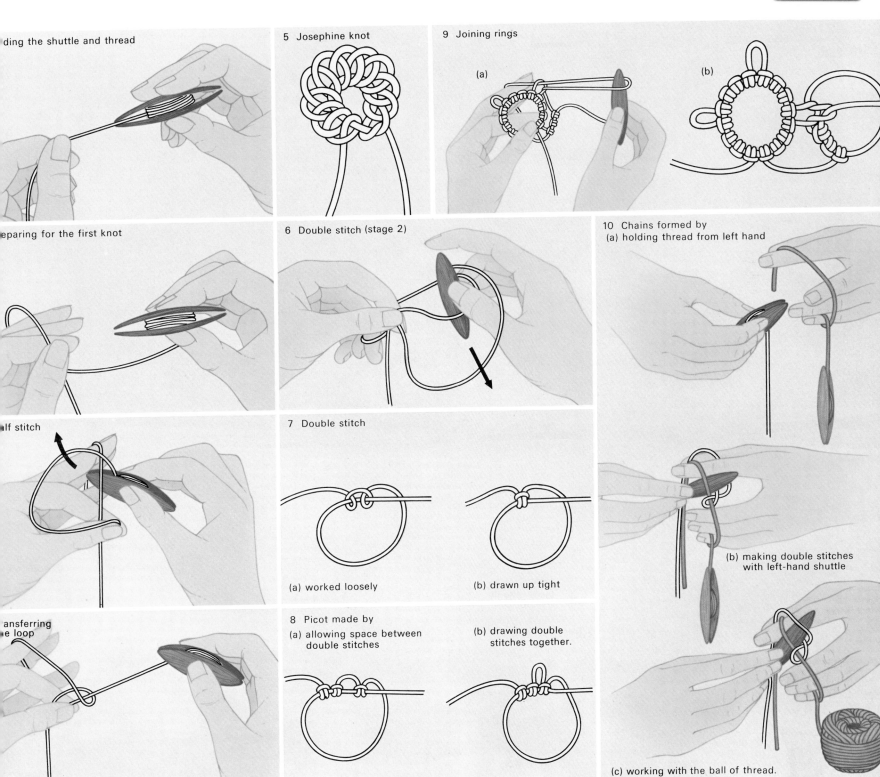

...ding the shuttle and thread

5 Josephine knot

9 Joining rings

(a)

(b)

...eparing for the first knot

6 Double stitch (stage 2)

10 Chains formed by
(a) holding thread from left hand

...lf stitch

7 Double stitch

(a) worked loosely

(b) drawn up tight

(b) making double stitches
with left-hand shuttle

...ansferring
...e loop

8 Picot made by
(a) allowing space between
double stitches

(b) drawing double
stitches together.

(c) working with the ball of thread.

Picots (fig.8). Make a double stitch. Leave a space of about 0.5cm ($\frac{1}{4}$in), then make a second double stitch. Draw the two double stitches together so that the thread between arches to form a picot. The size of the picot is determined by the length of the space between the two knots.

Joining rings (fig.9a and b). Rings are joined at a picot. Usually a ring will have a picot at the top and at each side. Make the second ring to just before the first picot. Insert the hook through the picot of the previous ring, draw the ring thread through to form a loop and hold it in the thumb and index finger of the left hand. Pass the shuttle through this loop and draw up the thread. Make the second half of a double stitch to lock the join. The join takes the place of the first half stitch.

Chains (fig.10a,b and c). These are made with two shuttles and the knots remain in straight lines or curves. Because there are two threads, it means that the tatting can

be done in two colors. If both threads are of the same color, it will help—especially if you are a beginner—to have different colored shuttles.

Hold the end of the thread from the first shuttle between the thumb and index finger of the left hand, pass the thread behind the middle two fingers and wind it around the little finger. Allow the shuttle to hang loose.

Hold the end of the thread from the second shuttle together with the first thread between the thumb and index finger of the left hand. Make double stitches as before but around the thread from the left-hand shuttle. After the tug which transfers the knot, the thread from the right-hand shuttle becomes the running thread and this is usually the thread which has made any previous rings. The left-hand shuttle is usually the extra one, and often this thread can be used straight from the ball and not wound onto a shuttle at all.

Two pretty edgings for lavender bags
Lavender bags make deliciously fragrant gifts and look especially pretty when trimmed with a homemade edging. Here are two which are easy to make and quickly enable the beginner to grasp the basic principles of tatting. The edging for the round bag is made with one shuttle and is approximately 1cm ($\frac{3}{8}$in) wide; that for the square bag is made with two shuttles and is about 2cm ($\frac{3}{4}$in) wide.
Abbreviations: ds, double stitch; p, picot; RW, reverse work.

Circular lavender bag
You will need:
1 ball lightweight mercerized crochet cotton □ shuttle □ small hook.
Making the edging. Ring of 4ds, 5p separated by 2ds, 7ds, close. *Ring of 7ds, join to last picot on previous ring, 2ds, p, 4ds, 3p separated by 2ds, 2ds, close. Join shuttle thread to 3rd picot from the end of

last ring, being careful to keep the thread at back of work. To do this, insert hook in picot and draw thread through, pass shuttle through loop just made and adjust knot. Ring of 4ds, join to previous ring at picot left free between the previous picot join and shuttle thread join, 2ds, 4p separated by 2ds, 7ds, close.** Repeat from * to ** for length required. Finish off.

Making the bag. Cut a circle of fabric measuring approximately 26cm (10¼in) in diameter. Turn under a small seam allowance and make neat with zigzag stitching or by hand. Trim the edge with the tatting neatly. Place a generous handful of lavender in the center of the fabric, then gather it up in your hand and tie with a narrow, attractive ribbon.

Square lavender bag

You will need:
1 ball lightweight mercerized crochet cotton □ 2 shuttles □ small hook.

Making the edging. Tie the shuttle threads together. With shuttle A, ring of 5ds, p, 5ds, p, 5ds, p, 5ds, close, RW. *With shuttle B over left hand, shuttle A in right hand, chain of 6ds. With shuttle B, ring of 2ds, 5p separated by 2ds, 2ds, close. With both shuttles as before, chain of 6ds, RW. With shuttle A, ring of 5ds, join to last picot of 1st ring, 5ds, p, 5ds, p, 5ds, close, RW.** Repeat from * to ** for length required, allowing ease at corners. Join the final ring to the first, and tie the final chain to beginning of work. Finish off.

Making the bag. Cut 2 pieces of cotton fabric approximately 10cm (4in) square. Stitch together allowing space for turning. Turn to right side, press and fill with lavender or herbs. Close the opening with slip stitching. Trim with the edging neatly. Finish off.

Floral mat

Although this design looks complicated, it will be no trouble once you are reasonably experienced in tatting. Worked in a soft creamy color, it will look equally at home on a table or chest. Note that the center daisy motifs are made with one shuttle only; the inner chain border is made with one shuttle and the ball thread; and the outer floral border is made with two shut-

tles. The mat measures approximately 24 × 33cm (9½ × 13in).

You will need:
2 balls medium-weight mercerized crochet cotton □ 2 shuttles □ small hook.

Making the center. Ring of 6ds, p. 6ds, p, 6ds, p, 6ds, close. *Ring of 6ds, join to last picot of previous ring, 6ds, p, 6ds, p, 6ds, close.** Repeat from * to ** 4 times more. joining the last picot of the 6th ring to the first picot of the 1st ring. (This can be done more easily if the 1st ring is folded forward to the left to insert hook.) Tie ends and finish off. Work 58 motifs altogether, joining them during working to make an oval shape (ie the center row consists of 10 motifs, the rows on either side have 9 motifs, flanked by rows of 8 and 7 motifs respectively).

Making the chain border. Tie ball thread and shuttle thread together (or leave uncut if winding a new shuttle), and join on at any corner picot on outer edge of center piece.

1st round. Chain of 10ds, join with shuttle thread to next picot on center piece (to do this, insert hook at picot and draw shuttle thread through, pass shuttle through loop just made and adjust knot). *p, 10ds, join as before to next picot.** Repeat from * to ** all around, ending by joining to the first picot to which threads were attached.

2nd round. Continue with chain of *p,

11ds, join with shuttle thread to next picot on previous round.** Repeat from * to ** all around, ending by joining to 1st picot.

3rd round. Continue with chain of *p, 12ds, join with shuttle thread to next picot on previous round.** Repeat from *. to ** all around, ending by joining to 1st picot. Finish off.

Making the floral border. Tie both shuttle threads together. With shuttle A, 1st ring of 12ds, p, 4ds, p, 8ds, close. *2nd ring of 8ds, join to last picot of previous ring, 2ds, p, 2ds, p, 2ds, p, 2ds, p, 8ds, close. Make 3rd, 4th and 5th rings as 2nd, RW. With shuttle B over left hand, shuttle A in right hand, chain of 12ds, RW.

1st leaf. With shuttle A, ring of 12ds, join to last picot of 5th ring, 4ds, p, 8ds, close, RW.

2nd leaf. With shuttle B, ring of 8ds, p, 4ds, join to (any) picot on edge of chain border, 8ds, close.

With shuttle B over left hand, shuttle A in right hand, chain of 12ds, join to following picot on chain border, 8ds, p, 12ds, RW. With shuttle A, 1st ring of 12ds, join to free picot on 1st leaf, 4ds, p, 8ds, close** Repeat from * to ** all around, but on every following repeat, join the 1st picot of 2nd leaf to the free picot on opposite chain. On the final pattern repeat, join the 1st leaf to the 1st ring at beginning of round, and join the final chain to leaf at beginning of round. Tie ends and finish off.

Lacemaking

Detail from a late 19th-century French fan mount in black Chantilly bobbin lace, showing a garden scene with peacocks, inside an intricate border of flowers and leaves.

According to a Bruges legend the beauty of a spider's web inspired the first attempts at making pillow lace, so it is quite significant that the word "lace" comes from the Latin *laqueus* meaning a snare, or *lacere* to entice.

Evidence of meshes made from twisted threads does, in fact, date back some 6,000 years to the Egyptian "Mummy lace," which was made on a frame. The free ends of thread were wound onto small shaped pieces of stone, wood or bone, which served as bobbins. Traditional lacemaking, however, is thought to have developed from the ornamental plaitings and braidings of the Middle Ages, and it is possible that the similarity between ancient and modern bobbin worked lace is mere coincidence.

By the mid-15th century, pillow lace—worked on a firm cushion or pillow, with pins to keep the threads in position—was well established in Venice and Flanders and spreading to other parts of Europe. In England, lacemaking centers in Devon and the Midlands were set up in the 16th and 17th centuries by refugees from religious persecution in Europe.

The use of finer linen threads encouraged more complicated and decorative designs of leaves, flowers, sprays and birds, with a variety of fancy fillings. Some fine patterns entailed over a year's work to produce one yard of lace using a thousand or more bobbins!

Other interesting developments included the outlining of individual sections with a thicker thread or "cordonnet" as in Buckinghamshire and Lille laces, or working motifs separately and then joining them with bobbin net needlepoint or appliquéing them by hand.

By the 18th century, there was an enormous demand for the finest laces for shawls, bonnets, cravats, flounces, collars, parasols, fans, handkerchiefs and christening robes. Heavy taxes and import prohibitions were adopted in England and France to protect the home lace industry. As a result, smuggling became quite a common practice and laces like Brussels, which was especially prized, were sometimes taken across the frontier to France packed in coffins, with or without a body! Lacemaking was generally a badly paid occupation and conditions were tiring and hard. Valencienne lace, for example, could only be made in damp rooms, as a moist atmosphere was necessary to prevent the gossamer threads from breaking.

The 19th century saw the introduction of machine-made nets and laces and cotton threads. Cheaper laces were in demand and the handmade lace industry tried in vain to compete with machines by using thicker threads and simpler Torchon, Cluny and Maltese patterns. By World War I, Britain was producing very little handmade lace and the craft was gradually dying out in the rest of Europe. Thankfully, interest in lacemaking has now been revived and the craft continues as an absorbing hobby.

Equipment

Making pillow lace is a fascinating hobby which requires little equipment, much of which can be made at home or improvised.
Pillow. Lacemaking areas each have their traditional shape of pillow. Some, for example, are bolster pillows supported on a stand or "horse"; others incorporate a rotating cylinder, which is useful when

Above: Traditional Maltese lace.

Below: Collection of bobbins from different lacemaking areas of Europe. The bobbin with beads attached is English and is made of glass. The one immediately below it dates from Henry VIII's reign (1509–47), the three metal rings indicating that his third wife, Jane Seymour, was then queen.

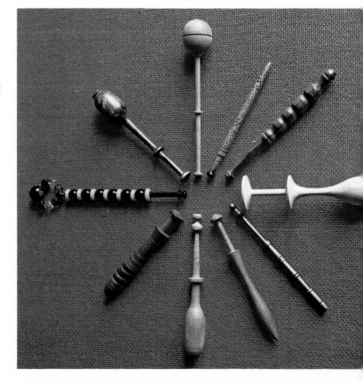

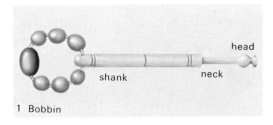

1 Bobbin

making edgings. You can make your own square pillow quite easily.

You will need:
a 46cm (18in) square of hardboard or plywood □ 2 pieces of closely woven fabric, 47cm (18½in) square (plain green or blue should be chosen as these are the most restful colors.) □ large quantity of sawdust, straw or hay.

Making the pillow. Make a square bag with the fabric by seaming three sides. Put the hardboard into the bag to form the base and pack the bag tightly with the sawdust, straw or hay. (If straw or hay is used, cut into 5cm (2in) lengths and hammer to flatten any knots.) Bang the surface hard with a rolling pin to compress the filling and continue packing and beating until the

Lace border in progress using 8 pairs of bobbins.

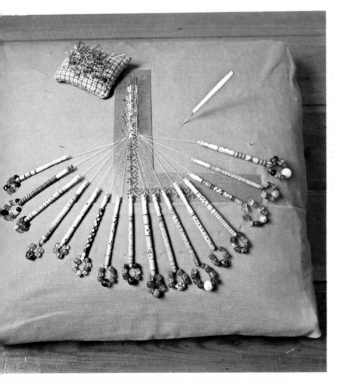

filling is firm and the surface smooth. Seam the fourth side by hand to complete the pillow.

Note: the pillow must be sufficiently firm to hold in place a partially stuck-in pin when a pair of bobbins hanging from it is pulled for working.

Bobbins. Old bobbins, although beautiful, are expensive to buy and difficult to obtain. They may be made of wood or bone and vary in shape from district to district. Some English types are decorated with inset wood or metal or are incised with colored inscriptions and enhanced with beads. Plain modern wood or plastic bobbins can be bought, or you may be able to carve or make some from 10–11.5cm (4–4½in) lengths of 1cm (⅜in) dowel. Drill a hole at the base to take the wire for the beads as shown in fig.1.

Lacemaking pins. These hold the threads in position until the pattern is completed. Long brass or stainless steel pins are essential as they will not rust or mark the lace.

Parchment or pricking card. The parchment or card stock used today is glazed and is a guide for the pattern. A beginner can use smooth, thick cardboard.

Pricker. You can improvise a pricker by pushing the head of a needle very firmly into a cork or a 7.5cm (3in) length of dowel.

Thread. In the past the best laces were made from linen, silk or even gold and silver thread. Fine linen thread is now difficult to obtain, but the wider variety of cotton threads available inspires a new approach and modern designs.

Basic techniques

With a little practice you will soon master the techniques involved in preparing the pillows for working and the basic steps in making lace.

Making prickings. From the patterns given for the projects trace accurately onto tracing paper the dots representing the pinholes and the lines showing the direction of the threads. This is the template from which you can make the prickings. Place the pricking card centrally onto the pillow and position the template over it as shown in fig.2. Secure both to the pillow by pinning at the corners. Holding the pricker in

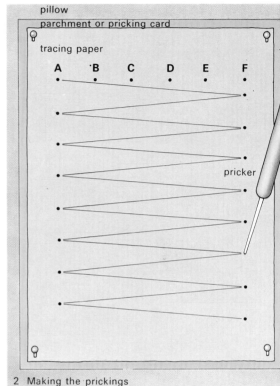

2 Making the prickings

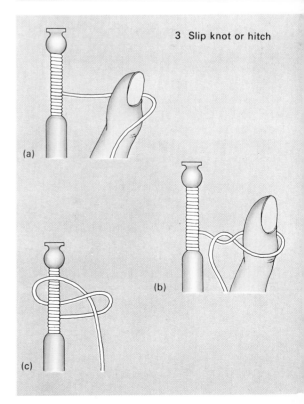

3 Slip knot or hitch

Basic techniques and stitches

an upright position, prick through each of the pinholes. Remove the tracing paper. Mark in the lines of the pattern onto the pricking card using non-smear ink.
Note: pencil and ballpoint pen are not suitable as these rub off and dirty the threads.

Dressing the pillow. Place the pricking card onto the upper section of the pillow. Fix it in place with a pin at each corner and another halfway down each long side. Cover the lower half of the pricking card with a piece of closely woven green or blue fabric approximately 30cm (12in) square and secure in position with pins to prevent the threads from the bobbins from catching the edges of the pricking card or the fixing pins.

Winding bobbins. Lace is worked with the bobbins wound in pairs. Hold a bobbin in your left hand and wind the thread around the neck of the bobbin in a clockwise direction three or four times. Continue winding by turning the bobbin in your fingers until the neck is filled. Use your right hand to guide the thread into place. To prevent the thread from unwinding, you need to make a slip knot or hitch (fig.3). This type of knot will allow the thread to be released gradually when working the lace. Make a loop over the index finger of your right hand (a), twist the loop twice by turning your finger around (b), then put the loop over the bobbin neck and gently tighten the knot to the bobbin head by pulling the free end of the thread (c). Now wind sufficient thread for the second bobbin over the filled neck of the first one. Break the thread and wind the thread from the first bobbin onto the second bobbin using the same winding method as before. Secure with a hitch knot. You should now have two bobbins attached to one length of thread ready to hang over a pin for starting work as shown in fig.4.

Handling bobbins. Hold the bobbins between your fingers and thumbs or your knuckles. With practice you will discover which is the most comfortable way to handle the bobbins and how much thread to leave between the pins and the bobbins. About 10cm (4in) is a suitable length for beginners. To release thread for working, turn the bobbin, keeping the thread taut.

4 Pair of bobbins wound for working

1 2 3 4 1 2 3 4
(a) cross   (b) twist
5

Note: the threads are easily soiled so try to avoid touching them with your fingers.
"Putting up" pins. When putting the pins into the work, insert them so that they lean slightly backwards, and outwards at the edges. This will ensure that the lace has a good outline. This process is known as "putting up" pins.
Stitches. These are formed by using two pairs of bobbins and are made with the movements called "cross" and "twist" (fig.5a and b). By adding crosses and twists and putting up pins as you proceed, you will be able to work different patterns and variations. Some of the pairs of threads travel across the pattern and are known as "workers" or "leaders," while others work down the lace and are called "passives."
Cloth or whole stitch (fig.6a–d). This is the basic stitch and is worked by using two

pairs of bobbins (a). Cross the second thread over the third (b). Twist the new second and fourth threads over the new first and third. Move the bobbins at the same time by holding one bobbin in each hand (c). Cross the new second thread over the third (d).
Half stitch. This is a variation of cloth or whole stitch using two pairs of bobbins in the same way. Work as shown in fig. 6a, b and c, but *omit* stage d.
Joining threads. Threads can be joined onto a passive by hanging a new bobbin from a pin stuck in at the top or side of the pattern so that the new thread lies next to that being lengthened. Put a rubber band around the bobbins holding the old and new threads and work the two as one for about 1cm ($\frac{3}{8}$in). Put the old thread over the finished lace and continue working with the new thread. Ends can be sewn in later. If a worker needs more thread, change it to become a passive by working an extra twist in a cloth stitch section and then join in a new thread as described.

Lace bookmark
This unusual bookmark is designed to use interesting combinations of basic stitches with variations, and is simple enough for

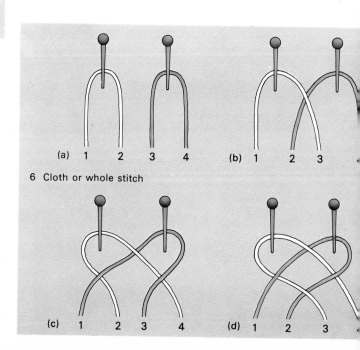

(a) 1 2 3 4   (b) 1 2 3
6 Cloth or whole stitch
(c) 1 2 3 4   (d) 1 2 3

Lace bookmark

Note: all pairs are numbered from left to right. The instruction "close the pin" (shortened to "close" in the text) means that a stitch should be worked around the pin.

1st section. This is worked in cs, and when the pin is put up the ws are twisted

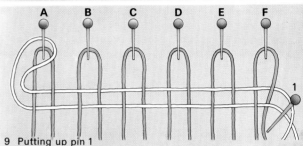

8 Hanging on the bobbins for the bookmark

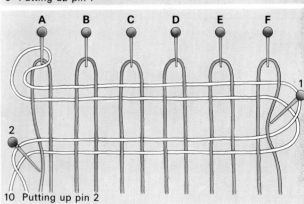

9 Putting up pin 1

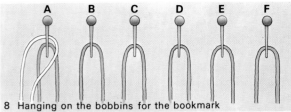

10 Putting up pin 2

the beginner to tackle as a first project. By using two colors the progress of the workers and passives is clearly shown through the lace and creates attractive patterns in five sections.

You will need:
lace pillow □ 8 pairs of bobbins □ lace-making pins □ a 6 × 20cm (2½ × 8in) piece of pricking card □ tracing paper □ 1 ball of brown pearl cotton no. 5 □ 1 ball of cream pearl cotton no. 5.

Preparing the work. Make the pricking using tracing paper and a pricking card as described earlier. Follow the chart as shown in fig.7. Dress the pillow. Wind 6 pairs of bobbins in brown for the passives and 2 pairs in cream for the workers.

Hanging on the bobbins (fig.8). Put up 1 pin at each of the points A,B,C,D,E and F. Hang a pair of brown bobbins from each and a cream pair from A to the left of the brown pair.

Abbreviations: w, worker; ws workers; p, passive; ps, passives; cs, cloth stitch; hs, half stitch; tw, twist; lh, left hand; rh, right hand; rep, repeat; cont, continue.

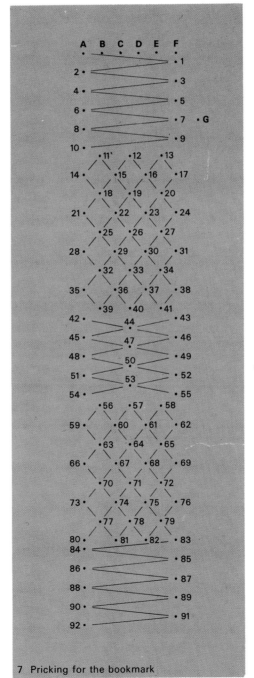

7 Pricking for the bookmark

*Using the cream ws and the brown ps hanging from A, make a cs. Push the brown ps to the left and bring the next pair of brown ps to the ws. Make a cs and push these ps aside. Cont taking the ws through the next 4 pairs of brown ps in the same way. Tw the ws once with your rh. Put up a pin between the ws and ps in pinhole 1 with your lh (fig.9). Holding the ws taut with your rh, smooth the p bobbins downwards so that the threads are straightened. The ps should have traveled to the left of the pillow and the ws to the right. The reverse will take place with the next line. Close by working cs between pairs 6 and 7. Although the ws are traveling in the opposite direction, the movements of cs remain the same. Cont by taking the ws through the ps with cs. Tw the ws once. Put up pin 2 between the first and second pair (fig.10) ** Rep from * to ** putting up pins 3,4,5,6,7 and 8.

Traditional handkerchief border

Take the ws across to the right edge in cs. Put up pin G. Hang from it a pair of cream bobbins down beside the ps. Work cs between the 2 cream pairs. Tw the ws and put up pin 9.

Close with cs. Remove pin from G. Allow the loop to come to rest on the threads of the ws in the completed lace. Cont working across and put up pin 10. Do not close this pin.

2nd section. This is worked in hs. Pairs travel diagonally to one edge of the lace and then the other. At each pinhole where pairs intersect, a sequence of hs, pin, hs is worked.

Tw all the pairs except the ws which are already twisted.

*Work hs with pairs 2 and 3. Put up pin 11. Close with hs. Repeat with pairs 4 and 5 at pinhole 12 and pairs 6 and 7 at pinhole 13. Work hs with pairs 1 and 2. Put up pin 14. Close with hs. Rep with pairs 3 and 4 at pinhole 15, pairs 5 and 6 at pinhole 16 and pairs 7 and 8 at pinhole 17.**

Rep from * to ** completing pinholes 18 to 38. Work pinholes 39 to 41 with hs, pin, hs. Remember to pull the threads up at intervals to keep the work neat. If necessary, move the cloth covering the lower part of the pricking card down the pillow to give extra working space.

3rd section. This cs section has 2 cream ws which meet in the center of the lace at a pinhole.

Work hs with pairs 1 and 2. Put up pin 42. Close with hs. Rep with pairs 7 and 8 to work pinhole 43. The cream ws should be in positions 2 and 7.

Bring the lh ws to the center by passing them through pairs 3 and 4 in cs. Bring the rh ws to the center by passing them through pairs 6 and 5 in cs. The 2 ws should now meet in the center of the lace.

*Tw each w once. Work cs with the 2 pairs of ws. Put up pin 44. Close with cs. Tw both pairs. Take the lh ws to the left side by working through pairs 3,2 and 1 in cs. Tw the ws. Put up pin 45. Close with cs. Return ws to the center by working through pairs 2 and 3 in cs.

Take the rh ws through pairs 6,7 and 8 in cs. Tw and put up pin 46. Close with cs. Bring the ws back to the center through pairs 6 and 5 with cs.**

Rep from * to ** to complete pinholes 47 to 53. Take the ws through to pinholes 54 and 55 to complete the section and close.

4th section. This is similar to the 2nd section but is worked in cs, tw, pin, cs and tw. Tw all pairs once.

*With pairs 2 and 3 work a cs. Tw both pairs. Put up pin 56. Close with cs. Tw both pairs. Rep at pinhole 57 using pairs 4 and 5 and pinhole 58 with pairs 6 and 7. Rep with pairs 1 and 2 at pinhole 59, 3 and 4 at pinhole 60, 5 and 6 at pinhole 61 and 7 and 8 at pinhole 62.**

Rep from * to ** to complete pins 63 to 80 and then work pins 81 to 83 in the same way. Keep the threads well pulled up so that the lace is neat.

5th section. In this part a pair of cream and brown ws are used alternately to form 2 different edges and a striped pattern. Work a cs with pairs 4 and 5. *Using pair 7 as the ws, bring to the lh side by working through pairs 6,5,4 and 3 with cs. Tw the ws. Make a cs with pair 2. Tw both pairs once. Make a cs with the first pair. Tw both pairs once and pair 1 twice more. Put up pin 84 between pairs 2 and 3.

Take pair 2 as the ws. Work cs with pairs 2 and 3. Tw both pairs once. Take the ws through pairs 4,5,6 and 7. Tw the ws. Cs pairs 7 and 8. Tw both pairs. Put up pin 85. Work cs. Tw both pairs.**

Rep from * to ** to complete pins 86 to 91. Bring the ws through to complete pin 92. Straighten the threads.

Finishing. Unwind each thread so that there is about 15cm (6in) from the pins to the bobbins. Cut the threads. Using an overhand knot (fig.11), join the threads from pairs 1,2 and 3. Join pair 4 with the first thread from pair 5 and the second thread from pair 5 with pair 6. Join pairs 7 and 8. Trim the fringe to 1.5cm ($\frac{1}{2}$in).

Traditional handkerchief border

This handkerchief border is adapted from a traditional lace design. The lace has a cloth stitch trail running through it, forming a pretty shell edging; the pattern incorporates ideas used in the bookmark. The edging is for mounting onto a handkerchief 28cm (11in) square.

You will need:

lace pillow □ 8 pairs of bobbins □ lace-

A selection of borders, corners, floral and butterfly motifs, in a variety of traditional lace patterns.

making pins □ piece of pricking card cut to an L-shape 7.5cm (3in) wide and 20cm (8in) along each outside edge □ 1 ball of lightweight white mercerized crochet cotton □ white handkerchief measuring 28cm (11in) square.

Preparing the work. Wind the bobbins with white thread. Fig. 12 shows the pricking for the corner and part of the sides of the edging. The pattern repeat or "point" is shown between lines I-I and II-II. Trace the design. You will need to make a pricking of 10 points running vertically, the corner and 10 points running horizontally, so after pricking the design on the tracing, move the tracing paper along to finish pricking the correct number of points. Dress the pillow.

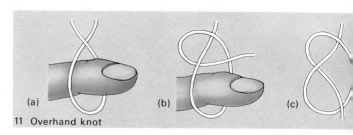

(a)   (b)   (c)

11 Overhand knot

Traditional handkerchief border

ricking for the handkerchief border

Hanging on the bobbins. Hang 3 pairs of bobbins from pins A and B and 2 from pin C.

Making the handkerchief border. The abbreviations used are the same as for the bookmark. The second point from the top on the pricking card will be used as the guide for working the first point of lace.

Working the first point. Work cs stitch with pairs 7 and 8. Tw both pairs twice. Take the ws, pair 7 through pairs 6.5 and 4 in cs. Tw the ws. Cs pairs 1 and 2. Tw each pair and pair 1 twice more. Cs pairs 2 and 3. Tw each pair.

†Cs pairs 3 and 4. Tw both pairs and put up pin 1. Close with cs and tw both pairs, joining the straight edge with the shell. Take the lh pair, pair 3, to the straight edge. Cs pairs 2 and 3. Tw each pair. Cs pairs 1 and 2. Tw each pair and pair 1 twice more. Put up pin 2 between pairs 2 and 3. Cs pairs 2 and 3. Tw both pairs.

Remove pins A and B. Pull pairs 2,3,5,6 and 7 gently downwards so that the loops come to rest on the threads of the ws in the completed lace.

*Using pair 4 as the ws take-through pairs 5,6 and 7 in cs. Tw the ws twice. Cs the ws and pair 8. Tw both pairs. Put up pin 3. Close with cs and tw both pairs twice. Take the ws through pairs 7,6 and 5 in cs. Tw the ws and put up pin 4.**

Working from * to ** put up pins 5,6,7,8 and 9 and work to pin 10. Check that the ws are twisted. Before putting up pin 10, make a cs with the ws pair 4 and pair 3. Tw both pairs and put up pin 10. Close with cs. Tw both pairs. Cs pairs 3 and 2. Tw both pairs. Work a cs with pairs 1 and 2. Tw both pairs and pair 1 twice more. Put up pin 11 between pairs 2 and 3. Work cs with pairs 2 and 3. Tw both pairs.

Take the ws, pair 4, through pairs 5,6 and 7 in cs. Tw the ws twice. Work a cs with pair 8. Tw both pairs and put up pin 12. Close with cs and tw both pairs twice.

Using pair 3 as ws, take the ws through pairs 4,5 and 6 with cs. Tw the ws. Put up pin 13. Take ws through pairs 6,5 and 4 in cs. Tw the ws. Cs pairs 2 and 3. Tw both pairs. Cs pairs 1 and 2. Tw both pairs and pair 1 twice more. Put up pin 14 between pairs 2 and 3. Cs pairs 2 and 3. Tw each pair once. Take the ws, pair 7, through pairs

6.5 and 4 with cs. Tw the ws. †† Rep from † to †† 7 more times to complete 8 points in all. Work through the 9th point in the same way, until pin 13 has been put up. Work pin 13 as before but leave pair 1 twisted *once* only before putting up pin 14.

Making the corner. Pinhole 14 of the pattern is the same as pinhole A shown in the corner section of fig.12. At pinhole A, work cs with pairs 3 and 4. Tw both pairs. Put up pin B. Close with cs. Tw both pairs. Working from * to ** put up pins C,D,E,F,G,H,I,J and K and work to pin L. Make sure the ws are twisted, and work a cs with pair 3. Put up pin L. Close with cs and tw both pairs.

Note: as you work the corner, turn the pillow to continue working downwards. Work cs with pairs 2 and 3. Tw both pairs once. Work cs with pairs 1 and 2. Tw both pairs and pair 1 twice more. Put up pin M between pairs 2 and 3. (M is the same as pinhole 11 of the basic pattern.) Complete as for pins 12, 13 and 14 to finish the corner. Rep from † to †† to make 10 points of side 2.

Moving the lace up. As there are 18 points in each side of the lace edging but only 10 points marked out on the pricking card, you will need to move the lace up to complete the second half of the second side and the first half of the third side. Fold the sides and bottom of the cloth covering the pricking card over the bobbins. Pin the bottom half of the cloth to the top half. Move the cloth and bobbins up the pillow slightly so that the threads are slackened. Remove the pins from the lace and gently lift the lace, cloth and bobbins up the pricking. Reposition so that the worked points 9 and 10 of the second side are over points 1 and 2 on the pricking card. Replace the pins in the last two worked points. Unpin and replace the cloth. Straighten and correct the positions of the threads.

Finishing the lace. Continue working the sides and corners to complete a square.

Cutting off and joining. Unwind the bobbins and cut the threads as for the bookmark. Lay the border out flat and work the join by weaving each thread by about 2.5cm (1 in) with a needle from the finishing end of the lace to the starting point.

Mounting. Mount the border onto the handkerchief with fine overcast stitching.

Using color

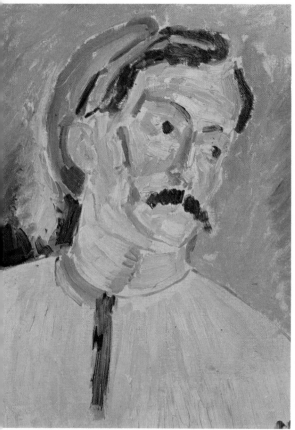

Portrait of André Derain by Henri Matisse, one of the many artists to experiment with unusual color combinations.

Certain rules were laid down in the past as to what particular colors might or might not be used together. Van Gogh, Gauguin and Seurat, among others, contributed to the development of modern art by their bold use of color, which was further developed by Matisse, while Seurat laid dots of bright hues side by side so that they mix in the eye of the spectator to make a shimmering effect of color.

These artists laid the foundation of modern painting by showing that any combination of color is permissible. You should not therefore have preconceptions about color harmonies and clashes but rather train your eye to see and choose those color effects which are suitable for your work, for color is not merely intended to represent reality but also to express originality and subjectivity of perception.

Understanding color

All visible color consists of light direct from a source or reflected from a surface. White light or daylight is made up of all the colors of the rainbow—the spectrum. Rainbows are in fact white sunlight broken into its constituent colors by passing through raindrops (see fig. 1).

Colored surfaces are seen as such since they absorb some of the colors of light and reflect others; for example, a green surface is one that reflects green light but absorbs the rest. This is why a colored fabric may look very different in artificial light, since it is itself a different color from daylight. An object that absorbs all the light is black, and one that reflects all the light is white.

Mixtures of colored pigment are subtractive, that is, they absorb all the light that the two original colors each absorbed, so that the mixed color is always darker than either of the originals (fig. 2). Colored pigments can be classified in two ways as described below.

Hues. Hues are colors equivalent to those of the rainbow. There are six key hues— red, orange, yellow, green, blue and violet. These gradate into each other and may be arranged in a circle or "color wheel" as shown in fig. 3. Red, yellow and blue are called *primary* colors since theoretically, all other hues may be produced from mixtures of these. Orange, green and violet are called *secondary* colors as they should be the result of mixing adjacent primaries. Unfortunately, manufactured pigments are never as pure as light and as pigment mixtures are subtractive, it is very difficult to achieve, for example, violet by mixing red and blue. For the purpose of designing and experimenting, it is advisable to buy the six main hues as well as black and white. As an experiment, make a color circle and create at least three gradated steps between each primary and secondary color. Then make scales in which you gradually change the tone of hues by adding white and black.

You will notice that some colors are opposite each other on the color wheel; these are called *complementaries* (fig. 3). Placing complementaries side by side creates particularly vivid effects since they seem to intensify each other. Mixing complemen-

taries gives an interesting range of browns and grays. Combinations of hues which are near to each other are less startling, although very close hues may create a visual tension of their own. A line drawn across the color circle as in fig.3 divides the hues into "warm" and "cold." This distinction between "warm" and "cold" is logical since we associate red with fire and blue with ice. As in almost everything else to do with color, this effect is however relative; a green-blue may look cold against a red but warm against a blue.

Tones, tints and shades. The lightness or darkness of a color is known as its *tone.* Some of the pure hues on the color wheel

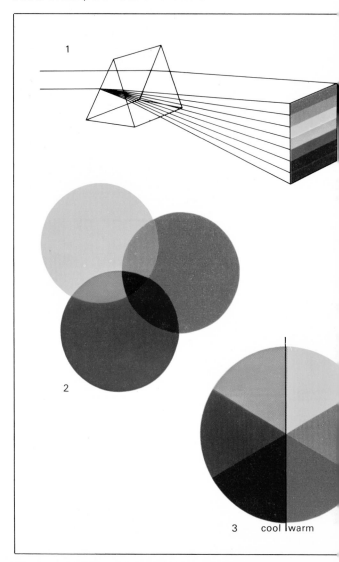

are seen to be darker than others when compared with a scale of grays (fig.4). You can change the tone of a color by adding black, white or gray, but this always reduces the intensity of the hue. Adding white, which increases the amount of light the hue reflects, gives *tints*. Adding black, which absorbs nearly all the light, gives *shades*. Fig.5 shows a range of tints and shades that can be made by adding white and black to red.

Further experiments with color
Apart from juxtaposing complementaries or adjacent hues there are other ways of achieving effect with color. The appear-

ance of hues, tones or colors of varying intensity are always modified by surrounding or adjacent colors. For example, a particular hue will look brighter against black but darker against white, more intense against gray than against black or white, and more luminous against its complementary. Even the area of a patch of color will appear to vary according to its surroundings. Large areas of color will look more intense than small areas. A combination of a large number of small areas of color will create an effect of luminosity, particularly if they are high in tone. This effect was much used by the Impressionist painters. You can use patches of colored

paper or material to show how colors are influenced by their surroundings. Fig.6 may surprise you because the central squares in both (a) and (b) are the same color. And in fig.7 you can watch the gray lines seeming to change color as they cross into different backgrounds.
Colors also have a spatial effect, this aspect being greatly explored by Cézanne and subsequently by Matisse. It has become a major preoccupation of 20th-century art. Warm colors will advance, less intense ones will recede. However, these effects are again relative, as, for example, a cold but intense color may appear to advance in front of a warm but less intense one.

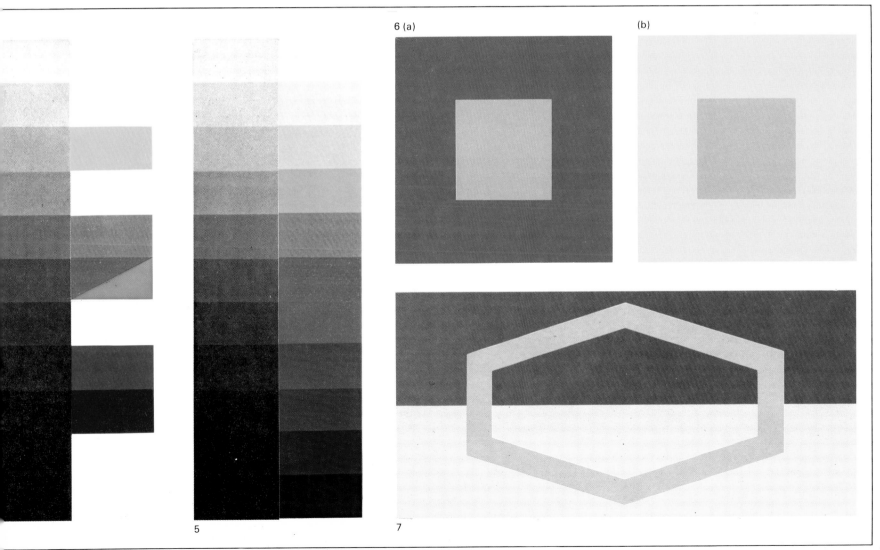

6 (a)

(b)

5

7

Patchwork

"It's foolish work," said Maggie, "tearing things to pieces to sew 'em together again." This is the way Maggie Tulliver, one of the characters in George Eliot's novel *Mill on the Floss*, written in 1860, chose to regard patchwork. However, her view should be taken to be the exception rather than the rule! Patchwork is an age-old household craft that has thrived as a symbol of friendship for centuries, as needlewomen both collected and exchanged small bits of colorful cloth, plain and patterned, in a neighborly way, using them to form a final piece of patchwork. This was certainly the case in America where, from the 18th century onwards, "friendship" quilts were put together by communities to honor a special occasion. The "freedom" quilts were made as mementoes for young men on their 21st birthdays, and traditionally a "marriage" quilt was made for a bride by her girl friends as a wedding gift. Indeed, it was considered a bad omen if a bride made her own wedding quilt, although prior to her engagement she would probably have worked the traditional 13 quilts for her bottom drawer.

But what exactly is patchwork, and how did it develop as a creative craft? Basically, all patchwork items consist either of numerous pieces of material joined together with stitching to form a decorative mosaic effect, or, alternatively, various pieces of cloth applied to some sort of backing material in such a way as to form a picture or design.

The ancient craft no doubt first arose out of sheer thrift—the need to be practical and to patch as a means of repair. But even in more prosperous times patchwork remained popular, since certain fabrics were far too beautiful to be thrown away and offered the opportunity for creative use. A few ancient examples of primitive patchwork were discovered by early explorers in Egypt and other Eastern countries. In the Boulak Museum in Cairo, for instance, there is a patchwork canopy of gazelle hide dating from c. 908 BC which was probably used for grand ceremonies. Medieval European paintings and manuscripts also provide evidence of patchwork banners, hangings and costumes. But

practicality was clearly the operative word, at least as far as the very early days of patchwork were concerned.

After the 16th century, cottons from India became available and gradually, with a wider range of fabrics and greater prosperity, patchwork played quite an important part in the social life of female society. Generally, the finished work was used for coverlets or quilts but it was used at times for other furnishings, too. There is, for example, a magnificent four-poster bed with patchwork coverlet, valances and curtains at Stranger's Hall, Norwich, England.

The craft was first introduced to the United States by cost-conscious Dutch and English settlers, and soon spread inland from the east coast. Various attractive names were coined for the traditional patterns worked, and these commonly changed as the continent became colonized.

By the 19th century, a veritable craze had developed for patchwork, both in Britain and America, sometimes producing the most elaborate designs in taffeta, silks, velvets, cottons and various other fabrics. Many patchwork pieces were made as heirlooms, and women produced numerous large quilts during their sewing lives. Jane Austen is known to have worked on a large patchwork piece with her mother and sister in 1811, and the resulting coverlet is today at the Austen family house in Hampshire, England.

The great prison reformer, Elizabeth Fry, is said to have taught the craft to female prisoners in London's Newgate Prison: even those deported to Australia were presented with sufficient fabrics to patchwork during the journey so that the resulting work could be sold for charity on arrival.

The art of patchwork was also taught to children in Victorian times, since it enabled them to practice stitching. Various items

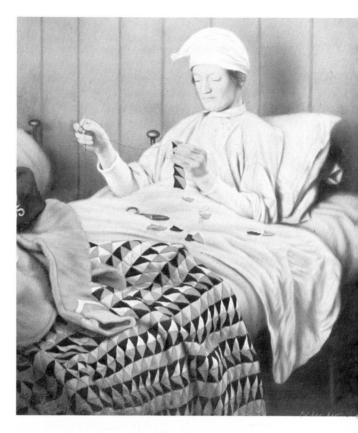

Above: Patchwork was encouraged in English hospitals during the Crimean War as a form of therapy for convalescing soldiers.

Right: A three-dimensional effect is created in this patchwork of a christening. Completed in 1876, the picture shows the West Window of Holy Trinity Church at Stratford-upon-Avon, England.

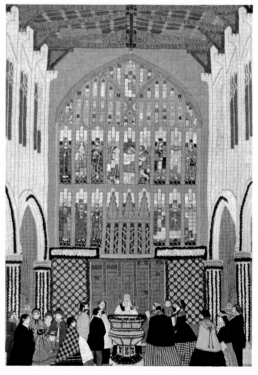

such as pincushions and pillow covers were fashioned from a variety of fabrics and in this way young girls soon learned how best to handle their materials.

The possibilities for creative patchwork are endless and certainly the early examples provide a wealth of pattern ideas—everything from combinations of flower designs, bows, diamond shapes, rectangles, squares and shell patterns to triangles, hexagons, zigzags and the "log cabin" effect where strips are arranged in squares according to shade.

Patchwork today

Patchwork is essentially a very personal craft: each piece is unique, the overall pattern, color and design owing much to individual skill and creativity. The recent revival of interest in this craft has seen the return of the family "rag-bag"—all those odd bits and pieces collected and saved from years of home dressmaking and sewing. As for the techniques, these have hardly changed at all, although the sewing machine has obviously speeded up the process considerably. The many stitches possible with modern machines allow for potential development in the field of decorating patchwork. However, most people enjoy patchwork because it is relaxing, and prefer to work by hand.

Equipment. The most basic of sewing kits will contain all that you need for patchwork. Use the finest needle you have and choose a thread that matches the main background color of the fabrics you are using: black or brown for dark colors, white for light cotton prints. Although ordinary dressmaker's pins are adequate, shorter ones will prove more suitable when working out the arrangement of patches on a board, rather as a jigsaw is pieced together. For a board, use anything suitable on hand: heavy cardboard, or even cork tiles—anything that the pins will go into easily and yet hold the patches securely in place while you arrange them. You will also need dressmaker's chalk to draw around the template onto the fabric.

Fabrics. Sources for patchwork pieces are numerous. Remember that it is essentially about saving money, not spending it, so the rag-bag should be your first choice.

Many stores sell small inexpensive remnants from the ends of rolls; some even sort them out into bundles especially for patchworkers. Friends and neighbors, too, are a likely source as they would probably be happy to hand over remnants and old clothes they no longer need.

Try not to mix different types of fabric in one piece of patchwork: choose fabrics of a similar weight and weave and try to cut them so that the grain of the fabrics runs in the same direction. Mixing them could result in one patch of a loose weave stretching, another shrinking, and then all your hours of work will be wasted when the patchwork becomes puckered and out of shape.

Note, too, what the fabric is made from. Natural fibers such as cotton are still the best and most reliable, and they wear better, too. Closely woven fabrics are the most suitable: check they do not fray. Also

A mid-19th century example of log cabin patchwork, a technique that became popular in America and England during that century and is described later in this section.

check the fastness of the dyes before beginning to work. If you intend to make something that will get a lot of wear and therefore need constant cleaning, it is vital that the fabric will not shrink and that the dyes do not run. Wash samples beforehand as a preventive measure. Some fabrics are better dry-cleaned—just in case. Rich materials like velvet and brocades are often used in crazy patchwork but they will not wear well unless they are lined and cared for. Finally, if two fabrics *are* very different in weight, line the lighter with a bonded material.

Templates. A template is, very simply, a pattern. In patchwork, it is used to cut shapes of the same size from fabric, and of course, the variety of these shapes is numerous. The most basic shapes are squares, diamonds, triangles, hexagons, octagons and church windows. These shapes can be cut to any size. Trace the shapes given in fig.1 for a set of average-sized templates for the beginner. There are many other shapes for templates too, and as you become more interested and experienced in the subject, you will begin to

Patchwork

Materials and equipment

discover other sources around you in tiling, mosaics and even parquet flooring. The main consideration when deciding the shapes to use for your patchwork is that when assembled together they form solid areas of fabric.

Templates are easy to make in cardboard, but they must be accurate and they will not last as long as purchased templates. These can be bought from most stores in plastic or metal. They come in pairs: one template is for cutting out the paper lining for the patch (fig.2a) and is the actual size of the finished patch, while the other often has a transparent window (also the actual size of the patch) with a metal edge indicating the width of seam allowance (fig.2b). This window enables you to see the pattern of the fabric.

Lining patches. Individual patches are made by stretching and basting a patch of fabric over a paper lining. This lining helps to keep the shape of the patch while several are being sewn together, so always use good quality paper for this purpose. Interfacing can be used too, and this can be left in the patch to form a firm lining if required. If paper is used, it should be removed after the patchwork has been assembled. The linings can be re-used several times if removed carefully enough.

Color schemes. Begin by using only two or three effectively combined colors. Plain fabrics are best to start with, but you will soon want to introduce patterns for more complex results. A random selection of fabrics can work together very well, but you must have a basic understanding of color, design and balance.

Your real skill will develop and reveal itself when you come to plan an overall design in

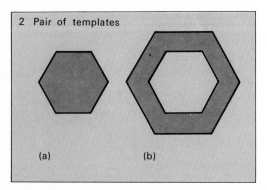

2 Pair of templates
(a)   (b)

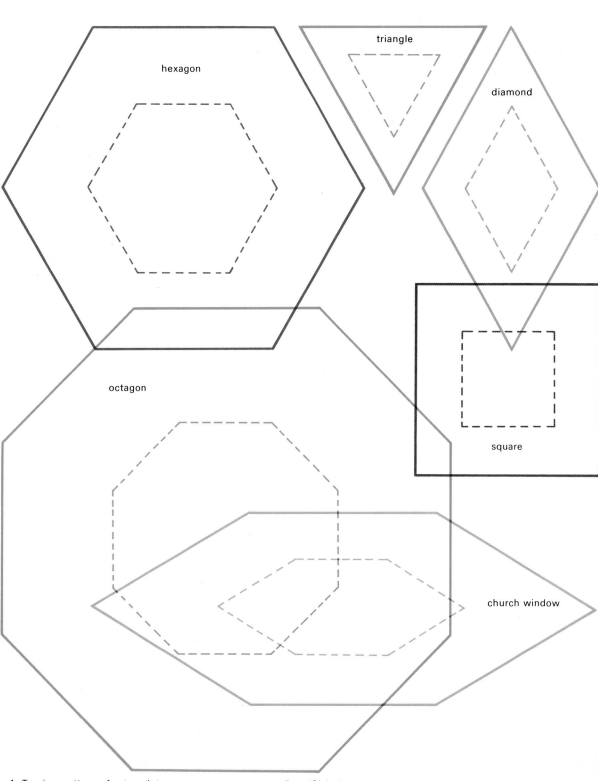

triangle

hexagon

diamond

octagon

square

church window

1 Tracing patterns for templates - outer measurement 5cm (2in), inner measurement 2.5cm (1in)

you can sew by hand and know how to cut out, baste, overcast and hem neatly, you will have no problems.

Small patches are always better sewn by hand. Use the template patterns given on the previous page and trace the shape onto tracing paper and transfer onto cardboard or strong paper. Cut out the shape. This will be the size of the completed patch. Cut out a lining for the patch in paper the same size as the template. Then position your template on the wrong side of the fabric, draw around with dressmaker's chalk and cut out. Pin the lining paper to the wrong side of the fabric so that the center aligns precisely, as shown in fig.3a. Then fold the seam allowance over to the back and baste down neatly as in fig.3b, taking particular care with the corners. The prepared patch should now look as in fig.3c. To join the patches, place two sides together with their right sides facing, then overcast neatly by hand, beginning and finishing as neatly as possible (fig.3d). Continue to assemble all the patches in this way. Fold in the corners of sharply-angled patches as shown in fig.4.

Making the patchwork. Once the patchwork is complete, remove the basting threads and the lining.

Finishing depends on the eventual use of the patchwork. The work may need to be lined, or straight or curved edges bound or piped. Always allow for seams. For garments, simply place the paper pattern onto the patchwork as with an ordinary length of fabric and continue making the garment in the usual way.

Lining patchwork. Patchwork is generally strong once it has been stitched and the thread ends neatened and secured firmly in the work. However, it can become distorted if the grain of the fabrics does not run in the same direction, in which case a lining will be necessary.

Place the patchwork and lining together, wrong sides facing, and then catch the two layers together every other patch or so all over the work. Having done so, baste around the outside and then treat the fabric as if it were one layer only. This applies to furnishings and clothing, and in the case of the latter an additional body lining is usually required.

Virtually any color combination lends itself to patchwork, as this collection effectively demonstrates. The girl's trouser suit is an amusing interpretation of "instant" machine-stitched patchwork, whereas various templates have been used to create the other designs.

plain and patterned fabric. Colors often work with each other, even if at first glance they might appear to clash. Use your intuition to decide whether a selection of patterns and colors will combine happily.

Sewing patches together by hand

Anyone who can sew can do patchwork. If

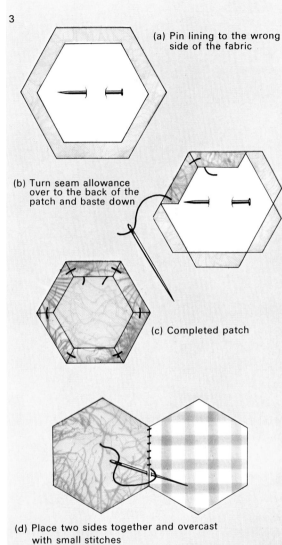

3

(a) Pin lining to the wrong side of the fabric

(b) Turn seam allowance over to the back of the patch and baste down

(c) Completed patch

(d) Place two sides together and overcast with small stitches

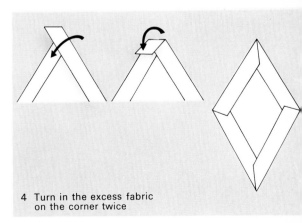

4 Turn in the excess fabric on the corner twice

Patchwork bag

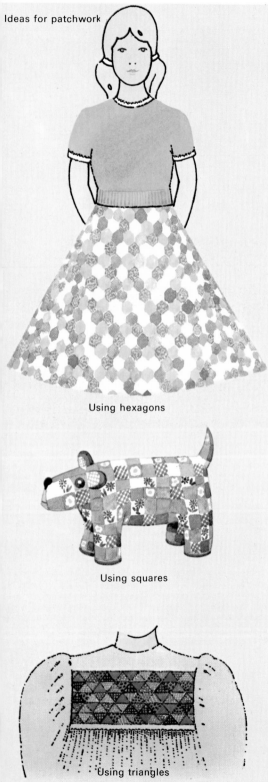

Ideas for patchwork

Using hexagons

Using squares

Using triangles

Patchwork bag

This patchwork bag uses three basic templates: the triangle, hexagon and square. When finished it is ideal for storing knitting, needlepoint or simply as a fashion accessory.

You will need:

0.25m ($\frac{1}{4}$yd) of red, white and patterned cotton fabrics, 90cm (36in) wide □ 0.75m ($\frac{3}{4}$yd) blue cotton fabric □ matching thread □ 2 lengths of 43cm (17in) dowel, 1.5cm ($\frac{1}{2}$in) in diameter □ 2 strips of iron-on interfacing □ lining papers.

Making the patchwork. Cut out the lining papers and fabric for 72 red triangles, 42 hexagons, 36 white squares and 30 blue squares. Baste the patches to the linings, turning in the edges neatly. Stitch the triangles to the hexagons making sure that the edges match exactly. Stitch the white squares to the red triangles and the blue squares to the hexagons. Continue in this manner until there are 3 rows of 7 hexagons and 3 rows of blue and white squares.

Make the other side of the bag in the same way. Iron the patchwork on both sides and remove the linings.

Making the bag. Trim the excess fabric from the sides of the hexagons to form 2 rectangles of patchwork fabric. Cut out strips of blue fabric the depth of the bag and 6.5cm ($2\frac{1}{2}$in) wide. Stitch them to each short side of the bag pieces. Press open the seams. Cut out 2 rectangles of blue fabric to match the size of the patchwork pieces for lining. Stitch the 2 bag pieces together around the sides and along the bottom edge. Repeat with the lining. Slip the lining into the bag, wrong sides facing, and baste the top edges together. Cut 2 strips of blue fabric 9.5cm ($3\frac{3}{4}$in) wide by the length of the bag, allowing 3cm ($1\frac{1}{4}$in) seam allowance on all edges. Iron the interfacing onto the strips 1.5cm ($\frac{1}{2}$in) from one long edge. Stitch the 2 strips together along the short edges to form a circle. Press open the seam allowances. Stitch one long edge to the top edge of the bag, right sides facing. Press as before. Fold in half lengthwise to the inside, turn in the seam allowance and slip stitch to close. Cut 4 strips of blue fabric for the handle loops 5 × 12.5cm (2 × 5in). Fold in half lengthwise with right sides facing

(a)

(c)

Sewing patches together by machine

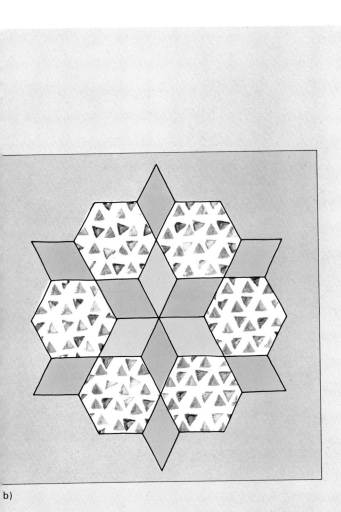

Combining shapes in patchwork

(a) rectangles, squares and octagons

(b) diamonds and hexagons

(c) hexagons, octagons, diamonds and squares

and stitch the long sides together. Turn to right side, press flat with the seam in the center. Turn in the short ends and stitch to the bag with the seamline to the inside. Top stitch as required.

Slip the dowels into the loops and stitch under the loops to hold the dowels in place.

Sewing patches together by machine

If you have a sewing machine, you will be able to produce "instant" patchwork in no time at all. A zigzag stitch on a machine will enable you to make machine embroidery on the patchwork too, and so add a new dimension to the finished piece. You can even use gold or silver thread to create an exotic effect on the material.

The larger your patches, the more suitable they will be for assembly by sewing machine. Prepare the patches in the usual way as for hand sewing, but use interfacing rather than paper linings if the patchwork is to be made into clothing.

Use a needle suitable for medium-weight work and check the point of the needle more often than usual as paper tends to blunt its sharpness. Cut squares and strips of fabric to make "instant" patchwork; in

Clamshell patchwork

this way, you can make up large areas very quickly (see fig.5a,b, and c). To stitch more complicated shapes together, a zigzag stitch is best. Adjust to a medium-length stitch. Loosen the tension on the top of the machine and thereafter alter the machine to cope with the individual demands of the work. Press machine-stitched patchwork on the wrong side with either a damp cloth or a steam iron before finishing it.

Clamshell patchwork

Using the shaped template provided (fig.6a) you can make patchwork with attractive scalloped lines. It is also known as scale or shell patchwork. The patches are usually stitched in rows and look rather like overlapping fish scales.

Begin by cutting patches in fabric and paper in the usual way. Check that the grain of the fabric runs down the center of each shape. Pin a lining paper to the wrong side of the fabric as shown in fig.6b. Turn in the seam allowance around the upper

Opposite: Simple patchwork items such as this doll's crib cover and the cushion cover on the previous page can be machine stitched in a matter of minutes.

Right: A detail from an 18th-century wall hanging worked in clamshell patchwork. The fabrics — mainly printed cottons and linens — were collected from many countries, including India.

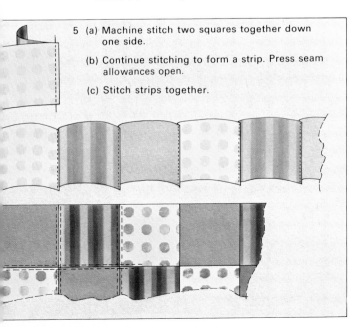

5 (a) Machine stitch two squares together down one side.

(b) Continue stitching to form a strip. Press seam allowances open.

(c) Stitch strips together.

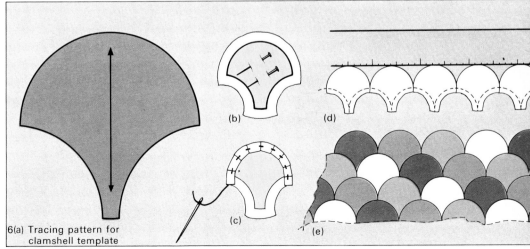

6(a) Tracing pattern for clamshell template

155

Cathedral patchwork

curved edge, making small pleats and tucks where necessary (see fig.6c). Baste in place, then remove the pins and press from the wrong side. Prepare all the patches in the same way.

To create the basic clamshell design, assemble the patches in rows and build up the pattern as shown in fig.6d and e. Place the top edge of the top row along a ruler to get the first row as straight and accurate as possible. The second row overlaps the first, the third overlaps the second, and so on. Baste in place and then sew with small hemming stitches. Continue adding rows, adding one extra patch to the end of each succeeding row, until you have a size of patchwork suitable to use. Then remove the lining papers and basting stitches and press lightly on the right side. Clamshell patchwork is most effective when made into cushions and other fairly large items, but it can also be very interesting when used decoratively: an insertion of clamshell looks pretty on a dress, and it can also be used in groups for accessories and small furnishings.

Cathedral patchwork

Cathedral patchwork is particularly interesting as it uses scraps of fabric to their fullest advantage. It is reputed to date from the 17th century with the pioneers who left England on the *Mayflower* to start colonies in the New World. The settlers created a method of showing off each precious piece of fabric in a window formed from the base fabric of sacking or canvas. The effect was almost three-dimensional, and the small areas of color looked like stained glass, so winning the affectionate name of "Cathedral" patchwork. The magnificent bedspread illustrated here fully demonstrates the technique.

Making a window
You will need:

pieces of base fabric cut to measure 15cm (6in) square □ pieces of printed cotton cut to follow the grain of the fabric and measuring 4cm (1½in) square □ thread to match the base fabric □ needle.
Note: as several layers of fabric are involved, choose a base fabric that is fairly

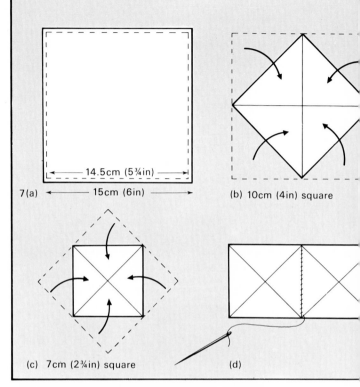

7(a) 15cm (6in)   14.5cm (5¾in)   (b) 10cm (4in) square

(c) 7cm (2¾in) square   (d)

Left: No doubt several women combined their efforts to produce this fine American 19th-century cathedral patchwork bedspread where each window is made from a different fabric.
Above: A section of the bedspread shows the remarkable detail of the individual windows.

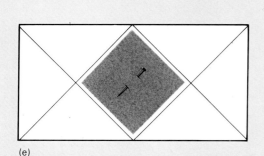

(e)

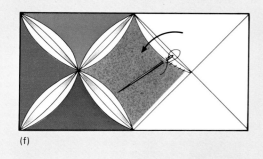

(f)

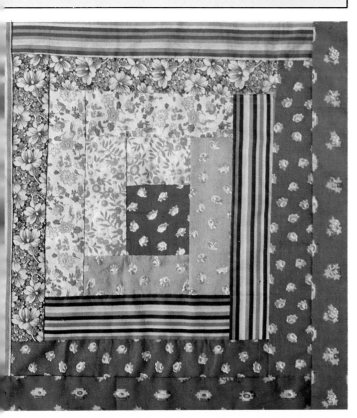

A modern example of a log cabin patchwork.

soft and easy to handle. Medium-weight cotton or muslin (calico) would be ideal.

Making the patch. Fold a narrow hem around 1 square of base fabric so that it measures 14.5cm ($5\frac{3}{4}$in), see fig.7a. Fold each corner to the center and pin in place (fig.7b). The square should now measure 10cm (4in). Fold each corner to the center again, re-pinning as you go, so that the square measures 7cm ($2\frac{3}{4}$in) (fig.7c).

Make a second square in the same way. Sew the 2 squares together down one side by overcasting neatly (fig.7d). Open out the squares to lie flat, then take a square of printed cotton measuring 4cm ($1\frac{1}{2}$in) and pin it over the seam joining the 2 base squares together (see fig.7e).

Take the folded edge of the base fabric and turn it back over the raw edge of the cotton square, then sew in place neatly with small running stitches, taking the needle through all layers as you do so (fig.7f). Repeat on all 4 sides, then work two or three small stitches across each corner for a firm finish. Continue in this way to build up as large or as small a piece of patchwork as desired. Do not press the finished piece or it will lose its texture. There is no need to line this type of patchwork. With the simplest of techniques, time and patience, you will have a family heirloom to be proud of.

Log cabin patchwork

Log cabin patchwork was very popular in England and America during the late 19th century. The pattern consists of strips of fabric built outward from a center square with their edges overlapping for a step-like effect.

By using a range of dark and light colors, attractive designs can be created. Originally, the light colors on one side of the patchwork represented the firelit half of the cabin, and the darker colors the part of the room in shadow.

By sewing the patchwork onto a base, a selection of fabrics can be used very successfully. Refer to fig.8a,b, and c to start working, then see the photograph for the type of effect you can very easily achieve.

8 Log cabin patchwork

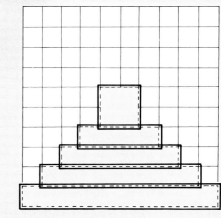

(a) Cut a set of five templates

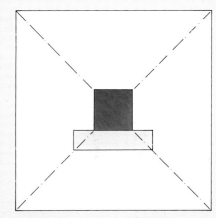

(b) Baste the central square into the middle of the base square and stitch in the first strip

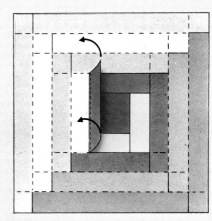

(c) Continue to fill in the whole area

Crazy patchwork

Crazy patchwork

As the name suggests, in crazy patchwork virtually anything goes. Again, a base fabric is used so that you can mix velvets with cottons, brocades with woolens and so on. Shapes can be irregular and sewn in place with virtually any stitch—the more decorative the better: blanket, chain, herringbone and feather stitch are all excellent. Begin by basting one corner in place and then continue to build up the design, turning in seam allowances and basting the shapes down as you go. Once the patchwork is all in place, you can sew them down. Sequins, buttons, gold thread or any other decorations can then be added—there are no rules!

Above: This Welsh coverlet, made by Jenny Jones in 1884, is a good example of traditional crazy patchwork.

Right: The detail from the coverlet shown here illustrates how decorative embroidery stitches in contrasting colors can be used to emphasize the "crazy" effect.

However, a minimal amount of planning is sometimes very helpful. If you are working on a very large piece of patchwork, such as the coverlet illustrated here, you may find it easier to construct it in sections which can be joined together afterwards. You can also see that the colors on this patchwork have been carefully balanced, so that no one area is either too light or too dark.

Appliqué

A Spanish early 17th-century example of appliqué. Part of a cope, the figure of John the Evangelist is embroidered on satin and applied to a velvet background with additional gold thread decoration.

Appliqué, as the name suggests, is the art of applying shapes cut from a variety of fabrics onto a different background material. As a form of needlework, it can be traced back at least as far as the time of the Crusades when the knights wore appliquéd heraldic insignias. There is also evidence of a much earlier type of decorative appliqué dating back to the Ancient Egyptians. Excellent examples of appliqué which have survived in good condition can be found on many of the early embroidered Church vestments; the appliqué was worked in velvets and silks and embellished with gold and silver threads. Appliqué was also used to decorate wall hangings: often linen was richly embroidered and then applied to a background of heavy velvet.

The art traveled from Europe to America with the early settlers, and some of the finest designs can be seen on coverlets and quilts of the period. The women used every scrap of material to create fascinating patterns which reflected their homes and surroundings. Sometimes these bedcovers were made up in sections, each decorated with a different appliqué design.

Appliqué work is still very popular today, perhaps because it relies more on imagination and creativity than sewing skill. It can be used to decorate furnishings and any number of garments, and is an ideal way of rejuvenating worn or old items.

Fabrics and equipment

Fabrics. The fabrics you choose will depend on what you wish to make and how much wear it is likely to receive. Dress-weight cotton is ideal to begin with: it has a crisp finish and does not fray easily. Felt is very easy to use as it does not fray at all and comes in a large selection of colors, but remember that it shrinks if washed. Wool is not ideal as it tends to stretch out of shape, but it is very suitable as a background material. Unless you are stitching by machine, it is best to avoid very thick fabrics which are difficult to sew. Layers of fine fabric can be used to build up interesting "shaded" effects.

Equipment. You will need sharp scissors for cutting into difficult areas; shears for cutting out the shapes; sewing and embroidery needles (the size will depend on

This appliqué quilt's place of origin is easy to determine since two of the chintz cutouts depict the figure of Liberty and the American eagle. It forms part of a friendship quilt, completed in 1862.

the fabrics and threads you are using); basting and sewing thread and an assortment of embroidery yarns. An embroidery frame is useful as it keeps the fabrics taut and prevents wrinkles from developing in the background fabric.

Designs

The best way to create an appliqué design is to look around you—ideas quickly present themselves in the form of trees, animals, flowers and buildings, and you can either portray them realistically or build them into an abstract design.

Start by planning the design on paper. Then either trace the shapes onto paper to use as patterns, or trace them directly onto the wrong side of the fabric with a soft pencil. You will find that some shapes overlap others in the overall design, so start by basting down the shapes from the bottom layer upwards.

Appliqué

Basic techniques

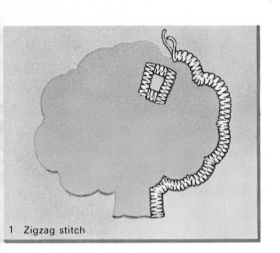

1 Zigzag stitch

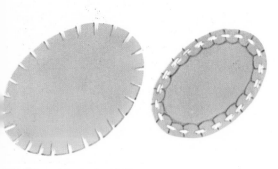

2 Clip and baste turnings

3 Mitering corners

Basic techniques

Stitching by machine. The simplest and quickest appliqué technique is to machine stitch the shapes to the background using zigzag stitch (fig. 1). This eliminates the need for turnings on more difficult curved shapes. The stitches should be small and close together so that the finished article

A highly colorful interpretation of a traditional heraldic fashion, is this modern banner decorated with applied emblems.

will be able to withstand frequent washing if necessary, without fraying.

You can also use a small straight machine stitch, but it is more time consuming and you will need to allow for turnings around each shape unless you are working in felt. Clip into the turnings on curved shapes to keep them flat and then baste to the wrong side of the fabric (fig.2). Miter corners to avoid a lumpy appearance (fig.3). Press each shape before basting it to the background fabric. Then machine stitch around each shape, keeping close to the folded edges. Take the ends through to the wrong side of the background fabric and make

Basic techniques
Flowered
cushions

Note: the addition of an iron-on interfacing, cut to the same size as the individual shapes, helps to keep the shapes smooth and also provides a firm edge for turning over the seam allowances.

Flowered cushions
Two of these satin cushions have been made by handstitching and two by machine, using the techniques already described. You can, of course, make them all by one method and vary the colors and fabrics.

You will need:
0.5m (½yd) gray satin, 90cm (36in) wide □ 0.5m (½yd) dark green satin, 90cm (36in) wide □ 0.5m (½yd) cream satin, 90cm (36in) wide □ 0.5m (½yd) dark brown satin, 90cm (36in) wide □ scraps of lime green, emerald green, pink, blue and beige satin for the appliqué flowers □ sewing thread □ standard embroidery floss (cotton) □ 25cm (10in) iron-on interfacing □ cushion pad 30cm (12in) square □ cushion pad 35cm (14in) square □ rectangular cushion pad 30 × 40cm (12 × 16in) □ circular cushion pad 35cm (14in) in diameter.

Note: in the graphs for all the cushions 1 square equals 3cm (1¼in).

Making the brown cushion. Draw the pattern pieces for the appliqué design from the graph (fig.5). Cut out each piece in an appropriately colored satin, allowing for small turnings all around. Clip into the curved edges. Press the brown satin and cut out two 38cm (15in) squares. On the right side of one square, position the stem then the leaves of the flower. Stitch around the leaves turning in the allowances on each edge and stitch each in place with small, close hemming stitches. Work along the stem and then the petals in the same way. The raw edges at the center are covered by the flower center so there is no

---

raph pattern for brown cushion   1 sq = 3cm (1¼in)

---

edges neat. You can attach the fabric using a decorative braid to hide any raw edges: baste the braid around the shape first and then stitch it in place using a straight machine stitch on both edges or a wide zigzag stitch.

Stitching by hand. Appliqué can be done by hand using the same basic steps. When working with fabrics which are liable to fray, turn under a narrow seam allowance around each shape. Baste the turnings to the wrong side after clipping into any curved sides, or turn them under and pin them down as you stitch. Attach the shapes with very small hemming stitches which

should be as invisible as you can make them from the right side.

On very fine fabrics, such as organdy, it is best to cut out the pattern shapes allowing 0.5cm (¼in) for turnings all around. Stitch each shape to the background with fine blanket stitch (fig. 4), and then trim off the excess fabric very close to the stitching with sharp embroidery scissors. Embroidery stitches can be used to secure the applied shapes. Embroidery can also be used effectively to add depth and texture to appliqué and you can use a variety of stitches to fill in any parts of the design which would be impractical in fabric.

4 Blanket stitch

161

Appliqué

Flowered cushions

need to make them neat. Stitch the flower center into place. Press the work on the wrong side. With right sides together, stitch around the cushion with a 1.5cm (½in) seam allowance. Leave an opening to insert the cushion pad, clip into the corners (fig.6a), and turn the cover to the right side. Insert the cushion and slip stitch the opening to close.

Cream cushion. From the cream satin, cut out 2 circles 38cm (15in) in diameter. Draw the pattern pieces for the appliqué design from the graph (fig.7). Cut out each shape from the interfacing, and iron these onto the wrong side of the appropriately colored fabrics. Cut out the fabric shapes around the edge of the interfacing. Working in towards the center of the circle, baste the leaves, stem and then the petals into place. Finally baste on the flower center. Using either matching embroidery floss or sewing thread, stitch around the outside of the center with satin stitch or blanket stitch. Stitch around the petals, stem and leaves in the same way. Press the work on the wrong side. With right sides together, stitch around the cushion with a 1.5cm (½in) seam allowance. Leave an opening to insert the cushion pad, clip into the curves (fig.6b), and turn the cover to the right side. Insert the cushion and slip stitch to close the opening.

Green cushion. Draw the pattern pieces for the flower design from the graph (fig.8). Cut out the appliqué shapes allowing small

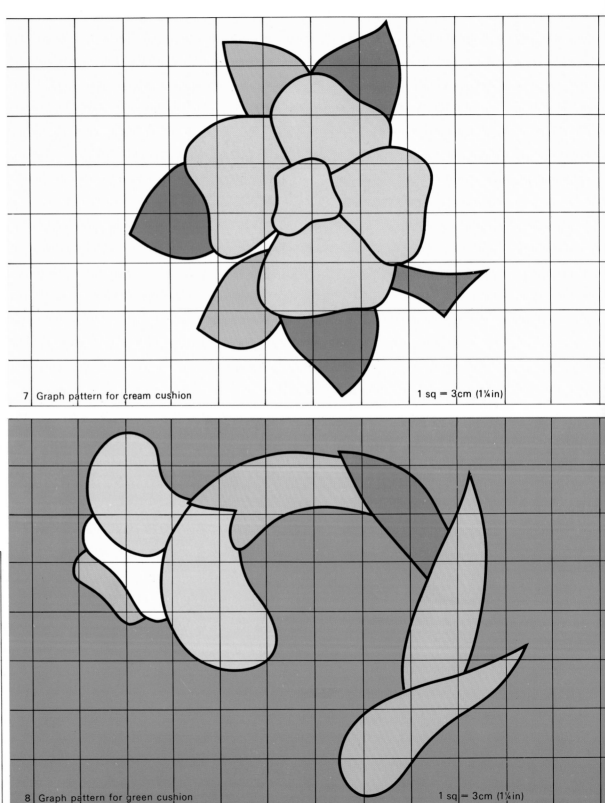

7 | Graph pattern for cream cushion   1 sq = 3cm (1¼in)

8 | Graph pattern for green cushion   1 sq = 3cm (1¼in)

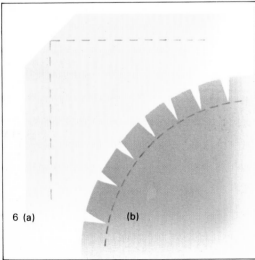

6 (a)   (b)

turnings all around. Press the green satin and cut out two 42cm (16½in) squares. Clip into all the curved edges of the appliqué shapes and baste the turnings to the wrong side. Press each piece before basting them to the green satin. With small, straight machine stitches, work around the shapes in matching thread, close to the edge. Take the threads through to the wrong side and make neat. Press the work and make the cushion as previously described.

Gray cushion. Draw up the pattern pieces for the appliqué design from the graph given (fig.9). Cut out 2 pieces of gray satin, 33 × 42cm (13 × 16½in). Cut out the shapes for the petals, leaves and stems from the interfacing and iron these to the wrong side of the appropriate fabrics. Cut out the individual shapes around the edge

of the interfacing. Baste the pieces to the right side of 1 rectangle. Set the machine to a small, close zigzag stitch and sew around the edge of each shape with matching thread. Make sure that the outer edge of the stitch takes in the edge of the fabric so that it secures the shapes. Fasten off each thread on the wrong side of the work and make the cushion as before.

San Blas or reverse appliqué
San Blas appliqué is worked by cutting *away* pieces of fabric and for this reason it is also known as reverse appliqué. The women of the San Blas Islands off the Panama coast are experts in this art: their bold and vividly colored designs represent gods, animals and plants, local personalities and sometimes loosely adapted and apparently meaningless English words

A fine example of traditional San Blas appliqué, made up into a typical mola and worn by a native woman of the islands.

Graph pattern for gray cushion   1 sq = 3cm (1¼in)

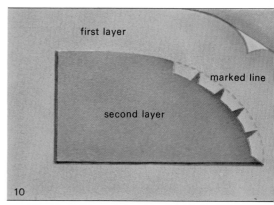

first layer

marked line

second layer

10

Appliqué
San Blas or
reverse appliqué

Basic technique

and letters. These gay and stylized designs are made up into short sleeved blouses known as molas.

Originally, when the Indians moved to the islands in the mid-19th century, these molas were simple garments made from dark blue fabric with just a narrow single band of color around the bottom. It was the arrival of the traders who supplied brightly colored fabrics that led to the development of the elaborate multi-layered designs that are worn today. Molas have become an important status symbol and as such are often included as part of a young girl's marriage dowry.

Basic technique

You will need several layers of different colored fabrics. On the finished work each of these colors will be revealed. This form of appliqué is most successfully done with lightweight cotton fabrics. Silk and shantung are also ideal but it is better to practice with less expensive fabrics first.

Cut out the fabric layers 5cm (2in) larger all around than the required finished size. Press each layer and then baste them together, one on top of the other. Mark the desired shape on the top layer of fabric. Keeping inside the marked lines to allow for turnings, cut away this layer with sharp scissors.

Clip any curved edges. Turn under the cut edges and neatly hem stitch in place with matching thread (see fig.10). The stitches must go through to the bottom layer to secure all the fabrics. If you prefer, pin the turnings under before stitching. Follow the same techniques on the second layer to reveal the fabric beneath. You can, of course, cut away more than one layer, in which case trim away the underlying edges to avoid bulk. Continue in the same way until all the colors have been revealed and your design is complete. Remember, though, that the last layer of fabric must remain uncut. If you do cut away the wrong area of fabric by mistake, it can easily be disguised by stitching an additional patch underneath the fabric that has been cut.

Some attractive and unusual ideas for using this type of appliqué technique are shown here.

Collage and Découpage

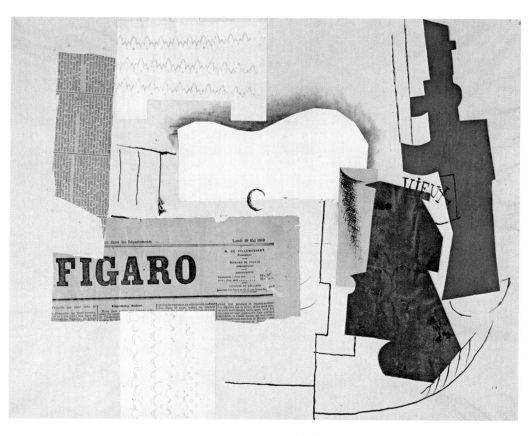

gardens make ideal subjects for collage.

Fabric collage
This is perhaps the most popular type of collage, mainly because of the rich variety of fabrics available and also because it can be combined with the traditional skills of embroidery to great effect.

You will need:
various fabrics ☐ sturdy cardboard for backing ☐ thick fabric for backing ☐ fabric adhesive ☐ paper for drawing out the designs ☐ scissors (large and small) ☐scraps of yarn, thread, ribbons, string, beads, sequins and braid for decoration.

Creating a fabric collage. Apply a thin coat of fabric adhesive to the cardboard backing and cover with a thick fabric cut slightly larger than the cardboard. Turn back the edges of the fabric, miter the corners and glue down the raw edges to the back of the cardboard. If you are working on a large project you may find that the cardboard

Left: Guitar, glass and bottle (1913) by Picasso, a collage made from newsprint, wallpaper and baize.

Below: A charming example of fabric collage.

The term *collage* comes from the French word meaning "glueing." In the 19th century collages were made from various papers which were cut out and applied to a background to form compositions known as *papiers collés.* During their Cubist period, Pablo Picasso and Georges Braque made use of collage, combining such materials as paper, wood, linoleum and newspapers with oil paint on canvas. As the art developed, other "found" materials were used — fabrics, cork, wood, metals and natural objects — to create decorative designs. It is the materials that inspire the picture, and these can be used individually or in combination to create a two- or three-dimensional effect. Much of the appeal of collage lies in the "accidental" nature of a successful composition: just by juxtaposing unusual materials, exciting representational or abstract designs emerge. To get ideas for pictures, keep a file of magazine photographs and illustrations, and postcards; and remember to look out of your window — street scenes, animals and

Lace collage

tends to bend, in which case you should reinforce the reverse side with an additional layer of sturdy paper, cardboard or fabric. If possible, choose non-fraying fabrics for the collage shapes. If they are likely to fray, seal the edges with clear adhesive or turn the edges under and press.

Draw the designs for the shapes onto paper. Cut these out to use as patterns. When you are more experienced you may prefer to cut directly from the fabrics as this imposes fewer restrictions on your eventual picture, but it can result in confusion if you have not planned your finished picture beforehand! Press all the fabric shapes. Place them on the mount and pin into position. Remember to allow for a border if you are going to frame the collage.

Make light pencil marks to indicate the position of each shape. When you have composed the picture, glue each piece into place. Use a toothpick or matchstick to apply adhesive to small areas. Add braid and any other ornamentation last.

Note: if you are using sequins, iron the work before adding them.

Lace collage

Attractive collages can be made from scraps of lace, discarded placemats and left-over trimmings. The technique is similar to that for fabric collage, with one or two variations.

You will need:
various lace remnants □ clear fabric adhesive □ cardboard for backing □ paper fabric or felt for backing □ coloring agents: cold water dyes, poster or water colors or inks □ paintbrushes □ toothpick or matchstick □ scissors.

Creating a lace collage. Cover the cardboard with paper, fabric or felt as previously described. Cut out selected lace motifs. Trim the shapes to remove frayed or worn areas. Either draw out a rough design on paper first or compose your picture simply by moving the lace pieces around on the cardboard until they form a pleasing overall design. With a pencil, lightly mark the position for each piece on the cardboard.

You can color the lace as you progress. Mix dyes or water colors (do not make the solution too thick as this will clog the surface

and texture of the lace) in bowls or saucers. Immerse the lace pieces in the color and stir with a paintbrush. Blot the lace on a rag or absorbent paper and allow to dry. Alternatively, you can color the lace in batches (this saves time if you are working on a large project), allow it to dry and then compose your picture from the colored pieces. Iron the lace and then stick the pieces

down applying the glue sparingly with a toothpick or matchstick.

Culinary collage!

Attractive and unusual collages can be made from seeds, beans, lentils and pasta. These "ingredients" should be stuck onto a firm non-pliable base or they will tend to fall off.

Making a natural collage: the materials being used include eucalyptus bark and leaves, birch bark, wild mustard and lily seeds, flowering heath, moss and lichens.

When you have completed the picture allow to dry overnight.

Collages from other natural materials
Dried flowers, leaves, grasses, ferns, small pieces of bark, pebbles and shells are all suitable materials for collage. The procedure is the same as for the techniques previously described. A carefully chosen colored background will often complement the subtle shades of plant material. You may also want to highlight flowers and leaves with water colors. Hang a plant collage away from sunlight and, ideally, protected behind glass.
If you use pebbles or shells a final coat of polyurethane varnish will give an attractive finish.

The finished collage is now assembled and is ready for framing.

You will need :
selection of seeds, beans, lentils, pasta □ a firm non-warping base such as plywood □ water-based paint (emulsion) —white will show off the natural color of the collage materials effectively □ clear adhesive □ tweezers.
Assembling the collage. Paint the board with water-based paint. Allow to dry and then make a faint pencil outline of your design to use as a guide. Apply adhesive to small areas at a time and position the beans, lentils and pasta; use tweezers for the seeds and for building up densely filled areas. There is no need to cover the board; in fact, you should leave areas of the background exposed to obtain the best results from your design.

Part of a 19th-century English nursery screen decorated with découpage.

wise you are likely to need a great many applications of varnish to achieve an even finish. You may be able to remove a greeting card illustration from its backing by soaking it briefly in water and then carefully peeling apart the two layers. If you want to color black-and-white prints, use water colors, acrylic paint or crayons.

Materials

The basic materials and equipment for découpage are a good assortment of prints and illustrations, sealer, adhesive, sharp scissors (large and small) and paintbrushes. You will also need fine sandpaper, wet-or-dry paper (fine abrasive paper that is used with water), a sanding block, steel wool for finishing and a polishing cloth.
Sealer. Prints and illustrations must be sealed to prevent any glue or varnish from seeping through. Suitable commercial products are available in either liquid or spray. Alternatively, make your own by mixing equal parts of turpentine and varnish. If you

Create an individual coordinated look to your room by using matching or toning fabric cutouts to decorate a piece of furniture.

Découpage is derived from the French *découper,* "to cut out." The craft was first practiced as a form of furniture decoration during the 17th century in both France and Italy. Engravings were cut out, colored, glued to the surface of items of furniture and then "sunk" under numerous coats of varnish or lacquer so that the finished effect closely resembled that of fine inlay work. As découpage traveled through Europe in the 18th century, it was enthusiastically adopted by the women of the courts who amused themselves by imitating the then fashionable Chinese lacquerwork. Découpage became a popular pastime for gentlewomen and it was applied to a wide variety of objects — often made from papier mâché — ranging from hairbrushes and tea caddies to elaborate paneled screens.
The techniques for découpage have not changed much over the years; the only real modification is that quicker-drying varnishes are now available.
Découpage can be applied to virtually any

firm and durable surface: wood, metal, glass, ceramic and even hard plastic, are all suitable bases. The objects you can decorate with découpage, again, are numerous — trays, boxes, picture frames, screens, lampshades and bookends are just a few ideas.

Choosing your cutouts

There are plenty of sources for decorative cutouts. Browse around junk shops and second-hand bookstores and you are certain to find old but inexpensive illustrated books and magazines. Victorian illustrations make particularly attractive découpage designs. Keep decorative gift wrap, odd scraps of wallpaper, postcards, Christmas and other greeting cards; thin fabrics can also be used. When you are planning a découpage design, try to use paper cutouts of a similar thickness, other-

lacquer or polyurethane varnish. You can also buy a clear liquid plastic which is thick, gives a hard finish and is crystal clear.

Basic techniques

First of all you will need to prepare the object to be decorated. Fill in any holes or cracks in wood and sand down. New wood can be stained and sealed or primed and painted with water-based paint. New metal should be primed to prevent rusting and then painted. Remove paint and rust from old metal and then prime and repaint. If you are decorating a hinged object, such as a box or cupboard, remove the lid or doors and treat these separately.

If you are working on a picture frame, as shown in the illustration, make sure that you have cleaned and treated all the recesses of the moldings thoroughly.

Cut out your prints, having sealed them first. Cut large areas first and then cut into the details with small sharp scissors; use a craft knife for really intricate work. Lay the cutouts onto the surface and lightly mark their positions in pencil. Apply adhesive evenly to the back of the cutouts and press down, working outwards to the edge to remove any excess adhesive. Wipe off the excess with a damp cloth and make sure that all the edges are firmly stuck down. If any air bubbles remain, prick them with a pin and press down firmly.

Varnishing. Work in a good light and, ideally, a room temperature of around 21 °C (70°F) to hasten drying. Clean off any dirt

An old frame (above) is given a new lease of life (right) after being decorated with découpage.

are using magazine illustrations where the print on the reverse side shows through, you will need to seal both sides. If the print is particularly heavy, try painting the reverse side with a coat of white acrylic paint. Always seal your illustrations before cutting them out as it is much easier to cut them accurately when they are stiff.

Adhesive. The adhesive you use depends on the surface of the subject you are decorating. It should be clear and non-staining and should preferably be slow drying as you will need time to maneuver your cutouts into position. White glue (PVA) adhesive is suitable and so is a fairly stiff mixture of cellulose wallpaper paste, though give the latter plenty of time to dry out before applying varnish. A general purpose adhesive can be used for metal and glass.

Varnish. Craft suppliers sell special quick-drying découpage varnishes which are clear and do not discolor. But if you happen to like a yellowish finish — and it can look very attractive — use either a traditional

Autumn leaves have been used imaginatively to decorate this set of traveling cases and hatbox.

or dust from the surface and then apply the first coat of varnish. Do not overload your brush as too much varnish will cause drips. Check for drips, particularly at corners and catch them with a brush before leaving to dry. If they do appear after the varnish has dried, sand them smooth before applying the next coat of varnish.

The number of coats of varnish you apply depends to a certain extent on the effect you wish to create : to achieve an embedded finish more coats will obviously be necessary. If you are using a traditional lacquer or polyurethane varnish, apply 10 coats before sanding, and thereafter sand down with fine sandpaper, preferably wrapped around a sanding block for even pressure, between each subsequent coat of varnish. Always make sure that the varnish is completely dry before sanding and be careful not to sand down to the prints themselves. Special découpage varnishes can usually be sanded between each application, but follow the manufacturer's instructions. Always clean the surface thoroughly before applying the next coat of varnish. To finish, rub down with wet-or-dry sandpaper, followed by fine steel wool. Then wax the surface with furniture paste wax and buff with a clean dry cloth.

Decorated stones

Pebbles are often collected for their shape, color, or some fault such as a quartz line, that makes them interesting and different. Decorating pebbles will transform their surface appearance to make them into attractive and unusual ornaments, and the intrinsic beauty of their shape will be enhanced.

Pebble hunting

A stroll in the country or even in your garden can reveal a wide variety of pebbles and stones. But the most successful place for pebble hunting is on the beach. Beach pebbles are clean and smoothly polished by the sea and therefore provide good painting surfaces. Next time you walk along the sea shore, look carefully for pebbles that are especially round or smooth, or oddly shaped ones that bring to mind an image. Though initially you will probably be attracted to stones that look and feel perfect, you will soon look for more unusual specimens as your experience in painting and decorating them grows. You will learn that some stones are porous, absorbing the paint easily, while others are so smooth that the paint literally sits upon the surface. With practice you will find that it is the shape and form of each stone that dictates the painting and mode

of preparation. The more distorted or oddly shaped the stone, the wider the scope you have for originality and the more interesting the resulting painting. Look for forms that suggest something sensual, sinister or amusing—it is your interpretation of the basic material that makes for original and personal work.

Preparing the pebbles. If the pebbles are collected in the country, wash them until clean in liquid detergent and hot water. Scrub off the mud and grime with a nail brush. Beach pebbles are already cleansed by the action of the sea, but, to remove all traces of salt, soak them in warm water three or four times.

Leave the pebbles to dry out completely for at least a day, if possible in the sun. Any dampness left in the stones will cloud the varnish. Use this period of time to study them and to consider various visual ideas before definitely deciding on an approach. An idea may spring to mind quickly; another may take several days to formulate. Center your design around the image formed by the shape of the pebble. Occasionally, some accidental process in nature shapes a stone to resemble the features of an animal, bird, face or profile.

Painting. Unless the color of the pebble is incorporated into the design, apply an

undercoat of white water-based paint (emulsion). Paint one side of the pebble and leave to dry. Turn it over and paint the other side. When both sides are dry, draw the outlines for the design with a fine brush (a sable brush is best) using black paint. Create shapes that sit excitingly on the surface as the aim is to make the stone come alive and demand attention. Always work on one side or surface at a time if more than one side is to be painted.

Filling in the design. Designer's gouache and water color paints provide a wide range of colors and are suitable for beginners. After some practice in pebble decorating, you will find that oil and acrylic paints give the best results. Clean brushes after use with water for water-based paint, warm soapy water for acrylics and turpentine (white spirit) for oil paint.

Finishing. Leave the design to dry. Then paint on 3 or 4 coats of polyurethane varnish by working on one side or surface at a time, and letting each coat dry before applying the next. The varnish will safeguard the intensity of colors and add a deep, clear glaze to the surface.

When the surface is completely dry, glue a piece of felt to the base of the stone to prevent it from scratching table tops or other display areas.

Jewelry

These silver rings are examples of Viking art, dating from the 9th century.

An Inca legend relates that on the day the world began, three magnificent eggs fell from heaven. One was golden, one silver and one copper. As they fell they cracked open and from them all the royalty, nobility and more ordinary peoples of the world were born. Apart from being a charming interpretation of the Creation, this story clearly expresses the Peruvian appreciation of mineral wealth. The Incas treasured gold, believing it to hold the power of the sun. Their craftsmen produced some of the most spectacular examples of jewelry ever known. The Aztecs of Mexico were also master goldsmiths. Mexico was rich in copper, lead, silver and tin, so rich in fact that earrings, necklaces and bracelets were worn by women at all levels of society. Men also wore jewelry, including pierced nose pieces, and chin ornaments.

Jewelry of some kind is as old as the human race itself. The very earliest form of jewelry consisted of strings of attractive pebbles, shells, fish vertebrae or teeth worn around the neck. The earliest of these date back to around 25,000 BC. Besides being worn for pure decoration, jewelry seems to have acquired magical properties quite early on. Brooches were worn as amulets in an attempt to ward off evil spirits and appease the gods. Women wore necklaces of particular shells to guard against infertility; the Egyptians and Sumerians wore gold and silver ornaments for their protective properties. Sometimes the material as well as the form of the amulet was considered powerful. In Arabia, Persia and China, green stones were placed in the mouths of the dead, as it was thought they contained life-giving substances. Even today, people wear lucky charms.

The techniques for working both gold and silver have changed very little since ancient times. By 3000 BC craftsmen in the Middle East were making headdresses, bracelets, necklaces and other jewelry from gold. The main source of gold was Nubia, in Egypt; it was a metal much loved and much used by the Egyptians, both for the living and for burial with the dead. Their goldsmiths developed the technique of repoussé, in which a raised relief design was punched on the metal. Some tomb paintings depict this technique in detail. Soldering was also mastered early on. Stamping was another skill; by this technique exact copies of a design were made, in an ancient form of mass-production. Though styles have been through a wide variety of changes, the basic techniques seem to have been in use almost unceasingly since these early times. Precious metals are rarely used in their pure state for making jewelry, as they tend to be too soft. Other metals are added during the molten state to produce an alloy.

Metals

Gold. Gold is a beautiful metal to work being extremely malleable and ductile. However, it is extremely expensive and in many countries a special licence is legally required in order to buy it. Pure gold is known as 24 karat. Different metals such as copper or platinum are added to produce different colors and karats. Alloys are made in karats of 22, 20, 18, 14, 12 and 10.

Silver. Unalloyed silver is known as fine silver. In its pure state it is very soft, so it is alloyed with copper to harden it. Sterling silver is 92.5% pure silver and 7.5% pure copper. It is extremely ductile. It can be bought from silversmiths in sheets, strips and as wire in a range of sizes and thicknesses. Sheet silver ranges from 12mm ($\frac{1}{2}$in) thick to 0.3mm ($\frac{1}{64}$in) thick. Wire, square or round, ranges from 25mm (1in) to 0.3mm ($\frac{1}{64}$in) thick. It can be bought

also in flat strips of patterned silver, called gallery silver. Different countries have different gauge systems to measure the thickness of silver. The American system is Browne & Sharp (B & S), the most common British the Birmingham Metal Gauge (BMG).

Copper. Copper is a good metal for jewelry making, being easy to saw, file, bend and solder. It can be polished to a high finish, but in its pure state tends to tarnish very quickly. It can be bought in sheets or as soft wire.

Other metals. Bronze is an alloy of copper and tin, reddish-yellow in color, and harder than brass or copper. It can be bought in sheets and as round wire. Brass is an alloy of copper and zinc. Alloys containing 55% or more of copper are malleable, and only slightly harder than copper. Besides sheet and wire form, it can be obtained in very thin sheets, called brass shim.

These Byzantine earrings are made of gold, with a delicate design of birds and trees worked into them. They date from the 7th century.

Nickel silver is an alloy of copper, nickel and zinc. It can be highly polished. Pewter is an alloy of copper, antimony and tin, and is a rather soft metal. It can only be obtained in sheet form.

Basic processes

Sawing and cutting. Very thin sheet metal can be cut with a pair of tinsnips (fig.1). Otherwise, use a jeweler's saw (fig.2). This is like a fret saw; the nuts at the top and bottom can be adjusted to change the length of the blade. A frame with a distance between the blade and the frame of 76–100mm (3–4in) is a good general size. Blades are available in a number of sizes; no. 2/0 is a coarse blade, 4/0 is very fine. A no. 1 blade is a useful general purpose size. To attach the blade, loosen the nuts at both ends of the saw frame. With the teeth of the blades pointing downwards towards the handle, insert the blade all the way into the top nut and tighten it with your hand. Then place the handle of the frame against your body and the other end of the frame against the work bench. Press hard against the bench, and maintain this pressure while you put the other end of the blade into the nut at the handle end and tighten it. Release the tension gently to prevent snapping the blade which should be quite rigid

in the frame. Use beeswax or paraffin wax to lubricate the blade occasionally. Sawing is done on a sawing table or bench pin (see fig.2). This can be bought from a jeweler's supplier. It is clamped to a table with a carpentry clamp. First mark out the design by scratching it lightly on the metal with dividers or a metal scriber, or draw it on with a pencil. Support the metal securely with your spare hand as you saw.

To cut sheet metal, move the saw vertically, putting more pressure on the downward stroke. Move the metal, rather than the saw, to form the design. To saw out an enclosed area, start by drilling a hole with a hand drill through the metal. Detach the saw blade and pass it through the hole. Then re-attach it to the frame and saw out the enclosed area.

Filing. For filing you will need a selection of large hand files and needle files as shown in fig.3. A detachable handle can be bought which is interchangeable and used on all large files. File in one direction only from the tip to the handle. Do not file consistently in exactly the same space, or you will make rough grooves in the metal surface. Hold the metal in the hand or in a ring clamp (fig.4), depending on its size. Use a large file for the rough outside edges of the work and a finer needle file to work on the

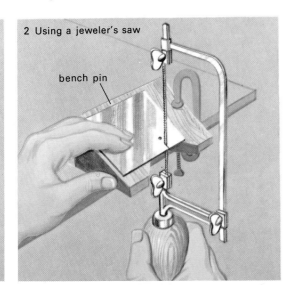

Tinsnips

2 Using a jeweler's saw

bench pin

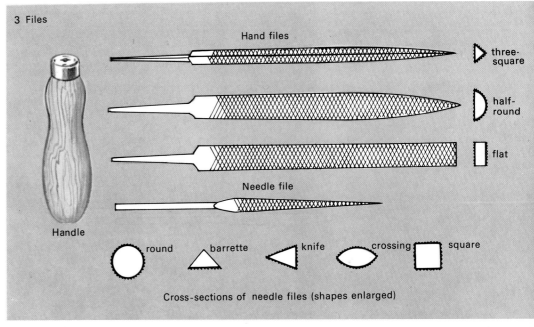

3 Files

Hand files

three-square

half-round

flat

Needle file

Handle

round   barrette   knife   crossing   square

Cross-sections of needle files (shapes enlarged)

Basic processes

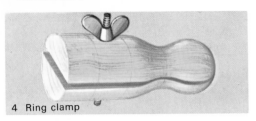

4 Ring clamp

more delicate and final areas where smoothness and precision are necessary. Choose a file according to the shape of the work. For example, the barrette-shaped needle file is triangular with two smooth surfaces. This will allow you to file an angle without cutting into the rest of the work. Keep files meticulously clean with a file brush and place them where they will not rub against each other when they are not in use. Always be sure to remove every trace of the metal from files used on lead or lead solder, as any particle contacting another metal will cause damage.

Annealing. Annealing is the process of softening metals by heating them to make them malleable. Alloys of metals cannot be shaped without first being annealed. For this you will need a charcoal block, asbestos block, soldering tweezers (usually made of sprung steel), and a blowtorch. Small blowtorches can be bought for the purpose from jewelers' equipment shops. Place the piece to be annealed on the charcoal block and place this on top of the asbestos block. Adjust the blowlamp to give a medium soft flame. Pass this over the whole piece heating it evenly until the metal turns a dull red color. If you are annealing silver, yellow-red is a danger sign, indicating that the metal is on the point of melting. If you heat the metal too much, firescale (firestains) may result. Firescale (firestains) appears as a dull gray covering the metal and is difficult to remove.

Cool the piece by dipping it immediately in water, and always use soldering tweezers to handle hot metal.

For some metals, this basic process must be modified. Brass must be allowed to air-cool. Copper and bronze must be heated to a bright red and immediately quenched in water as previously described. All metals must be kept malleable during shaping or

bending, otherwise they are liable to crack. If metal becomes hard while you are working it, anneal it again.

Bending metal. To bend smallish pieces of metal, use a pair of pliers. These have different shaped noses, and the ones most frequently used are round-, half-round and flat-nosed (fig.5). For bending heavier pieces of metal, use a wooden hammer, or one with a rawhide head.

Hard soldering. Solder is an alloy of the metal on which it will be used with small amounts of other metals added. Whereas soft solders are made of lead and tin, and melt at low temperatures, hard solders are made of alloys of silver with a range of melting points. There are three grades of solder available, hard, medium and easy. If more than one soldering is necessary to complete a piece of jewelry, use hard solder for the first join, as it has the highest melting point, medium for the second, and easy for the third. Medium grade solder is the most widely used. Solder can be bought in strip form. Hard soldering is essential for silver articles as it gives a strong joint. The materials needed for hard soldering are solder, flux and iron binding wire. You will also need charcoal and asbestos blocks to place the work on, a blowtorch, a fine sable brush to apply the flux, soldering tweezers and files. To make a strong join, all processes in soldering must be carried out with care and precision. The surfaces to be soldered must fit exactly at their contact points and any dents or irregularities must be filed away. Solder will run into the junction of joins but will not bridge any gaps. The join to be soldered must be placed at the top of the work. Support the work if necessary with pieces of charcoal or asbestos. First clean the work by sanding the joins with a clean piece of fine emery paper. Solder will not flow onto a dirty or greasy surface. Do not touch the joins after sanding or the silver will become greasy again. Now apply hard solder flux. Flux is made from a mixture of borax and water, and can be bought ready-made either as a paste or as liquid. Flux prevents the metal from oxidizing at the join and helps the flow of solder. Paint flux fairly thinly on and around the edges of the join, but avoid getting any of it beyond the edges of the

join as melted solder will follow the flux. Make sure that the pieces to be soldered do not slip while you are soldering them. Use iron binding wire to hold the pieces together if necessary. To tighten the wire twist the ends together.

To make small bits of solder, which are called paillons, out of the sheet, fringe the end of the strip with tinsnips, making cuts very close together. Then cut across the fringe again, thus forming tiny squares (fig.6).

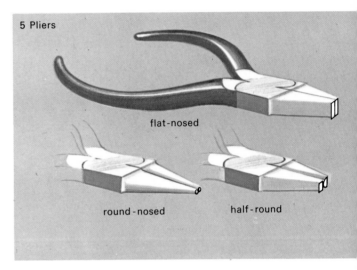

5 Pliers

flat-nosed

round-nosed

half-round

After fluxing the join, place paillons at intervals along the seam. Pick each one up with the tip of the flux brush and place it on the join into which you want it to flow (fig.7). Place the paillons about 3mm ($\frac{1}{8}$in) apart. You will have to learn the exact amount of solder required. Too much will make a lump over the seam and have to be filed away, while too little will not fill the seam correctly. To heat the work, take a blowtorch and adjust it to a soft blue flame. Heat the whole article gradually first before concentrating on the join area. Heat the area around the flux until the flux turns white and forms a crust. If you heat the join too rapidly the paillons will jump out of position. If this happens reposition the solder with soldering tweezers. After the flux has formed a crust, heat the join area evenly until the solder melts and flows into the join. If the paillons are concealed, for example, if one piece of metal is on top of

another, watch for the top piece to drop or look for the gleam of solder between the two layers. As soon as all the solder has melted, remove the flame. Allow a few moments for the solder to solidify. Then pick up the piece with tweezers and immerse it in water. Allow the work to cool. Remove the binding wire and then pickle the work as described below.

Solders for other metals. You can use the same solders for copper, brass and bronze as for silver, but an alloy of copper and zinc is closer in color. This solder is called a spelter. Take care not to overheat the work when using a spelter. If you are soldering brass or bronze to silver, they may collapse into the silver as their melting temperatures are lower. Use the lowest melting solder or spelter and heat it carefully. Gold has three grades of solder as silver does; for pewter there is pewter solder.

Pickling. This is the process of thoroughly cleaning the metal after it has been annealed or soldered. If you are making a complicated piece of work you may need to pickle it after each soldering to remove excess oxides and old flux from the work. Pickle can be bought as a granular compound which you then mix with water. If this is unobtainable, you can make a pickle. For silver, gold, copper, brass and bronze, pickle is composed of one part sulphuric acid to ten parts water. Place the water in a deep earthenware bowl and gently add the acid to it, trickling it slowly and gently down the side of the container.

Warning: Always add the acid to the water, *never* the other way round.

There should be enough liquid in the container to cover the work.

Cutting paillons of solder

7 Positioning the solder

Make sure the work is cool before dropping it into the pickle. In cold solution the work will take about twenty minutes to clean. When clean, silver is a dull white, copper is pink. To remove the work, use copper or brass pickling tongs. Never use iron or steel tongs or the acid will change in composition, which could be dangerous. Hold the work under cold running water. Brush it gently but thoroughly with a soft brush to remove all traces of acid, and dry it with a clean cloth. If the work you are pickling has grooves in it, rinse it in hot water and boil in a solution of sodium carbonate and water.

Important: If you burn your skin or clothing with acid, rinse the area immediately with cold water and sprinkle sodium bicarbonate (baking soda) over the burn. When using acid, work in a well-ventilated area.

Finishing and polishing. Good machine polishers can be bought from jewelers' suppliers, but they are very expensive and not essential for the beginner. After soldering and pickling, finish the work by smoothing away all scratches and blemishes. Do this with a series of abrasives, ranging from coarse files, Scotch stone (Water-of-Ayr stone), felt and lambswool buffing sticks, jeweler's rouge, a burnisher and tripoli. Remove surplus solder with a file, and use a finer file to remove coarse file marks. Then take a piece of Scotch (Water-of-Ayr) stone and work over the surface of the work using a circular motion. Dip the stone in water occasionally to moisten it. Then wash the work thoroughly in detergent and warm water to remove all traces of the abrasive. If the work is complicated and pieces might get stuck in corners boil it for a few minutes. Dry the work thoroughly. Now take a felt buffing stick. To make one, take a piece of wood $177 \times 12.5 \times 6.5$mm ($7 \times \frac{1}{2} \times \frac{1}{4}$in) and glue a strip of felt or soft leather 125×38mm ($5 \times 1\frac{1}{2}$in) to one end. Rub the felt with tripoli and buff the work. Tripoli is a very fine abrasive mixed with wax and sold in blocks. After buffing, boil the work in detergent and water and dry thoroughly. Then for gold and silver work use a lambswool buff dipped in jeweler's rouge. This buff can be bought or made in the same way as the felt stick. Mix the rouge with water to form a thick paste. Polish difficult areas with a highly polished

steel tool called a burnisher. Rub the burnisher over the surface, pressing firmly; the tool will move the top layer of metal across the surface of the work, filling out irregularities. The burnisher can be better controlled if you wet the piece of metal with soapy water first. When the work has been polished to a high finish, give it a final wash to remove all traces of grease.

Making a ring band

Measure the circumference of the finger for which the ring is intended by taking a strip

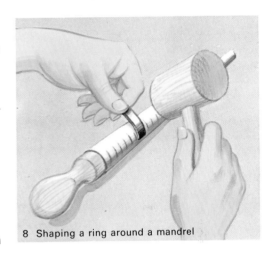

8 Shaping a ring around a mandrel

of thick paper of the required width and bending it around the knuckle. Mark the measurement, where the paper overlaps. Take a piece of silver and mark the dimensions by drawing along the edges of the paper. Allow a little extra at the end for cutting, filing and adjusting ends. Cut out the shape with a jeweler's saw. Anneal the metal. File the ends so that they are exactly squared off, in order to ensure a good join. To shape the ring, use a ring mandrel. This is a tapered, hardened and polished steel bar used specifically for making rings. Hammer the strip around the ring mandrel with a wooden or rawhide mallet, which will not damage the surface of the metal (fig. 8). Hammer one end first, then the other, then the middle. Press the ends together with half-round pliers, bringing one slightly over the other, pulling them apart and then closing them together. The next stage is to bind the shank firmly with binding wire and put the ring on a charcoal block with

Free-formed ring
Ring geometry

the join on top. Support it with small pieces of charcoal. Put flux along the join, and paillons of hard silver solder. Solder, cool in water, and pickle the ring as already described. Make sure both sides of the ring are absoutely parallel, and file down as necessary. Slip the ring onto the mandrel until it fits exactly, and hammer it into a perfect circle. As the mandrel is conical, the ring will stretch slightly at the lower end. To avoid this, slide the ring off the stick, put it on the other way around and hammer again. Finish by polishing as previously described.

Free-formed ring
An unusual ring whose irregular edges make it an ideal first project. Copy the design exactly or draw your own version.
You will need:
12mm ($\frac{1}{2}$in) wide strip of silver 1.20mm ($\frac{3}{64}$in) thick and long enough to fit around your finger □ jeweler's saw □ vise □ round needle file □ emery paper □ binding wire □ charcoal block □ hard solder □ flux □ blowtorch □ pickling solution □ ring mandrel □ rubber cement.
Making the ring. Measure your finger for the length of the silver as previously described using a piece of paper 12mm ($\frac{1}{2}$in) in width. Mark the silver with a pencil. Cut out the silver with a jeweler's saw. Trace the design (fig.9) onto paper. Cut this out and stick it on the silver with rubber cement, making sure the surface of the silver is perfectly clean. Mark around the edge of the pattern with a pencil or metal

scriber. Hold the silver with one edge over the V of the bench pin, and cut out the design, making sure that you keep the saw at a right angle to the metal. Take a round needle file, and smooth the outside edges of the design, so that there are no sharp edges. Remove all scratches with fine emery paper. Anneal the metal and cool it as previously described. With a ring mandrel form the ring shape. Bind the shank firmly with binding wire and place it on a charcoal block, with the join to be soldered at the top. Solder using hard solder, then pickle and polish as previously described.

Ring geometry
The cut-out edges of this ring are used to decorate the surface. Make a precise edge as described here, or cut a freer pattern.
You will need:
9mm ($\frac{3}{8}$in) wide strip of silver 1.50mm ($\frac{1}{16}$in) thick and long enough to fit around

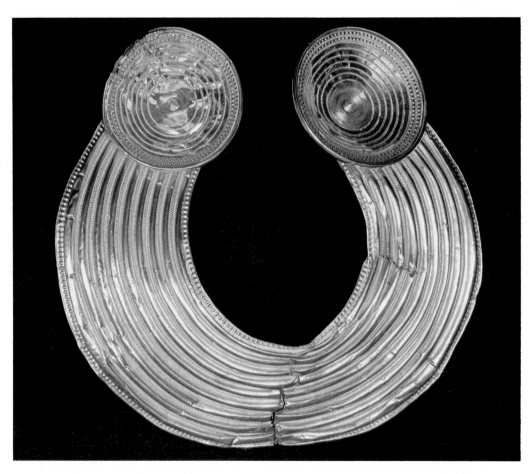

This gold torchet, made in Ireland in the 7th century BC, illustrates the bold effect of repoussé work.

your finger □ jeweler's saw □ files □ emery paper □ binding wire □ hard and medium solder □ flux □ blowtorch □ pickling solution □ ring mandrel □ rubber cement.
Making the ring. Make a pattern for the ring as previously described by tracing the design (fig.10). Saw out the squares with a jeweler's saw. Anneal the silver. Put the cut-out squares carefully to one side. Keeping the piece of silver flat position the squares, using a fine brush with flux on it. Put tiny pieces of hard solder at the sides of the squares. Solder them on. File off excess solder, and clean all scratches with fine emery paper. Shape the ring on a ring mandrel. Bind with binding wire. Flux the join and put paillons of medium solder on it. Solder, pickle and polish the ring.

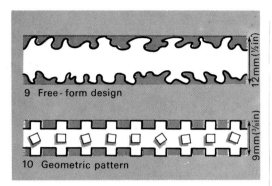

9 Free-form design

12mm (½in)

10 Geometric pattern

9mm (⅜in)

Decorative techniques

Repoussé. This is the technique of forming a relief on sheet metal, working from the back with hammers and punches. It is a technique that can be used on most metals. The work has to be held on a surface both firm and yielding, and a metal bowl filled with pitch is used. Besides this you will need an assortment of steel punches and a chasing hammer (fig.11). First clean the reverse side of the piece of metal with fine emery paper. Draw the design onto the reverse side with a pencil or metal scriber. Anneal the sheet of metal, cool and pickle it. Smear a thin film of oil over the right side of the metal and place it, right side down, onto the pitch. The oil will make it easier to remove the metal later. Gently warm the metal with a blowtorch until it sinks very slightly into the pitch. Leave it to cool. When it is cool and the pitch is firm, outline the design with the blunt chisel-shaped punches. Hold the punch as shown in fig.12. Tap the punch lightly and regularly with the hammer, following the shape of the design. This will produce a raised line on the other side of the metal. If you feel the metal beginning to resist the punch, heat the metal gently to soften the pitch and remove the work with tongs. Clean off all traces of pitch with a cloth dipped in paraffin. Anneal, cool and pickle the work. Dry it thoroughly and replace it in the pitch, making sure it is evenly supported before continuing the design. When the design is complete, remove the work, anneal, pickle, rinse and dry it. The form can now be defined and detailed with chasing tools.

Chasing. Chasing is a method of imprinting more detailed designs on metal, working on the right side. You will need a hardwood block, headless nails, a chasing hammer and chasing tools. Tools can be bought or simple ones can be made by filing the tips of household nails into different shapes with an ordinary file to produce different results. After filing, polish the tool with tripoli and rouge. Beading tools are used to make circular indentations and matting tools produce a more complex textured effect (fig.13). Scratch the design on the surface of the metal very lightly with a metal scriber. Fix the metal onto the hardboard block by holding it in place around the edges with headless nails to prevent it moving around. Hold the chasing tool in the same way as the repoussé punch. Then, keeping the sides vertical, tilt the tool at a slight angle away from the direction in which you wish to move. This will cause the tool to work forward with each blow of the hammer, forming the line with the corner rather than the whole edge of the tool. Strike the tool steadily and continuously with the chasing hammer to make an even smooth line.

Straight lines and very gentle curves can be chased with a straight "liner" (fig.13). Make the curves by rotating the straight liner very gradually as you hammer it. For more definite curves use a curved "liner."

Embossing and dapping. Embossing is a process in which small punches are used to stamp simple forms into the sheet metal

Made about 1920, this chased Art Nouveau pendant is the work of W. Augustus Steward.

Chasing hammer and steel punches

lips

Holding the repoussé punch

repoussé punch

ch
ch
wl

13 A selection of chasing tools

curved liners

straight liners

beading tools

matting tools

This Roman jewelry is typical of the sophisticated embossed work of the period.

Wire jewelry

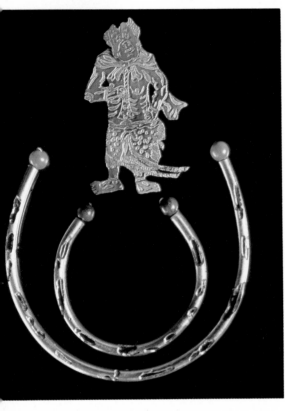

Examples of etching: the necklace and bracelet reveal resin where copper has been etched away.

from the back. Place the work on a pitch bowl, on wood or on a lead block. Dapping punches are traditionally used to form hollow beads. Place two equal disks of sheet metal about 1cm (⅜in) larger than the finished half-bead size you require on the dapping block (fig. 14a). Make hemispheres with a round-headed dapping punch (fig.14b) by moving the disks into increasingly smaller depressions in the dapping block, and hammering them with the punch. When they are the required size, drill a small hole into the middle of one of the hemispheres to allow hot air to escape and then solder the two halves together. Cool and pickle the work. Then boil the beads in soapy water to remove all traces of pickle, and dry the beads by warming them gently with a blowtorch.

Etching. Etching is a technique for leaving a raised design on a sheet of metal by protecting it with a "resist," (a substance which will not be eaten away by acid) and

dissolving the rest of the metal with acid. You will need a resist such as wax, varnish or gum; an acid solution, called a mordant, which for copper or brass is composed of a mixture of one part nitric acid to ten parts water. You will also need an etching bath; a pyrex dish is suitable or a porcelain or glass container at least 10cm (4in) deep with a flat bottom, large enough to take the metal plate, and wooden tongs to remove the work. Choose a design in which the contrasts are clearly defined and which does not have too much intricate detail. Trace the lines of the design with a metal scriber. Before applying the resist, clean the metal by dipping it into a pickling solution. Rinse and dry. Wear gloves or hold the metal with a piece of cloth to prevent it from being covered in fingermarks. Cover the areas which are to remain high with the resist using a brush, and coat the back of the metal as well. Leave it to dry completely, preferably overnight. Make up the etching fluid. Always pour the acid gently into the water, *never* the reverse; wear gloves and do it in a well-ventilated area. Mix the acid only in glass or porcelain containers, and stir gently with a glass rod. Immerse the metal in the etching bath by lowering it into the acid on a cradle of cotton string. After a few minutes tiny bubbles will appear and light fumes will be thrown off – do not stand over the acid bath, or inhale these. Large active bubbles and heavy fumes indicate that the mordant is too strong. If this happens, add a little water very slowly and mix it in carefully, using the glass stirring rod. The acid is sufficiently diluted not to react too violently. After about 30 minutes, inspect the metal by lifting it out of the bath with wooden tongs, and running it under clear water to rinse off the acid. Use a pointed steel tool to examine the depth of the etched lines. If they are not deep enough, return the plate to the bath. If any bits of resist become detached from the metal, remove the work from the acid, rinse it, remove the resist and re-apply. When you consider the plate ready, remove it, and rinse it well in running water to clean off the acid. Remove the resist with turpentine and polish the metal with fine emery paper and finish with rouge.

Wire jewelry
Wire plays an important part in much jewelry making, being twisted into patterns or soldered onto more solid metal to provide decoration. It can itself be formed into attractive bracelets, necklaces, cuff links and other pieces. You can buy wire ready-made in half-round, round or square sections, in a wide variety of standard gauges. It is also obtainable in round and square hollow tubes. You may find it more practical to buy heavy gauge wire and reduce it to your own requirements.

Working wire. First anneal the wire by coiling it, binding it with iron binding wire and laying it on an asbestos mat. Make sure that

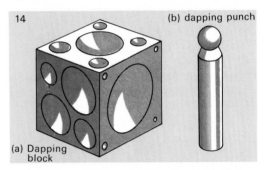

14   (b) dapping punch

(a) Dapping block

you anneal the wire evenly. Cool it after annealing by immersing it in water. A drawplate enables you to reduce the thickness of wire or to change it into other shapes. This is a plate made of high grade steel, perforated with round, triangular or square holes. These holes are graded in size and taper from the front to the back. You will also need a vise, draw tongs or pliers, and a beeswax block. Fasten the drawplate horizontally in the vise, with the smaller tapered end of the holes facing you. Clamp the vise to a heavy bench, since pulling the

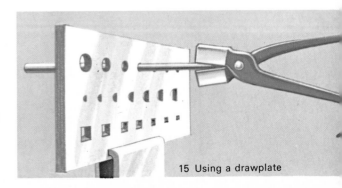

15 Using a drawplate

wire through is a strenuous job. Draw the wire across the wax block to make it easier to draw through the plate. File one end of the annealed wire to a point so that it will go far enough through the largest hole for you to take hold of it with the pliers. Pull the wire through the plate (fig.15). Then pull it through the next hole down in size, and continue doing this, grading down through the holes until the required gauge is reached. Pull the wire through smoothly and continuously. If you stop half way you will produce a kink in the wire.

Fastenings

Ring and clip fastening. The simplest fastening for a bracelet or necklace consists of a twisted piece of wire that clips onto an oval ring. Take a piece of wire and shape it into an oval ring. You will have to judge the size of the clasp in relation to the piece of jewelry. Solder the ends together. Take 2.5cm (1in) of round wire and fold it in the center, using round-nosed pliers. Twist the wire each end as shown in fig.16a. To make a secure fastening, clip the curled wire ends over the long edge of the oval ring, and push it around to the short curve (fig.16b).

Jump rings. Jump rings are round or oval rings which can act as connecting links or be formed themselves into lengths of chain. Take a dowel or a steel rod whose diameter will be the inner diameter of the jump rings. Clamp one end of the rod or dowelling in a vise, and clamp one end of the wire in as well. Hold the other end of the wire in your hand and wind the wire around the rod. Wind each curve of the wire close to the last. Then cut down the length of wood

Copper wire necklace, bracelet and earrings.

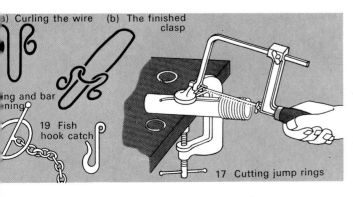

(a) Curling the wire   (b) The finished clasp

ng and bar ning

19 Fish hook catch

17 Cutting jump rings

Copper wire necklace
Silver choker

with a jeweler's saw as shown in fig.17. Solder the ends of the rings together.

Ring and bar fastening (fig.18). This is a slightly more complicated fastening. Take a very small jump ring and solder it to the center of a short rod of wire. Solder another small jump ring to a larger metal ring. To make the fastening, thread the bar through the metal ring and turn it vertically, locking the two ends together.

Fish hook catch. Using round-nosed pliers, make a loop one end of a small piece of wire. This loop will be attached to one end of the jewelry. Hook nose the other end as shown in fig.19. Make sure that the end of the hook touches the back of the wire. Attach a jump ring to the other end of the piece of jewelry, and make the fastening by slipping this ring over the hook nose.

Copper wire necklace

Intricate looking chains linked together make attractive bracelets and necklaces. This necklace is 50.5cm (20in) long and consists of 49 twists of thin copper wire.

You will need:

49 lengths of 15.5cm (6in) long copper wire ☐ piece of copper wire 6.5cm (2½in) long for fastening ☐ round-nosed pliers ☐ flat-nosed pliers.

Making the necklace (fig.20a–d). Take a length of copper wire and using the round-nosed pliers make equal spirals on either end until the wire measures 4cm (1½in) end to end (a). Hold the wire in the center with a pair of flat-nosed pliers and bend the spirals to touch each other (b). Squeeze the wire just above the spirals and at the top of the loop to form a V shape. Now bend the V shape back so that the other end of the chain is on a level with the middle of the two spirals (c).

Make 48 more links in the same way. Assemble the chain by hooking the links over each other as shown (d).

Making the fastening. Take a 5cm (2in) piece of copper wire. Leaving 2.5cm (1in) free, form 2 small rings next to each other and twist the rest of the wire around the first 2.5cm (1in) as shown in fig. 21. Take a small length of copper 1.5cm (½in) and form a jump ring between the fastening and the first link of the chain. Fold the twist of wire in half to make a loop which can then

be attached to the first link of the other end of the necklace.

Making a matching bracelet. Take 24 lengths of wire and form them in links in exactly the same way. Take a piece of wire 2.5cm (1in) long and make a fish hook fastening, looping the round end to the last link of the bracelet. Attach it to the first link the other end.

Earrings. These are made of four links of twisted copper. To make a fastening for pierced ears, twist a tiny jump ring at the curve of the first link. Attach a small piece of gold or silver wire to this and shape it into a fish hook with the round ended pliers. Alternatively, you can buy earring screws.

Silver choker

This delicate choker has spirals of silver wire hanging from a chain of silver tubing. A detachable pendant can be added: you can make the simple shape described here or design a more elaborate one of your own.

You will need:

35cm (17½in) silver tubing ☐ 90cm (36in) silver wire ☐ 31cm (12¼in) round silver wire 1mm ($\frac{3}{64}$in) thick for the pendant ☐ 36cm (18in) nylon thread for threading the necklace ☐ torpedo clasp fastening ☐ jeweler's saw ☐ round-nosed pliers ☐ flat-nosed pliers ☐ wooden hammer.

Making the choker. Take the tubing

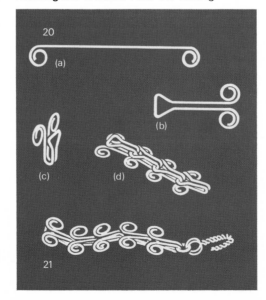

and saw it into equal lengths 0.5cm (¼in) long, cutting at right angles. Clean the ends with emery paper. Cut the silver wire into 12 lengths 7.5cm (3in) long. Using round-nosed pliers make a spiral at one end and a small loop for threading on the wire at the other. Thread 13 pieces of silver tubing onto the thread, and then 1 spiral. Then thread 4 silver tubings and 1 spiral until all 12 spirals have been strung. Thread 13 more pieces of silver tubing. Tie the thread on securely at each end to the loops of the torpedo clasp.

Making the pendant. Take the round silver wire and twist it into a flower shape as shown in the photograph, leaving 2.5cm (1in) free at the beginning. Hammer flat the end of each loop. Solder the first and last loops together with medium solder. Cool and pickle.

Then hammer flat the end of the spare 2.5cm (1in) of wire, and coil it over at the end with pieces to form a loop to fit over the necklace.

Above: A portrait by Sir George Hayter of Queen Victoria in her coronation robes and crown. The Black Prince's ruby can be clearly seen.

Right: The "Imperial Crown" which was made about 960 AD for Otto the Great and was used at the coronation of Holy Roman Emperors.

In the Tower of London, closely guarded by those famous British figures, the Beefeaters, is housed the most magnificent collection of jewelry in the world. It is reputed to be valued — if indeed any true valuation is possible — at over $60,000,000. The crowns are the main focus of interest. Among them is the St. Edward's Crown, which was made for Charles II in 1661 after Cromwell had destroyed the previous English crown. It is a copy of King Edward the Confessor's crown and is adorned with sapphires, rubies, emeralds, diamonds and pearls. It is still used when a sovereign is crowned, but as it is unusually heavy, it is replaced by a lighter version fairly early on in the ceremony!

The next most important crown is the Crown of State, made for Queen Victoria in 1838. It is decorated with many famous jewels: the Black Prince ruby, worn by Henry V at the Battle of Agincourt; the St. Edward's sapphire, which comes from the coronation ring of Edward the Confessor and the Lesser Star of Africa, the second largest diamond in the world. To these are added thousands of other diamonds, pearls, sapphires, emeralds and rubies. The most famous stone of all, the Koh-i-noor (meaning "mountain of light") diamond, is also part of the collection of the Crown Jewels. This remarkable stone was presented to Queen Victoria by the army of the Punjab.

Throughout history different precious and semi-precious stones have been popular.

For instance, emeralds, rich dark green in color and softer than diamonds, have been widely used in jewelry making since around 3000 BC. They are found mostly in Colombia, Russia and South Africa. Rubies, deep red and among the most precious of stones, are next hardest to diamonds and are regarded as sacred in Burma where the very best examples are found. Coral, from the sea bed, has been known since the Bronze Age. It was particularly popular with the Victorians who carved it to produce attractive brooches and necklaces decorated with flowers and birds. These were usually given to children and young girls. Amber is the fossilized resin of pine trees and is very rare. It was valued by the Greeks and Romans who revered it for its supposed medicinal powers.

Jewelry
Lapidary

Lapidary is the art of working gem stones. It is a craft in that the basic skills of cutting and polishing the stones must be learned, and an art in that these skills must be applied with an understanding of color and form to produce the best results from the raw material.

A wide variety of equipment is now available to help you. The lapidary units described below may be purchased separately or in combination. Either way, the basic requirements are a slab and trim saw, grinding wheels—rough and fine—and interchangeable sanding and polishing disks or drums. If you are beginning lapidary and want to try out the craft first before committing yourself to the expense of buying equipment, it is a good idea to enroll at a class at your local college or school where you will be able to try out the tools and receive advice about the suppliers in your area. The rough gem material may be bought from suppliers who specialize in collecting the material from all over the world.

The scale used by lapidary workers to show the relative hardness of minerals is the Moh's Scale of Hardness:

1	Talc	6	Orthoclase (Feldspar)
2	Gypsum	7	Quartz
3	Calcite	8	Topaz
4	Fluorite	9	Corundum
5	Apatite	10	Diamond

This selection of rough cut and polished stones includes amethyst, quartz, citrine, azurite, malachite, emerald, aragonite and aquamarine.

As a general guide for the amateur lapidary worker, stones that are used in settings where they will receive a certain amount of rough treatment, such as rings, should be of a hardness of 7 or higher. Other jewelry which is less exposed to wear — brooches or earrings, for instance — can be made from stones of a hardness of 4 or more. Some of the gem materials you may wish to use with their comparative ratings on the Moh's scale are listed on the right.

Amber	2.5	Tourmaline	7.5
Beryl	7.5	Turquoise	6
Corundum	9 (rubies and sapphires)		
Feldspar	6 (moonstone, sunstone, labradorite, amazonite)		
Garnet	7	Synthetic stones	(the range of synthetic stones includes rubies, sapphires and emeralds. The two most commonly available synthetic materials are yttrium aluminum garnet 7.5 (available in a variety of colors) and Strontium titanate 6.5 (used as a substitute for diamond, but much softer).
Jadeite	7		
Lapis Lazuli	5		
Malachite	4		
Obsidian	5.5		
Opal	6		
Quartz	7 (Amethyst, Cairngorm, Citrine, Rose quartz, Aventurine, Carnelian, Chalcedony, Jasper, Bloodstone, Agate, Tiger's eye).		

Basic lapidary techniques

Sawing. Gem materials must first be cut into useable slabs by feeding the material into a saw. This saw is a thin disk of steel with diamond grit set into the rim. The blade may be either a notched or a sintered segment type. The notched blade is lightly chiselled on the edge and then rolled in diamond grit. The notches are hammered to hold the grit and the edge is heated to combine the grit with the blade. Sintered blocks are made by mixing diamond grit with powdered metal and then fusing the mixture into small blocks which are soldered into recesses cut into the steel disk. There are two types of diamond saw — a slabbing saw which should measure about 25cm (10in) in diameter to slice large lumps of stone, and a trimming saw measuring between 10.5 and 21cm (4—8in) in diameter to cut the slices into smaller pieces. The saw should be cooled by running it through a cooling bath to prevent cracking the stone or dulling the edge of the blade. This bath should contain a mixture of soluble oil diluted in about 10 parts of water. The sludge that collects at the bottom of the bath should be cleaned out regularly to avoid wear on the blade. The gem material is fed into the slabbing saw by clamping it onto a platform that moves forward automatically. Hold the stone firmly using just enough gentle pressure to allow the saw to cut the stone without bending the blade. Allow the blade to contact the stone lightly at first to make a "step" to guide the drill. After the main slab has been cut, use the trimming saw to complete the sawing. To cut out an oval cabochon from the main slab, mark out the shape on the slab using a template and an aluminum or bronze pencil (fig.1). Next, mark out the first lines for cutting leaving a 1.5mm ($\frac{1}{16}$in) clearance of the template mark (fig.2). Holding the stone, cut along the lines with the trimming saw until you have a rectangle enclosing the oval mark (fig.3). Finally saw off all four corners (fig.4).

Grinding. The cabochon is now ready to be ground into shape on a rough grinding wheel. The wheels are usually of 21cm or 15.5cm (8 or 6in) diameter and come in two grit sizes. The most useful are a coarse

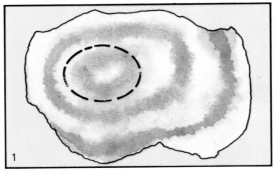

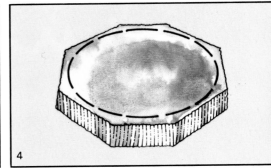

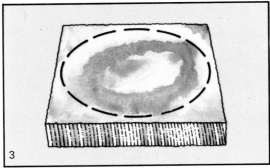

100 grit wheel and a fine 220 grit wheel. Grinding wheels are always marked with a maximum safety speed and this should never be exceeded. A general guide for cutting speed is 2,000 rpm for 21cm (8in) wheels and 2,600 rpm for 15.5cm (6in) wheels.

Water should always drop into the forward surface of the wheel when grinding as the heat caused by the friction may crack the stone and the air will fill with particles of dust if it is ground dry. However, never leave a stationary wheel standing in water as this will saturate part of the wheel and throw it off balance, making it extremely dangerous to use. As always, treat tools with respect and keep fingers clear of the wheel. Check that the saw is running smoothly by switching it on and allowing it to run for a few minutes — standing to one side as a safety measure. Begin by making a smooth shape on the coarse grinding wheel moving the stone from side to side on the face of the wheel. To avoid chipping the stone, grind a slight bevel on both edges, repeating as the edge is ground away. When you have ground down to the basic template line, move to the fine grinding wheel to make a smooth surface.

Amethyst crystals (*above*) and after cutting, grinding, shaping and faceting (*below*).

Dopping, shaping and sanding

Dopping. Before grinding the top rounded section, the stone has to be mounted on a dopstick to facilitate control over the stone. Dopsticks can be bought ready-made in metal or wood or they can be made from 15.5cm (6in) pieces of dowel rod. The most frequently used diameters are 6mm to 19mm ($\frac{1}{4}$ to $\frac{3}{4}$in) although you may require extra sizes for smaller or larger

Lift the stick with the stone upright. Wet your fingers in cold water and mold the wax around the stone. Check that the stone is centered and at right angles to the stick. Correct any errors in positioning immediately — you have about half a minute to do this before the wax hardens. Place the stick on a rack to harden completely for several hours.

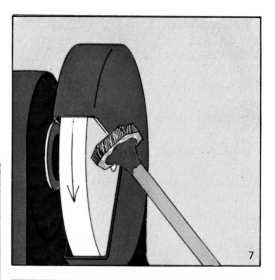

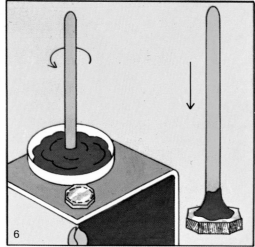

stones. If you make your own, round one end so that it will fit comfortably in the hand leaving the other end flat for the stone. Dopping wax, used to stick the stone to the dopping stick, can be purchased from a lapidary shop. To warm the stone and the wax you will need a small alcohol lamp and a piece of aluminum or steel bent at the top and the bottom (fig.5). The top shelf should be about 2.5cm (1in) above the height of the lamp and about 10.5cm (4in) square. Break up a stick of wax and place it in a small metal container —the lid of a screw-top jar is fine—on the shelf above the flame. Warm the flat end of the dopstick in the flame and insert it 10mm ($\frac{1}{2}$in) into the melted wax. Rotate the stick in the wax, then remove it and stand it on a smooth, clean metal sheet. Place the stone to be dopped on the shelf beside the container and put a small piece of wax on the base of the stone. When.this wax melts the stone is warm enough for dopping. As this occurs, take the dopstick and warm the wax at the end until soft. Then press the stick vertically on the stone (fig. 6).

Shaping. Return with the dopped stone to the coarse grinder. Using one hand to support the stick and the other to rotate it, form a small chamfer around the edge of the stone, leaving approximately 0.80mm ($\frac{1}{32}$in) at the base. Change the angle of the stone and make another chamfer (see figs.7 and 8).

Now move the stone across the wheel in smooth curves to round off the angles and remove the flat top (fig.9).

The small area left at the base helps to ensure that the original shape of the cabochon is retained.

On the smoother grinder remove any irregularities on the stone, checking carefully for symmetry as you proceed. This is the last step in the process of actually shaping the stone and none of the later processes will alter it so it is essential to take plenty of time at this stage to make sure that the stone is perfectly smooth and symmetrical.

Sanding. A sanding machine removes the scratches left by the grinding machine. The two machines are similar, but in sanding, the side of the wheel is used, so it is un-

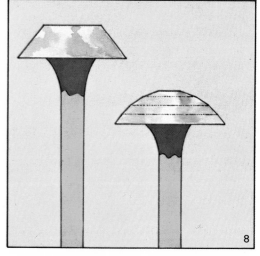

covered (fig.10). Sanding disks are disks of waterproof "wet and dry" silicon carbide with grit surfaces graded from rough to smooth and different ones can be attached to the machine. The most suitable for sanding stones are 220, 400 and 600 grits. The disks are backed with a padding for resilience when sanding the smooth curves of a cabochon cut stone. The wheel must be run wet, so use either a hand or foot

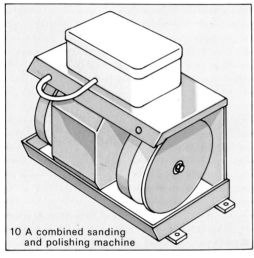

10 A combined sanding and polishing machine

operated spray. Rotate the sanding wheel at about 2,000rpm. Use the 220 grit disk first and spray it before you start, respraying as it dries.

Hold the dopstick in both hands and move the stone across the disk against the direction in which the wheel rotates. Turn the stone as you work so that all parts are sanded evenly. Check the stone for progress under a magnifying glass. Continue sanding until all traces of the grinding wheel are removed. Then repeat the process with the medium and then the fine grit. Wash the stone thoroughly with soap and water.

Polishing. The polishing wheels of a sanding and polishing machine must be kept completely free from any traces of silicon carbide from the sanding wheel. A single grain can scratch the stone and send it right back to the fine grinding stage. Always wash your hands, the stone and dopsticks before beginning to polish.

Polishing buffs are usually made of felt or leather. The most common agents for polishing are cerium oxide or tin oxide. Some stones polish better with one, while others look better with the other. Tin oxide is particularly recommended for hard materials. Never use both oxides on the same wheel. If you are polishing several stones and have two wheels you can use cerium oxide on one and tin on the other. If you have only one wheel, change the polishing buff when changing the agent.

Always use and mix the powders separately. Mix the powder with water to a creamy consistency. Spray the polishing buff with water and paint a coat of the oxide mixture on it. Wash the brush before using it in another mixture.

Rotate the wheel quite slowly at 450—800 rpm. Hold the dopstick with both hands and move it against the wheel with the same curving strokes as for sanding. Apply considerable pressure. The whole process should not take longer than half a minute. If the heat of the friction softens the wax on the dopstick, allow it to cool before working it again. If the dopping wax melts, the stone will fly off the stick. At best you will have to repeat the dopping process, and at worst the stone will crack as it hits the workroom wall.

Once you have finished polishing, remove the stone from the dopping stick by warming the wax over the dopping lamp until the stone will pull off easily. Alternatively, put the stick in the freezer until the stone slips off the wax easily. Scrape residual wax off the stone with a knife, or dissolve it with alcohol. Refine the surface of the base of the stone if necessary, by holding it against the smooth grinding wheel as it rotates. Wash the stone in warm soapy water to remove all traces of polishing powder.

Drilling. Drilling holes through gem stones to turn them into beads or pendants is straightforward but time-consuming. Use a high-speed (4,000—5,000 rpm) electric press drill or an electric hand drill mounted on a press stand and fitted with a fine metal tube drill. Fix the gem stone to a block of wood a little larger than the stone with dopping wax or beeswax. Make a box or fence around the area of the hole with plastic clay (plasticine), or fix a large metal nut with dopping wax over the area to produce the same effect. This will keep the abrasive slurry in place around the hole during drilling (fig.11). Clamp the block of wood with the stone and fence to the bed of the drill so that the drill will constantly touch down at the same point. Mix up a pinch of 220 grit silicon carbide with a few drops of thin oil and place it inside the fence to form an abrasive slurry.

Turn on the drill and check that there is no wobble on the tubing which would cause inaccurate drilling. It is most important to use a light up-and-down touch. Bringing

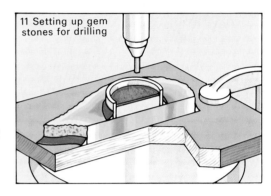

11 Setting up gem stones for drilling

the drill down into the slurry-filled fence, hold it in place for a few seconds, then lift it out of contact with the stone. Continue until you have almost drilled through the stone, and use even lighter strokes to finish. To bevel off the edges of the hole use a countersinking bit of brass or mild steel. Use the same abrasive slurry.

For drilling a large number of holes you will need a diamond drill. A fence is unnecessary with this as no abrasive mixture is used. Keep the stone wet by adding water with a small brush. As the diamond drill works much faster than the tube drill, many lapidaries prefer to hold the stone by hand, holding it in position on the wood block. When the stone is almost drilled through, it is turned over and drilling completed from the other side. This avoids the risk of damage as the drill breaks through. Other diamond drills that may be useful are the core drill and double core drill. The first of these makes holes of more than 4.76mm ($\frac{3}{16}$in) in diameter. The double core drill is used for making rings out of solid gem stone material such as jade. It produces a ring ready for grinding and a round cabochon ready for dopping at the same time.

Facet cutting. Faceting is the art of putting faces or facets on transparent gems to make

Methods of setting stones

them sparkle. It is a very precise and complex craft and much of the equipment is extremely expensive. The basic equipment is a lap or wheel that revolves horizontally. The stone is mounted onto a dopstick and fixed into the faceting head. This has a fixed arm which is set by a protractor. It is tightened at the correct angle required and locked in place (fig.12).

After cutting each facet the gem is polished on a polishing lap. The stone then has to be reversed accurately on a special piece of equipment called a transfer jig.

Methods of setting stones

Choose a setting that will show the stone to its best advantage and hold it firmly in place. Some settings are more suitable than others – for instance, a setting which requires chasing the metal against the stone is unsuitable for soft or brittle stones as they may crack or become scratched. For soft stones take care that the setting protects it as much as possible.

Closed setting. This is the setting most frequently used for cabochons and irregularly shaped stones. A fine band of silver (known as the bezel) which will fit around the stone, is soldered onto a base. The stone is then fitted inside and the bezel pushed against the side to hold the stone firmly.

To make the setting, cut a strip of sterling silver 0.356mm or 0.406mm (0.014 or 0.016in) thick, slightly higher than the proposed height of the setting to allow for filing level and rubbing over the stone. Take care when you are determining the height of the bezel. If it is too high it will hide most

of the stone and if too low it will not secure the stone correctly (fig.13a,b and c). With a narrow strip of paper, measure around the stone to find the exact length required for the bezel.

Cut out a strip of silver to the correct dimensions, anneal it, and bend it around the stone so that it fits closely, but not so tightly that the stone will not fit in easily. Remove the stone. Snip off any extra metal with tinsnips or a saw. File the ends smooth and true. Tie binding wire around the bezel so that the ends meet. Check that they fit well together. Place it on a flat charcoal, paint the join with flux and solder using a paillon of hard solder on the join. Cool and pickle the bezel then rinse it in hot water to remove all traces of flux. Check that the bezel fits around the stone. It should be just tight enough to allow the stone to pass through without tilting. If it is too tight slip it on a ring mandrel and roll it on a wooden block using pressure to stretch the bezel. If the bezel is too large, cut it again on either side of the original join and resolder it.

The top and bottom edges of the bezel should be parallel. File them true with a fine flat file and then smooth inside and outside with a file and emery paper. Now take a piece of backing metal which you have cut to the diameter of the stone, plus the width of the silver gauge of the bezel. Solder the bezel onto the backing metal. If the stone is translucent, saw and file a hole in the backing silver the same shape as the stone and about three quarters of its diameter to let the light through. For an opaque stone a small hole drilled in the backing will help in case it becomes necessary to remove the stone.

Place the bezel on the backing sheet around the hole. Flux and place paillons of easy solder on the inside of the band (fig.14). Play a small flame around the outside of the bezel to draw the flow of solder to the lower inside edge.

If the stone has a convex base, or if the backing metal is curved – for instance with a ring or bracelet – it will be necessary to make a bearing inside the bezel to hold the stone off the backing metal. This bearing is a kind of ring inside the bezel, which forms a shelf on which the stone will sit (fig.15).

A closed setting made out of gold is a fine contrast to the dark blue lapis lazuli stone.

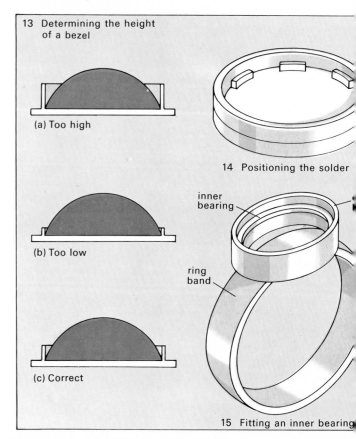

13 Determining the height of a bezel

(a) Too high

(b) Too low

(c) Correct

14 Positioning the solder

inner bearing

ring band

15 Fitting an inner bearing

12 Faceting equipment

elevation angle indicator

gear wheel

lap wheel

dop arm

stone

Claw settings display the diamonds to best effect in this flower-like gold brooch.

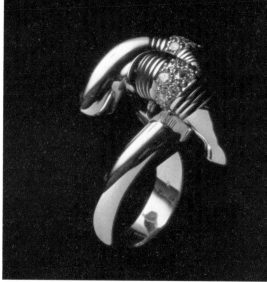

Sculptured twists of gold form this ring, with diamonds enclosed in pavé settings.

Use rectangular wire to make this bearing and solder it in place before the bottom of the bezel is filed to fit the curve of the backing metal.

Pickle the bezel, cool and polish it.

Then set the stone. Place it in the bezel and press the bezel around the stone with a burnisher. Wedge the ring against the edge of a table or shelf to do this as quite a lot of pressure is necessary. Press one small piece over the ring, then turn the ring around and press the silver over on exactly the other side. Repeat this, opposing the pressure points in order to keep the stone centered. Make at least eight main points. Then work around the bezel pressing inwards evenly with the burnisher. Finish by using the burnisher to rub the bezel smoothly against the stone and remove any traces of tool marks.

Claw setting. The number of claws made for a claw setting depends on the size of the stone, and is usually four, six or eight. Make a closed setting with an inner bearing as already described. Use a heavier gauge metal 1.016–1.295mm (0.04–0.05in) depending on the size of the stone. The setting should be high enough to allow the claws to reach up to and over the edge of the stone. Measure equal distances be-

tween the claws with dividers (fig.16). Cut away the metal between the claws with a jeweler's saw with an 0 blade or file away with a needle file. Use folded emery paper to remove saw and file marks. Solder to the backing silver, finish and polish the setting. Place the stone in the setting and, holding it firmly in place, press the claws over the

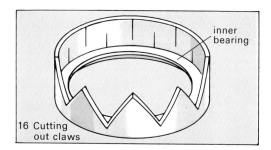

16 Cutting out claws

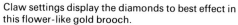

17 A scorper

stone. Apply pressure from opposing points as before.

Paved setting. In a paved setting the stone is set into a cavity cut or drilled into solid metal. The surrounding metal is then chased over the edges of the stone to hold it in place. For this type of setting the stone should be fairly hard, no softer than No. 6 on the Mohs Scale. The metal must be thick

enough for you to cut away half its thickness, leaving sufficient to protect the stone. To cut out the setting, mark the outline of the stone on the metal with a metal scriber, and carefully cut away the metal with a special steel tool called a scorper (fig.17), or with a chisel used with a chasing hammer until the stone fits exactly (fig.18a). Then cut a groove around the edge of the hole sloping outwards with the scorper with the highest part around the stone (fig.18b). Clean and polish the work and set the stone by burnishing the metal against the stone to hold it in place (fig.18c). Another method of making a paved setting is to drill or saw a hole through the metal the exact size of the stone. This method is useful when using thinner metal. Then cut a disk of silver slightly larger than the stone

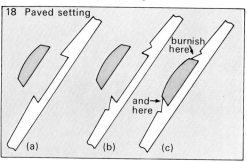

18 Paved setting

burnish here

and here

(a) (b) (c)

Silver-hearted brooch

sterling silver strip for the bezel □ 44mm (1¼in) long German silver or sterling silver wire for the pin, 0.8mm (1/32in) in diameter □ 1 revolver catch and 1 fichu joint for the fastening in sterling silver □ 1 oval cut cabochon coral □ jeweler's saw □ half-round needle file □ emery paper □ binding wire □ cotter pins □ flat charcoal □ hard, medium and easy solder □ borax flux □ blowtorch □ pickling solution □ tripoli □ jeweler's rouge □ 2 soft cloths for final polishing.

Making the brooch. Trace shapes A and B from the pattern (fig.19) and transfer them onto the sheet of silver. The shaded areas show where the two shapes will overlap. Place the stone in the position marked on the drawing and draw a line around it, leaving a margin of at least 1mm (3/64in) around it for the bezel setting. Cut out shapes A and B with a jeweler's saw, using a medium blade. Smooth down the edges with a half-round needle file and get rid of all file marks with successive grades of emery paper. Measure the height of the thin strip of silver against your stone. A low cut cabochon will need only about 2.5mm (7/64in) high bezel. Mark the height all along with a metal scriber and cut off excess metal, leaving a little over for safety.

Make the bezel as previously described. Put it in position on A and hold it in place with a cotter pin (fig.20). Solder with medium solder, heating the base, not the bezel. Cool and pickle. Then put the stone in to check the height of the bezel. Remove the stone and file down the bezel if it is too high. Cut off excess silver from around the bezel. File the side smooth and finish with emery paper (fig. 21). Check the inside curve of shape B by putting it on top of A, with the edges of either side of the corner matching. File the area on shape B that follows the bezel so that it forms a smooth curve (fig. 22).

Attaching the two shapes. Make sure that the overlapping surfaces of A and B are clean, paint them with borax and clip them together with a cotter pin.

Using a thin piece of charcoal, support shape B in its place on shape A. Prop tiny strips of easy solder against the side of the join (fig.23). Solder, clean and pickle, then rub out scratches with fine grades of emery

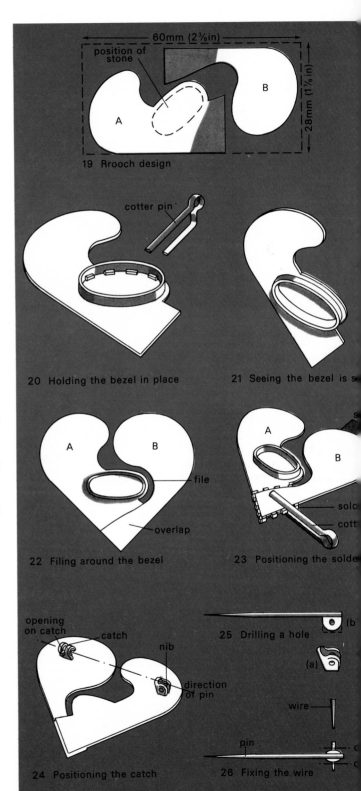

19 Rrooch design

cotter pin

20 Holding the bezel in place

21 Seeing the bezel is s

22 Filing around the bezel

23 Positioning the solde

24 Positioning the catch

25 Drilling a hole

26 Fixing the wire

and solder this under the hole to support the stone. Then make a groove around the stone and burnish the setting as described above.

Silver-hearted brooch

This pretty heart-shaped brooch has a cabochon cut coral set into a closed setting.
You will need :
28 × 60mm (1⅛ × 2⅜in) sheet of sterling silver 0.95mm B & S gauge 18–20 (BMG gauge 13) thick □ 6 × 50mm (15/64 × 2in)

Silver pendant

paper. Now position the joint and catch on the back of the brooch as shown in fig 24. Solder them at the same time with easy solder.

Set the stone in position as previously described. Polish the brooch using tripoli on a soft cloth. Wash in warm soapy water and repeat the process with jeweler's rouge and a new cloth. Wash again.

Making the pin. Cut a piece of silver sheet 3mm ($\frac{1}{8}$in) square, and round it down to fit the joint. Cut a piece of wire 36mm ($1\frac{7}{16}$in). Solder the sheet to the end of the wire. Make a mark on the sheet through the hole in the fichu joint, take it out and drill a small hole through the mark (fig.25a and b). Take a piece of wire 6–8mm ($\frac{15}{64}-\frac{5}{16}$in) long and taper it so that it will fit through the fichu joint and the pin. Push it into position and cut both ends to 1mm ($\frac{3}{64}$in) each side of the joint (fig.26). Cut the pin so that it is 2–3mm ($\frac{5}{64}-\frac{1}{8}$in) longer than the catch and taper the end gently to a point.

Silver pendant

This unusual pendant is made from two pieces of flat silver decorated with an amethyst and two pearls. It measures about 15cm (6in) in length.

You will need:
28×100mm ($1\frac{1}{8}×4$in) sheet of sterling silver 0.95mm B & S gauge 18–20 (BMG gauge 13) thick □ 3.17×1.59mm ($\frac{1}{8}×\frac{1}{16}$in) rectangular sterling silver wire 700mm (28in) long □ 1.22mm ($\frac{3}{64}$in) diameter sterling silver round wire 300mm (12in) long □ 3.15mm ($\frac{1}{8}$in) square hollow sterling silver tubing 40mm ($1\frac{1}{2}$in) long □ 1 square cut amethyst 6mm ($\frac{15}{64}$in) square □ 2 cultured pearls 6–8mm ($\frac{15}{64}-\frac{5}{16}$in) in diameter and half drilled □ jeweler's saw □ round needle file □ three square needle file □ emery paper □ cotter pins □ steel pins □ flat charcoal □ hard, medium and easy solder □ flux □ blowtorch □ pickling solution □ tripoli □ jeweler's rouge □ 2 soft cloths □ rubber cement □ round wooden rod 6.5mm ($\frac{1}{4}$in) in diameter for making jump rings.

Cutting out the silver. Trace shapes A and B from the pattern (fig.27) and transfer them onto the sheet of silver. Cut them out. Mark the approximate center of the small holes. Drill a hole in each, insert the blade

Jewelry
Lapidary

Silver pendant

of the jeweler's saw and cut out the holes. Drill a hole where the center of the stone is marked and, using the saw, cut out a square with sides measuring about 3mm ($\frac{1}{8}$in). File away the edges of the square at an outward-sloping angle, enlarging the size gradually (fig.28a and b). Check the size of the hole and the angle frequently with the stone. The stone should rest comfortably in the hole (fig.29). File down all rough edges of the 2 pieces of silver and smooth them down with successively finer grades of emery paper.

Cut out 2 edging strips from the rectangular wire, 60mm ($2\frac{3}{8}$in) long. Straighten them with a hammer and smooth them down.

Soldering on the edging strips. Place snipped off straight lengths of small cotter pins on the charcoal. Place shape A on top of these so that it is about 1–1.5mm ($\frac{3}{64}-\frac{1}{16}$in) above the surface. Position the 2 edging strips against the long sides of Shape A so that they extend beyond its straight end by 5mm ($\frac{13}{64}$in) as shown in fig.30. Bend cotter pins around this arrangement as shown in fig.31. Make them tight enough so that the pieces are pressed together. Drive the cotter pins into the charcoal to keep them upright. Make sure that the edging strips and sheet are tightly fitted together with straight, continuously touching sides or you will have a nasty split between the strip and the sheet. Secure the ends of the vertical strip in place with steel pins as shown in fig.31. Solder with medium solder, putting small paillons of solder alongside the join. Pickle and rinse. For shape B cut edging strips 68mm ($2\frac{11}{16}$in) long for the left side and 78mm ($3\frac{1}{16}$in) for the right side (fig.32). Repeat the process, using new cotter pins to hold the pieces in place.

Setting the stone. To make claws for the stone take the piece of square tube and make a diagonal cut from one corner to a point 7mm ($\frac{9}{32}$in) from the top at the next corner (fig.33). Cut from the opposite corner to the same point, to cut out a wedge shape. Cut out a similar piece on the opposite side. Then saw across the tubing at the 7mm ($\frac{9}{32}$in) line and 2 more identical pieces will have been formed (fig.34). Put your sawblade through the square hole

of shape B. Cut through the corners diagonally outwards, 1mm ($\frac{3}{64}$in) beyond the edge of the hole. Cut corners 2mm ($\frac{5}{64}$in) parallel to the sides of the square in both directions (fig.35). Enlarge these corners until the claws can be wedged in, with the narrow part poking through the other side. The claws should be held tightly in place. If they are too large to fit, file them down a little. Check the position of the claws with the stone. The claws should be 1mm higher than the corner of the stone in position. Make 4 small balls (called shots) of different sizes, the biggest being 1.5mm ($\frac{1}{16}$in) in diameter, by heating up snippets of silver until they curl into balls. Position them as marked on B in fig.27. Mark the positions well and make small indentations with a scriber so that the shots stay in place. Prop up the sheet in the same way as for the first soldering, and solder claws and shots in their places with easy solder, making sure you heat the sheet rather than the shots or claws so that they do not melt. Pickle and rinse and then check the position of the claws with the stone. Bend them slightly if they are out of place. Cut and file the protruding claws on the underside of the silver. Then file down the height of the claws, and thin the top edge of the claws that will fit over the stone.

Making jump rings. Smooth down the ends of the edging strips and drill holes 1.5mm ($\frac{1}{16}$in) in diameter for the links and 1mm ($\frac{3}{64}$in) from the end, at equal distances from the sides (fig.36). Check that the round wire can move fairly loosely in the hole. Enlarge it with a round needle file if necessary.

Drill a hole at all 4 ends of both A and B. Clean and smooth down both side pieces with a file and emery paper. Then anneal the round wire. Wind it around the wooden rod 6 times, so that a length of wire at least 5mm ($\frac{13}{64}$in) protrudes from each end (fig.37). Cut along the coil in a straight line, making 6 jump rings. Save the first and last of these for fastening the pearls. To make these, file into the wire where the curve touches it about halfway through with a three-square needle file (fig.38a). Then bend the end out at right angles (fig.38b). Check the depth of the hole of the pearl with thin wire and snip off the peg

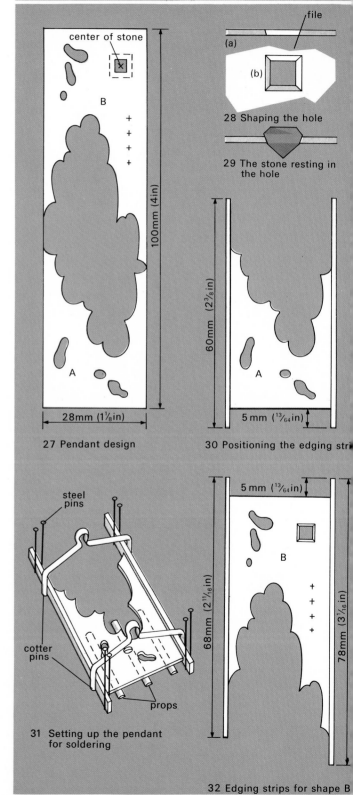

27 Pendant design

28 Shaping the hole

29 The stone resting in the hole

30 Positioning the edging strip

31 Setting up the pendant for soldering

32 Edging strips for shape B

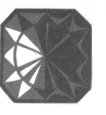

Silver pendant

to that length. File around it to slim it down until it will push fully into the pearl. Make a second one in the same way, but do not attach the pearls yet.

Making the neck fastening. Cut an oval shape from the leftover sheet of silver as shown in fig.39. Drill and cut out the middle. Clean the edges, smooth and polish it. Cut the rectangular wire into 2 equal lengths of about 215mm (8½in). Round one end of each with a file and bend these ends at 18mm (⁴⁵⁄₆₄in) as shown in fig.40a. Bend the ends as shown in fig. 40b, one with the end upturned and a slight gap, the other closely to the wire to trap the oval link. The fastening works as shown in fig.41.

Soldering the jump rings in place. Drill the other end of both straps in the same way as the edging strips. Attach the jump rings in their places starting at the top of the pendant (fig.42). Open them slightly sideways to fit them through the holes. Press the jump rings very tightly once they are in position. Solder them one by one with easy solder, making sure that the whole piece is steady but the link is resting loosely. Make sure that the join to be soldered is away from the other parts, preferably on the outside. Fit the bottom 2 jump rings through the holes in the same way, with the peg hanging down.

Shaping the strap. Bend both straps symmetrically to form an oval shape, with a distance between the 2 of 120mm (4¾in) at the widest point. Then bend a downward curve to follow the shoulder line (fig.43). Clean and smooth down all surfaces, taking out scratch marks with emery paper.

Setting the stone. Set the stone by fitting it in the hole and pushing the top of the claws over the stone. Work on them bit by bit all around rather than trying to finish one, otherwise the stone might jump out or end up lying crooked. If the claws are too thick, thin them down with a needle file at the corners. File and smooth the tops of the claws carefully when the setting is finished.

Finishing the necklace. First polish the pendant with tripoli, then clean it thoroughly with warm soapy water. Then use jeweler's rouge to give it a final sheen. Wash that off with warm soapy water. To fix the pearls, use a drop of clear strong glue.

---

33 Cutting the tubing — 7mm (⁹⁄₃₂in)

34 The cut out claws

35 Cutting corners for the claws — 1mm (³⁄₆₄in), 2mm (⁵⁄₆₄in), 2mm (⁵⁄₆₄in)

36 Drilling holes for jump rings

37 Cutting jump rings — cut

38 Making pegs for the pearls — (a) file (b)

39 Pattern for the oval fastening — 22mm (⁵⁵⁄₆₄in), 18mm (⁴⁵⁄₆₄in), 6mm (¹⁵⁄₆₄in), 10mm (²⁵⁄₆₄in)

(a)

(b)

Making the fastening

The finished fastening

42 Placing the jump rings

43 Bending the strap — bend, bend, side view, 120mm (4¾in)

For millions of years pebbles have been polished naturally by the action of sand and sea. Artificial polishing — by hand or with a polishing machine — emulates this natural process, and would also, with time, reduce all stones to sand.

Equipment

Polishing machine or tumbler. This machine consists of a small motor which turns one or more barrels containing the pebbles to be polished, water and a polishing agent. To accelerate the polishing process, use a machine that turns more than one barrel, so that each barrel holds pebbles at a different polishing stage. The barrels are made from plastic or rubber; the latter last longer and are easier to open.

Polish. This is an abrasive ranging from the coarsest grit to the finest oxide. Use separate barrels, clearly marked, for each grade of abrasive, as a few grains of coarse grit left in when using a fine oxide will scratch the pebbles. Start with the coarsest grit and continue with finer polishes until the pebbles are completely shiny. The polishing agents are, in their order of use: silicon carbide No.80 or 120 grit; silicon carbide No.220 or 320 grit; silicon carbide No.400

or 500 grit; tin oxide, cerium oxide or levigated alumina plus additives; detergent for the final polish.
These polishes can also be used for hand-polishing with glass.

Pebbles. Pebbles can be picked up from beaches, river beds, the countryside and mountainous areas and will vary considerably depending on their locality. Their shiny appearance when immersed in water is an indication of how they will look in their final, polished state. Alternatively, obtain rough stone from a supplier. This will probably have to be broken up. Wrap the stone in newspaper and crush with a hammer. Check before collecting stones to make sure it is allowed.

Techniques

Hand polishing. This is preferable for large or soft specimens. Place a small amount of the coarsest grit onto a sheet of glass. Add a few drops of water and rub the pebble continuously in the grit until it is smooth. Wash the pebble and glass thoroughly in running water. Successively use finer grits and rinse the pebble and glass after each grit. Finish by rubbing the pebble with cerium oxide.

Machine polishing. Sort the pebbles into different grades of hardness. A rough guide to their hardness is:
A scratch mark left on the stone by a fingernail = up to hardness 2 which is not suitable for polishing.
A scratch mark left by a copper coin = up to hardness 4.
A scratch mark left by glass = up to hardness 5.
A scratch mark left by a steel knife = up to hardness 6.
Many pebbles are conglomerates, that is, a mixture of hard and soft areas. These must be polished carefully or the soft areas will wear away, leaving cracks and holes.
Stage 1. Fill the barrel with pebbles to approximately $\frac{5}{8}$ of its capacity. Add the following proportion of 28.4g (1oz) of the coarsest grit to 0.5kg (1lb) of pebbles. Add enough water to just cover the stones so that the barrel is now two-thirds full. Seal the lid, place the barrel on the rollers and switch on. A continuous rumbling sound indicates correct running of the machine;

an intermittent rumble indicates that there are not enough pebbles in the barrel; if the barrel does not turn, there are too many pebbles.
Let the machine run day and night. Water smoothed pebbles will take about seven days; rough stones take two to three weeks. Remove the lid once a day to release gases which might otherwise build up. These gases are not toxic, but if left to accumulate they could cause the barrel to burst. Also, inspect the progress of the stones and extract any stones which appear too soft. Re-seal and continue tumbling. For rough or hard stones add an additional amount of No.80 or 120 grit—since the grit breaks down with coarse stone. The run is complete when all the stones have lost their rough texture and edges. Remove the stones and wash out the sediment from the barrel. Rinse the pebbles in a colander or sieve until free from sediment. Dispose of the sediment outside—not in a household drain as it will harden to form cement and block the drain. It is often necessary to do two consecutive barrels using No.80 or 120 grit in order to complete barrel loads for the following stages, since the barrel must be kept two-thirds full throughout the process.
Stage 2. This stage can be left out if Stage 1 produces fairly smooth surfaced pebbles. Place the pebbles in the barrel, add 28.4g (1oz) of No.220 or 320 grit to 0.5kg (1lb) of pebbles. Cover with water until two-thirds full. Proceed to tumble and inspect every 24 hours. Stage 2 takes one to two weeks. Then rinse the pebbles and barrel.
Stage 3. Proceed as before, using No.400 or 500 grit. Stage 3 takes four to seven days. Then rinse the pebbles and barrel as before.
Stage 4. This is the final polishing stage. Place the pebbles in the barrel and add 14g ($\frac{1}{2}$oz) of a polishing agent such as tin oxide, cerium oxide or levigated alumina to 0.5kg (1lb) of pebbles. Take care at this stage not to bang the stones together as they will scratch each other. To soften the impact, add small pieces of felt, sole leather, plastic granules or vermiculite. Cover the load with water until two-thirds full. Proceed to tumble. Stage 4 takes four to seven days. Inspect the load every 24

hours and remove one or two pebbles each time to check whether they have a good polish. Do this by washing them and allowing them to dry. If they still appear wet and shiny when dry, tumbling is complete. Remove and rinse the pebbles. Wash out the barrel thoroughly. Replace the stones and add two tablespoons of detergent, and water to cover to two-thirds full. Tumble for six to eight hours. Finally, rinse the pebbles and barrel.

Sometimes after polishing, the stones have small cracks in an otherwise attractive surface. Fill these with paraffin wax and then rub with a cloth.

From pebbles to jewelry

A variety of traditional jewelry bases called findings are readily obtainable. Alternatively make your own and set the pebbles to your own design.

Glueing. Remove all traces of grease from the pebble and finding with carbon tetrachloride. Leave them to dry for half an hour.

Note: work in a well-ventilated room when using the grease solvent.

To hold the pebble and finding in place for setting, fill a small dish with sand and press down firmly until compact. Insert the pebble: it is now in a steady position for the finding to be attached. Glue the pieces together with an epoxy glue, using a matchstick as an applicator. Wipe off the excess glue with a wet tissue.

Horseshoe nail jewelry

Due to their natural silvery color and delicate shape, horseshoe nails are ideal to use for making unusual chunky jewelry. They can be bent to numerous different shapes to stand alone, or combined to form intricate designs, as in the photograph.

Basic materials and tools

Nails. These are available in a variety of different sizes, the most appropriate for jewelry being between sizes 2 and 8. The nail will have a trademark stamped on it, so when creating a design make sure that, if on display, the trademarks balance to form a pattern.

Wire. Use copper or tin wire, 1.22mm (0.05in) thick (16,17 B&S). The wire can

be either straight to bind nails together into a design, or coiled to serve as rings forming a chain.

Pliers. These are used for bending the nails to shape. Use pointed jewelry pliers with a textured surface on the inside of the points so they grip the nails firmly.

Cutters. Use wire cutters for cutting straight and coiled wire to the appropriate length.

Basic techniques

Shaping a nail. Using the pliers, bend the pointed end of the nail once to form a half loop (fig.1). Then bend again to form a whole loop (fig.2). Now bend the nail back the other way—upon itself—to form a second curve (fig.3).

Making a pendant. Cut a length of straight wire. Hold the wire vertically, gripping it with the pliers at the top. Tension it from below and twist once to form a loop. This loop fits over the nail and so enables you to bind the nail or several nails together to form a pendant (fig.4). Thread the pendant onto a leather thong.

Making bracelets and earrings. Cut a loop from the coiled wire. Thread on two bent nails and close the loop with the pliers (fig.5). If you wish to make a chain holding several nails, then add another loop, attach a nail, close the loop, add another nail, a loop and continue to the required length.

Jewelry from natural objects

Since the earliest times in history, natural objects have been used to adorn the body. Strings of beads made from seeds, nuts and bones were used as decorations in the Stone Age and are still worn today by some tribes, especially during religious ceremonies since many natural objects have assumed a symbolic value.

From natural objects to jewelry

Nuts, seeds, twigs, shells, leather, feathers and even bones can be used to make attractive and original jewelry; some ideas are shown in the photograph opposite. These objects can be joined by first piercing holes through each and then threading together on waxed linen thread. Seeds from melons, pumpkins, apples or citrus fruit are easy to thread and simply require the piercing of holes before they dry out. Dried beans, peas and chick peas need soaking until softened, whereas bamboo and fish vertebrae only need cleaning before piercing holes. Hard substances like nuts, shells, twigs, bones and hard seeds such as date stones require drilling to make the holes. Simple rachet or Archimedian fretwork drills are easy to use. Hold the object to be drilled steadily either in a vice or in a lump of plastic clay (plasticine). Proceed carefully with shells as they are difficult to drill without cracking. Once drilled or pierced, natural objects need little finishing. Twigs and bamboo are more attractive if sandpapered, other materials can be polished or varnished.

Bead jewelry

Bead jewelry is simple to make and involves only a few basic materials and techniques. Make the jewelry with ready made beads or make your own using such materials as clay, wood and paper to achieve original shapes and designs.

Thread

Thread must be fine enough to pass through each bead yet strong enough to support the weight of all the beads together. A

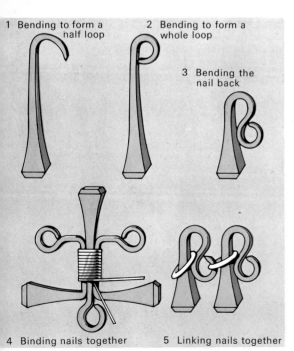

1 Bending to form a half loop
2 Bending to form a whole loop
3 Bending the nail back
4 Binding nails together
5 Linking nails together

variety of threads can be used for both necklaces and bracelets. Threads should be generally invisible on the finished piece, although decorative threads such as embroidery threads, knitting yarns and leather thongs are very attractive when used as an integral part of the jewelry. Use nylon, synthetic or linen carpet thread for small beads. Shirring elastic is useful for bracelets which are slipped over the hand.

Knots and fastenings

Knots are used to space out beads or to secure each bead, so that if the thread breaks the beads will not slide off. Fastenings are used to attach the ends of the thread together.

Knots. Make an overhand knot (fig.1) using double thread to space out and secure the beads. If this knot is not large enough to prevent the bead from sliding through, make a loose double overhand knot (fig.2). Ease the knot up to the bead with a needle and then pull it tight. Overhand knots are used in tie and pull closures, which are the simplest fastenings.

Tie closure. Check that all the beads are in the center of the thread. Fasten each end by making an overhand knot close to the first and last beads as shown in fig.3. Leave a space of a few centimeters (inches), make an overhand knot, thread on a single bead, make a final knot and cut the thread.

Pull closure. When all the beads except three are in position, thread both ends through a tightly fitting bead. Separate the threads. Finish off each end with a bead placed between overhand knots as in fig.4.

Metal fastenings. Metal fastenings or findings are obtainable in a variety of shapes and sizes. They include screw and box clasps which are usually used on necklaces, bracelet clasps and bolt and split ring clasps. Attach findings in the same way as the bolt and ring clasps.

Bolt ring. This is a metal ring which opens to hold another ring. Thread the yarn through the eye attached to the ring. Tie an overhand knot with double thread close to the ring. Thread the loose end through the first few beads, knot the threads tightly together. Snip the loose end neatly so that, as the rest of the beads are threaded on they will hide the knot (fig.5).

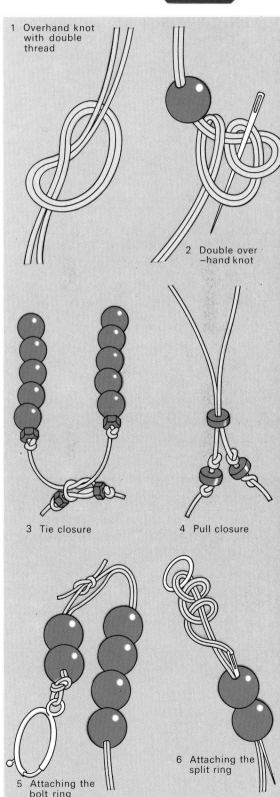

1 Overhand knot with double thread

2 Double over-hand knot

3 Tie closure

4 Pull closure

5 Attaching the bolt ring

6 Attaching the split ring

Four clay necklaces

Split ring. This is the plain ring of metal that accompanies a bolt ring. To finish off a necklace, loop the thread around the ring, pulling it up close to the last bead. Tie a knot and thread back through a few beads before cutting the thread (fig.6).

Making clay beads

Pinch off small pieces of self-hardening clay and roll them between your palms to make beads. Keep a bowl of water beside you so that you can smooth the clay with wet fingers as you work. Decide roughly on the thickness of yarn or thread you will be using before making holes in the beads. If you wish to make fairly large holes for a cord or leather thong to pass through, pierce the beads with, first, a darning needle. Then increase the size of the hole progressively with a medium sized knitting needle until the holes are large enough for the thread. This technique prevents the beads from being pushed out of shape. Leave the clay to dry overnight at room temperature. Large solid beads may take up to three days to dry completely. If you have made flat beads, inspect the pieces regularly, making sure that they do not turn up at the edges. Once dry, file the beads smooth with an emery board.

Sketch designs onto the beads with a pencil. The most efficient method of painting the beads is to position them first and stand them in a lump of plastic clay (plasticine). Then, using water or poster paints and a fine brush, paint half of the bead and leave to dry. Turn the bead around, replace it in the plastic clay (plasticine) and paint the other half. As the self-hardening clay is absorbent apply two coats of paint.

Four clay necklaces

Ice cream and candies. Roll out a piece of self-hardening clay into the shape of a cone. Make a hollow approximately one third of the way down from the base and put in two balls of clay. With wet fingers pull the balls down the sides of the cone to resemble scoops of ice cream. Cut the ice cream cone down the length so that it lies flat on the reverse side. Pierce a hole through each ice cream scoop. Make indentations over the cone with the blunt end of a needle.

To make the candies, roll out a piece of clay and, with a knife, cut four diamonds, four circles and two squares. Then mold four round and two oval beads between your fingers. Pierce all the shapes with a needle to make holes for the thread. Then smooth the shapes with wet fingers. When the clay is dry, smooth any rough edges with an emery board. Draw the inside squares, circles and diamonds lightly with a pencil. Paint the shapes in a variety of pastel colors and varnish. Thread the necklace on waxed linen thread, with the round and oval beads nearest the clasp and the ice cream cone in the center.

Bluebird, hearts and flowers. Trace the bluebird and heart shapes (figs.7a and b) onto card and make templates. Roll out a thin sheet of clay and using a sharp knife, cut out a bluebird and 6 hearts from the templates. Pierce 2 small holes in the bird, and 1 in each heart as indicated on the tracing pattern. To make the flower, roll a small ball of clay and pull it into 4 rough petal shapes, picking away the clay between the petals with the point of a knife or a needle. Press a small ball of clay into the center of each flower, smoothing the join with a wet knife blade. Prick the center all over with a needle and make a hole in 1 petal. Curve the petals upwards. When the clay is dry, file any rough edges around the petals. Paint and varnish. Make 4 flowers in this way.

Thread each side of the necklace separately, starting from the bluebird. Using nylon thread, push the needle through 1 hole in the bird, thread on a clear glass bead and bring the needle back through the hole (fig.7c) so that the bead rests on the hole and secures the thread. Pull the thread through and double it by threading the loose end through the needle. Use double thread for the rest of this side. Thread on 6 red glass beads, then 1 heart. Make an overhand knot, take the thread back through the last red bead and thread on 8 red beads and a flower. Make an overhand knot and take the thread back through the last bead. Continue in this way, threading 8 beads, then a heart until there are 3 hearts and 2 flowers on this side of the necklace. After the final heart is in place, thread on 55 glass beads and attach the clasp. Repeat in

Painted wooden beads

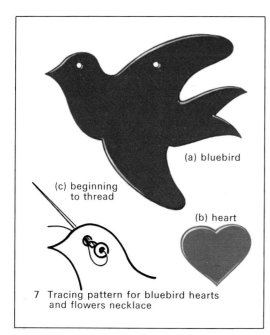

(a) bluebird

(c) beginning
to thread

(b) heart

7 Tracing pattern for bluebird hearts
and flowers necklace

the same way for the other side of the necklace, finishing with the clasp.

Butterfly necklace. Trace the butterfly
wings (fig.8) onto cardboard. Using the
templates cut out the shapes from thin clay
with a sharp knife. To make the body section roll out a cone and 2 small balls, one
slightly larger than the other. Fit them together to represent the head, thorax and
abdomen. Place the body part between the
wings, blending the reverse side of the
wings into the body with a knife. Make 2
holes at the top of the wings as in fig.8. Be
careful at this stage as the butterfly is fragile, but if the body is well smoothed into the
back of the wings it will be rigid and secure
when dry.
Roll out 40 small beads; 20 for each side
and slightly decreasing in size. Make the
beads oval in shape, the largest bead about
2.5cm (1in) in diameter and the smallest
0.5cm ($\frac{1}{4}$in). When the clay is dry, file
down any rough edges on the butterfly and
beads with an emery board. To achieve a
jewel-like effect, first paint the butterfly
and beads with white poster paint, allow to
dry and color with felt-tip pens. Finally,
varnish both the butterfly and beads.
Thread each side of the necklace separately, as for the bluebird necklace, securing the thread on the front side of the wing.
Alternate a glass bead with a clay bead,

then thread 21 glass beads. Repeat in the
same way for the other side. Knot the
thread in the middle and hide the loose
ends inside the beads.
Ethnic necklace. To make the central pendant, roll out a ball of clay and with wet
fingers, pull it out into a double cone shape
5cm (2in) long and 2.5cm (1in) across the
widest point. Incise designs of your choice
on the pendant with the blunt end of a
needle. Make 2 oval beads about 1.5cm
($\frac{1}{2}$in) long to hang beneath the pendant.
Make 36 fairly flat round clay beads; 4
large (about 2cm ($\frac{3}{4}$in) diameter), 14
medium and 18 small. Make 200 very flat
beads; 20 large (about 2cm ($\frac{3}{4}$in) diameter), 120 medium and 60 small. The beads
need not all be exactly the same size, and
they need not all be regular in shape. The
edges of the flat beads will crack as you
press them between your fingers so file
them smooth when dry or leave uneven.
When the clay is dry, paint all the flat beads
cream; half of the round beads orange and
the other half dark blue. Paint the 2 oval
beads orange and the pendant in all 3 colors. Leave all the beads unvarnished. Pull
the thread across beeswax to strengthen it,
knot one end and thread on 1 oval bead
and the pendant. Tie a knot in the thread.
Decide on the arrangement of the other
beads. Divide them in half—for each side
of the necklace—and group them according to color and size. To do this, place the
beads on a table and move them around

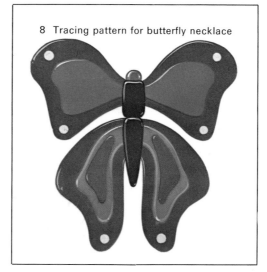

8 Tracing pattern for butterfly necklace

until you have the groups of color, shape
and size you wish. Thread on all the beads,
then tie a knot, take the thread through the
pendant and secure the other oval bead
with a knot at its base.

Painted wooden beads
Unpainted wooden beads are available
from craft shops and can be decorated with
your choice of design. Shapes can be
drawn onto the wood with a hard pencil
and then painted.
Sky necklace. This bold colorful necklace is
painted with a bright sun, silver moons,
stars and clouds with silver linings. It is
composed of 26 unvarnished wooden
beads: 1 × 5cm (2in) diameter, 2 × 4cm
(1$\frac{1}{2}$in), 2 × 3 (1$\frac{1}{4}$in), 2 × 2.5cm (1in) and
19 × 1.5cm ($\frac{1}{2}$in). With a compass draw a
line around the middle of the bead from
hole to hole. Then draw a circle with a
2.5cm (1in) radius on each face of the
bead. Draw in the rays of the sun from the
edge of the circle to the central line around
the bead so that there is a sun ray shape on

Papier mâché and nuts and washers

each side with the points of the rays touching on the central line.

Using a compass, draw half moon shapes on both 4cm (1½in) beads and draw 6 point stars around the moons. On the 2·5cm (1in) beads draw 5 point stars. Draw clouds on both 3cm (1¼in) beads.
Paint 10 small beads blue and 9 silver. Now paint the designs on the other beads, using poster paint first and then the silver enamel. Using a fine brush, paint a silver strip around the top of each cloud. Varnish each bead if you want.
Make a cord by doubling 6m (6½yd) of knitting yarn, twisting it and then doubling and twisting it again. Set aside 2 small and 1 silver bead. Thread the rest of the beads on the cord, making an overhand knot between each bead. You will need to make double overhand knots between the largest three beads. Finish off by making a pull closure with the three remaining beads.

Paper bead necklace
Make the long oval beads from rolled up triangles of paper. On a sheet of green wrapping paper mark out 6 triangles 5cm (2in) wide at the base and 45cm (18in) long; then mark out 12 triangles 2cm (¾in) wide and 37.5cm (15in) long. On a sheet of sturdy red paper mark 6 triangles 4cm

(1½in) wide at the base and 45cm (18in) long. On a sheet of sturdy blue paper mark 12 strips 1cm (⅜in) wide and 15cm (6in) long, to make the tubular beads. Cut out the triangles and strips with a craft knife and steel ruler. To roll up the beads, start at the base of the triangle and roll once around a knitting needle. Glue the rest of the strip and slowly roll up the paper. Proceed in the same way with the strips of blue paper to make the tubular beads. Thread the necklace on shirring elastic, beginning with a red bead, a small green bead, a blue bead, a large green bead, a small blue bead, a small green bead then another red bead, and so on. Finally tie a knot in the elastic and push it into a bead.

Papier mâché necklace
Papier mâché is ideal for making large bold pieces of jewelry as it is a light and tough material when dry. This unusual necklace is taken from Pueblo Indian pottery designs.
Making the necklace. Mold 6 rectangular hollow beads and the pendant from papier mâché, using the layering method (see page 227). When it is completely dry, sandpaper any rough edges. Pierce a hole in the pendant and then paint and varnish both the pendant and beads, copying the patterns of fig.9a and b.
Make a cord with embroidery thread. Thread the pendant in the center and wrap a bright contrasting thread around the 2 pieces of cord from which the pendant suspends. Use a needle to pull the loose end of colored thread into the cord under the wrapped embroidery thread. Thread 2 beads on either side of the pendant, tying knots between each bead. Leave a space of 4cm (1½in) on each side and knot. Then thread a bead and knot. Wrap colored thread around the cord after the second bead, and before and after the third bead. To attach the findings, loop the cord through the rings, knot and secure by wrapping tightly with the colored thread.

Nuts and washers jewelry
Jewelry from brass nuts and washers is simple to make. Choose a selection of interesting shapes and sizes, arrange them attractively and thread them onto a leather thong.

The necklace. Use 1 large and 2 medium sized brass balls; 2 coils; 4 large and 80 small washers; 4 large, 4 medium and 10 small nuts. Thread the large ball onto the center of a thong which is approximately 60cm (24in) long. Then, on each side, thread a medium sized ball, 2 large washers, a coil, 2 large nuts, 2 medium nuts, 4 small nuts and 40 washers. Position the pieces in the center of the thong and tie an overhand knot after the last washer. Finish off with 1 small nut knotted at each end of the thong to make a tie closure.
The bracelet. Use 1 large and 4 small brass balls; 4 large and 40 small washers; 10 small nuts. Thread the large ball onto the center of a thong which is approximately 45cm (18in) long. Then, on each side, thread on 2 large washers, 25 small washers, 1 small ball, 4 small nuts and 1 small ball. Position the pieces in the center of the thong and tie an overhand knot after the small ball. Finish off with a small nut at each end of the thong to make a tie closure.

Sequin jewelry
Sequins make delicate jewelry, ideal for evening wear. Choose any number or combination of colors

9 Designs for the papier mâché necklace

(a) pendant

(b) bead

Sequin jewelry

Beads and sequins choker. Attach one section of the clasp onto waxed linen thread. Thread on a silver bead, then thread on alternately, 65 green cup sequins, a silver bead, 65 black cup sequins, a silver bead and so on. Make sure the faceted cups of the sequins all face the same way. Attach the other section of the clasp.

Center bead and sequin choker. Attach the clasp onto waxed linen thread. Thread on 20 blue sequins, 40 silver, 15 pink, 5 blue, 15 pink, 40 silver, 60 pink, 20 blue, 30 silver, 10 pink, 5 blue, 10 pink, 30 silver, 20 blue, 30 pink, 10 silver, 30 pink, 60 blue, 20 silver, 10 blue, 5 pink, 10 blue, 20 silver, 60 blue, 15 pink, 10 silver, 15 pink, 40 blue, 20 pink, 10 blue, 20 pink, 10 blue, 20 silver, 10 blue. Thread on a glass bead to form the center and repeat the sequence in reverse. Finish off by attaching the other section of the clasp.

Matching bracelet. The bracelet is designed to fit tightly around the base of the wrist. Therefore, to ensure a correct fit, do not attach the clasp first—as on the choker—but first thread on the complete sequence of sequins, then check for fit and add more sequins if required. Thread on 5 silver sequins, 10 pink, 5 silver, 60 blue, 40 pink, 50 blue, 20 silver, 10 blue. Thread on a glass bead to form the center and repeat the sequence in reverse.

Enamelwork

This late 13th-century reliquary is a fine example of medieval French enamelwork; the technique used is champlevé enamel on copper gilt.

with the cloisonné method. Between the 6th and 12th centuries Constantinople was a flourishing center, producing crosses, altar screens and other religious items, all incorporating elaborate and exquisitely intricate cloisonné designs on gold.

Many new enamelwork techniques were developed during the Middle Ages all over Europe, and especially in France. The craft reflects the French influence of this period in its use of terminology to describe different processes and methods of enameling. Limoges in France, for example became well known as a center for painting in enamel. In Limoges work, finely ground enamel is used for delicate painting and the master enamelers of this city also perfected a similar technique, known as *grisaille*, in which the enamel is painted onto the metal in several layers to suggest sculpted features.

The French enamelwork style continued to dominate throughout the 16th and 17th centuries and the techniques of painting in enamel spread as far afield as China, where they were introduced by French missionaries. The Chinese, who had been producing cloisonné enamels since the begin-

This Dutch pendant locket made in 1630 shows the fine and delicate effects that can be achieved by painted enamelwork.

Fine enamelwork is beautiful to look at and enticing to touch, the brilliant fluid color being rivaled only by that of precious stones.

For centuries, goldsmiths and coppersmiths have inlaid pieces of glass into ornaments to increase the color and splendor of their work in the same way as they used precious stones, coral and lapis lazuli.

In true enamelwork, however, glass is fused onto metal by means of heat. This technique is known to have been used by the Ancient Greeks in the 5th or 6th century BC and a few remnants survive from this period of gold ornaments decorated with colored enamel.

The two basic techniques used for early enamelwork were *champlevé* and *cloisonné*, although these particular names were not used until the 17th century. Champlevé means literally "raised field"

and for this method, channels are cut out of the metal and infilled with glass and fused. Cloisonné is a method whereby thin strips of metal are soldered onto a base-plate to hold the enamel in the design. The metal strips are known as *cloisons*, meaning "divisions" or "cells." Both methods are still widely used today.

The champlevé technique was especially favored by the Celts in the British Isles and parts of Northern Europe from the 3rd century BC until the 2nd and 3rd centuries AD. The metal used was generally bronze and the predominant color for the enamel was red, which was produced by using copper oxide. Enamelwork was typically found on articles such as buckles and brooches and formed the basis of decoration on helmets, shields, horse harnesses and drinking vessels.

Enamelwork of the Byzantine period, on the other hand, reflects a preoccupation

ning of the Ming dynasty in the 14th century, developed the painted enamel techniques for decorating both copper and porcelain.

By the middle of the 18th century, however, enamelwork had suffered a decline. Enamelworkers turned their attention more and more to small articles such as snuffboxes, watchcases and portrait miniatures, but very few of these items could compare with the fine craftsmanship and magnificence of earlier work. Battersea enamelware, produced in England in the 1750s, is perhaps the most interesting work of this period.

Nineteenth-century jewelers such as the Russian goldsmith Carl Fabergé, brought new inspiration to the craft. Fabergé is especially remembered for the enameled gold Easter eggs he created, the first of which was commissioned by Emperor Alexander III in 1884.

Over the past few decades enamelwork has been used, not only for jewelry, but also for large-scale architectural work, incorporating a wide range of naturalistic, stylized and abstract designs.

In the past the art of enameling was shrouded in mystery and secrets were passed down from master to apprentice. Color formulas and the development of new techniques and designs were jealously guarded. Nowadays, however, just as the painter no longer has to make his own paints nor the weaver spin his own wool, so the modern enameler has recourse to commercially made and milled enamel. Easily controlled electric kilns mean that work that once would have taken many hours of labor can now be completed quickly and safely.

Tools and equipment

It is important to have the correct tools and equipment for enamelwork, especially as you will be dealing with high firing temperatures and handling dangerous substances such as acid. Always wear heatproof gloves when using the kiln and make sure you have a clear working area, with heat-resistant surfaces.

Jars and dishes. Store powdered enamels in airtight glass jars. Always dry enamels before storing and keep colors separate.

A selection of basic tools and equipment, including a pestle and mortar, tongs, a spatula and sifters.

When preparing to work, keep the enamel in ceramic dishes. You will also need an acid-proof dish when preparing and using cleaning solutions.

Pestle and mortar. A porcelain mortar is the best type of vessel to use when washing enamel and the pestle is used for grinding enamel if this is bought in chunk form.

Sifters. Sifters or strainers are used to dust dry enamel powder onto a piece to ensure fine even coverage. You will need several fine coppermesh or stainless steel sifters, mesh 60, 80 and 100.

Supports. There are various kinds of support available and these are used to hold the piece in the kiln during firing and afterwards during the cooling process. Use flat steel, marinite or metal mesh tray supports when enameling one side of a piece only and steel pointed trivets (star stilts) supported on a flat tray when enameling is to be done on both sides. You can also make your own stilts by

embedding steel pins (pre-fired before use) into a fire-clay base.

Tongs. These must be metal and have non-conductive handles and be fairly long. Use tongs to grip the tray support or trivet when you are inserting or removing work from the kiln.

Spatulas. It is important to avoid tilting or jarring a piece and you will therefore need a long spatula for lifting or setting it down. An additional smaller spatula or palette knife is also useful for handling powdered enamel.

Abrasives. Fine steel wool, pumice powder, abrasive (emery) paper and medium and fine carborundum stones are essential for leveling or rubbing down surfaces or smoothing off edges of a piece. You will also need a fine wire brush and a stiff bristle

The kiln
The metal

Metal mesh tray supports and steel pointed trivets are essential pieces of equipment for enamelwork.

brush for cleaning the metal.

Wire cutters and jeweler's pliers. These are used for cutting and shaping copper wire.

Paintbrushes. You will need soft paintbrushes for applying enamel in some cases and also a separate brush for applying a binder.

Sharpened quill or point. This is used for inlaying wet enamel. A sharp point is also used for engraving designs directly onto the metal.

Binder. A binder helps the enamel to adhere to the metal during firing, especially on curved or raised areas. Buy a ready mixed binder or mix gum tragacanth or a little wallpaper paste with water to produce a thin solution.

Drying cloth. Use a lintfree cloth that will not deposit particles of dust onto the piece.

The kiln
Electric enamel kilns are available in a wide assortment of sizes. Small kilns suitable for jewelry work are relatively inexpensive to buy and use little electricity.

Note: a kiln must be properly earthed and there should be no exposed wires.

All enamel kilns are designed so that they can be opened frequently before, during and after the firing process. When buying a kiln check that the door opens easily and also that it closes tightly to prevent heat loss. The kiln should be capable of reaching and maintaining a temperature of up to 1000°C (1832°F). A pyrometer, which measures high temperatures, is very useful and if not built into the kiln, can be purchased separately.

Small pieces can also be fired by means of a blowtorch. Support the piece on a laboratory tripod and apply the flame from underneath. Do not allow the flame to come into direct contact with the enameled

surface. This method is especially suitable for metals of a thicker gauge and dispenses with the need for a counterenamel (enamel applied to the underside of a piece).

The metal
The most easily worked and effective metals for fine enameling are gold, silver and copper. Gold and silver, however, are expensive materials and the following directions relate to copper only, which is a more suitable metal for a beginner to work with. Copper will easily take high firing temperatures and has a very pleasing warm color.

The gauge of metal used depends on the overall size of the piece. For small objects, which will be counterenameled, gauge 20 is suitable. Use gauge 18 and 16 for larger pieces and engraving. For cloisons use copper wires of gauge 20 or 18.

Cleaning the metal. Enamel will only fire clearly and evenly if the surface of the metal is completely free of grease. Clean the metal by immersing it very briefly in a "pickle" solution ("brightening dip"). This solution can be bought ready mixed and is usually made up of 10% nitric acid, 65% sulphuric acid and 25% water.

Do not mix your own solutions until you have gained some experience of using acids. Commercially prepared pickle solutions vary in strength but are generally safer to use. Always follow the manufacturer's instructions carefully.

Warning: acid should always be used with extreme care as contact with eyes and skin and inhalation of fumes is highly dangerous. It is advisable to wear protective clothing, such as a canvas apron, and goggles. Always add acid to water to avoid splashing, *never* vice versa.

Remove the piece from the pickle solution with metal tongs and wash it under running water to remove acidic residue. Avoid touching the surface that is to be enameled with the fingers. Finally, scrub the piece with a fine wire brush or steel wool and dry with a cloth.

You can also clean metal by soaking it for about half an hour in a solution of 0.5 liter (1 pint) of vinegar with 2 tablespoons of

Enamel and enamelwork techniques

table salt. Remove the piece, then brush with steel wool and pumice powder.

Cleaning copper after firing. When copper is fired an oxidized layer (known as "fire-scale") forms, which darkens and flakes off during cooling and re-firing. As a result, specks may become embedded in the enameled surface. After each firing, therefore, all fire-scale should be cleaned from the exposed parts of the metal. To do this, allow the piece to cool, then immerse it into a pickle solution of 2 parts sulphuric acid to 8 parts water for about 15 minutes. **Warning:** never put a hot piece into acid as this will cause splashing, which is highly dangerous, and will also cause the piece to warp.

Remove the piece from the pickle solution with tongs, brush well with a stiff bristle brush under running water and dry with a cloth.

The enamel

Enamelers refer to a finished piece as "an enamel" and also use "the enamel" to mean the actual glass used to coat the metal. The enamel (glass) is manufactured to fuse easily onto metal, and colors are produced by the addition of different metallic oxides. Enamel is made in slabs and has to be reduced to fine powder to be used. It can be bought crushed into chunks (called "frit") or ready milled to powder. Grind enamel chunks to the required fineness in a porcelain mortar. Cover the enamel with water and pound with a pestle. Transparent enamels give a stronger color when coarser grains are used.

In powder form, the enamel is spread onto a metal base and when fired the grains melt into a glassy coating which fuses permanently to the metal. The thinner the layer of enamel the better, but if put on too sparsely, bare patches will be left after firing, as the grains shrink a little.

A piece is fired several times before the design is complete. Some colors improve after several firings, but others may burn out or shrink from the edges.

Counterenamel. To reduce the tensions due to expansion and contraction of metal and glass, the underside of the metal is also covered with enamel: this is known as the counterenamel.

Types of enamel

Enamel colors vary widely according to the type of chemicals and processes used by different manufacturers. It is always advisable to experiment at first by firing each color on a test piece in order to discover what the final effect will be.

Transparent enamel. This allows light to pass through when fired, so that underlying colors and patterns in the metal show through. Transparent colors are improved by washing the powdered enamel. Place the enamel in a dish and cover with water. Stir and then pour off the resulting cloudy precipitate until the water remains clear. On copper, transparent enamels are usually fired over a layer of clear flux for greater translucence. Flux is the clear enamel-glass base to which metal oxides are later added. It can be used alone under other colors.

Opaque enamel. This gives a brilliant dense colored coating.

Opalescent enamel. This type of enamel produces a milky opal-like effect.

Painting enamel. For really delicate work, the most suitable material is painting enamel, which is ground to a very fine powder.

Enamelwork techniques

Certain techniques are for the professional craftsman only and other methods will give greater rewards after practice, but it is possible to obtain pleasing and artistic results right from the beginning.

When using enamel on metal, two elements with different physical properties have to be maintained in balance and it is important therefore to follow certain rules and routines. The inherent nature of the enamel glass will partly decide the choice of design and colors. The actual firing process is very exciting – as the materials re-arrange themselves under the intense heat, they take on an ordered beauty which is beyond direct control.

Basically, enameling can be divided into traditional and modern techniques.

Traditional techniques

Champlevé. The design is engraved into metal and the channeled areas infilled with enamel to the level of the metal.

Basse-taille. A low relief design is chased

Enamelwork is ideal for all kinds of jewelry, but pendants and lockets have always been especially favored. The blue pendant on the left could easily be tackled by a beginner.

or engraved into metal and the surface is covered with transparent enamel so that the underlying design shows through.

Cloisonné. Thin strips of metal known as "cloisons" are soldered onto a metal base and the cells formed are filled with colored enamel.

Plique-à-jour. The design is built up as for cloisonné but the wires are soldered to each other without a base, and transparent enamels are used to create a "stained glass window" effect.

Grisaille. Enamel is used in successive coats on a dark ground to create a relief effect.

En résille. The design is engraved into glass or crystal, then inlaid with gold and enamel.

Limoges. The enamel is very finely ground and is used for paintings.

Modern techniques

Some of the following techniques are adapted from traditional methods, while others have evolved with the development of modern materials and equipment.

Champlevé. The design is engraved, acid-etched or die-stamped into the metal and the channeled areas are filled with enamel. A champlevé effect can also be achieved by cutting the design into a thin metal sheet, soldering or embedding it onto the base-plate, and filling the cut-away areas with enamel.

Applying the enamel
Drying and firing

Cloisonné. Flattened wire is bent to the design and hard-soldered onto the metal base. Alternatively, the wires can be embedded into a layer of enamel flux. The cells formed by the cloisons are filled with colored enamel.

Dry sifting or dusting. Dry powdered enamel is dusted evenly over and fired onto the metal. The design is developed in subsequent firings.

Stencil or template. A silhouette design is made by first coating the metal base with a layer of enamel, then dusting over the stencil with a contrasting color.

Sgraffito. A prepared enameled surface is coated with binder and a contrasting color of enamel sifted over. A design is scratched through to the underlying enamel surface and fired.

Scrolling or swirling. Small lumps of enamel are fired to melting point on a prepared enameled surface and the viscid enamel lumps drawn into a "scroll" design with a steel point.

Crackle enamel. Very finely ground enamel is brushed onto a prepared surface giving a crazed pattern when fired.

Decorative effects. Different designs and textures can be produced by using transfers, enamel threads, beads or other decorations. They are used on prepared enameled surfaces.

Foils. Gold or silver foils are very thin sheets of metal, handled between layers of paper to prevent damage, which are cut to shape ("paillons") and used under transparent colors on the enamel surface.

Lusters. Lusters are painted onto an enamel surface before the last firing to add highlights.

Applying the enamel

For champlevé and cloisonné work use wet powdered enamel. Place the enamel in a mortar or dish and cover with water. Pour off excess water and support the dish in a tilted position so that some of the powder is just above the water line and is not too wet or too dry. Work the enamel into the channels in the metal or cloisons, taking a little at a time from the mortar or dish with a pointed quill, palette knife or spatula. For a flush surface, fill in to just above the level of the cloisons or metal to allow for shrinkage. Place in the kiln on a flat mesh tray support for the first firing, then allow the piece to cool. Clean as described earlier. Add more enamel to level off the surface and fire the piece again. Remove the piece and allow to cool. Rub down the piece with carborundum and water until the surface is level. Brush with a stiff brush and water to remove carborundum particles and re-fire to achieve a glossy finish. Powdered enamel can also be used dry. Coat the piece evenly with a binder and place on a sheet of paper. Partly fill a fine-mesh sifter with dry enamel powder and hold it over the piece, gently tapping the sifter until the surface is covered with a thin even layer of enamel. Avoid leaving bare or sparse patches as the grains will shrink when fusing. As the binder will tend to dry more quickly at the edges of the piece, work from the outside in towards the center. When the piece is covered, lift it gently with a spatula onto a support.

Drying

Whichever method of enameling you use, a piece must be completely dry before it is put into the kiln. Moisture from water, binder or luster will bubble and spoil the surface during firing. Always test by holding the piece on a support in front of an open kiln for a moment. Rising steam indicates that moisture is still present.

Firing

It is important that the piece is held firmly and in a level position during firing. When only one side of a piece is to be enameled, use a flat mesh tray support. If you are enameling both sides of a piece use the tray as a base for a stilt support. Set the kiln to reach the correct firing temperature before putting in the piece. A temperature of 850°–950°C (1562°–1742°F) is required for large pieces and transparent colors and 800°–900°C (1472°–1652°F) for smaller thinner pieces and red and orange colors. Firing times vary from under one minute to two or three minutes depending on the size of the kiln and the thickness of metal being used.

When the piece reaches the red-hot stage, the grains will have fused into the required smooth glossy surface. It is im-portant to watch the progress of firing in order to judge precisely the right moment to remove the piece. You will only acquire the necessary skill and judgment with practice and experience, but the following hints and remedies should be noted.

Under-firing. If the surface of the piece is not quite smooth then it has probably been under-fired. Either re-insert it immediately before fire-scale forms or allow it to cool, then clean as described earlier, touch up with fresh enamel and re-fire.

Uneven surfaces. A combination of some smooth areas and bare rough patches is an indication that the enamel was unevenly applied. Allow the piece to cool, clean it thoroughly, apply a fresh layer of enamel and re-fire.

Bubbles. Tiny bubbles due to trapped air will disappear with subsequent firings. If the bubbles are large, burst them and fill in with enamel before re-firing.

Over-firing. Over-firing, unfortunately, damages the enamel and cannot easily be remedied. The signs of over-firing are blackened edges and burning-out of some colors, especially red. If the piece is not too badly over-fired, rub down with carborundum and clean. Apply fresh enamel, then re-fire.

Pendants

These attractive pendants can be made in two different ways—either by using a stencil or by following the standard

just under a minute. At this stage the piece will be bright red.

Open the kiln door to check that the enamel layer is completely fused and if so, remove the piece on its support with the tongs and place on a fire-proof surface.

Counterenameling. When the piece is cool, clean it and then apply the blue counter-enamel to the reverse side of the pendant. Support the pendant, bottom side up, on a trivet so that only the edges of the piece are touching it and place on a flat mesh tray support. Allow it to dry, then fire. Remove the piece and allow it to cool, then clean the edges of the pendant and brush the top surface with binder.

Applying the stencil. Place the stencil in position, making sure it lies smooth and flat. Sift opaque red enamel onto the area not covered by the stencil, but overlapping it at the edges. Allow a few moments for the binder to dry a little, then lift off the stencil by pulling it up vertically by the tape tag. Remove any stray specks of enamel with a fine brush. Support the pendant right side up on a trivet and when it is completely dry, give the piece a final firing, taking care to set the piece down in the kiln without jarring.

Finishing. Remove the piece and finish when cool by cleaning the edges with a fine carborundum stone and fine steel wool.

Second method: Champlevé

Making the design. Clean and dry the copper pendant and inscribe the design with a point and then engrave it to a depth and width of approximately 1.5mm ($\frac{1}{16}$in). Clean the pendant and dry it.

Applying the enamel. Put the blue enamel powder into a dish and cover with water. Pour off excess water, then support the dish in a tilted position. With the enamel moist but not too wet, take up a little enamel at a time on a small palette knife or spatula and work it into the engraved channel, using a fine brush or point. Fill in to just above the level of the copper surface. Allow the pendant to dry, place it on a flat mesh tray support and fire it. After cooling and cleaning, add enamel to any parts not level with the copper surface and refire the pendant.

champlevé technique. Both methods are described below.

You will need:
shaped copper pendant 6 × 3cm ($2\frac{1}{2}$ × $1\frac{1}{4}$in) or 6cm ($2\frac{1}{2}$in) in diameter, with a small hole drilled at the top □ powdered opaque blue enamel □ powdered opaque red enamel (blue only if following the second method) □ binder □ tweezers and paper for stencil or sharpened quill or point for champlevé design.

First method: using a stencil

Cutting the stencil. Draw the design and cut out a stencil from paper. Attach an adhesive tape "tab" to the upper side so that the whole stencil can be lifted up later.

Preparing the base. Clean and dry the copper pendant base, then brush the top surface with binder solution. Dust the blue enamel powder over the whole surface to form a close and even but fairly thin layer. Make sure that the hole is not clogged with powder.

First firing. Lift the pendant with a small spatula and place it onto a flat mesh tray support. Check that the piece is thoroughly dry, then place the support gently on the floor of the kiln using firing tongs. Close the kiln door carefully and fire the piece for

Sifting the blue enamel.

Lifting off the stencil.

Setting the piece down in the kiln.

White and silver dish

If there are any areas that are raised above or overlapping the copper, rub these down with a carborundum stone to leave a level sharp outline. Brush out any traces of carborundum. Re-fire the pendant to give a final even surface. Clean and polish all the bare copper areas and edges, using a jeweler's buffing wheel or with tripoli or red rouge and a soft leather cloth.

White and silver dish

This dish incorporates a design that can be used for playing tic-tac-toe (noughts and crosses) with each player using colored enamel pieces. As the dish is heat-proof it can also serve as an ashtray.

You will need:
shallow copper dish, gauge 18, approximately 11cm ($4\frac{1}{4}$in) in diameter □ 9 copper disks, gauge 18 or 20, 2cm ($\frac{3}{4}$in) in diameter □ 4 narrow strips of silver foil, approximately 9.5cm ($3\frac{3}{4}$in) long and 0.5cm ($\frac{1}{4}$in) wide, tapering to a point (flattened silver wire or copper foil can be used if preferred) □ powdered white enamel for dish □ any good powdered opaque color such as royal blue for the counterenamel □ powdered opaque green and orange-red enamel for disks □ lacquer □ binder □ tweezers.

Enameling the dish. Clean and dry the copper dish and brush the inside with binder. Sift white enamel over the entire surface of the inside of the dish by rotating and tilting the dish with one hand and holding the sifter with the other hand—using one finger to tap the sifter gently. Work quickly, beginning at the rim and working towards the center, so that all the enamel is applied before the binder dries. Dry and fire the dish—white-enameled side up—supporting it on a flat mesh tray support. Take care not to over-fire or the edges will sink down.

Note: most white enamels will produce some greenish veining giving a pleasant marbled effect, as a result of contact with the copper.

Clean the fired dish and check that the surface and edges are perfect. If necessary, build up any thin patches or untidy edges and re-fire.

Turn the dish upside down, brush with binder and sift on the counterenamel.

Allow to dry, then lift carefully with a spatula and place on a flat mesh tray support, bottom side up. Fire just to fusing point (any under-firing can be corrected in later firing) and cool and clean the dish. Check that the edges are completely covered and add a little more counterenamel and re-fire if necessary.

Brush the top (white) surface of the dish with thin binder solution and, using tweezers and a brush, position the four strips of silver foil carefully to form the grid design. Smooth out any air bubbles under the foil. Support the dish on a trivet placed on a flat mesh support, bottom side down. Dry and fire the dish at not more than 940°C (1724°F) to protect the silver foil.

Enameling the disks. The disks are enameled with green and counterenameled with orange-red. Clean and dry each of the copper disks. Working on 1 or 2 disks at a time, brush with binder and sift on the green enamel. Lift them up with a spatula and place them onto a flat mesh tray support, green-enameled side up. Dry and fire. When you have covered all disks with green, clean them and counterenamel with orange-red in the same way. Support on a trivet by the edges only, orange-red side up. Dry and fire. Enamels of this color type tend to burn out if over-fired, so remove the disks from the kiln immediately on fusion. The disks may look blackened at first but as the pieces cool the true orange-red color will begin to appear.

Finishing the dish and pieces. Clean the edges of the dish and the 9 pieces with fine

Sifting the red enamel.

The piece is now ready for drying and firing.

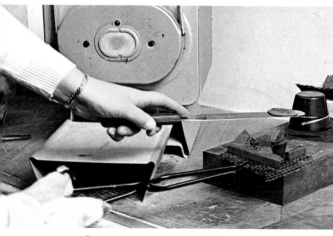
Removing the piece after firing.

Square plaque

abrasive (emery) paper or steel wool. Lacquer the silver strips to prevent them from tarnishing.

Square plaque

The cloisonné design on this plaque is very simple and can be duplicated on other pieces so that a large surface can be covered, using the squares as mosaics or tiles. Squares of 15cm (6in) are suitable for mural decoration, those of 7.5cm (3in) can be incorporated into a coffee table top, box lid or mirror frame and smaller pieces 2.5cm (1in) square will make cufflinks, earrings or brooches. Use gauge 20 metal for pieces up to 7.5cm (3in) square and gauge 18 for larger pieces

You will need:
copper square ☐ flattened copper wire ☐ flux ☐ transparent enamel in light blue, light green and light turquoise ☐ counter-enamel ☐ tweezers.

Preparing to enamel. Wash the transparent colors and the flux. The colors will be used wet, but pour excess water from the flux and allow to dry in a warm place. Clean the copper square.

Making the cloisons. Anneal the copper wire by heating to dull red in the kiln or over a flame, then plunging it into cold

water. Bend the wire to the required shape or shapes and clean.

Enameling the plaque. Sift a thin even layer of dry powdered flux onto the copper square (a little binder can be brushed on the edges but too much may cause air bubbles), then lift very carefully onto a support. Dry the piece if binder has been used, then fire in the normal way.

When cool, clean the square and apply a good coating of counterenamel to the reverse side. Support by the edges only, on a trivet and fire just to fusion point to avoid over-firing. Cool and clean the edges. Apply very thin binder solution to the top surface of the square and sift on a second very fine layer of flux to help keep the cloisons in position. Holding the cloisons with tweezers, place each one carefully in position. Allow the binder to dry, then lift the square onto a support and avoid any tilting or jarring. Support by the edges only. Put the supported piece into the kiln and watch the progress of firing. As soon as the surface melts, remove the piece from the kiln and, before it hardens, gently press the flat side of a spatula onto any wires which are not well embedded in the flux. Allow to cool and clean the square.

Fill in the design with the wet colored enamel, taking it up bit by bit on the tip of a small palette knife or spatula, pressing it into the various spaces according to the pattern. Fill up to the level of the cloisons. Each color can be fired individually or the whole piece can be filled with enamel and fired in one operation. Allow to dry completely before inserting into the kiln. For transparent colors a heat of 950°C (1742°F) or a little above will give a good hot firing.

When cool, clean the piece and examine the surface. It should be smooth and level. Use a carborundum stone to grind down any raised uneven areas. Fill in any areas that have sunk with more enamel and re-fire. If there are a lot of air bubbles in the enamel, re-fire to increase the transparency.

When cool, clean the edges for the last time, and either immerse the square in pickle to clean the cloisons, or rub the exposed edges of each cloison with very fine abrasive (emery) paper.

Festive decoration

Christmas table decorations

The decoration (left) is made from plastic flowers and holly, and dried magnolia leaves sprayed with silver and gold paint from an aerosol spray. The support which holds the arrangement in place is made of chicken wire patterned into a triangular shape which is tightly packed in the middle and less densely on the outsides.

The candle holder (right) is made from dried magnolia leaves and plastic holly leaves sprayed in silver and gold. The candle, leaves and flowers are inserted into a plastic clay (plasticine) base with the leaves and flowers fully covering the base and encircling the candle.

Berry and holly cushions

The berries and holly leaves are both made from soft fabrics. About one meter (one yard) of green lining material is needed for each holly leaf. The leaf shape is drawn onto newspaper and cut out to serve as a pattern. Two leaf shapes are then cut out from the material and the veins and outer edges of one piece are top stitched in pale green cotton thread. The pieces are sewn together, with a small opening left at the base for stuffing; they are pulled the right side out, stuffed with old bits of soft materials and finally neatly oversewn at the opening. The berry is made from 0.5 square meter ($\frac{1}{2}$ square yard) of fluffed nylon. A pattern like a segment from an orange, 7.5cm (3in) at its widest point, is drawn onto newspaper and cut out. Six pieces of material are cut from this pattern and sewn together inside out, with an opening left for stuffing. The berry is pulled the right side out, stuffed with bits of material and neatly oversewn at the opening.

Halloween decorations

Here are some easy to make Halloween decorations which are sure to pacify witches, demons and eerie spirits on their commemorative day!

Witch's hat. The black witch's hat is made from a cone of heavy black paper which is glued and stapled down the back. A cir-

Traditional Christmas decorations using glass balls, ribbons and tinsel can be expensive to buy, and making your own from natural materials which wither and die within a few days is a disheartening task. Here are some ideas for table decorations that can be used over and over again, not only for each party during the Christmas season, but also for subsequent years as the materials can be packed away without damage.

Cushions in traditional holly leaf and berry shapes make unusual and colorful Christmas decorations and the berries are especially popular with children since they can be used all year round as indoor soccer balls.

Festive decoration

Halloween

cular strip of paper is glued to the inside of the base and forms the brim. Halloween symbols, painted in silver paint, complete the hat.

Lanterns. The jack-o'-lantern is made from a hollowed out pumpkin. The eyes, ears, nose and mouth are carved out and a candle placed inside. The black strip lantern is made from a cylinder of heavy black paper which is cut at regular intervals down the center to form strips. It is then glued, stapled and pushed into shape so that the light from the candle shines through the slots. The square and round lanterns are made from heavy black paper with large rectangles cut out and covered with cellophane, to serve as windows. The besom broom is made from twigs attached with twine or wire to a long stick.

Eastertime

Painted eggs. Eggs and newly hatched chicks are closely associated with the pagan rites of spring and have become a major symbol of Easter festivities. The freshness and happiness of this season can be captured successfully by decorating eggs with personal and colorful designs. Fresh eggs can either be boiled until hard, or else emptied by blowing. To do this,

pink satin ribbon is attached to the lace to cover the stitches.

The ribbon is stitched in place at the back of the hat and the loose ends are left to flow freely. Pink and mauve pom-poms and flower shapes, made from scraps of wool, feathers and fabric leaves, are combined with larger fluffy feathers and flowers made from scraps of pink satin, and sewn onto the ribbon and lace. Finally, a chick emerging from a shell — made from plastic — is glued onto the lace. A decorative trimming overstitched onto the brim completes this bonnet.

The highly colored Easter bonnet (top) is made from heavier straw weave. A band matching the color of the straw is stitched around and paper flowers supported by wire stems are stitched on until the band is fully covered.

Papier mâché hen

This paper sculpture of a hen brooding over her colorful eggs makes an unusual centerpiece for your table. The body part of the hen is made from papier mâché modeled over a balloon using the layering method (see pages 227 and 234). The extra details are made from cardboard and stuck onto the papier mâché. Then using poster paints the hen's body and wings are painted and, finally, the whole sculpture is coated with polyurethane varnish. To complete the effect, the hen is placed on some straw pulled into the shape of a nest, and surrounded by candies.

make a hole with a pin at each end of the egg. Then carefully enlarge one of the holes and blow through the smaller hole. Designs can be painted onto the eggs with felt tip pens or poster paints and coated with polyurethane varnish. Almost any surface decoration technique can be used to ornament the eggs; fabrics and wool can be used, and even pieces of string can be plaited and wound around the egg to achieve an unusual effect, as in the top right egg.

Easter bonnets. These Easter bonnets, with their gaiety and color, confirm the arrival of spring!

The bonnet (bottom) is made from a fine straw weave which blends with a soft color combination. A piece of delicate lace is sewn around the hat and a length of dark

Toymaking

Basically the same kinds of toys have served as playthings for thousands of years. Balls, marbles and tops, rattles and whistles, pull-along toys, dolls, puppets and miniature animals and kites — all have remained popular with children throughout the centuries.

The ball, probably the very earliest form of toy, was originally made of stone. With time, balls of leather stuffed with papyrus, straw or hair were also widely made for children. Early 16th-century tennis balls were made from white goatskin stuffed with hair. And much later, of course, the now universal rubber ball bounced its way into popularity. Early forms of marbles were just simple smooth round pebbles to begin with, but later were fashioned from agate and other attractive materials until the 18th century, when marble was actually used and a new name was coined.

Rattles, meanwhile, have been used for a variety of purposes: to frighten away evil spirits, as simple percussion instruments or merely to keep infants amused. They have ranged from those made of wood with seeds or beads inside, to the elaborate gold and silver rattles made for the children of the aristocracy during Renaissance times. No toy collection would be complete without a doll or a cuddly animal and these too have always been firm favorites. One relatively recent innovation, however, is the much-loved teddy bear, which has its origins in the United States. Named after President Theodore Roosevelt, the first "teddy" was manufactured soon after it was reported that the President had refused to shoot a bear cub while hunting.

Given the wide range of toys now available, choosing something suitable for a child can be difficult, especially if the aim is to provide an opportunity for truly creative play. Building blocks, hoops and hobby horses, boats and windmills, trains, planes and spacecraft can all be made at home, even those with clockwork mechanisms of a simple kind. And often it is the specially created and individual plaything that gives lasting pleasure, rather than the more expensive mass-produced item.

Soft toys

Soft toys are always loved by young child-

Bruegel's *Children's Games* presents a fascinating if somewhat riotous picture of toys in use during the 16th century.

ren. They are easy to make and many suitable materials, such as velvet, corduroy, tweed and upholstery fabrics can be bought cheaply as remnants. The important points to remember are that the material must be able to withstand a good deal of wear and tear, and at the same time be pleasant to touch. Very fine fabrics are unsuitable as the texture of the stuffing will show through. It is also advisable to use washable material and stuffing when making soft toys for very young children.

Felt is a very useful material as the edges do not fray and can simply be overcast or blanketstitched together.

Fake fur fabrics, many of which are washable, make the most realistic animal toys. Cut the material so that the pile lies in the same direction on each piece, otherwise the small animals will not "stroke" properly

when finished. Ordinary pins are easily lost in the pile of the fabric and could mistakenly be left in a toy, so use pins with colored plastic heads. Never press or steam fur fabric.

Kapok, foam rubber and synthetic batting are the most common types of stuffing for cuddly toys. Fine wood shavings and sawdust are usually used for more solid toys. You can make your own stuffing materials by using old panty hose or knitted garments, washed and cut into small pieces or unraveled. Discard any elastic or other parts likely to make the stuffing lumpy. For economy, these homemade stuffings can be mixed with bought ones.

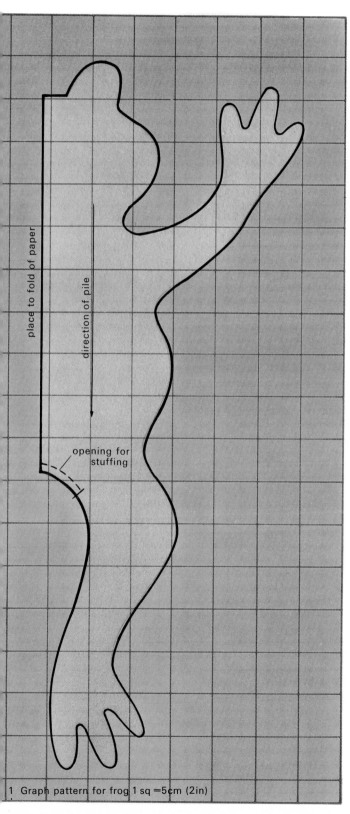

1 Graph pattern for frog 1 sq =5cm (2in)

Labels on pattern: place to fold of paper · direction of pile · opening for stuffing

Freddie the frog

This brightly colored and very huggable frog is particularly easy to make as the pattern is made up of two pieces only. Fake fur fabric in two colors has been used but it could be made just as successfully in felt.

You will need:

1 yellow and 1 green piece of fake fur fabric, each measuring 85 × 65cm (33½ × 25½in) with the pile running down the length of the fabric □ scraps of black, white and red felt for features □ matching cotton thread □ stuffing □ paper for the pattern.

Cutting out the pattern. Draw the pattern from the graph (fig.1) in which 1 square equals 5cm (2in) and cut out. Lay out 1 piece of the fake fur fabric, wrong side up, and lay the pattern on it, checking that the pile lies in the direction indicated by the arrow on the graph. Chalk or mark with a ballpoint pen around the edge of the pattern. Cut out the frog shape 2cm (¾in) outside the marked line to allow for turnings. Repeat with the second piece of fabric.

Making the frog. Place the frog shapes, right sides together, and pin at right angles to the cut edge. Stitch all around the frog, leaving an opening as indicated on the graph for the stuffing to be inserted. Snip and trim the seam allowance carefully

Freddie the frog
For all ages

around all the curves, particularly between the "toes" and "fingers." Turn the frog right side out. Ease out any fake fur caught in the seams with a pin or by brushing gently.

Cut out the eye and mouth shapes from the felt and stitch to the face of the frog. Before stuffing a fur fabric toy, it is advisable to baste a piece of thin material around the opening in order to protect the fur pile when the stuffing is inserted.

Stuff the frog, starting with the fingers, toes, arms and legs, then the head and lastly the body. Insert small amounts of stuffing at a time to prevent lumps from developing. Stitch up the opening. Add a ribbon or felt bow tie.

If you make the frog from felt, seam allowances are not necessary. Place wrong sides together and stitch all around the outside of the frog 3mm ($\frac{1}{8}$in) from the cut edge.

For all ages

This dachshund will become a friend of all the family. It can also be used as a bolster cushion as well as a toy. The body is made of fake fur fabric and the soles of the feet and the inner ears are in narrow wale corduroy (needlecord). Other fabrics such as velvet, tweed or printed upholstery fabric would work equally well. The dog is 130cm (51in) long and 45cm (18in) high. A smaller dog could be made by drawing the pattern to half size.

You will need:
2m (2yd) fake fur fabric, 140cm (54in) wide □ 30cm (12in) narrow wale corduroy (needlecord), 90cm (36in) wide □ 2 glass or plastic eyes □ black felt for nose □ matching cotton thread □ stuffing □ paper for pattern.

Cutting out the pattern. Draw all the pattern pieces from the graph (fig.2) in which 1 square equals 10cm (4in), and cut out.
Note: make sure you have a pattern piece for each side of the body and underbody, *not* 2 body pieces for the same side or 2 underbodies for the same side.

Lay the fake fur fabric, wrong side up, on a table and place all the pattern pieces (except the soles of the feet and 2 inner ears) onto the fabric, checking that the pile is running in the direction indicated on the graph. Mark carefully around the pattern with chalk or ballpoint pen, marking the points for the openings for stuffing. Cut out, leaving 2cm ($\frac{3}{4}$in) for turnings. Cut out the 2 inner ears and the soles from the corduroy in the same way.

Making the dog. Place the underbody pieces onto the body pieces, right sides together, C to C and D to D. Stitch around the bottom edge of the dog, leaving the feet open for the soles. Sew these in next. Now join the forehead to one of the body pieces, placing A to A and B to B. Stitch along this seam.

Next, join the body pieces together. Placing right sides together, start by joining C to C and D to D, and match up the A and B positions. Stitch around the upper dog shape from C to D. Finally, sew the under-

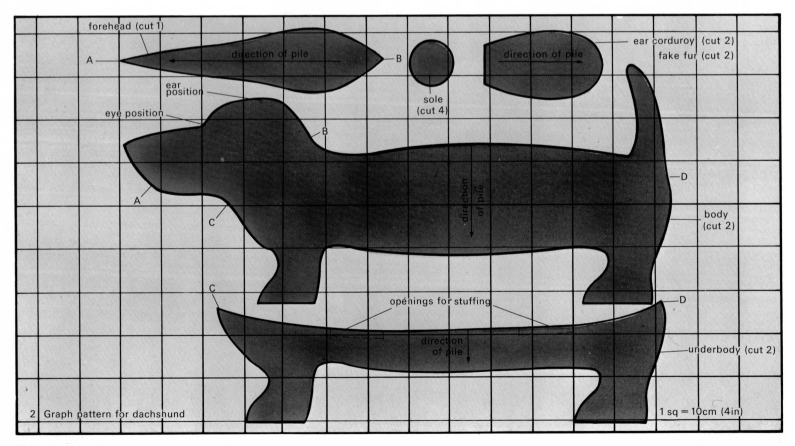

2 | Graph pattern for dachshund   1 sq = 10cm (4in)

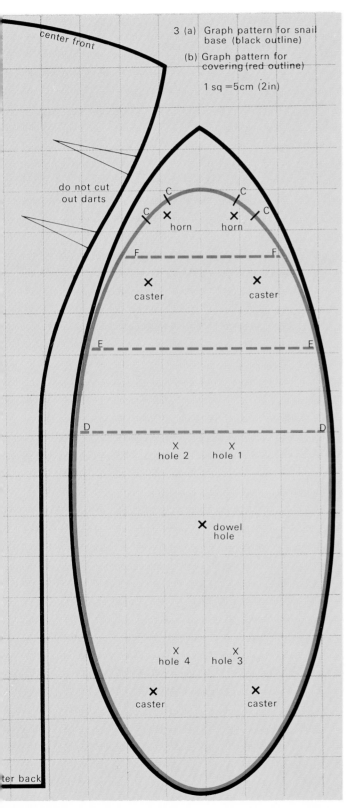

3 (a) Graph pattern for snail base (black outline)

(b) Graph pattern for covering (red outline)

1 sq = 5cm (2in)

center front

do not cut out darts

C C
C X X C
horn horn

F F

X X
caster caster

E E

D D

X X
hole 2 hole 1

X dowel hole

X X
hole 4 hole 3

X X
caster caster

ter back

body pieces together, leaving the 2 openings for stuffing as marked. (Only one opening is needed if you are making a smaller dog.)

Snip and trim the seam allowance carefully around all the curves. Turn the dog right side out. Ease out any fake fur caught in the seams. Fix the eyes in position. Now stuff the dog, starting with its tail and paws, then the head and front. Sew up the front stuffing opening, and finish stuffing the rear end of the dog. Sew up the rear stuffing opening.

Make the ears, each from 1 fake fur and 1 corduroy shape. Place right sides together and sew together, leaving the top edge open. Turn right side out. Turn in the top edge and stitch. Gather or pleat the ear so that the top edge measures 8cm (3¼in) across. Sew in position. Sew on a felt nose or embroider one in black yarn.

Finally, make a collar of felt, ribbon or scraps of leather.

Speedy snail

This sturdy toy can accommodate two children at a time, one on top of the shell and another behind the horns.

You will need:

piece of 16mm (⅝in) plywood, 82 × 33cm (32½ × 13in) □ piece of 2cm (¾in) dowel, 1m (39in) long and cut into 2 pieces 36cm (14in) long for horns and 1 piece 28cm (11in) long for shell support □ 2 wooden balls 4cm (1½in) in diameter □ 4 casters □ 1m (1yd) red cotton fabric, 90cm (36in) wide □ 1.75m (1¾yd) dotted cotton fabric, 90cm (36in) wide □ 1.10m (1⅓yd) narrow red upholstery braid □ 1.75m (1¾yd) synthetic foam, 5cm (2in) thick □ 1kg (2lb) kapok or similar stuffing □ scraps of black, red and white felt □ fine string □ toymaker's needle or large carpet needle □ dressmaking shears □ all-purpose adhesive □ woodworking glue □ strong thread □ tacks □ upholstery tacks □ sturdy paper for pattern □ paint: undercoat and top coat (any color for the underside of the base and white and black enamel for the horns.)

Making the snail base. Following the graph (fig.3a) in which 1 square equals 5cm (2in), draw up the pattern for the base onto sturdy paper, marking in the points for drilling as shown. Place the pattern onto

the plywood, draw around and saw around the shape. Drill 4 holes large enough to take the toymaker's needle and 1 hole for the shell support dowel where indicated. Drill 2 holes to take the dowels for the horns; angle the drill so that the horns will slope outwards.

Note: the side on which you have just been working becomes the upper side of the base.

Turn the base over and mark on the positions for the casters. Paint this side with an undercoat and a top coat. When the paint is dry, screw in the casters.

Making the body covering. Draw up patterns for the body covering from the graphs (fig.3b and 4) in which 1 square equals 5cm (2in). Ignore the dotted lines D, E and F for the moment but mark in the 4 points C on either side of the front. Cut pattern 3b in red cotton fabric, adding 1.5cm (½in) seam allowances. Cut 2 pieces from pattern 4 in red cotton fabric, one for the left-hand side and the other for the right-hand side of the body, adding 1.5cm (½in) seam allowances. Mark in the darts but do not cut them out.

Join the center back and front seams of the 2 pieces from pattern 4 and stitch darts in the sides where marked. Fold in 1.5cm (½in) on the long straight sides, and press the folds and all seams. Matching the center back and front on the piece from pattern 3b to the seams on the pieces from pattern 4, pin and baste, leaving points C to C open at each side of the front to enclose the horns later. Clip into the curves on the seam allowances and press these seams open.

Foam padding. The foam padding is built up in 4 stepped layers (fig.5). Mark the dotted lines D, E and F onto pattern 3b. Place the pattern on the foam and mark around it using a felt tip pen. This will be the base layer of foam. Cut out with dressmaking shears. Cut across the paper pattern along line D to D. Take the smaller front part of the pattern and cut a piece of foam to size. Cut out pieces E to E and F to F in the same way. Using all-purpose adhesive, glue the pieces one on top of the other as shown in fig.5. Snip off the edge of each layer to taper. Apply glue to the upper surface of the plywood base and stick down the stacked

Speedy snail

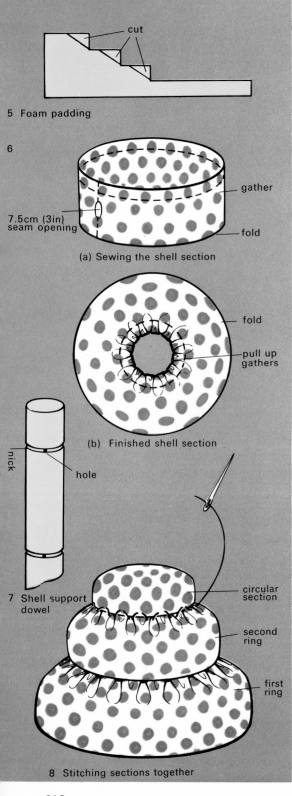

5 Foam padding

6

gather

7.5cm (3in)
seam opening

fold

(a) Sewing the shell section

fold

pull up
gathers

(b) Finished shell section

nick

hole

7 Shell support
dowel

circular
section

second
ring

first
ring

8 Stitching sections together

foam padding. Cut a slit in the foam padding with the point of the scissors to allow for the dowel for the shell support and also in the front for the 2 horns. (The foam will spring back around any inaccurate cutting.)

Fitting the dowels. Drill 2 holes through the shell support dowel, the first hole 4cm (1½in) from the top and the other 15cm (6in) from the top. With the underside of the base facing you, apply woodworking glue around the drilled holes. Turn the base right side up and insert the dowels. Paint the horns with white undercoat and top coat.

Finishing the body covering. Cut 2 slits crosswise in the body covering to fit over the shell support dowel and lower it onto the foam padding, at the same time pushing the horns through the openings allowed at the front. If the edges of the foam need to be evened out, pad with scraps. Hammer tacks at intervals to hold the folded edge of the body covering to the edge of the base. Fasten the braid around the edge with upholstery tacks. Close any excess opening around the horns with overcasting.

Drill holes in the 2 wooden balls, paint them with undercoat and black enamel and glue them on top of the horns.

Making the features. Cut 2 large oval eyes from white felt and 2 smaller ovals from black felt for the pupils. Sew the pupils to the eyes. Cut 2 red eyelids and overcast them to the eyes, inserting some padding underneath. Sew the eyes in place and add black felt curves to emphasize the upper shape of the lids. Sew on a curved strip of black felt for the mouth.

Making the shell. Cut 2 pieces of red dotted cotton fabric, one measuring 45 × 114cm (18 × 45in) and the other measuring 45 × 90cm (18 × 36in). From the remainder of the red dotted fabric cut out 2 circles, each measuring 25cm (10in) in diameter. (You can use a plate for a good circle shape.)

Working with the longest straight piece, join the 2 shorter sides together, right sides together, and leaving a 7.5cm (3in) opening at the center of the seam. Press and turn the work. With the wrong sides together, fold the work in half lengthwise and stitch

along the raw edges with a 1.5cm (½in) seam allowance. With strong thread used double, run a gathering thread close to the last line of stitching (fig.6a). Pull up the gathering threads as firmly as possible (fig.6b), tie securely and trim the ends. Repeat the procedure with the second straight piece of material.

With right sides together, sew around the edge of the 2 circular pieces to within 1.5cm (½in) and leave a 7.5cm (3in) opening in the seam. Press and turn the work. Stuff all 3 sections of the shell with kapok, making sure the padding is firmly compressed. Close the openings with overcasting stitches.

Assembling the shell. With a sharp knife, cut nicks in the shell support dowel on each side of the drilled holes as shown in fig.7. Put the larger ring over the dowel. Thread the toymaker s needle with string and attach the ring firmly by passing the needle several times through the bottom hole drilled in the dowel. Wind the string around the nicks in the dowel and tie securely to finish. Attach the second ring in the same way.

Place the circular section on top of the second ring and sew them together with fine string. Take a large stitch through the underside of the circular section and one near it through the top of the second ring where the two touch (fig.8). Continue working all the way around in this way. Pull the string up firmly and tie and trim the ends to finish off. (The first and second rings can be made more secure by stitching them in the same way.)

Attaching the shell to the base. Thread the toymaker's needle with a length of string and, working from the underside of the base, push the needle through hole 1 of the 4 small holes. Leave a length of string hanging below the base. Bring the needle up through the body and take a stitch through the under part of the first ring of the shell. Withdraw the needle and rethread it onto the free end of the string. Bring the needle up through hole 2 and make a stitch in the first ring as before. Tie the ends of the string under the first ring very securely and trim. Repeat the procedure through holes 1 and 2, then secure the shell through holes 3 and 4 in the same way.

Dolls

Most societies, it seems, have produced dolls or models of the human form in miniature, either as play things or as objects imbued with sacred or symbolic significance. Some of the oldest surviving dolls have been found in Ancient Egyptian tombs, dating from around 2000 BC, and were made of carved wood with strings of clay or wooden beads for hair.

All kinds of materials were used, including wood, terracotta, alabaster, ivory and bone, and dolls of wool or leather with straw or sawdust stuffings have also been found.

The first "fashion dolls" appeared in Europe in the late 14th century. Many of these were made as models to show off the new styles of dress and this practice continued until well into the 19th century. Dollmakers

An assortment of miniature articles fill the stall of this mid-19th century English pedlar doll who stands 24cm (9½in) high.

Egyptian painted wooden doll found at Thebes, dating back to the Middle Kingdom. The doll's hair is made of clay beads.

then began to experiment with different materials and techniques to create dolls with wax, papier mâché or fine porcelain heads, topped with wigs of real hair, and dressed in the elaborate and splendid silks, satins and laces of the day. This period too, with its fascination for clockwork and mechanical toys, was responsible for introducing dolls which could walk, open and close their eyes and utter cries or sounds to represent speech.

By the beginning of the 20th century rub-

more complicated. Legs and arms are made separately and then attached to the body. Seams running down the front and back of the legs allow more shaping, and foot gussets enable the doll to stand. For a more realistic effect, lines of running stitch can be worked down the hands to represent fingers.

The head can be cut in one with the body or made separately, and hair is usually yarn, which should be stitched very securely to the head. Faces can be drawn on using non-toxic crayons or felt tip pens, or the features can be appliquéd or embroidered. (Buttons or eyes that can easily be pulled off should never be used on a doll intended for a very young child.) It is possible to buy ready-made plastic faces to stitch onto the head. The join can be disguised by stitching the hair over it.

If you wish to make a doll that can be moved into different positions, you will need to use a wire frame. Bind the frame tightly with rags so that no sharp edges protrude.

Large as life
This life-size rag doll is made from two main pieces and makes a perfect playmate for any child. The doll measures 152cm (60in) from top to toe and will wear your children's outgrown clothes quite happily.

You will need:
3.5m (3½yd) flesh-colored closely woven cotton fabric, 90cm (36in) wide □ matching sewing thread □ approximately 1.5kg (3lb) kapok or other stuffing □ 45.5cm (18in) length of dowel (optional) □ 300g (11oz) yarn for hair □ non-toxic felt tip pens □ cardboard.

Cutting out the pattern. Draw the pattern from the graph (fig.1) in which 1 square equals 12.5cm (5in) and cut out. Note that 1.5cm (½in) seam allowances are included.

Making the doll. Fold the fabric in half across its width and pin the pattern in place with the straight edge on the fold. Cut out 1 pattern piece and mark the gathers in the feet. This will be the back body piece. Remove the pattern and pin it to the remaining half of folded material, again with the straight edge on the fold. This time, mark the darts in the feet, and cut off at the dot-

ber dolls were quite common, and then molded plastic and other synthetic materials were used for the now familiar baby dolls and glamour dolls.

Rag dolls
The simplest type of rag doll is made from two pieces of fabric for the back and front and stitched together all round. The curved seams are clipped and the doll is turned right side out and stuffed. "Joints" are made by stitching across the tops of the legs and arms. A reversible doll can also be made in a similar way. The doll has two heads, each with a different facial expression, and two body tops joined at the waist. A reversible long skirt hides the underneath head when the doll is turned upside down.

Dolls made from several pattern pieces are

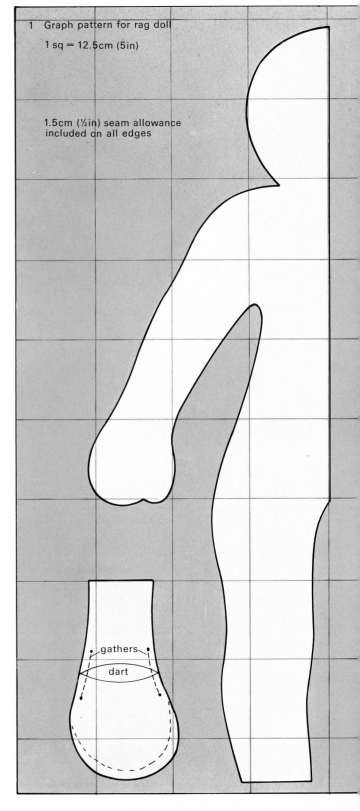

1 Graph pattern for rag doll

1 sq = 12.5cm (5in)

1.5cm (½in) seam allowance included on all edges

gathers

dart

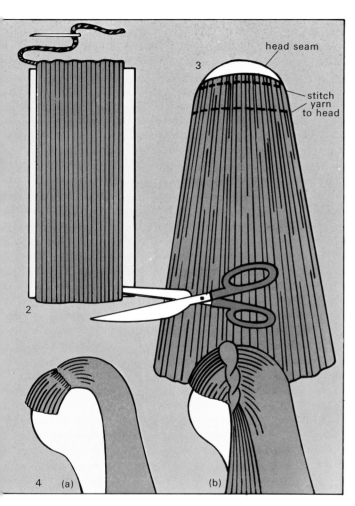

Stitching the joints. When you reach the thigh level, stitch across the top of the leg with small running stitches to stop the stuffing from escaping and to make a leg joint. Do exactly the same with the other leg and the arms. For extra support insert a dowel into the body and up through the neck to the head. Finally, stuff the head and body firmly and stitch up the side opening. Make a row of gathers around the neck to pull it up slightly.

Attaching the hair. Cut a piece of cardboard about 61cm (24in) long and 25cm (10in) wide. Wind all but 2 balls of yarn around the *length* of the cardboard. Work back-stitch along the top edge of the cardboard to secure the loops together, but do not stitch through the cardboard. Cut along the bottom edge as shown in fig.2.
Position the hair across the back of the head, just below the head seam. Stitch it firmly in place using matching yarn (fig.3). For the bangs (fringe) wind all but half a ball of the remaining yarn around the *width* of a piece of cardboard 10cm (4in) wide and 25cm (10in) long. Stitch and cut as before. Place the bangs across the front of the head so they overlap the hair join (fig.4a). Stitch the bangs in position. Make a 25cm (10in) braid with the remaining yarn, leaving a tassel at both ends of equal length. Stitch the braid over the hair and bangs join (fig.4b).
Draw the features onto the face and color them in using non-toxic felt tip pens.

Victoria

In complete contrast, here is an exquisitely detailed yet relatively easy to make Victorian-style rag doll. She has her own set of clothes and is 51cm (20in) high.
You will need:
0.5m (½yd) cream cotton fabric (lawn) □ 0.25m (¼yd) white cotton fabric (lawn) □ 1m (1yd) flower print cotton □ 0.25m (¼yd) white eyelet embroidery (Broderie Anglaise) □ 1m (1yd) pink velvet ribbon, 0.5cm (¼in) wide □ 0.75m (¾yd) pink velvet ribbon, 1.5cm (½in) wide □ 0.5m (½yd) brown velvet ribbon, 1cm (⅜in) wide □ 0.5m (½yd) cotton lace, 1cm (⅜in) wide □ 1.25m (1¼yd) white cotton lace, 1.5cm (½in) wide □ 2 hanks fine brown string or cord (candlewick cotton) for hair □ 66cm (26in) pink satin ribbon, 0.5cm (¼in) wide □ matching sewing thread □ pink, dark blue, black and cream stranded embroidery floss (embroidery cotton) □ small pieces of black leather □ 1 gray and 1 white pearl button □ kapok or other suitable stuffing □ paper for patterns □ long metal knitting needle □ fabric adhesive.

Cutting out the pattern. Draw the pattern pieces for the doll from the graph (fig.5) in which 1 square equals 2.5cm (1in) and cut out each separate piece. Place the cream cotton on a flat surface and arrange each section along the grain of the fabric as indicated. A seam allowance of 0.5cm (¼in) is included on all pieces.
Note: where 2 or 4 sections are to be cut, fold the fabric right sides together and cut as one. Trace around each piece with a sharp pencil and mark the darts with small dots. Cut out all pieces.

ted line. This will be the front body piece. Baste both foot darts on the front body piece and make the gathers on the back body piece between the lines indicated. With right sides together, baste the 2 pieces of the doll around the edge, leaving a 1.5cm (½in) seam allowance. Make sure that the dart falls in the center of the gathers on each foot. Using a small machine stitch, stitch carefully around the doll, leaving an opening in one side at waist level for stuffing.
Clip into the seam allowances all around the curved edges. If the seam is not clipped enough, you will find that the pieces become "square" and misshapen when stuffed. Turn the doll right side out. Starting with the feet, push the stuffing, small handfuls at a time, into the feet and continue to work up the legs.

Toymaking
Dolls

Victoria

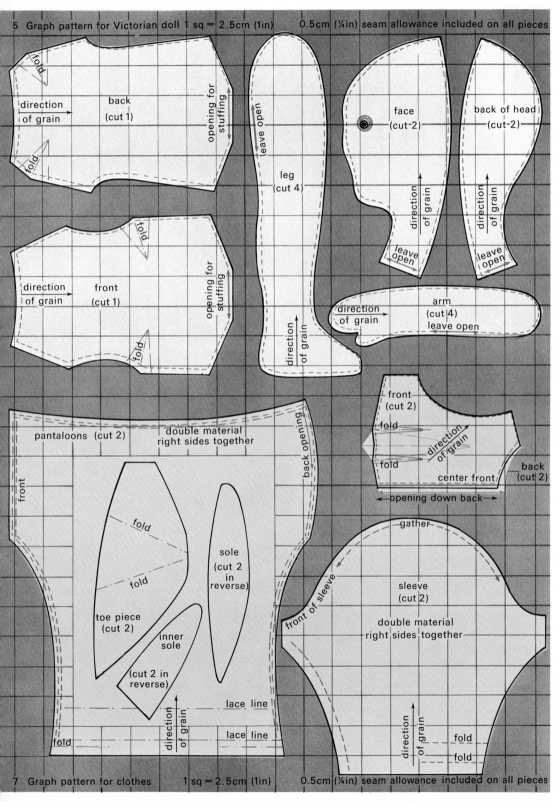

5 Graph pattern for Victorian doll 1 sq = 2.5cm (1in)   0.5cm (¼in) seam allowance included on all pieces

direction of grain | back (cut 1) | opening for stuffing

leave open

face (cut-2)

back of head (cut-2)

leg (cut 4)

direction of grain

direction of grain

leave open | leave open

direction of grain | front (cut 1) | opening for stuffing

direction of grain

arm (cut 4) leave open

pantaloons (cut 2) | double material right sides together

back opening

front (cut 2) | fold | direction of grain | fold | center front | back (cut 2)

opening down back

front

fold | fold | sole (cut 2 in reverse)

toe piece (cut 2)

inner sole

(cut 2 in reverse)

gather

front of sleeve

sleeve (cut 2)

double material right sides together

lace line | lace line | direction of grain

fold | direction of grain | fold | fold

7 Graph pattern for clothes   1 sq = 2.5cm (1in)   0.5cm (¼in) seam allowance included on all pieces

Making the doll. Stitch both darts on the front and back pieces of the body and press each one downwards. Put right sides of the body together and stitch around, leaving an opening for stuffing where indicated at the neck. Turn inside out.

With right sides together, stitch around each of the limbs in the same way. Clip curves and turn inside out. Join the 2 face pieces of the head together, paying particular attention to shaping a good profile. Sew the 2 back pieces of the head together. Stitch the seam, joining the front to the back, in one continuous movement. Press the seams open, clip curves and turn inside out.

Fill each separate piece firmly with stuffing. Use only small teased-out pieces and push into shape with the knitting needle. Fill the arms and legs and overcast the openings together. Fill the head and about 2.5cm (1in) of the neck very firmly. Sew across the bottom and trim. Insert the neck into the top of the body and slipstitch firmly in place.

Attaching the limbs. Thread a long needle with 6 strands of cream embroidery floss and take it through the base of the body, return, pull tight and knot. This forms the sockets for the legs. Attach the legs at either side by passing the needle through the leg, body and far leg and returning it. Insert the return needle the length of a small stitch away, pull tight and knot. Attach the arms by sewing each one to the outside shoulder seam. With 6 strands of cream embroidery floss make a small stitch in the upper arm about 1.5cm (½in) from the top. Take the needle through to the shoulder, return and knot.

Attaching the hair. Using the flat surface of an ironing board, mark the corners and the center of the hair shape with pins as shown in fig.6.

Cut lengths of fine string or cord and lay them in parallel lines to cover the area. Cut a thin strip of cream cotton fabric allowing a small turning at either end and glue it along the center. Leave to dry. Turn, and with matching thread, machine stitch down the center of the hair. Run a thin line of fabric adhesive down the head and glue on the hair. Turn in both ends and glue down. Take 12 strands from either side of the front

and braid. Cross them at the back of the head and secure each end with a little glue. Tie a brown velvet ribbon bow at the back of the head to cover the braided ends. **Embroidering the features.** Measure and mark the center of each eye with a pin. With a single strand of black embroidery floss, work a small double cross for the pupil. With a single strand of dark blue embroidery floss work straight stitches for the iris radiating from the black center. For the mouth use single strands of pink and work stem stitch and straight stitch.

Clothes
You will now be ready to make the clothes and dress the doll. Draw all pattern pieces from the graph (fig.7) in which 1 square equals 2.5cm (1in).

Pantaloons. Place the pantaloon pattern on the straight grain of the white cotton fabric and cut 2 pieces. Cut a bias waistband measuring 21.5 × 2.5cm (8½ × 1in). Mark the back opening and the top row of lace with a pencil dot. Turn the bottom of the legs over once, to the right side, and baste a length of 1.5cm (½in) lace to each leg. Baste a length of 1cm (⅜in) lace onto each top row, then machine stitch all 4 rows into position.

Make a small seam down the front for about 7.5cm (3in) and below the opening at the back for about 5cm (2in). Join the legs together in the same way, making a continuous seam around both inner legs. Sew down the turnings on the back opening. Gather across the top, allowing equal fullness at the front and back so that the doll will sit easily. Attach the waistband to the wrong side of the gathered waist first, press upwards, then fold over. Turn under a narrow hem and machine stitch on the right side. To fasten, sew a small white pearl button onto the waistband and make a buttonhole to correspond.

Petticoat. Cut 2 pieces of eyelet embroidery (Broderie Anglaise) as shown in fig.8. Make small seams down both sides. Turn the hem over once towards the front and baste. Gather the remaining length of wide lace, approximately 1m (1yd) and baste on to cover the hem of the petticoat. Stitch into position and remove the basting. Make a 0.5cm (¼in) casing at the waist and

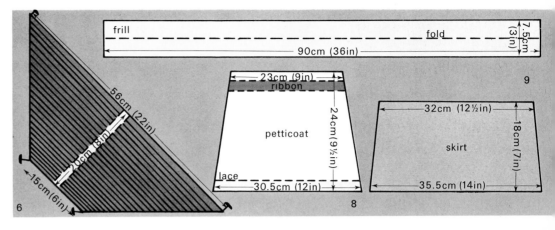

machine stitch. Thread with pink satin ribbon. Make an eyelet at either side of the seamline on the outside of the waist or utilize 2 holes from the eyelet embroidery and thread the ribbon through. Gather and tie in a bow.

Dress. Place the dress material on a flat surface, right sides together, and arrange the sleeve and bodice pattern pieces on the straight grain of the fabric, as indicated. Measure and mark out the skirt with pins as shown in fig.9. Cut out all these sections. Stitch the 2 bodice pieces together at the center front and press open the seam allowances. Stitch the darts on the front and the back 2 sections and press outwards. Turn in and stitch the hem on the back opening. Stitch the shoulder seams together and press open. Gather the top of the sleeve in between the points indicated, allowing slightly more fullness at the back of each sleeve. Machine stitch a line just above the gathers to hold them in place. With right sides together, pin and baste the sleeves in position. Machine stitch, then remove basting. Turn over the bottom of the sleeve once and sew.

Cut a long strip of fabric for the frill measuring 90 × 7.5cm (36 × 3in). Sew the short ends together to form a circle and press the seam allowance open. Fold the strip in two and press flat. Using a long stitch sew a line 0.5cm (¼in) in from the raw edges and gather. Adjust the gathers to fit the bottom of the dress and knot the threads. Shorten the stitch and machine stitch a line just above the gathers to hold them in place. With right sides together, baste the frill onto the

bottom of the dress and stitch about 0.5cm (¼in) in from the edge. Press the seam upwards. Baste narrow pink velvet ribbon over the seamline and slip stitch along both sides. Turn the bodice inside out. Make a small flat seam to join sleeve and bodice together in one continuous line. Turn in the bottom edge of the sleeves, about 1.5cm (½in) and catch on the seam. Set the machine for a larger stitch size and sew around the top of the skirt. Gather and fit to the bodice. With right sides together, baste the bodice to the skirt and stitch.

Turn in the neck edge and baste. Stitch a length of narrow lace along the basting. Remove all basting stitches. Sew on a small gray button to fasten at the neck and make a buttonhole to correspond.

Cut two 23cm (9in) lengths of narrow pink ribbon and catch them at either side of the center front seam. Take them over the shoulders and catch at the center back. Tie the length of wide pink ribbon around the waist making a bow or knot at the back. Make a tiny pleat in the center of both sleeves (at elbow level) and catch with a single stitch.

Shoes. Place each pattern onto the leather and cut 2, reversing for left and right. Cut the sole with the suede side outside. Shape the toe piece to form a cone. Apply fabric adhesive to the bottom part and glue it to the sole. Glue the inner sole in position. Glue a small flower made from a circle of gathered ribbon to the toe. Repeat for the other shoe in reverse.

Glue the shoes onto the toes of the doll with fabric adhesive.

Children playing with marionettes, a detail from *The Hundred Children*, a 17th-century Chinese handscroll.

Puppetry as a dramatic art form has a long history in both the East and the West. Shadow plays featuring two-dimensional figures moving behind a screen have been traditionally performed in China, Java and India since the 11th century. Rod puppets and marionettes were also used in many parts of Asia and it is possible that these were brought from Southern India, perhaps by Gypsies, to Persia and Western Europe. There is also a great deal of evidence to suggest that puppets were an established feature of the culture in Ancient Greece. Herodotus, for example, writing in the 5th century BC, mentions puppet statuettes operated by priestesses during certain religious festivals, and Plato likened the human race to marionettes, with the gods working the strings.

The word "marionette" is a diminutive form meaning "little Mary" and in the Middle Ages in Western Europe, puppet figures representing Jesus and Mary were quite common. Several examples of such puppets remain housed in museums — the Cluny museum in France, for instance, where there is a figure of Christ with eyes that move. One of the very earliest depictions of a puppet show is to be found in the illustrated Flemish manuscript *Li*

Romans du bon Roi Alexandre by Johan de Grise, dating from around 1344 and now in the Bodleian Library, Oxford, England. From the 14th century onwards puppeteers took traveling shows through Europe, mainly in Italy, France, Spain, Poland, Germany and England, visiting fairs and festivals and playing to the aristocracy in noble and royal households. The Italian scientist, Hieronymous Cardanus, records with great enthusiasm, one performance that he witnessed:

"I have seen two Sicilians who did real wonders with two wooden figures which they made to move. A single string was carried through both. It was attached on one side to a fixed post and on the other to the leg which the showman moved. . . There is no kind of dance which these figures could not execute. They made the most astonishing movements with their feet, legs, arms and head . . . they play, fight, hunt, dance, blow trumpets . . ."

Sicilian puppets were traditionally used to tell the story of Roland and Charlemagne, but each country tended to develop its own repertoire of stories and stock characters. By the end of the 17th century, for example, the most popular puppet figures in England, and later in America, were undoubtedly Punch and Judy, who were not marionettes but hand or glove puppets. Performances were usually given by traveling puppeteers from portable red and white striped booths. Punch or Punchinello was probably modeled on Pulcinella, one of the stock buffoon characters of the Italian *Commedia dell'arte*. The same figure was adopted as Polichinelle in France and as Petrushka in Russia. Stravinsky's ballet *Petrushka* (1911) is built around this character and the three principal roles — Petrushka, the Ballerina and the Moor — are performed by dancers to resemble puppets. The practice of presenting puppet plays or *fantoccini*, common in Italy and England since the 15th century, became widespread in the rest of Europe somewhat later. Haydn, for example, composed the music for a special puppet opera for his patron Prince Esterházy in 1773: *Philemon und Baucis* was produced with puppets performing on stage and singers positioned out of sight in the wings.

A puppet show in progress, from the 14th-century Flemish manuscript *Li Romans du bon Roi Alexandre*.

Audiences were already familiar with many dramatic and operatic works especially adapted for puppets. Mozart's delightful opera *Bastien und Bastienne*, written in 1768 when he was 12 years old, was particularly popular, as were the various versions of Shakespeare's plays. The Salzburg Marionette Theater, established in 1913, continues to present operas, ballets, plays and pantomime in this style.

Though puppet performances in theaters have declined in recent years, puppets have been used to great effect in television shows and films for children and have found a permanent place in the repertoire. Pinocchio, the lovable story-book puppet originally created by Carlo Collodi in 1880, for example, achieved universal fame in 1940 when he was immortalized on film by Walt Disney.

Shadow puppets

Shadow puppets are flat figures seen in silhouette through an opaque screen, which has a light source behind it. A screen, a few puppets and props can easily be made and be ready to use in one afternoon. You can make a simple shadow puppet from cardboard by drawing and cutting out a single shape in one piece. The witch in the illustration, however, has one basic body piece with the addition of movable arms and lower jaw.

You will need:

piece of thin but sturdy cardboard □ thin stick or length of galvanized wire for the rod □ lengths of thinner wire for movable parts □ 3 rivet-type paper fasteners □ adhesive tape or glue □ sheets of colored cellophane, tissue paper or acetate for decoration.

Making the puppet. Draw the outline of the puppet onto the cardboard from the graph (fig.1) in which 1 square equals 5cm (2in). If movable parts are required, draw these separately. Cut out the pieces. The puppet is held by means of a rod. Attach the thin stick or length of galvanized wire to the main body area with adhesive tape or glue. The rod should extend below the base of the puppet. Join all movable parts to the body with paper fasteners, then make a hole in each part and attach a thin wire by threading it through the hole and bending the top of the wire over to form a loop.

Experimenting with color. Colored shapes can be used to suggest features or clothing by cutting out holes in the puppet and glueing the paper over them.

Making the screen. A simple screen can be made by using an old picture frame and a piece of white cotton fabric. Stretch the cotton over the back of the frame and fix it in position with tacks (drawing pins) or staples. Screw angle-brackets to the base of the frame so that it stands upright on a flat surface. Use a table lamp or light from a window to light the screen. Adjust the light or the screen so that the shadows of the puppet operators do not fall on the screen. Make a temporary screen by stretching a cotton sheet over a doorway or open window.

Decorating the screen. Scenery for the puppet shows can be made by making shapes from the same basic materials of cardboard and colored paper and then propping them up against the screen or sticking them to it with adhesive tape or glue.

1 Graph pattern for shadow puppet
1 sq = 5cm (2in)

rivets

rod

wire

Finger and glove puppets

Finger puppets

Make a handful of finger puppets to delight a toddler or small child. They are simple to make and great fun to play with. An international theme is shown in the photograph but it is just as easy to create characters from a children's story or rhyme. To allow scope for individual ideas, the basic pattern only is given (fig.2).

You will need:

10cm (4in) square of felt for each puppet base ☐ colored scraps of felt for clothes and features ☐ fabric adhesive ☐ thread to match the body felt.

For all the puppets. Trace and cut out 2 basic shapes and stitch them together close to the edge, leaving the bottom open. Cut out and glue on 2 hands and a face. Then, from the scraps of felt, cut out and glue on individual features and clothes to suit each puppet.

Glove puppets

Glove puppets are a very simple form of puppetry. They are especially suitable for children because they are so easy to operate and can become a companion as well as a toy; through their puppets children will often find a way to express themselves by acting out stories and fantasies.

Felt puppets. The basic teddy bear glove shape illustrated opposite should fit most hands although it may need adjusting for a small child. The shape of the head can easily be adapted to make many different characters, two of which are shown. As an alternative, the bear could also be made very successfully from fake fur fabric.

Teddy bear

You will need:

gold or brown felt for body ☐ brown or black felt for paws and ears ☐ black buttons or felt for eyes ☐ black yarn for nose ☐ ribbon for bow tie ☐ fabric adhesive ☐ construction (cartridge) paper for the pattern.

Making the bear. Draw the pattern from the graph (fig.3) in which 1 square equals 5cm (2in). Cut out 2 teddy bear shapes. Cut out the paw and ear shapes and glue or sew in position on one of the teddy bear shapes. Glue or sew the eyes in position and embroider the nose. Sew the 2 halves of the

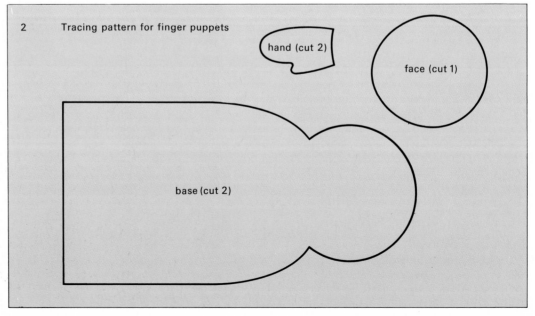

2   Tracing pattern for finger puppets

hand (cut 2)

face (cut 1)

base (cut 2)

puppet together, following the dotted line. Tie a ribbon in a bow around his neck.
If using fake fur fabric, cut out the 2 teddy bear shapes with a 1 cm ($\frac{3}{8}$in) seam allowance. The features must be sewn on. Place the fur sides together and sew 1 cm ($\frac{3}{8}$in) from the edge. Snip the seam allowance with scissors around the curves and into the corners. Turn right side out and ease out any fur caught in the seam with a pin.
Sock puppets. These are popular with children and they have the added advantage of being made from materials which can generally be found at home.
You will need:
an old sock, plain or patterned ☐ pair of old panty hose with the elastic removed ☐ elastic thread ☐ felt for the features ☐ yarn for the hair ☐ scraps of fabric for accessories ☐ glue or nail polish.
Making the puppet. To form the head of the puppet, stuff the toe of the sock with panty hose (or another sock) rolled up into a ball. Using a blunt needle with a large eye, sew a line of running stitch with elastic thread where the neck will be (fig.4). Draw up the elastic just tight enough to push your forefinger into the head (fig.5). Wind the elastic round the puppet's neck 2 or 3 times and tie securely.
With the puppet on your hand, mark where the arms will be. Remove the puppet and

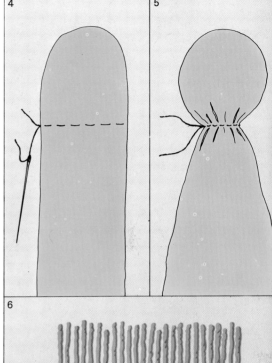

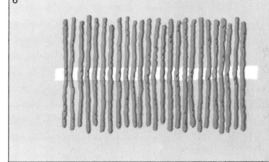

snip slits to allow your finger and thumb through. Smear glue or nail polish around the edges of the holes on the inside of the sock to prevent fraying.
Make a wig from yarn lengths sewn onto a tape (fig.6) or by stitching loops of yarn onto the head. Sew or glue on felt eyes, nose and mouth or draw them on with felt tip pens. Sleeves can be made from felt or from the cut-off ribbing of the sock. Cut 2 pieces approximately 6 × 4cm ($2\frac{1}{2} \times 1\frac{1}{2}$in). Sew the long edges together to form a tube. Sew up one end of the tube, rounding it a little to fit the end of your finger. Turn it right side out and sew the open ends into the finger openings in the puppet.
Wearing a glove on your hand under the puppet also gives it sleeves.
Sleeve puppets. These are another great success with children and are very easy to operate. The main expressions come from

pattern
r
5 cm
(2in)

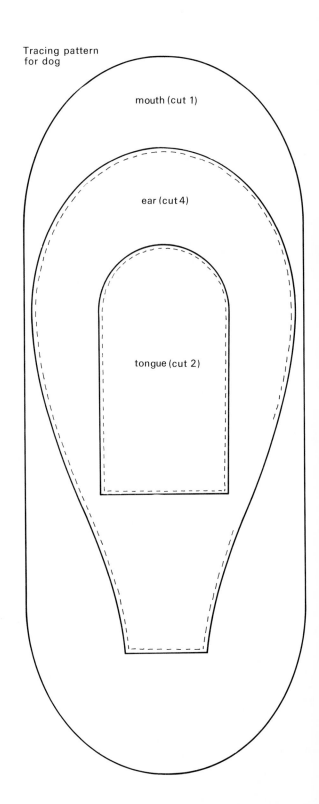

Tracing pattern
for dog

mouth (cut 1)

ear (cut 4)

tongue (cut 2)

opening and closing the puppet's mouth and tilting its head.

Oscar the dog
This puppet is made from a brightly colored sock. Synthetic foam enables the puppet to be very expressive but could be replaced by a double thickness of felt for the mouth lining. Different types of material such as velvet and corduroy could be used for ears.

You will need:
long sock □ brown felt for ears □ bright pink felt for mouth □ red felt for tongue □ black felt for nose □ 2 plastic eyes or scraps of black and white felt □ synthetic foam 5mm ($\frac{3}{16}$in) thick □ black wool or embroidery floss for whiskers □ glue or nail polish.

Making the dog. Cut open the toe seam at the foot of the sock and extend the opening on each side 5cm (2in) further into the foot to form the opening for the mouth (fig.7). Carefully turn the sock inside out and apply glue or nail polish along the raw edge to prevent fraying.

Trace the pattern and cut 2 tongue shapes out of red felt and stitch them together. Cut

1 mouth shape from pink felt and 1 from synthetic foam. Stitch the tongue along its top edge to the center of the felt mouth shape (fig.8). Now turn the mouth shape over and baste the foam onto the back of it. With the sock turned inside out, pin the mouth shape into the mouth opening, with the pink felt and the right side of the sock together (fig.9). Stitch all the way around. Turn right side out and sew or glue on the eyes and nose. Embroider a few whiskers with the black yarn. Cut out 4 ear shapes, 2 for each ear. Place 1 pair together and sew along the dotted line leaving the opening for turning. Turn right side out, sew up the opening and iron. Repeat for the other ear, then stitch in position.

Papier mâché heads
Papier mâché is ideal for making puppet heads because it is light, strong and durable. There are two ways of making it.
1. By pasting torn pieces of paper in layers over a model or object. This method gives a fairly smooth finish.
2. By making the paper into a pulp, which can be modeled like clay. This method

Papier mâché heads

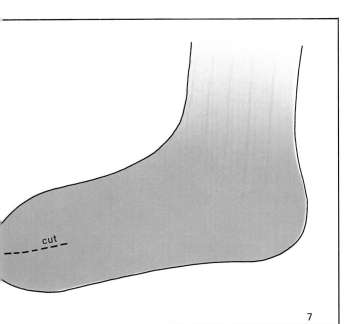

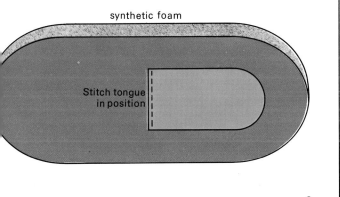

synthetic foam

Stitch tongue
in position

8

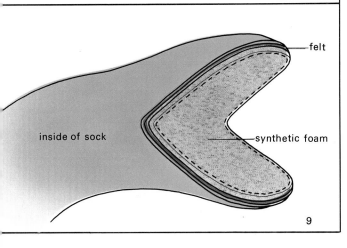

felt

inside of sock

synthetic foam

9

gives a rugged texture and is suitable for monsters.

Rough paper is essential — newspaper, comics, sugar paper, corrugated paper and egg cartons are all very good. Never use smooth shiny paper as it does not absorb moisture properly.

Making a puppet head using the layering method

It is easier to ensure even coverage when layering if a different color paper is used for alternate layers.

You will need:

tissue paper □ wallpaper paste □ newspaper □ plastic putty (plasticine) □ petroleum jelly.

Form an "egg" shape with plastic putty, approximately 10cm (4in) high for the basic head. Roll a piece of plastic putty a little thicker than your forefinger and 2cm (¾in) long. Attach it to the head to form the neck. Build up the features with pieces of plastic putty, keeping them fairly bold. Smear petroleum jelly over the head to prevent the newspaper from sticking to the plastic putty. Tear (never cut) the newspaper into small pieces.

Using wallpaper paste, paste on the first layer of newspaper, overlapping the pieces all over the head. It is very important to smooth the newspaper down as you go, to remove any excess paste and air bubbles. Continue with alternate layers of newspaper for 6 layers. Finish with 2 layers of tissue paper, carefully smoothed down. Leave in a warm place to dry out. This will take between 24 and 48 hours.

When the head is completely dry, cut through the papier mâché shell, splitting the head in half so that the front is separated from the back. Pull the 2 halves apart and carefully ease out all the plastic putty. Glue the 2 halves of the head together again. Paste over the join with 2 layers of newspaper and 1 of tissue paper and put aside to dry. Make a finger tube from a piece of thin cardboard about 2cm (¾in) longer than the length of the puppet head. Wind the cardboard around your forefinger, then making sure the tube is not uncomfortably tight, glue the edges together. Glue the tube in position around the neck hole of the puppet head.

Making a puppet head using papier mâché pulp

The best way to use pulp is to model it onto a base such as a cardboard tube, a box or basic head shape made by the layering method.

You will need:

cardboard egg cartons or newspaper □ wallpaper paste □ bucket of water □ loosely woven cloth for straining.

Tear the egg cartons or newspaper into small pieces and leave to soak in a bucket of cold water overnight. Strain handfuls of the soaked pieces through a loosely woven cloth and squeeze out as much water as possible. Put the pulp into a bucket and add wallpaper paste, a little at a time, until the pulp can be manipulated like clay. Take care not to make the mixture too wet. Mix thoroughly. Pulp takes between 3 and 7 days to dry according to its thickness. Baking it in a low oven will help to speed up the process.

Painting puppet heads

Having prepared the papier mâché head, the next step is to paint on the features which give the puppet its individual appearance. Ordinary white water-based (emulsion) paint provides a very good base for most other types of paint. Poster or acrylic paints can be used for the features but if you intend to varnish the puppet head, poster colors should not be used as they become dull under varnish. If you use acrylic paints, varnishing is a good idea because it protects the paint and generally strengthens the puppet head.

Mr Punch

This puppet has finger tubes in the hands and feet as well as in the head so that it can be operated either as an ordinary glove puppet using one hand, or by using both hands, his feet can be made to move too.

You will need:

red felt for body, hat, collar and legs □ yellow felt for trimmings □ black felt for boots and club □ pink felt for hands □ cotton print for smock □ thin cardboard □ synthetic foam or kapok for stuffing □ matching cotton thread □ pipe cleaners.

Making Punch. Make the head from papier mâché by the layering method and paint it.

Punch, derived from the traditional 15th-century *Commedia dell'arte* character Pulcinella, is still highly popular with children today.

Cut out pattern pieces from the graph (fig.10) in which 1 square equals 2.5cm (1in), adding a 1cm ($\frac{3}{8}$in) seam allowance for the basic glove, smock and hat.

Hands. Overcast all around the hand shape, marking the divisions between the fingers with back stitch. Cut short lengths from a pipe cleaner to fit into each finger, folding over the end of each piece to prevent them from piercing the felt. Dab the pieces with glue before pushing them inside the fingers. Make the finger tubes from pieces of thin cardboard approximately 8 × 4cm ($3\frac{1}{4} × 1\frac{1}{2}$in). Roll each piece to fit inside the wrist of both hands. Pinch together one end of each tube and fix with adhesive tape before glueing them into the hands.

Legs. To make the legs, sew the upper leg to the boot by overlapping the pieces by 5mm ($\frac{3}{16}$in). Sew the leg and boot together along the front edge from the toe to the top of the leg. Pin the sole of the boot in position and overcast around the edge. Cut 2 boot soles from thin cardboard and place 1 inside each boot. Cut cardboard 8 × 5cm

($3\frac{1}{4} × 2$in) for finger tubes for the legs and make in the same way as for the hands. Stuff the boot firmly with foam or kapok. Glue the finger tube to the front edge inside the top of the leg — the top edge of the tube should be even with the top edge of the leg. Finish stuffing the leg and sew up the top edge on both sides of the finger tube. Glue yellow bands of felt around the top of each boot.

Basic glove shape. Cut the slit indicated on 1 of the glove shapes and sew around the edge. This is the back piece of the glove. Place the 2 glove shapes together and sew 1cm ($\frac{3}{8}$in) from the edge, leaving the neck, armholes and hem open. Turn right side out. Insert the wrist of each hand into the openings in the glove and pin in position. Try the glove on to adjust the position of the hands if necessary. Overcast around each of the wrists. Sew the legs to the bottom front edge of the glove as indicated.

Smock. Place the 2 smock pieces right sides together. Sew the shoulder and side seams, as marked on the pattern, 1cm ($\frac{3}{8}$in) from the edge. Turn right side out. Hem-stitch around the armholes and the hem. Put the smock onto the glove and sew it to the glove around the neck edge.

Hat. Place the 2 hat shapes together and stitch 1cm ($\frac{3}{8}$in) from the edge, leaving the hem open. Snip into the seam allowance and turn right side out. Stuff the hat with foam or kapok so that it fits closely around the head. Adjust the hat to the position you want and mark in a light pencil line around the head. Glue inside the hem and also on the puppet head above the pencil line, then glue the hat onto the head. Make the tassel by snipping the piece of felt as marked on the pattern. Glue along the uncut edge and roll it up. Sew the tassel onto the hat.

Collar. Sew or glue the ring of yellow felt around the edge of the collar shape. Slip the collar onto the neck of the puppet with the yellow rim facing upwards. Glue the neck of the puppet head into the neck opening in the glove.

Club. Place the 2 club pieces together and stitch along the dotted line shown on the pattern, leaving an opening for stuffing. Stuff with foam or kapok and sew up the opening. Sew the club to the palm of the right hand and bend the fingers over it.

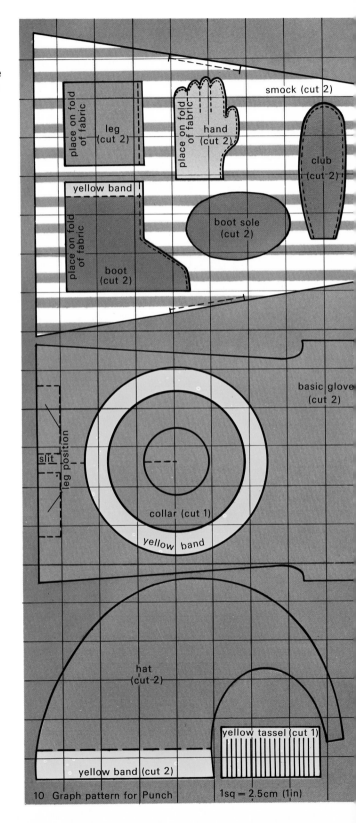

10 Graph pattern for Punch   1sq = 2.5cm (1in)

Structure

A marionette is basically a jointed doll on strings. The traditional material is wood but paper, cardboard, wire and cloth can also be used. If you use these lighter materials, you will need to insert weights into the head, hands, hip base and feet so that the limbs will drop correctly when the strings are released. Lead dress weights or fishing weights are ideal, but anything small and heavy will do just as well. The minimum joints needed are the neck, shoulders, elbows, tops of thighs and knees. Joints at the waist, wrists, ankles and jaw can also be added for greater flexibility. The ideal height for a puppet is between 30cm (12in) and 45cm (18in). Anything smaller will be difficult to see from a distance and will be a problem to dress and anything larger will be too heavy to handle comfortably, especially for a child. Human body proportions are shown in fig.11. Alter these if you wish to make a more eccentric puppet figure.

Slithery snake

This snake is made from fabric and is stuf-

fed with kapok. It is operated by means of a very simple control made from two lengths of dowel.

You will need:
70×32cm (27½×12½in) light green jersey □ 70×16cm (27½×6¼in) dark green jersey □ 1m (1yd) velvet or fancy braid □ small scraps of felt, gold material, sequins, etc., for decoration □ 2 ping pong balls for eyes □ 2 black buttons □ poster paints □ length of fine flexible wire for tongue □ 1 pipe cleaner □ kapok □ 5 dress weights or other weights □ glue □ contact adhesive □ 50cm (20in) length of thin dowel or strip of wood □ strong thread □ paper for pattern.

Cutting out the pattern. Draw the top body from the graph (fig.12a) in which 1 square equals 2.5cm (1in).

Note: the tail, head and one curve only are given. To elongate the snake, repeat the section between the dotted lines twice more or as many times as you like.
Draw the pattern for the underbody (fig.12b) in the same way.

Making the body. Cut one top body piece for the left-hand side and another for the

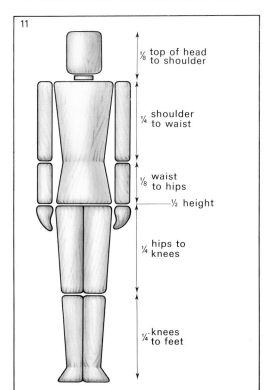

11

½ top of head to shoulder

¼ shoulder to waist

⅛ waist to hips

½ height

¼ hips to knees

¼ knees to feet

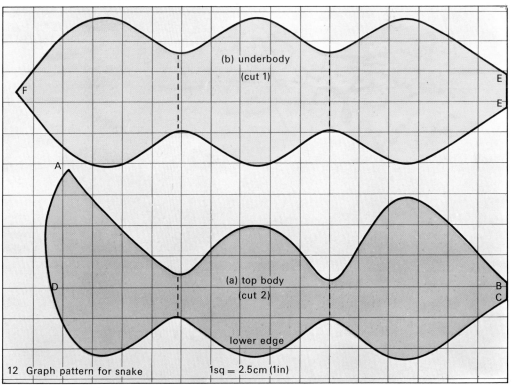

(b) underbody
(cut 1)

F

E
E

A

D

(a) top body
(cut 2)

B
C

lower edge

12 Graph pattern for snake   1sq = 2.5cm (1in)

Slithery snake
Come to the circus!

right-hand side from light green jersey and one underbody from dark green jersey, adding seam allowances of 1.5cm ($\frac{1}{2}$in) on all edges. With right sides together, stitch the seam from A to B on top bodies, leaving about 2.5cm (1in) open on each curve to allow for stuffing later. With right sides together, pin E and E of the underbody to C on either side of the top body. Match F at the end of the tail on the underbody with D on the top bodies and pin curves in between. Baste carefully. Seam, leaving the section at the front of the head open to insert the tongue later. Turn right side out. Stuff the body and head firmly but leave the narrow part between each curve unstuffed to give the snake flexibility. Insert a weight into each section, using lead dress weights, large bolts or anything that will make the snake hang well. Sew up the stuffing openings along the curves.

Decorating the snake. Sew the velvet braid along the center back. Cut circles from felt or fabric and sew or glue in place.

Eyes. Paint 2 ping pong balls with fluores-

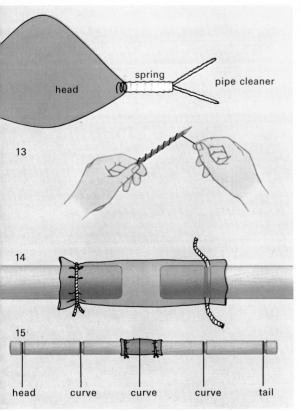

head   spring   pipe cleaner

13

14

15

head   curve   curve   curve   tail

cent poster paints. Stick black buttons in the center then paint black rings around them. For eyelids, cut a length of felt to encircle each ball, fold in half lengthwise, join the short ends and then gather one side. Glue around the eye. Sew the eyes to the head, piercing through the balls.

Tongue (fig.13). Wind flexible wire around a pencil for about 5cm (2in) to make a spring. Fold a pipe cleaner in half and cover with fabric for the forked tongue. Cover the spring with a tube of material, attaching the fork to one end. Push the other end inside the head at C to C and overcast firmly to close the opening.

Mouth. Cut 2 curved strips of black felt and sew in place on either side of the tongue.

Control. Saw the strip of wood or dowel in half. To make a hinge, nick one end of each piece with a sharp knife. Push these ends into a tube of material and tie firmly around the nicks (fig.14).

Stringing the snake (fig.15). Cut a nick at each end of the rejoined control and one half way along each portion. Attaching the

thread by sewing to the body, take one length from the tip of the tail and the top of each curved section and tie around the corresponding nick in the control. Sew the center string to the material joining the 2 halves of the control.

Come to the circus!

These two puppets team up to make an entertaining vaudeville act and will amuse young children for hours.

Sammy seal. This marionette's main string is elastic thread and the head moves independently on a spring.

You will need:

black velvet, wool or other suitable fabric □ small piece black satin □ material or ribbon for ruffle □ 2 black buttons for eyes □ scraps of red and black felt □ thin white cord for whiskers □ adhesive interfacing □ small glass bottle (or plastic bottle half filled with sand) about 17cm (6$\frac{3}{4}$in) high including cap and 5.5cm (2$\frac{1}{4}$in) in diameter at the base □ old sock □ fine string □ thin cardboard □ ab-

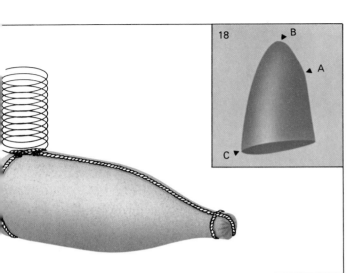

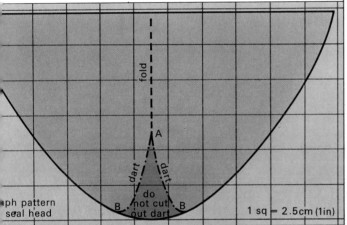

ph pattern
seal head

fold

A

dart dart

do
not cut
out dart

B B B

1 sq = 2.5cm (1in)

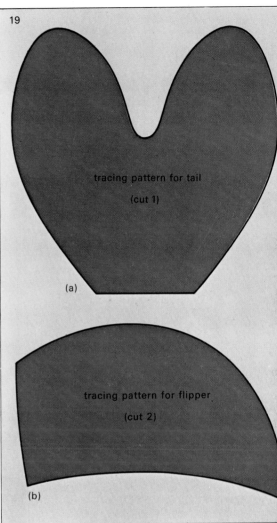

18

B

A

C

19

tracing pattern for tail

(cut 1)

(a)

tracing pattern for flipper

(cut 2)

(b)

2 nuts, washers or lead weights and tie or glue them down firmly to the top end of the spring. Cover the bottle with black fabric.

Making the head. Draw the pattern for the head from the graph (fig. 17) in which 1 square equals 2.5cm (1in), noting the fold. Cut out the head in the body fabric, adding seam allowances of 1.5cm ($\frac{1}{2}$in). Do not cut out the dart. Trim the dart on the paper pattern and cut it out in the interfacing (without seam allowances), then iron or stick it onto the wrong side of the black fabric. With right sides together, fold the head in half and sew from A to B to C (fig.18). Leave the straight edge open. Trim the material here so that it is the same size as the stiffening, or turn in and stitch. Turn the work right side out.

Making the features. Sew a piece of black satin cut on the bias onto the tip of the head for a nose and stitch narrow strips of red felt underneath for a smiling mouth. Cut 2 ovals of white felt for eyes and sew buttons on top for pupils. Add 5 double lengths of fine white cord to either side for whiskers. Sew a gathered length of ribbon or decorative fabric around the bottom of the head for a ruffle.

Finishing the head. Draw a circle 23cm (9in) in diameter on the cardboard and mark off just over a quarter section. Cut out and then glue, straight edges overlapping, to make a cone with a diameter of 7.5cm (3in) across the bottom. Cut 2.5cm (1in) from the tip of the cone. Try the cone inside the head to check the fit, then remove it and stuff the tip of the nose firmly with absorbent cotton. Glue a little more stuffing inside the back of the head if it needs more support. Smear the outside of the cone with glue and press it into the head. Spread contact adhesive generously over the top of the spring and the weights, and slip the cone over it. The head should move freely and is not attached in any other way.

Making the flippers and tail. Cut a tail and 2 flippers from medium thickness card, following the tracing pattern (fig.19a and b). Spread glue on one side of each piece and stick to the wrong side of black satin. Cut out, allowing about 1.5cm ($\frac{1}{2}$in) all around. Snip into the turnings and glue them to the back of the cardboard. With contact adhesive glue a weight on the uncovered

sorbent cotton (cotton wool) □ spring (eg from a hair roller) 1.5cm ($\frac{1}{2}$in) in diameter □ 5 small weights □ 53cm (21in) strip of wood approximately 2.5cm (1in) wide □ black elastic thread □ strong thread □ painted ping pong ball or hollow plastic ball.

Making the body. Cover the bottle firmly with 2 thicknesses of an old sock. Sew the ends together and trim off any excess. Pull the spring so that the coils are stretched out to measure about 9cm (3$\frac{1}{2}$in) long. This makes it more flexible. Tie the spring very firmly to the bottom end of the bottle with fine string and stitch the string to the sock covering around the length and width of the bottle as shown in fig.16. Pull the spring over at a slight angle and weight the top on opposite sides so that it trembles easily. Use any small heavy objects, such as

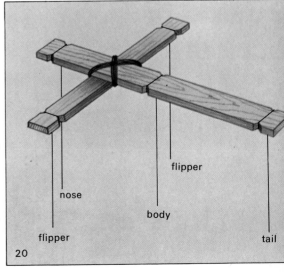

nose

flipper

body

flipper

tail

20

side of each cardboard piece. Pad lightly with absorbent cotton and cover the weighted side with body fabric, stitching the edge to the cardboard. Sew the flippers to the body attaching them at an angle near the underside, with the satin below. Stitch the tail to the end of the body.

Control (fig.20). Saw the wood into 2 pieces measuring 33cm (13in) and 20cm (8in) in length. Glue or screw the smaller piece at right angles, 7.5cm (3in) from one end of the longer piece. Cut nicks 0.5cm (¼in) in from the end of each piece. Cut more nicks in the longer piece, 12cm (4½in) down from the crossbar end.

Stringing the seal. Find the point of balance on the seal's body. To do this, tie a string around it, just behind the flippers. Check that it balances evenly when it is held up by the string, adjusting backward or forward as required. Mark this point then remove the string and sew a length of elastic thread to the top center of the body at the marked point. Tie the other end of the elastic around the nicks behind the crossbar. Take string 2 from the tail, and strings 3 and 4 from the flippers. Thread string 5 through a ping pong ball and sew to the tip of the seal's nose.

Comic clown. This clown puppet is made very simply using blocks of wood and dowels, jointed by screw hooks and eyes. No carving is necessary and facial features are glued in place. The finished height is approximately 46cm (18in).

You will need:
Wood blocks: 9 × 5 × 4cm (3½ × 2 × 1½in) for head; 10 × 7.5 × 4cm (4 × 3 × 1½in) and 7.5 × 5 × 4cm (3 × 2 × 1½in) for torso □ 2.2cm (⅞in) dowel, 66cm (26in) long for limbs □ 0.5cm (¼in) dowel, 2.5cm (1in) long for control peg □ strip of wood 19 × 16mm (¾ × ⅝in), 79cm (31¼in) long for feet, hands and control □ 7 pairs smallest size hooks and eyes, preferably plastic-coated □ 4 smallest size eyes only □ 4 hooks 1.5cm (½in) for joints □ strong thread □ old panty hose □ large round wooden bead for nose □ 2 black buttons for eyes □ egg carton □ 4 pipe cleaners □ 1 used wooden matchstick □ absorbent cotton (cotton wool) □ orange knitting yarn □ paint: white undercoat and white, red and black enamel □ white felt for

gloves □ black felt for shoes □ brightly colored fabric for clothes □ 2 buttons □ fabric adhesive □ contact adhesive □ scissors □ small hacksaw □ bradawl □ pliers.

Making the head. Take the wood block for the head and make a preliminary hole with a bradawl to insert 3 small screw eyes as shown in fig.21. Drill a hole in the center of the "face" to take about 1.5cm (½in) of matchstick. Cut ears and a mouth from sections of egg carton and glue them in place with contact adhesive. Cut the bases from 2 egg sections of the carton for eyes, padding the insides with paper or cardboard. Glue them to the face. Give the head a white undercoat and top coat. For the nose, insert a matchstick into a large wooden bead and paint it with white undercoat and a red top coat. Glue the matchstick into the hole in the face. Glue 2 black buttons to the eyes and paint the rest of the face.

Making the hair. Bend 4 pipe cleaners in half, apply adhesive and glue absorbent cotton around each one to form a cone. Leave about 2.5cm (1in) of the ends projecting. Wind the cones with orange yarn, then fray the ends of the pipe cleaners. Stick 2 cones to each side of the head, using the screw eyes to anchor the top two. Glue loops of orange yarn to the top of the head.

Note: do not fasten the head to the torso until you have dressed the clown.

Making the torso. Take the 2 wood blocks and insert the hooks as shown in fig.22. Link the large hooks at the waist and close firmly with pliers. Cut 2 pieces, each about 17.5cm (7in), from the leg of an old pair of panty hose and cover the torso with a double thickness, making sure that the joined blocks hang properly. Run a gathering thread through both layers of material at top and bottom, and pull up to enclose the wood, adding adhesive under the gathering thread where necessary. Attach the large hooks for the arms to the sides through the panty hose (fig.23).

Making the feet. Cut two 8.75cm (3½in) lengths of dowel and two 7.5cm (3in) strips of wood. Glue, nail or screw one strip of wood to one end of each dowel as shown in fig.24

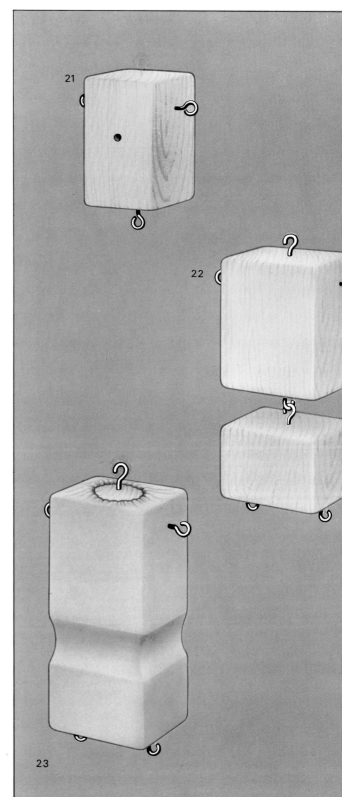

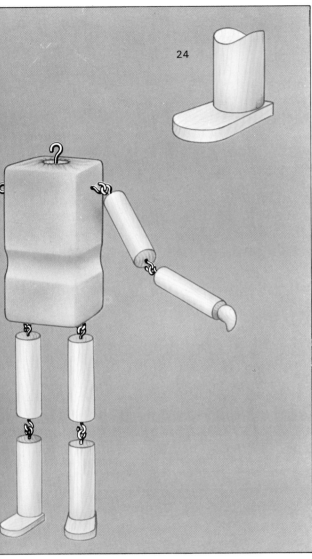

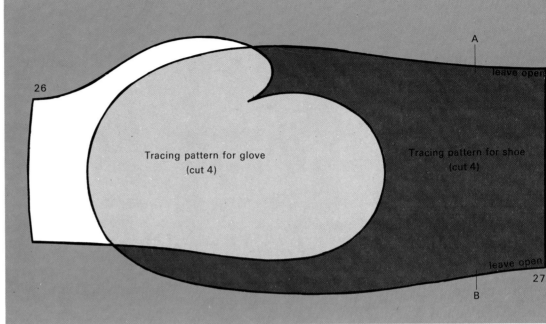

Tracing pattern for glove
(cut 4)

Tracing pattern for shoe
(cut 4)

Making the hands. Cut two 6.25cm (2½in) lengths of dowel. Drill holes 0.5cm (¼in) in diameter across each, within 1.5cm (½in) of the end. Make 2 parallel saw cuts in the end of the dowel to the hole. The wood in between the saw cuts will drop out. Cut two 4.5cm (1¾in) strips of wood and glue them into the slots between the saw cuts in the dowel.

Jointing the limbs (fig.25). Cut four 8.75cm (3½in) lengths of dowel for upper arms and legs, then attach to lower limbs with screw hooks and eyes. Secure by closing the hooks with pliers.

Dressing the clown. Having completed the puppet sections, you will now be ready to make the clothes. You will need to make a shirt front, trousers, vest (waistcoat) and coat. Make each garment separately and attach to the puppet by sewing through the panty hose covering the torso.

Shoes. Trace the pattern for shoes (fig.26) and cut 4 pieces from black felt. Overcast in pairs from A to B. Turn. Stuff lightly with absorbent cotton then pull over puppet's feet. Gather around the upper edges and glue to the lower leg dowel.

Gloves. Trace the pattern for gloves (fig.27) and cut 4 pieces from white felt. Overcast in pairs leaving straight edges open. Turn, then stuff with absorbent cotton and pull over the hands, binding at the wrists by taking thread through the dowel hole.

Hat. Take a small cylindrical box or make one from cardboard and cover with black paper or felt. Add a brim and felt flower as shown. Sew to the hair.

Fix head to torso at neck and add a collar and bow tie made from cardboard or felt.

Control (fig.28). Take the remaining strip of wood and saw it into 2 pieces, one measuring 25cm (10in) and the other 30cm (12in). Insert a small cup hook into one end of the longer piece. Drill a hole to fit the control peg, 2.5cm (1in) from the cup hook end. Drill another hole big enough to fit easily over the dowel in the center of the other strip of wood. Cut nicks in the center of the longer piece, in the end opposite the cup hook and in either end of the shorter piece. Glue the peg in place.

Stringing the clown. Take strings 1 and 2 from the hooks at either side of the head, using strong thread. Wind the end around the cut nicks and tie firmly. Sew string 3 to the center base of the back hip, stitching through the clothes. Attach strings 4 and 5 to the front knee hooks and a continuous string 6 to 7 running through the cup hook and stitched to the top of each hand.

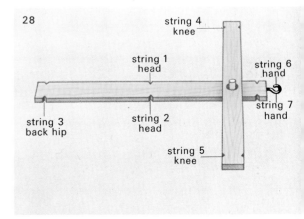

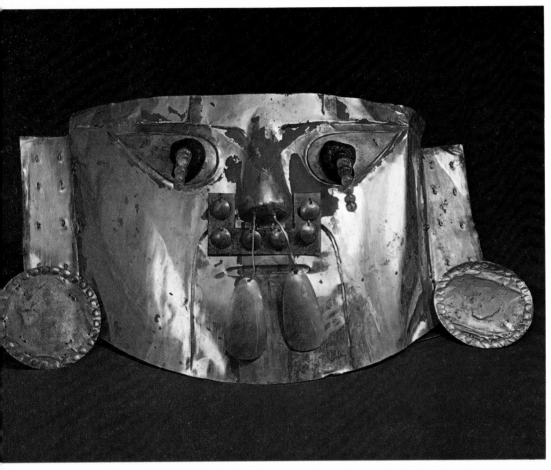

Designing and making masks can be a good outlet for the imagination. Putting on a mask creates an instant disguise or enables the wearer to assume a different personality when acting in a play. Masks are most effective if their expressions are exaggerated; this is particularly important if they are to be used on stage and seen from a distance.

Warning: before putting on any mask make sure that it is sufficiently ventilated so that you will be able to breathe freely. Never use plastic bags, containers with sharp edges or any other potentially harmful objects as masks.

Making masks

Masks from paper bags and boxes. You can make very simple and effective masks from paper bags and boxes.

To make a paper bag mask, find a plain paper bag that will fit over the head easily. Hold the bag against your face, the sealed end at the top, and mark the position of your eyes, nose and mouth with a pencil. Cut openings at these positions. Paint the mask boldly with poster paints.

Body masks can be made in the same way from very large paper bags such as the type used for refuse collection. Cut openings in the sides of the bag for the arms.

To make a box mask use a whole box to cover the head or half a box to cover just the face. Make in the same way as for a paper bag mask.

Add features by glueing smaller boxes, cardboard tubes, egg cartons, corrugated cardboard etc., to the mask. Decorate by painting, spraying, or covering the mask with colored paper.

Masks from balloons. Papier mâché masks modeled on balloons are easy to make and will stand up to fairly harsh treatment. A standard-sized balloon will make a face mask and a large balloon will make a head mask. Glue features onto the balloon and cover with papier mâché layers or add them afterwards and cover the joins with papier mâché or paint over them.

Modeled masks. Modeling is the most precise method for making masks, and although time-consuming, it is the best way to go about creating a specific character in the exact size required.

Masks are associated not only with carnivals, processions, masquerades and the theater, but also with many different forms of religious practice and ritual.

A mask is not necessarily just a form of simple disguise, but may be used in many societies either to frighten or placate evil spirits. As worn by the Japanese *samurai* or Chinese warriors, a mask became an awesome device for instilling terror into an enemy.

Whether worn by a medicine man or *shaman* for purposes of exorcism or curing disease, by West African tribesmen during initiation rites or by Hopi and Zuni Indians of North America during rain-making ceremonies, masks play an essential practical and ritualistic role in the cultural life of peoples all over the world.

The connection between ritual and theater is a close one. Non-literate societies often use elaborate masks and costumes to de-

Peruvian gold funerary mask from Mochica decorated with emeralds and dating from between the 4th and 9th centuries AD.

pict human or animal ancestry when re-enacting the story of the origins and history of their culture. This practice is not so far removed from the wearing of stylized masks by actors to represent the gods and goddesses who were the principal subjects of Ancient Greek or Roman drama. Similarly, Japanese Nō masks of lacquered wood fulfilled the same kind of function. Masks can be made from all kinds of different materials — wood, bark, paper, papier mâché, dried grass, palm fiber, animal skins or fur, feathers, clay, ebony, bronze and gold. Some of the most splendid examples of gold masks survive from the Inca civilization, and gold was also used for the funeral mask of the Egyptian Pharoah Tutankhamen (C1350 BC).

Robot mask

The robot mask pictured overleaf is particularly easy to make. If you want to add the body mask as well, simply use a larger carton.

You will need:
cereal box □ yogurt container □ egg carton □ 3 boxes (eg large matchbox sections) for ears and mouth □ large piece of fairly sturdy colored paper for face □ small piece of silver paper □ colored paper shapes for decoration □ elastic cord □ enamel paint □ poster paints □ glue □ scissors.

Making the mask. Cut the back and top flaps off the cereal box, leaving the front, 2 sides and bottom. The bottom of the box will be the top of the mask. Hold the box against your face and mark the position for the eyes and nose inside the box with a pencil. Cut out 2 circles about 2.5cm (1in) in diameter for eyes and a rectangle about 2.5×4cm ($1 \times 1\frac{1}{2}$in) for the nose. Glue the colored paper onto the front, sides and top of the mask and cut out the holes for the eyes and nose.

Adding the features. Take 2 egg carton sections and cut out the circular base. Place the wide end of an egg section onto the silver paper and draw around it. Cut out the paper and make a neat hole in the center the same size as the eye hole in the box. Make a second eye-surround from silver paper in the same way. Glue the paper pieces onto the front of the mask over the eye holes and glue an egg section on top of each piece.

Make a small triangular hole just below the rim of the yogurt container. (This will enable the wearer to breathe more easily.) Paint the container with enamel paint and glue to the face over the nose hole, with the breathing hole in the "nostril" position. Paint the boxes for the ears with poster paint and glue in position on each side of the mask.

Cut an oval or rectangle from the left-over back of the cereal box for the lips and open mouth. Paint it and glue it onto the center of the "mouth" and glue onto the face. Stick colored shapes onto the face for decoration. Pierce a small hole above and below the ears on each side of the box and thread a length of elastic cord between the top holes and another between the bottom holes.

Devil mask from Oruro, Bolivia worn at "La Diablada" a dance performed by Bolivian Indian miners: the ceremony enacts the conquest of the devil and his minions by angels. Note the ingenious use of painted electric lamp bulbs!

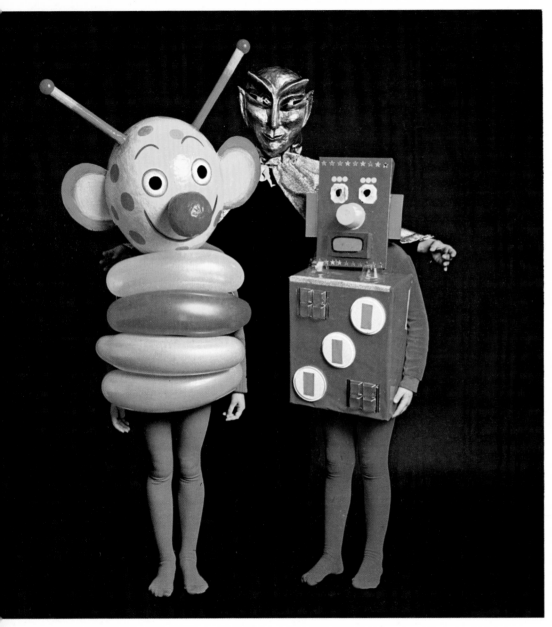

places that seem thin with more paper and paste.

Cut out 2 ear shapes from the cardboard and make 2 cardboard tubes for antennae. Glue or tape these in position and stick a ping pong ball onto the end of each antenna. Cover the joins with one or two more layers of papier mâché.

Cut out holes for the eyes and around the bottom of the mask so that it will slip over the wearer's head easily. Paint the mask with a primer coat of white water-based paint (emulsion) and a top coat of poster or acrylic paint, then varnish.

Demon mask

This papier mâché mask would make an impressive disguise at a children's Halloween party.

You will need:

piece of strong cardboard 40cm (16in) square □ plastic putty (plasticine) □ petroleum jelly □ wallpaper paste □ newspaper □ white water-based paint (emulsion) □ silver, green and purple enamel and spray paint □ elastic cord □ craft knife.

Making the mask. Draw an outline of your face onto the cardboard, marking the position of the eyes, nose and mouth. It is important to mark these accurately to ensure a good fit later. Build up the mold for the mask onto the drawing with plastic putty. Make the features bold, exaggerating the eyebrows, eyelids and cheeks.

When the mold is complete, smear it thoroughly with petroleum jelly and cover it with papier mâché, using the layering method as described on page 227.

When the papier mâché is completely dry, slip a knife under the edges of the model and lift it carefully off the cardboard with the plastic putty still inside. Gently ease out the plastic putty and patch any thin places with more paper and paste. Trim around the edges of the mask and carefully cut out holes or slits for the eyes, mouth and nostrils.

Painting the mask. First coat the mask with a layer of white water-based paint, then spray and paint with silver, purple and green enamel paints for a "metallic" effect. Pierce a small hole inside each ear section and thread with elastic cord.

Yellow space creature

This jolly space mask will delight small children.

You will need:

large balloon for head □ small balloon for nose □ wallpaper paste □ newspaper □ adhesive tape □ glue □ thin cardboard for ears and antennae □ poster or acrylic paints □ white water-based paint (emulsion) □ 2 ping pong balls □ varnish.

Making the mask. Blow up the large balloon and place it in a small bowl or box so that it is supported while you paste. Blow up the small balloon and attach it in position onto the large balloon with adhesive tape. Tear strips of newspaper about 10 × 4cm (4 × 1½in) and paste 6 layers of these over both balloons, using the layering method of papier mâché as described on page 227.

When the papier mâché is thoroughly dry, burst the balloons with a pin. Patch any

Making and assembling a kite

A 19th-century print of Japanese kite fliers. Many Japanese kites represent symbols of good fortune; the carp kite, seen here, is thought to be a particularly good omen.

Kite-flying has been popular in China, Japan and Korea for over two thousand years. Kites were usually made of bamboo and silk or paper and many were shaped like a dragon, a bird, or a centipede. Others were decorated with traditional symbols, such as the crane, which represents longevity. The Chinese word for kite, *fen cheng*, means "wind harp" and kites were sometimes fitted with strings or pipes, which produced musical sounds when air passed through them.

In Japan, kite fights — the object being to destroy or bring down an opponent's kite — became a national pastime. But kites have not only been made for sport or regarded merely as playthings. They have been used as a means of divination, flown in order to ward off evil spirits or created as symbols to bring good fortune. Japanese carp kites, for example, are traditionally flown during the Boys Festival, celebrated on May 5th. The carp is a fish believed to be able to overcome disaster and such a kite is therefore considered a good omen.

Special kites have also been developed in both the East and West for purposes of military observation or for meteorological investigation. In 1752, Benjamin Franklin used a kite to conduct a scientific experiment that determined the nature of lightning and led to the use of lightning rods or conductors. He risked his life by flying a kite in a thunderstorm and noted that sparks were discharged between parts of a key that he had attached to the bottom of the flying line, thereby proving that lightning was in fact a form of electricity.

Kites have never been a significant feature of cultural life in the West, but as a sport kite-flying has enjoyed something of a revival in the past few years and has become a source of simple enjoyment for adults and children alike.

Making and assembling a kite

Kites are made from three basic parts: a frame, a sail or cover and usually a tail. A kite also has a bridle (strings attached to the frame) and a flying line.

Frame. Frames are usually made from split bamboo as this is light, strong and flexible and can easily be bent to the required shape. The safest way to split bamboo is to lay the cane on the ground and insert the point of a knife into the center of the width of the cane, near one end. Press hard so that the knife point comes out on the other side. Stand the cane on end and tap sharply so that the knife cuts down to the bottom. Reverse the cane and use the knife to split the other end. By using this method your hands do not come into contact with the knife blade. If necessary, split the half canes again for a lighter stick. The smaller the kite, the thinner the sticks need to be. Hazel, willow and poplar branches are also suitable if they are straight and completely dry.

The horizontal part of the frame must be perfectly balanced. After cutting the stick for the horizontal, mark the center with a pencil and balance it at this point on one finger. If the stick dips at one end, shave a little wood from this end and test again. The vertical stick should be a little heavier at the bottom than the top.

Sail or cover. A wide assortment of materials can be used for sails, such as closely woven fabric, different types of paper, and vinyl.

Note: do not use any kind of perforated materials.

Tail. Almost every kind of kite, with the exception of a box kite, needs a tail to stabilize it. Make one from the same material as the sail or cover and tie extra strips to the bottom of the kite as streamers. Alternatively, make a tail by cutting strips of paper about 20 × 5cm (8 × 2in) and tie them along the tail string about 20cm (8in) apart. The length of the tail is determined by the size and shape of the kite. Generally, a tail should be about five times the length of the kite.

Bridle. A bridle is essential as a means of tilting the kite at the right angle to meet prevailing air currents. It consists of two or more strings threaded through a towing ring and tied to the frame.

Flying line. A flying line must be both light and strong: the best thing to use is thin string or nylon. Do *not* use wire. The line must be firmly anchored to the reel. Three different types of reel are shown in fig.1. Attach one end of the line to the towing ring.

Decorating the kite. Dyes or oil-based paints are suitable for fabric, water colors or

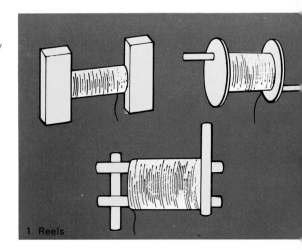

1. Reels

ink for paper and water-based acrylic paints for vinyl or plastic. You can also cut out colored paper shapes and glue them onto the kite.

Flying the kite. Choose an open field. If there is a hill do not stand on the top, but stay halfway up on the side facing the wind.

Warning: do not fly a kite near buildings or overhead power cables or in the vicinity of an airfeld. It is not safe to fly a kite when it is raining.

To launch a kite stand with your back to the wind, and holding the kite by the towing ring at arm's length, allow the wind to lift the kite into the air. It should not be necessary to run with the kite.

Cutter kite
This simple but effective kite can be made from paper, plastic or fabric. It measures 61 × 40.5cm (24 × 16in).

You will need:
2 split bamboo canes 61cm (24in) long

☐ large sheet of strong light paper or large piece of fabric ☐ quick-drying wood glue ☐ string ☐ curtain ring ☐ knife ☐ scissors ☐ ruler ☐ pencil ☐ needle and thread if fabric is used.

Making the frame. Trim one of the canes to 40.5cm (16in) and balance it as described earlier. Place this cane across the long one at right angles about 20cm (8in) down from the top. Bind the canes together

where they cross, by winding string over, under and around. Finish with a double knot to secure. Cover the binding with wood glue and leave to dry for 20 minutes. When the glue is dry, cut a small notch at each end of the canes (fig.2). Cut a piece of string long enough to go around the kite from one cane end to the next to form the cutter shape. Slot the string into each notch and secure with a double knot at the bottom of the vertical cane.

Making the sail or cover. Place the frame onto the cover material and draw around the shape of the frame with a ruler and pencil, leaving a margin as shown in fig.3. Cut V shapes at each corner. Remove the frame and decorate the kite as desired, then replace the frame in the same position as before. If the cover is made of paper or vinyl, turn over the margin and glue down. If you have used fabric, stitch down with needle and thread.

Attaching the bridle. Place the kite on a flat surface, decorated side upwards. Cut a piece of string equal to the length of 1 long and 1 short side of the kite. Cut a second piece of string equal to 2 short sides. Tie the longer piece of string to the top of the kite and the other to the left-hand end of the horizontal cane. Thread both strings through the curtain ring, looping them over twice, then tie the end of the longer string to the bottom end of the vertical cane and the other to the right-hand end of the horizontal cane as shown in fig.4. Make a tail as described earlier and attach it to the bottom end of the kite.

Air testing. Start with the towing ring at the center of the horizontal string, just level with the point where the canes cross. Secure the ring in this position with adhesive tape. The kite should ideally fly at an angle of 45°. If the kite does not rise correctly try moving the towing ring upwards. If it flutters or dips, move the ring downward. If it falls to the left, move the ring a little to the right and if it veers to the right, move the ring a little to the left.
A kite may also fail to rise if the tail is too long and spinning or looping will occur if the tail is too light or too short. The tail may have to be lengthened or shortened according to the strength of the wind.

Experimenting with kite shapes
There are many designs that are suitable for kites, from simple flat shapes to more complicated bird shapes. Some alternative designs are shown below. Instead of making a covered kite, try cutting a kite shape from polystyrene foam and use cane for supports.

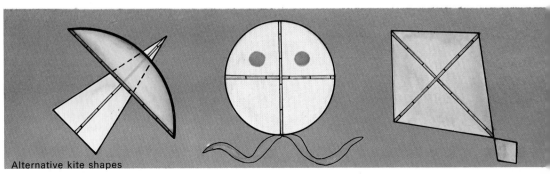

Alternative kite shapes

Basketry

A tribal basketry hat from British Columbia, depicting a whale hunt.

Basketry is one of the oldest and most widespread crafts in the world and ancient techniques used thousands of years ago are still practiced today. Coiling, which is one of the basic methods used for baskets, is also known as Indian basketwork and many Native American tribes had their own distinctive styles and designs. Simple weaves, diagonal combinations for a herringbone effect, triangular groupings and other geometric designs are all forms that have important symbolic significance in Indian basketry. Color too has a special place, achieved by the highly skilled use of various dyes or deriving from the natural color of materials. The Hopi, for example, use mainly yucca, which has yellowish-green leaves, while other tribes use cedar bark, spruce roots and willows.

As well as having many obvious practical uses, baskets may have a specially important role to play in domestic and religious ceremonies. One type of Navajo basket, for instance, is made of aromatic sumac and used during a sacred meal. This same tribe uses a certain type of basket as a ceremonial drum or tom-tom. Tribal baskets are also an important feature of a women's ceremony in which both basket dancers and basket throwers take part in an intricate ritual.

Basketry has been said to be "the poetry of Indian women" and legend tells how the first woman lay asleep and prayed in her dream for help in pleasing her companion. In reply she was given a tiny basket containing a magical element which she could not see, touch or smell. This magical element however, enabled her to possess all the skills of basket-making.

Most societies in fact have developed their own basketry skills and all have their fair share of stories or legends and traditions. It is a fascinating craft offering endless possibilities for experiment and innovation.

Basketry is a craft which varies all over the world, being closely linked to the types of plant that are available in any particular country. Useful materials can range from pliable strips of split wood to rushes, leaves or grasses.

The techniques fall roughly into two groups, although the dividing lines are blurred. They are "hard" basketry, which is worked with fairly rigid materials such as thin branches or cane, and "soft" basketry, for which you can use rushes, iris leaves and similar plants.

Above: Gathering and preparing materials.

Left: A Victorian perambulator with canework.

Collecting your material

Cane, willow or rush can be bought, but you will find it quite possible and very satisfying to gather your own material. For soft material, gather in summer or when the plants are fully grown. Cut full-length rush, reeds, long grass, or any leaves of a strap-like nature, from bullrush to garden plants such as iris, gladiolus or even crocus. Lay the materials out in the open air to dry, turning occasionally, or hang them up in bundles. (They will keep much of their green color if this is done out of direct sunlight). They will shrink a great deal when dry, so collect as many as you can. As soon as they feel dry and papery, tie them in bundles and store in an airy place. For hard material, gather in winter when the sap is down, from plants such as wil-

Coiling
Braiding or
plaiting

low, hazel and dogwood. Try any thin, one-year old shoots, and if they kink rather than crack when gently bent over, they can be used. Long strands which taper very little can be cut from honeysuckle, bramble and some ivy and garden climbers. Most of these materials will need to be left outside on grass or under a hedge for two or three weeks to mellow and shrink a little without drying out completely. After this period use them right away to enjoy the colors at their most vivid or peel away the bark if you prefer a paler whitish shade.

Soft basketry
Preparing the material. The dry plant materials need to be made pliable again, so dip enough for a day's work in water, then wrap them in a cloth to mellow. This may take from half an hour for thin leaves to eight or ten hours for thick rushes; the time needed for mellowing will depend on weather conditions as well as on the plant itself. When the leaf is pliable when bent, it should be ready to use. If necessary, redip, but never allow it to become waterlogged. Keep the bundle wrapped up while working and draw each leaf out by the thick or butt end.

Basic techniques
There are three main ways of working: coiling, braiding or plaiting, and weaving. These are all distinct techniques.

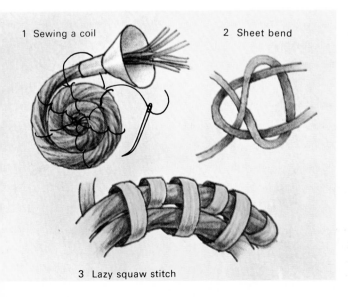

1 Sewing a coil   2 Sheet bend

3 Lazy squaw stitch

Coiling
This is done by guiding the material through the neck of a funnel and sewing the coil with fine string or twine (fig.1). Practice at first with a funnel having an opening with a diameter of about 1cm ($\frac{3}{8}$in). The funnel will act as a gauge, so push in enough leaves by the butt ends to fill the neck comfortably, then as the work progresses, insert more as needed to keep the thickness even. Trim the end of the bunch to a slant, then start wrapping it firmly, past the slant, for 3—4cm (1$\frac{1}{4}$—1$\frac{1}{2}$in) with string threaded into a curved packing needle or upholsterer's needle. Work from right to left, holding the neck of the funnel in your left hand and twisting the bunch slightly as you work, to keep the strands together. Bend the beginning into as small a coil as possible and continue binding over the slant to hold it together, sewing from the back to the front.
Make a second round of close stitches, going over the new coil, and inserting the needle on the back at the right of a stitch and through to the front on the left of the same stitch. On the next row, the stitches will be more widely spaced and, as the spiral widens to about 2.5cm (1in), start an extra set of stitches halfway between the others to keep the work really firm and secure.
To join in a new length of string, tie it with a sheet bend to the old length as shown in fig.2 and continue sewing.
Finishing. Gradually flatten off the coil until it merges with the previous row, then sew back from left to right into the same stitches to form a waved lined. Cover the coil with raffia, fine rush or strong pliable leaves for a different effect.
Try a figure eight stitch, working alternately around the new coil and the previous round. Lazy squaw stitch (fig.3) is a short stitch wrapped around the top coil from front to back, followed by a long stitch taken over the top coil again and coming out below the lower coil.
If the raffia or leaves are dry, wipe them with a damp sponge or cloth while working. Dry off any unused material, and allow the air to circulate around the work to prevent mold from forming. Before the next working session, when dampening the

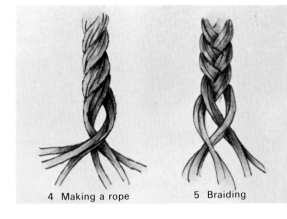

4 Making a rope   5 Braiding

material, wrap a damp cloth around the unfinished ends of the mat or basket so that everything will work pliably together.
To join in new material, lay a new working strand along the coil under the stitches, then lay the short end of the old material under the following stitches. To make a stronger article, twist the raffia or leaves as you work.
Making a rope (fig.4). Hang up a bunch of leaves from a nail or hook, divide into two even groups, twist the right-hand bunch to the right and cross it over the other to transfer it to the left hand and repeat.

Braiding or plaiting
With braiding or plaiting you can make a long length of very strong material from individually weak leaves. Different braids may be used for wide, narrow, flat, round or square effects. A very useful simple method to try first is the same as is generally used for braiding hair. It is a good way of using material of varied thickness and length.
Tie up a small bundle of rushes or leaves very firmly by the base or butt and hang from a hook. Divide into three bundles of equal thickness and braid as shown in fig. 5. Continue working in this way from side to side, forming a wide angle each time for a close firm braid. As soon as one bundle begins to feel thin, add a new butt near the center of the braid and twist it in with the rest of the group. This keeps all the ends at the back for trimming off later. Make sure that the thickness of the braid stays the same by slipping a ring of a suitable size over the braid to act as a gauge.

Weaving

For sewing, use soft strong string and a small packing needle. The needle will slip through more easily if the braid is completely dry. Use a sailor's palm if the braid is thick. This is a special leather pad worn over the palm of the hand to prevent the needle from digging into the skin.

Flat circular base. For a neat start when braiding, fold the leaves or rushes over a loop of string secured over a hook or nail. Make a long length of braid, then start sewing. Bind firmly for about 2.5cm (1in) with the end of a long length of string, then press into a tight little circle to form the center for a flat base. Stitch through the middle once or twice, making sure that the wrong side of the braid with the trimmed-off ends is on the inside of the coil. If you are right-handed, coil in a counterclockwise direction (fig. 6) and if left-handed in a clockwise direction. Do not take stitches over the edge of the braid where they will show, but through the middle of two rows of braiding, inserting the needle on the same side each time. When you get near the ends, dampen them and braid another length until the article is the right size. On the last row, the stitches will sink invisibly into the braid as it is gradually flattened down to merge into the previous round.

To join the new lengths of string, tie to the old end with a sheet bend as shown in fig.2.

Bowl shape. Make a flat circular base as described, then hold each succeeding

6 Sewing up a braid

round slightly tighter and over the edge of the previous row until the braid is lying horizontally over the base. Make handles by extending a row slightly on either side and leaving a gap when sewing up. For an oval mat or bowl, start with a straight line down the center instead of a circle.

Scrolls. To make scrolls, mark the middle of a braid about 1m (1yd) long, sew up one end as for a flat base until you reach the middle point, then start again from the other end, coiling in the opposite direction to form an "S" shape. Sew up until the two circles meet.

Turk's head mat. A length of braid worked into a flattened knot or Turk's head shape will make a very effective mat. For the Turk's head, complete five loops as shown in fig. 7 and then continue alongside the original line two, three or four times depending on the size of braid. Finish at the back beside the beginning and stitch the ends neatly to the main braid. Take a few stitches through the sides of the braids to keep them in position if necessary.

Weaving

This will produce a very lightweight basket which shows off the variety of colors in the dried plant material. Because of their soft nature, woven baskets and similar articles need to be made on a smooth mold, preferably of wood or pottery.

Woven mat

This simple mat incorporates the basic techniques of weaving (checkweave) and pairing and measures 15cm (6in) across. Use freshwater rush if available as these are strong, pliable and even in width.

You will need:
10 rushes, 1.5cm ($\frac{1}{2}$in) wide for stakes ☐ a handful of thinner rushes for weaving ☐ awl or rush threader for weaving strands ☐ rolling pin or straight-sided bottle ☐ ruler ☐ cloths for dampening and wiping ☐ scissors.

Preparing the rush. Prepare 10 rushes 1.5cm ($\frac{1}{2}$in) wide and a handful of thinner rush. Cut stakes 35cm (14in) long from the butts of the 10 rushes, putting aside the other ends for weaving.

Woven (checkweave) center. Lay 5 stakes side by side horizontally, and as they taper

gradually from butt to tip keep the work even by laying a butt first at one end then at the other. Find the middle by folding one of the stakes in half and place a ruler straight across the stakes, about 3cm (1$\frac{1}{4}$in) left of the center, so as to give a clean first folding line.

Place the side of your left hand firmly on the ruler and lift stakes 2 and 4, holding them behind your left thumb as shown in fig. 8. Lay the first vertical stake across 1, 3 and 5 as close as possible to the ruler. Lift up 1, lay down 2, lift up 3, lay down 4 and pick up 5. It is most important not to drop 2

Soft basketry items. Working clockwise: braided oval mat with scrolls, shoulder bag being worked on a wooden mold, Turk's head mat, scroll mat, bowl with handles and (center) mat with woven (checkweave) center.

and 4 before picking up the alternating stakes as they will tend to drift apart and they must be kept as close as possible. Place the next vertical stake in position, lift up 2 and 4 and lay down 1, 3 and 5. Repeat with the 3 remaining stakes.

Pairing (fig.9). Select a long strong rush for the weaver. Pull off the weak tip and loop it around the first stake on the left to

make two working ends. Take the left-hand weaver in front of stake 1, behind 2 and lay it diagonally in front of 3. Anchor it there with your left thumb. Take the new left-hand weaver in front of stake 2, behind 3 and lay it in front of 4, pulling it slightly to the right to draw the stakes together. Repeat this pairing all the way around, giving the mat a quarter turn when you reach a corner so that the working stakes are always upright. After the first round, check that the center is square. If necessary ease into shape with the awl or threader and adjust the length of any short stake by pulling on it gently.

After the second round, fan out the stakes to resemble the spokes of a wheel while continuing with the pairing. Stakes have a tendency to slope to the left, so hold them carefully in position as you work.

Note: flatten lightly with the rolling pin or bottle after every few rows of work to improve the finish.

To join in a new weaver, overlap for several movements and trim so that the ends are hidden under the pairing. When the mat measures about 15cm (6in) across, end off the weavers by pushing the awl or threader up through 5cm (2in) of pairing over the stake on the right of the weaver and threading the weaver and drawing the threader down. Turn the mat over and check that the circle shape is satisfactory and dampen the stakes again before making either of the following borders.

First border (fig.10). Using the awl or threader as for ending off a weaver, draw each stake down in front of the next, working closely and firmly. Trim the ends very closely, put the mat under a weight overnight and dry off in a current of air.

Alternative border. Using the threader, draw each stake down in front of the *second* stake to the right to give a more visible ropelike edge.

Further weaving techniques

Adding stakes (fig.11). Sometimes extra stakes are required, for example to make a square mat. To fill in each corner, fold a new stake into a right angle and lay it close to the corner, using the top half only, on the first round. This will make the join less visible. Repeat in each corner every two

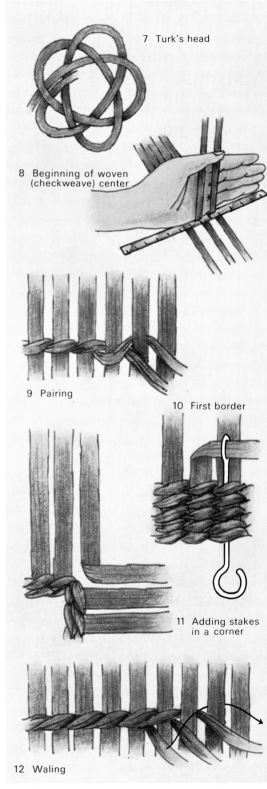

7 Turk's head

8 Beginning of woven (checkweave) center

9 Pairing

10 First border

11 Adding stakes in a corner

12 Waling

Shoulder bag

rounds, finishing off with at least four plain rounds.

Broken stakes. Sooner or later one of the stakes is bound to break. Push the threader up through several rows of weaving below the break and draw down a new length of stake over the broken end so that they overlap. Trim when the article is complete. Use this method to add an extra stake alongside another.

Waling (fig.12). Waling is a method of making a firm thick line of weaving. Place three (or four) weavers in a similar way as for pairing, but work in front of two (or three) stakes instead of one.

Simple weaving (randing). This is a method of weaving using a single rush or twist of thin leaves, taken in front of one stake and behind the next.

Shoulder bag

This attractive shoulder bag with a braided handle is worked on a mold to produce the basic shape.

You will need:
cigar box measuring 21 × 18 × 5cm (8¼ × 7 × 2in) for mold □ rushes about 1cm (⅜in) wide for stakes □ thinner rushes for weaving □ leaves such as iris for handle □ awl or rush threader □ cloths for wiping and dampening □ scissors □ fine string.

Preparing the stakes (fig.13). You will need 2 sets of stakes. Cut 5 stakes for the first set to measure about 85cm (33½in) to be taken lengthwise along the base of the mold and up the sides and allowing 10–15cm (4–6in) at each side for the border. Cut 22 stakes for the second set to measure about 90cm (36in) to be taken from the front to the back of the mold, allowing for a border at the front and for the flap at the back.

Positioning the stakes. Turn the mold upside down and lay the first set of stakes in position along the length of the base, matching the centers of the stakes to the center of the base. Tie the stakes down with string at the center point.

Making the base. Introducing the second set of stakes, work weave (checkweave) from the center to the right-hand edge of the base, then turn the mold around and work the other half in the same way. Secure this section firmly to the mold by adding another string tie across the first. Lay the mold on its side, insert an extra short stake at one corner to make an odd number and work a round of waling very carefully along the edge of the base. Smooth the stakes against the sides of the mold as you work.

Working the sides. Continue with simple weaving (randing) with a twist of thin leaves, adding in new leaves to keep the work even. Check every few rows to ensure that the lines are straight. When you reach the top of the mold work a few rows of pairing to finish off the front and sides.

Working the flap. Working with the stakes at the back, continue with simple weaving (randing) to cover the top of the bag, then change to waling for the front of the flap, gradually reducing the stakes used at either end to make a curve. Finish off the flap with 2 rows of waling all the way around and the alternative border as described earlier, worked from the inside.

On the other 3 edges work the border from the outside.

Put the flap in position under a weight while still damp and leave overnight. Remove the mold and allow the work to dry out.

Note: never leave the work wrapped up for more than a day and when redampening only wet the unused portion of the stakes.

Making the handle (fig.14). Work a 285cm (112in) length of three-stranded braid from leaves and sew to the bag.

Making the loop. Thread 2 or 3 leaves behind one of the central stakes on the front flap and work a thin length of rope with both ends. Take the ends behind the next stake on the flap and secure through the weaving at the back.

Making the button. Make a length of fine braid about 70cm (27½in) long and no more than 0.5cm (¼in) wide, and shape into a turk's head. Ease the shape into a small solid ball instead of a flat shape.

Hard basketry

Cane or rattan is a climbing palm that grows in the jungles and swamps of the East Indies. Inside the rough outer bark, which is removed, is the hard glossy cane. Palembang is a reddish-brown pliable cane graded as "thick" or "thin" and used unsplit, while pulp cane or center cane comes from the center of another cane whose glossy bark is stripped off and used as a chair seating cane.

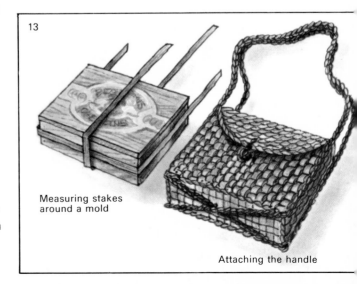

13

Measuring stakes around a mold

Attaching the handle

Palembang ball

This Palembang ball, which is a simple version of the Javanese football, makes an ideal toy for a child. Alternatively, with a small bell tied firmly inside, it can be converted into a baby's rattle.

You will need:
4 lengths of cane, each measuring 175cm (69in) □ shears or basketmaker's side cutters □ fine string or cellophane (clear adhesive) tape □ piece of cloth.

Preparing the cane. Soak the cane for about 6 hours (water does not penetrate it easily) wrap in a cloth and leave overnight.

Making the ball. The ball is made of 4 interlocking circles to form spaces of triangles and squares. Lay 3 canes across each other to form an interlaced triangle then weave the fourth cane around in a circle once as shown in fig.15, and then once more. This forms half the ball. Pull it into a cup shape to measure about 8.5cm ($3\frac{1}{2}$in) across and tie with string or secure with cellophane (clear adhesive) tape to stop the circle shape from springing loose. Complete a second circle by taking the end of one cane and bringing it over to join up with itself on the far side of the circle, following its own path through the first half. Adjust the size to 8.5cm ($3\frac{1}{2}$in) and tie or secure with tape. Take another cane as it comes from inside the first circle, take it over the second circle and join it up by weaving through to complete the third circle. Adjust the size. Take the last cane as it comes from inside the first circle and weave it over the third circle and under the second to join up with its other end. Continue weaving to complete the circle and, after adjusting the size again, repeat the same routes until each circle consists of 6 strands. Remove the string or tape and trim the ends on the inside.

After you have practiced making balls with 4 circles and can easily visualize the shapes needed, try making one with 6 circles, which will form triangles and pentagons. Start with an interlaced five-sided figure, weave the sixth cane into a circle around it (fig.16), and ease into the half ball shape as before.

Weaving methods for baskets

Simple weaving (randing). The method used is the same as for soft basketry described earlier. Take the weaver in front of one stake and behind the next. Always bend the weaver around the stake without distorting it. A weaver must be smaller than a stake unless the stakes are double. With an odd number of stakes, one row will alternate with the next and with an even number of stakes use two weavers, one starting in the space behind the other, but never passing it. Join in new cane so that old and new ends lie behind the same stake.

Double weaving (slewing). This is a method of simple weaving using two or more weavers together.

Pairing and waling. Use the methods as described for soft basketry.

Reverse pairing and waling. Work as for ordinary pairing and waling, but take the left-hand weaver *under* the other (or others) instead of over.

Chain pairing or waling. Work as for ordinary pairing or waling but reverse the second row of a pair. Join in new cane so that the old and new ends lie side by side in the same space, one pointing out and the other in.

Footing (trac border) (fig.17). Weave each stake (or pair) in turn diagonally through successive stakes in the same sequence and thread through the last stakes to complete the pattern without a break. When worked with single stakes in an "over and under one" sequence, this type of border is unobtrusive and looks very like a continuation of the simple weaving. When worked with double stakes in a sequence containing a movement over two stakes, it gives a bolder ropelike effect.

Bowl-shaped basket

As cane is available in long lengths it is best to take advantage of this characteristic rather than cutting the cane into short pieces and using techniques more suited to willow rods. For this basket, the base stakes are taken up the sides, then down the outside to finish off at the base. It is made entirely in No. 3 cane.

You will need:
No. 3 cane cut into 16 stakes each measuring 85cm ($33\frac{1}{2}$in) and 2 stakes measuring 45cm ($17\frac{3}{4}$in) □ sharp knife □ shears or basketmaker's side cutters □

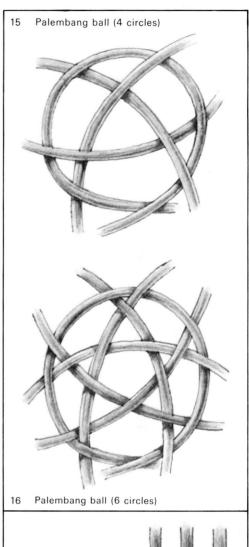

15 Palembang ball (4 circles)

16 Palembang ball (6 circles)

17 Footing (trac border):
behind 1, in front of 2, behind 1

awl or knitting needle □ piece of cloth.

Preparing the cane. Soak the cane in lukewarm water for several minutes, then wrap it up in a cloth for a few more minutes. Do not let the cane get too dry while working, but dry everything off at the end of the day.

Country baskets

Making the base (fig.18). Divide the long canes into 4 groups and mark the middle of each. Place one set over the other in the shape of a cross and the other 2 sets in the shape of an "X". Put one on top of the other to make 8 spokes to be used as stakes. Place the end of the short pair in the middle of the top group, with the ends projecting 5cm (2in) across the center. This will eventually give an odd pair of stakes and avoid the need for 2 weavers. Hold the canes flat on the table with the left hand, slip a weaver under the lowest group and weave (rand) all the way around. Start the second round, still working over and under the same groups, then pull the first round tight. Complete 3 rounds of the same weave, then slip the weaver under 2 groups instead of 1 to start the next 3 rows of alternate weave. Complete these 3 rows, then separate the spokes into 17 pairs of canes and weave (rand) 3 rounds to complete the base.

Making the sides. Work from the other side of the basket to weave the sides and begin shaping them with 1 row of pairing. When you reach the first stake again, change to reverse pairing for the second row, leaving the ends inside. (A row of ordinary pairing followed by a row of reverse pairing is the same as chain pairing.)

Thread the second end under one cane in the first space used to complete the row neatly. Holding the stakes in a shallow bowl shape, weave (rand) until the basket measures about 15cm (6in) across and 7.5cm (3in) high. Now hold the stakes in toward the center and weave (rand) until

the opening measures 12.5cm (5in) across. Work a row of footing (trac border), taking each stake pair over one and under one. Allow the stakes to lie in a comfortable curve, then turn the basket upside down and thread each pair through the chain pairing, using an awl or knitting needle to ease a space open. Work another set of chain pairing, holding the stakes away from the center, and finish off with footing (trac border) of "over two and behind one", working from right to left. Trim the ends, making sure that they spring against a stake and not through a gap.

To remove the cane whiskers, dip the basket into water and pass it quickly across a smokeless flame several times.

Country baskets

A basket made from materials that you can gather for yourself is fun to work and will cost nothing to make. The main thing to remember is that the thickest material should be used for the base and handle. Side stakes should be somewhat thinner and weavers must be thinner still and soft and pliable.

Round base. For a round base measuring 15cm (6in) in diameter, cut 6 stakes 20cm (8in) long. Sharpen the points of 3 stakes and pierce slits through the middle of the remaining 3 stakes. Put the 3 pointed stakes through the slits of the other 3 stakes to form a cross. Hold the cross in position by looping a length of bramble for example, around one group and pairing 2 rounds very closely. Now spread out the stakes so that they look like the spokes of a wheel and very carefully pair around each of the stakes separately as shown in fig.19. This opening out is one of the most important parts of the basket. Continue pairing until the base measures 15cm (6in) across, making it an inverted saucer shape for strength and steadiness.

Oval base. Cut 3 stakes 33cm (13in) long and 7 stakes 21.5cm (8½in) long. Insert the 3 long stakes through the short ones, placing 1 short stake in the middle, 1 on each side, 3cm (1¼in) away, and then a pair on each side, the same distance away (fig.20). Hold these in place by binding with a split rod, wrapping between the

Hard basketry items: Palembang balls, bowl-shaped baskets and oval country basket.

short rods, and starting and finishing with a cross over the pairs. These, with the long sticks, will be opened out in the same way as half a round base, while the 3 center short stakes will remain straight. However, as an oval base has a tendency to warp, this must be counteracted either by working it in chain pairing (perhaps

18

Oval country basket

more suited to canework) or by working one third of the base in pairing and the rest in reverse pairing.

Oval country basket

This sturdy basket is made with an oval base from a combination of garden willow and dogwood, but other suitable materials can be substituted as available.

You will need:

3 stakes 33cm (13in) long and about 0.5cm ($\frac{1}{4}$in) thick and 7 stakes 21.5cm (8$\frac{1}{2}$in) long and about 0.5cm ($\frac{1}{4}$in) thick for base □ 32 stakes about 50cm (20in) long for side stakes □ 7 or 9 sturdy rods about 80cm (32in) long for handle □ 12–15 rods for waling □ 32 rods for weaving (randing) □ sharp pointed knife □ garden shears or secateurs.

Making the base. Work an oval base as previously described.

Making the sides. When the base measures 17 × 28cm (6$\frac{3}{4}$ × 11in) trim the base stakes closely and insert the sharpened butts of the side stakes for 6cm (2$\frac{1}{2}$in) 1 at each end of the straight base stakes, and 2 for the fanned out ends in the semicircles (fig.21). To accommodate the handle, add a second stake at each end of the short central stake, but treat them both as one during the weaving (randing), keeping them at the right distance apart with temporary rods.

Bend up each stake over the point of a knife, close to the base, and hold firmly in position while working 3 rows of waling. Work firmly as this is the most important part of the shaping of the basket. Work with tapering rods requires a slightly different weaving (randing) technique (known as French weaving or French randing). Place a rod in one space, work in front of one stake and behind the next, leaving the end outside. Repeat in each space to the left until the round is complete, then continue the next rows in similar steps to the left. If a second set of weavers is needed, start the first round in front of 2 stakes all the way around, to give the effect of waling. Continue for 13cm (5$\frac{1}{4}$in), then complete with 3 rows of waling.

Finish off the basket with footing (trac

border) or work a 3-rod border (fig.22), as follows: bend stake 1 behind 2, 2 behind 3 and 3 behind 4. Take 1 in front of stake 4 and behind 5, and bend 4 down to lie closely behind 1, making a pair in front. Work stakes 2 and 3 in the same way, making 3 pairs. Now it will always be the 5th rod from the right which is taken in front of one standing stake and behind the next. Thread in the last stakes to complete the pattern. The ends may be cut off outside, or taken through in a follow-on row of footing (trac), by taking each rod past 2 stakes and underneath the border to the inside of the basket.

Making the handle. Remove the temporary rods in the handle space and insert a handle bow pointed at each end as far down as the waling. Insert 3 or 4 long rods on the left of the rod in the same space. Twist them all to the right in front of the handle and under it, ending at the other side by going over the handle and under the waling, crossing the border again before securing the ends. Repeat with 3 or 4 more butts inserted on this side and twisted over the handle bow, filling the gaps to the other side.

Trim all the ends with a slanting cut against a stake.

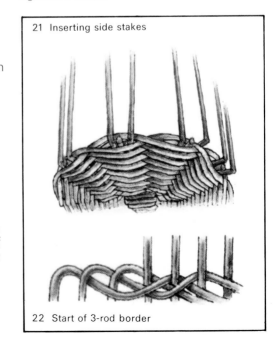

21 Inserting side stakes

22 Start of 3-rod border

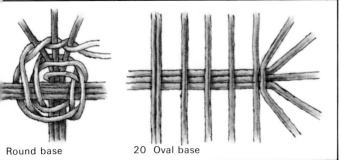

Round base   20 Oval base

Basketry
Canework

Chair caning

As well as being used traditionally for making all kinds of baskets, cane has proved its versatility as an ideal material for certain types of furniture. Cane is usually used for chair seats and for the backs and sides of chairs and sometimes couches, within a wood or bamboo frame. Canework for this purpose originated in China and other parts of the Far East and was introduced to Europe by the Dutch colonizers of the East Indies during the 17th century.

Chair caning

Chair caning is a method of weaving a firm fabric inside a frame, using the glossy bark of climbing palms such as *Calamus rotang*. The cane is graded according to strand width from No. 1 to No. 6—about 1–5mm ($\frac{1}{16} - \frac{3}{16}$) wide—and should be selected according to the spacing of the holes in the frame and the pattern to be woven.

Patterns

Canes are worked in four directions: vertically and horizontally (giving a grid of squares), and diagonally in two directions.

Standard patterns. In the standard pattern the diagonals lie on either side of the corners of each square formed by the verticals and horizontals. A four-way pattern uses one set of canes in each direction, a five-way pattern incorporates a second vertical set and a six-way pattern (fig.1) includes a second horizontal set as well. The six-way pattern is the one

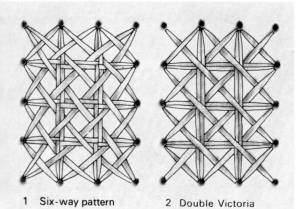

1 Six-way pattern   2 Double Victoria

Antique daybed made from carved walnut and cane.

most commonly used.

Victoria patterns. These are quicker to work than the standard patterns and are best suited to rectangular frames. The diagonals lie over or under the corners of each square and a single Victoria pattern uses one set of canes in each direction, while a double Victoria (fig.2) has two vertical sets, two horizontal sets laid on top, one diagonal set laid over the top of these and the last diagonal set woven under the corners of each square.

Re-caning a chair

It is rare to find a home these days without at least one chair which needs re-caning or which has had its original cane replaced with some form of upholstery. The patterns achieved with canework are very attractive and you will find restoring a chair to its original state a rewarding and satisfying task.

Re-caning
a chair

You will need:
straight piece of metal rod or "clearer", slightly smaller than the frame holes, to knock out the old caning □ pointed awl □ small hammer □ pointed craft knife □ 6 or more cane or wood pegs, about 7.5cm (3in) long, tapered at one end and slightly larger than the holes at the other □ length of cane or wood to be split for the permanent plugs at the end □ about 90g (3oz) of cane.

Clearing the chair. Turn the chair upside down and cut the cane between each hole. Knock out the plugs with the clearer. Keep the old seat for reference in case you wish to reproduce the same or a similar pattern.

Flat rectangular shapes. The easiest type of chair to start with is one with a flat square or rectangular frame. Practice the weave on a small sample frame before starting on the chair itself. It is usually easier to work with one hand above and the other below the seat.

First vertical course (fig.3). Dampen the cane for a few minutes to mellow it. Select one of the longest strands and thread half of it through the middle hole at the back of the frame. Peg the cane so that its shiny surface is visible when the top half is brought over to the front rail of the chair. Thread the cane down through the middle hole on the front rail, pull firmly and peg, then take the cane up through the next hole on the same rail. Repeg and take the cane over to the corresponding hole on the back rail.
Note: the glossy side of the cane should always face outwards, both above and on the underside of the frame.
Continue working the vertical lines until the corner holes are reached. These will not be used until the diagonal sets are worked. Complete the second half of the frame as for the first half, using the end of cane left under the frame at the center hole on the back rail.

Joins (fig.4). To join in a new length of cane, take the short end of the old length of cane down one hole, peg it and bring it up through the next hole. Put the new cane down the same hole, with the wrong side against the right side of the old cane. Take the new cane under and over the old cane on the underside of the rail as shown. Adjust the new cane to lie flat and peg on top.

First horizontal course. Take the end of cane from the first vertical course under the corner and bring it up through the first hole on the side rail. Take it across to the corresponding hole on the other side rail and continue working from side to side to produce a grid of even squares.
Note: to work a standard four-way pattern, now move onto the first diagonal set.

Second vertical course. Work as for the first vertical course, taking the strands over the horizontal course. There is no need to start in the center of the rail, but pull the top strands slightly to the left of the first set and make sure that the new strands on the underside fill the gaps between those already in position.

Second horizontal course (fig.5). For this set the cane is woven. Take the cane over

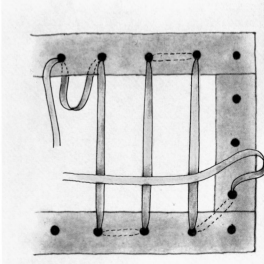

3 First vertical course

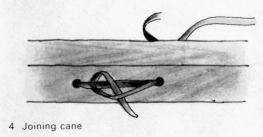

4 Joining cane

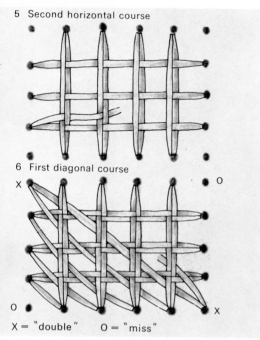

5 Second horizontal course

6 First diagonal course

X = "double"   O = "miss"

the second vertical course and under the first vertical set, weaving the cane in this course so that it is above that of the first horizontal course. Work with a short end of cane for a third or half way across before pulling the whole length through: this will be quicker and will help to prevent the cane from twisting too much. Fill in the gaps on the underside and keep the lines straight and even, pulling the cane down with an awl at the end of each row if necessary.

First diagonal course (fig.6). Work this set with the cane dry and dampen slightly only if it starts to split. A diagonal must be able to slide slightly into the corner of each square of the grid as it passes. Begin near the center of the front rail and working from the bottom right to the top left, pass the diagonals under the verticals and over the horizontals as shown. Work with short lengths of cane—two or three rows are enough to do at a time—pulling the cane through only when it gets too tight.

Note: when starting or ending a row, always make use of the short ends of the verticals and horizontals. Do not weave straight in and out of a square but pass the cane under the end of a vertical pair

on the left of a hole and take it in a series of "steps" up and along before taking it over the end of a horizontal pair and down through the hole above. When working the first diagonal course you will have to "miss" the bottom left-hand and top right-hand holes and "double" the top left-hand and bottom right-hand holes as shown. For the second diagonal set these "misses" and "doubles" should be reversed and, if your weaving is correct, you will end up with a "double" in each hole, including the corners.

Second diagonal course. Starting in the center of the front rail, work the second diagonal course from bottom left to top right. Begin by weaving under a diagonal to the right of the hole, work over the verticals and under the horizontals, taking the cane up and along in a series of steps and finish by weaving over a diagonal and threading the cane down through the hole above. Always make use of the end of a first diagonal at the beginning and end of each row.

Plugging. Having completed all vertical, horizontal and diagonal courses, cut plugs of a length shorter than the depth of the rail and knock them into alternate holes, missing out the corner holes and each adjacent hole on either side of the corners. Alternatively, plug every hole and omit the later finishing stages if preferred.

Trimming. With a pointed knife cut all ends of cane slightly below the level of the holes and all longer strands passing over one or more holes on the underside.

Binder (beading). Cut a length of No. 6 cane to measure about 15cm (6in) more than the length of one rail. Mellow the cane and insert one end into either of the right-hand corners and peg it. Take the lacing cane and thread it down through the next hole and secure it on the underside or bring it up through the corner hole and hide it on top under the binder cane (beading). Pass the long end of the lacing cane over the binder cane and take it down through the same hole. Continue lacing into each unplugged hole, taking up the slack underneath and making sure that the binder cane lies closely and evenly over the holes. Use the awl to make a space in the hole if

necessary. If the binder cane is to lie over a curved rail, gradually stretch the well-mellowed cane into a curve before beginning to weave it in.

Different shapes

Many chairs are wider at the front than at the back and when this is the case, evenly spaced short verticals must be taken from the extra holes on the front rail. This will cause a diagonal "double" or "miss," usually in the first or second hole below the top of the short vertical as shown in fig.7. The "doubles" will be on the left and the "misses" on the right in the first diagonal set and vice versa in the second diagonal set.

Bowfronted or round frame. If you are using this type of frame, you will probably need to work short horizontals as well as short verticals. These will also require a "double" or "miss" at either end as shown in fig.8. Weave each diagonal as fully as the correct weaving sequence will allow so that no bare areas of wood will show inside the binder cane. If preferred, work the diagonals from the center outwards towards the edge of the frame and rearrange the ends after a few rows if necessary.

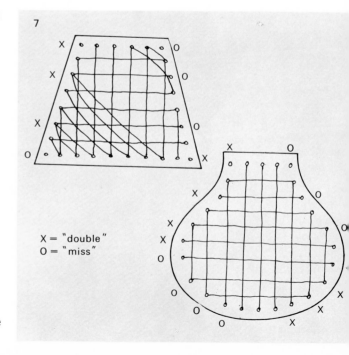

7

X = "double"
O = "miss"

Replica of a corn dolly found in France and following a traditional Arabic design. The center medallion is worked in oats and the scrolls and outer fringe are made of wheat.

Ever since crops have been grown, straw has been used for decorative as well as for practical purposes. Agricultural communities all over the world have created straw objects which play a central role in rituals connected with the harvest and fertility. In England and many other countries for example, the corn dolly is a traditional harvest symbol. A corn dolly is made from the last sheaf to be cut. This is regarded as being the resting place of the corn spirit and has therefore to be preserved throughout the year until the next harvest.

But there are other dimensions to straw work. Straw can be used to make jewelry, bags, baskets and workboxes, hats and fans. In the 17th century, the French mastered the art of straw marquetry, while in Italy the making of straw pictures was highly fashionable.

Straw work, however, remains essentially a country craft, though with the widespread use of reaping machines and combine harvesters and the introduction of new varieties of wheat and other crops, which are

Straw marquetry box made by a French prisoner-of-war in England during the Napoleonic Wars. Each compartment and drawer is lined with straw, a small star forming the center. The motif on the main lid shows Forde Abbey, Dorset; the motifs on the front two lids portray the Aesop Fable of the fox persuading the crow to sing and so drop the cheese from its beak.

unsuitable for straw work, the craft has naturally suffered.

Much of the fun of straw work comes from selecting and gathering your own materials. Experiment with what is readily available and use the following techniques to make articles of your own design.

Selecting materials. Look for spring-sown wheat, which is long, flexible and hollow and ask permission to cut some while it still shows a touch of green at the base. Other sorts of wheat may be suitable for some types of straw work and rye and barley are very useful for fine work. Oats have a beautiful shine and will add contrast of texture to your work, while wild grasses can be used to introduce variations of color. Whatever materials you gather, use them immediately or preserve them by spreading them out to dry for several days to prevent mold from forming. Then tie into

251

Stars and crescent moon

a loose bundle and store in an airy place.
Preparation of materials. If the materials have been freshly gathered, the only preparation needed is to cut each stem below the grain and above the first joint before removing the sheath. If the straw is dry make it pliable again by immersing in water for half an hour, then wrap it in a cloth to mellow. Alternatively, pour boiling water over the straw and it will be ready for use almost immediately. Always dry off any unused straw after finishing work.

Stars and crescent moon mobile

Practice the basic techniques of strawcraft by making this delicate mobile. The crescent moon uses the technique of five straw spiral braiding, which forms the basis for working most types of corn dolly.
You will need:
selection of stems of oats, rye and grasses for stars □ handful of prepared wheat and a piece of cane, 75cm (29½in) long and about 3mm (⅛in) thick for moon □ strong fine thread (preferably linen) in scarlet and a natural color □ blue nylon thread □ pointed craft knife □ scissors □ ruler □ thin paper □ glue.
Tying the straws. Tied straws are most easily held in place with a clove hitch (fig. 1). Make 2 loops of thread, place the second behind the first and slip the loops over the ends of straw.
Tied bunch. Cut 20 lengths of fine straw or grass each about 6cm (2½in) long. Divide these into 2 equal bundles and tie each bundle very firmly at the center with scarlet thread (fig.2). Place one bunch across the other so that the ends are evenly spread out and tie them in position with scarlet thread, leaving a long end for attaching to the moon.
Six-pointed star (fig.3). Cut 6 straws, each about 8.5cm (3½in) long. Make 2 triangles and tie close to the ends with scarlet thread. Place one triangle on top of the other to make a star shape as shown and tie them lightly together at 3 of 6 intersection points. Adjust the position of the triangles into the correct star shape, tighten the ties and complete the last 3 ties.
Five-pointed star (fig.4). Cut 5 straws each about 8.5cm (3½in) long, and tie 4 of these into the shape of an "M". Take each

leg of the "M" across to the opposite side as shown and join the fifth straw to complete the star shape. Tie with scarlet thread at each intersection, leaving a length from one of the points for attaching to the moon.
Double five-pointed star (fig.5). This star needs careful measuring to keep it even. Take 10 straws each about 10cm (4in) long and tie very tightly with natural colored thread in the center so that they fan out above and below the middle. Take 2 straws which are lying side by side and bring together the upper and lower halves. Tie these 4 halves together with scarlet thread 1.5cm (½in) from the center tie. Repeat with the remaining 4 pairs. Take 2 straws from one group to meet 2 straws from the next group and make a point by tying them together close to the ends with scarlet thread. Repeat for the other 4 points, leaving a length from one of the points for attaching to the moon.
Crossed star with weaving thread (fig.6). Cut 4 pieces of very fine straw or grass each about 7.5cm (3in) long and 4 pieces of oats or rye each about 5.5cm (2¼in) long and about 3mm (⅛in) wide when flattened.
Trim each end to a sharp point. Place 2 of the fine straws in the shape of a cross. With 2 wider straws, form an "X" and place it over the cross, matching the centers. Take a scarlet thread and weave it over and under each straw, all the way around, pulling firmly. Secure the ends. Repeat with the other set of straws, then lay one star on top of the other and weave over and under the 16 ends. Having secured the ends, leave one for hanging up and thread the other away invisibly.
Solid star. For this star use oats, rye or grass straws. Split them down one side and flatten with a hot iron. Continue ironing until the straw is slightly scorched to give the contrast of a darker shade.
To mark out a five-point star without using drawing instruments, cut a strip of thin paper to measure 5 × 33cm (2 × 13in) and fold it into an overhand knot by taking the left end over the right end and pulling the original left end down through the loop created. Draw the paper through gently until it is flat and forms a five-pointed

shape (fig.7). Cut off the ends of paper to leave just the pentagon shape. Place the pentagon shape onto a piece of paper and draw around it. Using a pencil and ruler, join up the points of the pentagon to produce the star shape. Cut out the star. This will be used as a base. Cut out 2 more star shapes in the same way. On each of these 2 star shapes draw a straight line from each point to its opposite "notch". Cut out each of the 5 sections from both stars so that they will fit together again as shown in

Stars and crescent moon

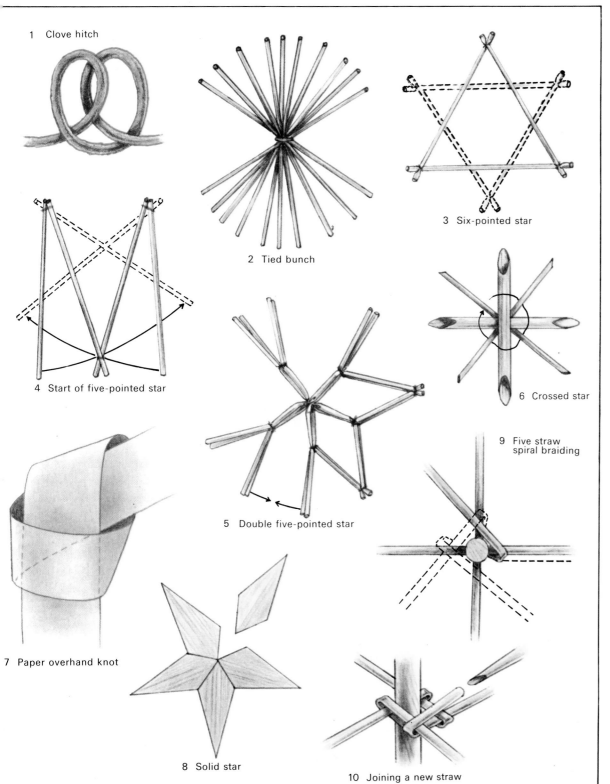

1   Clove hitch

2   Tied bunch

3   Six-pointed star

4   Start of five-pointed star

5   Double five-pointed star

6   Crossed star

7   Paper overhand knot

8   Solid star

9   Five straw spiral braiding

10   Joining a new straw

fig.8. Glue a straight strip of straw onto the top of each section, put under a weight to dry and then trim the edges. Glue these sections onto both sides of the base star, enclosing the end of a length of scarlet thread inside one of the points. Put under a weight to dry.

Crescent moon. Cut the cane into 2 pieces, one measuring 42cm (16½in) long and the other 33cm (13in) long. From the prepared bundle of wheat, select 5 evenly matched straws. Tie the tapered ends tightly around the end of one of the canes with natural colored thread. Keep 2 straws side by side and the others evenly spaced out. Bend the straws at right angles to the cane so that they point N(orth), S(outh), E(ast) and W(est), with the extra straw at E. Take one straw from E and lay it over N as shown in fig.9. Hold these 2 straws with the right hand and turn the cane clockwise with the left hand for a quarter turn so that they both now lie at E. Bend the new E straw (the lower one) to lie across the new N straw as before. Make another quarter turn in a clockwise direction and repeat. Slide the left thumb down the cane to hold the fold in position each time to make it close and firm. The section of straw between each fold should be a straight tube, lying close to the previous row.

Joining in a new straw (fig.10). Cut the old straw so that it projects just beyond a corner and insert the tapered end of a new straw. The next fold over that corner will hide the join.

Having worked to the end of the cane, tie all the straws and cane together as at the beginning, leaving long threads. Cover the second cane in the same way and trim each end to a point. To make the cane pliable, leave in water for 10 minutes. Using the long threads tie each piece into an arc, which should be slightly more curved than the required finished shape. Leave to dry so that it keeps this shape, then cut the threads and tie the arc together very firmly with scarlet thread into the shape of a crescent moon.

Attaching the stars. Attach a length of blue nylon thread to each end of the crescent. Hang 1 star from each end and 2 from each curve, varying the lengths of thread as desired.

Pottery

No-one knows exactly how the process of making pottery was discovered. Perhaps fires were made in holes in the ground lined with clay; or maybe baskets were lined with clay to waterproof them, and as the clay dried and shrank away from the sides a simple pot was formed. Whatever the answer, pottery has been found in many parts of the world dating from the New Stone Age onwards. Before the invention of the wheel, pottery was made entirely by hand. In the earliest societies women made the pots; only with the evolution of urban societies and the use of the wheel did pottery become highly specialized work done by men.

Some time during 4500—4000 BC, two important technological discoveries were made—the kiln and simple glazes. Perhaps the most beautiful examples of early pottery are those from Crete. The Minoans exported oil and wine in pottery jars, which they decorated with delightfully naturalistic designs of flowers, birds and fishes. In contrast, the Mycenaean designs that followed, lacked charm.

The Greeks perfected both the forms and decoration of pottery, bringing both to the state of high art. They developed the technique of black and red pots, decorating their work with battle scenes, races and processions, or more peaceful illustrations from everyday life. Sometimes instead of black figures on a red background they used a white background. As this produced a more fragile clay, such pots were used as perfume bottles or funeral urns. The Romans were less interested in the aesthetic qualities of pottery and their pots tended to be purely functional. Pottery centers were established throughout the vast Roman Empire and local variations of style were generally ignored.

This prosaic approach to pottery was not confined to the Romans. In the 18th century in England, the great Doctor Johnson called the East Indians barbarians. Boswell—clearly a little shocked by this—asked him:

> "You will except the Chinese, Sir?"
> "No, Sir," replied Johnson.
> "Have they not arts?" enquired Boswell.
> "They have pottery," said Johnson.

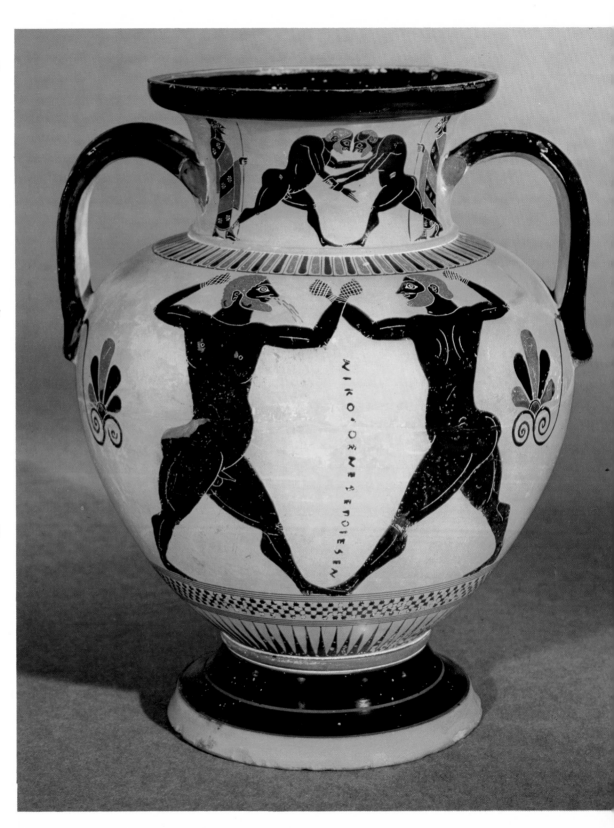

Above: This delightful engraving of a pottery in Staffordshire shows the type of earthenware that was being made in England at the beginning of the 19th century.

Left: Early 6th-century Greek vase decorated with scenes of boxing and wrestling. The inscription reads: "Nikosthenes made me."

Above right: Handpainted 17th-century porcelain plate from Fukien Province, China.

This contemptuous attitude is no longer in vogue and it is recognized that the Chinese were master potters. The Chinese, in fact, always had a completely different attitude to pottery from that of their contemporaries. From the earliest times, pots were highly regarded by both religious and secular leaders in China, being used in Buddhist and other religious ceremonies. The Chinese produced stoneware, which is clay fired to a higher temperature than that needed for terracotta, and also made porcelain. They produced white, blue and green glazes, many of which were intended to simulate jade. One lyrical description of such glazes describes them as "blue as the sky after rain, clear as a mirror, thin as paper, resonant as a musical stone of jade." The Islamic people admired the Chinese art and copied it. They spread the techniques throughout Europe, bringing styles into Spain and from there to Italy and elsewhere. However, the secret of making porcelain was one that eluded Europeans until early in the 18th century when Böttger in Germany discovered the secret and founded the Meissen factory to produce it. Throughout the rest of Europe tin-glazed ware was widely used. Then in 1765 Josiah Wedgwood flooded the market with his cream-colored ware. The factory production of this enabled him to sell it at re-

markably low prices, and by the end of the 18th century tin-glazed ware had virtually ceased to be produced in Europe. In North America, too, there was very little manufacture of pottery. Until late in the 18th century porcelain from Europe and China was considered a great luxury. Ordinary pottery too was scarce, and Wedgwood's cream ware found a huge market for many years in the United States. It was not until the 19th century that the industry really developed. By the mid-19th century in England, reaction had set in against the cheap, machine-made pottery. George Moore, the writer, fulminated against it: "Look at these plates; they were painted by machinery. They are abominable. In old times plates were painted by the hand, . . . and a china in which there was always something more or less pretty, was turned out . . ."
William Morris and his friend William de Morgan started the movement back to small potteries and individual craftsmanship, a movement which has co-existed with mass production techniques from that time to this.

Clay

Clay is a natural material found in abundance on the surface of the earth. It is usually found mixed with water which makes it a plastic, pliable material which can be easily shaped.

Most clays were formed over millions of years from the breaking down of granite. This extremely hard rock is composed of mica, quartz and feldspar and it is the feldspar which was vulnerable to disintegration caused by pressure and the effects of hot chemical gases present during the active periods while the earth was formed. The largest clay deposits are therefore found in areas where there was once an outcropping of granite. These deposits of kaolin or china clay are found on the site of the mother rock, granite.

China clay. China clay, which is also called primary clay, is very white and is chemically inert. It is made up of flat, hexagonal particles and therefore feels gritty to the touch (fig.1). It is non-plastic when mixed with water. The rain of centuries has washed these particles of china clay away and carried them along into streams and finally to

rivers to the sea. On meeting salt water, the fresh water deposited the china clay particles. This is why large clay deposits are found at river estuaries.

During this process, the clay particles became worn down and rounded (fig.2). These sedimentary or secondary clays which are found at the mouths of rivers are

therefore a smooth and plastic material. Because of its qualities, this is the clay used by the potter.

Since every terrain through which the china clay particles traveled on its way to the sea is different, so all secondary clays vary. Most of these clays are red, although some clays are gray, yellow, orange, brown,

Above: Modern pot from Ghana.

Left: Nineteenth-century Jutland pot.

Below: Modern slab sculpture.

green or even blue. The coloring in the clays is due to the presence of iron. When most clay is fired in a kiln, it will become orangy red.

Clay which contains a lot of sand is known as "short" clay. More water is needed when working with this type of clay to keep it from cracking. A clay which is composed of only fine particles is known as "lean" clay. A good all-purpose clay should be half-way between the two. But you can use different types of clay for different purposes. A lean clay can be rectified by adding sand to it, but it is difficult to correct clay which is short.

Types of pottery

Pottery is described generally as earthenware, stoneware or porcelain.

Earthenware. This is used for crockery and flowerpots and other fairly rough pots. It is made of porous, reddish clay and is fired at a comparatively low temperature. Glaze is needed to make it watertight.

Stoneware. This type of pottery is made from finer grained clay and can be fired at higher temperatures. At these temperatures, the clay becomes completely impervious to water. Glazes are therefore only used on stoneware pots to make the surfaces smooth and for decoration.

Porcelain. Porcelain, which is fired at even higher temperatures, is made of pure china clay. It is extremely strong and can therefore be made very thin. Porcelain is almost translucent and is resonant when tapped with a finger. It is used for fine work and for tableware.

Digging for clay

If you want to dig your own clay, ask a local builder or surveyor where to find a good deposit, or ask workmen who have been digging holes in a road. They will have encountered clay deposits. If there is no clay in your area, there is sure to be some at the mouth of the nearest river. The only equipment you need for digging clay is a shovel and a plastic bucket or plastic bag for carrying the clay. Once you have located a source of clay, dig in an area free from tree roots. Dig down as far as you can to get at clean clay. Often the clay is pure enough to use straight out of the ground.

Preparing the clay

Break the clay into pieces about the size of a walnut and put it out where it can dry thoroughly. It is important that it be absolutely dry before you proceed.

Fill a plastic bucket three-quarters full of water and drop the dry knobs of clay into it until the bucket is nearly full. Leave overnight without stirring and do not move the

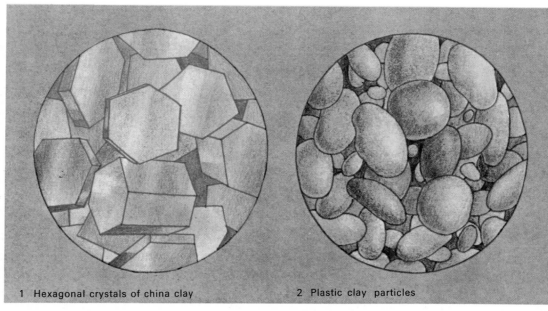

1 Hexagonal crystals of china clay   2 Plastic clay particles

Pottery

Wedging clay
Hand-built and
thrown pots

bucket. If the clay is disturbed at this stage, particles of dissolved clay will collect around the solid pieces and seal them off, thereby preventing them from dissolving. The clay will dissolve to form a thick liquid called "slip." On the next day, stir the slip thoroughly with a stick and remove all pieces of debris from the surface of the water. Stones and large particles will settle on the bottom of the bucket. The heavy clay will form the next layer, then finer particles of clay and then a layer of water (fig.3). Strain off the water, disturbing the clay as little as possible. Then leave the bucket of clay to dry out. As it dries, you will notice the clay shrinking and coming away from the sides of the bucket.

When the clay is moist but not soggy, invert the bucket on a clean sack and let the clay slide out, as if you were making a sandcastle (fig.4). Then take a wire and holding an end in each hand, pull it horizontally across the clay cylinder at the point where pebbles and debris meet clean clay, to cut off this section. The remaining clay is now ready to be mixed and kneaded to make it more workable and to remove air bubbles.

You can of course buy clay suitable for pottery if you do not want to dig your own.

Wedging the clay
All clay must be wedged before it is used for pottery. Some store-bought clays are already mixed, but it is still a good idea to wedge the clay before you begin. If the clay is uneven, it will be difficult to use, especially on a potter's wheel, and it will contain air bubbles which can cause distortion in drying and even cause a pot to burst during firing.

Wedging should be done just before the clay is to be used so that it does not dry out. You can wedge a large mass by applying sufficient pressure and having enough patience.

Wedging clay is very much like kneading dough. Always work on a strong bench or table with a smooth surface. Place the clay on the workbench and cut it in half with a rustproof wire (fig.5a). Bring down one half of the clay on top of the other so as to force out air bubbles (fig.5b). Lean into the clay with the heel of your hands, pressing hard with the weight of the torso. Press down on the clay and fold the clay over itself as you progress, to form a roll. Continue kneading the clay until it is even and pliant. Continue to check whether you have successfully removed all air bubbles by cutting the clay mass in half as before. If

there are still holes in the clay continue wedging. The length of time this takes will depend on the condition and type of clay you are using. Finally, pat the wedged clay into a compact shape.

To wedge a small piece of clay, slice it in half with the thumb of one hand against the fingers of the other hand. Then bang the wedged shape piece against the flat piece in the other hand in a clapping motion. It does not pay to scrimp on this preparation stage as it will affect the later stages of making a pot.

Hand-built and thrown pots
Once the clay is prepared, it can be used to make hand-built pots or thrown on a potter's wheel. Hand-built pots are made completely by hand by forming clay into shapes such as coils or slabs which are joined together or simply by hand-molding the clay into shape.

Thrown pots are formed on a potter's wheel and are therefore more regular and uniform in shape. The method you use depends on the effect you want to achieve, the number of pots you are making—and your skill. You may find it best to start with hand-built pots and progress to thrown pots when you have got the feel of the clay.

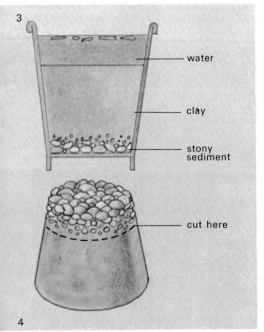

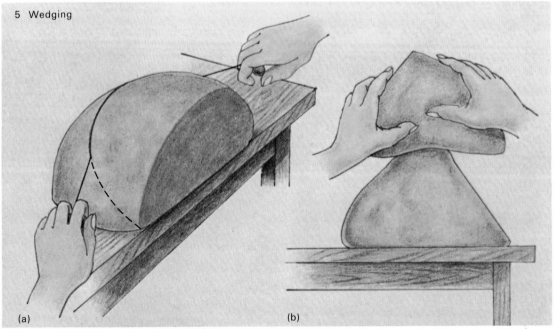

5 Wedging

(a)　　(b)

Wedging a small piece of clay

Hold the clay in one hand.

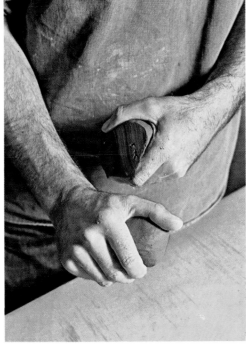

Separate the piece into two halves.

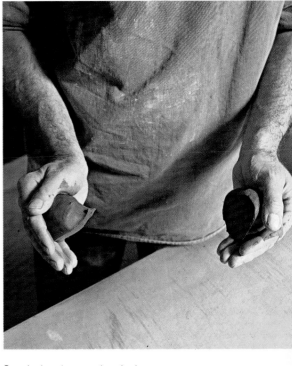

Cup the hands around each piece.

Bring both hands together.

Press both halves of clay firmly together.

Pinch pots (thumb pots)

One of the simplest shapes to make is the pinch pot. Always keep your hands wet when working with clay so that it does not get too dry.

Making a pot. Take a piece of clay the size of a golf ball and form it into a sphere. Put the ball into the palm of your hand. Apply gentle pressure with the thumb of the other hand in the center of the ball to make a depression. Rotate the ball, continuing to apply pressure so that the circular depression is even and the pot has been opened out. Turn the pot on its side in your palm and continue pressing on the sides of the pot, turning it as you work until the walls are of the desired thickness.

If the rim of the pot starts to crack, the clay is getting too dry. You can correct this by running a wet finger around the rim of the pot. To make the walls thinner, put the pot on a table and squeeze the walls with thumb and forefinger, beginning at the base of the wall and working up and around in a spiral. Pat the pot on the table to flatten the bottom.

Pottery

Pinch pots
(thumb pots)

Make a small depression in the ball of clay.

Make the depression wider and deeper.

Turn the pot and press on the sides.

Continue pressing until the pot is formed.

Moisten the rim of the pot.

Decorate the pot by marking with a stick.

To make a square or triangular pot by this method, pat the sides of the pot on the table. Put the pot aside to dry before firing.

Coiled pots

Pots of nearly any shape or size can be made by the coiling method. This method of hand-building is as old as the craft of pottery. A sandy or short yet plastic clay is best for making coiled pots. Test the clay by rolling a coil and bending it around. If the coil cracks, the clay is too sandy and will be difficult to use.

Making the base. Take a piece of clay the size of a tennis ball and place it on a sheet of newspaper, supported by a tile. It helps to use a stand which turns so that the pot will be more even. With the flat of your hand beat the ball of clay into a disk the same thickness as you intend the base of the pot to be.

Making a coil. Take a handful of clay and roll it roughly into a long sausage shape. Working on a clean, smooth surface and with the fingers of both hands extended, roll the coil backwards and forwards with your fingers, moving your hands outwards from the middle as you work. Don't use your palms as this will flatten the coil.

Note: keep your hands wet while working so the clay does not dry out.

When the coil is about half as thick as you want the finished wall of the pot to be, place it around the perimeter of the disk and mold it into the disk, pressing down into the base with a finger. Do this on the inside edges of the coil so that it stays firmly in place.

Building up the pot. Take another length of coil and place it on top of the first, spiraling

Selection of coiled pots.

Beat a ball of clay into a disk for the base.

Roll the first coil.

Pottery

Coiled pots

Mold the first coil onto the base.

Add the second coil.

Build up the sides of the pot.

Shape the inside with the edge of a protractor.

Remove the ridges with a hacksaw blade.

Smooth the surface with a knife blade.

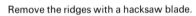

upward. Support the clay on the inside of the pot with one hand, revolve the pot and mold the coil onto the one below it as the pot turns. Again be sure to do this inside and outside the pot. If you continue adding coils on top of each other, you will create a cylindrical shape. If you place the coils each slightly to the outside of the last one to make a slightly larger circle, the pot will curve outwards. With a smaller circumference, the pot will curve inwards.

To give the pottery shape fullness, stroke the inside of the pot with a plastic protractor held against the support of one hand as you build the pot upwards.

When you are happy with the shape of the pot, allow it to dry until fairly firm. If it is not even, push it back into shape with a flat stick.

Finishing off. To remove the horizontal ridges created by the successive coils, comb the pot evenly with a hacksaw blade, using diagonal strokes from right to left and then back around the pot from left to right. Then smooth the surface with a knife blade. Finish the rim of the pot with a wet chamois or wet finger. Put the coil pot aside to dry before firing.

Slab pots

Sandy clay is best for making angular slab pots. This enables the clay to dry without too much shrinkage and prevents the distortion and cracking that would be caused by using a lean clay. Remember to keep your hands wet while working.

Making the slabs. The easiest method of making slabs is to roll out the clay on a cloth with a rolling pin. Moisten a dish cloth or similarly textured surface to prevent it from taking up too much moisture from the clay. Take a handful of clay and beat it out as flat as possible on the surface, using a clenched hand. Place a strip of wood on either side of the clay cut to the thickness you want the slab to be. Use these wood strips as guides to prevent the rolling pin from flattening the clay too much. Do not make the slabs too thin to support the pot. Roll the clay evenly and firmly with the rolling pin. Then cut out slab shapes with a strong pin or knife. To make

Selection of slab pots.

Pottery

Slab pots
Drape pots

Cut the slabs to the correct size.

Join the side slabs to the base.

Add a coil of clay to strengthen the joins.

a small box accurately, cut paper shapes to the exact size you want the box sides to be, remembering to subtract the thickness of the two sides that are joined to the ends. Cut out the pieces accurately and then cut the base slightly larger than needed. Put the slabs aside to dry until they are firm. This is an important step, and is vital to making strong and accurate slab pots. Soft slabs would be pushed out of shape when the box is assembled.

Meanwhile, take a spare piece of clay and push your thumb into the middle to make a thick-walled pot. Put a little water in this pot and stir around with a brush. This will give a thick slip in its own container, and should be used when assembling the slabs.

Assembling the slabs. Cross-hatch the sides of the slabs that are to fit together with a needle and apply thick slip to these

surfaces with the brush or your finger. Begin to assemble the pot, holding the joins together firmly. Wipe off any excess slip.

Make a thin clay coil and push it into the corners of the joins inside the pot to strengthen the structure. Continue assembling the parts until they are all in place. Cut away any excess from the base of the box in line with the walls with a knife.

Two small slabs can be attached to the underside of the pot to act as feet if required, for example for a plant holder or flowerpot. Trim off the sharp corners of the outside of the box with a knife. Leave the box upside down to dry before firing.

Note: when the slabs have been cut and before the pot is assembled, textures and designs can be impressed on the surface using wooden or metal implements.

Drape pots

The method for making these pots is similar to that used for a slab pot. Roll out a sheet of clay as described, leaving it as a free-form shape or cutting it into a desired shape and size. Allow the clay sheet to dry out slightly and then drape it over an appropriately-sized smooth surface such as a stone. Press the clay around the stone so that it takes on the same shape. Leave the clay to dry until it is firm. When it is firm enough to move, slide it off gently and put it aside to dry. The clay sheet can be decorated with slip before being draped over a shape so that when the pot is dried it is already decorated. (For slip decoration see page 272.)

Plaster molds can be made in any shape and covered with a clay sheet in a similar way.

Press molding
Throwing pots
on a wheel

Press molding

To make hollow molds you can use any support such as a pie plate or a ready-made plaster of Paris mold. This can be cast over a clay shape or it can be cast over a previously made dish.

Roll out a sheet of clay as before. Lift the sheet with the rolling pin and push the clay gently but firmly into the bottom of the mold with a damp sponge. When you have pushed the clay into place all around the mold, take a thin wire and cut off the edge, flush with the top of the mold.

Leave the pot in the mold to dry. It will come away from the sides of the mold as it does so.

To make feet for the pot, attach three little balls of clay to the bottom with slip.

Throwing pots on a wheel

The potter's wheel is one of the oldest forms of machinery known to man, and the basic principle of how it works has changed very little.

When pots are thrown on a wheel, the spinning clay is acted upon by centrifugal force which allows the potter to create cylindrical shapes easily. Many modern wheels are operated by motors so there is no work required to make them revolve. But a kick wheel, operated by foot power, is quite adequate for any type of thrown shape. Some potters prefer a non-mechanized wheel, which they feel gives them more control over the clay.

Wheels can go either clockwise or counterclockwise, depending on whether the potter is right- or left-handed. The speed at which the wheel revolves can be controlled with both a kick wheel and a powered wheel. Every potter has his own method of throwing, but there are three essential stages to throwing any pot.

Centering the clay. The first stage of throwing a pot is to center the clay mass on the revolving wheel. Place a prepared lump of clay firmly on the center of the wheelhead. Start the wheel revolving. Then with wet cupped hands, exert even pressure on the spinning clay to form it into a balanced shape. This cone-like shape is then pushed down with one hand while the other hand acts as a control, and the clay is pushed down onto the wheel as a round and more centered mass. Repeat this action three times to center the clay and make it more workable.

The success of centering depends to a large extent on the position of the potter's body. Lean over the clay as it revolves and keep your elbows close to your body, bringing the weight of your torso to bear on the clay. Keep your hands wet during this process.

Place the rolled sheet of clay over the mold.

Push the clay into the mold with a damp sponge.

Trim the edges with thin wire.

Don't take your hands away from the clay too quickly as this will throw it off balance. Test to be sure that the clay is centered by holding a finger on the outside of the revolving pot. It will touch evenly all around if the pot is centered.

Opening the clay. As the centered clay spins on the wheel, press your wet thumbs into the middle of the mass, making a depression almost through to the wheelhead. Then open out the mass with a gradual horizontal movement of the thumbs until what is virtually a thick-walled pot is formed. Be careful not to make the hole off center by sticking your thumbs into the clay too quickly and be sure to keep your hands and the clay well-moistened. Do not open out the clay too quickly in relation to the speed of the wheel. At this stage, the bottom of the pot has been formed, but the walls are still very thick.

Raising the wall. Reduce the speed of the wheel by half. Wet your hands and place the fingers of one hand inside the pot with the fingers of the other hand outside the pot. Steady your hands by putting the thumb of the hand outside the pot firmly across to the other hand. With two fingers opposite each other on either side of the pot, apply even pressure to the base of the clay wall. Squeeze gently and slowly and lift the fingers slowly upwards as you do to thin out the walls. When you have reached the rim of the pot, start at the base again and repeat this process. You will get to know from the feel of the clay exactly how much pressure to apply and in which places. Do not spin the wheel too quickly and be sure to keep the clay wet. Practice throwing simple cylinders until you have mastered throwing and can go on to more complicated shapes.

Taking the pot off the wheel. Cut the finished pot from the wheel by pulling a wire under the pot and flush with the surface of the wheel as it spins very slowly. Stop the wheel and slide the pot to the edge of the wheel supporting it evenly. Place it on a wooden board to dry before firing.

Drying the pots

All pots, whether thrown or hand-built, must be dried evenly and thoroughly to minimize the chance of cracking. You can

Form the cone-like shape.

Press the clay into a round shape.

Press your thumbs into the clay to open it.

Apply pressure to the sides of the pot.

wrap pots in air-tight plastic between working sessions to keep the clay moist, but it dries out slightly nevertheless and you should try to finish a pot in as few sessions as possible.

The term "leather-hard" is used to describe clay that has dried to the point where it is still moist, but is firm enough to be handled without damaging the shape of the pot. This is the first stage in the drying process. At this point, a pot can be decorated by carving or incising and then put aside to dry completely before the first kiln firing stage. Dry pots on a surface covered with plastic or newspaper so they can dry and shrink without sticking to the surface. As the clay dries, and the water in it evaporates, it becomes a lighter color.

Burnishing

Just before the clay is dry, you can burnish the surface to produce a smooth and shiny finish. Take a hard smooth implement like a spoon and rub it firmly against the surface of the pot. All the particles on the surface are pushed down flat and tight and the surface is smoothed and polished. Burnish

Shape the rim.

the whole pot or parts of it to make a pattern. Finish drying the pot before firing.

Firing pottery

Pottery is called *greenware* before it is fired. It is fragile and will eventually dissolve in water turning back into slip. Firing the clay hardens and strengthens it and changes its composition so that it will not dissolve into slip. Most pottery is fired twice.

First firing. This is done very slowly and at a relatively low temperature. This first firing is called *biscuit* or *bisque* firing. At this stage the greenware can be stacked in the kiln as the pots will not stick to each other. The heat of the kiln drives out the chemically combined water from the clay and the clay particles melt and join together. It is essential that pots be dry before they go into the kiln for biscuit firing or the steam created by the evaporation of water in the clay will cause them to burst.

After the firing period, the kiln is turned off and allowed to cool for about six hours before it is unpacked. The pottery is now quite brittle and fragile but it will no longer disintegrate in water.

Lift the pot off the wheel with wire.

Second firing. After the first firing glaze can be applied to decorate the pottery and make it smooth. For the second firing, care should be taken to ensure that the pots placed inside the kiln are not touching one another.

Types of kiln

A kiln is a special oven designed for firing pottery. Modern kilns, whether fueled by electricity, gas, oil, wood or coal, are made of special bricks which can withstand very high temperatures. With most kilns, potters use pyrometric cones to check the progress of the temperature. Numbered cones, made to melt at specific temperatures, are placed in the kiln so that the potter will know what temperature the kiln has reached by checking when the cones melt.

Electric kilns. These are designed so that they switch off automatically when the correct temperature is reached. Electric kilns are safe, clean and straightforward to use indoors, provided there is adequate electric current and good ventilation.

Gas and oil kilns. These tend to be larger than electric kilns, and are more economical to operate. Whereas the electric kiln produces an oxidized atmosphere which restricts the colors obtainable in the firing, gas and oil kilns can both produce a reduced atmosphere where there is little or no oxygen. This in turn affects the color qualities of the various substances used to glaze pots.

Wood and coal kilns. These are usually built outdoors as they tend to be more difficult to control and the fuels produce more fumes and dirt. Like gas and oil kilns, wood- or coal-fueled kilns produce a reduced atmosphere.

Sawdust kilns

A sawdust kiln operates on the combustion principle and fires at a relatively low temperature. It is easy to construct one yourself using ordinary materials.

Making a kiln. Find an old oil drum or very large can. Pierce around the side with a chisel to allow air in through the sides (fig.6). You will also need a large bag of sawdust. If you use fine sawdust, the resulting pots will be darker since the denser sawdust allows less oxygen to reach the

Electric kiln with a selection of glazed pots.

Sawdust kiln with a selection of pinch pots.

pots. By mixing the sawdust with coarser chips, you may get pots with mottled tones. But the result of firing in this primitive sort of kiln is only approximate and it is not possible to predict results accurately.

Do not fire a sawdust kiln on a windy day as the kiln will burn too quickly and the pots may shatter as a result.

Packing the kiln (fig.7). Put 10cm (4in) of sawdust in the bottom of the kiln. Make sure the pots are perfectly dry, then fill them loosely with sawdust and place them onto the layer of sawdust in the kiln, making sure that they do not touch each other. Fill in the spaces around the pots and over the top to a depth of about 1cm ($\frac{1}{2}$in). Add more pots putting them in layer by layer. Keep the pots away from the sides of the kiln and make sure there is enough sawdust packed in between the pots. Continue packing until you are near the top, then finish with a 5cm (2in) layer of sawdust.

Firing. Put some newspaper and wood twigs on top of the kiln and light a fire. The sawdust will ignite and will continue to burn downwards through the pots.

The kiln can be left overnight and in the morning you will find a heap of black pots and sawdust ash in the kiln. Take out the pots and rub them with a cloth. If the pots have been burnished, they will need to be polished with a fine cloth.

You will find that some pots have broken, but then our ancestors would not have been motivated to produce better kilns if pots fired in this primitive way came out

269

Glazing

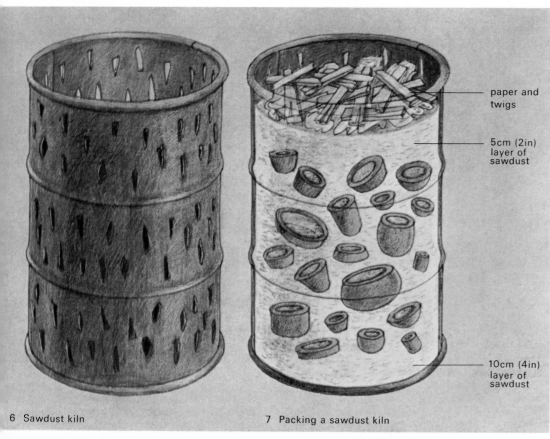

paper and twigs

5cm (2in) layer of sawdust

10cm (4in) layer of sawdust

6 Sawdust kiln

7 Packing a sawdust kiln

perfect. Black pots fired by this simple method are still produced in many parts of the world.

A larger sawdust kiln can be made by placing house bricks in a rectangle on a foundation of bricks. Leave little gaps between the bricks when stacking. You can get higher temperatures in this type of sawdust kiln, and sawdust can be thrown on top of the pots throughout the firing to prolong the process.

Decorating pottery

The earliest pots were fired in open fires and were therefore black when they emerged. Sometimes shapes were pressed into the soft clay for decoration but usually the pots were left plain. In some societies a sharp tool was used to incise and cross-hatch the surface. In Jutland, for example, primitive pots were burnished with a pebble to make a design which showed up as a shiny line after firing. This technique is still

used today in parts of Africa. Pots in Peru were traditionally decorated by using a light-colored clay slip over a darker clay body. A light clay is brushed on over a red body to form a decoration that is later burnished. Slipware in England used a similar method. By Medieval times metal oxides were being used in the slips. These react with the covering glaze and produce a brighter color than clay slips alone. The most common way of coloring pottery surfaces today is to apply a glaze after biscuit firing and before the second firing.

Glazing

Glaze is a thin layer of clear or colored glass which adheres to the surface of a pot, giving it different colors and textures and making it smooth and watertight. If you think of it as ordinary window glass ground very fine and suspended in water, this gives a good idea of the glazing process. If you dip a porous biscuit-fired pot into this liquid, the

water will be sucked up by the pot and the particles of glass will remain on the surface. Glaze is applied as a colorless liquid which dries quickly to a powder on the surface of the pot. It is the consistency of cream and it should not be stirred before applying. Do not leave prepared glaze standing too long or it will tend to crack on the pot. You can buy glaze ready-made with the correct firing temperatures indicated, or you can mix your own glazes.

The temperature necessary to melt the glaze must correspond with the correct temperature for the type of clay you are using. You will learn to coordinate these two factors successfully. If the firing temperature is too high, the pottery will become over-fired. The glaze will burn out and muddy or even run off the pot.

All glazes contain three basic ingredients: flux to make the glaze melt at a specific temperature, silica and a hardening agent, and clay to fuse the glaze onto the pot. Metallic oxides added to these create the color of the glaze.

The color of the glaze will vary depending on the amount used, the temperature at which the pottery is fired, the type of clay used and an element of chance. Glazing pottery is a trial and error procedure and it takes practice to know what effects will result from each glaze mixture.

Experimenting with glaze recipes and firing test pieces will allow you to build up a selection of colors and textures. Be sure to pack the kiln with glazed pots so that they do not touch each other or they will fuse together when the glaze melts.

Metal oxides used in glaze. Certain types of metal oxides are used to produce different colors. The strongest coloring agent is *cobalt oxide* which fires blue. It is very stable at high temperatures and if it is over- or under-fired, it still shows through clearly as blue. This is one reason why there is so much blue and white ware made all over the world. It tends to be a little strong on its own and is often used with other oxides. *Cobalt carbonate* is another popular blue oxide.

Copper oxide is used in lead glazes for earthenware throughout the world. In an

"Peruvian bull"—unglazed with slip decoration.

Slip decoration

Pour white slip into the dish. Allow to dry.

Pipe dark brown slip into the dish.

Pour off excess slip.

ordinary oxidized firing under a lead glaze, copper oxide will produce beautiful greens. As the temperature rises, the color tends towards red. If copper is applied too thickly it produces black.

Manganese oxide gives brown at ordinary earthenware temperatures but its color will vary according to the nature of the glaze with which it is used. In alkaline glazes, it produces violets and purple brown colors. It will withstand high temperatures. *Iron oxide* is the stoneware potters' favorite oxide as it can produce many variations from pale blues through greens to bright orangy reds and blacks. There are many other less common coloring oxides used in glaze to create other colors and different effects.

Majolica decoration

Tin glazes—sometimes called stanniferous glazes—are used to make a transparent glaze opaque. *Tin oxide*, which is very ex-pensive, is the basis of majolica decoration which is still a popular technique today. The Babylonians were the first to discover the use of tin oxide around 1000 BC, but they used it only to make glazes white without other decoration. The development of porcelain in China encouraged the Islamic potters to use tin glaze which was the nearest imitation to porcelain they could achieve. The technique spread across Europe and was named for the island of Majorca off Spain.

Slip decoration

The same metal oxides used in glaze are also used for slip decoration applied before the pot is biscuit-fired. They are added to white clay slips so that a pot made in brown clay can be dipped in a slip which will produce a blue pot when it is glazed and fired. Once the leather-hard pot has been dipped into slip, you can scrape away areas with a flat-ended tool to expose the clay underneath. When fired the piece will be patterned. This process is known as "sgraffito."

Slips of light and dark clay can be used to decorate leather-hard pots by simply pour-ing or dribbling slip over the pot, pouring off the excess and allowing the slip to dry before firing the pot.

Slip can also be piped onto a pot in the same way as you would decorate a cake and allowed to dry before firing.

Another simple but effective method of decorating with slip is to use a masking technique with pieces of newspaper ripped into strips. Moisten the strips with water and stick them down on the leather-hard pot. Then spoon a creamy consistency of slip over the dish, pour off the surplus and leave to dry. When the newspaper dries, it will be easy to peel off the strips, which leave behind shapes in the color of the original underlying clay. Interesting free-form effects can be achieved in this way.

Stick wet strips of newspaper onto the dish.

Spoon slip over the surface of the dish.

Pour off excess slip.

Remove strips of newspaper.

Plastics and resins

The use of plastics as an art form still has a long way to go: for they have been regarded as substitutes—in appearance or function—for other materials such as metal, glass and wood. But plastics should be explored for their own potential since their glossy surfaces, clear texture and ability to reflect light provide lots of scope for artistic expression. When experimenting with plastics, use shapes to reveal these characteristics. Do not, for example, add engravings and decorations to the surfaces as these will detract from the intrinsic surface beauty of plastics.

Understanding synthetic plastics

Synthetic plastics are a group of new materials of major importance in the 20th century, their common characteristic being that they can be molded into a desired shape. Each plastic has its own properties and characteristics and may appear to have no relation to other products referred to as plastics. For example, polyethylene is different in appearance, texture and rigidity from acrylic sheet, and both of these are very different from nylon, fiber glass or synthetic fabrics. However, they all come under the definition of plastics, which is essentially a commercial rather than a scientific term. Most plastics are made from resins. To make the liquid resin set, a hardener or catalyst is added. Heat is also generated in the resulting chemical reaction and the resin solidifies into a translucent product. Plastics can be divided into the following two main groups.

Thermoplastics. These are materials which soften when worked and shaped in the presence of heat but they regain their original properties and rigidity when cooled. The heating and cooling process can be repeated any number of times in order to remold the material. Acrylic and nylon are examples.

Thermosetting plastics. These solidify in the presence of heat and, once hardened, cannot be remolded. Polyester is an example.

Safety precautions

Work in a well ventilated room since the fumes formed by the chemical reaction of resin and hardener are toxic.

Three modern lamp designs which reveal the natural beauty of plastics.

Clear cast embedding

Keep the resin away from a naked flame and do not smoke while working.
Avoid contact with eyes.
Remove spilled resin from skin with soap and water and use a barrier cream on hands as a protection while you work.
Cover the working surface with paper.
Wipe away spilled resin with acetone or nail polish remover.
Always replace cap on resin and hardener; store in a cool dark place away from food.

Clear cast embedding
This is a process of covering an object already placed within a mold with liquid resin and hardener. The mixture is poured in layers and each layer must have time to harden before the next layer is poured. The first layer or pour covers the bottom of the mold and will constitute the top or upper surface of the finished cast; the second pour embeds the object and also makes up the back or base of the cast. Two pours are generally sufficient if only one object is to be embedded. If you wish to embed more than one object, use several pours depending on the number of objects and the way they are spaced within the mold. Always pour to the depth required to provide a foundation layer for the next object.

Basic materials
Readily available clear cast embedding kits are excellent for beginners. The kit contains all the necessary items such as resin, hardener, stirring sticks, mixing cup, pigments, mold release wax and molds which vary in shape and size and are accordingly suitable for paperweights, ashtrays or jewelry. Each item of the kit is also available separately so that you are not limited to the scope of the kit alone but can improvise on certain materials. For example, use household objects instead of rubber molds for casting. Avoid objects with complicated shapes as it is difficult to get the solidified plastic out of them. The surface of the cast will only be as good as the finish of the mold. A mold with a smooth, highly polished surface gives the best results. Glass is suitable, as is metal. Plastic containers are also appropriate unless made from polystyrene, a light brittle plastic, since the resin will dissolve it. If you

are not sure of the constituency of the container, test it beforehand by covering a tiny patch on an inside surface or base with a mixture of plastic and hardener. Generally, soft plastics are suitable.
Using hardeners. Most proprietory products are similar in that they consist of liquid resin and accompanying hardener, but they may vary in the amount of time needed for the resin to set. However, the setting time is also relative to the amount of hardener you use. The greater the quantity added, the quicker the liquid sets. But, if the resin sets too fast, it will shrink and if it shrinks too quickly, it will form cracks and become useless. Usually the slower the resin sets the better the results.
You will need:
clear cast resin □ appropriate hardener □ pigment (optional) □ mold □ mold release wax □ measuring cup □ paper cups □ stirring sticks □ object to embed.
Preparing the first pour. Each pour is prepared individually prior to use. To measure the amount of resin required for the first pour, fill the mold with enough water to cover the bottom. Transfer this to the measuring cup and note the quantity. This quantity will be the amount of resin you need. Throw away the water and dry the cup and mold. Measure out the quantity of resin. Then transfer it into the cup. Add the pigment if you wish to use it. Mix well for at least a minute. The mixture might contain air bubbles so wait a few minutes until they disperse.
Apply mold release wax to the surfaces of the mold and allow to dry. Although waxing is not essential, it will facilitate the release of the finished cast from the mold.
The first pour. When the air bubbles have dispersed from within the mixture of resin and color pigment, add the appropriate amount of hardener by following the manufacturer's instructions. As a general guide, 15 drops of hardener to about 30ml (1fl oz) is needed. For 60ml (2fl oz) you will need to use less hardener (9 drops) in order to prevent cracking, since more heat will be caused by the hardening process. If substantially more than 60ml (2fl oz) is needed, use 3 drops of hardener only. Stir the mixture thoroughly and pour into the mold. Leave to set about 1 hour. Place the

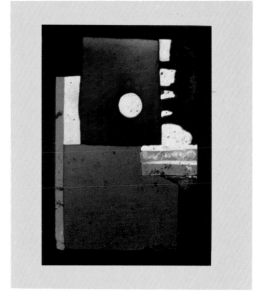

An abstract panel of plastics. The background is made from formica while the geometrical designs are made from walls of plastic clay (plasticine) filled with resin.

cast in a warm place as extra heat will speed up the setting process.
Preparing the object to be embedded. If the object has an irregular shape, for example a bunch of dried flowers, dip it into resin and hardener before embedding, then leave to set. This technique prevents air bubbles from forming in the mold as well as sealing the surface of the object. Make sure that the object is dry since any dampness will cloud the plastic.
Second pour. Place the object face down onto the set surface of the resin. If necessary, hold the object in position with a clear plastic adhesive. This is also advisable with very light objects which would otherwise float to the top of the pour. Prepare the second pour of resin and hardener as for the first pour. Pour the mixture into the mold until the object is completely covered. Leave to set for 1 hour. Air trapped in the resin will cause bubbles. Remove these by pricking with a pin before the resin sets.
Finishing. Air inhibits the curing or hardening of the resin so any exposed area, such as the surface at the open end of the mold will remain tacky. This tacky surface must be finished once the resin has set.

Liquorice candies embedded in clear plastic make up this colorful piece of pop sculpture.

Cover the surface with a thin layer of resin mixed with slightly more than the usual amount of hardener. Leave to set until extremely hard, preferably overnight. Once set, rub the tacky surface down with "wet and dry" paper (an abrasive cloth made to be used wet). For a very shiny finish, rub with metal polish. Alternatively, stick a piece of felt to the surface with plastic adhesive to form a protective base.

Removing the cast. The resin will shrink slightly as it sets so it is usually easy to remove the cast from the mold. However, if the cast does stick, hold the mold under running hot water for a few minutes and then plunge it into cold water. If necessary, repeat this hot and cold water method several times. Do not chip away at the casting; the mold will drop out of its own accord. Remove small marks and scratches on the surface of the cast with metal polish.

Acrylics

Acrylic is a brittle thermoplastic material and its main characteristic is the capacity to transmit and reflect light. It can be brilliantly translucent, luminous or colored, opaque or transparent. It is available in sheets of varying sizes and thickness as well as in the form of rods and tubes. Be careful not to mark the surface of the acrylic as you work. It comes covered in a protective paper to prevent scratching. Do not remove this paper until it is absolutely essential, preferably until the work is completed.

Being a thermoplastic, acrylic can be remolded under heat. However, methods of heating plastics are complicated and involve too many dangers for the amateur. It is advisable therefore, not to use these techniques but rather, the simpler methods of cutting and glueing.

Tools. Cut the acrylic with woodworking and metalworking tools. Cut thin sheets with a paper cutter or metal cutting shears. For acrylic thicker than 2mm ($\frac{5}{64}$in) use a sharp hack saw. Do not exert a lot of pressure on the saw but use light quick strokes. For curved edges, use a coping saw or a jeweler's piercing saw. Drill holes with drill bits. The worked surface will have a matt finish. Rub with metal polish to restore a shiny surface. Smooth any rough edges with a file or sand with fine grade "wet and dry" paper.

Joining. Pieces of acrylic can be glued together very successfully to provide a new shape. Use a clear acrylic adhesive and apply to the surfaces which are to be joined together. Wipe away excess adhesive and allow to dry.

Laminating acrylic. This process is the bonding together of thin sheets of acrylic with clear adhesive. Acrylic is attractive if different colors are laminated, especially if you use luminous colors. Use small laminated surfaces for items such as jewelry. You will need 4 or 5 strips of acrylic. Check that the surfaces are clean and free from dust. Apply a clear plastic adhesive onto the surfaces to be joined. Stick the pieces together, one on top of the other. Protecting the outer surfaces with cardboard or plywood so as to prevent scratching, secure the laminate in a C (G) clamp so that the vise rests on the piece of cardboard (or plywood). Leave to dry for an hour.

For bracelets and necklaces, drill small holes with drill bits into the acrylic to hold a jump ring. To make earrings and brooches, glue jeweler's findings to the surface with clear adhesive.

Flowercraft

Throughout the ages, man has been fascinated by the elusive qualities of flowers and has sought to preserve their perfect color and form long after the natural bloom is over. For centuries flowers and leaves have been dried and pressed and these crafts are still practiced today.

In an attempt to capture the various moods of nature, and even to elaborate on them, highly decorative artificial flowers, buds, leaves and fruit have been created using a wide assortment of materials—everything from paper, beads and sequins to delicate fabrics and silver foil. The Victorian era saw particular inventiveness in this respect and many examples remain of pictures of flowers and fruit fashioned from fabrics. Natural objects such as rocks, tree bark, pebbles and shells were also used creatively to form designs.

One of the most satisfactory ways of imitating the physical, almost opalescent appearance of certain flowers and leaves has always proved to be waxing. Again, the Victorians were perfectionists in this form of flowercraft.

Ordinary household candles were melted down, and painted paper flowers were individually dipped into the wax. The flower was then lifted out quickly, but extremely carefully to prevent the wax from cracking and left to cool. The Victorians also knew how to make certain appropriate leaves appear shiny. They were dipped for just a second or two into a bowl of cold water as soon as they were removed from the wax and immediately lifted out again. Perhaps because it demands a fair amount of care and patience, waxing flowers has rather lost favor over the years, but the results can be so exquisite and realistic that it is well worthwhile reviving the art. Read the sections on paper flowers and candle-making and you may be tempted to try!

Pressed flowers

Pressing flowers is a revived, gentle Victorian art that requires patience and skill. As a craft it is especially rewarding as the beautifully colored, perfectly preserved

"Spring", one of Giuseppe Arcimboldo's famous allegorical heads. Arcimboldo (1530–1593) used a skillful combination of flowers, fruits, vegetables and other everyday objects to create his fantastic portraits.

Memories of summer
Flower-scattered table

Wild flowers and leaves gathered from the hills of Jerusalem, pressed and mounted into a book.

specimens can be displayed in numerous decorative ways.

Materials. Select perfectly shaped wild and cultivated flowers, leaves and grasses and pick them in their prime. Flat plant material like ferns and leaves, and flowers like hydrangeas, pansies and primroses are ideal for pressing. Some bulkier flowers with hard thick centers can be dissected, pressed and re-assembled. Yellow and orange colored specimens retain their color best; blues—with the exception of delphiniums—tend to lose color; reds turn brown; delicate rose colors merge into cream.

Equipment. All you require are blotting paper, books, large weighty objects like bricks, garden scissors, tweezers and paintbrushes for gently lifting and moving the pressed material.

Method. Cut the blooms around midday when the morning dew has dried and the flower is fully open. Place the blooms on a base sheet of blotting paper, then press the corolla (the flower center) hard to set the flower correctly. Lay each bloom out very carefully making sure that they do not touch. Cover with another sheet of blotting paper. Position this blotting paper sandwich carefully between the pages of a book and place a heavy weight on the top. Leave for at least 6 to 10 weeks, preferably in a light, dry and airy room. An alternative method is to use a special flower press which works by compressing the material between boards that are tightly screwed together.

Arranging the flowers. The best way to arrange an attractive composition is simply to play around with your pressed specimens until the whole looks well balanced. The first step is to select a focal point and pin-point it with a splendid, largish bloom. From this point, work upward and outward using material that either creates directional straight lines or curves to take your eye around the total arrangement.

To fix the final composition to the background, lift each flower in turn, dab with a rubber-based glue along the strongest stem or vein of the specimen and then gently replace it in position. Never apply glue to the middle of a delicate petal as it will show through: apply just a small amount to the center tip of the petal.

Memories of summer

Carefully pressed flowers and leaves can be beautifully and skillfully worked into a picture, designed specifically to conjure up summer memories.

You will need:

pressed violets ☐ pressed carrot leaves ☐ long reeds or grasses ☐ sheet of paper ☐ cream cardboard mount ☐ frame ☐ glass ☐ hardboard or stiff cardboard for backing ☐ clear-drying glue ☐ tacks.

Making the woven basket. Cut the reeds or grasses while they are green and weave them into a flat length, then press them in this woven state. Remove carefully when pressed and lay on a flat surface. With a fine brush, poke small amounts of clear-drying glue between the interwoven layers to hold them all firmly together. Place a weight on top until the glue is dry. Draw a simple basket shape onto paper. Cut this out and, using it as a pattern, place it on the woven leaves and cut around it.

Arranging the picture. Place the basket shape centrally at the bottom of the mount and then add the single leaf basket handle. Arrange the violets and carrot leaves as though they were emerging from the basket top, moving them around until they appear well balanced and "natural". Carefully lift each specimen and stick into place, dabbing glue into the strong stem part. Continue to lift, glue and replace each flower and leaf. Finally glue down the basket.

Framing the picture. Have pieces of glass and hardboard or stiff cardboard cut to fit the frame. Clean the glass thoroughly, place the picture face down on it and then put the hardboard onto the back of the mount. Drop this sandwich into the frame. Hold firmly in place with tacks all around the sides of the frame.

Flower-scattered table

This is an individual and attractive way of giving an old table a new look.

You will need:

characterful secondhand table ☐ selection of pressed flowers ☐ felt for the backcloth

Secure at the corners with a dab of glue on the reverse side. Arrange the flowers and leaves, glue into place as described earlier. Position the well-cleaned glass or acrylic sheet carefully on top. Tack the beading around the edges to hold the top firmly in place.

Pressed flower paperweights

Pressed flowers that have been collected on vacation or from a summer garden can be perfectly preserved in a clear plastic paperweight.

You will need:
plastic dome-shaped mold □ casting plastic □ catalyst □ mold release wax □ measuring beaker □ small pressed flowers and leaves.

Embedding the flowers. Coat the inner surface of the mold with mold release wax and allow to dry. Mix the manufacturer's recommended proportion of casting plastic and catalyst thoroughly together and pour into the mold so that it is one third full. Allow this to set for two or three hours.

Meanwhile, mix a further small amount of casting plastic and catalyst and dip each pressed specimen into the mixture and leave to set. When the plastic in the mold has formed a fairly firm surface, carefully place the pressed flower and leaf specimens face down. Mix together casting plastic and catalyst for the next layer and pour into the mold. Allow to set well before easing the paperweight out of the mold.

Greeting cards

Homemade greeting cards are often more appreciated because of the care and thought that goes into them. Here are two arrangements of delicate pressed flowers.

You will need:
cardboard or thickish paper □ pressed flowers □ glue.

Making the cards. Cut the cardboard or paper to the size required. Fold the cardboard in half. Carefully arrange the flowers on the front of the card, then glue each bloom firmly into place. Place a flat weight on top until they are firmly set.

□ cut-to-measure acrylic sheet (perspex) or glass for the table top □ wooden beading □ scissors □ pinking shears □ sandpaper □ stapler □ fabric glue □ tacks.
Preparing the table. Prepare the surface of the table top by rubbing down with sandpaper until it is smooth. Make a paper template of the table top to use as a cutting guide for the felt. This template is also used to measure the glass or acrylic sheet, but reduce the measurements by half the width of the beading to allow room for tacks.
Making the new top. Place the felt back-cloth on the table top and staple securely along all the edges. Cut strips of felt 4cm (1½in) wide, using pinking shears to trim one edge. Place these cut-to-size strips along the outer edges to form a frame.

Techniques

Gather and harvest flowers, leaves and grasses at the end of the growing season, then carefully dry and preserve them to retain their natural autumnal shades.

Materials. Most varieties of leaves, grasses, seedheads and flowers can be dried successfully. You will need glycerin for the first method and sand, borax or silica gel and lidded cardboard boxes or plastic storage containers for the third method.

Glycerin and water method

One of the best ways of preserving flowers and leaves is by using the glycerin and water method. The flowers are stronger and more pliable and so tend to last longer. You will need a solution of one part glycerin and two parts water, a tall glass jar and a sharp knife.

Technique. Mix the solution very thoroughly and pour into the jar. Scrape and split the base of hard woody stems. Place the plants in the solution so that it reaches about 5cm (2in) up from the base of the stem. Store the jar in a dry place to avoid mildew. The time taken to absorb the solution depends on the type of plant, but you can generally judge the progress fairly accurately by noting the color change through the plant. If too much solution is absorbed, drops of excess glycerin will appear on the leaves and should be removed as they could damage furniture when the flowers are arranged.

Drying flowers by hanging

Flowers that are dried by hanging tend to be brittle and consequently more fragile than the glycerin-preserved specimens. They do, however, dry to delicate pale neutral shades that blend beautifully with natural decoration schemes.

Plants to choose. The following are some of the plants that lend themselves to this method: spiraea, golden rod, delphinium, yarrow, lavender and baby's breath (polygonum); grasses and cereals of all kinds; everlasting flowers (flowers that actually produce papery everlasting growth) such as statice, helichrysum and Chinese lanterns. Seedheads from poppies, cow parsley, allium, honesty, sorrel, globe thistle, hollyhocks, clematis and acanthus are all suitable.

Technique. Cut the flowers and grasses on a dry day when the bloom is young and not fully open. Seedheads can be cut when they have started to dry on the plant. Tie the material in loose bunches taking care not to crush the flowers. Hang them, heads down, in a dry airy space for about three weeks.

Preserving flowers by desiccation

This method results in perfectly preserved, well-colored specimens.

Flowers to choose. Roses, daffodils, lilies, daisies, primroses and marigolds are all suitable.

Drying agents. Use sand, borax or silica gel.

Technique. Place the flower heads carefully on a bed of sand, borax or silica gel in a box or storage container. Make sure that they do not touch each other. Cover them com-

A selection of dried flowers and leaves including Chinese lanterns, poppy fruits, hydrangea, beech leaves, teazel, various grasses, ferns and bracken.

pletely with the same drying agent, taking care to add it gently so that no petals are damaged. Close the boxes or storage containers and place them in a warm dry place for two to seven days.

Wiring dried flower heads and leaves

Dried flowers and leaves can be handled and arranged more easily if their brittle stems are replaced with flexible florist's wire. This wiring method allows greater freedom of arrangement—flower heads can be used to decorate domes of floral foam, or they can be wound securely into place for a formal centerpiece. Push the wire through the center of a dried flower

head, turn a small hook over at the top and draw this back down into the flower center. If the wire stem is likely to show you can disguise it with green tape or by slipping a real, hollow stem over it (see fig.1).

Feather flowers

The craft of curling, dyeing and assembling feathers into pictures and flowers initially gained popularity in Europe in the 18th century. Today, with the increasing interest in crafts, especially those with a thrifty something-from-nothing aspect, the art of turning feathers into decorations is having an understandable revival.

Materials. If you can, get some feathers from a farmer. You can, however, purchase packs of ready-dyed, prepared feathers at most hobby and craft stores. You will need florist's wire and fine wire to make flowers, and pads of felt or buckram for hat decorations.

Cleaning, curling and dyeing feathers. Untreated feathers need to be cleaned before they can be dyed and worked. All that most feathers need is a thorough washing in soap and water, followed by a good rinsing. Dry them with a hair drier or something similar; the air current will help to restore the natural fluff.

Many feather arrangements, especially hat decorations, need curls and movement to get the best effect. To curl feathers, draw the center spine over the back of a blunt knife, applying pressure as you do so.

In Victorian times feathers were dyed with vegetable dyes. Today more varied and subtle colors can be obtained by using hot-water dyes.

A feather flower spray from Rio de Janeiro made in 1877.

To dye approximately 230g (8oz) of dry weight feathers, you will need hot-water dye and a heatproof bowl or bucket. Wash the feathers first in soapy water to remove grease and dirt. Rinse very thoroughly. Mix the dye in 0.5 liter (1 pint) of boiling water, add the solution to 4.5 liters (1 gallon) of warm water in the bucket or bowl. Immerse the wet feathers in the dye solution, heat to about 90°C (194°F) and simmer for about 10 minutes, stirring continuously.
Rinse the dyed feathers thoroughly until the water runs clear. Dry as before.

Trimmed with a feather flower . . .

This feather flower trimming for a hat is simply made yet it can turn a plain or old hat into a splendid creation.

You will need:
a selection of small, medium and large feathers in toning colors □ an oval pad of felt or buckram measuring 7.5 × 5cm (3 × 2in) □ all-purpose glue.

Making the flower. Place the oval pad on a flat surface. Sort through the feathers and group them into colors and then similar sizes. Take 4 of the largest feathers—about 9cm (3½in) in length at the most—and place them, quill into the center, in a cross shape. Glue these firmly into place. Take the next size down and in the same way form a cross in the gaps created by the first layer. Continue in this way, placing decreasing sizes of feathers until the pad is covered and ending with a small feathered center. Place a small weight in the center until all the plumes are fixed securely in place. Position the flower onto the hat and stitch to secure.

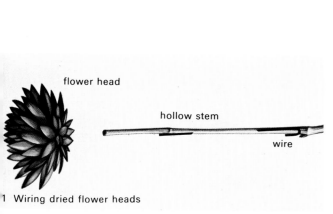

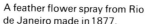

1 Wiring dried flower heads

flower head

hollow stem

wire

Feather flower arrangement

Feather flowers can be grouped together or combined with dried or natural flowers to form a delicate, fluttering decoration.

You will need:

feathers that are similar in size and type in blending colors □ florist's wire □ fine wire □ scissors.

Making the individual flowers. Make the stem with florist's wire; bend over a small hook at the top. Sort the feathers into colors and sizes. Select three or four small or spiky feathers for the centers and larger ones for the outside. Curl the feathers so that they lean outward. Arrange them around the stem and secure with fine wire around the base (this can be disguised with florist's tape or green or brown adhesive tape). Trim the feather tips into pointed petal shapes with small sharp scissors. Make all the flowers in the same way, using different color combinations.

Paper flowers

Paper flowers are one of the most colorful ways of brightening up a room. They can be made to look realistic or stylized and in any shape, size or color.

Materials. Use papers of various kinds— tissue, crepe, gift wrap, construction (cartridge) and even paper doilies. The choice of paper decides the character of the flower.

Equipment. You will need sharp scissors (small and large), pinking shears, pliers for bending wire, florist's wire for stems. fine wire for fastening flower heads to stems, rubber-based glue, paper and cardboard.

Basic technique. All paper flowers are made by attaching petals and a flower center to a wire stem. Make the centers from tufted paper, beads, buttons, paper-covered corks, absorbent cotton (cotton wool) or artificial stamens. Fix the flower centers to the wire stem either by binding them to the stem with fine wire or by pushing the wire into the center and then glueing the base to the stem.

Making the flower. Whatever kind of flower you are to make, you will need to decide first on the petal shape and then draw it out accurately on paper. From this paper pattern you can make a cardboard template. The type of flower will obviously determine the petal's shape and size, also the method of attachment. For some flowers like tulips, roses and lilies you will need to make and attach each petal separately, while daisies and peony-type flowers require complete circles of petal shapes. Poppies and simple stylized flower shapes can be made from petal-shaped strips and then rolled into a flower head.

Individual petals. Draw a petal shape onto paper and use this as a pattern (fig.2). Take the first petal, dab a little glue onto the base and stick to the wire stem just below the center. Apply the next petal in the same way, placing it so that it overlaps the first. Continue to work around the center core in this way until all the petals have been attached. For a more interesting shape, position some of the outer petals fractionally further down the stem. Gently but firmly ease each petal out to give the flower fullness. Bind the wire stem with a narrow strip of crepe paper and glue into position.

Whole flower shapes. To make the flower shape shown in fig.3, draw and cut out a circle, fold in half, halve again, and again, until the circle is folded into eighths. Round off both corners to make eight petals.

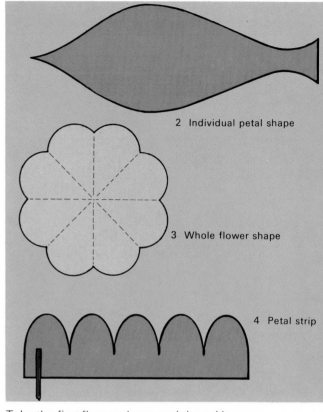

2 Individual petal shape

3 Whole flower shape

4 Petal strip

Take the first flower shape and thread it onto the wire stem pushing it well up the center core. Pinch the paper around the stem to create a cone shape and glue into position. Apply the remainder of the shapes in the same way, adjusting the position so that the petals overlap. Bind the neck of the flower with fine wire and cover this and the stem with crepe paper.

Petal strips. Cut paper strips to the depth of the whole flower. Fold into two or more petal widths. Trace the petal outline across the top and cut out the shape through the total thickness. Place the stem at the start of the strip (fig.4), glue into position and wind the roll around the stem pleating the base of the petals and glueing as you go. Continue to wind the strip around and down the stem. Gently ease each petal shape out to give fullness. Bind the stem with strips of crepe paper.

Larger than life

Oversized, outrageously colorful paper flowers are an extravagant and sensational way of brightening up a home. Make one

Dahlias and peonies

or a mass of blooms to cheer up a dark corner.

You will need:

crepe paper □ tissue paper □ decorative gift wrap □ brown wrapping paper □ wire for stems □ thin wire for binding and supporting leaves □ pliers □ scissors □ glue.

Gift wrap dahlias

Prepare a wire stem with florist's wire about 76cm (30in) long and bend one end into a hook. Take a pack of folded crepe paper (they are usually about 10cm (4in) wide), and, keeping it folded, cut through it twice to make 2 strips 20cm (8in) deep. Join the strips together to make a double length. Refold this strip into a length of between 38cm (15in) and 46cm (18in), depending on the size of the original pack. Cut a fringe down to about 4cm (1½in) from the bottom. Roll this fringed strip around the looped top of the stem and bind firmly into place with thin wire. Cut 12 petals from decorative gift wrap using the tracing pattern given (fig.5). Glue each onto a sheet of brown wrapping paper and cut out these reinforced petals. Glue the petals around the crepe paper center. Curl the petals back.

Tissue or crepe paper peonies

Cut out about 15 squares of tissue paper, each measuring 50cm (20in). Fold each diagonally into a triangle, fold again, and again, and finally fold across the resulting triangle to form an irregularly shaped cone (see fig.6). Crease the edges sharply. Draw and cut 2 petal shapes across the wide part of the cone as shown in fig.7. Open out the resulting petal-shaped circles, dab a little glue into the center of each and stick each one to the next, being careful to keep the creases in place. Weight the center and leave to dry. Push the wire stem through the center of all layers and turn over a hook at the top. Draw the hook down into the center, pinch the petal circles into the base and bind to the stem with fine wire. Separate and ease the petals gently outward from the base.

Stems and leaves

The leaves are made from two layers of crepe paper reinforced with a wire spine. Cut the leaves from crepe paper using the same pattern given in fig.5 for the petals. Cut fine wire the length of the leaf plus an extra 5cm (2in). Glue the wire to the center of one leaf, then glue another leaf on top.

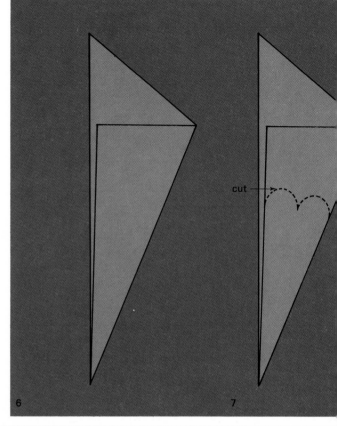

6

cut

7

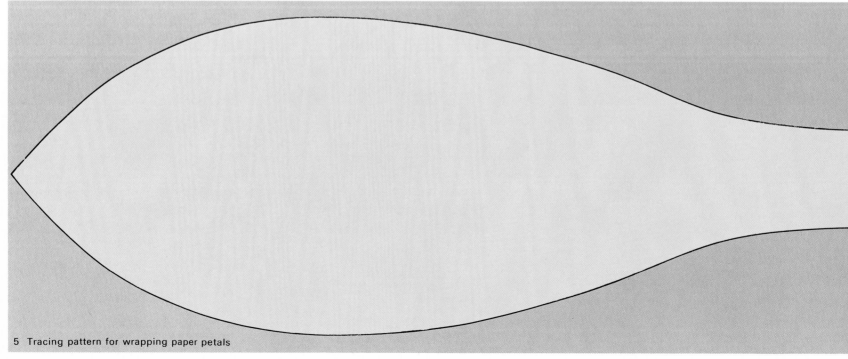

5 Tracing pattern for wrapping paper petals

Wrap the projecting leaf wires around the stem at appropriate intervals. Cover the stem with strips of matching crepe paper, starting at the top and winding tightly down the length of the stem, glueing at intervals from top and bottom.

Fabric flowers

Fabric flowers have always been thought of as a fashion accessory, something to add an individual touch of style to a plain dress or hat. Today, fabric flowers, although still a fashion success, are also popular in the home as attractive and longlasting flower arrangements that are particularly appreciated during the winter months.

Materials. The following fabrics are the most suitable: plain or printed cottons, taffeta, satin, silk, organdy and velvet. Use absorbent cotton (cotton wool) for the flower centers or, alternatively, artificial stamens which are obtainable from the notions (haberdashery) counter of most department stores or from hobby shops. Use medium-weight wire for stems and fine wire for binding. You will also need a suitable fabric glue, coloring, fabric stiffener, paper for cutting out petal patterns and cardboard for templates.

Equipment. The only tools necessary are a bradawl for making neat holes to take the stem, wire cutters, a small pair of scissors, a teaspoon, a metal knitting needle and a knife.

Making petal patterns. Fabric flowers are made from either lots of separate petals or from several petal-shaped circles. Most flowers start with small petals near the center and work out to larger shapes. Draw out the petal shapes onto paper, adjusting them until the size and shape looks right. For individual petal shapes, draw out a circle, divide into quarters, cut out each quarter separately and round off the corners. For a circle of petals start by drawing and cutting out the circle, fold in half, halve again, and again, until the circle is folded into eighths, then round off one corner of the resulting triangular shape (see fig.8). Trace around the paper pattern onto cardboard to make a more permanent template. To scale down the petal shapes, simply trim down the paper pattern and again transfer the shape onto cardboard.

Flower centers. Flower centers are made from balls of absorbent cotton (cotton wool) fixed to the wire stem and then covered in fabric, or by rolling a triangular length of fabric cut on the bias into a cone shape, or simply by inserting artificial stamens.

Stiffening fabrics. Before you cut out petal shapes, stiffen the fabric as this helps to prevent fraying. Spray-on starch and clear varnish work well on most substantial fabrics, but you may find that very fine fabrics like silk and organdy will stiffen better with a two-part glycerin to one-part water mix. For spray-on stiffeners, hang the fabric on a wire coat hanger in a well-ventilated space and then spray evenly from top to bottom. Fabrics requiring the glycerin and water treatment need to be dipped into the boiling solution and then hung to dry. If you use clear varnish, lay the fabric out flat over layers of protective newspaper and a top layer of tissue paper; apply the varnish evenly with a clean dry brush.

Painting petals. Painting petals adds a touch of realism to a fake flower, giving it form and character. Use ordinary water color paints for subtle shading on fine fabrics, or food coloring and fabric dyes for a more colorful result. Mix the paints and dyes well and then apply to the petal with a fine paintbrush; the paint should flow on quickly and evenly to avoid streaking.

Making and molding petals. Trace the

Ruched ribbon flowers and silk embroidery decorate this early 19th-century velvet book cover.

petal shapes onto the stiffened fabric using the cardboard template as a guide. Make sure that the center of the petal is laid across the grain. Mold the center of each petal shape separately by using the back of the bowl of a heated spoon (fig.9). Curl the outer petal edges in the same way but use a

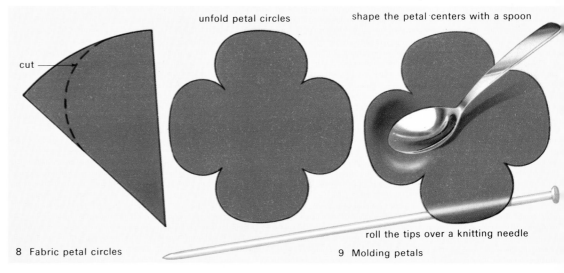

unfold petal circles

shape the petal centers with a spoon

cut

roll the tips over a knitting needle

8 Fabric petal circles

9 Molding petals

green fabric cut on the bias or purchased bias binding. Secure this to the neck of the flower with glue and a circle of fine wire, then wind it down the length of the stem. Tuck the end neatly into the fabric coil and glue into place.

Fabric poppies

These plain and printed cotton flowers can be used to create a distinctive arrangement, either on their own or combined with natural plant material, as shown in the photograph.

You will need:

remnants of fine small print and plain cotton fabric □ spray-on starch or stiffener □ absorbent cotton (cotton wool) for centers □ fine wire □ fabric glue □ florist's wire □ pinking shears □ scissors □ pair of compasses □ teaspoon □ knitting needle □ paper □ cardboard.

Preparation. Pin the fabric lengths onto wire coat hangers. Hang in a well-ventilated space and spray evenly with starch. Leave to dry.

Making the petals. With the compasses, draw 3 circles onto paper with diameters measuring 13cm (5$\frac{1}{8}$in), 11cm (4$\frac{3}{8}$in) and 7cm (2$\frac{3}{4}$in) respectively. Fold and cut the circles as described previously. Trace the petal shapes onto more permanent cardboard templates. Use these as patterns for cutting out the fabric petal circles. With the pinking shears, cut the smallest petal circles from the printed fabric; cut out the second and third from plain fabric using ordinary scissors. Make a hole in the center of the circles with a bradawl. Using the heated spoon and knitting needle method, mold each petal to form a bowl in the center and curl the edges over. Cut out as many "sets" of petals as you will need for the final arrangement.

Making the centers. Turn a hook over at one end of the wire stem, cover with a ball of absorbent cotton (cotton wool) and fabric, and bind together with fine wire.

Making a flower. Slip the first circle of petals onto the stem. Apply a dab of glue to the center and pinch into the stem at the base. Thread on the second and third petal circles in the same way, making sure that the petals overlap. Pinch, glue and finally wire into place.

heated knitting needle to give a fine roll.

Making the flower. Start with the smallest petals, and place these one by one so that they overlap slightly around the flower center and stem. Secure with a dab of glue at the base and bind with a twist of fine wire. Continue in this way until all the petals have been attached. Thread the individual petal circles onto the wire stem through a small hole made in the center with a bradawl; secure with a touch of glue and fine wire. Position each layer of petals so that it overlaps the previous one. The final step is to cover the wire stem with

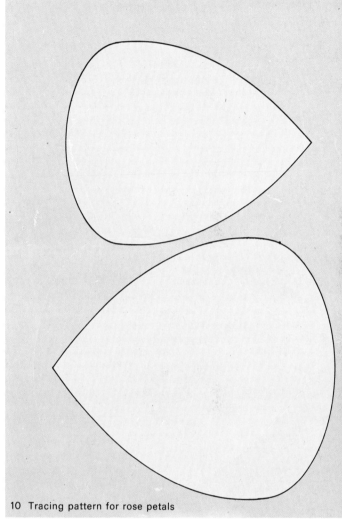

10 Tracing pattern for rose petals

A single rose

Make a single rose in pale creamy satin to add a touch of style to a plain dress or jacket.

You will need:

11cm ($4\frac{1}{4}$in) satin, 90cm (36in) wide, green bias binding □ florist's wire □ fabric glue □ fine wire □ spray-on starch or stiffener □ needle and thread □ tracing paper □ spoon □ knitting needle.

Making the petals. Begin by stiffening the length of fabric with spray-on starch or stiffener and leave to dry. Make paper patterns for 2 sizes of petal—7.5cm (3in) and 6.5cm ($2\frac{1}{2}$in) respectively—using the tracing patterns given (fig.10). Cut out 4 petals in each size.

Using the heated spoon and knitting needle method as previously described, carefully mold each individual petal into a realistic shape.

Making the center bud. Cut a 17cm ($6\frac{3}{4}$in) triangular length of satin on the bias measuring 3cm ($1\frac{1}{4}$in) at the narrow end graduating to 9cm ($3\frac{1}{2}$in) at the widest. Fold in half lengthwise. Starting at the narrow end, coil the fabric around and around to form a layered cone shape; then hold firmly in position by stitching through all layers.

Forming the flowers. Feed approximately 15cm (6in) of florist's wire for the stem into the center bud and secure with a touch of glue and bind the base with fine wire.

Attach each petal to the stem individually, starting with the smallest size. Apply glue to the base tip of each petal and place each in turn around the base of the bud, making sure the petals overlap fractionally. Attach all the petals in the same way.

Bind the complete flower to the bud with fine wire.

Covering the stem. Glue one end of the bias binding to the neck of the flower and from here wind it around the complete stem so that all the wire is concealed.

Tuck the end into the last coil and glue into place.

Stripping and decorating furniture

There are many ways in which a cheaply bought piece of secondhand furniture can be renovated and given a completely new lease of life. The first and most important thing to do when buying a piece is to make sure it will be suitable for your purpose.

White pine. If you want a stripped pine finish, the furniture must be made of white pine. You will never achieve the same effect with wood such as oak or mahogany. White pine is an even textured wood and often has "knots" along the surface. Look inside drawers and doors for these qualities. Scrape off a tiny patch of paint or varnish somewhere where it will not show on the piece of furniture. Press your thumbnail into this patch. If this leaves a slight indentation, the piece is likely to be of pine, which is a soft wood.

Woodworm. Check all furniture for telltale woodworm holes. The larvae are still active if the holes are lighter in color than the rest of the wood and if a whitish dust falls out of the holes when the wood is scraped. Isolate the piece from the rest of your furniture to prevent the woodworm from spreading. Treat the surface of the wood with woodworm fluid, then fill the holes with plastic wood. When dry, rub level with fine sandpaper. If, on the other hand, the holes are dark and clear, it is unlikely that the woodworm larvae are still active, but treat the furniture in the same way as a precaution.

Veneered furniture. Avoid working on furniture with a veneered surface (this is where a thin layer of wood has been glued to the surface) as the process of stripping off the old finish may well cause the veneer to warp—a fault difficult for the amateur to correct. Also, if parts of the furniture have been replaced with plywood or hardboard, this will call for extra preparation.

Stripping

Many professionals strip furniture by completely immersing it for several days in a large tank containing a strong solution of caustic soda. After this the softened paint is hosed off. However, this method is impractical for use at home because of the size of the tank, the amount of caustic needed and the danger to children and pets. This technique also tends to "fur" the surface of the wood and destroy the glue that holds moldings and joints together. The more painstaking method of hand stripping described below results in a much better finish.

You will need:
bottle of commercial paint stripper □ old tin can to hold stripper □ old paint brush to apply stripper □ warm water □ scrubbing brush □ scouring powder containing bleach □ rubber gloves □ medium and fine sandpaper □ newspaper to work on □ paint scraper.

Stripping the furniture. Pour some of the paint stripper into the tin can and brush on to a small area of the furniture at a time.
Note: paint stripper is corrosive and should not be allowed to come in contact with the skin or clothing. Wear rubber gloves and old clothing.

Keep the area being stripped in a horizontal position so that a maximum amount of stripper remains on the surface. Leave on for about 5 minutes or until the paint starts to bubble. Do *not* leave until the stripper dries hard. Remove the stripper and as much of the paint or varnish as you can with warm water and a scrubbing brush. The number of applications necessary depends on the number of layers of paint that have been applied to the piece over the years. There is usually a layer of white or pink primer immediately next to the wood. This is stubborn but can be removed in the same way. Work over the entire surface, using the paint scraper to remove paint or varnish from ridges and grooves. Wearing rubber gloves, use the scouring powder as an abrasive and bleaching agent. When dry, sand all over with medium sandpaper and remove any remaining flecks of paint. Finally rub the entire surface with fine sandpaper to provide a very smooth surface to which wax or seal can be applied. This final sanding is most important because if the surface is not sanded properly to a silky smooth finish, the seal or wax will tend to collect on porous areas and leave a patchy dark effect.

Repairs

With a little imagination and ingenuity, missing parts can be replaced or improvised. The plant stand illustrated, for exam-

Plant stand and mahogany table before renovation.

ple, once had a gallery or rail around the top. This was replaced with a rail made from basket cane to create a different but entirely satisfactory edge.

Replace missing beading with new wood. Stain with cold tea to match the old wood and stick with wood adhesive.

Correct any differences in color with oil paint or shoe polish carefully applied with a fine brush. Fill in small chips, cracks or nail holes with plastic wood filler and sand smooth with fine sandpaper.

Sealing or waxing

This is the final stage and should be done after stripping and when all repairs are completed. Polyurethane sealer, which is available in gloss and matt finishes, has the advantage of giving the piece of furniture a very hardwearing surface which will not be damaged by heat and water, or alcohol or oil. For this reason, furniture that will receive heavy wear—for example, in a kitchen or bathroom—is best treated this way. Apply the sealer sparingly with a brush to avoid an uneven surface.

Waxing with a colorless pure beeswax furniture polish gives a more vulnerable but more delicate finish to a surface. Use waxing for furniture that will not receive such hard wear. Apply the wax with a soft cloth. This will absorb the wax and help spread it evenly over the surface. Both sealing and waxing finishes will slightly darken the wood. You can test just how much darker the surface will be by wetting the wood with a finger. The darkening of the finishes will be approximately the same.

Below: The "new" plant stand with the missing beading replaced with basket cane.

Below right: The mahogany table restored to show off the deep rich tones of the original wood.

It is important to remember that the success of both these finishes depends on the care taken in the preparation and sanding beforehand.

French polishing

A mahogany piece, like the table illustrated, which had a scratched, stained and ringmarked surface, can be successfully restored with French polish. When buying furniture to French polish, scrape off a tiny patch of varnish or paint to check that the wood really is the rich color it appears and not a lighter wood stained to look like mahogany.

You will need:

French polish ☐ raw or pure linseed oil ☐ denatured alcohol (methylated spirits) ☐ sandpaper: medium, fine and very fine ☐ soft cloth ☐ absorbent cotton (cotton wool).

Preparation. Strip the old varnish from the piece as described earlier, but omitting bleaching agents. The aim of French polishing is to enhance the rich color of the wood and not to give a stripped effect.

Finishing. Sand the surface smooth with medium and fine sandpaper. Make a pad of absorbent cotton and cover this with a cloth. Pour approximately a tablespoon of

Stripping and decorating furniture

Decorative painting

New chairs for old!

French polish and a few drops of linseed oil onto the pad and apply to the surface with light sweeping strokes. Leave the surface to dry for about half an hour. Sand with very fine paper. Apply 3 to 4 coats of French polish and linseed oil mixture, drying and sanding between each coat. This sanding is important since it prevents a buildup of polish and creates a smooth surface. For the final coat, dilute the polish with denatured alcohol (methylated spirits) to give added gloss to the surface. The beautiful finish achieved in this way can be damaged by heat and scratches easily, so must be treated with care.

Decorative painting

When choosing a piece to paint, look for solid surfaces which are not veneered and an interesting shape that can be incorporated into the design.

Painting the furniture. Strip the piece of furniture as described earlier. Give it a coat of wood primer and an undercoat. Before painting the furniture, work out a design on paper. A light natural touch only comes with practice. Do not put too much paint on the brush as this will cause drips. Let one color dry before applying the next. Use additional moldings and carvings to enhance the design further.

Surface decoration

Above: A 19th-century engraving by Thomas Bewick entitled *The Peacock.*

Right: Fabric printing at its very best. This print was designed by William Morris.

The use of block printing as a method of decoration dates back thousands of years and was certainly practiced in ancient Babylon and China. Carved wooden blocks were among the first stamps to be devised for printing, not only on fabrics but also on items of pottery.

Modern block printing now also includes printing with found objects, such as corks, lids and paper doilies, potato printing and linoleum cutting. The object common to all these methods is to obtain an impression on paper or fabric from a block which has been coated with ink or dye. A block may be printed singly or may be repeated many times to produce a complex pattern. If translucent inks are used, another dimension can be added to give further colors by overprinting. For example, by using three different colors on a block, eight colors, including the background, can be produced.

General equipment
Printing table. An even level surface is essential for good printing. Use a table or wooden board covered with a blanket and a piece of clean cloth. Alternatively, use a folded sheet or newspapers for padding and cover them with a sheet of plastic (polythene) or oilcloth.

Materials and inks
Printing on paper. Choose paper or cardboard that is slightly absorbent. There are many suitable inks available or you can use a paint which mixes to a thick consistency, such as powder paint.

Printing on fabric. Natural fabrics such as cotton, linen and silk are the most suitable. They should be closely woven. Always wash the fabric before printing to remove any substance that might resist the dye. There are basically two kinds of ink that can be used for fabric printing: oil-based block printing inks, which are fixed by ironing, and water-soluble block printing inks, which are usually more liquid in consistency and require special fixatives.

Printing with found objects
With a little imagination, almost any object can be used in this method of printing. Unlike potato or linoleum printing, the object is used in its natural form so you should choose something with an interesting outline or pattern or an unusual texture. A smooth surface gives a solid print whereas only the raised parts of a textured surface will print. Wine bottle corks, bottle tops, lids, paper doilies and embossed wallpaper are all excellent materials for this type of printing.

Basic techniques
Some blocks can be used as they are, others are better mounted onto wood or cardboard. Mount them singly or make a composite block from a number of objects arranged together.

Inking the block. Apply the ink to the block using a brush or paint roller or press the block onto a sponge soaked in ink.

Printing the block. Stamp the block onto the fabric by placing the block face down and applying pressure. Do this by rolling the back with a hard rubber roller, by hitting with a mallet, or simply by pressing with your hands.

It is essential to make trial prints from your block. Use newspaper for economy before experimenting on scraps of the fabric to be printed.

Surface decoration
Block printing

Autumn leaves

Autumn leaves
This very effective example of found object printing uses autumn leaves in October colors on a natural background.

You will need:
adhesive tape ☐ length of unbleached cotton fabric ☐ sponge roller and tray ☐ hard rubber roller ☐ variety of leaves ☐ newspaper ☐ blotting paper ☐ brown, red, yellow and orange water-soluble block printing inks ☐ fixative.

Printing the fabric. Tape the fabric to the printing table. Mix the color in the tray and prime the roller. Place a leaf on the newspaper and cover the leaf with color using the roller. More than one color can be used on the same leaf. Place the leaf in position face down on the fabric, cover with a piece of blotting paper and print the leaf by pressing with the roller. The blotting paper will absorb any dye that spreads around the edge of the leaf. Use the same leaf a number of times until it begins to break up. Start printing at the bottom of the

openers □ 2 bottle tops □ 4 pieces of wood, 10 × 2.5cm (4 × 1in) for blocks □ hammer and 2 nails □ masking tape □ strong glue □ 2 squares of sponge □ graph paper □ felt tip pen □ 3m (3yd) red bias binding □ 5.5m (5½yd) turquoise ribbon or tape for straps □ mallet □ turpentine □ turquoise and red oil-based block printing inks.

Cutting out the apron. Draw up the pattern from the graph (fig.1) in which 1 square equals 5cm (2in). Cut out the apron pieces.

Printing the pockets. For the design on the pockets, draw around the bottle opener onto the graph paper with a felt tip pen, following the patterns shown in fig.2a and b or creating your own design. The exact spacing will depend on the size of the bottle opener but the graph paper will help you to achieve a symmetrical design. Glue each bottle opener flat to a piece of wood and nail each bottle top to the end of a piece of wood. Put the paper design onto the printing table and keep the pocket piece in position over it with masking tape so that the design shows through. Squeeze some color onto a square of sponge and spread evenly. Try a few prints on a spare piece of fabric first by pressing the opener on the pad several times so that it is coated evenly and then pressing it down onto the fabric. To get a really clear impression hit the block with a mallet. Print all 3 pockets using 1 bottle opener and 1 sponge pad for each color.

Printing the main apron. Put a large piece of graph paper onto the printing table and fasten the main apron piece over it with masking tape. Print the bottle top over the whole of the fabric, using the squares on the graph paper as a guide. Print the first row in one color and the second row in the other color, moving the design along half a width for a staggered effect. This method of lining up a print (called "registration") is fairly quick and very accurate but is only possible with fabrics thin enough to allow a design to show through.

Making the apron. Bind the main apron piece with red bias binding and each pocket piece with turquoise ribbon. Sew the pockets in position and sew ribbon straps to the bib and sides of the apron.

1 Graph pattern for apron   1 sq = 5cm (2in)

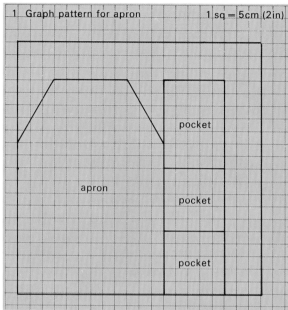

2 Designs for pockets

fabric, using the largest leaves and the darker colors. As you progress use smaller leaves and lighter colors. Continue printing until you are satisfied with the balance of colors and shapes. Fix the dye according to the manufacturer's instructions.

Kitchen apron

This striking apron was printed with bottle openers and bottle tops. It is not a difficult project but does require time and patience.
You will need:
1m (1yd) strong cotton fabric □ 2 bottle

Potato printing

Potatoes are ideal for printing, though certain other vegetables are also suitable. The gourd, for example, is still used for printing cloth in West Africa.

Basic technique

Cut the potato in half so that you have a flat surface. Cut out the design using a sharp craft knife. Ink the potato with a paint brush or by pressing onto a pad impregnated with color. Print by stamping the potato onto the material. Interesting effects are obtained by printing in rows

down on the cut surface of the potato. Transfer the design to the potato by cutting around the main lines through the paper onto the potato with a sharp knife. Remove the paper and cut away the unwanted parts of the potato with a craft knife. The design will be reversed on the potato but will print the right way around. Mix some color and print by painting the potato surface and pressing it onto the paper. Apply only enough pressure for a good print otherwise the potato surface will become damaged. The same potato can sometimes be used for more than one color if the paint can be washed off. Registration can be done by eye or by drawing faint pencil guidelines on the paper that can be erased later.

Snail gift tag and invitation
This endearing design was printed with a minimum of effort using plastic sheet (polystyrene). This method is ideal for printing any small line drawing or silhouette.
You will need:
sheet of plastic (smooth polystyrene) ☐ colored paper ☐ ballpoint pen ☐ pencil ☐ ☐ sheet of glass ☐ hard rubber roller ☐ water-soluble ink ☐ tracing paper.
Printing the snail. Trace the snail design (fig.4) and draw it onto the plastic sheet (polystyrene) with a ballpoint pen so that an even groove is made. Squeeze some color, a little at a time, onto the sheet of glass and spread with the roller to make an even, sticky surface. Ink the plastic sheet (polystyrene) with the roller. Print the snail by placing it face down onto the paper and pressing by hand. Print the balloons by using the end of a pencil and complete the invitation by drawing in the balloon strings and a border.

4

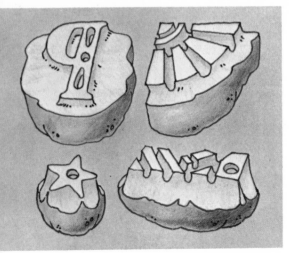

and rotating the potato 90°. A potato cut deteriorates quickly, so all printing should be done in one session.

Stationery motifs
Potato printing can be used very effectively to print your own personalized stationery. The easiest motifs are those made from straight lines, but more complicated designs are also possible. Use the ideas shown here (fig.3) or create your own.
You will need:
potatoes ☐ sharp craft knife ☐ palette ☐ paint brushes ☐ any water-soluble ink that is not too thin ☐ tracing paper.
Printing the motifs. Draw the design on tracing paper and place the tracing face

Hand block printing cannot compete commercially with machine techniques but is nevertheless an exciting craft. Wood or linoleum blocks are not only more permanent than potato or other vegetable blocks, but allow finer and more accurate lines to be cut. Linoleum cutting is a relatively modern printing technique dating from the beginning of this century. The first exhibition of linoleum cuts was held in London in 1929.

Tools and equipment
Cutters. For linoleum cutting you will need a variety of blades, which will fit into one handle or, alternatively a number of separate tools. Three blades are usually adequate: a wide shallow gouge for removing large areas, a small V-cutter for cutting thin lines and a large V-cutter for wider deeper lines. A sharp knife such as a stencil knife can also be useful.

Technique
Trace the design onto the linoleum; the design will of course print in reverse. If possible press the far edge of the block against something solid to steady it. Hold the cutting tool with the handle fitted comfortably into the palm of your hand and cut away the unwanted area. Always cut away from the body and keep both hands behind the cutting edge. For very accurate work use the stencil knife to cut the outline before removing the linoleum with the appropriate tool.

Printed table linen
This matching set of tablecloth, tea cozy, napkins, placemats and curtains was printed with two linoleum blocks in only one color from a single tracing. The teapot motif is ideally suited to this medium but the stems on the smaller block are more difficult to cut accurately and could be omitted for a simpler design if preferred.
You will need:
plain cotton fabric in the following quantities: 4m (4yd) for tablecloth, 0.6m ($\frac{5}{8}$yd) for tea cozy, 38×48cm (15×19in) piece for each table napkin and placemat and an appropriate length for curtains □ foam padding for tea cozy □ bias binding for edgings □ paper for patterns □ 2

linoleum blocks, one measuring 18×12.5cm (7×5in) and the other measuring 7.5×11.5cm (3×4$\frac{1}{2}$in) □ 2 pieces of plywood of the same size for mountings □ sheet of glass or acrylic (perspex) □ hard rubber roller □ mallet □ linoleum cutting tools □ stencil knife □ masking tape □ glue □ oil-based block printing ink □ tailor's chalk □ string □ tracing paper.
Preparing the blocks. Trace the teapot design (fig.5). Tape the tracing face down onto the larger of the 2 linoleum blocks and cut around the whole outline with a stencil knife. Remove the linoleum surrounding the teapot, the section inside the handle and also the linoleum inside the flower motif.
Trace the flower motif and transfer the design to the smaller linoleum block in the same way, again cutting away the

surrounding material. Make a few trial prints on spare paper and when you are satisfied, glue each block onto a plywood mounting. Sketch the design onto the back of the blocks to avoid printing upside down and to help in positioning them correctly.
General instructions for printing. Roll out some color to an even consistency onto the glass sheet and coat the block evenly using the rubber roller. Tape the fabric to the printing table and print by placing the block face down onto the fabric. Hit the back of the block sharply with a mallet to ensure a clear print.
Cutting out the tablecloth. Measure the radius of the table. Decide how much overhang you want and add this to the radius. Draw a circle of this size onto the fabric using an improvised compass of string and tailor's chalk. If the table is large or the fabric is narrow, you may need to cut

2 semicircles as shown in fig.6. In this case, sew the center seam before starting to print.

Print layout for the tablecloth. The exact layout will depend on the size of the tablecloth, but to achieve even spacing, fold the tablecloth in half and mark the point for the base line of the smaller block in tailor's chalk, 4cm ($1\frac{1}{2}$in) from the edge at both ends of this fold. These lines will be guides for printing. Open out and fold again, placing these chalk lines together. Mark in 2 more base lines. Continue in this way until you are satisfied with the spacing of motifs in the border. Print the border and edge with matching bias binding to finish.

Making the tea cozy. Make a pattern for the the tea cozy, drawing it up from the graph (fig.7) in which 1 square equals 4cm ($1\frac{1}{2}$in). Cut 4 pieces of fabric and print the teapot motif centrally on 2 pieces. Cut 2 pieces of foam padding using the same pattern but cutting to the seamline. With right sides together, sew the bottom seam of the lining and the front. Turn right side out and place the layer of foam padding between them. Repeat for the back of the cozy. Place the front and back together with the motifs inside and stitch along the curved seam. Finish the edges and turn right side out.
Edge and decorate with matching bias binding if desired.

Making the table napkins and placemats. For the napkins, print a row of 4 flower motifs as shown in fig.8 and for the placemats print a teapot as in fig.9. Positioning or registration can be done by drawing lines lightly in tailor's chalk or by making guidelines with masking tape. Finish the

5 Tracing pattern for table cloth

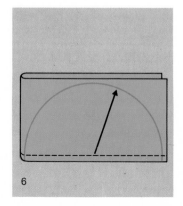

6

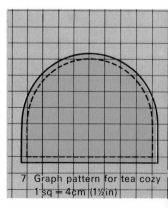

7 Graph pattern for tea cozy
1 sq = 4cm (1½in)

Pineapple surprise

...sition of motifs for napkins

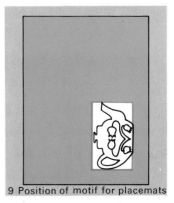

9 Position of motif for placemats

edges with a rolled hem of 1cm ($\frac{3}{8}$in).

Printing the curtains. Draw a base line or mark with masking tape 8cm ($3\frac{1}{4}$in) from the bottom of the curtain. Print a line of flower motifs above the guideline. Print the next line by moving the block half a width to one side. Continue printing in this way until the depth of border is compatible with the overall size of the curtain. Finish the curtain by taking a 5cm (2in) hem to leave a plain border of 2cm ($\frac{3}{4}$in) below the pattern.

Pineapple surprise

The sarong originates from Indonesia and is the simplest type of skirt, made from a rectangular piece of cotton fabric wrapped around the waist. This design has an exotic oriental influence with pineapple and palm tree motifs. The finished size is about 114 × 152cm (45 × 60in).

You will need:

For making the blocks: 1 piece of linoleum 8 × 9.5cm ($3\frac{1}{4}$ × $3\frac{3}{4}$in) and 1 piece of linoleum 8 × 2.5cm ($3\frac{1}{4}$ × 1in) for the pineapple motif □ 1 piece of linoleum 17 × 24.5cm ($6\frac{3}{4}$ × $9\frac{3}{4}$in) and 1 piece of linoleum 13.5 × 24.5cm ($5\frac{1}{4}$ × $9\frac{3}{4}$in) for the palm tree motif □ 4 blocks of wood, 2.5cm (1in) thick and the same size as linoleum pieces □ linoleum cutting tools □ craft knife □ 2 sheets of paper the size of the palm tree and pineapple motifs □ tracing paper □ pencil □ ballpoint pen □ black wax crayon □ contact adhesive.

For printing: 1 piece of cardboard, 27.5 × 31cm ($10\frac{3}{4}$ × $12\frac{1}{4}$in) for palm tree motif □ 1 piece of cardboard, 15 × 18.5cm (6 × $7\frac{1}{4}$in) for pineapple motif □ piece of yellow cotton fabric, 114 × 152cm (45 × 60in) plus seam allowance □ small rubber roller □ orange, green and brown oil-based block printing inks □ sheet of glass or metal □ turpentine (white spirit) □ mallet □ needle and thread □ pins.

Making the blocks. Make 4 separate blocks, 1 for each color in both motifs, in the following way. Draw up the palm tree motif from the graph (fig.10a) in which 1 square equals 2cm ($\frac{3}{4}$in) and trace the pineapple motif (fig.10b). Transfer each motif to a separate sheet of tracing paper and wax the back of each sheet heavily with a wax crayon.

Take the piece of linoleum measuring 17 × 24.5cm ($6\frac{3}{4}$ × $9\frac{3}{4}$in) and place the palm tree motif tracing on it, lining it up at the top edges. Draw over the outlines of the *leaves* of the palm tree with a ballpoint pen, to make an impression on the linoleum with the wax crayon.

Using the same method trace the *trunks* of the palm trees onto the linoleum measuring 13.5 × 24.5cm ($5\frac{1}{4}$ × $9\frac{3}{4}$in), lining it up at the lower edges.

Next trace the *base* of the pineapple onto the linoleum measuring 8 × 9.5cm ($3\frac{1}{4}$ × $3\frac{3}{4}$in) and the *leaves* onto the linoleum measuring 8 × 2.5cm ($3\frac{1}{4}$ × 1in). Glue each piece of linoleum onto the appropriate wood block with contact adhesive and leave to dry.

Cutting the linoleum blocks. Use the sharp cutting knife to cut along the shapes in each motif, then start to cut away the linoleum with a narrow cutting blade. Use a wider blade to remove the linoleum surrounding the motif. The linoleum block should have clearly defined edges and

10 (b) Tracing pattern for pineapple motif

297

Surface decoration
Linoleum cutting

Pineapple surprise

10 (a) Graph for palm tree motif
1 sq = 2cm (¾in)

Further design ideas for linoleum blocks

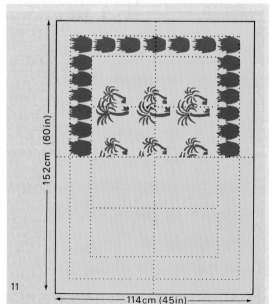

11

152cm (60in)

114cm (45in)

should be in sharp relief. Mark an arrow for the top of the design on the back.

Positioning the linoleum blocks. Hem the cotton fabric. Baste lines as indicated in fig.11 and refer to positions of motifs when printing. This will enable you to position the blocks correctly. Take the piece of cardboard 27.5 × 31cm (10¾ × 12¼in) and draw a rectangle 24.5 × 21.5cm (9¾ × 8½in) on it, leaving a margin around the edge. Cut this rectangle away so you have a cardboard frame to use when printing the palm trees.

Repeat for the pineapple motif on the cardboard measuring 15 × 18.5cm (6 × 7¼in) cutting out a rectangle measuring 8 × 12cm (3¼ × 4¾in).

Printing the fabric. Place the yellow fabric on the printing surface, and pin flat. If the printing surface is smaller than 114 ×

152cm (45 × 60in) print one area first and then move the fabric across.

Print the border of pineapples first, starting with the orange area of the motif. Place the cardboard frame in the first position at one corner, positioning it on the basting lines. Squeeze some orange printing ink onto the glass or metal sheet, and roll it with the roller until evenly covered. Roll the ink onto the surface of the block so you have an even layer all over the motif.

Note: if any ink touches the background areas you have probably not cut the linoleum away enough. Cut away the excess linoleum or it will print on the fabric. Position the block face down on the fabric, inside the cardboard frame, lining up

298

Stenciling

Stenciling has been used to decorate paper, fabric, walls, floors and many other objects since civilization began. The most common example of present-day stenciling unfortunately seems to be restricted to the use of stenciled letters on the sides of crates and packages. However, stenciling was once used extensively in churches during the Middle Ages and reached its peak as an art form in America at the turn of the 18th century. Early American settlers brought with them memories of expensive furnishings, intricately carved furniture and elaborate wallpapers. Their attempts at reproducing this luxury have left behind some of the best examples of stenciled interiors in existence.

Materials

Stencil paper is most suitable to use because it is oiled, but any heavy paper or cardboard can be substituted if not too

Stenciled wallpaper and bedcover, originally from the Joshua La Salle house, Windham, Connecticut.

many images are needed. For cutting use a stencil knife or any small, sharp knife or blade. Either oil-based or water-soluble printing ink can be used, provided it is not too thin. You will also need stencil brushes or a sponge roller and tray. Traditional stencil brushes are efficient but a sponge roller enables you to work more quickly especially when printing onto fabric.

1 Cutting a stencil

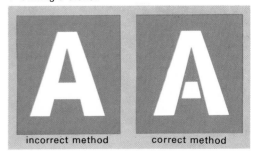

incorrect method   correct method

the lower edge of the block to the lower edge of the frame. Tap the block firmly with the mallet, holding the block carefully in position so that it does not move. Give a final press and lift. Apply more ink to the block, and continue to print the rest of the border. Clean the roller and block with turpentine (white spirit). Repeat the process, printing the leaves of the pine-apple with green ink, and positioning the block inside the frame at the top edges this time.
Next, print the palm tree motif, starting with the palm tree trunks in brown and again positioning the lower edges of the block inside the other cardboard frame. Then print the palm tree leaves, registering at the top edges.

Surface decoration
Stenciling

Stenciled cushion covers

Technique

When designing a stencil make sure that there are no "floating" pieces such as the center of a letter. Fig.1 shows how this problem should be tackled.

Unlike block printing, stenciling does not reverse the image so draw or trace your design onto the stencil paper the right way around. Cut out the stencil, rotating the paper so that you are always drawing the knife toward you to avoid buckling the stencil. Hold the stencil in place with masking tape and then apply the paint or dye.

Stenciled cushion covers

The mushroom and toadstool designs for these cushion covers make ideal subjects for stenciled decoration. The fabric was printed with five separate stencils used singly and together.

You will need:

unbleached muslin (calico) or similar fabric for cushion covers ☐ double-sided adhesive tape ☐ sponge roller and tray ☐ large paint brush ☐ shredded foam or kapok for stuffing ☐ stencil paper ☐ stencil knife ☐ tracing paper ☐ crimson and brown printing ink ☐ newspaper.

Stenciling the fabric. Wash and iron the fabric. Cut out each cushion square in turn and tape it to the printing table. Trace each mushroom design (fig.2) onto the stencil and cut it out. Fasten the stencil to the fabric with small pieces of double-sided adhesive tape and also tape along the edges so that the stencil lies completely flat. Squeeze plenty of color into the roller tray and ink the roller thoroughly. Apply the color, putting newspaper around the border of the stencil in case you roll too far.

2 Tracing pattern for mushroom stencils

Peasant skirt

Two bordered skirts

These two skirts, very different in style, both have stenciled borders, illustrating the diverse effects you can achieve with this simple technique.

Peasant skirt

You will need:

3m (3yd) blue denim □ stencil paper □ stencil knife □ tracing paper □ small pieces of sponge □ palette □ masking tape □ crimson, blue and green printing ink.

Stenciling the skirt. Wash and iron the denim. Copy the design (fig.3) and cut the stencil leaving a 3cm (1¼in) border at the bottom and a generous border at the top and left-hand edge. Cut the right-hand edge as shown in fig.4. Mask out the flower heads and tape the stencil in position on the fabric with the bottom edge against the selvage. Soak the end of a piece of sponge in the green ink and color the leaves and stems on the denim by pressing the sponge down on the unmasked areas. Reposition the stencil for the first repeat,

3 Flower design for peasant skirt border

working right to left and lining up the right-hand edge of the stencil with the last clump of grass, as shown.
Continue working right to left until you have stenciled the green border for the full length of the fabric. Unmask the flower heads and put masking tape over the leaves and stems closest to the flowers. Position the stencil over the green design and color the flowers. Use fresh pieces of sponge for each new color. When all the flowers have been colored make up the skirt with a single hem of 1cm (⅜in).

4

5 Graph for flared skirt border   1 sq = 0.5cm (¼in)

Flared skirt

You will need:

suitable pattern for a four-gore flared skirt ☐ light brown heavy cotton fabric ☐ stencil paper ☐ stencil knife ☐ tracing paper ☐ small pieces of sponge ☐ masking tape ☐ palette ☐ white, green and red printing ink.

Stenciling the fabric. Cut out the skirt pieces following the pattern instructions and sew the front and back seams. Draw up the motif from the graph (fig.5) in which 1 square equals 0.5cm (¼in). Cut the stencil. Make 6 paper cutouts from the stencil. Put the skirt front flat on the table and position 3 paper silhouettes on each panel. Adjust their positions to obtain the correct even spacing. Place the stencil over each silhouette and mark the corners of the stencil on the fabric with masking tape. Using the same cutouts, repeat this spacing on the skirt back remembering to leave a seam allowance. Mix the ink by adding a very small amount of red and green to plenty of white in a palette. Test the color on a piece of spare fabric making sure you let it dry. Position the stencil on the skirt panel and apply ink with a sponge as for the peasant skirt. Print alternate designs so that the color dries before stenciling adjacent motifs.

Stencils can be used in an ingenious way to enhance the interior of a room. Here the same motif has been used on the wooden cabinet and on both walls to create an unusual effect.

Screen printing is a process which evolved from stenciling in the 18th century. A traditional stencil requires tabs to hold floating pieces in place. These tabs were replaced by hairs so that they were barely perceptible in the final print. This idea was developed further until the whole stencil was held in place by a grid of hairs attached to a frame. Finally, by the middle of the 19th century the grid was replaced by a fine mesh of silk stretched taut over the frame. Silk-screen printing gives more rapid and detailed repeats than other forms of stenciling and its commercial possibilities were soon realized. During World War I for example, the technique was used to make flags in America and nowadays it is used widely for fabrics and patterned paper.

Equipment
Silk-screen. A silk-screen consists of a flat rectangular wooden frame with a fine mesh stretched over it. The mesh can be silk, nylon, organdy, Dacron (terylene) or a similar fabric. Fix the mesh to the screen with tacks or staples along the side of the frame in the order shown in fig.6. It is important to get the mesh as taut as possible. Block the screen on the outside to the required size with masking tape. This masked area acts as a reservoir for the ink.

A modern example of screen printing showing how a repeat design can be used to advantage.

For a more permanent screen, paint the tape with varnish both inside and outside.
Squeegee (fig.7). This is a thick piece of rubber set in a piece of wood. Make it wide enough to cover the print easily and about 2cm ($\frac{3}{4}$in) narrower than the inside of the frame. Add a bar so that the squeegee can rest on the frame.
Printing ink. There are many ready-mixed inks which are suitable. If they dry too quickly the mesh becomes clogged and will not give a good print. If they are too thin the paint will run under the stencil.
The stencil. To produce the image, block the screen with a paper stencil, or shellac varnish. A manufactured film stencil, which is a thin sheet of lacquer on backing paper, can also be used.

Technique
Screen printing any design needs a number of trial runs. Use old newspaper for test prints. Place the blocked screen on the newspaper and pour some ink into the masked reservoir. Fig.8 shows the screen ready for use. Draw the squeegee towards you with a firm even pressure holding the screen with your other hand. When using a larger screen you will need both hands on the squeegee and someone else to hold the screen for you. Depending on the surface and ink used, it may be necessary to pull the squeegee back across the screen to get a perfect print.

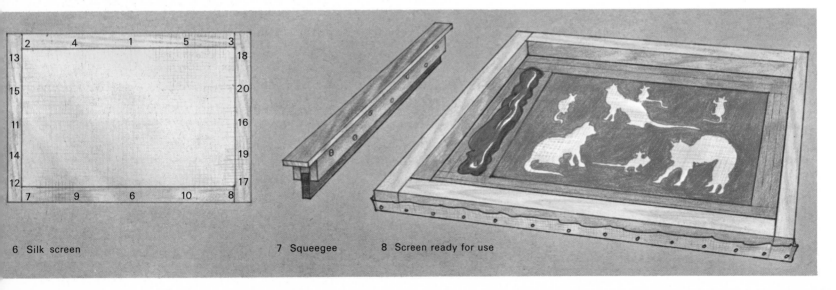

6 Silk screen   7 Squeegee   8 Screen ready for use

Cutting the stencil. Draw up the cat and mouse design from the graph (fig.9) in which 1 square equals 1cm ($\frac{3}{8}$in) and fasten it to the cutting board with masking tape. Tape the film stencil on top of the tracing, shiny side up, so that the design shows through. Cut all the lines of the design with a stencil knife. Make the cut through the varnish but *not* through the backing sheet. Remove the areas to be printed, that is the cats and mice, by sliding the stencil knife under the varnish and peeling it off.

Printing the fabric. Wash and iron the denim. Place the screen over the film stencil, shiny side up. Iron the stencil onto the screen with a cool iron and peel off the backing sheet. Mask the screen at the edge of the stencil and make a few test prints. Tape the denim to the printing table and mark out into rectangles with cotton thread as shown in fig.10. Print alternate lines of the fabric in the order shown, making sure that each print is completely dry before making an adjacent print.

Rearrange the cotton thread so that the rectangles are cut in half as shown in fig.11. Now make 2 whole and 2 half prints in each row. Print in the order shown. Fix the ink if necessary and wash and iron the fabric.

Sew up the dress in the usual way.

Cat and mouse dress

This delightful print was made in one color from a single screen; the very professional result is surprisingly easy to achieve.

You will need:

screen measuring 30 × 45cm (12 × 18in) □ 23cm (9in) squeegee □ 3m (3yd) pink denim □ large jar for mixing and storing ink □ tracing paper □ cutting board □ cotton thread □ manufactured film stencil □ stencil knife □ masking tape □ red printing ink □ fixative.

9 Graph for cat and mouse stencil   1 sq = 1cm (⅜in)

10

1		3		5		7		9		11
13		14		15		16		17		18
2		4		6		8		10		12

11

19		21		23		25		27		29
31		33		35		37		39		41
20		22		24		26		28		30
32		34		36		38		40		42

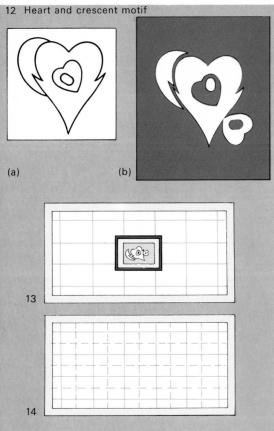

12 Heart and crescent motif

(a)   (b)

13

14

Length of fabric.

This striking modern design was printed using only one screen and two colors on plain white cotton fabric.

You will need:
screen measuring 45 × 61cm (18 × 24in) □ 36cm (14in) squeegee □ 2.75m (2¾yd) white cotton fabric □ 2 large jars for mixing and storing ink □ scissors □ old newspaper □ printing paper □ masking tape □ cotton thread □ blue and brown fabric printing ink □ fixative.

Making the stencil. Draw a heart and crescent motif onto a piece of old newspaper as shown in fig.12a. Cut a circle from the heart and a further circle from this piece. Arrange the paper pieces on a clean piece of printing paper as shown in fig.12b. Mask the screen so that the print will measure 30 × 45cm (12 × 18in). Place the screen over the stencil and make a test print using the brown ink. This will make the stencil stick to the screen where it will stay for the duration of printing.

Printing the fabric. Wash and iron the fabric. Fasten it to the printing table with masking tape, leaving a border of 10cm (4in). You will need this space for positioning the screen. Measure a trial print and mark out the fabric in rectangles using cotton thread held in place with masking tape. Make a few more test prints on paper until you are satisfied that the screen is thoroughly inked and is not clogged anywhere. Place the screen in position by lining up the edge of the masking tape on the screen with the cotton threads as shown in fig.13.

Make a print and reposition the screen on the next rectangle. Continue printing until all the fabric on the printing table is covered. Always clean the masking tape on the front of the screen between each print. It is impossible to position the screen exactly on the fabric so you will have either a narrow white line or a darker brown overlap. Remedy this by rubbing in the ink on the joins immediately after each print with your finger. Finish printing the brown by taping the rest of the fabric to the table and marking out as before. For best results fix, and then wash and iron the fabric before printing the second color. This is more important the larger the area of color

being printed as the dye makes the fabric shrink causing small puckers. Unless the fabric is perfectly flat overprinting will be inaccurate. To print the blue, mark out the fabric in rectangles with thread as shown in fig.14.

Sponge out the remaining brown in the screen taking care not to move the stencil. Run test prints on newspaper using the blue until the color is clear. Print the blue with the screen turned 180°. To print half the width of the screen put a piece of paper under the edge of the fabric before making the print. Finally, fix, and then wash and iron the fabric.

15 Graph for windmill design   1 sq = 5 cm (2 in)

This rural scene is a five-color repeat on unbleached cotton fabric.

You will need:
screen measuring 90 × 61 cm (36 × 24 in) □ 45cm (18in) squeegee □ old newspaper □ 3 jars for mixing and storing ink □ 3m (3yd) unbleached muslin (calico) or similar fabric, 180cm (72in) wide □ masking tape □ tracing paper □ shellac □ denatured alcohol (methylated spirits) □ paint brushes □ blue, yellow, red, brown and black printing ink □ fixative.

Designing the print. Draw the design from the graph (fig.15) in which 1 square equals 5cm (2in). Color the buildings in 3 colors—say red, brown and black— and then color the greenery. The darkest of the 3 colors will be the overprint from the other 2 colors. Use it for outlines and places where 2 colors meet. Make 3 tracings, the first of all areas that are red or black, the second of all that are brown or black and the third of all that are green.

Making the stencil. If you print using a single screen, you will have to remove the shellac with denatured alcohol (methylated spirits) after each color. Alternatively, use 3 screens, 1 for each color. Place the screen over the tracing and paint out with shellac all the areas not to be printed.

Printing the fabric. Make the green by mixing together blue, yellow and a little black. The light brown is a mixture of red and brown, and the darker brown a mixture of the green and brown. Mix the colors thoroughly and store them in airtight jars. Wash and iron the fabric before printing, then tape it in place on the table. Print the light brown first. Positioning for this is very simple: put a piece of masking tape every 61cm (24in) at the edge of the material and line up the bottom of the screen with it. Print the length of fabric by which time the the first prints should be dry so that the adjacent ones can be made. Line up the rows by eye. Print the darker brown in the same way, placing the screen over the light brown print and adjusting for the best effect. When both these colors are dry, print the green, again positioning by eye. Finally, fix the colors and wash and iron the fabric.

Tie and dye is one of the oldest dye crafts. Although no-one can be sure of its exact origin, tie-dyed fabrics were known to have been produced in India, Japan and China during the 6th century AD. In India, tie and dye was known as "bandhana" and traditional designs were created by tying hundreds of rice grains into fine muslin or silk to produce intricate patterns made up of minute dots of dyed fabric surrounded by tiny undyed rings that stood out against the background. The "bandhani"—women who practiced this delicate craft—grew the nails of their thumbs and forefingers very long to enable them to tie the points of fabric with fine thread.

The Japanese developed their own version of this technique, known as "shibori," using mainly silk and cotton fabrics. During the Middle Ages, China exported tie-dyed fabric to many neighboring and more distant countries, including parts of West Africa where the craft still flourishes today.

Dyes

Modern dyes have opened up a whole new world of color and there is now a dye for virtually every kind of fabric, including many of today's synthetics. Always choose the dye that is appropriate for the fabric. Multi-purpose and liquid dyes are suitable for a wide range of synthetic and natural fabrics and can be used in very hot water. For really deep dark colors the water must be simmering. Natural fabrics such as cotton, linen, wool and silk, however, are best dyed with cold dye—a colorfast cold water dye which is extremely easy to use. Cold dyes can also be used for polyester-cotton blends. The resulting colors will be pretty pastels as only the cotton content of the fabric will absorb the dye.

For the best results, fabrics should be white or pastel-colored. Always be sure that the fabric is perfectly clean and stain-free and avoid anything with a drip-dry or other special finish which will not absorb the dye well. It is advisable to test dyes beforehand on a spare piece of fabric. When using several dye colors, always start with the lightest and where two colors overlap to produce a third, make sure that they will all blend well.

Containers

Select a container for the dye that is large enough to allow the fabric to move around freely. If too small a container is used the dye will be prevented from penetrating the fabric thoroughly and untied parts may dye patchily.

Use a large saucepan or rust-free metal bucket on the stove for multi-purpose and liquid dyes when dyeing. For cold dyeing use a plastic bowl, metal bucket, the kitchen sink or the bathtub.

Tie and dye patterns

The beauty of the tie and dye method is that an infinite variety of patterns can be created and no two designs are ever exactly alike. The manner in which certain areas of fabric are protected from the dye produces a specific pattern. More intricate designs can be produced by using different colors together. Dye with the lightest shade first, then move the bindings to a different position or refold or retie the fabric and dye with the second color and so on. Some of the first dye color will be retained while exposing new areas of fabric to subsequent colors.

Marbling. Of all patterns, marbling is the easiest effect to achieve. Crumple the fabric into a ball or sausage shape and bind tightly at intervals with string. Wet thoroughly and dye. If using more than one color, rinse the fabric well, undo the string, crumple again and retie.

Knotting. Depending on how the knots are formed, knotting can produce a variety of different patterns from intermittent undulating bands to unusual freeform flower shapes. Roll the fabric diagonally, knot tightly at intervals and dye. Rinse fabric thoroughly, undo the knots and re-knot below the original knots. Rinse, untie the knots, rinse again and wash the fabric. To produce a broken wavy pattern, fold the fabric three or four times lengthwise and tie into several regularly spaced knots before dyeing. Freeform designs can be created by knotting the fabric at random, although the areas of pattern can be determined by first marking the position of each knot.

Clump tying. A very attractive pattern can be made by tying small stones into the fabric at intervals. Dye the fabric, then rinse

Marbling

Knotting

Gathering (ruching)

Sunburst circle

Clump tying

Tie and dye techniques

Pleating

Tritik circles

Tritik stitchi

it. Remove the string and stones and wash the fabric thoroughly.

Pleating. Pleat or fold the fabric to produce colored stripes. Several variations are possible : fold the fabric lengthwise for vertical stripes, widthwise for horizontal stripes or diagonally for diagonal stripes. Every fold denotes a stripe, so for an evenly spaced design, measure the distance between each fold and tie the string bindings at regular intervals. By refolding and retying the fabric between several dyeings, a multicolored criss-cross design can be created. Always tie the new bindings before removing the old ones so that the pleats are not disturbed.

Gathering (ruching). Lay a length of string over one corner of the fabric and roll the fabric diagonally around it. Form a circle with the rolled fabric, gather tightly along the string and tie the ends. Dye the fabric, then rinse, remove the string and rinse again. When dry, repeat the process but roll the fabric from the opposite corner and dye in the same or a different color.

"Sunburst" circles. Circles and especially "sunburst" patterns are always effective and can be varied in size and complexity according to the number and position of the string bindings. Pick up a point of fabric to form a peak (this will be the center of the circle) and arrange the fabric into even folds as it falls away. For a circle measuring 2.5cm (1in) in diameter bind the fabric tightly 1.5cm ($\frac{1}{2}$in) from the top of the point and for one measuring 5cm (2in) bind 2.5cm (1in) from the point and so on. To create a specific design, mark out the position of each circle beforehand. Add more circles with each dyeing or alter the bindings to create a more colorful pattern. Two evenly spaced sets of bindings will produce a circle within a circle and by developing this technique a stage farther, it it is possible to create a large radiant circle called a "sunburst." Pick up the fabric to form a peak, furl like a closed umbrella and bind tightly at regular intervals. Refold or reposition the bindings through several dyeings.

Tritik circles. Sewing or "tritik" is used to produce a precise and controlled design. To create a circle using this method, pencil the shape onto the fabric. Knot a length of

strong thread firmly at one end then stitch around the penciled outline on the fabric. Gather the fabric tightly along the stitches and secure with a knot. Add random thread bindings to some of the gathered fabric and dye. Rinse, remove the bindings and rinse again. When dry, remove the stitches and rinse and wash the fabric.

Tritik stitching. For more intricate designs, such as paisley shapes, flowers, geometric patterns, names or initials, draw onto the fabric in pencil either freehand or with the aid of a stencil. Make a double row of stitching around the outline, using strong thread. For an outline design, gather the fabric along the stitches and secure tightly. To produce a bolder relief design bind the gathered fabric. Rinse, remove the binding and rinse again. When dry, remove the stitches, rinse and wash.

New look for bed linen
Tie-dyeing is shown off to best effect on large areas of fabric, so demonstrate your skills by brightening up a set of bed linen. The set illustrated consists of a coverlet (duvet cover) and dust ruffle (valance), a

bottom sheet and pillow cases.
You will need :
3 plain white sheets □ pillow cases □ several lengths of cotton about 38cm (15in) wide for dust ruffle (valance) □ cold dyes in orange, red and brown □ elastic □ tape with snaps (popper tape).

Bottom sheet. Dye the sheet with a marbled pattern in 3 colors. Crumple the fabric as described previously and dye with the lightest color first, progressing to the darkest. Change the position of the binding with each dyeing.

Dust ruffle (valance). Dye the lengths of cotton as for the bottom sheet then make the dust ruffle (valance) by stitching the lengths together to form a circle. Turn up a hem at the bottom and make a casing for the elastic at the top.

Pillow cases. The pillow cases are marbled on one side and have a paisley design on the other. To make the pattern, stitch around the paisley shapes as described in the tritik stitching section. Then bind the inner and surrounding areas for a marbled effect. Change the position of the bindings for each of the 3 colors.

Coverlet (duvet cover). Dye one of the sheets plain brown. Draw paisley designs on the other and dye using the same method as for the pillow cases. To make the cover, sew the 2 sheets together around 3 sides with French seams. On the remaining side, make the raw edges neat, stitch a single seam for about 28cm (11in) in from each corner and stitch tape with snaps (popper tape) along the remaining open edges.

Further ideas for tie and dye fabrics
As well as bed linen, tie and dye can be used to pattern tablecloths, cushion covers and garments of all kinds. Decorate a whole area of fabric or just part of it, for example, the hem of a skirt with a shirt to match or the edges on sheets.
If you make your own clothes, why not design your own fabrics too ? Choose the colors and pattern to complement the garment; narrow stripes, produced by pleating and binding the fabric before it is dyed, provide an attractive background for smocking, and random circles or marbled patterns look stunning highlighted with beading or embroidery.
You can produce localized tie-dye designs by patterning certain pieces of the cut-out fabric before they are sewn together, and then perhaps dyeing the remaining fabric, zipper and trimmings in a plain color to match. Similar results can also be obtained on ready-made articles by tying all but the areas to be patterned into plastic (polythene) bags. This method can also be used if a certain color is only required on a specific area of the fabric, for example, a deep border pattern at the hem of a dress. Tie up the hem to make the pattern and seal all the untied fabric in plastic (polythene) before dyeing it. Most of the dress will remain the same color as it is protected by the plastic (polythene), but there will be a pretty pattern around the hem.
With economy in mind, remnants and, for instance, the good parts of sheets that have worn thin can be utilized to make tie-dyed cushion covers, clothes for the children or cuddly toys. Even small left-over pieces of fabric can be used to make a colorful and unusual collage.

Batik is an Oriental craft with origins in India, China and Indonesia. The word itself is Malay and means literally "writing on wax." The craft is probably most highly developed in Indonesia, especially on the island of Java, where it is the task of the women to draw the design outlines onto cotton or silk cloth with charcoal and to carry out the waxing process, while the men concentrate on the dyeing. Originally, however, the work was done solely by women of the nobility who passed on their skills from generation to generation.

By the time the Dutch traders arrived in Indonesia in the 17th century, batik had been established as a traditional craft for over 700 years. As the trade routes opened, batik fabrics were exported to the West. Traditional methods continued to be used until around 1850 when the whole waxing process was considerably speeded up by the introduction of the *tjap*. This is a block consisting of copper strips soldered together to form the design motif. The block is dipped into wax and then pressed onto the fabric before dyeing.

Elaborate flower, animal and bird motifs are still popular forms of decoration on fabrics used for garments such as the sarong, pandjang or slendang. The sarong is an ankle-length garment made from a rectangle of cloth and worn wrapped around the waist. The pandjang is a similar garment but longer than the sarong and a slendang is a long narrow shawl.

Although batik work is usually applied to fabrics, the techniques can also be used on any surface that will take wax and dye. In the Ukraine for example, eggs are decorated in this way at Christmas and Easter.

Traditional methods

Before work is begun, the cloth is measured and cut out, boiled to remove any surface treatment, then stretched over a frame, to facilitate waxing. The main lines of the design are drawn onto the cloth with charcoal, and then hot liquid wax is applied to the cloth with a *tjanting*. This is a small copper implement with a spout, fixed to a bamboo handle. The tool is dipped into the hot wax, then the spout is trailed along the lines of the design. The typical delicacy of batik relies on the worker's skill in using the

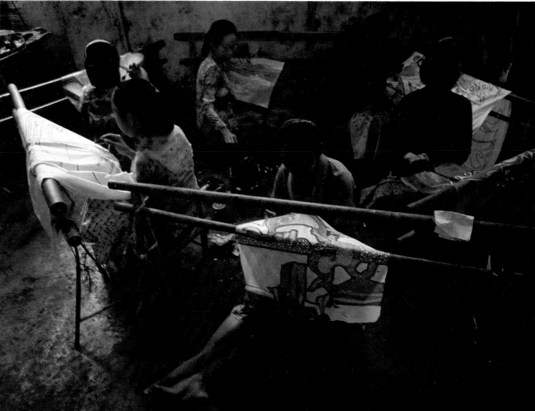

Indonesian women applying batik.

tjanting, and in designs where there are many lines or dots, a tjanting with two or more spouts may be used. The larger areas are waxed with a brush, and the cloth is then dipped into a cold dye bath. If a waxed area is to appear crackled in the design, the wax is hardened in cold water then crushed prior to dyeing. Traditionally, the white cloth is first dipped in a deep blue dye, then re-waxed to cover the blue areas, and then dipped into a deep brownish-black dye. The finished cloth, after wax is removed by boiling water, appears as an intricate and very delicate design in white, blue and brownish-black. The motifs are usually based on natural forms such as flowers, birds and patterns of flowing wavy lines and dots. The whole process, when done by hand in this way, can often take as long as 30 or 40 days.

Batik picture

This batik picture shows how an array of colors can be obtained by overdyeing. The selection used here is from white through green to brown, but white, pink and purple, or white, blue and dark green would also blend well together. The finished picture measures 25 × 32.5cm (10 × 13in).

You will need:

piece of unbleached cotton fabric, 25 × 32.5cm (10 × 13in) □ sheet of paper, 25 × 32.5cm (10 × 13in) □ wooden frame with an inside measurement of 25 × 32.5cm (10 × 13in) □ cold dyes in pale green, dark green and brown □ batik wax or 75% paraffin wax mixed with 25% beeswax □ medium-sized tjanting □ medium bristle paint brush □ tailor's chalk □ pencil □ black felt tip pen □ small can to hold the wax □ tin lid □ metal saucepan □ bowl or bucket for dyebath □ turpentine (white spirit) □ newspaper or absorbent paper □ tacks.

Drawing the design. Draw the design from

Batik picture

First stage

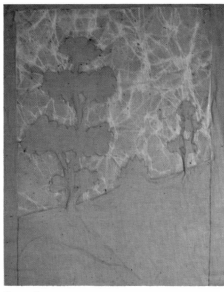

Second stage

Third stage

Fourth stage

1 = white   2 = pale green

3 = dark green   4 = brown

1   Graph for batik picture   1 sq = 2.5cm

the graph (fig.1) in which 1 square equals 2.5cm (1in). Draw the outlines clearly with a felt tip pen and number the areas for each color as shown.

Waxing the white areas First trace around the areas that will be white on the fabric with tailor's chalk. Stretch the fabric over the frame and secure with tacks.

Put the wax into the can and place the can inside the saucepan. Fill the saucepan with water until it reaches halfway up the sides of the can. Bring to the boil, and then keep the water simmering constantly so that the wax melts. Add more water if necessary.

Dip the tjanting into the hot wax and apply to the fabric around the lines of the area you have traced. Use the can lid beneath the tjanting to catch any drips. Fill in the larger areas with a brush. When this waxing is complete, remove the batik from the frame and put it in a bowl of cold water.

First dyebath. Prepare the pale green dyebath according to the manufacturer's instructions. Take the fabric out of the cold water and gently crush the waxed areas so that thin cracks appear. Open out again and submerge in the dyebath. Rinse the fabric and allow to dry.

Waxing the pale green areas. Trace the

Batik wall hanging

instructions already given, retouching waxed white areas where necessary.

Second dyebath. Prepare the dark green dyebath. Crush the fabric again and submerge in the dyebath. Rinse and allow it to dry.

Waxing the dark green areas. Trace the areas to be dark green onto the fabric, and wax these areas. Continue as before, and retouching all waxed areas where necessary.

Third dyebath. Prepare the brown dyebath. Crush the fabric again and submerge in the dyebath. Rinse and allow to dry.

Removing the wax. Iron the batik between layers of newspaper until you have removed as much wax as you can. The fabric may still be slightly stiff, and to restore its natural softness, put a little turpentine (white spirit) into a bowl, and squeeze the batik in it for about 2 minutes. Wash in mild soapy water and allow to dry.

Batik wall hanging or shade

Once you have acquired the skills of waxing and dyeing, you will be ready to attempt this more intricate design. The basic techniques are the same as for the batik picture. The finished size is 70 × 100cm (28 × 40in). Hang the batik on a wall for decoration or make up into a window shade.

You will need:

piece of unbleached cotton fabric, about 70 × 100cm (28 × 40in) □ sheet of paper the same size □ wooden frame with an inside measurement of 70 × 100cm (28 × 40in) □ cold dyes in pale pink, orange, red and purple □ batik equipment as for batik picture.

Drawing the design. Draw the design from the graph (fig.2) in which 1 square equals 10cm (4in). Draw the outlines of the design clearly with a black felt tip pen and mark the colors in the appropriate areas.

Waxing the white areas. The first area to be waxed is the background, which remains white. Draw around the background area onto the fabric with tailor's chalk. Stretch the fabric onto the frame and secure with tacks. Apply the wax as for the batik picture. Crush the wax for a cracked effect and put the batik in a bowl of cold water.

First dyebath. Prepare the pale pink dye-

areas to be pale green onto the fabric. As the fabric is now colored, it may be easier to trace the design by holding it against a window. Wax the areas which will remain pale green. Proceed as for waxing

2 Graph for batik wall hanging or window shade
1sq = 10 cm (4in)

First dyebath

Second dyebath

Third dyebath

Fourth dyebath

bath. Dye the fabric, rinse and allow to dry.

Completing the design. Wax the pale pink areas. Prepare an orange dyebath, dye and rinse the fabric and wax the orange areas. The third dyebath is red. Wax the red areas. The final dyebath is purple.

Note: remember to retouch all previously waxed areas if necessary as you proceed and crush the fabric before each dyeing. Remove the wax as previously described.

Surface decoration
Fabric painting

T-shirts galore!

Fragment from an Egyptian mummy cloth.

Before printing was developed, fabrics were individually hand-painted. Natural dyes were used, such as iron oxide for red and yellow, and malachite and azurite for green and blue.

Today, fabric dyes suitable for painting can be bought in bottles, mixed and ready to use. These dyes are water-soluble and need to be "fixed" into the fabric with fixing solution. Cold dyes used with a special thickener are also excellent for fabric painting. Add the fixative to the dye solution before painting. Both of these types of dye are recommended for use on natural fabrics such as pure cottons, linen and silk. Viscose rayon, which is made from wood pulp is suitable, but acetate rayon is not, and it is best not to use fabrics which are "drip dry."

T-shirts galore!

Everyone wears T-shirts and everyone will love to have one with a personalized design on the front.

314

Hand-painted kaftan

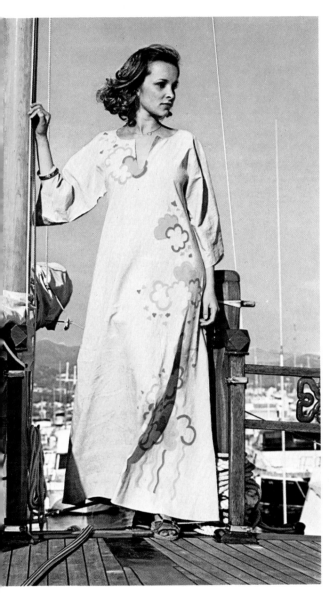

absorb excess dye and prevent dye from reaching the bottom layer of fabric.

Painting the T-shirt. Paint the design onto the fabric with a brush, being careful not to smudge the design with your hand. If you want to prevent the colors from running, allow a little drying time between color applications.

When the design is complete, allow the T-shirt to dry completely. If using ready-mixed dyes, fix the dye with the fixing solution according to the manufacturer's instructions. Wash the T-shirt again to remove excess dye and rinse until the water is clear.

Painting a length of fabric

Fabric is painted in exactly the same way as described for T-shirts, but before starting work on the design either pin the fabric onto a board with several sheets of newspaper underneath it, or stretch it over a picture frame to prevent the fabric moving or stretching.

Fabrics can be painted very successfully using your fingers, by spreading the paint onto the fabric sparingly with a palette knife, or by using a stencil.

"Tin can printing" is a very simple way of producing long unbroken lines. Simply remove both ends of a small tin can, leaving smooth edges. Place the can upright on the fabric and put a little dye into the can. Drag the can along the fabric to leave a trail of dye behind.

Fabric crayons are also very simple to use, although they are only suitable for synthetic fabrics such as nylon. Draw the design with the crayons onto thick paper, then place the design face down onto the fabric. Transfer this to the fabric by ironing the back of the paper.

Hand-painted kaftan

This simple kaftan is easy to cut out and sew and is made more individual by hand-painting a bold design onto the fabric with fabric dyes. Measurements given are for size 91cm (36in) bust and the finished length is 145cm (57in) but you can adjust these if necessary when drawing up the pattern.

You will need :

3.5m (3½yd) cream or beige cotton fabric,

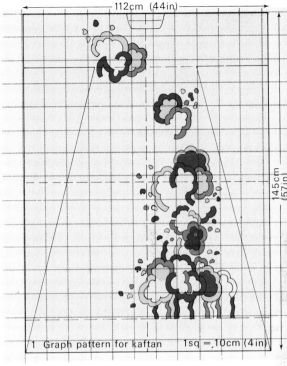

1 Graph pattern for kaftan   1sq = 10cm (4in)

115cm (45in) wide □ sheet of paper, 112cm × 145cm (44 × 57in) for pattern □ sewing thread □ pencil □ black felt tip pen □ tailor's chalk □ fabric dyes in deep yellow, orange and pink □ fine and medium sable paint brushes □ 2 or 3 sheets of paper.

Making the paper pattern. Draw the pattern from the graph (fig.1) in which 1 square equals 10cm (4in). Plot the design motifs onto the pattern clearly with a felt tip pen.

Cutting out the kaftan. Cut out the kaftan from the paper pattern following fig.2a–f, adding 1.5cm (½in) seam allowance at the sides and sleeves and 7.5cm (3in) at hem.

Transferring the motifs. Place the paper pattern flat on your working surface and lay the front of the kaftan on top. Trace the motifs lightly onto the fabric with tailor's chalk. If the design of the pattern will not show on the fabric, transfer the design by using dressmaker's carbon paper and a tracing wheel or by pricking through the paper pattern and drawing over the needle pricks on the fabric with tailor's chalk. Transfer the design to the back of the kaftan in the same way.

Painting the design. Hand-paint the motifs

You will need :

cotton T-shirt □ fabric dyes and fixative or cold dyes □ paint brushes □ pencil or tailor's chalk □ newspaper.

Preparing the T-shirt. Before starting to work on the design, wash the T-shirt to remove any substance on the fabric that would prevent the dyes from being absorbed well. When the T-shirt is dry, iron it, than draw on the design very lightly with a soft pencil or tailor's chalk.

Cover the work surface with several layers of newspaper. Slip two or three sheets of newspaper inside the T-shirt to

2 Cutting out the kaftan

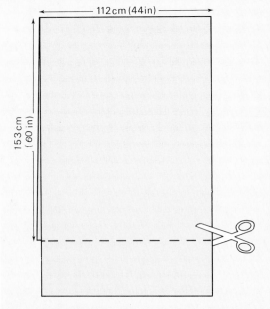

(a) fold fabric

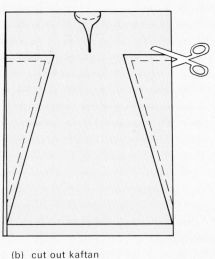

(b) cut out kaftan

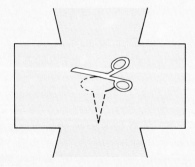

(c) cut neck area away

(d) cut fabric for neck facing

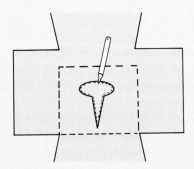

(e) draw neck facing shape from neck edge with fabric beneath kaftan piece

(f) cut neck facing at neck and outer edges

Fabric painting can be fun and create a pretty effect at the same time.

with the fabric dyes, using the fine brush to outline the shape and the medium brush to fill in. Apply the dye evenly to avoid patchiness. Allow the dyes to dry and then fix according to the manufacturer's instructions. (This is usually done by ironing on the back of the fabric for a few minutes on each area. Place a sheet of paper over the fabric to prevent scorching.)
Making the kaftan. Stitch the neck facing to the right side of the kaftan around the neck edges and opening at the front. Clip the curves, then turn to the inside, press and top stitch.
With right sides together, fold the kaftan along the shoulder line. Stitch along the sleeves and down the side seams. Double stitch at the underarm and clip the curves. Hem the sleeve edges and along the bottom of the kaftan.

One of London's Pearly Kings, with a shining suit decorated with thousands of pearl buttons.

Elaborately pearl-buttoned jackets and bodices, waistcoats simply smothered with pearl buttons, buttoned boots and gloves and wide-brimmed ostrich-feathered hats for the ladies: these costumes sound fit for nobility, yet they are in fact the traditional "uniforms" of London's *Pearlies*. Pearlies were originally street-traders who lived and worked in the East End of London, and who—in a late 19th-century craze—started decorating otherwise very simple clothes with rows and rows of sparkling pearl buttons. Today, the Pearly Kings and Queens of various areas within East London, together with their helpers known collectively as the "Pearl Pride", still dress in this way and collect money for various charities. Indeed, they constitute a uniquely British phenomenon.

Buttons, baubles and beads

With just a little imagination and a lot of buttons, sequins or beads, you can easily brighten up almost any kind of garment. Bags, pillows, cushions and a host of household articles can also be given a completely new look and a new lease of life.
Thread. Use strong fine thread to attach decorative buttons, beads and sequins. Silk is best but polyester or invisible nylon thread can be used, although nylon thread is slippery and difficult to knot and thread.

Strengthen silk or polyester thread by drawing it across a lump of beeswax before beginning to sew.
Frame. If you want to make a motif or cover an area of fabric solidly with small beads or sequins, it is best to work the motif separately on a piece of canvas stretched tightly over an embroidery frame and then stitch the motif to the garment. Use a light woven canvas or stiffening. Draw the outline of the motif onto the canvas using tailor's chalk or dressmaker's carbon paper and a tracing wheel. The frame must be larger than the complete motif as you will not be able to wind completed beading over rollers or push the top of a round frame over it. A square frame or a round frame with a stand is best as you will need both hands for the work.
Leave at least a 0.5cm ($\frac{1}{4}$in) border of canvas around each motif. When the work is complete, cut out the motif, turn under the raw edges of canvas and baste them down. Slip stitch the completed motif to the garment.
Buttons. There are various ways of attaching buttons for a decorative effect. Always sew with a double thread. You can use a contrasting thread for all the buttons, or sew on four-holed buttons as shown in fig.1 to make an attractive pattern. Fig.2 shows how small brightly colored glass beads can be used to attach buttons.
Beads. To attach beads singly, first secure the thread on the wrong side of the work, then thread up one bead after each stitch, as shown in fig.3. Fig. 4a, b and c shows how to attach a string of beads. Secure the thread and string on a number of beads; using another needle and thread, catch down the string of beads at intervals. You do not need to stitch between each bead, particularly if they are small but you should do so if stitching around a curve.
Sequins. Sequins can be flat or cup-shaped with a faceted surface. They have center or side holes and are measured across their diameter. These sequins should be stitched on singly. Sequins can also be bought in lengths, ready strung so that the holes overlap. Fig.5 shows how to sew a string of sequins. It is not necessary to stitch down after every sequin.
When sewing on sequins, the main

1 Sewing a four-holed button

2 Attaching a button with beads

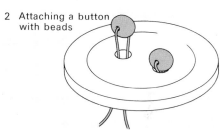

3 Attaching beads singly

4 Attaching a string of beads

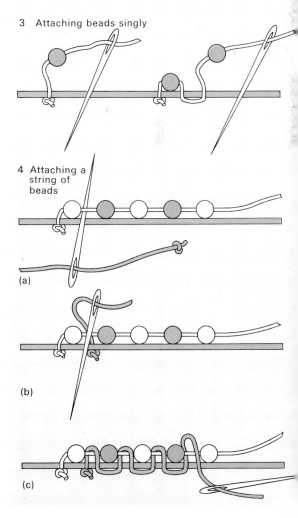

(a)

(b)

(c)

Surface decoration
Buttons, baubles and beads

Decorative pincushions

object is to hide both the hole and thread. With strings of sequins this is done for you. Sequins that have to be applied individually can be attached in two ways. Fig.6 shows how to attach sequins using a bead and fig.7 shows the method used to attach sequins by overlapping each one by at least half to cover the center hole. This latter method is the one to use if you want to cover an area solidly with sequins. If you are filling in a motif with sequins, you can work up and down, or around, filling in from the outside edge or outwards from the center. The direction of overlap will affect the finished appearance of the motif and the way in which the sequins catch the light.

Sequins can also be stuck down with glue, although this is not a satisfactory permanent method of attaching them. Put a blob of glue onto a toothpick, apply the glue to the fabric and stick down each sequin individually.

Studs. Studs can be bought cheaply in many shapes and sizes. Metal studs have either a brass or chrome finish, others have

colored glass attached. They are easy to apply as the back of each stud has small spikes around the edge. Simply position the stud and push the spikes through the fabric and bend the spikes back. Hammer the spikes flat for a more secure hold.

Decorative pincushions
Any one of these three pincushions would make an attractive gift. They are simple to make and look very decorative. Each pincushion when finished measures about 12.5cm (5in) square.

Pearl button pincushion
This pincushion is made of black velvet decorated with pearl buttons of various sizes for a dramatic effect.

You will need:
2 pieces black velvet 14.5cm (5¾in) square □ pearl buttons in the following quantities and sizes: 4 buttons 2cm (¾in) in diameter; 12 buttons 1.5cm (½in) in diameter; 16 buttons 1cm (⅜in) in diameter; 24 buttons 0.5cm (¼in) in diameter □ steel pins □ 170g (6oz) dried sifted sawdust □ knitting needle □ white linen thread □ 61cm (24in) black velvet ribbon 0.5cm (¼in) wide.

Making the basic cushion. Lightly iron the velvet on the wrong side. With right sides together, baste and then machine stitch around 3 sides 1cm (⅜in) from the edge. Fold over the turnings on the open edge and baste. Trim the seams to 0.5cm (¼in) and cut the corners across. Turn right side out.

Fill the cushion with sawdust. Pack tightly and use the blunt end of the knitting needle to force the sawdust into the corners. Smooth out any wrinkles and slip stitch the opening to close, using double thread. Remove the basting stitches.

Decorating the cushion. Following the chart (fig.8), pin the buttons onto the cushion, starting with the largest buttons first. Measure the distance between each button carefully before pinning. Starting in one corner of the cushion, sew each button in place using double thread. Take the thread underneath the surface of the velvet after sewing on each button in order to move on to the next one without breaking the thread.

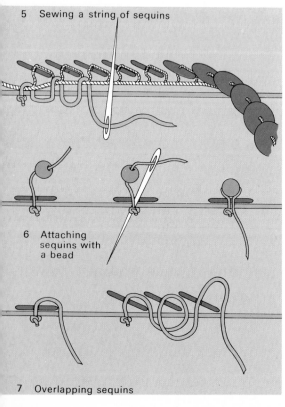

5 Sewing a string of sequins

6 Attaching sequins with a bead

7 Overlapping sequins

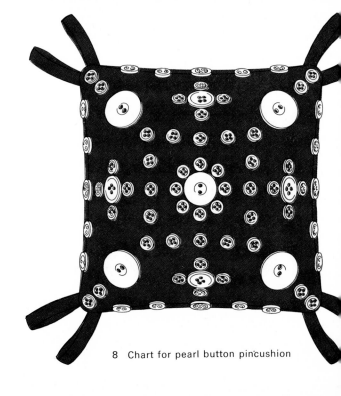

8 Chart for pearl button pincushion

Cut four 15cm (6in) lengths of ribbon, make each one into a double loop and attach underneath each corner of the cushion with a pearl button.

Blue and silver
Silver pins on a pale blue background combine to produce this delicate pincushion.

You will need:
4 pieces blue silk 14.5cm (5¾in) square ☐ steel pins ☐ 170g (6oz) dried sifted sawdust ☐ knitting needle ☐ tracing paper ☐ sewing thread.

Making the basic cushion. Press the silk pieces on the wrong side with a cool iron. Using 2 pieces of silk to form a double thickness for both top and bottom, make the cushion following the previous instructions.

Decorating the cushion. Insert 1 pin into each corner of the cushion and wind sewing thread around them. Take the thread diagonally across the cushion to form 4 equal triangles. The lines will be used as a guide to placing the design centrally. The chart (fig.9) gives one quarter of the design. Trace the design and place the tracing over one corner of the cushion. Push the pins through the paper following the design outline. Tear away the paper and repeat for the 3 remaining corners. Finish off with a double row of pins all around the seamed edges of the cushion, avoiding the extreme tip at each corner where the pins would not cross correctly inside. Fill in the small motif in the lower half of the cushion on each side.

Brown and orange sequined cushion
A geometric design creates a more modern look on this pincushion decorated with sequins on a satin background.

You will need:
1 piece brown satin 14.5cm (5¾in) square ☐ 1 piece brown satin and 1 piece orange satin 15 × 7.5cm (6 × 3in) ☐ two 28cm (11in) lengths of sequins in each of the following colors: gold, bronze and blue ☐ 4 gold sequins 2cm (¾in) in diameter ☐ 8 sequins 0.5cm (¼in) in diameter ☐ 170g (6oz) dried sifted sawdust ☐ steel pins ☐ knitting needle ☐ contact adhesive ☐ sewing thread.

Making the basic cushion. Cut the small pieces of brown and orange satin in half and join them together to make a square for the top section, matching the colors in opposite corners. Use the larger piece of brown satin for the bottom section and make the cushion as described previously.

Decorating the cushion. Glue the 4 large sequins in position in the center of the cushion where the seams cross. Glue the bronze sequins along the seamlines on top of the cushion to form a cross, securing at the beginning with a pin underneath the cushion in the center. Glue the gold and blue sequins in the same way to overlap the large gold sequins slightly and form a grid pattern. Slide the blue sequins under and over the gold sequins to create an interwoven effect. Finally, glue the small gold sequins in a circle around the center on top of the 4 larger sequins to complete the design.

Denim jacket motif
The back of this denim jacket is covered with an impressive array of buttons, beads, sequins and studs.
To reproduce the design shown in the photograph, follow the accompanying chart (fig.10). The central sequin motif is worked on canvas as previously described and uses 1,000 each of pink, blue and mother-of-pearl 10mm (⅜in) cup sequins. You will also need 0.5m (½yd) lengths of silver, blue and purple sequins.

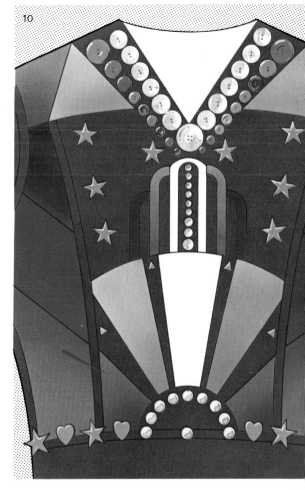

9

10

Brass rubbing

Although there is evidence that the Chinese were making rubbings of incised copies of writings and paintings from at least the 7th century AD, such rubbing techniques can only be documented in Western Europe from the 17th century. As a hobby the collecting of rubbings of medieval monumental brasses became very popular towards the middle of the 19th century and is once again being revived as an original form of interior decoration. The most popular rubbings are those of church brasses, but equally good results can be achieved with facsimiles, as it is not always possible to obtain permission to rub in churches, cathedrals and museums. Apart from rubbing from the more traditional monuments, try experimenting from a variety of different sources, such as plaques, rare coins or even embossed wallpaper. Any textured surface with flat relief or incised design can be used to produce unusual motifs, as in the collage illustrated, made from rubbings of various bookcovers.

You can make rubbings using a black wax (heelball) on white paper to produce a negative impression of the incised image. A positive impression is obtained by rubbing in white wax and then inking in the incised lines and mounting on colored or textured paper. There are many colored waxes available if you prefer a colored rubbing. You can also achieve a beautiful luminous effect by using gold wax on white paper, and coloring the background with water colors following any traces of enamel which might have remained on the brass.

Basic materials

The materials you need for rubbing are simple: a good quality rag paper, scissors, soft duster, wax sticks (or heelball if you are making a negative impression), masking tape and paper. Use a thin paper such as detail paper—this is obtainable in stores specializing in architect and drafting materials—as thick paper will obscure fine incisions.

A negative impression (*top*) and a positive impression (*bottom*)—rubbings made at Blickling Church, Norfolk, England and believed to be of James de Holveston (d. 1378).

Making the rubbing

Make sure that the brass is very clean before you start rubbing, as small pieces of grit or fragments of heelball under the paper may tear it as well as scratch the surface of the metal. Then place the paper over the surface of the brass and fix it in place with strips of masking tape. Press the

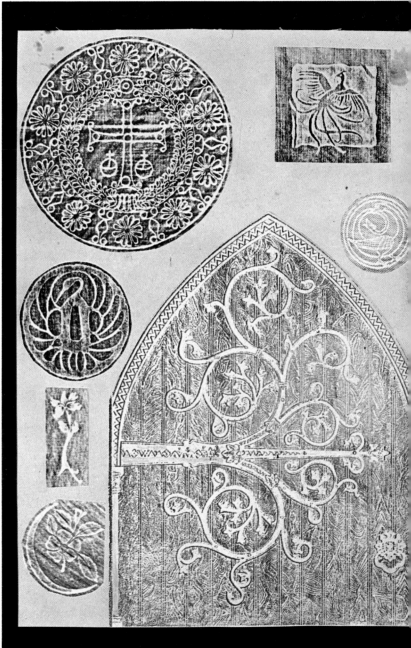

paper gently into the surface and outline the edge of the brass. This will prevent you from going over the edges and rubbing the stone.

The most successful method of outlining is to hold the wax in one hand and let it follow the forefinger of your other hand. An old stick of wax worn to a point is ideal for outlining. Then rub the whole area of the brass using short firm strokes, pressing hard on the wax.

When you have finished rubbing, polish the paper lightly with a duster or soft nylon cloth to remove any loose flakes of heelball. Remove the masking tape and then the rubbing. Finally, wipe the brass clean.

Above left: Rubbing of a panel depicting Marguerite de Scornay (1443–62), Abbess of Nivelles. Color has been added according to traces of enamel found on the original brass.

Above right: A colored collage made from different book covers.

321

Leatherwork

Colonel John Russell, one of Charles I's officers in the English Civil War, displaying a fine leather jerkin. Portrait by J. M. Wright.

As early as the Ice Age, man was wearing clothes made out of untreated leather. By the Stone Age, methods had already become more sophisticated: leather was treated with animal fat, and pieces sewn together with bone tools.

Leather was an important item of trade in ancient times. The Phoenicians spread the influence of Babylonian embroidered and decorated leatherwork to Mediterranean countries, and themselves dyed leather such a distinctive reddish purple color that it became known as Phoenician Red.

In Roman times leather became a status symbol and a man's rank in society was immediately apparent from the workmanship of his boots, shoes and belts. When the Romans invaded the cold north of Europe, they discovered the inhabitants far more suitably dressed for the weather than they were; they shocked their fellow Romans by returning home wearing leather breeches or "braccae" The Emperor tried to ban this outlandish fashion, but failed: the custom spread. In medieval Europe the most coveted leather goods were made in Cordova by the conquering Moors. They specialized in softly tanned goatskin dyed many colors and often perfumed. Their techniques spread all over Europe, and leather became widely used for gloves, boots, shoes, purses, belts and jackets. On the North American continent, native Americans had independently developed the art of tanning and working leather, making beautiful red, yellow and white buckskin, as the early colonists discovered. They allied the Indian methods of tanning to those they already knew, setting up tanneries throughout the colonies. During the settlement of the American West, frontiersmen adopted many native American garments for comfort and protection, such as fringed buckskin jackets, gauntlets, boots and hats—styles which have come back into fashion today.

Leather is a beautiful and rewarding material to work with. It has an infinite variety of uses, for it can be smooth and soft as velvet or as hard as wood. Skins can be expensive to buy, but they are much cheaper than ready-made leather garments, and give you the opportunity to design and make exactly what you want.

Tools and equipment

The simplest clothes and accessories can be sewn by hand. Otherwise the most essential piece of equipment is a sewing machine. Ideally this should have a zigzag needle and some alternative stitch patterns, to enable you to create decorative effects on the leather. There are also other tools you will need.

Cutting shears. A good pair of cutting shears is essential. You will need a pair that can easily cut all types of leathers, both thick and thin. Special leatherwork scissors can be bought for this purpose.

Punch pliers. These are very useful for making holes for thonging and creating decorative effects.

Light hammer. You will need this for opening and flattening seams. Pad the head with absorbent cotton (cotton wool) and cover with coarse cotton fabric.

Adhesive. Choose an adhesive that is suitable for leatherwork, for glueing together seams and applying decorative bindings. Rubber adhesive is best, as it does not become rigid when dry, and can be washed if used on washable suede.

Pins. If you are cutting out leather on a wooden surface use plastic-head map pins to hold the pattern in place while marking around the shape with tailor's chalk. Do not use chalk if it is likely to show on the finished article. Instead, use the end of a sharp pointed instrument such as a knitting needle, to draw around the pattern. Place weights on the pattern if pins cannot be used, or if pin holes might show.

Thread. Cotton, silk or any strong thread may be used. If embroidery is to be used for decoration, a thinner thread is sufficient.

A ham. This is a formed padded shape for sewing curved seams used in the tailoring profession. It is available from specialist tailoring equipment stores. You may find that the curved edge of a sleeve board (as used for ironing), or the arm of an armchair is adequate, but if you plan to specialize in leatherwear, it is a very useful piece of equipment.

Types of suede and leather

Most leather is processed from animals which also provide man with food. The outside of the skin is the grain side, and the inside the flesh side. The grain side is known as leather, the inside, suede, the flesh having been buffed to a fine finish.

Calf skin. This is good quality leather with a fine grain and smooth surface. It is supple and hard-wearing, ideal for all types of clothes. Thicker calf hide can be used for belts, hats and bags.

Persian suede. This comes from the hair sheep which live in the sub-tropics. It is a superior quality suede, light in weight and often soft to the touch, with a good fine grain that makes it suitable for all types of leatherwear.

Sheepskin. This is obtained from wool sheep and is inferior compared to the Persian suede. Generally, where the quality and density of wool covering an animal is high, the quality of the leather is low.

Choosing, sewing and embroidering leather

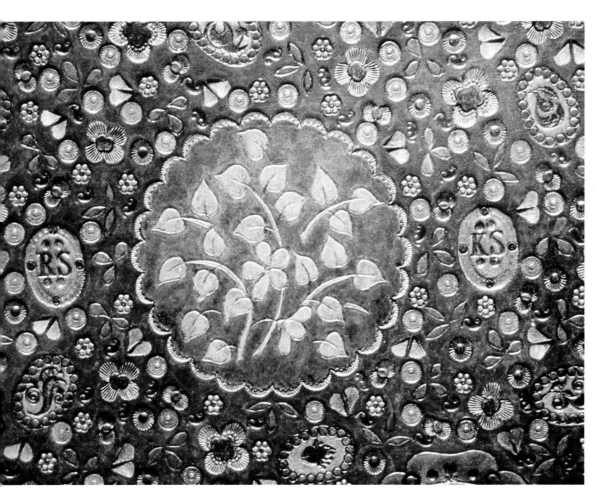

A modern example of embossed and painted leather, with an irregular design of flowers and leaves.

Pigskin. Tanned from the domestic pig, pigskin can be found as soft suede, as hard-grained leather, or as washable leather that is both soft and pliable. It has a characteristic marking caused by the way the hair grows, in clusters of three.

Chamois. In the leatherwear trade chamois is used as a lining for small leather goods. Its great advantage is in being washable. However, it is not suitable for making slacks and skirts (unless using a patchwork technique) as it is too thin and too supple.

Morocco. This is goatskin and is produced in both soft and hard grains. It is the leather most widely used for belts, bags, hats and other fashion accessories.

Choosing leather

To be sure of buying enough leather, take your pattern with you. Try to select a skin the same quality and thickness all over.

Though skins are usually thinner around the edges, they should not be so thin that they will wear out easily. When buying skins of the same color, check that they match as dye lots can vary considerably. Always hold the skin up to the light to look for holes. Avoid skins with holes or any other obvious defects.

Making a patch. If, despite careful scrutiny, you find you have overlooked a hole in the middle of a pattern piece, you can make a patch in the following way. Take a thin piece of leather slightly larger than the hole and, with a sharp knife or blade, pare away the leather around the edges to half its thickness. Apply adhesive around the edges of the hole on the wrong side, apply the patch and press it down lightly.

To avoid having to patch a skin, place the pattern so that the defect is on the edge of a seam, or inside a waistband, or on a seam line where a decorative strip can be applied to hide the hole.

Using a pattern

Dressmaker's patterns are suitable for leather clothes, as long as they are of simple design. The individual pattern pieces should not be too large, or you will not be able to find skins big enough.

Laying out a pattern. Lay out all the skins right side up. Never cut leather folded. Instead, cut out the pattern piece on a folded piece of paper to achieve the right dimensions. Use the firmer part of the skin for the part of the garment that will have most wear. When making sleeves, always cut them from the lighter part of the skin, as it will be easier to fit them into the armholes and they will be more comfortable to wear. Some suede has a grain that is obvious to the eye. This alters the tone of the skin, so it is important to ascertain the direction of the nap and place all pattern pieces the same way.

Hold the pattern in place with weights or map pins. Mark all notches. After each piece is cut out, take a pencil and mark on the back which part of the garment it is to avoid confusion when making up.

Cutting out. Always cut the leather with sharp shears or leather scissors, using a sliding action. Never close the scissors fully when cutting, or jagged edges will result. Open the scissors, close down on to the leather to be cut, but before reaching the end of the cut, open the shears again and slide them forward.

Sewing and embroidering leather

Using adhesive. Although it is an invaluable aid to sewing, if too much adhesive is used it will leak from the seam, causing ugly stains which are very difficult to remove. When working over a ham on a curved cut edged seam, apply adhesive to one seam edge only. Place the other seam over it, gently molding the shape of the seam with your fingertips.

Sewing leather. There are special needles for sewing leather, but in most cases a medium-sized sewing needle is sufficient.

Pretty chamois tunic

As you sew leather it becomes perforated and may tear if the holes are too close together. It is therefore important never to sew leather with any stitches smaller than 0.5cm ($\frac{1}{4}$in). Leather needles cut the skin as they sew, so be careful not to tear the material.

Before making a garment, always test the tension and stitch of your sewing machine on a scrap of leather. A firmer foot pressure is often needed to push and ease the material along. For thicker leathers a special leather foot is useful.

If you tighten the foot pressure and still have difficulty sewing, it may be that the foot and foot plate are sticking to the suede or leather. Sprinkle French chalk lightly onto the foot plate, or put tissue paper between the suede and the foot. Some machines have a slower speed control which helps when sewing thicker seams.

When machine embroidering seams or bindings, always sew first the seam that will show up least. By the time you sew the front seams you will have perfected the technique.

Fasteners. There are many types of fasteners for suedes and leathers. Zippers and buttons are suitable and ties, loops, buckles and snaps (pop fasteners) can also be used.

Pretty chamois tunic

This child's tunic is made attractive by the use of thongs and fringes. It is handsewn throughout, and worn with a tiny purse.

You will need :

1m (1yd) square of chamois leather □ sharp dressmaker's or leather scissors □ tailor's chalk □ mapping pins or weights □ rubber adhesive □ darning needle □ ruler preferably 61cm (24in) long □ pencil □ punch pliers.

Cutting out. Draw the pattern pieces from the graph (fig.1a) in which 1 square equals 2.5cm (1in). Arrange the pattern pieces carefully on the right side of the skin (fig.1b).

Take the chalk and trace around the pattern sections. Mark "center front" (CF) and "center back" (CB) on the wrong side of the pattern pieces. Mark all the notches, then cut out each pattern section separately.

Pretty chamois tunic

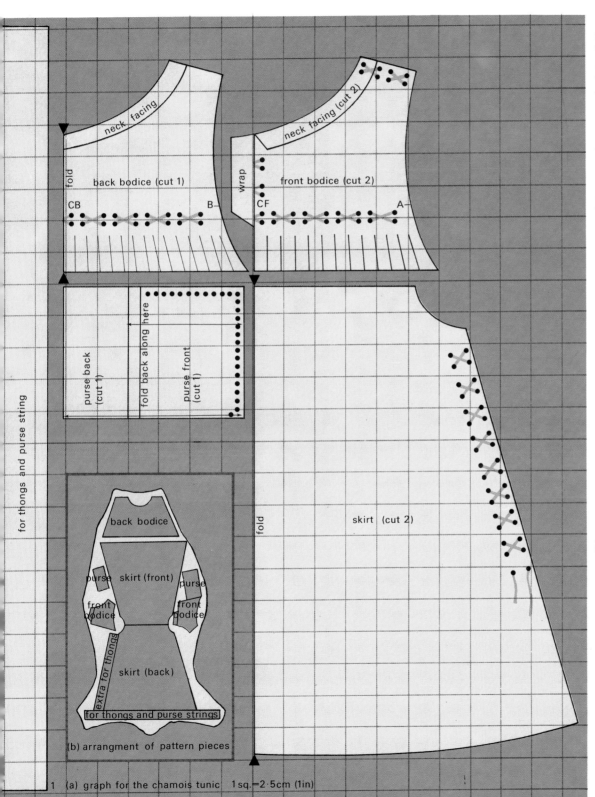

1 (a) graph for the chamois tunic   1 sq.=2.5cm (1in)

for thongs and purse string

neck facing

fold

back bodice (cut 1)

CB   B—

neck facing (cut 2)

wrap

front bodice (cut 2)

CF   A—

fold back along here

purse back (cut 1)

purse front (cut 1)

fold

skirt (cut 2)

back bodice

purse   skirt (front)   purse

front bodice   front bodice

extra for thongs

skirt (back)

for thongs and purse strings

(b) arrangement of pattern pieces

Making the tunic. Using rubber adhesive, stick the front and back neck trims around the edge of the neck hole, on the wrong side of the chamois. Fold back the center front facing and glue it down (fig.2). Take the back and the 2 front bodice pieces and mark the fringes on the wrong side with a pencil. They should be 4cm (1½in) from the edge, and 0.5cm (¼in) in width. Cut along these lines with scissors. Take the back bodice pieces, and, with chalk, mark 2.5cm (1in) from the bottom edge on the right side. Apply a small amount of adhesive to the right side of this edge and place the back of the dress up to notch B on either side. Use the same procedure for the front bodice with the front of dress placed up to notch A. Punch holes in the front and back bodices where indicated.

Cut 4 thongs 38cm (15in) long and 3mm (⅛in) wide. Starting from the top left punch-hole, thread the thong through to the right-hand side (fig.3a). Thread the other thong through from the top right-hand side (fig.3b). Tie the ends firmly. Cut one more thong 51cm (20in) long and 3mm (⅛in) wide and thread this through the front opening, leaving 2 long strips at the top.

Side seams. With chalk mark 2cm (¾in) in from the edge of the back piece. Apply adhesive to the right side of the back side seams. Place the front dress over the back. Punch holes where marked and thread thongs through, leaving 10cm (4in) thong ends at the bottom.

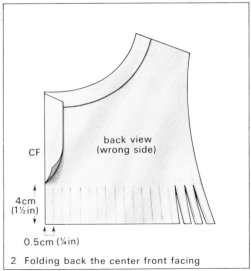

back view (wrong side)

CF

4cm (1½in)

0.5cm (¼in)

2 Folding back the center front facing

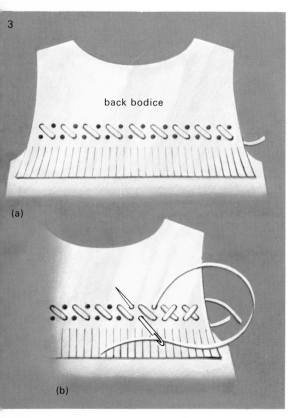

3

back bodice

(a)

(b)

Burning. You can make marks by burning into hide, either with a soldering iron, a knitting needle or meat skewer. Heat the tool and apply it gently to the hide, leaving it for only a few seconds before a mark appears.

Painting. You can make patterns by painting on hide with dyes. There are several kinds of dye which can be used on leather. The most easily available are dyes sold as shoe dyes or shoe color. Shoe color will give an opaque finish, shoe dye a more translucent sheen. You can also use special leather dyes. These are powder based, and have to be mixed with alcohol (methylated spirits).

Make a stencil out of thick cardboard as shown in fig.4. Place the stencil over a strip of the hide. Take brown dye and apply it with a paintbrush through the stencil. Move the stencil along, applying color until strips of brown are formed along the length of the sample. Leave to dry. Paint red dye through the stencil alongside the brown strip. Leave to dry. Paint thick yellow lines between the brown and red blocks, thinner yellow lines across the length of the strip. Finally, paint fine red lines across the thinner yellow lines and after each thick red strip.

You can also paint freehand designs like the floral design shown here.

Embossing. To make patterns in relief you will need a metal stamp, fancy punch or thonging tool (as used in the leather manufacturing trade). Make diamond shapes with a thonging tool (fig.5). With a soft pencil mark out diamonds on the hide, each side measuring 1.5cm ($\frac{1}{2}$in). Take the thonging tool and a hammer and stamp the top and bottom of the diamond, then the middle, then each side.

Embossing and painting (fig.6). Embossed patterns can always be painted afterwards. Cut a strip of hide approximately 5.5 × 11cm ($2\frac{1}{4} \times 4\frac{1}{2}$in). Draw semicircles along the edge of the hide 1.5cm ($\frac{1}{2}$in) in diameter and 1.5cm ($\frac{1}{2}$in) apart. Dampen the hide, then take the fancy punch and stamp out the pattern around the edge of the semicircle. Using dye, paint around the edge of the embossed motifs. Keep the brush horizontal so that the color does not sink into the embossed images.

Shoulder seams. Glue and place the front bodice shoulder seams over the back bodice. Punch where marked and thread thongs through. Secure ends with adhesive.

Making the purse. Mark and cut the fringe 2.5cm (1in) from the flap edge in strips 0.5cm ($\frac{1}{4}$in) wide. Apply adhesive to the top edge of the front and fold down. Apply adhesive to the other 3 edges and place the pieces over the fringed section. Punch holes with pliers where indicated on the pattern. Cut thongs 3mm ($\frac{1}{8}$in) wide and 38cm (15in) long and overcast the purse edges. Secure the ends of the thong with adhesive. Finally, cut a thong 0.5cm × 61cm ($\frac{1}{4} \times 24$in) long for a purse string. Thread ends through the holes punched on the purse and tie firmly. Trim ends.

Decorative techniques

The samples of cowhide photographed here illustrate three basic decorative techniques: burning, embossing and painting. In some cases the three techniques are combined.

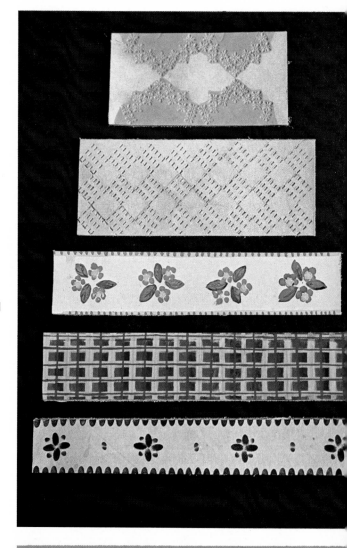

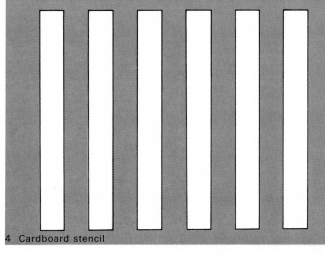

4 Cardboard stencil

Rawhide belts
Narrow embossed belt

Rawhide belts

Belts are frequently made from raw cowhide, which is approximately 3mm ($\frac{1}{8}$in) in thickness. To use this kind of leather you will need some special tools.

Knives. Perfect straight edges are obtained with the use of a "clicker" knife. This is a narrow thin knife with detachable blades. The blades have straight or curved edges according to the type of leather being cut. Curved blades are more suitable for cutting thick hides. If you cannot get a clicker knife, a craft knife will do. Sharpen the knife frequently on a sharpening stone.

Cutting board. Leather cutting boards are made up of small blocks of endgrain wood to prevent the knife from following the grain. As alternatives, sheet zinc or good quality plywood can be used.

Gripper pliers. These are a form of pliers adapted for attaching studs to leather.

Steel ruler. This is essential for cutting belts.

Two attractive rawhide belts

Practice your skills embossing and painting these two rawhide belts.

Narrow embossed belt

This embossed belt, which is about 91cm (36in) long and 2.5cm (1in) wide, has a design stamped out along each edge.

You will need:

piece of hide for belt □ small pieces of hide for experiment □ steel ruler □ cutting board □ clicker knife □ fancy punch □ punch pliers □ light hammer □ 1 stud □ gripper pliers □ buckle with a 2.5cm (1in) bar and prong □ leather dye □ needle and heavy duty thread.

Cutting out. Place the hide right side up on the cutting board. Taking ruler and knife, cut a length 91 × 2.5cm (36 × 1in). If you are right-handed, place the leather so that you are cutting from a position in front of your right arm; if left-handed, cut from in front of your left arm. Insert the point of the knife into the hide and draw towards the body. Avoid cutting longer than the length required. Turn the knife inwards towards the ruler.

Making the belt. Rub over the strip of hide with a damp cloth. Take a fancy punch and position it on the edge of the hide. Bring the hammer down sharply to emboss the hide. Continue this process along both edges of the strip.

Dyeing the belt. Pour dye onto a plate. Cover one end of the ruler with a cloth, and dip this into the dye. Drag it firmly along the hide keeping the ruler upright. Continue until the color of the dye is as dark as you want it to be. By using this method the color will adhere to the flat surfaces but leave the embossed pattern colorless. Apply the dye to the sides and back of the belt with the applicator provided with the bottle.

Attaching the buckle. Mark a hole for the buckle prong 3cm (1$\frac{1}{4}$in) from the end of the strip with a pencil. Punch 2 medium-sized holes either side of the mark about 1cm ($\frac{3}{8}$in) apart with a pair of punch pliers. Take the knife and cut away the 1cm ($\frac{3}{8}$in) of hide in between, thus making one large hole. Push the prong of the buckle through, and fold back the end of leather Take your gripper pliers, stud and secure (fig.7). If

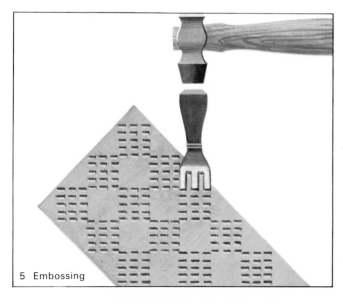

5 Embossing

6 Embossing and painting

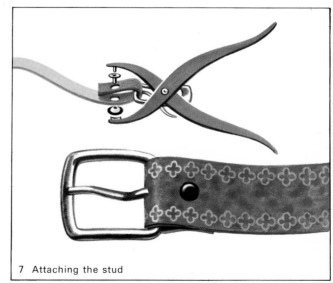

7 Attaching the stud

Wide hand-painted belt
Woven paneled sleeveless jacket

you do not have gripper pliers and studs, take punch pliers and punch out small holes. Sew these together with heavy duty thread.

Punch 3 holes for fastening at the opposite end of the belt, in the middle of the belt width. Trim the end of the belt to a V-shaped point. Finally, to make the belt loop, cut a strip of hide 0.5cm ($\frac{1}{4}$in) wide and long enough to go around the belt easily. Punch 2 holes at either end, then take needle and thread and sew them together.

Wide hand-painted belt

This striking belt is painted in four colors, with a blue buckle to give it extra impact. It is 91cm (36in) long and 7cm (2$\frac{3}{4}$in) wide.
You will need:
piece of hide for belt □ brown leather dye □ blue, red and pink shoe dye □ cutting board □ clicker knife □ steel ruler □ paintbrush □ leather buckle with a 5cm (2in) bar □ tracing paper □ needle and heavy duty thread.

Cutting out. Cut a strip of hide 91 × 7cm (36 × 2$\frac{3}{4}$in) as described for the narrow belt.

Making the belt. Apply brown dye smoothly along the length of the belt with the applicator. Leave to dry. Trace the pattern (fig.8) and transfer it to the belt, penciling over the tracing paper to leave an impression on the leather. Begin with the blue dye and paint the design. Add the pink. Finish with the red. Leave to dry. Paint the buckle with blue dye and attach it by threading it through one end of the strip, and pressing in 2 studs, one above the other, 0.5cm ($\frac{1}{4}$in) from the edge of the strip. Attach a belt loop as previously described.

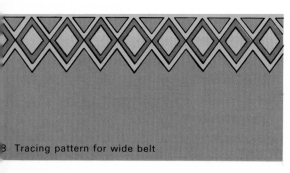

8 Tracing pattern for wide belt

Woven paneled sleeveless jacket

You will need a certain amount of experience in handling leather before tackling this jacket. Machined embroidery and punch work give it an unusual finish. The jacket will fit a 91cm (36in) bust.
You will need:
0.78m (2$\frac{3}{4}$ft) square of lilac suede □ 0.6m (2ft) square cream suede □ sewing machine with a zigzag needle □ sharp

**Woven paneled
sleeveless jacket**

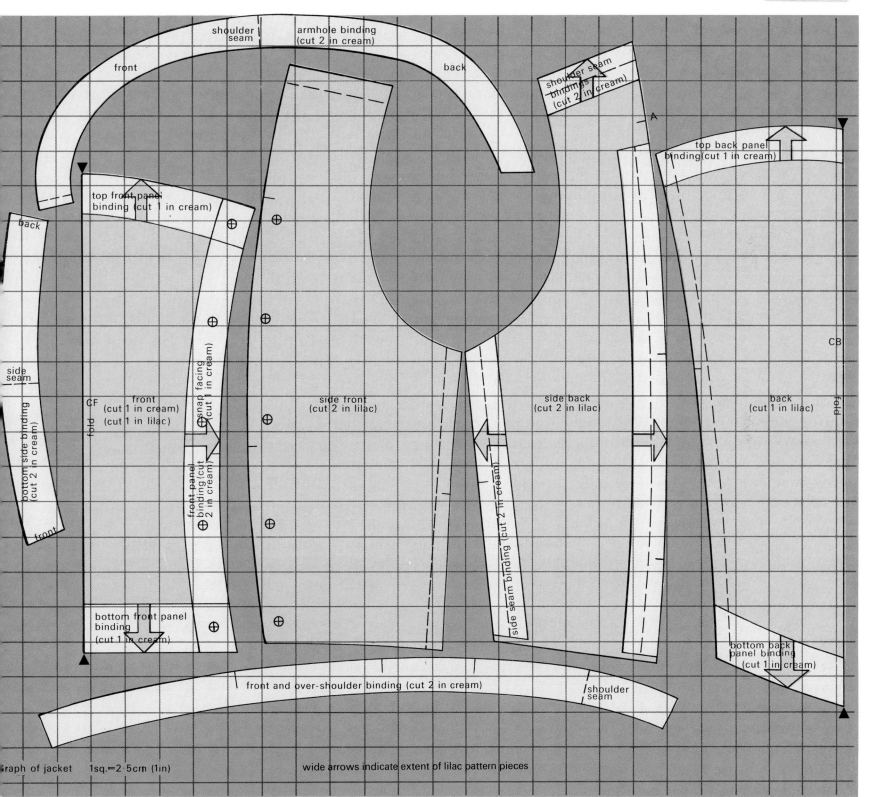

shoulder seam

armhole binding
(cut 2 in cream)

front

back

shoulder seam
bindings
(cut 2 in cream)

A

top back panel
binding (cut 1 in cream)

top front panel
binding (cut 1 in cream)

back

CB

side
seam

bottom side binding
(cut 2 in cream)

CF
fold

front
(cut 1 in cream)
(cut 1 in lilac)

snap facing
(cut 1 in cream)

side front
(cut 2 in lilac)

side back
(cut 2 in lilac)

back
(cut 1 in lilac)

fold

front panel
binding (cut
2 in cream)

side seam binding (cut 2 in cream)

front

bottom front panel
binding
(cut 1 in cream)

bottom back
panel binding
(cut 1 in cream)

front and over-shoulder binding (cut 2 in cream)

shoulder
seam

graph of jacket   1sq.=2·5cm (1in)

wide arrows indicate extent of lilac pattern pieces

Woven paneled sleeveless jacket

dressmaker's or leather scissors □ metal knitting needle □ rubber adhesive □ tailor's chalk □ sewing thread to match both suedes □ small hammer with a padded head □ stapler □ punch pliers □ gripper pliers □ 5 large snap fasteners □ ruler □ pencil □ map pins.

Cutting out. Draw the pattern pieces from the graph (fig.9) in which 1 square equals 2.5cm (1in). Fold the pattern pieces, not the suede. Arrange the pattern pieces on the right side of the suede. Secure with weights or pins. Take a sharp-edged instrument, such as a knitting needle, and trace around the pattern pieces. Mark on the back CB, CF etc.

Making the jacket. On the side backs snip the seam back to 1.5cm ($\frac{1}{2}$in) where it meets the top edge of the back panel, on the seam line underneath notch A. Hold the seam secure by stapling edges together and then sew with straight stitch in matching thread. Tie and glue off ends. Remove the staples, open out the seams and gently hammer them flat. Secure in place with adhesive.

Making the woven front panel. Take the lilac front bodice and mark parallel lines in pencil across it, 2cm ($\frac{3}{4}$in) apart. Cut these with scissors up to 3mm ($\frac{1}{8}$in) from the right-hand edge.
Take the cream front bodice and with chalk mark parallel lines down 2cm ($\frac{3}{4}$in) apart on the right side of the suede. Set your sewing machine for a close buttonhole stitch and, using lilac thread, stitch

machine embroidery 0.5cm ($\frac{1}{4}$in) in from the parallel lines (fig.10).
Note: it is a good idea to test the tension first, also the width and closeness of the stitch, on a scrap piece of suede. The stitch should be 3mm ($\frac{1}{8}$in) wide and close enough to give the appearance of a thick line when seen from a short distance away. Cut along the drawn lines to within 3mm ($\frac{1}{8}$in) of the bottom edge of the panel. Take punch pliers and punch out semicircles along the edges of each strip (fig.11). Take the lilac bodice and pin the uncut edge to a flat surface with map pins. Place the cream bodice over the lilac one, matching all edges, and secure it with pins along the uncut bottom edge. Weave the strips in and out of each other, starting at the top left-hand edge and working across to the right. When you come to the right-hand uncut edge, carefully snip the 3mm ($\frac{1}{8}$in) of strip free and apply a spot of adhesive to the underside to stick the lilac strip to the cream strip. As you continue to weave, secure the ends of the strips with adhesive. When you have secured all 4 sides, sew around all edges with straight stitch, 0.5cm ($\frac{1}{4}$in) from the edge.
To attach the woven panel to the side front, apply glue to the wrong side of the right-hand edge of the panel. Place the panel 2.5cm (1in) over the side front and sew with straight stitch. Staple, sew, hammer flat, and glue to side and shoulder seams.

Applying the bindings. With punch pliers,

punch semicircles out of the edge of the bindings. Place the binding for the shoulder seams over the center of the seam. Glue them on, embroider with close buttonhole stitch in lilac thread as previously described. Sew the bindings on in the following order: side seams, front and overshoulder binding, top back panel bindings, front panel bindings, bottom side binding and back bottom panel binding. Sew the armhole binding over the back as shown in fig.12.

Attaching the fasteners. Take a strip of suede as given on the pattern. Glue it to the wrong side of the front panel where snap fasteners are to be placed. Attach snaps where indicated on the pattern. Take the punched front panel strip, embroider it with buttonhole stitch as before, glue this over the snaps to conceal. (This strip must be embroidered first and then applied to the panel, as the snaps interfere with the path of the machine foot and tend to throw the stitch askew.)

Front bindings. For the front bindings, take the top panel bindings and embroider the end where a snap will be covered (fig.13). Apply adhesive to the back of the partly embroidered strip and attach to the top edge of the front panel. Stitch remaining embroidery along strip. For the bottom panel binding, work as for the top.
Finally, to make sure that the embroidery stitches will not come undone, put a small amount of adhesive at the end of each run of stitches on the wrong side of the suede.

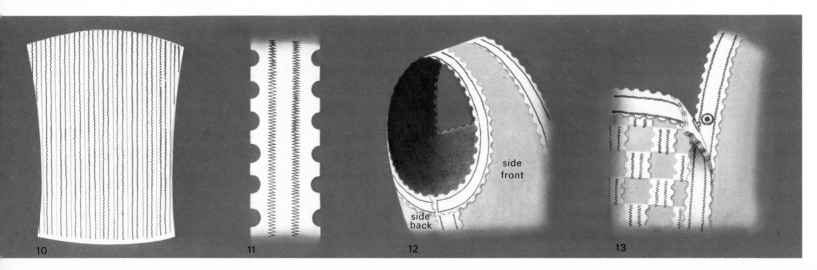

10   11   12   side front   side back   13

Candlemaking

Once primitive man discovered fire and the various uses to which it could be put he no doubt also soon noticed that animal fat burned particularly brightly. So it was probably not too long before he put this discovery to good use, and was able to illuminate his otherwise dark cave with flaming lumps of tallow.

It is difficult to date the origins of true candles exactly, but we do know from archaeological remains that candlesticks were used both in Egypt and in Crete around 3000 BC. However, it was the Romans who really developed the candle, using it both as an aid for traveling at night and for lighting their homes and temples. Candles are traditionally associated with worship, and in Europe during the Middle Ages the beeswax church candles were manufactured by the priests themselves. As their production for domestic use increased, candle guilds were formed, and in 15th-century England, during the reign of King Edward IV, it was the duty of a specially employed tallow-man to keep stocks of grease and fat taken from animals after slaughter to use in the making of candles. Ordinary candles were in fact known as "tallow dip" and were used to provide minimal artificial light after dark. The liquid tallow was drawn from a tub into another vessel. Then two rods known as "broaches" and strung with a number of wicks—in early days made of the peeled pith of rushes and later cotton—would be dipped three times into the tallow, drained and hung on a rack to dry. Once they had cooled, the wicks would then be dipped repeatedly until they had reached the thickness required.

The technique of molding candles probably began in France, during the 15th century. Several open-ended hollow cylinders, usually made of pewter, with small metal caps with a hole in the center for the wicks, were placed in a frame. The wicks were then passed through the molds and kept taut in the center by means of small wires. Once the molds had been filled with tallow, the wicks were pulled tight, the frames left to cool, and the wires pulled out.

The true craftsman bleached his tallow candles by fastening them to rods and hanging them out of doors for some 8–10

The mass production of candles became feasible in the mid-19th century. This contemporary engraving shows Price's Patent Candle Manufactory at Battersea in London, England.

days, screening them from rain and sunshine.

By the 1820s, as a result of research by Michel Eugene Chevreul into oils and fats, braided wicks were used in conjunction with candles of stearic acid, a component of tallow: the result—a perfect candle, requiring no snuffing at all. Spermaceti from the head cavity of the sperm whale also began to be used for candle stock. In time, paraffin wax almost completely took the place of tallow.

In 1834, a candle-making machine complete with moving pistons was introduced, but even in an industrial age there remained a place for the handmade candle, and many used by the Church are still individually made using early methods. Read on to find out how you, too, can create your own decorative, colorful candles.

Ornamental candles can be made for a fraction of the cost of bought ones and they are surprisingly easy to create once the

simple, basic rules have been mastered. Candlemaking is a very satisfactory craft too, for the shapes and colors of the candles you make will lead to other, even more exciting ideas until eventually you will find yourself with more projects in mind than time to do them!

Candlemaking is a perfectly safe occupation for older children as long as the materials are used sensibly. Remember that wax should not be heated violently over direct heat. Use a double boiler if possible; never fill a pan too full and use an asbestos mat with gas or an open flame.

If the wax does catch fire, smother it with a pan lid but *never* pour water over it.

If wax gets onto clothes, pick off what you

Candlemaking

Materials and equipment

can, place the cloth between pieces of absorbent paper, iron with a warm iron to lift the grease onto the paper and then wash thoroughly.

Paraffin wax. This is usually bought in the form of prepared granulated wax, which is very easy to use. It has a melting temperature of 57°–60° C (135°–140° F) and about 1 kg (2 lb) will melt down to enough hot wax for several good sized candles. You can also melt down old candles or buy wax in slabs, when it must be broken up into manageable proportions with a hammer.

Stearic acid (stearin). This special ingredient adds hardness to candles, makes them burn slightly longer, helps release them from their molds (because it makes the wax mixture shrink a little), develops their color and increases opacity. The proportion is usually 10% stearic acid to 90% wax.

Wax dyes. These are sold in the form of color discs or sticks or sometimes in powder or liquid form. Dyes are very concentrated, so it is best to work carefully when using them, for an overdyed candle looks very dark and lifeless. Colors can be mixed for more subtle shades. Usually the stearic acid is melted first in a separate pan, the dye is then sprinkled or scraped onto it and the mixture heated and stirred gently until all the dye is dissolved into a colored

Candlemaking is certainly a craft that can be enjoyed by all the family, but do remember to supervise young children.

liquid. This liquid is then added to molten wax.

Wicks. These come in various sizes depending on the height and diameter of the candle. If the wick is the right size for the candle, an even, non-smoky flame and a smooth-burning candle will result. If a wick is too small, it will not burn well; if it is too large, there will not be enough wax to burn and the candle will produce a smoky flame. If you want a candle to burn leaving a hollow shell of wax behind, use a slightly smaller wick.

Wick holder. This is a rod to go across the top of the mold to hold the free end of the

Basic candles (*left to right*): Cut-back dipping, chunky candle from rigid mold, embossed candle from flexible mold, lacy ice candle from improvised mold, two layered candles, carved sand candle, simple hand molded candle, multi-colored balloon candle.

wick while the wax sets. A pencil will serve quite well for this.

Thermometer. You need a thermometer with a range of up to 204° C (400° F)—a candy (sugar) thermometer will do very well. Do not overheat the wax. If it starts to smoke it is around 132° C (270° F) and much too hot for normal candlemaking. A good tip if working without a thermometer is to put a drip of water in the wax when

you heat it. When it starts to sizzle and spit, the wax has reached pouring temperature. But for advanced candlemaking, a thermometer is essential for really good results, for the temperature can be critical. If wax is poured too cold (usually below 77°C or 170°F), it will begin to set as you pour and an unsatisfactory surface will result. If it is poured too hot, it could ruin the mold.

Double boiler and/or various pans. To melt wax and dissolve stearic acid and dye.

Mold seal. To stop up the holes made by the wick. Use plastic putty (plasticine) or special sealer.

Deep enamel container or bucket. For dipping candles. The bucket can also serve as a cooling bath, which gives a better finish to a candle.

Molds. You can buy all kinds of ready-made molds, which are ideal for candlemaking. Flexible plastic or rubber molds enable you to produce beautiful embossed designs, and you can also buy rigid molds in plastic, metal and glass, which allow the candle to cool rapidly and so give a very good finish. Just for fun, try using improvised molds such as milk cartons, plastic food containers, plastic drainpipe, rubber balls, acetate and plastic bags and even balloons.

Improvised molds may lead to a few disasters, but you can learn a lot from them and anyway, the wax can always be re-melted and used again. The main difficulty with improvised molds (apart from the obvious one of remembering to use something that will withstand heat), is to position the wick centrally and to keep it tautly in place. If you are using a container which cannot have a hole bored in it, drill a hole in the wax with a hand drill or a hot metal knitting needle after the candle has set. Then dip the wick in wax, let it harden and thread it into the hole and top up with hot wax to secure. Alternatively, use a weight such as a button, or a piece of mold seal, to anchor the wick to the base of the mold while the candle is setting.

Paper. To protect work surfaces.

Roll of paper towels. For mopping up wax.

A knife. To cut up dye discs and carve candles.

Old spoons. To stir wax.

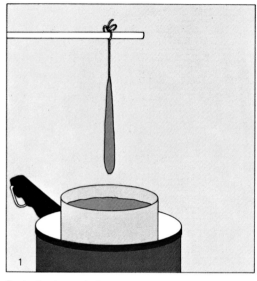

Basic dipping technique.

Dipped candles

Dipped candles are a good idea to start with, as they give you the feel of wax and make you familiar with its characteristics. Dipping is the oldest of all methods of candlemaking. All you need is a container slightly taller than the length of the candle you are to make, wax and wicks.

Fill the container with wax and heat to 82°C (180°F). If you are making colored candles, dissolve some dye in stearic acid and add it to the wax. Dip a length of wick tied to a stick into this wax as shown in fig.1, then remove it. Repeat the process at 30-second intervals which will allow time for each additional coat of wax to harden. The wax must be kept at the right temperature during the dipping process, so either use an enamel container and keep it on an asbestos mat at a low heat, or re-heat the wax at intervals.

When the candle is thick enough, hang it up to cool.

For a more interesting finish give white candles an outside coat of color by floating a 5cm (2in) layer of colored melted candle-wax on the surface of water heated to 82°C (180°F). Make sure the heat of the water and that of the wax are the same, then dip the white candle through the wax into the water and pull it out. Continue this until the required depth of color is obtained.

Variations on dipped candles

There are many variations on the basic dipped candle. Some of these are relatively easy to achieve by twisting for a spiral effect or braiding several together. Even more interesting though are the effects of cut-back dipping and combining dipping with hand molding and painting.

Cut-back dipping. One attractive form of dipped candle is made by building up various layers of different colors, each one about 3mm ($\frac{1}{8}$in) thick. When several layers of color have been added, one on top of the other, the candle is left to harden, then it is carved to reveal the bright colors inside. To get a rounded effect, as in the illustration on the previous page, use a long wick and hold from alternate ends as you dip.

Hand-molded fruits

This variation on dipping can be used to make these lovely and realistic fruit candles—oranges, apples and pears. Though the results are impressively professional, they are actually very easy to make, and when mixed with fresh fruit as a centerpiece for a dinner party, the effect is not only startling, but quite beautiful.

You will need:

113g (4oz) of white wax per fruit □ wick □ 340g (12oz) additional wax for dipping □ yellow, orange and green dye discs—1 disc is sufficient for up to 0.5kg (1lb) of wax □ egg poacher □ burnt sienna poster paint □ knitting needle □ wire brush □ 2 cheese graters □ paper clip or nail □ paintbrushes.

Making the basic candle. Allowing 113g (4oz) of wax per fruit, place the wax in the top half of a double boiler over hot water and melt at a low temperature. When the wax has melted completely, set it to one side until it is soft when prodded. Warm the pan slightly so that you can remove the wax easily, and then take a suitably sized lump in your hand. The wax will be firm but quite malleable at this stage, so mold into the required shape with both hands, and then make a hole for the wick by pushing a knitting needle through the center of the candle. Remove the needle cleanly and thread the wick through the candle, attaching it at one end to a paper clip or nail to keep it secure. The candle is now ready to

be dipped in colored wax.

Dipping the candles. Melt the wax for each color in separate containers over hot water in the usual manner, adding a quarter of a dye disc to each to make yellow, orange and green wax. Dip the candles into their respective colored waxes, lift them out and then allow to dry before polishing and adding surface color and texture.

Decorating the candles. To add surface color to the individual fruits melt small quantities of appropriately colored waxes in the compartments of an egg poacher over hot water. Place your paintbrushes in the warm waxes and leave them there until required. Paint the wax onto the surface of the candles one stroke at a time, returning the brush to the wax between each stroke. Having painted the candles as required, re-dip the oranges, apples and pears in their original colored waxes for a final coat. To decorate a pear, follow the basic procedure but, after painting the fruit, add texture by hitting the surface with a wire brush and then rub a little burnt sienna poster paint into the holes and re-dip as usual in yellow wax. To decorate an orange, rub the candle between 2 cheese graters for the effect of pitted peel and then re-dip in orange wax.

Casting candles

A cast candle is made by pouring wax into a mold where it will harden into that shape.

Casting an embossed candle from a flexible rubber mold. Choose a wick suitable for the diameter of the candle. Dip the wick into hot wax, pull it straight and when it has stiffened, thread the wick through the base of the mold with a large-eyed needle, making sure that it is positioned centrally. Tie the top end of the wick to a wick holder, pull the bottom end taut and seal with mold seal (fig.2). Flexible molds must be supported while the wax sets otherwise they will become distorted. Either make a "jacket" from corrugated paper fastened with adhesive tape and wrap it around the mold, or hang the mold from two sticks between a couple of chairs (fig.3). Melt the prepared wax, stearic acid and dye to a temperature of 98° C (208° F) and leave to stand until it is about 93° C (199° F). Gently warm the mold in front of

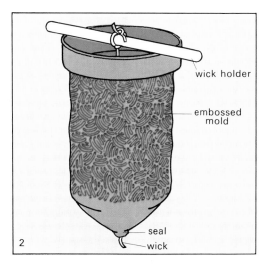

wick holder

embossed mold

seal

wick

a radiator or heater (never over a flame). Put the mold into its jacket or hang it as described and pour in the melted wax. When pouring, tilt the mold so that the wax trickles slowly down inside, thus reducing the number of air bubbles which can spoil the finished appearance. Slightly overfill the mold past the shoulder to create a lip. This prevents an unsightly wedge from appearing when the wax is "topped off." Lightly tap the sides of the mold to bring any air bubbles to the surface. Leave the candle to stand while the heat permeates through to the outside of the mold and then give the mold a final tap all over.

Wax contracts as it cools and it will be necessary to top off the well which will appear. You may need to do this several

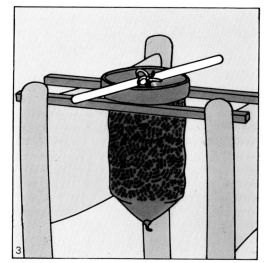

times in order to keep the surface flat. Remember to keep the wick in position. Release the candle when it is cold by rubbing the surface of the mold with soapy hands and warm water and then peel it off carefully. Wash and dry the mold and restore it to its original shape before storing it away from heat or sunlight. Trim the wick and stand the base of the candle in a heated pot until the shoulder flange melts away leaving a flat base.

To finish an embossed candle, paint the embossed areas with poster paint mixed with a drop of liquid detergent. Do not add too much liquid as this prevents the paint from drying. Rub off any excess with a damp cloth and buff the finished candle with a dry soft cloth.

Layered candle in a rigid mold. Layered candles are made by pouring different colored waxes on top of each other, allowing each layer to congeal before pouring the next. Make sure that the mold is clean and dry inside. Thread the wick, pull taut through the mold base and seal with a mold seal. Tie the other end of the wick to a wick holder. Prepare several different colors of wax and stearic acid. Pour the first layer at 82° C (180° F) for plastic molds, 104° C (219° F) for metal molds and 93° C (199° F) for glass molds. The smaller the quantity of wax, the hotter it can be because it will cool faster. Give the mold a tap to release air bubbles. Allow the wax to cool until the surface feels rubbery. Then pour the next layer at the same temperature and leave to set to the same consistency. Continue like this until the mold is full. Fill up the well with the last color. To be certain that the bands of color are even, measure the amount of wax being poured or use a transparent mold. By standing the mold at an angle, layers can be built up diagonally. Reverse the angle for each new layer of color (fig.4a and b). The speed at which the wax is cooled will affect the appearance of the candle. Very slow cooling will produce what look like air bubbles in the wax; rapid cooling in a bucket filled with cold water will produce an even finish. The more water there is, the faster the candle will cool. The water level should be the same as that of the wax. Wax must not be poured into a mold that is already in a

cooling bath as this will result in an unattractive scaly finish. The best cooling method for diagonally layered candles, which are difficult to prop up in cold water, is to aim a cold fan at them.

Chunky candle. Wax the wick and thread it through the bottom of the mold; seal at the base. Fill the mold with chunks of left-over wax of different colors or chunks of wax made in ice cube trays. Arrange them around the wick, making sure that the wick is still central. Heat up either white or colored wax and stearic acid to 115° C (239° F) and pour it over the chunks. Use a cooling bath to prevent the chunks from melting too fast thereby coloring the molten wax. After the candle is released from the mold, it can be carved to reveal the shapes and colors of the chunks inside.

Lacy candle in an improvised mold. Place a thin, ready-wicked candle as a core in the middle of a tin mold. Place crushed ice in the mold around the candle and pour hot wax—104° C (219° F)—over the ice. The ice will melt and when the wax has set the candle can be taken out and the water poured away.

Carved sand candle. Fill a box or bucket with slightly dampened sand. Any type of sand will do, but remember that its texture and color will form the outside of the finished candle. Level off the surface of the sand but do not compress it. Press a suitable shape—such as a bowl—into the sand, then bang the bucket to settle the sand. Remove the shape and smooth off any roughness in the sand. Additional impressions can be made by pressing with the back of a spoon.

The thickness of the sand around the candle will depend on the amount of moisture in the sand (which stops the wax from spreading) and by the temperature of the wax which, if heated to below 93° C (199° F) will not pick up the sand. Gently heat the wax to about 126° C (259° F). A thermometer is essential as the temperature is above boiling point [100°C (212°F)] and so a double boiler cannot be used. Melt plenty of wax as quite a lot will be lost in the sand. Remove the wax from the heat, having first turned off the stove. Pour it carefully into the sand mould and top it off after about three minutes. While the wax is

soft, push a knitting needle into the middle and then insert a waxed wick. Use a smaller wick than usual so that the candle will burn hollow. Top off the well taking care not to knock any sand into the wax. When completely set, dig the candle out of the sand. It will look shapeless at first but brush off the loose sand and carve back to the original shape; you can add carved holes for a special dramatic effect.

Balloon candle. This is quite difficult to do, but produces a most attractive candle. Partly fill a round balloon with cold water until it is distended to a diameter of roughly 7.5cm (3in). Heat some wax to about 77°C (171° F) and repeatedly dip the well-dried balloon into it up to the same level about 10 times, allowing 30-second intervals between each. When the last coat has set, pour the water carefully out of the balloon which should then pull easily away from the inside of the wax shell. Melt three different colored dyes with stearic acid in the compartments of an egg poacher or in three cups in a pan of boiling water. When the dyes have dissolved, put a teaspoonful of one color into the shell and quickly rotate it as though it were a glass of brandy. Empty any surplus color at once. Repeat with the other colors to coat the inside of the shell. Cool quickly, using a fan if possible. The shell must now be filled. Add a coating of wax, a tablespoonful at a time, heated to 87° C (189° F), rotating the shell so that it adheres evenly. Pour off the excess so that it does not form pools of hot wax which will distort the shell. Continue slowly filling, a tablespoonful at a time until a wall of 1.5cm ($\frac{1}{2}$in) is built up. Throughout, the shell must not be allowed to rest on a hard surface until the wax is completely hard. Slightly larger quantities of wax and stearic acid can now be poured in and allowed to cool. When the shell is three-quarters full, drill a hole for the wick or use a hot metal knitting needle. Insert the wick and top off the candle.

Casting your own molds

This is now a well-established technique in candlemaking and it offers the possibility of making an infinite variety of candle shapes. The only real consideration to bear in mind when you choose the object to be cast is

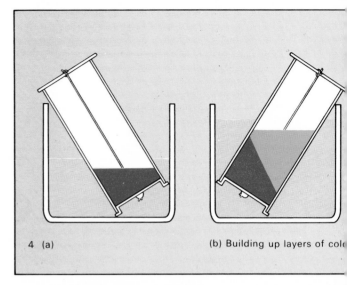

4 (a)　　　　　　　　　(b) Building up layers of colo

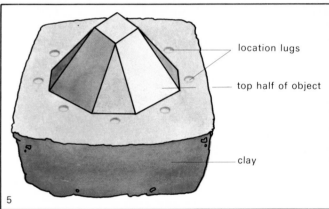

location lugs

top half of object

clay

5

that its surface should be non-absorbent and relatively firm.

Basic materials

Clay. This is used to form a firm base for the object, and to build a protective wall around it when making the plaster cast.

Molding material. There are various materials now on the market. Go to any good specialist candlemaking supplier or craft store and ask for a suitable product. The molding material is usually painted over the object in several layers (but individual manufacturers may differ in their instructions); it then hardens to form a removable and flexible mold.

Plaster. This is used to make a cast of the mold. It is necessary also as a rigid support for the mold when the candle itself is cast.

Cheesecloth (muslin). This may be ne-

Basic techniques
A touch of the macabre

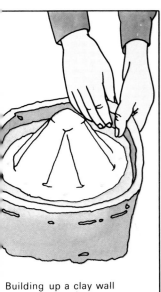

Building up a clay wall to house the plaster

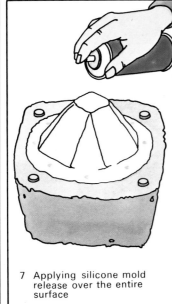

7 Applying silicone mold release over the entire surface

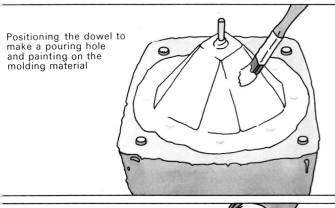

Positioning the dowel to make a pouring hole and painting on the molding material

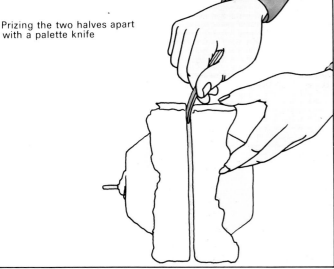

Prizing the two halves apart with a palette knife

cessary to make a further supporting jacket within the plaster cast.

Silicone mold release. This is obtainable in several forms and can be sprayed, rubbed or painted on. Soap will do just as well in an emergency.

Basic techniques
Making the first half of the mold. Form a solid square pad of clay and center your object on it. Build up a thick wall of the clay around the object to exactly half its total depth (see fig.5.) Make a series of holes in the clay around the object by pushing in a short length of dowel to a depth of about 2.5cm (1in), and with your finger make depressions at the four corners of the clay housing. These holes are known as location lugs and serve to fit the two halves of the final mold together. Paint a thin coat of the molding material over the surface of the projecting half of the object. You will notice air bubbles rising to the surface; this is normal and they will disappear in about 10 minutes. Paint several more layers of the molding material, so that it spreads to fill the location lugs. Allow to set.

Pinch up the sides of the clay to reach just above the height of the object so that it forms a well for the plaster (fig.6).

Casting in plaster. As your plaster will only remain workable for about 10 to 15 minutes, you need to have everything ready beforehand. Sift the plaster into a bowl or bucket of water; following the manufacturer's instructions as far as quantities are concerned, until the plaster forms a peak in the center. Knock it gently with a plastic or wooden spatula and stir thoroughly. When it is the consistency of thick cream, pour it into the sides of the clay well and flick and spread it thickly over the surface of the mold, making sure that it is even in depth.

You can also strengthen the plaster cast with a layer of cheesecloth, well soaked in wet plaster; work over the surface of the mold until no bubbles remain. Allow the plaster to harden, again following the manufacturer's recommendations for setting times.

Making the second half of the mold. When the plaster cast has set, remove the clay.

Turn the cast upside down to expose the section of the object previously embedded in clay. Note the protruding location lugs set in the mold. Remove all traces of clay from the object by washing in soap and water and allow to dry.

Spray, paint or rub a mold release agent over the entire surface of the object, mold and plaster, including the lugs (see fig.7). Apply your molding material as before, but this time stand a short length of dowel in the center of the object (fig.8) and build up the molding material around it. This will provide a "funnel" for pouring in the wax later on. Build up a clay housing around the object as before and pour in the plaster. Again, strengthen with cheesecloth if necessary and then set the whole cast aside to dry.

Removing the plaster cast. Remove the surrounding clay when the plaster is solid. Separate the two halves of the cast. This should be fairly easy if the mold release agent has been effective, but you may need to pry the two sections gently apart with a palette knife as shown in fig.9. You will now have two halves with the object and mold inside one of them. Remove the object in its mold from the cast. Note the protrusion formed by the dowel on one side. As well as acting as a funnel for the wax it will also enable you set in a wick. Peel apart the two halves of the flexible mold to reveal the object inside. The two halves key together by means of the location lugs, so you can push them together again in exactly the same position. You now have a flexible mold and a rigid mold to enable you to make perfect candles.

A touch of the macabre
When you have learned how to make your own mold from a solid object, try something startlingly "lifelike." To reproduce this remarkable candle is not as difficult as it looks, but it should not be tackled by a beginner. This is the type of project that takes skill plus a dash of confidence. The resulting candle, placed in an alcove or in front of a mirror, will resemble finely carved alabaster.

You will need:
425g (15oz) beeswax □ 425g (15oz) paraffin wax □ approximately 0.5kg (1lb)

A touch of the macabre

molding material □ wine bottle □ bottle cutter □ 2.5 liters (½ gallon) water □ 2 buckets □ spatula □ a willing model.

Casting the hand. Gather all the equipment together before you begin as the materials will set rapidly once you start working. Fill one of the buckets with water and stir in the molding material slowly. It will set within about 20 minutes, so work swiftly. Cut the bottle in half with the cutter and give the top (neck) section to your model to hold upside down.

When you have arranged the fingers in a satisfactory "holding" position, the model should place his or her hand downwards into the second bucket. There should be a small space between the hand and the bottle, and neither should touch the sides of the bucket. Pour in the molding material so that both the hand and the bottle are submerged and the bucket is almost full. Shake the bucket gently to release any air bubbles, then persuade your model to remain absolutely still for approximately 20 minutes.

When the molding material is firm to the touch, remove the hand in its mold from the bucket. Make a neat incision very carefully down one side of the mold to release the hand and bottle. Replace the mold in the bucket, aligning the cut edges as accurately as possible. This is important as an inexact join could result in a ridge down the side of the hand and other imperfections.

Prepare a quantity of plaster as previously described, then pour gently and slowly into the mold. To release any air bubbles trapped in the fingertips and other crevices, cover the opening of the mold with a piece of cardboard and pour it in the other way up. Hold it like this for about a minute and then leave the plaster model to dry out completely. This usually takes about 2 weeks.

Making the candle. When the plaster model is dry, stand the hand on its base and coat it with several layers of molding material. When this is dry, it should be treated as a solid object around which a plaster cast should be made as previously described. The only difference is that with an object of this complexity and detail, it is advisable to make the cast in 3 pieces rather than 2 halves. The technique is the same, but treat

product that is now generally available and has great potential for creative experimenting. It is a water-emulsified wax, which is used cold for decorating the surface of a candle. It can be used for a wide range of textured effects and can also be colored very successfully with special Whip Wax dyes.

A cool idea !
This cone, filled to the top with swirls of apparently delicious ice cream, makes a delightful gift or centerpiece for the table at a children's party.

You will need :
a beeswax sheet for the cone □ half a cupful of Whip Wax □ Whip Wax dyes if color is preferred □ cook's piping bag □ cake decorating tube □ egg beater.

Making the ice cream cone. With a compass draw a quadrant within one quarter of the beeswax sheet, as shown in fig. 10 and cut it out. Place it in a warm place to soften slightly so that it will bend into shape easily without losing its texture. Cut a length of wick measuring approximately 8cm ($3\frac{1}{4}$in). Use a wick that is slightly thicker and heavier than usual. Dip it into hot wax, allow it to harden, then place it along one side edge of the beeswax. Carefully roll the beeswax, together with the wick, into a cone. Seal the cone by heating the outside edges quickly in a flame and working the 2 surfaces together with your fingers. Leave it on one side to harden.

Preparing the ice cream. Put the half cupful of Whip Wax into a bowl and whip it up with an egg beater as though preparing egg whites for meringue. When the wax is stiff and stands in peaks, put it into the piping bag, making sure the decorating tube is firmly in place. Squeeze the bag, rotating the cone as you do so so that the wax falls into a spiral. Adjust the wick so that it is positioned centrally and finish off with a decorative swirl of wax.

The wax will remain soft for several hours. Support the cone in an upright position while the wax hardens. All decorative candles should be left for at least two or three days before being moved.

By using different colored waxes, there is no end to the "confections" that can be made by the same process.

The pièce de résistance of candle confectionery !

You can use Whip Wax dyes to make strawberry and chocolate ices, shaped with an ice cream or potato scoop and arranged in a tall glass as an ice cream sundae or a knickerbocker glory.

the plaster model as if it has 3 sides instead of 2, and remember to apply the silicone mold release to all the surfaces so that the plaster cast will separate easily afterwards.

Candlemaking is fun !
Candlemakers are increasingly experimenting with basic materials and techniques to produce new and exciting candle ideas. Whip Wax is a recently developed new

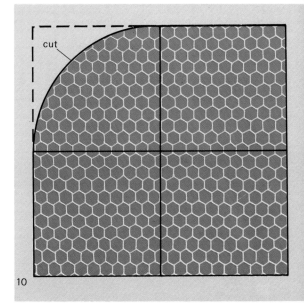

10

cut

Woodwork

Wood is one of the most versatile and accommodating materials of all, lending itself to an infinite variety of forms and uses. Woodworkers have traditionally played a vital role in any community, called upon to construct almost anything from sailing ships to musical instruments.

As with any highly valued material, the use of special woods, for example for furniture, has always been reserved for the wealthy and important members of society. The earliest kind of furniture tended to be public furniture—thrones for kings and tables from which the affairs of state were conducted. The Greeks, Romans and Egyptians used beds, chairs and other wooden furniture, though the Egyptians had so little wood that they imported cedar and sandalwood from abroad. These woods were so highly prized that they were often exacted in tribute from subordinate states. By the end of the Roman era many of the sophisticated techniques that had been developed fell into disuse and were forgotten. Furniture was made of roughly hewn boards attached by oak pins and nails. Saws were unknown—wood was cut with a wedge and a hammer, or with an adze.

In Europe until the 9th century AD, all carpenters' shops were attached to the monasteries and were controlled by them. Furniture, in fact was extremely rare outside the church and until the 14th century the nature of domestic life made furniture largely unnecessary. Hangings of all kinds were regarded as being more useful than heavy furniture. Most houses, too, had very few rooms. As late as 1301 the richest burgess in Colchester, England, had only three rooms in his house.

It was not until the 16th century that a general increase in domestic comfort led to more sophisticated furniture. The use of the hall declined and rooms were built with more specific functions.

In the 17th century ebony was introduced into England. This was a new and difficult wood to use, and craftsmen solved the problem by using thin sheets of it as a veneer. Its frequent use in the making of cabinets led to its users being labelled cabinet makers, or, in France, "ébénistes." The technique was such a skilled one that cabinet makers often had royal patrons. Furniture became increasingly elegant, with the work of Chippendale, Sheraton and Hepplewhite being the supreme

The Cosimo panel—a wood sculpture by the master 17th-century wood carver, Grinling Gibbons. Gibbons is generally regarded as being one of the finest craftsmen of his time.

Tools, wood and techniques

example. The 19th century saw a variety of styles, many of them extremely florid. It was only in the early 20th century that there was a return to more austere forms.

Wood carving

It is only when beginning to carve wood perhaps that one really learns to appreciate the many different qualities of the material. Look carefully around you and take inspiration from the many beautiful examples of carving that are to be found in churches and old buildings.

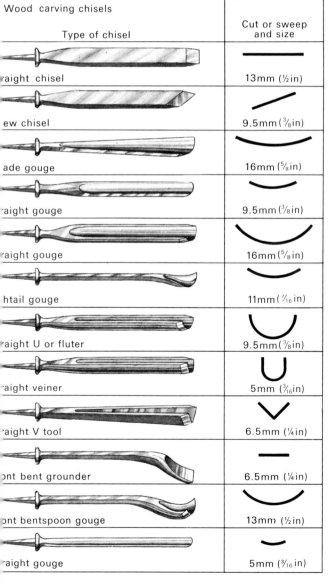

Wood carving chisels Type of chisel	Cut or sweep and size
raight chisel	13mm (½in)
ew chisel	9.5mm (⅜in)
ade gouge	16mm (⅝in)
aight gouge	9.5mm (⅜in)
aight gouge	16mm (⅝in)
htail gouge	11mm (7/16in)
aight U or fluter	9.5mm (⅜in)
aight veiner	5mm (3/16in)
aight V tool	6.5mm (¼in)
ont bent grounder	6.5mm (¼in)
ont bentspoon gouge	13mm (½in)
aight gouge	5mm (3/16in)

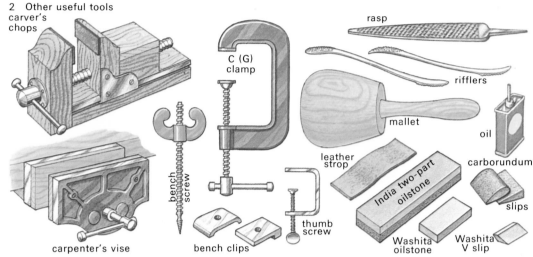

2 Other useful tools

carver's chops
carpenter's vise
bench screw
C (G) clamp
bench clips
thumb screw
rasp
rifflers
mallet
oil
leather strop
India two-part oilstone
carborundum
slips
Washita oilstone
Washita V slip

Tools

Chisels (fig.1). Wood carving chisels are perhaps the most important tools of all for the wood carver. The selection shown here is suggested as a basic set which can be added to as your skill develops. Really sharp tools are essential for successful wood carving. A good tool merchant will sharpen tools for you if they are sold rough ground. If you decide to sharpen tools yourself, get an expert to show you how.
Other useful tools (fig.2). As well as chisels you should have a selection of rifflers and files for carving in corners and awkward places. Rasps are used for smoothing the surface of the wood and carborundum for sanding down. Use various clamps as shown in fig.2 to hold the wood in position while it is being carved. A wooden mallet is essential to drive the carving tools into the wood. Keep your tools sharp with oilstone and oil.

Types of wood

When choosing the wood for carving, a number of things should be kept in mind. The natural color of the wood is important of course, but you should also take into account the grain (the structure of the wood fibers) and the figure, which is the pattern formed by the grain. In some woods, such as oak and walnut, the figure is generally well developed due to the rapid growth of the tree during the summer months. Different woods and their characteristics are illustrated in fig.3.

Wood finishes

Various finishes can be used to act as a protective sealer, and in some cases also to stain the wood.
Wax polish. Cut pure beeswax into small pieces, put into a can and cover with turpentine. Place in a pan of water and heat until the wax melts, allow to cool and then apply sparingly with a soft rag. Leave to harden for a day or two before applying a final polish.
Shellac. Natural shellac is orange-colored, which is fine for dark woods, but white shellac should be used for light woods. Apply in several thin coats, sanding down with very fine sandpaper (flour paper) between each coat. Dilute shellac with alcohol if necessary. Finish with wax polish.
Polyurethane varnish. This is useful for extra protection against heat or weather or for any utensils that will need constant cleaning. It can be bought in either matt or shiny finish and comes in colors.
Oil-based stain. This is difficult to put on evenly, so it helps to seal the wood first with a thin coat of shellac. Thin the stain with alcohol and apply until the required shade is attained.

Carving techniques

Basically there are two main types of carving—relief carving and carving in the round.
Relief carving. The simplest forms of relief carving are chip carving, and incision

3 Types of wood

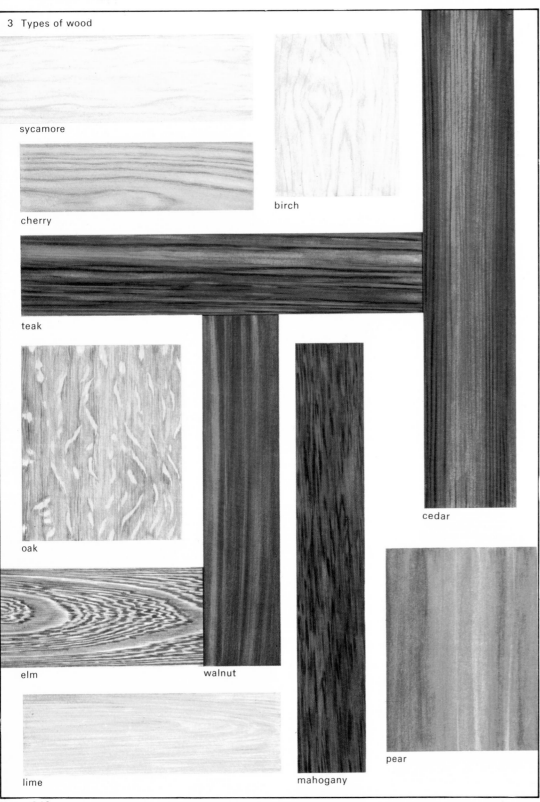

sycamore

cherry

birch

teak

oak

elm

walnut

cedar

mahogany

pear

lime

Sycamore. Light straw, close grain, soft figure, gives smooth finish, works well, hard.

Cherry. Yellow to pink, close grain, subtle marking, hard, good for fine work.

Birch. Yellow to brown, decorative figure good for bowls etc, medium hard.

Teak. Brown with dark streaks, close strong grain, good for outside work, medium hard.

Cedar. Many varieties, pink to red, lovely figure, hard close grain, perfumed.

Oak. Golden, strong grain, interesting figure, good for bold "off the tool" work, hard.

Elm. Yellow, dark grain, decorative figure, good for bowls etc and large work.

Walnut. Rich brown, close grain, English and Italian best in color and figure, medium hard, lovely to work with.

Lime. Light straw, close grain, delicate figure, soft to carve but firm.

Mahogany. Many kinds from light brown to red, usually close firm grain, lovely figure, medium hard.

Pear. Pink to yellow, close grain, little marking, good for fine work, hard.

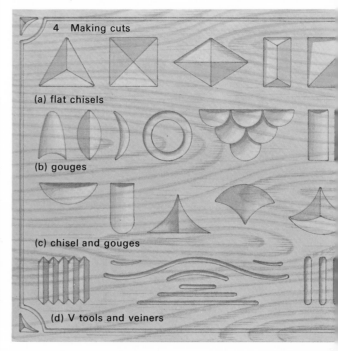

4 Making cuts

(a) flat chisels

(b) gouges

(c) chisel and gouges

(d) V tools and veiners

compact and that the dark holes of the cut-out background form a small and even overall pattern.

In high relief the form is much fuller and is sometimes almost three-quarters of the suggested shape.

All relief carving depends on the play of light on the facets carved on the surface, so you need a good cross light when doing this work.

Chip carving. This is a good method to start with and it will give you an opportunity to familiarize yourself with various carving tools. Select a piece of wood, such as lime, that is close-grained and not too hard, making sure that the surface is flat and smooth. Fix the wood to the bench with clamps. Lay out your tools with the handles away from you, so that you can see the cutting edges at a glance. Have your mallet on hand.

The flat chisels make straight-faceted cuts (fig.4a). The gouges make curved notches, scoops and channels (fig.4b). Fig.4c shows combined chisel and gouge cuts, while fig.4d shows cuts with V tools and veiners.

The technique is to make one, two or even more cuts (depending on the shape that is required) from different angles to free the wood in between the cuts. Try out some cuts with a chisel and mallet. By combining different cuts, an infinite variety of designs is possible.

Cheeseboard carved in relief

Relief carving is highlighted with color on the back of this cheeseboard. The board, which measures about 26.5 × 34.5cm (10½ × 13½in), will look as good on your party table as it does hanging decoratively on the wall.

You will need:

piece of 19mm ($\frac{3}{4}$in) close-grained hardwood such as walnut, mahogany or teak, 28 × 35.5cm (11 × 14in)☐selection of chisels☐matt polyurethane sealer☐ poster or acrylic paints.

Making the board. Make sure that both surfaces are flat and smooth. Draw the design from the graph (fig.5) in which 1 square equals 3cm (1¼in) and transfer it onto the wood. Have the outline machine sawn, or saw roughly by hand and carve to

the exact shape. File and sand the edges. With a chisel bevel the edges at the back and front 3mm ($\frac{1}{8}$in) wide by 4mm ($\frac{3}{16}$in) deep. Drill a hole at the top for hanging.

Carving. Carve a shallow channel around the background areas, using a small U chisel and keeping away from the design lines. Carve away the remaining wood with a small chisel. Repeat this process until the background is recessed by about 4mm ($\frac{3}{16}$in). Carving precisely to the line with a skew chisel, clarify the edges of the design. Smooth and even up the background. The decoration is made with a combination of chip carving and simple incision. The tail, leaves and branches should have shallow gouge cuts to give light-catching facets.

Finishing. If necessary, rub down carefully with fine sandpaper. You may prefer to leave the wood plain, but if a finish is required, wipe over all surfaces with white spirit and then apply a thin coat of matt polyurethane. If this raises the grain, rub down gently with very fine sandpaper (flour paper). To add color, start by painting the whole raised surface including the chip-carved areas, with the light straw color. Then add the other touches of color as desired. Seal the whole board with 2 more thin coats of polyurethane.

which is really a surface decoration, but if well done can look rich and effective.

In low relief the design or motif is left up and the background taken down. The surface can then be treated in a variety of ways, but should be kept more or less flat with the background level. Forms and details are indicated with subtle stylized tool cuts. A relief can be cut in the shape of the silhouette of a motif. Another variety of this kind is called pierced relief. Here the background is cut away and the surface is richly carved. It is important when designing this kind of relief that the motif is

5 Graph for cheeseboard design   1 sq = 3 cm (1¼in)

the carving "off the tool" ie with the even gouge cuts showing, or smooth the surface with rifflers or files and sandpaper (c). Always sand with the grain to avoid making deep surface scratches.

Sometimes a carving does not need a base or the base is part of the carving itself, but if you want to mount it on a separate base, drill a hole in the bottom of the carving and in the base and fix with a short dowel and glue.

Try a variation of this simple shape with the carvings shown in fig.7a and b.

This reclining figure, carved in the round, has a perfectly balanced form.

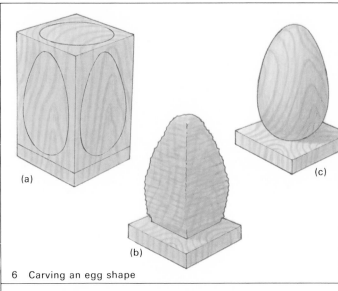

6   Carving an egg shape

Carving in the round

With this kind of carving, the form is free-standing and designed to be seen from all sides. It is important when preparing the design to remember that the balance of the silhouette, the mass and space, and the light and shade must work from all angles. It is a good idea to make a preliminary form in clay or plastic clay (plasticine). Make the forms fairly simple until you have some experience. Keep the form simplified and the changes of plane clearly defined until the required form gradually begins to emerge all around. Refining the forms, undercutting and detail should be left until the main form is finished.

Carving an egg shape (fig.6a,b and c). As an introduction to carving in the round, try a very simple shape, such as an egg, from a block of wood. Either leave enough wood to form a temporary base for holding in the carver's chops or vise, or try using a carver's screw (bench screw) to fix a separate base, then pass the other end through a hole in

the bench and tighten with a wing nut. Draw the silhouette of the egg on all four faces (a). Take a large shallow gouge (straight gouge) and begin to carve off the surplus wood. Carve all four faces down in flat planes to just outside the silhouette so that you are left with a squared-off egg shape (b).

Note: you will have to keep redrawing the silhouette as you carve.

Next begin to round off the form. Cut across the grain as much as possible. The grain should always run with the longest measurement of the carving. Take a shallower gouge (spade gouge) and begin to carve off the ridges left from the first gouge cuts, refining the form at the same time. Keep the cuts even, gradually perfecting the form to the true silhouette.

You will have to release the carving from the holding block to work on the bottom of the egg. Fix the egg in the carver's chops or vise, protected in some way to prevent bruising to the wood. You can either leave

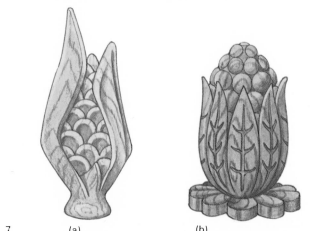

7   (a)   (b)

The decoration of both furniture and ornaments with rare and beautiful woods can be traced back as far as the 7th or 8th centuries BC, when the art of inlay was known to the Ancient Egyptians. *Inlay* is the adornment of solid wooden objects by the insertion into the surface of different shapes and types of wood, ivory and metal. *Intarsia*, which involves inlaying wood into wood was first practiced in Italy in the 13th century. However, marquetry as we know it, was not generally known until the 16th century. In marquetry the whole surface of an object is overlaid with thin decorative veneers.

Many items of furniture nowadays are veneered to give a look of expensive rare woods to objects made of more ordinary wood, but this is usually done using large sheets cut from the same log. Marquetry uses wood of different colors and grains specially cut and shaped to create beautiful designs and pictures. Marquetry can be used to decorate many items from cigarette and jewelry boxes to games boards and clock cases.

Marquetry pictures are an art in themselves using the grain and markings of the wood to suggest features such as grass and brick. By careful selection of the woods, a very realistic effect can be obtained.

Veneers

Veneers are cut from a solid log of wood, either by rotating the log against a blade, in which case large sheets of veneer are obtained, or by cutting across the log with the blade. The latter method is normally used for decorative veneers and shows up the beauty of the grain of the log. The number of types of veneer available is immense ranging from rare expensive woods such as bird's eye maple (with a very pronounced swirling grain), ebony and rosewood to the less expensive, but no less beautiful lacewood (plane tree) and sycamore. All have their own distinctive character. Veneers from handicraft shops are usually sold in 30.5 × 15cm (12 × 6in) sheets, although larger sheets are usually available from specialist suppliers.

Tools and equipment

Very few tools are required for marquetry.

The basic and most important item is the knife. There are many appropriate craft knives on the market with replaceable blades. Alternatively, use a surgical scalpel handle with very fine sharp blades to make cutting easy and accurate.

The veneer is cut on a cutting board, preferably made of plywood, which is soft and will not blunt the knife as it passes through the veneer. Hardboard can be used, but is harder and can form grooves which make accurate cutting difficult.

Tape is used for holding the design together as it is being assembled. Masking tape can be used although it must be treated carefully as it can stick so strongly that it may split the veneer or splinter the fibers as it is removed. Gummed brown paper is better as it can be removed by dampening.

A quick-setting glue such as balsa cement is also invaluable for holding the pieces of veneer together as the design is assembled. A thin layer of glue on the edges of the veneers to be joined will form a sufficiently strong bond.

Carbon paper is needed for transferring designs onto the veneer—use the black type as this will leave the finest of lines when used with a blunt-tipped awl (bodkin). The marking lines will hardly be visible when the veneer has been cut.

Basic techniques

Cutting. The best cutting methods to use are those where one cut piece of veneer is used as a template for the cutting of the neighboring piece; any irregularity in the cutting of the first pieces will then be transferred to the second and an exact fit will be achieved. This can be done by starting at one side of a design and working progressively across it (fig.1). Tape the two pieces of veneer together while making the cut, to ensure that they do not move out of position. Once the first cut has been made, cut the second sheet to the required shape and use it as a template for the third and so on.

Alternatively, use a sheet of "waste" veneer the same size as the overall design as a master template. Transfer the whole design to the master template using carbon paper and then cut out section by section.

As each section is cut out from the master, place this on top of the veneer and use it as a guide for cutting (fig.2). Again use tape to hold the two veneers in place as they are cut. Having cut out the new veneer, fit it back into the space in the template, securing it along the edges with balsa cement. Repeat this process until the whole design is assembled. The "waste" veneer can frequently be used as the background to a design.

When you have finished the cutting and assembling process, you will have a composite sheet of veneers held together with balsa glue and tape—this is now ready for glueing down onto the article to be decorated.

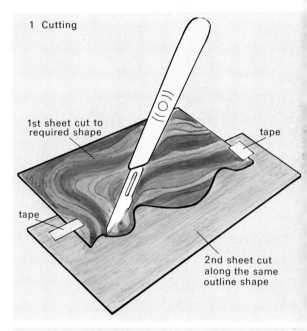

1 Cutting

1st sheet cut to required shape

tape

tape

2nd sheet cut along the same outline shape

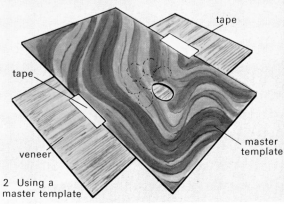

tape

tape

veneer

master template

2 Using a master template

immediately when the veneer and base are brought together, but this means that the design must be perfectly in position when it is placed on the base. Even after using a contact adhesive, keep the design under pressure with heavy weights for some hours afterwards.

Finishing. Remove any tape from the veneer and sand down using fine sandpaper and a sanding block. The block will ensure that the surface is absolutely flat and that you do not round the edges. Work carefully so that you do not sand through the veneer. When level, give the surface a final sanding with very fine (flour) sandpaper to polish the surface. Finish by applying a good quality colorless wax polish.

Box with a Japanese motif

A simple box is an ideal object for your first marquetry design—the one illustrated uses veneers of contrasting grains and colors to create a traditional Japanese motif.

You will need:

ready-made wooden box with a lid, and measuring approximately 15×14cm ($6 \times 5\frac{1}{2}$in) □ 1 sheet of mansonia, horse chestnut, harewood, ebony and walnut, each measuring 30.5×15cm (12×6in) □ knife and tools as described □ black carbon paper □ balsa cement □ contact adhesive.

Making the box top. Trace the design (fig.3) onto a piece of paper and transfer centrally onto the mansonia veneer. Cut out 1 of the sections of the mansonia and replace with the required veneer, using the method described previously. Using the diagram as a guide, continue placing the different veneers.

When the basic design is complete, insert the thin strips of veneer (these are known as "stringers"), which form the outer border as follows. Establish the area of mansonia to be actually stuck down onto the box lid, measure in 0.5cm ($\frac{1}{4}$in) from each edge and mark a pencil line parallel to the box edge. Then measure another 0.5cm ($\frac{1}{4}$in) and mark a 2nd line. Repeat for all 4 sides. Cut out the area between the 2 lines to give a rectangle containing the motif plus an outer mansonia border. Cut 4 strips 3mm ($\frac{1}{8}$in) wide from the ebony and horse chestnut for the stringers. The strips should be

Note: when cutting veneer, always hold the knife vertically and do *not* try to cut through the wood in one movement. Make a series of gentle cuts until the required piece is free—too much pressure on the knife will split the wood. When cutting a pointed shape, always cut *away* from the point to avoid splitting.

The baseboard. If you are decorating an existing object such as a box, then you have little control over the wood onto which the design will be glued. It should, however, be level and fairly thick. If the wood warps, the veneers will lift off the surface. If you are going to work on a new piece of wood, then the best material is plywood which, because of its layered

construction, is unlikely to warp. Do not use plywood that is less than 6mm ($\frac{1}{4}$in) thick.

Laying the picture. Before glueing the picture down, score the surface of the baseboard to provide a receptive surface for the glue. Use either resin wood glue or a contact adhesive to glue the veneer. Wood glue sets more slowly than contact adhesive, and this allows the design to be moved into position once it has been laid onto the board. However, considerable pressure needs to be exerted over the whole surface while the glue sets, to make sure that each piece of veneer is firmly stuck to the base. Contact adhesive overcomes this, as a strong bond is formed

Tracing pattern for Japanese motif

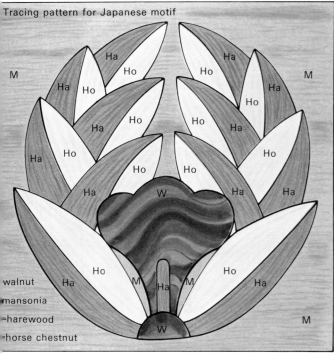

walnut
mansonia
=harewood
=horse chestnut

Positioning the stringers

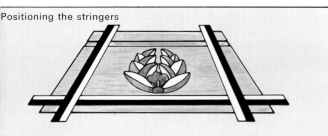

at least 1.5cm (½in) longer than the slots in the mansonia. Fix the strips into place with balsa cement as shown in fig.4. When all the stringers are in place, remove the excess by mitering the corners. Hold the knife blade absolutely vertically and chop diagonally through the stringers to form a 45° join. Glue the complete design to the box lid and sand down as described earlier.

Backgammon board

Marquetry need not be used for purely decorative purposes, as this splendid backgammon board proves.

You will need:

1 piece of 19mm (¾in) (13ply) plywood, 52 × 48cm (20½ × 19in) □ 30.5 × 15cm (12 × 6in) veneer: 6 sheets mansonia; 3 sheets wenge; 3 sheets sycamore; 4 sheets makore; 1 sheet horse chestnut □ knife and tools as described plus a steel straight-edge □ balsa cement □ contact adhesive.

Making the board. Mark out the baseboard using fig.5 as a guide to ensure the correct positioning of the pieces. Cut the mansonia along the grain into parallel strips, each 7cm (2¾in) wide. Join these strips together with balsa cement to form 4 sheets each measuring 21 × 30.5cm (8¼ × 12in) and each sheet consisting of 3 strips.

Note: if larger sheets of veneer were origi-

nally available, omit this process. Square off 1 end of each composite sheet of veneer. Measure 3.25cm (1¼in) down from the end and draw a line across. This line will be the "point end" line. From the same end, measure down 21cm (8¼in) and draw a line across. This will be the "point base" line.

On the "point end" line measure and make a mark, 1.75cm (1 1/16in) in from each side edge and then mark the veneer at 3.5cm (1⅜in) intervals from these points.

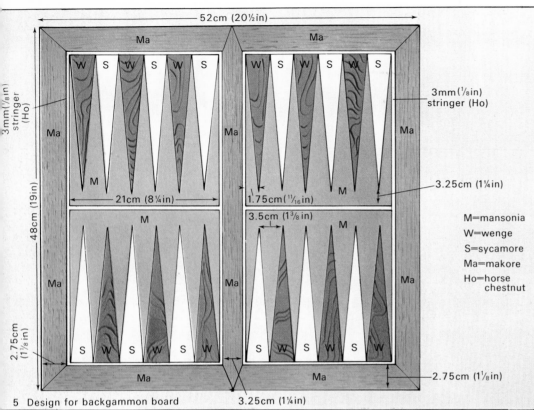

Ma

3mm(⅛in) stringer (Ho)

W S W S W S   W S W S W S

Ma   Ma   Ma

52cm (20½in)

M   M

21cm (8¼in)   1.75cm (¹¹⁄₁₆in)   3.25cm (1¼in)

3.5cm (1³⁄₈in)

M   M

Ma   Ma   Ma

S W S W S W   S W S W S W

Ma   Ma

48cm (19in)

2.75cm (1⅛in)

2.75cm (1⅛in)

3.25cm (1¼in)

M=mansonia
W=wenge
S=sycamore
Ma=makore
Ho=horse chestnut

5 Design for backgammon board

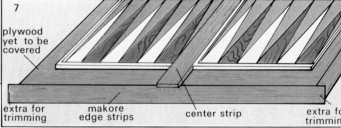

6 Cutting the wenge and sycamore points

"waste veneer"

allow this extra for trimming

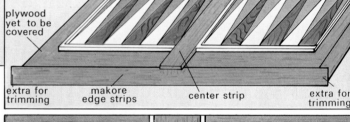

7

plywood yet to be covered

extra for trimming

makore edge strips

center strip

extra for trimming

This will give you 6 "point end" marks altogether.

On the "point base" line mark in 7 "point base" marks (including the side edges) at 3.5cm (1³⁄₈in) intervals.

Cut the veneer using the marks as a guide, running the knife gently along the steel straightedge until the veneer is cut through. Remember to cut away from the points. This will give a multi-pointed piece of mansonia which will be the "background" to the points. Repeat for the remaining 3 sheets of veneer.

Do not discard the waste veneer, but using it as a template, cut out alternate points of wenge and sycamore (fig.6) and fit them into the mansonia, using balsa cement. Repeat for all 4 quarters of the board.

Glue the sections of each board-half together with a 3mm (⅛in) wide stringer in between. Trim around each section to make sure they are perfectly square. Glue more 3mm (⅛in) horse chestnut stringers around all 4 sides, mitering each of the corners as described for the box top. Using contact

adhesive, stick down 1 board-half in the position marked on the baseboard. Keep under pressure while the glue sets.

Cut the makore lengthwise into 2 strips 3.25cm (1¼in) wide and 8 strips 2.75cm (1⅛in) wide. Square off the ends of the 2 wider strips and stick down next to the previously glued board-half to form the central bar. The makore should protrude beyond the top and bottom of the board to allow for trimming later. Stick down the 2nd board-half, butting it up against the central bar.

Cut the remaining sheet of makore into 8 strips 2.25cm (⅞in) wide and then, having squared the abutting ends, glue to the edges of the baseboard (fig.7). Trim the ends off and sand. Sand off the upper edge of the strips so that they are flush with the plywood. Shape the ends of the center strip as shown in fig.8 and glue down each of the 2.75cm (1⅛in) strips to fit all around, mitering the corners.

When all the glue has set thoroughly, sand and polish as for the box lid.

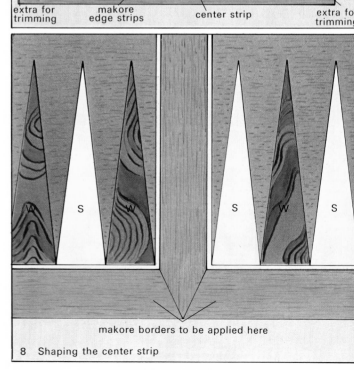

W   S   W   S   W   S

makore borders to be applied here

8 Shaping the center strip

A superbly ornate frame completes this miniature of Countess Frances Howard by Isaac Oliver.

In medieval times there were no distinct picture frames as such—pictures were part of Church decoration, integrated into the surrounding altarpiece or wall carving. Then in the 15th century paintings began to lose their solely religious function. Their use in home decoration meant that frames came to be regarded independently. At first frames were fairly austere in design, but gradually this gave way to rich carvings of foliage.

In Northern Europe frames were often of ebony or dark wood, lightened with the use of inlay. Gilded frames were also popular. During the 17th century, picture frames became extremely ornate, and veneers of many different woods and lacquers were used. The rich framed their pictures with silver; others imitated this with frames of silvered wood.

Since the beginning of the 20th century,

frames have generally tended to become much less elaborate in style.

Considering how expensive many picture frames are today, it is surprising that more people do not make their own. It takes very few tools and only a little practice to learn the basic techniques, and no matter how large or ornate the frame, these techniques do not vary.

Probably the most important step in framing a picture is the choice of color and style of the molding, and, if required, the color of the mounting board surround, all of which must complement and highlight the picture. The best way to get free advice is to visit frame shops or museums and galleries to study the way they treat their pictures. Pay particular attention to small drawings and paintings: how large the size or the surround is and the color of the frame and surround in relation to the picture.

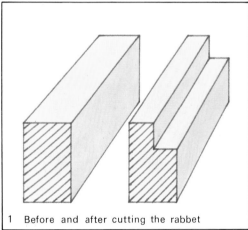

1   Before and after cutting the rabbet

A frame is made from moldings which are not, as the word implies, cast from molds, but are simply strips of wood which have been cut into various profiles. The rabbet (rebate) (fig.1) is a necessary part of all moldings as it provides a space at the back of the frame which conceals the edges of the glass, the picture and the backing boards. Today factories can cut the rabbet and the individual profile in one operation. Some of the styles generally obtainable are shown in cross-section in fig.2.

Traditionally, however, the framemaker would have cut the rabbet with a hand-

plane and would have used a variety of molding planes to shape the different profiles. Over the years he would have built up an impressive collection of these tools which were so finely made that many have now become collectors' items. In the example shown (fig.3) the bottom (a) of the plane would produce a half-round molding.

Constructing a frame
There are three basic steps in picture framing: cutting or mitering, joining and assembling.

Cutting (mitering). This stage is the most important. The ends to the four sides of the frame are cut off very accurately at an angle of 45°. This is made much easier by the use of either an old-fashioned miter box or one of the many devices on the market, all of which hold the piece of wood firmly and

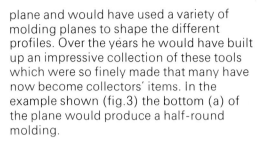

2   Types of molding

Scoop   Sloping   Flat

Reverse   Box   Half-round

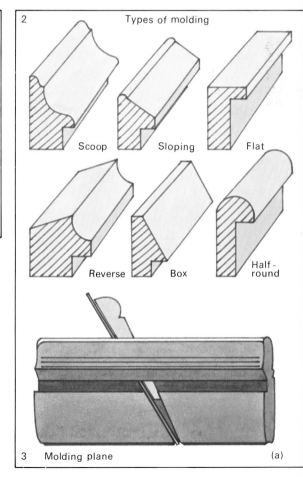

3   Molding plane   (a)

Framing your first picture

guide the saw at the correct angle at the same time so that the corners of the cut molding will fit flush together (see fig.4). The miter box you buy need not be expensive but it must have two sides and be at least 5cm (2in) high and with an inside width of about 7.5cm (3in). When you are working, mark the box by placing the saw in each of the slots in turn and pencil in the direction on the base of the box or make a light saw mark. You can use these as guidelines when measuring. The saw should be a tenon or back saw about 25cm (10in) long. It should have as many teeth as possible—at least 12 per 2.5cm (1in) for really smooth cuttings. If you are going to make several frames, it is well worth buying a really good saw with as many as 14 teeth to the same measurement.

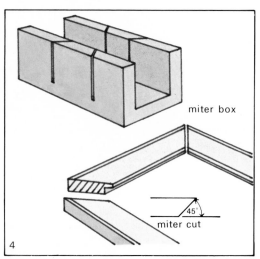

miter box

45°
miter cut

4

Joining. After the four pieces of molding have been cut to the correct length and the ends mitered, they must be joined together by glueing and nailing at the corners. The glueing is made easier if you tie a cord around the frame to hold it together while the glue dries. These cords can either be bought with special corner blocks to prevent them marking the frame, or you can easily make them yourself.
Once the adhesive has set, the corners should be reinforced with brads (panel pins) —small thin nails with narrow heads.
Assembling. This last stage requires less dexterity. To assemble the frame, pin the glass, picture and backing board into the

rabbet from the back, and finally add some hooks and a wire for hanging.

Framing your first picture
The basic components of a framed picture are the frame, glass, mounting board (optional), picture and backing board. The drawing (fig.5) shows the sequence in which these are assembled, but if the picture is quite large you may not need the mounting board.
Glass may be purchased from a glass shop. The mounting board should be a suitably colored cardboard to surround and complement the picture. The backing board should be thin hardboard or heavy cardboard.
You will need:
Tools and equipment: miter box □ steel ruler □ saw □ approximately 2m (2yd) nylon cord □ nail punch □ small hammer. Materials: frame molding (add 10cm (4in) to each dimension of the picture and add up the four lengths) □ mounting board □ glass to fit the rabbet 2mm ($\frac{1}{16}$in) thick □ backing board to fit the rabbet □ brads (panel pins) □ wire □ fine grade sandpaper □ wood adhesive □ corner blocks.
Making the frame. To determine the size of your frame, measure as shown in fig.6. These are the measurements for the rabbets and your glass and backing board will fit into this recess.
Cut off four lengths of molding to the required measurements. Check that the opposite sides are identical in length. Place the miter box so that the back of the molding is held firmly against the side of the box. Start sawing towards your body with the saw tilting slightly forward. As you begin to saw slowly and smoothly, level off the saw and then progress to the end with slow unhurried movements. Measure the required length of molding from the cut end and mark the other end ready to miter. Saw through the same way and repeat for the other lengths of molding. Check that the opposite pieces are identical and then lightly sand the ends with fine sandpaper (see fig.7). Place the adhesive on the cut ends and assemble the frame on a flat surface. Position the corner blocks. Tie a slip knot in the nylon cord as shown in fig.8 and pull one end to tighten it

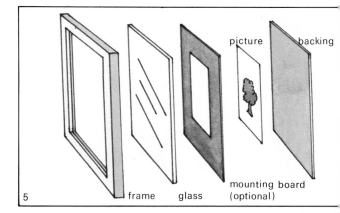

picture   backing

5   frame   glass   mounting board
(optional)

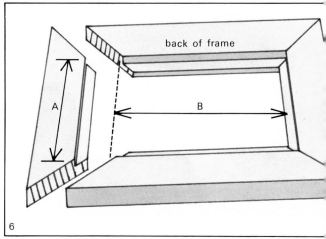

back of frame

A   B

6

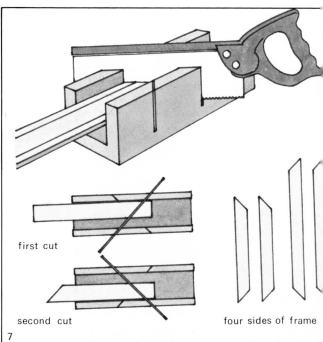

first cut

second cut   four sides of frame

7

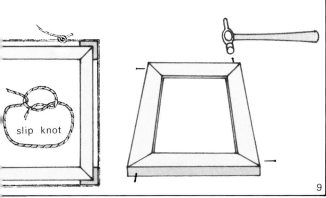

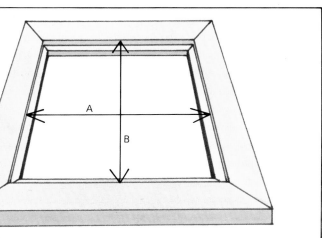

around the frame while the adhesive sets and dries.

Pin the corners carefully with small brads (fig.9). If possible, start the holes with a fine sharp tool such as a bradawl or a small drill bit. Use a nail punch to set the heads of the brads slightly below the surface of the wood. Measure the dimensions inside the rabbets at the back of the frame for a final check (fig.10). Deduct 2mm ($\frac{1}{16}$in) from this in each direction and cut the backing board to size. Order or buy glass to this size. Wax, paint or stain the frame as required. If using a mounting board, glue the picture to the front or cut a window into the board and glue the edges of the picture to the back (fig.11). The more fragile and delicate subjects can be simply held in position by pressing tightly between the glass and board.

Use small pins to hold everything tightly pressed against the glass. Drive these into the sides of the frame lightly but firmly. Cover the back with brown paper and make neat with brown adhesive tape to keep out dust and dirt. Finally add screw eyes and wire or cord to hang the picture safely (see fig. 12 : brown paper and tape are omitted for clarity).

This picture is the perfect example of choosing a mounting card that enhances the subject. Though the predominant color of the butterflies is white and pale yellow, the wing markings are orange and black, and it seems natural to choose the warmer color and emphasize this yet again in the choice of frame. A natural plain molding has been stained mahogany and then, for a touch of individuality, two fine lines have been etched into the wood with the point of a chisel.

As commercially made furniture becomes more and more expensive it is not surprising that carpentry has been taken up as a hobby by many people wishing to produce something that they are proud to have made themselves—and at a more realistic cost.

Carpentry or joinery is the craft of cutting and shaping wood so that it can be joined together to form furniture, fittings, etc. Although most items can be made using screws, nails and patent fixing methods, a real carpentry joint will usually prove both stronger and more attractive.

Types of wood
Wood falls into two types—hardwood and softwood. Hardwoods such as beech, oak and mahogany, come from trees with broad leaves, and as the name suggests, tend to be harder and more difficult to work than softwoods. They are more durable, have a better surface finish and will provide a better fit when jointed. Softwoods come from coniferous trees such as spruce, pine and Douglas fir and they all tend to have fairly pronounced knots. Wood bought from a do-it-yourself store will almost invariably be pine softwood. In general, softwoods are best for simple carpentry as they are easier to cut and work.

Tools
There are many different tools designed for carpentry, from the simple chisel and mallet to patent joint-making devices. With the following basic selection you will be able to tackle most joinery tasks.

Try square. This tool is used to make right-angled lines on wood. Line up the thick part with the edge of the plank, and the metal part will then give you an exact right angle.

Saws. The most useful types for normal joinery are the tenon saw and the panel saw. The more teeth a saw has per centimeter or per inch the finer the cut. All conventional saws have a "set", ie the teeth are slightly offset. This prevents clogging of the teeth when cutting and also means that the width of the cut made is greater than the saw blade itself. Remember this when cutting—always allow the width of the cut to extend into

the *waste* wood. The panel saw is used for cutting large areas, the tenon saw for making joints and for other accurate cutting. A pad saw is useful for cutting in awkward places such as curves.

Chisels. Chisels are for cutting wood, frequently across the grain, so it is essential to keep them sharp. A blunt chisel will split and fray the wood. The most useful for normal joinery are the bevel edge, mortise and firmer chisels and you will need two or three widths, for example 0.5cm ($\frac{1}{4}$in), 2cm ($\frac{3}{4}$in) and 2.5cm (1in). They can be used either with a wooden mallet or by hand pressure. By striking on the end with the palm of the hand, a good cutting action can be achieved.

Planes. Used for shaping and smoothing wood, planes are invaluable for reducing the width of planks.

Drill; brace and bit. Both are used for drilling holes in wood. A drill will make small holes, a brace and bit much larger ones.

Vise. This is a "must" for carpentry—a vise holds the wood steady while you work on it. A woodworking vise has wide flat jaws to prevent it from crushing the wood.

Ruler. This is an essential tool for accurate measuring. The traditional type for woodwork is made of wood and folds up with brass joints, but a steel tape or wooden ruler is just as effective.

Joints
The grain of the wood always runs along the length of a plank and it is important to remember this whenever you are working with wood, as chiseling or planing against or across the grain can cause splitting and cracking. Always chisel away from edges when cutting across the grain and in the direction of the grain when cutting or planing along the grain.

There are many different kinds of joint, all using for specific joining applications. The following two are the most useful for making basic shelving and storage units.

Mortise and tenon joint (fig.1a–d). This type is used to join horizontals to verticals and so is ideal for shelves. It employs a tenon formed in one of the pieces which slots into a mortise in the other, and is a very strong joint (a).

To make the mortise, measure the depth

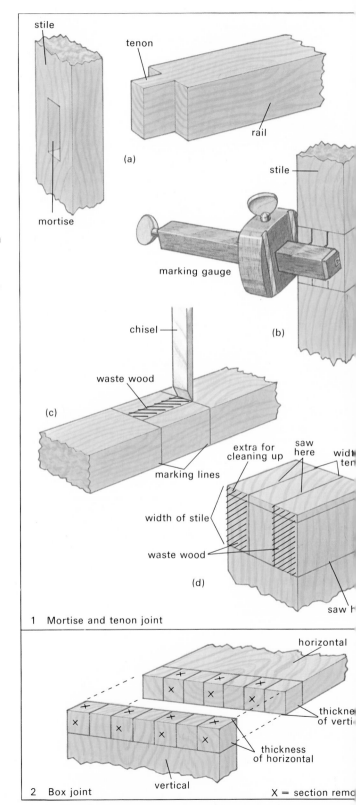

1 Mortise and tenon joint

2 Box joint

measuring, mark the width of the tenon along both sides *and* the end of the rail (d). With a tenon saw, cut down the sides of the tenon until you reach the shoulder line on each side. Cut along each shoulder cut, thus releasing the waste wood. If you have made the cuts accurately, the tenon will fit into the mortise easily but without being too loose.

Box joint (fig.2). This can be used for the corners of shelving units and is very strong. Measure along each plank the thickness of the plank which is to join it, plus an extra 3mm ($\frac{1}{8}$in) for cleaning up. Measure the planks and divide their width into an odd number of units of the same size. For example, divide a 17.5cm (7in) plank into seven 2.5cm (1in) units. Mark both horizontal and vertical joints with equally spaced lines extending over the end of the plank.

Using a tenon saw, cut vertically down the marked lines on each plank, allowing the thickness of the saw cut to extend into the waste wood. Cut down to the lines marked across each plank. Using a mortise or firmer chisel, remove the waste wood from alternate segments.

Cut both planks in this way to make an interlocking box joint.

Shelf unit

This simple, free-standing shelving system, using the joints described, can be adapted to whatever size you like. The shelf unit illustrated measures 66 × 56cm (26 × 22in) overall (without the small feet). To extend it, just add to the dimensions as you wish, remembering that the internal dimensions will be smaller than the exterior by twice the thickness of the planks. For a very large unit, you will need verticals at intervals of about 122cm (48in) to prevent the shelves from sagging under the weight of books etc. The diagram is for wood 170mm ($6\frac{3}{4}$in) wide by 19mm ($\frac{3}{4}$in) thick, but ask for 180mm (7in) by 25mm (1in) as planed wood is always smaller than its nominal size.

You will need:

3 planks of softwood 600 × 170 × 19mm ($23\frac{5}{8} \times 6\frac{3}{4} \times \frac{3}{4}$in) ; 2 planks 750 × 170 × 19mm ($29\frac{1}{2} \times 6\frac{3}{4} \times \frac{3}{4}$in) ; 1 plank 400 × 170 × 19mm ($15\frac{3}{4} \times 6\frac{3}{4} \times \frac{3}{4}$in) □ 4 small

head (lost-head) nails□tenon saw □2cm ($\frac{3}{4}$in) chisel□mallet□ruler□ marking gauge (optional)□try square□ woodworking adhesive□matt polyurethane sealer.

Making the shelves. Square off the planks to the dimensions shown in fig.3, remembering to allow a little extra for cleaning up the joints.

At B, make mortise and tenon joints as previously described. The horizontals should have 2 tenons at each end; each 3.75cm ($1\frac{1}{2}$in) wide (the waste wood is 3.25cm ($1\frac{1}{4}$in) wide.)

At A, make box joints as described with 9 units of 1.9cm ($\frac{3}{4}$in). The vertical (X) is not subject to sideways strain and can be fixed by glueing and driving 2 small head (lost-head) nails through the center and bottom shelves into the vertical plank.

When all the joints have been made, put the shelves together first without glue to make sure everything fits. If not, trim the joints as necessary. Glue the joints with woodworking adhesive and then assemble. Push the joints well in and keep under pressure while the glue sets, using clamps if you have them. Trim the surplus wood at the joints with a plane, chisel or by sanding all over. Finish by coating with matt polyurethane sealer.

of the rail and mark this on the stile, continuing the lines all around the wood using a try square. Then, using a marking gauge or by measuring, mark 2 parallel lines, the width of the tenon, on the inner and outer sides (b). Using a mortise or firmer chisel, chop out the waste wood, working from both sides (c).

Note: always cut vertically before you cut diagonally to remove a chip of wood.

To make the tenon, measure the depth of the stile along from the end of the rail and allowing at least 3mm ($\frac{1}{8}$in) extra to allow for cleaning up. Extend this line around the rail. Then, using the marking gauge or by

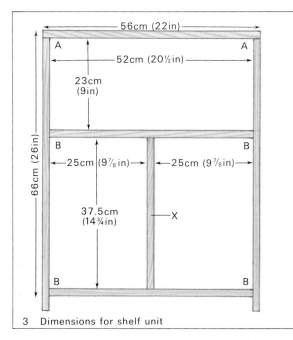

3 Dimensions for shelf unit

Pin art

Pin art is the art of creating pictures with nails and thread. With few materials and a small amount of time you can create a stylish wall panel, and even the first attempt can look astonishingly professional.

Basic materials
Board. Use a sheet of plywood or particle board (chipboard) which is at least 16mm ($\frac{5}{8}$in) thick. Paint it or cover it with felt, burlap (hessian), or any other cloth with an interesting texture. Cut the fabric at least 5cm (2in) larger than the board, and if it is likely to fray then also allow for a hem. Iron and hem if necessary.
Center the board onto the fabric and miter the corners. Spread fabric adhesive along both the edge of the board and the projecting edge of the fabric and allow it to dry. Then attach the fabric along one of the edges. When it is secure, attach the opposite edge, stretching the cloth as you go. Proceed with the other sides in the same way. Make the fabric absolutely secure by hammering in a few tacks around the glued edges.
Nails. The nails or "pins" should be at least 2cm ($\frac{3}{4}$in) long with small heads. Always buy more nails than the design requires as you may need to replace any that get damaged during hammering. Hammering is the most important part of the procedure. To make sure they are all straight and of equal depth, use a small block of wood of the required height as a gauge. Place it beside the nail and under the head.
Thread. Almost any kind of thread can be used—from crochet yarn and cotton to string, rope, raffia and even sisal. Make sure that the thread is the correct thickness for the size of the design and that the colors harmonize with the background. Scraps of knitting yarn may sometimes be used, although many designs require a long length of thread for a continuous threading pattern. Make joins and knots at the nail.

Experimenting with basic shapes
You can achieve a very pleasing geometric pattern with an arrangement of circles, curves and straight lines. Pictorial patterns can also be made with the same basic shapes, but it is advisable to practice with geometrical forms first until you are familiar

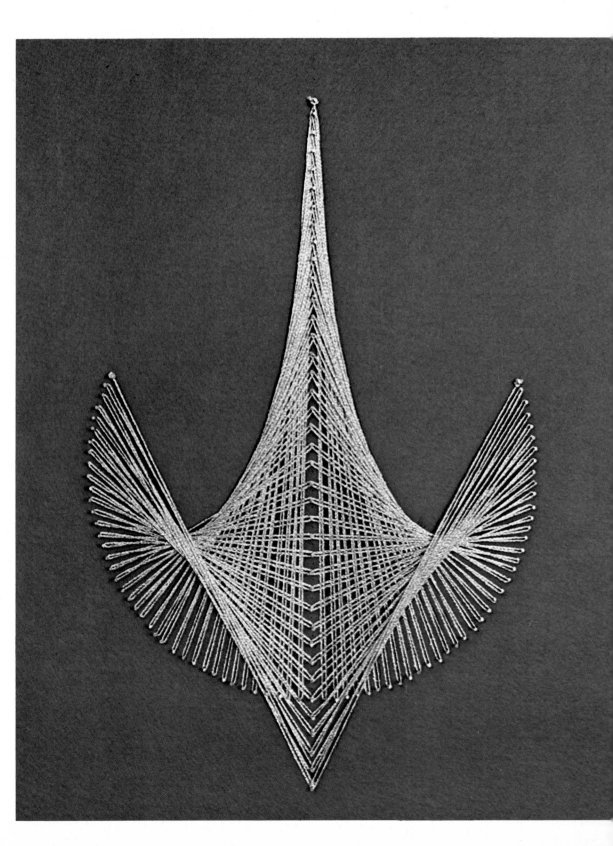

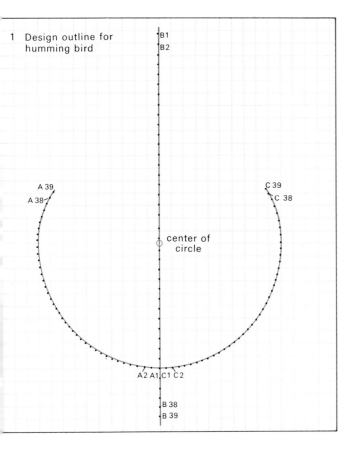

1 Design outline for humming bird

B1
B2

A 39
A 38

center of circle

C 39
C 38

A2 A1 C1 C2

B 38
B 39

Humming bird

This silver humming bird, mounted on a dark blue background, is a good example of how pin art can be used to produce a complex abstract design from a simple nail pattern and one of the standard threading techniques.

You will need:
46cm (18in) square board □ piece of felt 51cm (20in) square □ fabric adhesive □ graph paper for pattern □ 117 nails with small heads □ approximately 45m (50yd) thick silver thread □ compass □ ruler □ hammer.

Planning the design outline. Using fig.1 as a guide, make the pattern as follows. Draw a vertical line 38cm (15in) long down the center of the graph paper. Mark a point on the line, 17.5cm (7in) from the base, and with a compass, draw a circle with a radius of 12.5cm (5in). Mark off 39 points at 1cm ($\frac{3}{8}$in) intervals on the vertical line. Starting at the point where the line dissects the circle at the base, mark off 39 points at 0.5cm ($\frac{1}{4}$in) intervals in each direction around the perimeter of the circle, to give 79 points including that at the intersection.

Preparing the board. Cover the board with felt. Center the graph paper on the board and pin it to the felt. Carefully tap nails into all the points marked. When you have hammered in all the nails, carefully tear off the pattern.

Threading. Fasten the thread to B1, take it

Experimenting with nail patterns can produce imaginative designs such as the Chinese parasol (*above*) and the Roman galley (*below*).

down and around the outside of A1, take back to B2, pass around the outside and take to A2. Continue in this way until you reach B39. Take to A39 and fasten off. Fasten the thread to B1, take down to C1, pass around the outside, take back to B2, pass around the outside. Continue in the same way until you reach C39. Fasten off.

with the art and are able to visualize a picture from a bare skeleton of nails. Always keep the nail patterns simple and leave it to the thread to achieve a complexity of design. To begin, use an old board or piece of wood. For a simple arrangement, experiment with basic lines, curves and circles on a sheet of graph paper. Mark off the lines and circles into points of equal distance. Each line should have either the same number of points as the other lines, or a multiple number. For example if in three parallel lines one line is divided into three points, the other two lines must be divided into three, six or twelve points. Fix the pattern to a board with pins, then hammer nails through each point. Tear off the pattern and spend some time winding thread around the nails to make different designs. You will soon discover that different concentrations of thread can be used to create highlights and shadows, producing three-dimensional effects or variations in texture.

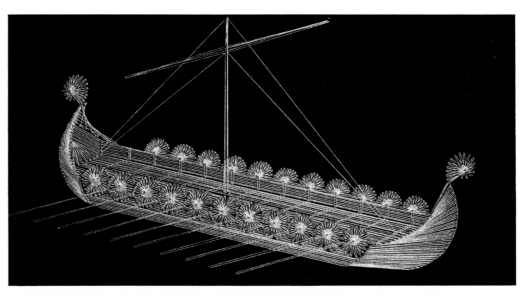

Glasswork

No-one knows exactly how glass, which is a mixture of sand, soda ash and limestone, was discovered, though the Roman writer Pliny has his own theory. He relates that some merchants were camping on a sandy estuary in Egypt. At night they placed their cooking pots on blocks of natron (a natural soda deposit) over the camp fire. Waking up in the morning, they discovered that the sand and soda had fused, forming a crude glass. Given that the temperature needed to fuse these two materials is very high, it seems unlikely that there is any truth in this story!

The earliest evidence of glass making dates from around 4000 BC when a turquoise glaze was applied to small clay ornaments. Not until 1500 BC were articles made entirely from glass, and then they were tiny items of jewelry, made exclusively for the luxury market. The main centers of production were in Egypt and Syria. The Egyptians developed the technique of "hollow

Selection of old glass bottles and jars.

The *Portland Vase*, dating from the 1st century AD, and displaying the superb technique of cameo cutting that was developed by the Romans.

ware," winding molten glass onto a core. Sometimes several layers were wound on, and the piece finally heated to fuse all the layers together.

The Romans were very interested in glass and established an industry in Rome itself employing craftsmen from Egypt. The early glassmakers worked glass as if it were gemstone, grinding it on a wheel. This was the method used for the Portland Vase. A layer of translucent white glass was fused onto a dark base and the cameo shapes were developed by grinding away the top layer.

About 50 BC came the greatest discovery in the history of glass making—the realization that glass could be blown like a soap bubble. This meant that glass now could be turned into shapes previously only possible with pottery and metal. This technique was never lost, though with the decline of the Roman empire many decorative techniques disappeared.

The glass produced in Europe during the Dark Ages was far less sophisticated in design and color. It was called *Waldglas* (Forest Glass) because the furnaces were wood-fired and a potash made from the ashes of woodland plants was used. From the 11th century, glass making was carried on in Italy, and by the 15th century Venice

Anglo-Saxon claw beaker, probably dating from the 6th century, and representative of the glassware known as *Waldglas*.

356

had become the European center for glass making, producing glass of remarkably beautiful colors and techniques. The trade was so competitive that craftsmen were condemned to death for treachery if they dared to leave Venice to practice their craft elsewhere.

Lampwork

Lampwork is the process of heating and manipulating glass tubes or rods over a flame. Until the introduction of the gas blowlamp in the 19th century, the traditional method of work was with an oil lamp and a pair of bellows.

Lampwork is especially suited to precision work, such as that required for making scientific and laboratory equipment. In 1665 Robert Hooke discovered that lenses could be made by melting glass in a flame. By 1690 many lampworkers were kept busy manufacturing glass eyes!

The discovery of borosilicate glass in 1914 was of great importance to lampworkers for it meant that this tough glass could be used extensively in mass production.

Equipment, tools and materials

The only equipment needed for lampwork is a gas cylinder and a burner or "lamp." Propane gas or natural gas cylinders are most commonly used. Make sure they are fitted with flash-back arrestors and if possible a set of non-return valves as well. The burner must be connected to the cylinder with the correct type of pressure tubing, fixed at both ends with hose-clips. You will also need an oxygen cylinder and regulator. Get an expert to check that the burner is working correctly before using it yourself.

Glass. A borosilicate "Pyrex" glass will give the best results, but almost any type of glass in tube or rod form is suitable as long as it will expand uniformly.

Tools. Your hands and eyes are the most important tools, but forceps can be used for holding the glass. Tools made from brass or steel sheet, or carbon rods or plates are used for shaping. Metal tools must be lubricated with beeswax before use to prevent them from sticking to the hot glass, but carbon tools can be used as they are. A glass-cutting knife is also necessary for trimming the rods to the size needed.

Basic techniques

Always work in a room that is well-ventilated but draft-free. Sit at a work-bench that is high enough to allow you to rest both elbows comfortably on it. The surface of the workbench should be fire-resistant. Wear a pair of dark glasses to protect your eyes from the sodium glare of hot glass. Keep a large metal bin beside you to take discarded bits of hot glass so that they are safely out of the way while you are working.

The basic glass tube or rod is held in both hands and rotated in the flame until the part to be worked becomes hot and pliable. The glass is then shaped while in this state, principally by blowing, bending, pushing and pulling. The skill of this type of glasswork lies in being able to rotate each end of the tube at the same speed so that the softened section of the glass will retain its cylindrical shape without becoming twisted or elongated, unless this effect is intentionally desired. It is essential to rotate the tubing uniformly to ensure even heating and to counteract the tendency of molten glass to droop. The glass should be rotated horizontally unless you deliberately want the glass to flow towards one end.

Left-hand hold. Support the weight of the glass in the left hand. With the palm of your hand facing downward, hold the glass rod with three fingers, and leave the thumb and forefinger free to rotate the glass. The second finger should be positioned at the point of balance, and the rod should be long enough to protrude from both sides of the left hand.

Right-hand hold. Hold the other end of the tube lightly in the right hand, this time with the palm facing upward. Support the glass with the second and third fingers at the point of balance. The thumb and forefinger are again left free to rotate the glass. Practice manipulating the rod, keeping the right hand and left hand synchronized.

Glass tree

This glass tree with twisted branches can be used as an ornament or as a stand for displaying rings and other jewelry. The gnarled effect is deliberate so that the many facets will catch and reflect the light. The finished piece is about 15cm (6in) high.

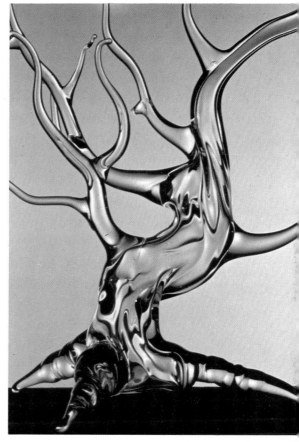

You will need:
0.6–1m (2–3ft) glass tubing with an outside diameter of 2.5cm (1in) □ equipment and tools as described.

Making the tree. Start with a length of tubing about 7.5–15cm (3–6in) and heat it in the flame to draw down strong "spear points" at each end so that you can hold it easily. Make grooves along the tube with a pointed tool in a random fashion. After grooving, twist and shape this main trunk section of the tree. Aim for a bold simple effect.

Note: the piece must be warmed gently in a softish flame after each separate stage of the work to ensure an overall strain release of the glass.

When the main trunk shape is done, add 3 root pieces to form a base for the tree so that it will be stable enough to stand on its own. Continue to shape the roots and add branches to complete the tree.

Joins must be strong where extra pieces

Drawing down the "spear points."

Making grooves along the tube.

Adding further grooves.

Starting to twist the main trunk.

Shaping the main trunk.

Adding the first root piece.

Shaping the root piece.

Shaping the branches.

are fused to the main trunk. Make sure that both surfaces are very hot before pressing together, and then allow a short pause or "freeze" before pulling the glass slightly to achieve the desired shape. Blowing the glass at this stage will help to give the correct shape and contours. Joins should not be sharply angled as these tend to be both mechanically weak and unsightly.

Ideally the piece should be annealed (cooled off) in a lehr, which is a special oven designed to allow the glass to cool at a controlled temperature. However, flame-annealing can be done quite satisfactorily without special equipment. To do this, heat the piece evenly all over to just below soft-

ening point and then allow to cool. It will help to place the piece in a tin box packed with special insulating material so that the piece cools very gradually and so is less liable to crack or shatter.

Engraving

Ever since glass was first made, ways have been found of decorating it. The Alexandrians are known to have used a wheel to cut designs on glass and the Romans applied many of the stoneworkers' techniques to glass with considerable skill. Cutting and enameling were the most common techniques used for decorating glass before the Middle Ages and the fine delicate work of the diamond point engraver that is so popular today did not appear until the 16th century. Venetian *cristallo* glass was ideal for diamond point engraving, being clear, colorless and very ductile. The Venetian craftsmen spread their engraving skills all over Europe and by the beginning of the 17th century many engraving centers had been established, the most influential being those at Hall in the Tirol, and at Nürnberg in Germany.

Cristallo glass at this time was the type of glass that most closely resembled natural rock crystal whose properties were so highly valued. Throughout the 17th century the search continued for ways of making glass that was even clearer and more brilliant. In the 1670s an Englishman, George Ravenscroft, found the answer. By adding lead oxide he was able to produce a lead crystal glass that could be made thicker and less brittle than *cristallo*, but was just as clear and brilliant. This new glass was suitable for wheel engraving as well as diamond point work. During the 18th century English lead crystal glass was being sent all over Europe and was especially favored by the Dutch engraver Frans Greenwood, who developed stippling as an engraving technique in its own right. The use of diamond point engraving declined during the 19th century, but from 1930 onwards the English engravers Laurence Whistler and William Wilson returned to the craft. Both men are self-taught and although their skill is the result of many years of patience, their work should be an inspiration to all beginners.

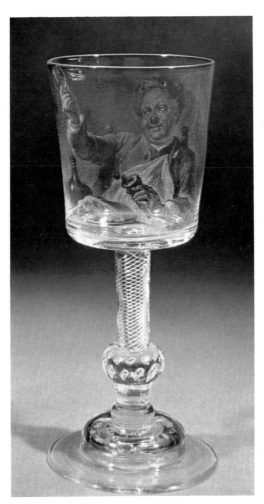

Goblet with a stippled design, engraved by the Dutch engraver Aert Schouman in 1751.

Glass

The first requirement is a suitable glass that is appropriate for engraving. The ideal glass is lead crystal as this has a soft texture which makes it responsive to the tools. Bottle and picture glass are both generally too brittle and do not have sufficient brilliance to take a good design. Soda glass, which has a small percentage of lead in it, can be used, although it will be more difficult to work on than crystal. It is, however, less expensive.

Practice first on a piece of sheet glass. Working on a flat surface to begin with will give you confidence in using different tools. As any engraving made on glass cannot be erased, you should then develop your skills by experimenting with techniques and designs on old glass jars.

Basic engraving methods

For most types of engraving you will need to work on a table or bench that is firm and has a flat even surface. The work area should be well-lit. Many engravers find that an adjustable lamp is best so that the direction of the light can be controlled so as to cause a minimum amount of reflection from the glass. A piece of black cloth, preferably velvet, should be placed under or inside the object being engraved.

It is advisable to wear a face mask for protection from the fine dust that is created during engraving.

Diamond or steel point pen. One common method of engraving is with a pen fitted with a diamond or steel (tungsten carbide) point. The advantage of a steel point is that it can be sharpened on a carborundum

Engraving with a diamond point.

Basic methods
Glass panel

Engraving with a dentist's drill.

block. Both types of point produce fine delicate effects and are therefore best suited to intricate designs covering a small area, especially fine linear work and crosshatching.

Stippling—a method of building up a shape from tiny dots—is usually done with a diamond or steel point pen. It will take many thousands of dots to produce an entire design, but the main thing to remember is that areas to be highlighted need more dots per square centimeter (inch) than those that recede or are in shadow. The pen should be held almost at right angles to the glass and tapped gently but firmly to mark the surface. Any force will chip the glass. Examine the work under a magnifying glass as you proceed to check this.

Dentist's drill. A dentist's drill is a popular tool as it is fitted with a flexible drive motor which runs at about 5,000 rpm, and results are therefore achieved relatively quickly. If possible, secure the motor on a strong hook above the workbench so that it is out of the way. The motor is controlled by means of a foot pedal and the drill itself has a chuck into which standard dental burrs are fitted. Use a carborundum burr for fill-

ing in areas of the design and a diamond burr for finer work and highlighting. The harder the glass the more quickly the burrs (especially the diamond ones) will wear out. Polishers are useful for giving a final satiny finish to an engraved area and can also be used to help disguise mistakes by smoothing over the surface of the glass.

Sandblasting. The principle of the sandblasting technique is to direct a jet of carborundum grit onto the glass at high pressure. Before the glass is sandblasted, particular areas are masked at different stages. This masking technique is explained more fully in the following project.

Sandblasters are standard equipment for most professional glassworkers and metalworkers, who can be approached to do the actual sandblasting for you.

Decorated glass panel

The decoration on this glass panel was done using a combination of drill engraving and sandblasting techniques. If you are unable to have the sandblasting done, a satisfactory design can still be completed by following the drill engraving instructions only. The finished panel should be 15—30cm (6—12in) square and can be used as a placemat cover or small table top.

You will need:

dentist's drill with 1 diamond burr and 1 pink carborundum burr □ sandblaster (optional) □ piece of glass at least 3mm ($\frac{1}{8}$in) thick □ 3 pieces of white self-adhesive fabric the same size as the glass □ piece of black paper the same size as the glass □ tracing paper for design □ carbon paper □ masking tape □ craft knife □ white crayon □ hard pencil.

Drawing the design. Copying the design from the photograph, make a detailed drawing in white crayon on black paper. Sketch in the various textures that you might use, for example on the bird. Mark in the shaded areas on the leaves so that it is clear how they overlap. The leaves will be sandblasted and the bird and foreground will be engraved with the drill.

If creating your own design, start with something fairly simple to begin with.

Preparing the glass. Cover one side of the glass with 3 layers of adhesive fabric. Smooth out any bubbles so that each layer

is perfectly smooth. Make a tracing of the drawing, marking in the outline of the shapes only. Number the leaves from 1 to 4, beginning with those nearest you.

Place the carbon paper face down over the adhesive sheet and tape the tracing face upwards on top. Draw over the outlines of the leaves with a sharp hard pencil. Remove the tracing and carbon paper. The design will now appear clearly on the adhesive fabric.

Sandblasting the leaves. Cut around the no.1 leaves with a craft knife and peel away the fabric sheet to leave the glass exposed on these areas.

Place the glass in the sandblasting machine and direct the jet at these cutout areas until about half the thickness of the glass has been worn away.

Cut away the fabric of the no.2 leaves and repeat the process but blasting less deeply than before. Use the tracing and carbon paper to renew any lines that have been

Columbine

eradicated. Continue with the no.3 and then the no.4 leaves. Each successive blast should be shallower than the previous one, and the final blast should be done to almost no depth.

Remove the adhesive fabric from the remaining areas and wash the glass thoroughly before engraving.

Engraving the bird and foreground. Begin with a diamond burr and lightly outline the bird, the grass and some of the stony foreground. Move on to some of the major feather patterns, particularly those of the wing and tail.

Using the carborundum burr, gradually fill in the bird. Work on the grass and the foreground next, lightly shading and filling in as appropriate.

Change back to a diamond burr and work on the highlighted areas, emphasizing the feathers that would be nearest you. This

will help make the bird look round.

Finishing the panel. Use the polisher to make finishing touches to the bird. Work lightly over the edge of the breast and the back, so making those parts recede to emphasize the solidity of the bird. Polish the stones in the foreground to give a shiny texture in contrast to the rough soil areas. If the sandblasted leaves require further detail, draw into them lightly with the drill.

Columbine

This beautiful columbine design was produced with a point using a combination of stippling and linear work. You can choose any flower or other suitable motif for the design. It is advisable to use a vase or glass with fairly straight sides.

You will need:

steel or diamond point □ vase or glass □ black paper for the design □ white crayon

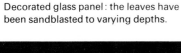

Decorated glass panel: the leaves have been sandblasted to varying depths.

After the sandblasting has been done the adhesive fabric is peeled off.

□ felt tip pen □ cellophane tape.

Drawing the design. Make a detailed drawing of the design with white crayon on black paper, carefully marking the shading to clarify the light and dark areas.

Tape the drawing to the inside of the vase or glass and trace around the outlines on the glass with a felt tip pen. Remove the drawing and keep it beside you for future reference.

Engraving. Begin by stippling the outlines so that they are established first before the tracing rubs off. Work carefully and slowly. Next stipple the most highlighted areas, remembering that several hundred dots per square centimeter (inch) will be needed. Considerably fewer dots will make up the darker areas.

Change to fine line work for details such as the stalk of the flower and the veins of the leaves. Some dark areas can also be emphasized by fine line work.

In around 300 BC the Romans made the first irons that were used for glass blowing to produce storage jars, bottles and drinking vessels. So began an ancient craft that is still carried on in much the same way today. Glass blowing is the art of controlling and shaping glass in a liquid form. It is unique as a craft material for you cannot touch it as you mold it.

To become a good blower you must acquire the skill of "reading" the glass and developing an ability to gauge the exact state of the glass as it is being formed and to match your movements with it. The glassworker's every action and the rhythm or "pace" of the glass must be coordinated precisely.

Glass blowing should only be attempted with adequate supervision in a properly equipped workshop. The main tools used during the glassworking process are described below.

Irons

Irons are used at different stages during the glass blowing process to support the glass while it is being worked. Irons are kept on a stand at the mouth of the furnace so that they heat up before use.

Blow iron or pipe. A blow iron is a hollow rod through which the glass worker blows after the glass has been gathered from the furnace.

Punty or pontil. This is a solid rod and after the glass has been blown it is transferred to the punty iron for shaping and finishing.

Gathering or bit irons. These solid rods are used to take extra glass from the furnace so that it can be added to the main piece. Handles and other pieces are added in this way.

Bench tools

Much of a glass blower's work of shaping and forming is done at a bench or "chair." The basic bench tools should be positioned on the bench in the order in which they will be used. Get into the habit of laying out the tools in the right order so that you can reach for them automatically and so concentrate on the process of forming the glass.

Jacks or tongs. These are the most useful tools of all and as well as being the main tools used for general shaping they are

used when "necking in" the shape just below the tip of the blow iron. This is where the piece will be "cracked off" when it is transferred from the blow iron to the punty.

Shears. These are used for trimming uneven edges.

File. This is used when cracking off on the necking-in line.

Tweezers. When extra glass is added to decorate or create patterns on a piece, tweezers are used for pinching and pulling the hot glass as it is being applied.

Blocks. These are not, strictly speaking, bench tools, but are generally kept in a bucket on the right-hand side of the bench. Blocks are usually made of wood and are used for centering and shaping the glass on the blow iron after each gather.

Basic techniques

Undoubtedly the greatest difficulty experienced by the beginner is that of keeping the molten glass under control and centered on the end of the blow iron. The first stage, however, is to gather the glass from the furnace.

First gather. When the tip of the blow iron is cherry red, put the blow iron into the furnace and lay it on the surface of the glass. Rotate the iron a couple of times and then still rotating it, withdraw the iron from the furnace. All manipulations are quicker when the glass is hot straight from the furnace, but should become slower as the glass cools and "stiffens."

Blocking. After withdrawing the iron from the furnace move across to the bench, still rotating the iron to prevent the glass from dripping and to keep it centered. Sit down at the bench. The next stage is to block the glass. The purpose of blocking is to reduce the thickness of glass around the end of the iron and to push as much glass as possible beyond the end of the iron. Blocking also forms the glass into an even ball and chills the surface of the glass so that it will acquire a "skin" which will contain the bubble when blown. The glass should not be overblocked as this will cool it down too much, so making it more difficult to blow.

First blow. Once a controlled shape has been achieved the first bubble can be blown. To do this hold the iron so that it

Blocking the glass.

Rotating the iron.

Reheating the piece.

Shaping the piece.

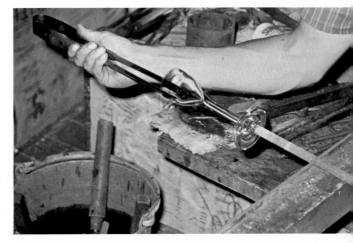
Shaping the rim.

cking in.

The second blow.

rther shaping.

Transferring the piece to the punty.

lding glass for decoration.

Trimming.

The finished piece ready for annealing.

points downwards at an angle. Use the arm of the bench for support so that you can rotate the iron while blowing and still keep the glass centered.

If the glass is at the proper working temperature at this stage very little pressure is required to blow the first bubble. The first bubble should be kept small and is only blown to the correct size after the second gather.

Necking in. This is done after the first blow. Necking in is important as the groove made will allow the piece to be transferred easily from the blow iron to the punty later. Roll the blow iron along the bench and use the jacks to indent a shallow groove on the bubble just beyond the end of the blow iron.

Second gather. A second gather is made when the glass is sufficiently cool. This moment can only be gauged with experience and practice, but if the second gather is made too early the bubble will collapse inside the new layer of hot glass. After the second gather, block as before and then blow again. The bubble should be bigger this time than before.

Reheating. The piece should be reheated frequently as it is being blown and shaped on the blow iron. If the piece is allowed to get too cool the glass will crack and fall off the blow iron. To reheat, place the piece in the furnace with the iron resting on the stand. Rotate the iron on the stand as the piece warms up to keep the glass centered.

Shaping. While the glass is on the blow iron it can be shaped in a number of ways. It can be formed by blocks, or a steel plate on a stand (known as a "marver") can be used to produce an effect similar to blocking. Tweezers and shears are used to decorate and trim the piece. If the iron is swung back and forth the piece will become elongated. Again the right temperature and the correct swinging action are needed to keep the glass under control. To achieve a desired shape it is necessary to integrate all these processes of blowing, blocking, swinging and necking in. There is no set way of manipulating the glass and all glass makers have their own methods of working, being ready to make adjustments as the glass dictates.

Transferring the piece to the punty. When

the glass is the required shape and size it is ready to be transferred to the punty. First flatten the bottom of the piece with the jacks or a wooden board. Heat the punty to below red heat and make a small gather from the furnace. This will help the punty to stick easily to the center of the base of the piece. The glass on the punty should stick firmly enough to allow the finishing process to be carried out, yet should be weak enough to break cleanly away from the form without damaging it when finished. There are several methods of creating this bond, the most popular being to cut two grooves in a cross shape in the glass on the punty to give four small points which at-attach the punty to the piece.

Guide the punty onto the base of the piece and attach it by pressing. A second person is usually needed to help with this. Pick up the file and score a line around the form where it has been necked in. Tap the blow iron with the file to break the glass away. With the piece now on the punty, reheat carefully. If the piece is put into the furnace too quickly it will usually crack around the neck. First place the punty in the mouth of the furnace to reheat gradually and then push it slowly into the body of the furnace. This gradual reheating has a valuable side effect in that it helps the glass to stiffen and so keeps the piece centered.

Further shaping. To make a closed or bottle-shaped form, most of the work is done on the outside of the piece. Use jacks to pinch the form in and to pull out the neck. For open shapes the tools are worked on the inside surface of the form. Close the jacks and place them inside the piece, rotating the punty at the same time. Slowly release the pressure of the jacks so that the arms open, and then push the lip or rim of the piece outwards. Further opening and forming can be done by pressing the jacks gently down on the rim from the inside.

Annealing. This is the process of cooling the finished glass at a controlled temperature. Once the piece has been knocked off the punty it is placed into a heated oven known as a "lehr" to cool evenly. If left in the open air to cool the surface of glass will contract more quickly than the rest and so cause the piece to shatter.

Decoration. When the piece has cooled

down sufficiently, remove it from the lehr. Various cold processes such as cutting and engraving can now be used to decorate the piece.

Stained glass

The term "stained glass" simply means any colored glass, but over the years it has tended to be applied almost exclusively to leaded windows of colored glass set in some kind of framework. Stained glass

Detail from the Jesse-tree window (C1145) at Chartres Cathedral, France.

windows were rare before the 12th century, but some of the finest work ever produced in the 100 years after 1145 can still be seen at Chartres Cathedral in France and Canterbury Cathedral in England. The *Five Prophets*—five pictorial windows in Augsburg Cathedral in Germany—are dated from about 1125 and are the earliest surviving examples of complete windows.

Glass and lead
Basic techniques

By the late 16th century, stained glass had begun to appear in secular buildings as well as in the cathedrals of Europe. These early secular pieces were mainly heraldic panels. The great period for domestic stained glass, however, began in England in the middle of the 19th century with the work of William Morris and Edward Burne-Jones and was continued in the United States by the designer Louis Comfort Tiffany and the architect Frank Lloyd Wright. Simple stained glass work can be done at home with the basic materials of glass and lead and a few essential tools.

Glass and lead
Machine-made glass. There are many different types of white and colored machine-made glass. White glass can be clear, frosted or patterned and colored glass can be plain or patterned.

"Antique" glass. This is another name for handmade glass. It is more expensive than machine-made glass and may be more difficult to obtain but it is a superior material to work with. Antique glass is made either in a single color (known as "pot") or can be one color fused onto white or another color (known as "flashed"). Antique glass can also be streaky—consisting of one or more colors—and with large or small bubbles in it.

Lead. Lead is commonly sold in lengths of approximately 1.5m (5ft) known as "calmes" or "cames." Widths vary from about 5mm ($\frac{3}{16}$in) to 12mm ($\frac{1}{2}$in). The calmes are I-shaped in section and are either finished square (fig.1a) or round (fig.1b).

Tools
Glass cutter and pliers. A simple glass cutter is needed to cut the basic glass shapes. For more difficult shapes and trimming, use a fine pair of pliers. Pliers are also used for bending the lead.

Lathekin. This is used for flattening the lead before it is cut. Make one yourself from a block of 6mm ($\frac{1}{4}$in) hardwood measuring 3×10cm ($1\frac{1}{4} \times 4$in). Shape one corner as shown in fig.2.

Cutting knife. The best kind of knife for cutting lead is a palette knife cut down to about 7.5cm (3in) and sharpened.

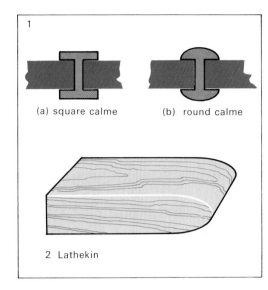

(a) square calme   (b) round calme

2 Lathekin

Soldering iron. When the lead has been cut it is soldered with an iron. This should not be too small as the lead and glass will soak up the heat. The soldering iron should be fitted with a 0.5cm ($\frac{1}{4}$in) diameter copper bit. You will also need a small flat file for cleaning and a tin can for "tinning" the soldering iron.

Horseshoe nails. These are obtainable from a blacksmith or farrier and are used to keep the glass and lead in position before soldering. A wire brush is used to clean them.

Basic techniques
Drawing the design. The first thing to be decided is the design. Draw this to full size on tracing paper and mark in the position for the leading, making sure that the correct width of the leads is shown. Mark in the center line on each lead. This should be 1.5mm ($\frac{1}{16}$in) thick and represents the heart of the lead. This center line or "cutline" is used when cutting the glass so that it will fit properly.

Cutting the glass. Practice cutting first on any scraps of glass other than plate glass or safety glass. Take the cutter and hold it between your index finger and second finger, supporting the underside with your thumb. Press your index finger down on the serrated top of the cutter. Make a score line by holding the cutter in a vertical position and drawing it firmly across the surface of the glass. Do not score too deeply or the glass will chip.

If you are cutting a straight line place the glass on a straight edge and apply even pressure on either side of the score line to break it cleanly. If you are cutting a curved line, tap the underside of the score line with the handle end of the cutter. Support both sides of the glass while tapping it with the cutter. When you can see and hear that the glass has broken through, pull both halves gently apart.

"Grozing"—cutting or trimming glass with pliers—should also be practiced on scraps of glass.

Painting the glass. If you intend to stain the glass yourself you will need paint medium which comes in powder form and is composed of glass dust and iron oxide, and a flux mixed together with gum and acetic acid. The glass is then fired in a kiln at about 600°C (1112°F) to make the color permanent. However, painting is a difficult job and because of the special equipment required, it is not recommended for beginners. Instead use colored glass as described earlier.

Preparing the lead. The calme of lead must be prepared before use. First straighten it out roughly by hand. Then bend the calme at right angles, 2.5cm (1in) from each end. Tighten one end in a vise and, holding the other end in a pair of pliers, pull the calme firmly and evenly. This should stretch the lead sufficiently.

Note: if you do not have a vise, stretch the lead by placing one end under your heel. Place the lead on the workbench and flatten all four flanges carefully with a lathekin. The lead is now ready for cutting.

Cutting the lead. Take a rough measurement from the drawing to find the length of each piece of lead and allow a little extra at each end. To cut the lead hold the knife vertically and rock it gently across the lead from side to side while applying pressure. The important thing is not to collapse the lead.

Assembling the glass and lead. For this you should work on a wooden board slightly larger than the finished piece. Place the pieces of glass in the correct position and fit each length of lead around the glass, taking care not to wrinkle the lead. Hold the lead in place around the glass by hammering horseshoe nails into the board at

Basic techniques
Hanging flower

strategic places. Put something such as a scrap of lead between the lead and the nail to avoid damaging the outer edge of the lead. Working outward from the corner, lead in each piece of glass, pushing the leads in tightly so that they fit firmly and butt neatly against each other.

Soldering. Before using the soldering iron, clean it with a file and "tin" it by rubbing it on a tin can. Heat the soldering iron and in the meantime clean the joins of the assembled piece with a wire brush. Apply flux to all the joins and then solder them. Judging the right amount of solder is a matter of practice. If too little is used the join will be weak but if too much is used the join will look messy. Make sure too, that the iron is not so hot that it melts the leads.

Remove the nails from the board, turn the piece over, and solder all the joins on the other side in the same way. Support the piece when turning it over so that it does not bend and become distorted.

Cementing. This is done to make the piece waterproof, which is particularly important if the stained glass is intended for a window. Make a mixture of putty and vegetable black and push it firmly under the flanges of the leads on both sides of the piece.

Blacking the leads. Leads are not intended to distract the eye, so to make them less conspicuous they should be made as dark as possible. The easiest way to do this is to apply grateblack with a cloth. Finish by brushing with an ordinary shoe brush.

Hanging flower

This stained glass flower will look most effective if hung in a window to catch the light. It measures approximately 25 × 16cm (10 × 6½in).

You will need:
streaky purple glass □ green "pot" glass □ 1 calme of 6mm (¼in) lead □ 1 calme of 5mm (3/16in) lead □ soldering iron □ 1 stick of solder □ 1 stick of flux □ tools as described □ wooden board slightly larger than the design □ tracing paper for design □ horseshoe nails □ wide felt tip pen □ short length of strong thick copper wire for loop □ length of silver chain.

Drawing the design. Draw the design from the graph (fig.3) in which 1 square equals 2cm (¾in). Mark in the center line of the

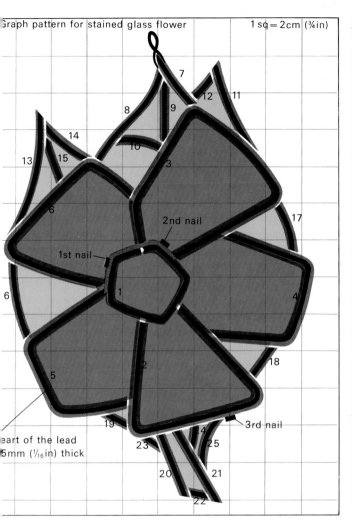

Graph pattern for stained glass flower   1 sq = 2cm (¾in)

7
12
11
8
9
14
10
13
15
3
6
2nd nail
1st nail
17
1
4
18
5
2
19
16
3rd nail
eart of the lead
5mm (¹⁄₁₆in) thick
23
24
25
20
21
22

A very effective use of stained glass is shown in this modern skylight designed and made by Michael King.

leads with a 1.5mm ($\frac{1}{16}$in) line as indicated, using a felt tip pen.

Selecting the glass. Take the design to your glass supplier so that you can choose the right quantity of a suitable glass. Select glass that is easy to cut accurately and bear in mind that the colors used for the petals of the flower should be stronger than those used for the leaves.

Cutting the glass. Place the glass on the drawing and, following the edge of the cut-line, cut out all the pieces as accurately as possible with the glass cutter. Trim with the pliers if necessary. As a final check, place all the pieces in position on the drawing. If any pieces overlap they will have to be "grozed" with the pliers. If there are any gaps greater than 1.5mm ($\frac{1}{16}$in) between the pieces, the glass should be recut.

Leading. Use the 6mm ($\frac{1}{4}$in) calme for the flower outlines (1–6) and the 5mm ($\frac{3}{16}$in) calme for the leaf outlines (7–25). The reason for this difference in width is that light will tend to flood around the leads, so making them appear thinner. The inner (thicker) leads will seem to be the same size as the outer (thinner) leads when the piece is hung.

Put the drawing on top of the wooden board face up and place the glass cut for the flower center in position. Measure and cut the lead as described earlier and fit it around the glass. The join will look neater if it is made at one of the junctions with a petal. Keep the lead in place with one or

two horseshoe nails.

Continue to fit the leads in the order shown in fig.3, repositioning the nails as necessary to keep the piece rigid. If preferred, the flower section can be soldered before you move on to the leaves.

Soldering. First clean the lead joins with a wire brush, then check that everything is in position. Apply flux and solder on both sides of the piece as described previously.

Making the loop for hanging. Bend a 4cm ($1\frac{1}{2}$in) length of copper wire into a loop. This will be attached to the piece at the tip of the middle leaf section as shown in fig.3. Clean the loop thoroughly, apply flux and solder in position, supporting the flower so that it is upright. Blacken the leads as described earlier and hang the piece from a silver chain.

Papercraft

The forerunner of paper was papyrus, processed from the papyrus reed, which grew abundantly along the River Nile in Ancient Egypt. Evidence of Egyptian papyrus, dating from the 3rd century BC, has been found in the form of numerous letters and documents preserved in sealed jars within tombs.

Papyrus sheets were made by removing the fibrous layers from the stem of the reed, and spreading them out side by side to form a sheet. More layers were placed at right angles to the first sheet and the two sets were glued together, probably by moistening with river water or with a paste made from wheat flour.

Papermaking as we know it today originated in China in about 105 AD, during the Eastern Han Dynasty. Under the Emperor Ho Ti, the Minister of Agriculture, T'sai Lun, began experimenting to produce a new material by breaking the inner bark of mulberry trees into fibers and then pounding them into sheets. This new type of paper replaced the traditional writing materials of bamboo and silk. T'sai Lun has been venerated by generations of Oriental artisans ever since as the god of the paper-makers. Later, the Chinese discovered that paper could also be made from cotton and linen rags, hemp and old fishing nets.

In the 8th century, an attack by the Chinese on the Arabs of Samarkand resulted in the capture of many Chinese prisoners. They were exhorted to teach their craft and thus the art of papermaking spread to the Arab world. By the 9th century, papermaking had spread to Egypt, thereby ending over 4,000 years of the use of papyrus. Papermaking was introduced to Europe in the 12th century with the Moorish conquest of Spain, and to North America with the Spanish domination of Mexico in the 16th century. The first paper mill to be established in the American colonies was in 1690, at Germantown, Pennsylvania. For several hundred years, paper was made by breaking down rags into fiber. It

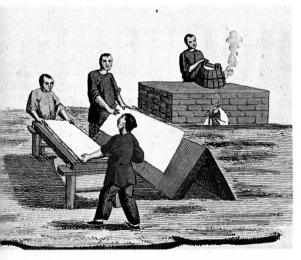

The process of papermaking in ancient China. Stage 1, bamboo shoots are stripped of the outer covering, cut lengthwise, pounded until flattened and soaked in water until the plant fibers dissolve. Stage 2, the fibers are pounded to a pulp. Stage 3, the pulp is heated and left to dry.

Early 8th century parchment manuscript; the art of papermaking was then still unknown in Europe.

was not until 1840, with the process invented by a German, Friedrich Keller, that paper was made by reducing logs into a fibrous pulp. This process was refined by 1867 by an American, Benjamin Tilghman, and so began the technique used in the modern paper industry today.

Types of paper
Paper is one of the most versatile materials available for craft work. It comes in many different qualities, finishes, thicknesses and colors. Construction (cartridge) paper, for example, is most commonly used for drawing and water color, whereas thicker paper with a rougher textured surface, is ideal for pastel and charcoal work. Both these types of paper can be used for paper sculpture. Smooth cover paper folds and holds a shape well and is suitable for

Three greeting cards

All colors and types of paper make up these decorative windows.

origami as well as paper sculpture. For paper flowers and all kinds of festive decorations, tissue paper and crepe papers are best, especially as they are generally available in many attractive colors. Lacy paper doilies and exquisite Japanese papers, which are often made with butterflies, leaves and other motifs set into the sheets, can be used for delicate effects. Use thin cardboard or thick paper for mounting and displaying finished work, or for paper sculpture and greeting cards.

Three greeting cards

A specially designed card is a pleasure to receive and fun to make. You can experiment with the classical flat-surfaced card or with pop-out and accordion effects.

Hearts and flowers

This romantic Valentine is decorated in an old-fashioned style with a collage of scrapbook cutouts. The finished card measures 25 × 20cm (10 × 8in).

You will need:
1 sheet of dark pink thick paper or thin cardboard, 50 × 40cm (20 × 16in) □ 1 sheet each of red, light pink, dark pink and

patterned paper for hearts □ scrapbook cutouts □ 2 paper doilies □ glue.
Making the card. If you are using thick paper, fold it in half, placing the two 40cm (16in) edges together. Then fold in half again so that the two 25cm (10in) edges are together and form a card. If you are using cardboard, mark in fold lines first in pencil on the reverse side. Using a ruler as a cutting guide, make a slight incision along the lines with the tip of a sharp knife. Press gently to avoid cutting through the cardboard completely. You will now be able to fold the cardboard so that it has sharply creased edges.

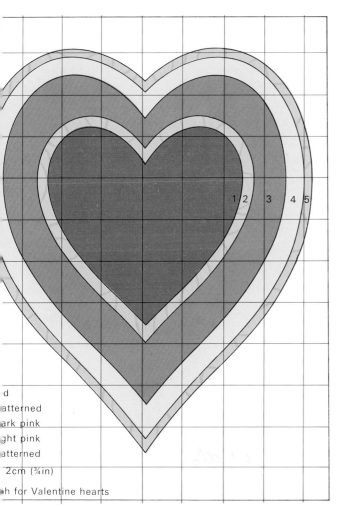

d
atterned
ark pink
ght pink
atterned

2cm (¾in)

h for Valentine hearts

You will need:
1 sheet of yellow thick paper or thin cardboard, 28 × 23cm (11 × 9in) ☐ 1 piece of fairly sturdy green patterned paper, 50 × 12.5cm (20 × 5in) ☐ tracing paper ☐ glue.

Making the card. Fold the sheet of yellow paper in half, placing the two 28cm (11in) edges together. Now fold in half again so that the two 11.5cm (4½in) edges are together and form a card. If you are using thin cardboard, score and fold as described for the Valentine card.

Making the cat. Cut a strip measuring 50 × 5.5cm (20 × 2¼in) from the green patterned paper. Mark points along the strip at 2.5cm (1in) intervals. Fold the paper sharply at these points, reversing the paper for alternate folds to form the accordion. Glue 1 end of the accordion to 1 side of the inside of the card, 2cm (¾in) up from the bottom edge and 6.5cm (2½in) from the center fold. Glue the other end of the accordion to the opposite side of the card so that it will open and close easily. Do this either by measuring carefully and then glueing the end of the accordion in position, or by glueing it while the accordion is closed, and then closing the card onto it.

Trace the cat's head, legs and tail (fig.2a,b and c) and cut out from the remainder of the patterned paper. Glue into position. Draw the eyes and nose or cut them from contrasting scraps of paper and glue on.

Birthday cake card
The birthday cake card has a simple pop-out cake shape on the inside fold. The design can easily be adapted to make a different pop-out such as a butterfly, a person, or anything of equal proportions along the sides. The finished card measures 15 × 14cm (6 × 5½in) when closed.

You will need:
1 sheet of white construction (cartridge) paper, 30 × 28cm (12 × 11in) ☐ water-color paints or felt-tip pens.

Making the card. Fold the paper in half, placing the two 30cm (12in) edges together. Fold the paper in half again so that the two 15cm (6in) edges are together and form a card.
Now open out the card completely and

2 Tracing pattern for accordion cat

(a)

cut 4

(b)

(c)

fold again, this time by placing the 28cm (11in) sides together. Copy the half cake shape (fig.3) and draw the design on the bottom half of the card and up to the folded edge as shown.

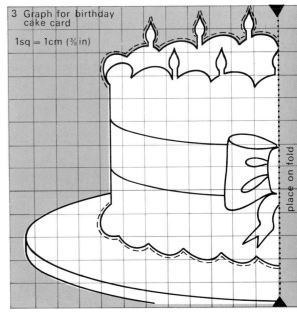

3 Graph for birthday cake card

1sq = 1cm (⅜in)

place on fold

Making the collage. The graph (fig.1) in which 1 square equals 2cm (¾in), gives 5 heart shapes. Draw each heart onto the appropriate paper to the size indicated, then glue heart shape 4 onto 5 and 3 onto 4 and so on. Cut the borders from the paper doilies and glue to the underside of the heart motif to form a lacy trimming. Glue a flower cutout in each corner of the card, then glue the heart shape in position in the center of the card. Finally, glue a cutout shape of flowers or linked hands in position in the center of the heart shape.

Accordion cat card
This charming card has an accordion fold of paper which forms the cat's body when the card is opened. The finished card is 14 × 11.5cm (5½ × 4½in) when closed.

Cut out the cake shape through both layers of paper along the top and bottom edges as indicated. Do *not* cut down the sides of the cake shape as these form the hinges for the pop-out.

Now open out the card again and fold as for the first time with the 30cm (12in) edges together and then the 15cm (6in) edges together. Fold out the cake shape creasing down each side. Color the cake and background with water-colors or felt-tip pens.

Paper sculpture

Although the folding of paper to form objects has enjoyed much popularity throughout the ages, it was not until the beginning of the 20th century that it became acknowledged as a serious art form.

Until the last century, modeling from paper had been considered merely an enjoyable pastime. It achieved its highest expression as a peasant craft in the Balkan countries, where paper shapes became part of the rituals of everyday life: decorations and toys were made to celebrate festive occasions, and paper flowers were made to adorn shrines. Modeling with paper also gained great favor with the Victorians, with such objects as doilies, woven baskets and tea caddies.

The German art movement, the Bauhaus, which achieved importance after World War I and was primarily concerned with the principles of artistic structure and construction, explored the potential of paper—especially in relation to architectural structures. They experimented with paper by folding it into three-dimensional structures to create different forms as well as to test the qualities of paper—such as strength, stress and tension—as a material for construction. The Bauhaus movement was also to have an enormous influence on the design of commercial products, packaging, advertising, home furniture and decoration. This development eventually led to the acceptance of paper sculpture as an art form. Cubist sculpture often took paper as its medium, and the early reliefs by Pablo Picasso in 1914 from cardboard and paper were major contributions to modern sculpture. Paper constructions by Braque also had a great influence, especially on the sculptor Henri Laurens.

In the Manifesto of Futurist Sculpture, 1913, Boccioni advocated, among other materials, the use of cardboard and the rejection of the traditional marble and bronze. Traces of Futurism, especially in regard to their preference of new materials, can be found in the Russian movement, Constructivism, especially in the works of Naum Gabo, whose constructions in cardboard were an attempt to define spatial volumes. Sculpting in paper was also incorporated into the Dada and Surrealist movements.

Due to the limitation of form and the techniques available, paper sculpture is at its best when removed from a naturalistic representation. Provided some care is taken with proportion, the simplification of form—to the point of becoming basic—at once produces an aesthetically pleasing and stimulating effect.

Basic materials

Paper sculpture in its purest form should be of white paper, using a variety of different thicknesses and textured surfaces to give interest to the design. However, colored papers come into their own on festive occasions such as Christmas, with decorations in gold, silver, red, blue and green for the tree or table. Colored paper is also suitable for fun sculpture, mobiles, toys, cake frills, flowers, lampshades and costume dolls.

Paper. Most types of paper, from fine Japanese rice paper to thick mounting cardboard, with all the varieties in between, such as crepe, tissue, embossed, grained, corrugated, perforated, laminated and metalized papers, are suitable for paper sculpture. Effective use can also be made of perforated computer tape, doilies, paper balls, streamers, paper napkins and paper straws. Always take into account the thickness, pliability and texture of the paper in relation to the design and structure of the sculpture. Paper sculpture can also incorporate plastics such as styrofoam and aluminum foil.

Tools. For cutting, a craft knife is best, especially if working with heavy paper or

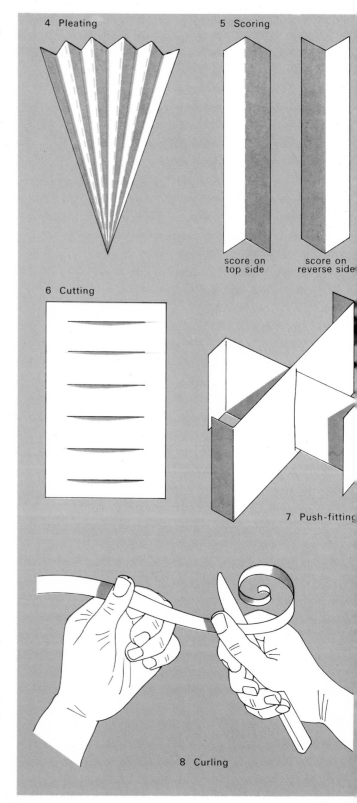

4 Pleating

5 Scoring
score on top side
score on reverse side

6 Cutting

7 Push-fitting

8 Curling

cardboard. Scissors are usually better for fine or delicate work on thinner papers. To score fine paper, however, use a steel knitting needle rather than a cutting tool. Various decorative effects can be produced with pinking shears, leather punches, tracing wheels and embossing dies. Use a small stapler or a strong clear drying adhesive to attach pieces of paper together as inside supporting pieces.

Basic techniques
Pleating (fig.4). Fold the paper at equal intervals, reversing the paper for alternate folds to form a pleating effect.
Scoring (fig.5). For thick cardboard, press on the top surface with a craft knife, using a metal ruler as a cutting guide. Then fold away from you so that the top surface is still on the outside. Bending the cardboard in this way will open the incision. For paper and thin cardboard, press on the reverse side with the point of a pair of scissors or similar tool, and again using a metal ruler as a guide. Fold the paper so that the top surface is on the outside.
Cutting. Cutting is used mainly within an area of paper as shown in fig.6. Cut slits on the top surface using a knife and metal ruler. When a second piece of paper is fitted through the slit, the technique is known as push-fitting (fig.7).
Folding. Follow the same technique as for scoring paper and thin cardboard. A concave crease is known as a "valley" fold and a convex crease is a "mountain" fold.
Rolling and curling. Roll paper by wrapping it around a cylinder or roller. The direction of the grain should run along the length of the cylinder.
Curling is a slightly different technique and can be done by gently stroking the paper towards you with the blade of a knife (fig.8).

Making a paper sculpture
Work out a rough sketch of a design on scrap paper. Keep in mind the size of the finished object and the type and weight of paper needed in proportion to the size and the character of the sculpture. Do not, for example, use a corrugated paper to represent a draped effect, but choose an easily workable construction (cartridge)

paper. The larger the sculpture, the heavier the paper should be. Break down your design into units and work out the sequences, making sure no construction aids will show after completion. Cut patterns or templates for the units, making design adjustments for proportion and shape. Number the units according to order of use. Cut out the final pieces of paper by marking around the pattern with a blunt point and then using scissors. Put the units

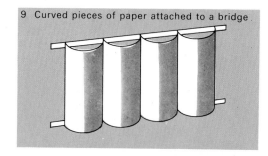

9 Curved pieces of paper attached to a bridge

together with staples, cellophane tape, or glue or by using push-fit pieces inserted into slots. Make use of paper tabs incorporated within the shapes to aid construction. Keep curved pieces of paper in place with bands of paper or "bridges" placed behind (fig.9).

Three designs
Here are three paper sculpture designs using the basic techniques already described.

Nice mice
As a first project, make one or a whole family of mice to amuse a small child. The design is very simple, involving only five units.
You will need:
gray flocked wallpaper □ scraps of pink construction (cartridge) paper □ scissors □ paper punch □ glue.

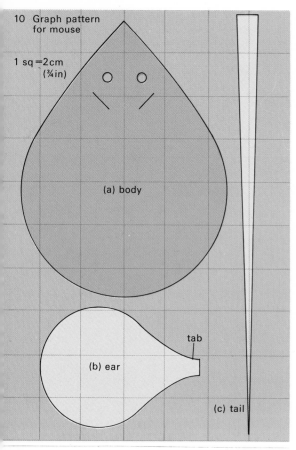

10 Graph pattern for mouse

1 sq = 2cm (¾in)

(a) body

(b) ear

tab

(c) tail

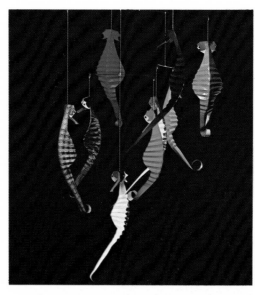

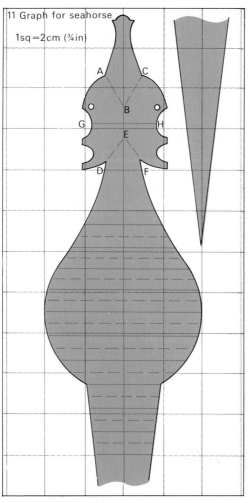

11 Graph for seahorse

1sq = 2cm (¾in)

A C

B

G   H

E

D   F

You will need:

green and blue construction (cartridge) paper, packaging paper and patterned paper □ scissors □ paper punch □ mobile wires □ nylon thread.

Making a seahorse. Draw the seahorse from the graph (fig.11) in which 1 square equals 2cm (¾in). Punch out 2 eye holes as indicated. Score along the spine and fold. Pleat the back for an accordion effect. Next score the fold across the head (G–H) and fold downward. Turn the paper over

Making a mouse. Draw the mouse shapes from the graph (fig.10a,b and c) in which 1 square equals 2cm (¾in). Using sharp scissors, cut out 1 body from gray flocked wallpaper and 2 ears and a tail from the pink construction (cartridge) paper. Score along the spine or center of the body piece and fold. Cut a slit in each side to take the ears. Roll the ear shapes around a pencil to curve them slightly, insert through the slits in the body and glue the tabs inside. Glue the tail inside the fold of the body and curl it. Punch a hole on each side of the head for the eyes. Make a tightly rolled tube from a rectangle of bright pink paper, 6.5 × 2cm (2½ × ¾in) and push the tube through the punched holes to make protruding eyes.

Swimming seahorses

These nine seahorses are made from a variety of different papers in blue and green and will look as though they are swimming when suspended from mobile wires.

and fold the snout toward the crown (B–A and B–C). Then fold from the neck to the crown (E–D and E–F). Push in the snout so that the crown of the head is slightly pointed. Curl the tail.

Make 8 more seahorses in the same way and suspend them by their heads with nylon thread from mobile wires.

White sunburst

This decorative wall fan is made entirely in white paper and involves pleating and some accurate measuring. It will take some time and patience to complete, but will look stunning mounted and hung in a modern setting.

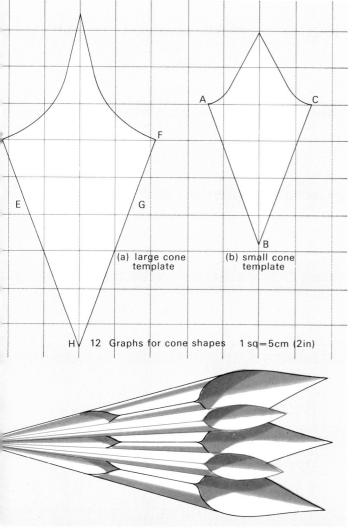

A

C

F

E

G

B

(a) large cone template

(b) small cone template

H 12 Graphs for cone shapes 1 sq = 5cm (2in)

You will need:
46 sheets of size A2 white construction (cartridge) paper □ scissors □ cardboard for templates □ compass □ strong thread or thin wire □ clear drying glue □ circular piece of 0.5cm ($\frac{1}{4}$in) plywood, 35cm (14in) in diameter for mounting.

Making the cones (fig.12a, b and c). Draw the 2 shapes for the cones onto cardboard from the graph (fig.12a and b) in which 1 square equals 5cm (2in). Using these cardboard templates, cut out 29 large cone shapes and the same number of small cone shapes in white paper. To make a small cone spread clear drying glue along the edges AB and CB then press together. To make a large cone glue from D to E and from F to G and press these edges together. Make all the cones in this way, then arrange the large cones to form a wheel. Glue the sides of the cones together. Place 1 small cone in between each large cone to form a smaller wheel on top (fig.12c). Secure with clear drying glue, spread on the sides and underside of each small cone.

Making the pleated circle (fig.13). Cut a strip of paper 50 × 29cm (20 × 11$\frac{1}{2}$in). Make 20 "mountain" folds to a depth of 1.5cm ($\frac{1}{2}$in). Tie a short length of thread or thin wire around the center as shown and then glue I to J and K to L to form a pleated circle.

Making the center piece (fig.14). With a compass draw a circle with a radius of 5.5cm (2$\frac{1}{4}$in). Cut it out and fold the circle in half and then twice more to form eighths. Unfold the circle, then make 8 "valley" folds as shown. Make V-shaped cuts around the edge of the circle at each fold.

Completing the fan. Attach the center piece to the pleated circle by means of a bridge glued in position. Be careful not to flatten the folds. Make another bridge to attach the pleated circle to the wheel of cones in the same way.

Mounting the fan. Glue the whole sculpture to a thin circular plywood backing.

Origami

Origami is the Japanese art of paper folding. Although paper folding most probably originated with the Chinese and was developed independently in other countries, the Japanese have established

This print by Kuniyoshi (C1798–1861), of a woman making fans, shows the art of paper folding as an integral part of Japanese culture.

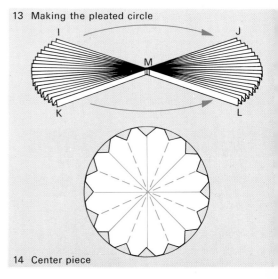

13 Making the pleated circle

I

J

M

K

L

14 Center piece

Basic techniques

the art and incorporated it into their social and religious traditions.

Paper folded into formal shapes has always been used in Shintu temples to mark the presence of the *kami* or temple deity. By the 13th century, the practice of folding shapes to attach to gifts and offerings was customary. The traditional subject matters included the crane and the tortoise, symbols of good fortune and long life; the carp, the symbol of aspiration; the frog, the symbol of love and fertility, and many other birds, fishes and animals. It became an essential part of every Japanese girl's education to know the correct way of wrapping gifts and also certain dry goods, such as rice and herbs, each of which had its own prescribed form of wrapping.

Paper folding has never developed to the same extent in Europe, though we know that Leonardo da Vinci used paper models to work out geometrical problems. Most Western knowledge of paper folding results from contact with Japan since the middle of the 19th century.

Origami has come to mean the practice of folding a sheet of paper, usually a square, into a variety of shapes, without the use of external aids such as scissors, glue or staples. Due to this strict requirement, origami is unlike other paper crafts. It has been described as poised halfway between art and game, bound by strict yet simple rules. It is linked with the world of parlor magic and children's play, while, because of its insistence on the medium of paper alone, it can be considered the purest form of paper modeling.

Paper

All you need for origami are a few squares of paper. Any paper which holds a crease is suitable, but packages of "origami paper" —colored on one side and usually about 15cm (6in) square—are the most appropriate. If you do not have any origami paper. cut some 15cm (6in) squares from sheets of poster paper, decorative wrapping paper or even old magazine covers. Experiment until you find a paper that suits you.

Basic techniques

By folding paper into several layers, a shape is created and further folding will

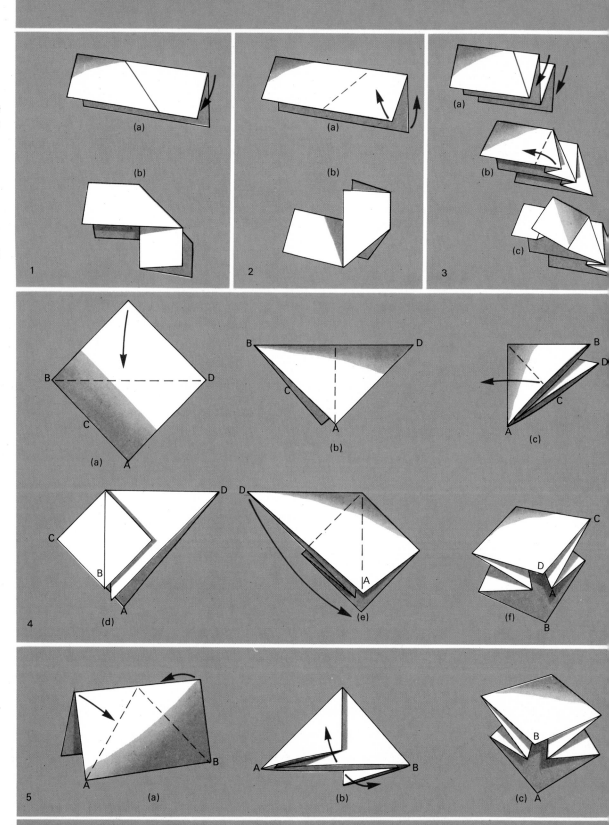

Preliminary base

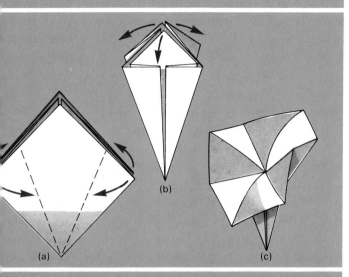

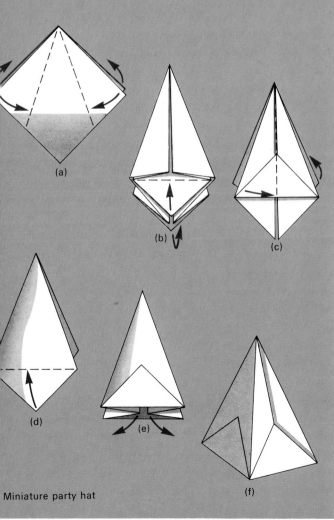

Miniature party hat

refine or develop that shape. Begin by folding a sheet of paper forwards (fig.1a). Now reverse one section of the folded paper between the two layers (fig.1b). Then reverse one section outside of the layers (fig.2a and b). Divide the paper into four layers by folding in half and then folding each half towards the center fold (fig.3a). Then reverse fold two points inside (fig.3b) and stretch the top layer to make a projection (fig.3c).

Preliminary base

A preliminary base is the point of departure for folding many origami models. It is a square of paper folded into two squares and two triangular flaps on a central axis. Here are two methods of folding the preliminary base. Both give the same result.
First folding method (fig.4a–f). Take a sheet of paper 15cm (6in) square. Place it in a diamond shape position in front of you (a). Fold the top point to the bottom point (b). Fold the left point to the right point (c). Now place a finger under the top layer of paper, letting the two layers making up the point of the triangle at A spread out into a square (d). Turn over. Bring the loose flap down to meet the bottom point, while letting the two layers making up the point of the triangle at D spread out into a square (e). The base is now complete (f).
Second folding method (fig.5a,b and c). Take a sheet of paper 15cm (6in) square. Fold the top edge to the bottom edge (a). Then fold the left side forward to the bottom edge and fold the right side back to the bottom edge (b). Place your thumbs between the two layers of the bottom edge and pull them wide apart so that the side points of the triangles come together (c).

Decorative shapes

The following exercises demonstrate the versatility of the preliminary base. Whenever a fold or series of folds is repeated on each of the flaps of the preliminary base, some sort of decorative arrangement will be achieved.
Flower shape (fig.6a,b and c). Take a sheet of paper 15cm (6in) square. Fold a preliminary base and place it before you with the solid point, that is, the center of the original square of paper, at the bottom

(a). Now fold the lower diagonal edges so that they meet on the center line (b). Turn over and repeat on the other side. Pull the top points apart. This will result in an attractive flower shape (c).
Experiment with this shape to make the petals narrower or wider. Try making a fold in any one flap and then repeat the technique with the other flaps to see what new shapes emerge.
Miniature party hat (fig.7a–f). Take a sheet of paper about 15cm (6in) square. Fold a preliminary base and place it in front of you with the solid point away from you (a). Fold the upper diagonal edges so that they meet on the center line (b). Turn over and repeat on the other side. Fold the bottom triangle up over the horizontal edges (c) and do the same on the other side. Fold the left upper triangular flap over to the right (d). Turn over and fold the left upper triangular flap to the right. Fold the bottom point up (e). Turn over and repeat behind. Put your finger in the opening and separate the surfaces. This will result in a miniature party hat (f). Try to alter the angles of the folds which make the party hat so that it will become a box instead of a hat.

Flapping bird.

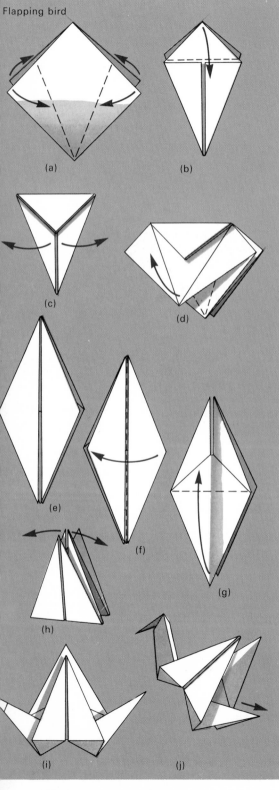

Flapping bird

(a)

(b)

(c)

(d)

(e)

(f)

(g)

(h)

(i)

(j)

Flapping bird

This paper bird, which flaps its wings, is a traditional and popular origami shape.
You will need:
1 sheet of red paper, 15cm (6in) square.
Making the bird (fig.8a–j). Take a sheet of paper 15cm (6in) square. Fold the preliminary base and place it in front of you with the solid point at the top (a). Fold the two lower diagonal edges so that they meet on the center line (b). Turn the paper over then repeat this move. Now fold the top triangle down over the horizontal edges (c). Release the 2 flaps (d), returning them to their original position in fig.8a. Keeping the little triangle in place, lift the large flap up, making a 180° movement (e). The 2 lower edges will come together and form the center vertical edges (f). Turn over and do the same on the other side.
Fold the left flap over to the right. Turn over and repeat (g). Fold the bottom point up to the top. Turn over and repeat (h). You now have a construction with 2 large flaps, which will form the wings, and 2 points between, which will form the neck and tail. Take hold of these two inner points and pull one to the left and the other to the right. Pinch new creases at the base so that the points will retain their new angle. Now push the head section down between the 2 layers of the neck, reversing the mountain fold into a valley fold (i). Hold the bird at the base of the neck. Pull the tail and the bird will flap its wings (j).

Origami necklace

This necklace can be made very quickly if you get several people to help you in making each of the 50 "beads".
You will need:
150 pieces of gold-colored paper, 4cm (1½in) square □ needle and nylon thread.
Making a bead (fig.9a–n). With the reverse side of the paper facing you (a), fold the top and bottom edges of 1 square to the center (b). Fold the bottom left edge to the top edge (c) and tuck under the flap (d). Fold the top right edge to the bottom edge and tuck under the flap (e). Fold the top left and bottom right points back over the folded edges (f). Fold the 2 flaps back so that you have a square, make a crease and then return to the same position as in fig.9f.

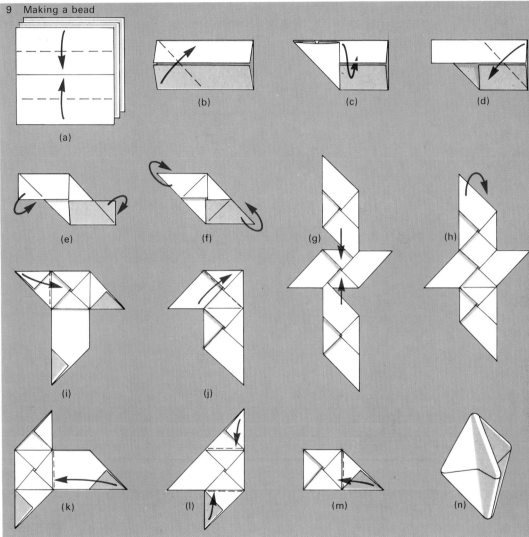

9 Making a bead

(a) (b) (c) (d)

(e) (f) (g) (h)

(i) (j)

(k) (l) (m) (n)

Fold 2 more squares of paper in the same way.

Arrange the 3 folded sections as shown in fig.9g. Slide the points of the top and bottom sections into the center section (h). Fold the upper square and triangle back. Turn over (i). Tuck the left point into the pocket and turn over (j). Swing the left point up to the top right point (k).

The original left flap will now be on top and the original bottom flap will now be on the right (l). Swing this right flap to the left. Tuck the top and bottom points into the 2 pockets (m). Turn over. Tuck the remaining point into its pocket. Hold the bead between your finger and thumb and apply gently increasing pressure until the bead pops into shape (n).

Making the necklace. Thread each bead through the middle with a needle and nylon thread and string the 50 beads together to form a necklace.

Wall streamers

Multi-colored wall decorations can be formed by making the beads described above on a larger scale and stringing them together. Cut 8cm (3in) squares from different colored paper. Follow the instructions for the necklace and string at least ten units together to form one streamer.

Mobiles

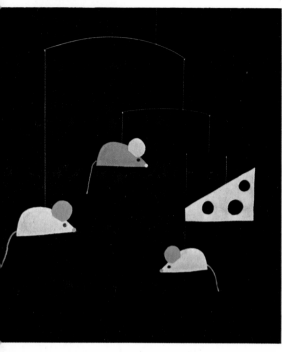

A mobile is a fascinating and graceful decoration whose constant slow movement can have a wonderfully soothing effect. The success of a mobile depends on very careful balancing, so that the suspended objects move around in the slightest breath of air. There is enough of a constant draft in most rooms to keep a mobile in motion continuously.

Popular themes for mobiles include birds, fish and boats all of which naturally suggest a peaceful floating movement. Mobiles can be as varied and imaginative as you wish: they can be realistic, abstract, humorous, sophisticated, and look attractive in the sitting room, bedroom or nursery.

Basic materials

Suspended figures. Use any material which is light enough to be suspended and move freely. Colored paper, foil, acetate, felt, straw, feathers, leaves and wood shavings produce light mobiles. Wood, metal, glass and plastic, although suitable, will make heavier mobiles requiring stronger support.

Supports. These are usually made of wire. The wire supports should not detract from the overall appearance of the mobile. Use the finest grade wire possible that does not bend under the weight of the suspended figure. Fine steel wire is suitable for suspending very light materials (paper, straw). For heavier objects (wood, metal), use brass, copper or galvanized wire. Ready-made wire supports which are cut into suitable lengths, are also available. For some mobiles such as those made with natural objects, the supports can become a feature. For example, fine twigs or lengths of cane or bamboo all make attractive supports.

Thread. This must be strong, and, unless part of the decoration, as invisible as possible. Thin nylon thread is ideal, although sewing thread may be used to suspend lightweight objects.

Making the mobile

Cut the wire supports to suitable lengths, ranging from approximately 12.5cm (5in) to 25cm (10in). Then bend the ends, either up or down, with fine-nosed pliers to form loops for hanging the thread which is attached at the other end to the mobile part.

Always begin hanging a mobile from the bottom and make sure that the figures cannot collide.

Long mobile (fig.1). Take the shortest length of wire and attach thread to each end. Suspend an object from each thread. Knot another length of thread around the wire and adjust the position until the wire support is balanced. Secure the thread in position with a blob of clear glue. Now tie this thread to one end of the next wire support, which is slightly longer than the first. Hang another object at the other end. Fasten a new thread around the second support and balance as before. Stick the thread in position with adhesive. Continue in this way until you have added the required number of supports. The top support will be the longest, with the whole mobile hanging from one of its loops, and the final object hanging from the other loop. This object should be on a very long thread to avoid colliding with the other objects, or, if it is sufficiently heavy to provide a counter-balance, on a very short thread.

Wide mobile (fig.2). As shown here, two similar constructions can be suspended from each end of a wide top support.

Variations. Basic mobiles can simply consist of a row of objects hung from one support as in the hearts mobile. Alternatively, two or three wires can be suspended one below the other, the largest at the top, the smallest at the bottom, as in the butterfly mobile.

A trio of mobiles

These three mobiles are all simple to make and show several possible variations of materials to use and methods of hanging.

Mice and cheese mobile

You will need:

scraps of felt in light pink, dark pink, yellow and black □ absorbent cotton (cotton wool) □ fabric adhesive □ sturdy paper □ 3 pieces of wire 26.5cm (10½in), 16.5cm (6½in) and 12.5cm (5in) long □ paper for pattern □ nylon thread.

Making the mobile. Draw 3 mouse shapes (body and ears separately) onto paper and cut out. Pin the paper pieces onto the felt and cut out 2 body pieces and 2 ears for each mouse. Cut 2 tapering strips for each tail and glue together. Spread a little glue around the outer edges of each mouse body piece on the wrong side. Spread out some absorbent cotton on one body piece up to the glued edge, then place the other body piece over the top and press together lightly, catching in the wide end of the tail. Glue on the ears and tiny circles for eyes and nose.

Draw a cheese shape onto sturdy paper, cut around the shape and cut out 3 holes as shown in the photograph. Pin the pattern

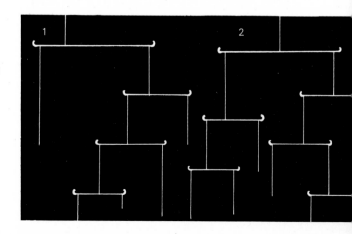

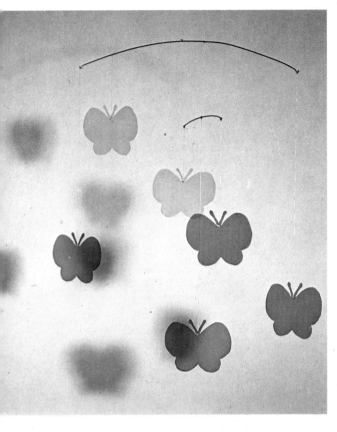

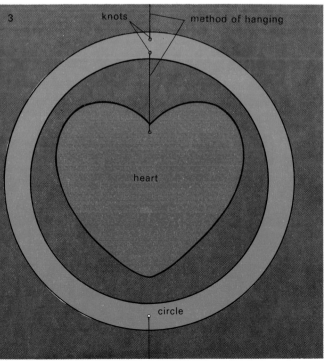

3 knots method of hanging

heart

circle

onto the yellow felt and cut 2 pieces. Cut out holes to match those in the pattern. Glue the 2 cheese pieces together with the paper pattern in between to stiffen them. Hang the mobile with nylon thread, as in fig.1, but using only 3 wire supports.

Hearts and circles mobile
You will need:

sturdy paper in red and green □ piece of wire 21.5cm (8½in) long □ compass □ cardboard □ tracing paper □ nylon thread.

Making the mobile. Trace the heart shape (fig.3) and make a template from cardboard. Cut out 9 hearts from red paper. Draw 2 circles onto cardboard with a compass, the outer circle measuring 8.5cm (3⅜in) in diameter, and the inner circle measuring 7cm (2¾in). Cut out the center

section, then cut out 9 outer ring shapes from green paper. String 3 lengths consisting of 3 motifs each. Thread the hearts inside the circles so that each part moves independently as shown in fig.3. Suspend from the mobile wire at equal distance.

Butterflies mobile
You will need:

sheet of acetate in blue, magenta and orange □ 2 pieces of wire 26.5cm (10½in) and 12.5cm (5in) long □ blunt-ended awl or bodkin □ tracing paper □ nylon thread.

Making the mobile. Draw a butterfly shape onto tracing paper, then place the tracing under the acetate and go over the outline with the awl or bodkin. This will leave an indentation in the acetate. Cut out 2 butterflies of each color, and hang as in the photograph.

Sculpture and modeling

The earliest evidence of human communities—in the cave dwellings of prehistoric man—includes examples of both painting and sculpture. Sculptures were not regarded as works of art in the modern sense, but served a useful function. An image of an animal was thought to give power over the animal it represented, and so increase the hunter's chances of success in the chase. These early ideas of the magical properties of sculpture developed into the idea of giving reality to powers men wanted to invoke by making sculptures of them—in Egyptian times statues were often thought to be the homes of spirits. They were also often related to ideas about the afterlife: it was believed that if the king's likeness was maintained then he would live for ever. The Greeks were influenced by Egyptian as well as Mycenaean and Minoan art. But in the few centuries from around 600 BC to 350 BC Greek art developed from a simple archaic form to a rich humanistic expression of man and woman—the beauty of body and movement expressed in stone and bronze. As the human form is imperfect, the Greeks applied intellectual principles of symmetry to correct these faults. In the 4th century BC Alexander the Great's conquests ruined the city state, but Greek art continued to be admired until the 3rd century AD. Reaction against Greek thought set in with Christianity—soulless human perfection was completely alien to Christian thought. What had been learned from the Greeks was never wholly lost, though, but a resurgence of their ideas on a large scale did not occur until the Renaissance in the 15th century. Interest in portraying human figures was revived, and a strong desire for scientific knowledge led to research into anatomical structure. A strong sense of individualism began to assert itself, so that the sculptor at last ceased to be just a craftsman, and became a master in his own right. The history of sculpture now has to trace the lives of individuals such as Pisano, Lorenzo Ghiberti, Donatello and Michelangelo. Italian sculptors took their work and ideas all over Europe, and the main subjects of their work—both human and animal—remained the prime inspiration of the high art tradition in Europe for several hundreds of years. Only in the 20th century did European sculptors begin to move away from natural to imagined forms. The Cubists exerted a powerful influence, with their discovery of "primitive" and African sculpture. They realised that it was a great art form, not merely an obscure curiosity. Artists developed a feeling for the modern age, with its accent on speed and its scientific inventiveness. This led sculptors to express ideas in new materials, such as metal, sheet iron, plexiglas (perspex), and concrete.

There are, roughly, two ways of creating sculpture. In modeling the sculpture is made by adding layer by layer onto a central core, building up from the center outwards. In carving the sculptor envisages a figure within a block of stone or wood and peels away the layers to reach it.

Modeling materials

These are necessarily softer materials than those used for carving.

Clay. This is the material most commonly used for modeling. You can buy it ready-prepared from good art stores or from specialist dealers. Clay has to be kept moist both for working and for storing, so keep it in a plastic container or in a plastic bag. Dampen it with wet cloths if it gets too dry. Before beginning to work squeeze the clay through your hands until it is of a fairly even consistency. Instructions for wedging clay are given on p. 258.

Self-hardening clay. This can be obtained from craft stores. It is satisfactory for experimenting and unlike ordinary clay does not need to be fired in a kiln. It does not shrink on drying, so it can be built on a rigid skeleton known as an armature, and allowed to harden. However, as it is liable to chip and crack if knocked, it is really only semi-permanent. Once this clay has hardened it can be made malleable again by wetting it and putting it into a damp plastic bag. Hardeners are available which are painted onto the clay once it is dry to prevent it getting damp.

Plastic clay (plasticine). This does not have to be kept moist when working, which is its main advantage, but it can be difficult to cast and is liable to be damaged from knocks. It does not harden.

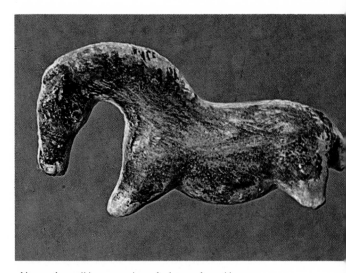

Above: A small ivory carving of a horse, found in Germany, which dates from about 30,000 BC.

Below: "The Slave" by Michelangelo, a masterpiece of Renaissance sculpture.

Modeling a clay relief

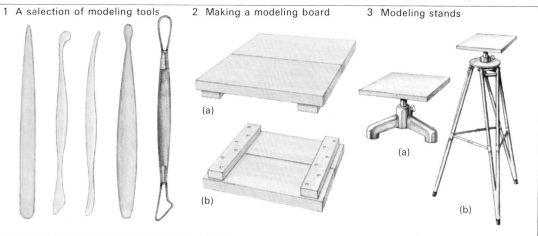

1 A selection of modeling tools   2 Making a modeling board   3 Modeling stands

(a)

(b)

(a)

(b)

A sculpture by Giacometti (1901–66) which stands in the new city of Brasilia in South America.

Modeling tools and equipment

You will need ordinary tools such as a hammer, pincers and pliers.

For modeling there are two kinds of tools—those used for adding and those used for taking away (fig.1). Tools for adding are the simplest. They are usually made of boxwood or a similar close-grained hardwood. They vary in size and can be as long as 30cm (12in) or more. An old kitchen knife, penknife or nail file may be used instead. The best tool for scraping or digging out modeling material is a wire loop on a wooden handle.

Modeling board (fig.2a and b). This is used for small sculptures and small reliefs. The standard size is about 30cm (12in) square. You can make a modeling board quite easily from two strips of 2.5cm (1in) board measuring 30×15cm (12×6in). Nail or screw them together with cross battens $28 \times 4 \times 2.5$cm ($11 \times 1\frac{1}{2} \times 1$in) as shown. Choose a wood that will stand up to constant wetting without warping. For larger reliefs, construct a board slightly larger than the relief.

Modeling stand (fig.3a and b). This is a stand with a horizontal plate on top, which can revolve freely and be adjusted for height. You can buy small table versions (a) or long-legged versions (b). Heavier models usually have a handle and screw for adjusting height and angle. The modeling board is placed on top of the stand.

Galvanized wire and chicken wire. You will need these to keep the work in place when making reliefs and armatures.
Clouts. These are nails with large flat heads, used to keep clay in place when making reliefs.

Modeling a clay relief

A relief is a sculpture that is flattened and intended to be looked at from one direction, as opposed to a sculpture "in the round," which can be looked at from any or most angles. A relief is *not* a figure in the round cut in half and fixed to a background—if you do that, it will never look satisfactory. The fact that it is flattened means that the top layer should include a good proportion of the relief, not just one or two high points. Fig.4a and b and the photograph above them show a relief, with the correct and incorrect ways of modeling it; they show the relief from above. A relief may be almost a drawing, very slightly raised from the background, or the figures may be raised very high.

Choosing and sketching a subject. To begin, it is wise to choose a subject that has few planes, or levels. A fish seen from the side, for example, will only have one level, whereas an animal seen from the side will have two or three—the nearer legs and the body, the head and the farther legs; a team of horses will have numerous levels of legs, heads and backs. Work out any problems initially on paper, then make a sketch model, which is a rough design worked in clay itself. For sketching models

Lysippus Junior made this medallion self-portrait in 1480; the drawings below show that the first impression—that it is a head cut in half—is an erroneous one.

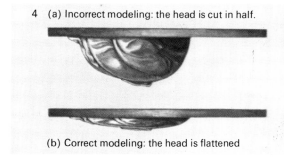

4   (a) Incorrect modeling: the head is cut in half.

(b) Correct modeling: the head is flattened

383

Sculpture and modeling

Mother and child relief

use a modeling board propped up as high as possible, so that the light will fall on it as you intend it to be seen. Do not spend too long on one sketch. Work it out and evaluate it, then do a second, correcting errors and varying design; and a third and fourth if necessary. Make drawings after your first sketch model if necessary, as a quick way of investigating variations.

Transferring the design onto clay. The best way to do this is by "squaring up." Make a drawing on paper and mark it with a grid of numbered squares. Mark the background layer of clay on the relief with a similar grid, to a larger scale. It is then easy to transfer the drawing to the relief.

Mother and child relief

This relief measures approximately 33 × 29cm (13 × 11½in) in size, and is worked in clay which can then be either fired, or cast in plaster.

You will need:

clay for the relief □ a modeling board with a margin 2.5–5cm (1–2in) around the relief □ 20 clouts; or 2.5m (2½yds) galvanized wire and nails, or chicken wire the size of the relief and nails □ rags, sacks or wood wool to support the relief □ knitting needle or thin pointed rod.

Preparing the board. Support the board as near vertical as possible. A painter's easel is an ideal support or you can lean the board against a wall or on a table against a pile of books. Make sure the top is secured back because the weight of clay may make it tip over. Fix it to the wall at the top with nails if it looks at all dangerous. There are several methods of preventing the clay from sliding off the board. Which you choose depends on whether you intend to cast the relief in plaster or fire it in a kiln. If you are going to cast it, any of the following methods is adequate. You can nail clouts in at intervals of 5–7.5cm (2–3in) all over the board, leaving the heads protruding. You can put nails in around the edges of the relief and take wire across the board and around the nails. Or you can attach the chicken wire to the board with nails. In each case the clay will completely cover the support. If you are going to fire the work, you will have to release the relief from the board while it is still damp, so the fixing should not be too

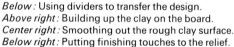

Below: Using dividers to transfer the design.
Above right: Building up the clay on the board.
Center right: Smoothing out the rough clay surface.
Below right: Putting finishing touches to the relief.

Sculpture in the round

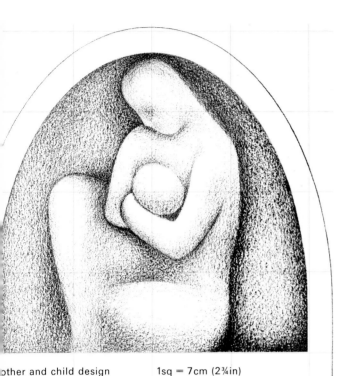

other and child design   1sq = 7cm (2¾in)

strong; support the work with clouts. The clay can easily be removed from these before it is dry.

Beginning the relief. Draw the design (fig.5) in which 1 square equals 7cm (2¾in). Press a layer of clay onto the board, making sure the clouts or chicken wire hold it securely. If the relief is to be fired later, be careful to avoid trapped air between the pieces of clay as this would result in damage during firing. If you are casting the work this is not important. Make the layer fairly smooth and transfer the main lines of the relief with a modeling tool.

Building up the relief. Pay attention to the levels as you build the relief, and ensure that one or two points do not stand out above the rest. Lay a strip of wood across the relief, and if you find any point getting too high, scrape or cut it off. Always work larger areas first, and get down to details right at the very end. In sculpture eyes, ears and nails are all details, only to be fixed when all the major elements are correct. Do not be afraid to draw on the relief with the modeling tool, even at quite a late stage. The discipline will force you not to be over indulgent with yourself, when you are

tempted to let mistakes and bad bits of modeling remain.

If the clay begins to get too dry, dampen it with a fine spray of water. When you stop work for the day put damp rags over it and cover it with plastic sheet (polythene) to make sure it does not dry out.

Finishing the work. The degree of finish is a personal matter, but the temptation to work to a perfect finish should in general be resisted. If the relief is of reasonable size it will usually be looked at from a distance and it should look satisfactory from there.

Preparing the work for firing. If you are going to fire the work, it must be hollowed so that its maximum thickness at any point is 2–2.5cm (¾–1in) and preferably less. Let the relief firm up, but do not allow it to get too dry. Remove it from the board and lay it face downwards on a fairly soft pad of rags, sacking or wood wool. Hollow it where necessary. Prick small or awkward places with a knitting needle or pointed rod. Try to avoid breaking through the surface at low points as you hollow, but if you do, patch the work first from the back then from the front, as long as the clay has not become too hard. If the relief is too large to fit into the kiln, cut it into sections with a knife— these sections can be rectangular or may follow some of the forms. It is difficult to keep large areas flat when drying.

Drying out the relief. Do this very carefully. Lay it face up on several sheets of newspaper so that it can move as it shrinks during drying, and keep it covered loosely with plastic sheet (polythene) so that it dries slowly; otherwise it will probably warp. Clay shrinks by 1/10–1/12 of its linear dimension between the wet and the fired state. When it seems to be quite dry, take it out and dry it further on top of the kiln until all moisture has gone. It is then ready to fire.

After firing. If the relief is in sections, glue them onto a wood or hardboard backing with tile cement and fill the joints with tile grouting or a thin mixture of fine sand and cement. You may color the former with poster paint or powdered clay to match the relief if you wish. Clay reliefs can also be painted and glazed.

Sculpture in the round

If you intend to model the human figure you will have to learn its simple basic proportions.

Adult proportions (fig.6a and b). For an adult man the halfway point is approximately level with the hip bones—for tall people a little lower (a). Women tend to be shorter in the leg than men so for them it may be a little higher, probably level with the top of the pubis (b). The head, from the

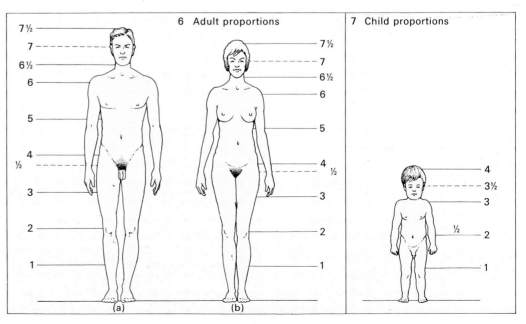

6 Adult proportions   7 Child proportions

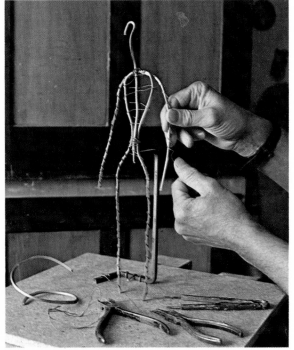

Binding wire around the armature.

Pressing small pieces of clay onto the frame.

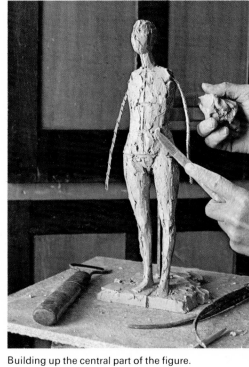

Building up the central part of the figure.

Re-marking the central line.

Smoothing out details.

The completed sculpture.

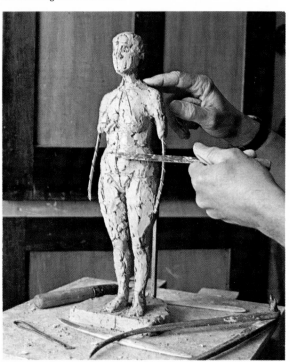

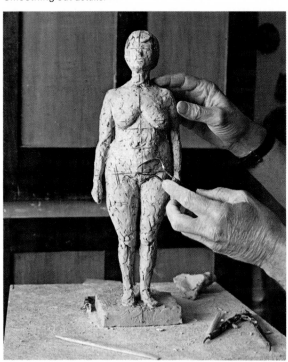

highest point to the chin, goes into the total height approximately seven and a half times. If you double your arm, your knuckles are level with your shoulder. The elbow tucks into the hollow between ribs and pelvis. If you kneel down, your heels touch your bottom.

Child proportions (fig.7). The proportions of a child are very different. The upper part of the head is relatively the biggest part of a young child and its proportions seem to get steadily smaller towards the feet. A young child has only four head lengths.

Facial features. These are crowded into the lower part of the head. The eyes of an adult are halfway between the level of the highest point and the chin.

Weight distribution and balance. When you stand, your weight is distributed around a vertical axis, so that you can keep your balance. This axis can vary quite a lot if the feet are well apart, but if the weight is on one leg, then the pit of the neck is usually vertically above the ankle. As weight is gradually thrown onto the other leg, so the axis will shift. With all movements there is a balance of tensions and corresponding relaxations. Note too how corresponding points on either side of the body relate to each other in various stances: knees, hip bones, wrists, elbows, shoulders, ears, cheeks. Observe yourself in a mirror and, if possible, get someone else to assist you.

Making a clay figure on an armature
Sculpture made in clay and then fired has to be self-supporting. Dry clay before firing is extremely fragile, so if you want to make, for example, a standing figure, it is more satisfactory to build it on an armature, and then cast it in plaster.

Making an armature. A back iron (fig.8a and b) can be bought or made. If you make one (b), bend it in a vise to get good clean angles. If you use mild steel bar, bend it by holding it in a vise and slipping a length of steel tube not much bigger in diameter than the steel bar over the end, using it as a lever to get a good clean right angle. Correct the angles with a heavy hammer before removing it from the vise. Attach the back iron to its base by banging in nails each side of the steel bar and bending them over it. The back iron should be of a height

such that the topmost point is between the middle of the back and the buttocks (fig. 9a). Allow for a clay base, even if you do not want one eventually. You may find while you are modeling that you need some more length in the leg. Decide the dimensions of the figure and make a sketch of it on paper. Arrange lengths of aluminum wire to support the limbs, torso and head and bind them with thinner wire to the back iron at the appropriate height (fig.9b). Wrap aluminum wire spirally around them to give the clay a key as shown in fig.9b. Galvanized wire can be used instead but it is less malleable.

Modeling the figure. Arrange the armature in the position you have decided, with the elements running down the middle of the limbs. Press a pad of clay onto the board at the bottom of the armature to hold the legs in position. Start pressing pieces of clay onto the armature, building slowly and steadily; avoid putting on too much which might then have to be cut away.

Work all over the figure. If you work on sections and carry them near to completion, while other parts are hardly started, you will find it difficult to relate the parts to each other to make a satisfactory whole. It is also tempting to work mainly from the front. Keep turning the figure to avoid this temptation, and do as much work from the sides and back. Draw in the center line, front and back, and other important horizontal points. Redraw and re-mark them whenever they get lost. Keep this up until almost the end. It is the only

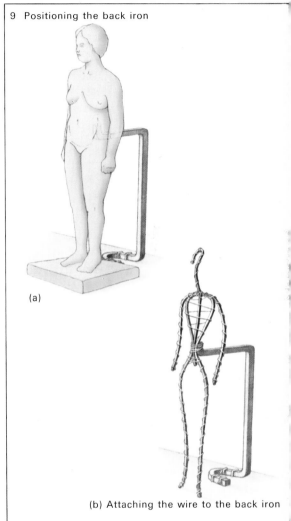

9 Positioning the back iron

(a)

(b) Attaching the wire to the back iron

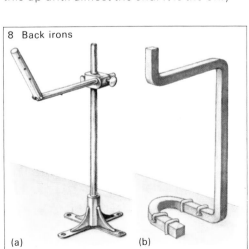

8 Back irons

(a)   (b)

way to ensure accurate relationships between the parts of the sculpture. Leave all detail to the end. Treat hair as solid form, not as individual strands. Even on the finished sculpture all details should be subsidiary to the total figure. Keep the figure damp by spraying with water and covering it with damp rags and plastic sheet, but do not make it so wet that the weight of the cloths damages it. When you have finished, the figure will have to be cast in plaster.

Casting in plaster
Casting consists of applying a layer of plaster over the clay sculpture to form a

mold. When the plaster has set, the clay is removed, and the void is then filled with a second lot of plaster.

When the mold is removed a cast of the original clay sculpture remains. The original clay model is destroyed, though the clay can be used again. The method is called "waste molding" because the mold is chipped away from the cast and can therefore only be used once.

Buying plaster. Buy good quality plaster, from a specialist supplier or from a good art store. It is best to buy it in smallish quantities of about 10kg (22lb) to start with. Store it carefully in a plastic sack or bin; it deteriorates very quickly as it easily picks up moisture from the floor and the air.

Mixing the plaster. Mix up a small quantity to practice with. Pour some water into a plastic bowl. Sprinkle plaster into it rapidly until it starts to appear through the surface (fig. 10a). In theory an equal volume of plaster to water is used, but with a little practice, you will learn the correct proportions. If you add too little or too much plaster, the resultant mix will be weak.

Let the plaster soak up the water for a minute or so and then agitate the plaster with an old table spoon so that it lifts up from the bottom of the bowl and becomes evenly distributed throughout the water (b). Keep the spoon near the bottom of the bowl and avoid splashing, as this will draw air into the plaster mix and make it porous. If the bowl is wide enough, agitate the mix with your hand by putting it into the water palm down and fingers spread (c). Use a side to side movement.

When the plaster is evenly distributed in the water, let it stand until it begins to thicken slightly. Then pour it out onto a sheet of plastic (polythene) and see how long it takes before it sets or "goes off." Try another small mix, with a little more or less plaster, and compare it with the first. Before you cast your figure, you should feel confident that you can control your mixes, that you know how thick to make them and how long it takes for them to go off.

Making the mold. Molds are usually made in at least two parts, sometimes many more. In the case of a standing figure it would be impossible to make the mold in a single section because the clay and armature

could not be removed from it. In this example, the front of the figure is in one piece and the back in three. There are two ways of dividing the figure to prepare it for sections of the mold. The first method is simpler, but if you cannot obtain brass shim, use the second method which uses clay.

First method. For this you will need thin brass sheet called brass shim, which can be bought from a good artists' suppliers or from a specialist supplier. By this method the whole of the figure is covered in plaster at one time. With a modeling tool or knife draw a light line up each side of the body, over the top of the head, and across the base to the board (fig.11). If there is a space between the legs, or between arm and body, do the same. Draw a line horizontally across the shoulders and on a level with the back iron. Cut the brass shim into strips about 2cm ($\frac{3}{4}$in) wide. Snip them into 2.5–4cm (1–1$\frac{1}{2}$in) lengths which taper slightly (fig.12). Make a vertical wall of shim around the line, pressing the pieces in firmly. For a figure 30–40cm (12–16in) high, the wall should be 1.5cm ($\frac{1}{2}$in) high. Kink three or four of them to make keys so that the sections of the mold will fit together correctly (fig.13). Trim so that the pieces of shim fit together neatly and do not overlap. Trim off projecting corners to make a smooth wall (fig.14a and b).

Second method. This method of dividing the figure uses clay. The plaster is applied to the figure section by section. Roll out clay to 0.5cm ($\frac{1}{4}$in) thick and cut it into strips 1.5cm ($\frac{1}{2}$in) wide. Build a vertical wall of clay along the line drawn around the figure as in the first method, pressing gently but firmly, and support the wall at the back with knobs of clay (fig.15a). Cut "V" shapes or hollows out of the wall to make keys for fitting sections of the mold together (b). Place the wall so that the front of the figure is molded first. Apply strips for the sections on the back later.

Preparing the mold. This is a messy process, so wear old clothes and protect surroundings from splashes. How you make the mold will depend on whether you are using brass shim or clay.

Using brass shim. Pour some water into a bowl and color it with powder paint or

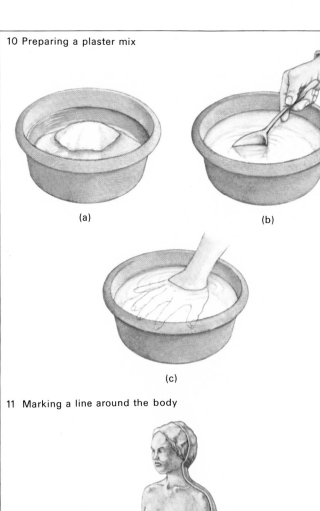

10 Preparing a plaster mix

(a)

(b)

(c)

11 Marking a line around the body

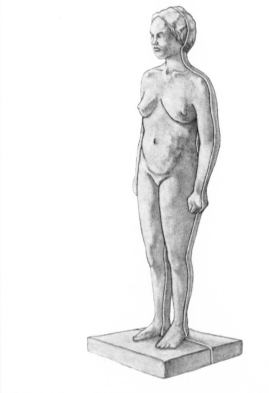

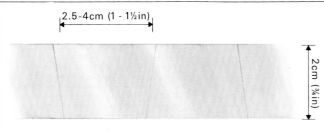

2.5-4cm (1 - 1½in)

2cm (¾in)

12 Cutting brass shim

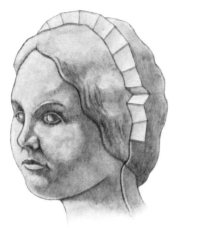

13 Making keys in the shim

correct   (b) incorrect

14 Making a smooth wall

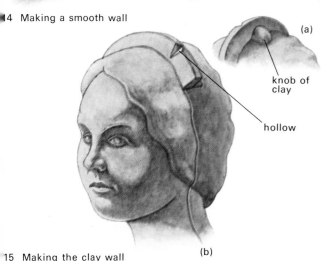

(a)

knob of clay

hollow

15 Making the clay wall   (b)

water-soluble dye. Prepare a plaster mix, slightly on the thin side, with this colored water. Leave it for a few minutes and then flick it all over the model with your fingers, making sure it covers the model, especially in corners and around the shim. Blow it into difficult corners. As it thickens, build up around the shim until it is supported by a thick layer of plaster. Before the plaster goes off completely, scrape gently along the shim wall to expose it, but be careful not to disturb the shim. When you chip off the plaster later on this layer of colored plaster will act as a warning that the sculpture is right underneath it. As soon as the plaster has gone off, prepare a mix of uncolored plaster and build up the mold to an even thickness, to approximately the same height as the shim wall or a little higher. Try to avoid creating thin or very thick points. Clean off the edge of the shim so that a bright line can be seen along its whole length.

Using a clay wall. The mold is made in four separate parts: the front, the back of the head and shoulders; shoulders to the level of the back iron; the lower half of the back. Cover the back of the figure with newspaper or plastic sheet, held in place with knobs of clay. Make a mold of the front part using the same method as for brass shim. When the plaster has gone off, peel away the clay wall and trim up the plaster edge. Paint this edge with a thin wash of clay. By doing this you will make a very fine seam of clay, instead of a thick one. Build a second clay wall along the level of the shoulders, and repeat the process, making the second mold of the back of the head and shoulders of the sculpture. Make a third wall along the level of the back iron. When you come to the back iron, stick a knob of clay around it, so that the hole in the mold left by it will be bigger than the iron itself. This will be patched up later. Make the fourth part of the mold in the same way as the first two.

Reinforcing. Sections sometimes need to be reinforced. In this case the front should be strengthened by plastering on strips of wood or iron (fig.16). Lay them on the mold and fix them with blobs of plaster, scrim or burlap. Scrim is an open-weave sacking material, which can be bought

from upholstery suppliers. Dip the strips in thickish plaster and lay them across the reinforcement, wiping the ends well onto the molded surface.

Removing the mold. If the sculpture is small enough, invert it in a bucket of water. Otherwise dribble water around the seam. As a slight gap begins to appear, gently ease the sections apart, taking care not to strain the mold as the plaster is not very strong. Take the sections off until you can remove the front. Support the sections upright against a wall or between wooden props to prevent them from warping and twisting. This is very important with long or heavy sections.

Cleaning and sealing the mold. Pick out lumps of clay from the inside and dab out smaller fragments with a piece of moist clay. With a soft brush gently wash out the sections, taking care not to stab the surface with the points of the bristle, as brushing will damage the mold. Prepare a strong solution of liquid detergent or soap flakes and brush a good lather into the mold. Rinse out with cold water and repeat two or three times. Rinse thoroughly. The surface of the plaster should now have a slight sheen and is sealed sufficiently to separate it from the cast.

Making an armature for the cast. Bend lengths of thick galvanized wire to fit into

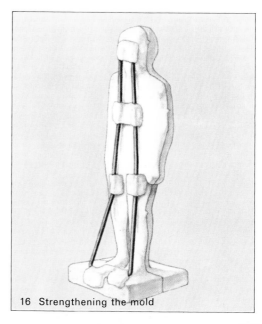

16 Strengthening the mold

Terracotta sculpture

the limbs and through the neck into the head (fig.17). See that the outside of the mold is thoroughly wet, but the surface well drained, and fix the armature in place with small dabs of plaster. Ensure that the wire in narrow parts will not impede the flow of plaster when it is poured in. The wire must not touch the surface of the mold or it will show on the finished sculpture. The wire can be supported on little knobs

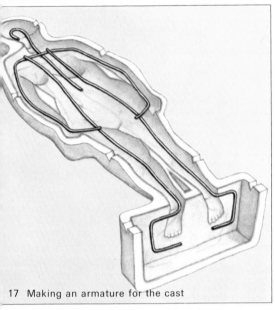

17 Making an armature for the cast

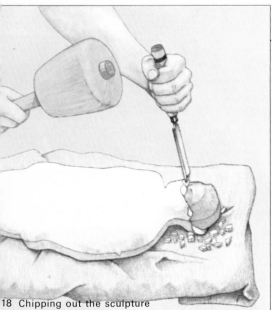

18 Chipping out the sculpture

of clay or plastic clay (plasticine) until the dabs of plaster go off. Be sure to remove them once they have. Put the sections of the mold back together and fix tightly in place, either with loops of wire tightened with pliers, or with strips of scrim or burlap dipped in plaster. Make a very small mix in a spoon and rub a little plaster around all the seams to seal them. Cover the hole left by the back iron with plaster and file off the resultant knob on the cast when the mold is removed.

Filling the mold. Make a mix, which is enough to fill the mold in one pouring if possible. Support the mold in a bucket or upside down between the legs of a stool and pour the plaster steadily down one leg of the mold. Stop and joggle the mold occasionally to ensure that all air bubbles are released. Continue to pour until the plaster stands slightly above the edge of the base and, as soon as it goes off, scrape the base flat with an old hacksaw blade, or something similar.

Chipping out and finishing. Leave for half an hour or more, then chip out the sculpture. Prepare a soft bed of rags to lay the mold on and remove wire or strips or scrim. Use an old, blunt chisel and mallet, starting at the top near the seam (fig.18). The plaster should be "stunned" off rather than cut, so hold the chisel at a fairly vertical angle. Chip away the white coat first of all, working steadily down from head to base, and working both sides until you come to the colored plaster. Do not pry pieces off. Ensure that the piece being chipped off is smaller and weaker than the one the chisel leans against.

Chip the colored coat very carefully, especially in complicated or detailed areas. Ensure that the cast is well supported by rags or wooden wedges at all times and that strain is not put on any weak points such as the legs. When the mold is clear, clean up any remnants with a small instrument such as a nail file. Carefully rub smooth any seams. Repair faults with plaster, dampening the area thoroughly first. Let the sculpture dry thoroughly. It can be left white or painted; water color will sink softly into the plaster. Alternatively seal it with shellac or clear polyurethane, and apply the required finish.

Terracotta sculpture

Terracotta sculpture is clay sculpture that has been fired like a pot in a kiln.

Preparing clay. The clay must be free from impurities. If you re-use clay used on an armature, it will be full of pieces of plaster. It should not be fired, or the plaster will expand during firing and blow pieces out of the figure, or even smash it completely. So keep your terracotta clay separate, and use a plaster-free board.

There are two basic clay colors, red and gray. The best clay is red clay with powdered fire clay added to give a coarser, more open texture. This is pleasanter to work with and allows trapped air to escape more easily. Ordinary pottery clay can also be used. Red clay fires to flower-pot color, gray clay fires white. Gray clay is probably best if you intend to paint or glaze the sculpture.

Clay must be carefully prepared by wedging and kneading to eliminate air bubbles, because trapped air will expand and crack or burst the figure during firing. Knead the clay as described on p. 258.

Firing. You can probably find studio potters in your area. If they are sure your sculpture is well made and will not be a danger to the other articles in the kiln, they will probably fire it for you for a small charge. Commercial potteries will do the same. If you want to buy your own kiln, take advice from a potter or sculptor. Some small electric kilns can be run from the ordinary power supply. Be sure the kiln is adequate for your purposes: your sculptures may grow as your skill and ambition increase.

Modeling figures for terracotta. Because you are working without an armature, and because thin limbs in wet or dry clay cannot support a heavy bulk, you must make a compact figure that can support itself. Make a series of sketches of sitting or crouching figures. Take a theme such as happiness, sorrow, dignity and try to make them express it. Keep these initial sketches very simple and undeveloped.

Building the figure. There are two ways of making a sculpture for firing: building it solid and hollowing it or building it hollow. If it is thicker anywhere than 2.5cm (1in) it will almost certainly break when fired, as pockets of air in the clay cannot escape through thick clay.

"Solid and hollowing" method. Take a board and on it press out a flat base of clay, 2.5cm (1in) thick. Make sure there are no air bubbles trapped in it, if you want it as part of the sculpture. Take a lump of clay and press it into a suitable shape to make a core for your sculpture. Leave it to firm up for a few hours. When it will retain its shape easily, but is not hard, continue to build the sculpture, ensuring that, as you add pieces, you do not entrap air. When you have finished, allow the sculpture to become firm but not hard. Begin hollowing from the bottom if possible. Otherwise, cut off a piece of the sculpture with a potter's wire or a thin knife, hollow underneath it and refix the cap with some thick slip—clay mixed with water until it is liquid (fig.19a–d). Press the join firm with a modeling tool and re-work it until it

2

4

our stages in modeling a terracotta figure.

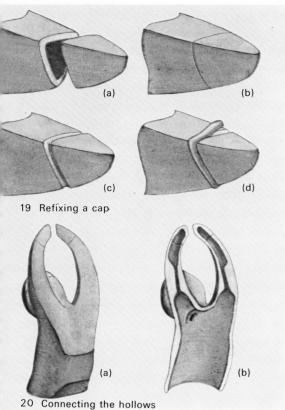

19 Refixing a cap

20 Connecting the hollows

disappears. If you make use of several caps, ensure that the hollows underneath them all connect up to the outside air or the sculpture may explode during firing (fig.20a and b). Prick smallish difficult parts, preferably from the inside, to leave channels for escaping air.

"Hollow" modeling (fig.21a and b). This is done by making a core figure out of coils, following a sketch model of your sculpture. Make a clay base. Build the figure with

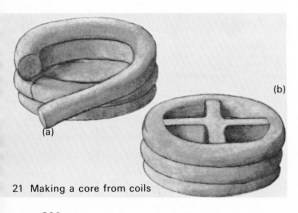

21 Making a core from coils

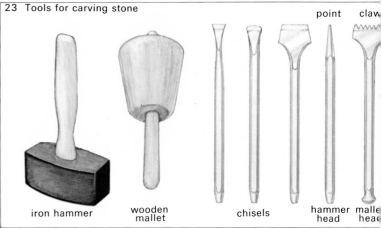

22 Tools for carving plaster

rasp   riffler   plaster rasp

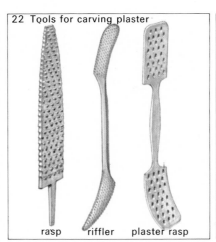

23 Tools for carving stone

point   claw

iron hammer   wooden mallet   chisels   hammer head   mallet head

coils about 1.5cm ($\frac{1}{2}$in) thick (a). Be careful not to press the figure out of shape as you join coil on coil. Incorporate a cross of clay inside the coils to act as a support, and extend it as the coils are added (b). Build only as much at a time as will support itself easily. After a few coils let the sculpture harden a little before continuing with the next section. When you have completed the basic shape in coils, you can begin work on the outside, adding clay in the usual way. If you have to press any part in, pierce it first to let air out. Make sure it does not become too thick at any point. Before firing, make an outlet for the air trapped inside, and dry out the sculpture thoroughly. If possible, fire at glaze temperature, but with the temperature rising slowly as for a biscuit firing.

Carving

Stone is the great traditional carving medium. It varies from chalk and very soft limestones, through sandstones and marbles to granites and diorites, which are extremely hard. The following are some of the more tractable materials.

Plaster. This is frequently used for working out sketch models, but finished carvings can also be made from it. Make a block of plaster of a suitable size, then leave it for a few hours before starting. Carve the broad shape first, using a knife, plaster rasp or suitable blade (fig.22). Move steadily in to the final shape, avoiding detail. Do not cut deeply anywhere until you are absolutely sure of what you are doing. For final

smoothing use sandpaper or glasspaper. If possible work on a bench or table, but if you have to hold the block in your hand or lap, be careful when using sharp tools. Always cut away from the body.

Concrete block. The only suitable type of concrete block is aerated concrete building block made from pulverized ash, sand and cement. Some blocks are fine, others contain largish holes. The material is quite fragile and will split easily, so use a good bed of sacking. Use stone carving tools or old wood gouges and rasps. Although soft, this material blunts tools quickly. The dust is dangerous, so wear a dust mask. Avoid wetting the block which would make it even more fragile.

Brick. This is not used very often for carving. Use bricks of a soft even consistency. If they contain stones or flaws they will break easily when vibrated. Work on sacking on a bench or heavy table and use stone carving tools and rasps. To make a brick relief, carve the bricks in the dry-clay state, fire them and join with mortar afterwards.

Soft stone. This includes soapstone, alabaster and soft limestone. Soapstone is dark and textured in appearance, but very smooth and soft, and works easily. Alabaster varies in color from translucent creamy white to opaque brown, as can be seen in the photo of a modern sculpture on the next page. It has a soft clean texture. Limestone carves very easily, but does not take fine detail. Most limestones can be put outdoors, though some will deteriorate in rain and frost.

24 Carving a sculpture

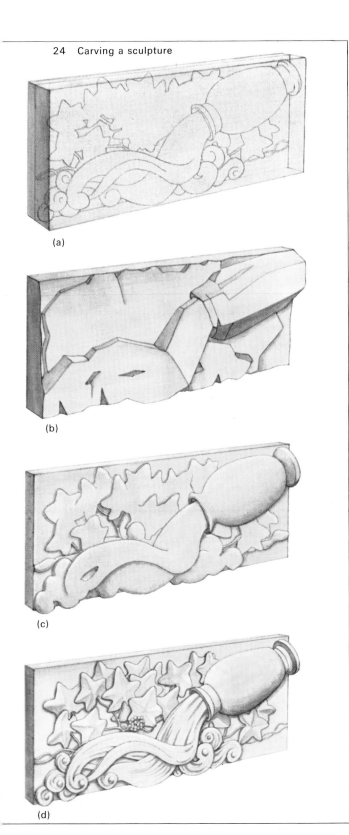

(a)

(b)

(c)

(d)

Carving soft stones. Use a heavy table or bench. Nail strips of wood to the table and use wood wedges to keep the work in place. Sacks and rags will prevent damage. You will need some special stone carving tools (see fig.23). Use a piece of gritstone, which is a fragment of natural paving stone or doorstep, or a medium Indiastone for sharpening tools. Once you have decided on your proposed form draw on the block with charcoal or chalk, indicating major volumes to be removed. Work these with a point, steadily cutting away only big volumes, until you get near the surface. Try to avoid making undercuts or making hollows for as long as possible. When the block looks like the sculpture you intend but as if it had a fine cloth tightly stretched over its surface, continue to develop the forms with a claw, moving onto chisels,

rasps and rifflers (fig.24a–d). Soapstone and alabaster may be finished with finer and finer grades of "wet or dry" abrasive (carborundum) paper used with water, until all scratches disappear. A finer rub with a slightly waxy rag will reveal the beautiful quality of these stones.

Hard stone. This includes some sandstones, gritstones and marble. The first two contain a lot of silica which makes the dust dangerous. Keep the stone wet or wear a dust mask.

Carving hard stones. These stones blunt tools very quickly, so you will need specially hardened tools. Tungsten-tipped chisels are available, which remain sharp much longer, but they are rather expensive. When your tools become too thick after many sharpenings they will have to be remade by a toolsmith.

Mosaic

Mosaic, the art of making pictures out of stones or small pieces of pottery or glass, has been practiced for over 5000 years. The mosaics of ancient Greece were largely created from uncut pebbles of natural colors. Used as floor or wall coverings, the most common subjects were birds, animals and flowers or scenes from mythology. The Romans evolved a more elaborate decorative style, using specially cut pieces of stone or marble known as tesserae (meaning "cubes" or "dice"). As well as scenes from nature and legend, geometrical designs and stylized floral motifs were characteristic features of mosaic pavements, ceilings and wall or vault panels. With the spread of Christianity, mosaic came to be used as means of telling the Christian story in pictures. The earliest examples (from the end of the 2nd to the beginning of the 3rd centuries) still show Christ looking like a Roman, but gradually the style known as Byzantine emerged. By the 6th century, in the city of Ravenna, some of the best examples had been produced, creating a totally new effect due to the extensive use of glass and gold mosaic. It is the glowing golden background of these mosaics that gives them their unique quality.

As fresco painting took over, from about the 12th century onwards, so the creative use of mosaic declined. It became the practice to make copies of paintings, as in St. Peter's in Rome. By the 18th century the stones used were much smaller; these later mosaics lack much of the boldness and originality of earlier works.

The present century has seen a great revival of the craft as modern glues and cements make it possible to apply mosaic to a wide variety of objects, such as tables, lamp bases and wall plaques, and to use it in domestic settings such as bathrooms and kitchens.

Paper mosaic

A good way of getting started is to experiment with paper mosaic, which does not require special materials or tools. Among the solemn saints and great glories of Ravenna there are also many charming and lighthearted details, such as the drinking doves in the illustration. By following the

grid you should have no difficulty drawing one of them.

You will need:
thick cardboard 36×26cm (14¼×10¼in) □ paper glue: rubber cement (Cow Gum) is ideal since it allows time for the pieces of paper to be adjusted or repositioned before setting □ tweezers □ pencil □ ruler □ 1 sheet of paper in each of the following colors: white, light gray, dark gray, pale blue, dark blue and orange □ 6 containers to keep each paper color separate.

Drawing out the design. Draw a grid of 1cm (⅜in) squares onto the cardboard with a sharp pencil, with 36 squares in one direction and 26 in the other. Number and letter the squares as shown (fig.1). Then draw in the outline of the bird by plotting the points from square to square. For example, the top of the head is in square 26 on the line between squares B and C, and so on.

Alternatively, the drawing can be done freehand if preferred. Once you have drawn the outline of the dove, you are ready to begin work.

Making the mosaic. You will need a stock of paper pieces, more of some colors than others obviously. First cut a few long strips 1cm (⅜in) wide and then cut them into squares. There is no need to be too careful about this as part of the charm of mosaic is the irregularity of the pieces. Keep the stock separated into colors. For paper mosaic, it is far easier to spread glue onto the card-

Above: Christ's summoning of the disciples Peter and Andrew, one of the famous mosaics from Ravenna in Italy.

Left: Roman mosaic dating back to the 1st century AD.

Right: This delightful mosaic of doves drinking from a bowl can be found in the so-called *Mauseoleum of Galla Placidia,* which was built in Ravenna in c.430 AD.

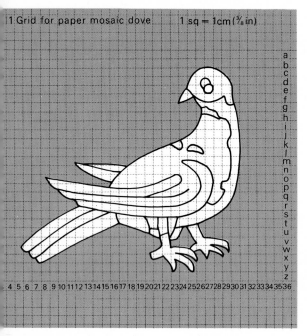

1 Grid for paper mosaic dove   1 sq = 1cm (⅜in)

board than onto each individual little square. The dark gray line of the wing is an ideal place to start. Spread the glue along it and then, by hand or using tweezers, position the row of squares carefully. Leave tiny gaps to represent the cement. The pieces should *not* be touching. The cracks are part of mosaic technique, though getting them exactly right requires practice. When you are satisfied with the spacing, press the pieces down firmly to secure them in position (corners tend to curl up) and then tackle the white line that is above the dark gray one. Continue in the same way, noting where the color changes to pale blue and so on, and finish with the dark blue background. In one or two places, pieces will have to be specially shaped but in paper mosaic this is no great problem.

Finishing the mosaic. If possible, leave the work flat and in a cool place to dry. If the cardboard begins to curl up, put it under weights for a few days. A shiny and more realistic finish can be obtained by applying a coat of polyurethane varnish, clear acrylic spray or paper varnish. A coat on the back of the cardboard, when the front has dried, will help to stop it from warping. If desired, the mosaic can be framed behind glass and

used as a tray. Real mosaic is usually too heavy to make a practical tray, but paper mosaic is ideal.

Working with real mosaic
Having tackled the paper mosaic, the next stage is to consider a project in real mosaic, for which a stock of tesserae is required. These are normally sold in parts of a square meter or by the square foot and may be supplied loose or attached to a paper or mesh backing sheet. They are available in three basic categories:

Smalti. These are small, handcut cubes of opaque glass, such as were, and indeed still are, used in the mosaic school at Ravenna and are available in a wide range of colors (plus gold and silver). However, they are rather expensive and not really suitable for beginners.

Glass tiles. These are the standard 2cm (¾in) squares available relatively cheaply at most craft suppliers. They are cut to a more regular shape than smalti and are therefore much easier to handle.

Ceramic tiles. These are the cheapest of all to buy. Usually they are available only in pastel shades and so are more suitable for bathrooms than artistic projects.

Mosaic tile
This attractive tile is in glass tile mosaic—the most suitable for the purpose. As you will probably have to buy more tesserae than you actually need for just the tile, both this and the more ambitious table top to follow will be in the same color scheme. Prices of colors vary, strong bright colors and metallics being the most expensive. Here four less expensive colors have been combined with one expensive one. If you choose a different range of colors, try to keep the tonal values the same, otherwise the balance of the whole design may be affected.

Just as it is necessary to practice spacing with paper mosaic, so it is very helpful to practice cementing tesserae on a small scale.

You will need:
piece of marine plywood 9mm (⅜in) thick and 24cm (9½in) square (ordinary plywood is likely to warp) ☐ small bag of Portland cement ☐ 1 liter (2 pints) concrete

bonding adhesive (polyvinyl acetate: PVA) ☐ rags ☐ plastic mixing bowl ☐ large jar and lid ☐ small mixing trowel ☐ palette knife ☐ wooden spoon ☐ hammer ☐ paper glue ☐ a 24cm (9½in) square of heavy paper ☐ about 30cm (12in) square of mosaic tiles in each of the following colors: green, black, sand, red and white.

Drawing the grid. Allowing for cement joints, 11 mosaic tiles will fit across the 24cm (9½in), so draw a grid onto the paper accordingly.

Glueing the mosaic. Mosaic tiles have a smooth side, which is the *front face*, and a beveled side (sometimes this has tiny grooves), which is the *back*. When glueing the mosaic tiles onto the paper work *in reverse*. This means that you pick up a mosaic tile, put a dab of paper glue onto the smooth face and put it, face down, onto the paper. Work methodically from left to right putting in the whole top row. Be careful not to apply too much glue or the tiles will slide around and the paper will buckle. Following the simple design, it should not take long to have them all in place. As with the paper mosaic, place the finished work under weights and allow to dry for a day or two.

Preparing the wood. Meanwhile, prepare the plywood by priming it with a coat of diluted concrete bonding adhesive (PVA). One measure of concrete bonding adhesive to 3 of water is sufficient. Mix enough to fill a large jar as it can be used again for cementing. When one side of the board is dry, prime the other side too. Always allow the board to dry flat rather than propped up at an angle.

Cementing the mosaic. Since cementing is apt to be a messy business, try to work somewhere where this does not matter and above all, where the cemented tile will not be disturbed for at least 48 hours. Wear rubber gloves to prevent irritation of the skin when working with cement.

By itself, Portland cement is not strong enough to bond mosaic tiles to wood, so mix it with concrete bonding adhesive diluted in water. Put about ½kg (1 lb) of dry cement in the mixing bowl and, very carefully, stirring all the time with a wooden spoon, begin to add the liquid. Although this is a simple process, it can be

quite difficult to get just right, especially the first time! The mix should spread like butter but not pour like cream. When you are satisfied with the consistency, spread it with a trowel or palette knife all over the backs of the tesserae just deep enough to cover the stones 2–3mm ($\frac{1}{8}$in) and pushing well down into the joints. Then, as quickly as possible, spread a thin, even layer of mix over the board and press the block and board together. The faster you do this, the less likely you are to have gaps between the two. Tap lightly all over with a hammer and if any mix squeezes out at the sides, push it back with the knife. Keep the edges as neat as possible for a good solid cement line, place weights on top and leave for at least 48 hours. Be sure to clean up all tools. Do *not* put any surplus mortar down the drain but scrape it onto old newspaper and throw it away.

Turning the mosaic. When the mosaic is ready to be "turned," take the weights off. Pick it up—you may need to loosen it a little with the palette knife, to separate it from whatever surface you have been cementing on—and dampen the paper "front" with a rag or sponge. After a few minutes of patient dampening, you should be able to peel the paper off. The mosaic will still be messy as some cement and glue on the surface is inevitable. Wash it carefully with warm water and rub off all surplus cement. Allow it to dry.

Grouting the mosaic. If there are any gaps between some of the stones, where the

Mosaic

Table top

cement has not quite reached the level of the mosaic, fill in with a little freshly mixed cement and concrete bonding adhesive using a palette knife. This "grouting" process is usually necessary and is a normal mosaic routine. Leave it to set for about half an hour and then, with an almost dry rag, rub the surface really clean. If washed too wet, mosaic always dries with a gray film on the surface. After a few days' further setting, coat with a colorless silicone wax to help bring out the colors and to protect the surface.

Framing and finishing. A plain wooden frame can be put around the mosaic (nailed onto, or glued to the plywood) and the base covered with felt. If the tile is to be used as a trivet the frame should be poly-urethaned to make it more heat resistant. Sand off any cement left on the plywood before applying felt with fabric glue. It is generally unwise to cut felt exactly to size as it tends to stretch or shrink in the glueing-on process, so cut a piece a little too large and trim it off with scissors when the glue is completely dry.

Mosaic table top

Having successfully completed the mosaic tile, you should be ready to try your hand at something more ambitious, such as this mosaic coffee table top. Cross-stitch designs always adapt very well to mosaic work and this one is based on a piece of traditional Yugoslav folk embroidery.

You will need:
piece of 19mm ($\frac{3}{4}$in) thick marine plywood, 80cm (31$\frac{1}{2}$in) sq □ sheet of brown paper of the same size □ pencil □ meter or yardstick □ rubber cement (Cow Gum) or similar adhesive □ concrete bonding adhesive (PVA) □ a 5kg (11lb) bag of Portland cement □ tesserae.
If you originally bought 30cm (12in) square of tiles in each color, there will be enough green and black left, but you will need a further 30cm (12in) square of the sand color and red and 60cm (24in) square of white.

Drawing the grid. The design consists of 37 squares in each direction. The easiest way to work out the spacing is to take 37 tesserae and see how they space out evenly across the 80cm (31$\frac{1}{2}$in). Mark the grid on

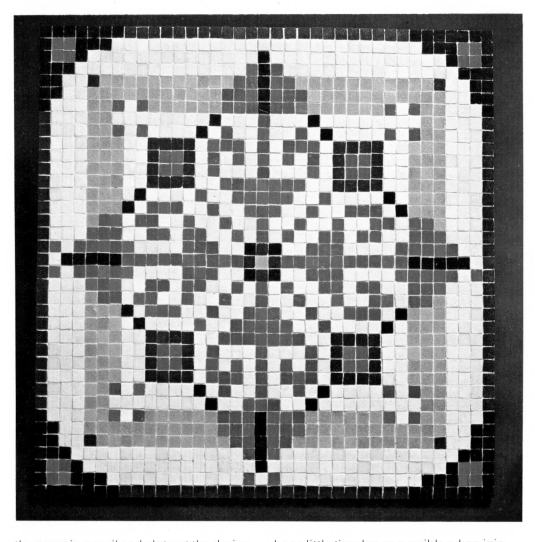

the paper in pencil and plot out the design by referring to the photograph. Fig. 2 gives an alternative mosaic design, which you may prefer to use instead.

Making the table top. The basic process is the same as for the tile. Prime the board on both sides and glue the tesserae onto the paper as before. When cementing, however, as the quantities are so much bigger, it is useful to get someone to help you. Five kg (11lb) of cement is too much to mix at one time and is quite hard work, so it is best to mix it in 2 batches. So while you are spreading the first mix over the backs of the mosaics, your helper can be mixing the second batch, which you both then spread as fast and as evenly as possible over the board. As already explained there should

be as little time lag as possible when joining the 2 cement surfaces. You will also need another pair of hands when trying to put such a large board down accurately on top of the mosaic. Put weights on top, clean the edges where the cement may have squeezed out and leave for at least a week. When turning the mosaic, the whole cleaning up and grouting operation should be done in a single session so that the work is even. Should any stones be loose, glue them in place with undiluted concrete bonding adhesive or tile setting mastic. Do the grouting—a small section at a time—with a palette knife and rags.

Finishing the table. The best way to complete the table is to put 3cm (1$\frac{1}{4}$in) wood beading all around and fit screw-on legs.

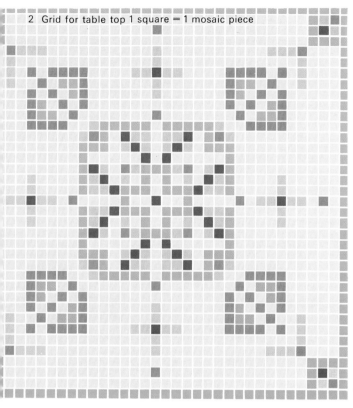

2 Grid for table top 1 square = 1 mosaic piece

Alternatively, an iron frame can be made, but this can be expensive.

Cutting mosaic

Clearly, a good book of embroidery patterns can be the source of an endless supply of mosaic motifs as long as you are happy to work in regular squares. If, however, you wish to attempt more intricate patterns in mosaic, you will need to master the technique of cutting. The tile design on this page for example, has hardly a square piece in it.

Mosaic cutters. These can usually be bought from a mosaic supplier or craft store. Being tungsten tipped, the cutters should never need sharpening.

Using the cutters. Begin by cutting some squares in half. Hold the cutters in one hand and hold the mosaic square firmly between the forefinger and thumb of the other, as shown in the photograph. Note that only about a third of the mosaic is actually in the jaws of the cutter. Glass breaks by vibration and as you bring the blades towards each other, a snapping sound will indicate that the mosaic tile has been split. If you let go of the pieces, they will scatter all over the room, hence the firm hold. Do not be disappointed if you have a few odd shapes, as they can probably all be used eventually. For obvious reasons, practice cutting on the cheapest colors. After an hour or so, you should be able to manage to cut halves fairly successfully. Next, try a few diamond shapes, then triangles, either by cutting the mosaic tile across at an angle or by taking a little from each side of a square. Try a simple design in paper mosaic or copy the one given here (fig.3). Try the simple leaf shapes and curved pieces they involve. If you find it very hard work, you are almost certainly holding the cutters wrong—either too far into the mosaic or too low down on the handles.

Mosaic for outdoor use

The process described earlier for cementing mosaic tiles onto a plywood base is suitable for any indoor mosaic, even a kitchen surface which will get wet. However, the expansion and contraction rates of wood and cement are so different that they will come apart when exposed to prolonged soaking or frost. So, for items that will be left outside such as a garden table, wall plaque or house number plate, a cement casting has to be made.

399

Mosaic

Cat wall plaque

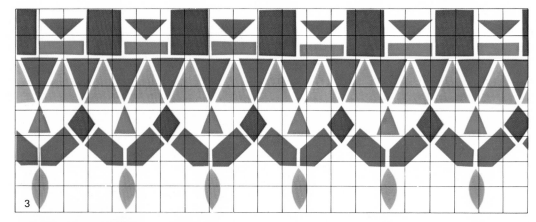

This mosaic can be made for indoor or outdoor use, but if you decide to display it outside, omit the frame shown in the photograph.

You will need:
hammer and nails □ sheet of tracing paper a little larger than the reproduction on this page □ wooden board for use as a work surface □ mosaic cutters □ adhesive tape □ 4 strips of 2 × 0.5cm ($\frac{3}{4} \times \frac{1}{4}$in) wood for a casting frame □ 15cm (6in) square piece of fine mesh wire □ loop of galvanized wire □ tesserae □ pencil □ small bag of sand and cement mix □ rubber cement (Cow Gum) or similar adhesive.

Tracing the design. Trace the design (fig.4), making a good clear firm line. Then tape the paper face down onto the board.

Beginning the work. To produce the design as illustrated, it is necessary, as in etching or setting type for printing, to work *in reverse*. Cut the mosaic tiles to the required shapes and glue to the paper, following the design and working methodically. It is important to continue working until a substantial area is filled in since tracing paper buckles more easily than thicker white or brown paper. Leave the mosaic under a weight overnight to settle.

Preparing the casting frame. Before beginning to cement, prepare the casting frame by nailing the pieces of wood around the mosaic as shown (fig.5), driving the nails firmly into the wooden board. The frame is used for shuttering or keeping the sand and cement mix from spreading. It is not part of the finished wall plaque.

Cementing the mosaic. Concrete mortar can be bought in bags already mixed to the right proportion of cement and sand. Rendering mix is the best material for such a small job. This time concrete bonding adhesive is not used, as sand and cement bind quite well when mixed with cold water. Put about 1kg (2lb) of the concrete mortar into a bowl, add water very gradually and mix. It should not be too wet. When you pick up a lump and squeeze it, a little water should come out but it should just about keep its shape. If water pours through your fingers, add some more sand and cement.

Spread the mix about 1cm ($\frac{3}{8}$in) thick across the tesserae, then press it all over

Cat wall plaque

4 Tracing pattern for the cat

too fast and leave it for a week.

Turning the mosaic. Undo the outer frame very carefully. If the cement still looks damp and crumbly, leave the edges to dry out until the next day and then turn. Wash and clean up as usual.

Exactly the same method can be used for a mosaic garden table except that it needs to be heavier, using about 3cm (1¼in) of cement. It should be left for at least 2 weeks before being turned and should be reinforced with heavier wire mesh.

Fixing the mosaic to a wall. Fix the plaque to the wall using a wall plug and screw of a suitable size. Drive the screw in until only 0.5cm (¼in) of the head protrudes. Mix a small amount of plaster of Paris. Hang up the mosaic by means of its inbuilt loop of wire onto the screwhead and pour a little plaster of Paris on from the top. Press the mosaic firmly into place and hold while it is setting. Then fill in the slight gap between the wall and mosaic plaque with mortar. On a brick wall, this picks up the color of the joins and looks very effective if neatly done. If the wall is plastered you may prefer to chip out a small area of plaster so that the plaque can be inset. Alternatively, frame the plaque and hang it as a picture.

Exterior mosaics can be set into a house or garden wall to add decorative interest.

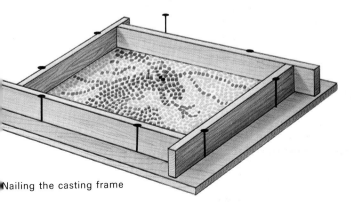

Nailing the casting frame

very carefully. This helps to compress the mortar and force it into the cracks. Pay particular attention to the corners. When this first layer is pressed well in, put on the wire mesh for strengthening, and add another layer of mortar. Fill the casting frame right up to the brim and level it off by drawing a well-dampened length of wood across it. This may take several attempts. Just before leaving it to set, take the wire loop and push it well in. This will set in the cement and will be the means of attaching the plaque to the wall. Cover the mortar with a plastic bag to stop it from drying out

Bookbinding

Bookbinding as a craft began to develop with the introduction of the codex or folded book, which had completely superseded the papyrus roll by the 4th century AD. The Romans were probably the first to use rudimentary bindings, which consisted of two pieces of wood, ivory or bone pierced with holes and linked with thongs.

The best examples of early leather bindings, however, were those produced in the 7th and 8th centuries by the Coptic Church in Egypt. These bindings were truly glorious with elaborate decoration of gold and jewels.

The Islamic bindings from the 11th century onwards continued to exploit the properties of gold, often combined with blind tooling, to create subtle effects of light and shade.

The Coptic and Islamic styles of decoration were in evidence throughout Europe during the 15th and 16th centuries, though different countries modified and refined the various techniques. In Elizabethan England, for example, fabric bindings embroidered in gold and silver thread were produced as well as the more usual full-leather bindings with gold-tooled emblems.

By the middle of the 16th century, French bindings were generally recognized as the best in Europe, Paris and Lyons being the major centers.

The advent of the printed book in the mid-15th century had of course increased the demand and scope for decorative bindings. It was at this time that books began to be stored upright and side by side rather than stacked flat as before. The boards of the book were now extended slightly beyond the leaves for extra protection. To prevent the distortion at front and back edges caused by the drag of the leaves, the back was rounded to a convex shape which in turn pulled the front edge to a concave shape. The extra thickness created by the thread at the folds meant that there was a need to distribute the swelling evenly. The back was beaten carefully with a hammer after rounding, to form a shoulder along each side of the folds, against which the boards could fit snugly. This technique formed the basis of craft binding as we know it today.

The fine individually tooled bindings of the 17th and 18th centuries gave way gradually to the heavily ornate bindings of the Victorian era. Painted or lacquered bindings, often inlaid with mother-of-pearl or butterflies' wings, were the fashion of the day. Cloth bindings, introduced in the 1830s, satisfied the demand for a material that was cheaper and quicker to work on than leather. Mechanical blocking presses were used to emboss the cloth with gold lettering and decoration. Casebinding—a method in which the covers or cases are made and decorated separately from the book sections—became the standard technique; by the end of the 19th century, machinery had been invented that could cater for every stage of this process. Unsewn binding, also known as perfect binding, is the method now used for paperback books. The single leaves are stuck together with glue and the cover is also glued, directly onto the spine. This method is obviously geared to mass production and suitable more for books that are not expected to last very long.

As with any other craft, the individually designed and handmade article cannot compete in the modern commercial market and craft binders today work to create bindings of a high quality, mainly for collectors or for exhibition purposes.

The hand method of case-binding provides a good starting point, as it requires very little special equipment. With this method you can produce your own books, make a new case for an old printed book or create a binding for magazines or journals.

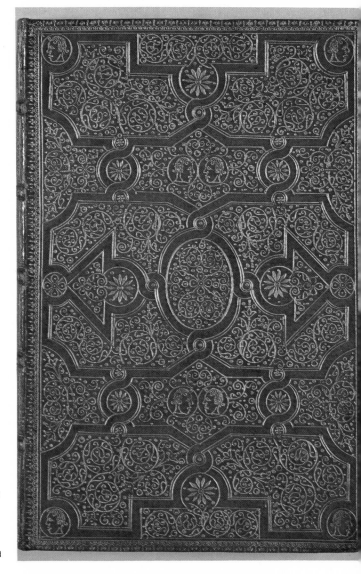

Basic equipment and tools

Presses. A craft binder uses four or five different types of press, all of which do different jobs. However, presses tend to be bulky and expensive, so if you do not have access to such equipment an improvised press using pressing boards can be made as described below.

Pressing boards. Used with a set of carpentry clamps, pressing boards make an adequate press. You will need two sets of boards, both of 16mm ($\frac{5}{8}$in) plywood. One set should consist of two boards slightly larger than the size of the book and the second pair of boards should be slightly larger than the area of the open book. Heavy iron weights are necessary to provide extra pressure during pressing.

Cutting tools. You will need one pair of shears—preferably bookbinder's shears—for heavy duty use and also a large pair of scissors. If you are not able to use a paper cutter (guillotine), bookbinder's plough or special board cutters for trimming and cutting paper and boards, use a craft knife fitted with sharp blades or a sharp penknife. A special saw (tenon saw) is used by bookbinders to make cuts in the back of the book sections to provide holes for sewing,

Above: A fine example of early 17th-century German craftsmanship, this elaborate book cover is richly decorated in gold and enamelwork.

Left: French binding in traditional red morocco with gold pointillé tooling, thought to be the work of Florimond Badier and dated C1640.

but you can pierce holes with a needle instead of using a saw.

Ruler. Use a long straightedged steel ruler. It is invaluable, not only for measuring, but also provides a firm edge which acts as a guide when you are cutting or trimming paper or boards.

Carpenter's square. This (or a set square) is essential for accurate measurement of right angles, for example when marking up the boards before cutting.

Bone folders. These flat pieces of bone, ivory or plastic are used to produce a neat crease when folding paper and other material and also to ensure a neat edge when the covering material is folded over the boards. You should have at least two bone folders—one small one with a tapered end and one larger one, rounded at both ends.

Brushes. For applying adhesive a round-headed glue brush is best, although a 5cm (2in) household paintbrush can be used instead.

Needle and thread. It is possible to buy special bookbinder's needles for sewing the sections of a book together, but an ordinary large-eyed needle will do just as well. The choice of thread, however, is important: use unbleached, two or three strand linen cord.

Materials

Paper. The type of book you want to make will determine your choice of paper. Colored or white medium-weight construction (cartridge) paper is ideal for many purposes but thicker paper may be preferred, for example for a scrapbook or album. Use thinner paper such as typing (bank or bond) paper for diaries and small notebooks. Use strong, colored paper for the endpapers. (These are pasted or glued to the inside back and front covers to secure the sections of the book firmly onto the cover.)

In addition to the paper needed to make the book, you will need sheets of wax paper for use when pasting and pressing the book. Two thin sheets of aluminum are also needed during the pressing process.

Boards. These are the hard covers of the book. A coarse, heavy type of cardboard (strawboard) or thin particle board (millboard) is usually used for boards and as a general rule, the larger the book, the thicker the boards should be. For the spine of the book choose a cardboard that is thinner and more flexible than the boards.

Cutting board. Always place a piece of strong cardboard underneath your work when cutting or trimming.

Tapes. Tapes are sewn in across the back of the book for extra strength. Unbleached linen tape is the best and is normally sold in rolls. The standard width is 1.5cm ($\frac{1}{2}$in).

Linings. Mull or stiffened cambric is used for the first lining and brown wrapping paper ("Kraft" paper) for the second lining.

Covering materials. Bookcloth is specially treated cotton or linen cloth; this varies in quality, buckram being the best but also the most expensive. Use bookcloth for the whole case or just for the spine of the book in combination with paper. Marbled paper is a traditional book covering material but you can also experiment with other types of patterned paper. The most common leathers chosen for bindings are morocco (goatskin) and vellum (calfskin) but it is advisable not to start using leather until you are reasonably skilled and experienced.

Adhesives

A really good glue or paste is essential for successful bookbinding. Always keep a damp rag or sponge beside you as you work to wipe off the excess glue and to keep your hands clean.

Glue. Some craft binders still prefer to use the traditional animal glues, but modern plastic glue (PVA) has proved a useful substitute. This glue is marketed under

Making a case-bound book

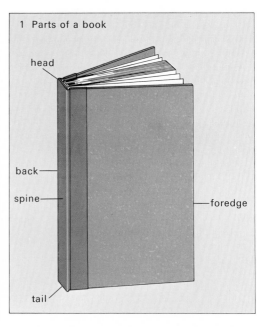

1 Parts of a book

head

back

spine

foredge

tail

The hand method of case-binding offers plenty of scope for using some of the many attractive patterned papers that are available.

various brand names and these do vary in quality. Choose a good one.

Paste. Paste takes longer to dry than plastic glue, but you may find it simpler to use as it can be cleaned off more easily. Either buy cold-water paste from a store or make your own as follows. Mix about 60g (2oz) plain wheat flour with 0.25 liters (16fl oz) water. Bring to a boil, stirring constantly, then allow to boil for about five minutes, still stirring. Remove from the heat and allow the mixture to cool to about 50°C (120°F). Add a pinch of crushed thymol crystals (these act as a fungicide) and beat the mixture well. Dilute the mixture with boiling water later if necessary, but allow it to cool before using it.

Making a case-bound book

The following instructions cover the basic techniques of making and sewing together

book sections and preparing and attaching the case. If you are rebinding a printed book or making a binding for magazines, you already have the sections but remember to keep them in the original order.

Before beginning to work make sure you are familiar with the different names used for various parts of a book; these are shown in fig.1.

Making the book sections

Checking the grain of paper. When using any sheet of paper it is important to check the direction of the grain first. All paper should be used with the grain running parallel to the spine of the book. A book sewn with the grain running in the right direction will open easily, whereas one whose sections have been folded against the grain will have leaves that open awkwardly.

When paper is made by hand the fibers are distributed in all directions as they settle. Handmade paper is usually very strong and since there is little noticeable

grain direction, it can be used in any way. However, most types of paper are now made by machine and during this process the fibers settle in one direction. The grain of machine-made paper is easily checked. Cut a small rectangle of paper measuring about 7.5 × 4cm (3 × 1½in) from the main sheet of paper. Dampen one side of the small rectangle. The paper will curl almost immediately and this will tell you the direction of the grain (fig.2). Mark a faint arrow in pencil on the main piece of paper to indicate the grain direction, then fold the sheet of paper once and then again at right angles. If you examine the sheet of paper carefully you will notice that the fold running along the direction of the grain is neat and regular. The fold across the grain will be irregular as the grain resists an even crease.

Note: if you want to use a whole sheet of paper without cutting off a small rectangle, check the grain direction by folding it both ways as described.

Folding and cutting the paper (fig.3a and b). Having checked the direction of the grain, take each sheet of paper and fold as shown in fig.3a or b, depending on the page size required. Measure and mark in the trim lines, then place a cutting board underneath the paper and cut along these lines, using a craft knife as a trimming knife

and a steel ruler as a cutting guide. Use a bone folder to crease the folded sheets more sharply, working with a stroking action along the fold.

Preparing the sections. The number of folded sheets suitable for one section of a book will vary according to the type and thickness of the paper and the required finished size of the book. You can get some idea of this by looking at other books and counting the number of leaves (folded sheets) per section and the total number of sections. Begin with a book that is not too thick—somewhere between 1–2.5cm ($\frac{3}{8}$–1in) is best.

To make a section for sewing, place the appropriate number of folded sheets, one inside the other, folded edges together. Make the remaining sections in the same way.

Note: if you are rebinding a book and the sections are already sewn, cut the thread carefully and gently pull the sections apart. If binding magazines, treat each magazine as a section and remove any staples.

Stack the sections, each one on top of the other, with folded edges together. Place between pressing boards and secure with clamps. Put a heavy weight on top and leave for a few minutes.

Cutting the boards. Two boards are used at this stage to help keep the book sections

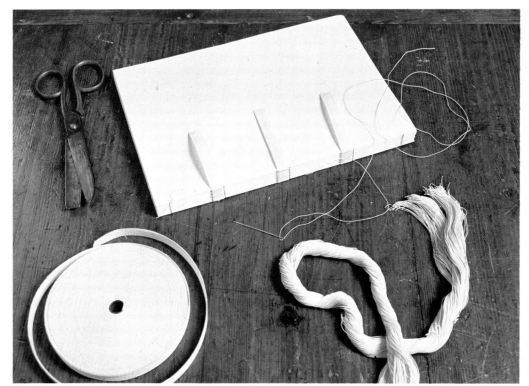

together. The same boards can be used later as covers for the book if you like. First test the grain of the board by bending it gently, first one way then the other. You will find that the board is more flexible in one direction, ie along the direction of the grain. Mark the board with a small arrow as a reminder. As with the paper, the grain of the boards must run parallel to the spine of the book. Use a carpenter's square to measure and mark up two boards, each of which should be the same width as the paper used for the book, but allowing 3mm ($\frac{1}{8}$in) extra at both head and tail. Cut the boards, using a craft knife and steel ruler.

Marking up for sewing. Keeping the sections of the book together, place one board on either side. Grip the whole book firmly, then tap first the head and then the back on the workbench to knock them square. Still gripping the book firmly, and without allowing the sections to move, place the book on a pressing board so that the back, which is facing you, is aligned with the edge of the board. (The head will be to the left and the side uppermost will be the front of the book.) Put a weight on the

Sewn book sections with tape and thread.

upper side of the book to keep it firmly in position.

Using a carpenter's square and a soft lead pencil, mark a line across the back 1.5cm ($\frac{1}{2}$in) in from the head and another the same distance in from the tail.

Cut a short piece of 1.5cm ($\frac{1}{2}$in) tape to use as a guide and mark off three bands so as to divide the back into four equal parts as shown in fig.4.

Remove the weight from the top of the book and, keeping the sections together, draw the book forwards slightly so that the back projects a little beyond the pressing board. Place a second pressing board on top and clamp securely. Make a shallow cut along each marked line with a special saw (tenon saw), drawing it once across the folds of the book.

Note: if using a needle instead, prick one hole on each section fold, following the marked lines.

Sewing. Cut three lengths of tape, each measuring 10cm (4in) plus the width of the back of the book. Keep the prepared sec-

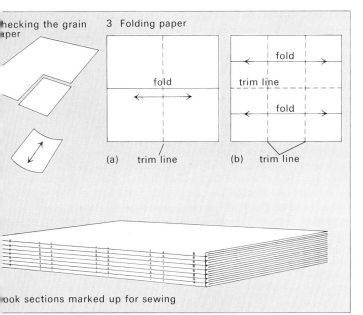

Checking the grain paper

3 Folding paper

(a) trim line

(b) trim line

ook sections marked up for sewing

Making a case-bound book

5 Threading the needle

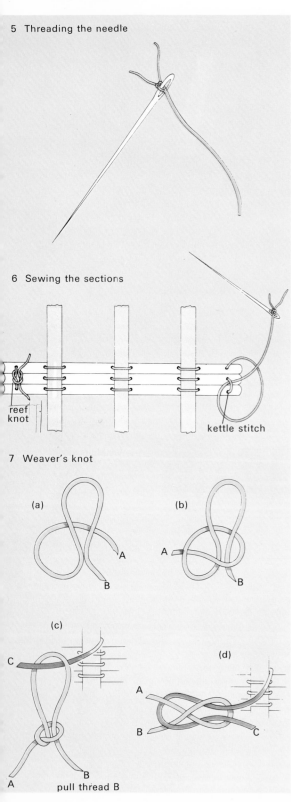

6 Sewing the sections

reef knot

kettle stitch

7 Weaver's knot

(a)

A

B

(b)

A

B

(c)

C

B

A

(d)

A

B

C

pull thread B

tions within easy reach. Position one of the pressing boards to the edge of the work-bench, and place the top section face down with the fold to the edge of the board. Place the tapes in position, tucking an end of about 5cm (2in) underneath the section. Take a length of linen thread about three or four times the length of the book and split one end. Thread the needle as shown in fig.5 and tie the split ends together to stop the needle from falling off as you are sewing.

Follow the diagram (fig.6) for sewing the first and subsequent sections. Push the needle through the first hole on the left, working from the outside through to the inside of the section. Draw the thread through gently, leaving an end of about 5cm (2in). Tie a small strip of paper around this end to stop the thread from being pulled through. Bring the needle through the next hole along, from the inside to the outside of the section, take it over the tape and push the needle through the hole to the right of the tape. Always pull the thread through firmly but gently in the direction of the sewing to avoid tearing the paper at the holes. Continue in this way until you reach the last hole. Bring the needle through this hole to the outside.

Place the next section face down on top of the first. Take the thread through the first hole on the right of the second section and sew as before.

At the last hole of the second section tie the short end of thread to the long length with a flat knot (reef knot) and, without cutting the thread, place the third section on top of the second and continue sewing. At the last hole on the third section bring the needle out and pass it between the sections under the thread link, making a loop. Pass the thread through the loop and pull up firmly. This special stitch is known as a kettle stitch.

Note: to keep the sections firmly together during sewing, tap down with the flat side of a bone folder after sewing two or three sections.

Sew all of the remaining sections together, making a kettle stitch at each end as described. At the last hole of the last section sew the kettle stitch twice for security and extra strength. Cut the thread close to

Trimming the edges.

the back. Place the book under a board with a weight on top.

Joining in new thread (fig.7a–d). A weaver's knot will lie flat and can be slipped in position on the outside. Make the join near a tape if possible so that it can nestle against the extra thickness where it is less noticeable.

Endpapers. Endpapers take the initial strain from the book at the joint whilst providing a pleasant transition from the cover to the inside. Using strong, colored paper, check the grain, then fold and cut in the same way as the main sheets to give two leaves — one each for front and back.

Take a thin strip of diagonally folded newspaper measuring the same length as the length of the book and place it not more than 3mm ($\frac{1}{8}$in) away from the back edge of the book. Hold it firmly in position with a ruler, then brush glue or paste carefully over the 3mm ($\frac{1}{8}$in) joint and onto the strip of newspaper. Remove the newspaper strip, and then place the folded edge of one endpaper over the glued section. Rub it through wax paper to secure. Turn the book over and attach the other endpaper in the same way.

Making a case-bound book

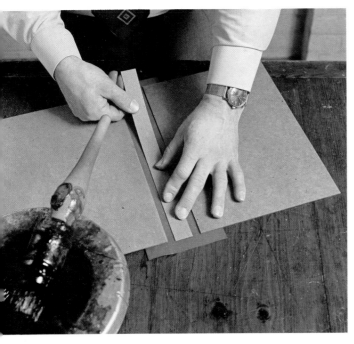

Quarter-bound case: positioning the boards and the cardboard strip for a hollow lining.

g line

1.75cm ($\frac{5}{8}$in)

1.75cm ($\frac{5}{8}$in)

3mm ($\frac{1}{8}$in)

4cm ($1\frac{1}{2}$in)

hollow lining strip

4cm ($1\frac{1}{2}$in)

1.75cm ($\frac{5}{8}$in)

1.75cm ($\frac{5}{8}$in)

1.75cm ($\frac{5}{8}$in)

3mm ($\frac{1}{8}$in)

asuring the bookcloth   9 Trimming the corners

Glueing the back. Tap the back of the book on the workbench to make it flat again, then place it on the board as before. Load the tip of a glue brush with adhesive (this should be of the consistency of thick cream) but make sure that it does not drip. Spread the adhesive along the back, between the tapes, and starting in the center and working outwards towards the head and then the tail. Be careful not to deposit any adhesive over the cut edges. Rub the adhesive well in between the sections with your finger.

1st lining. Cut a piece of mull or stiffened cambric slightly shorter than the length of the back and the same width plus 5cm (2in) on either side for flanges. Glue the back again carefully, then center the mull lining and rub down through wax paper to fix it.

2nd lining. Check the grain of a sheet of brown paper, then cut a strip the width of the back and the same length as the mull. Glue the brown paper strip sparingly, place on top of the mull and rub down carefully as before to force out any air bubbles.

Trimming the edges. If you are not able to use a bookbinder's plough or paper cutter (guillotine) to trim the edges of the book, use a sharp trimming knife or craft knife, together with a steel ruler.
Measuring from the back of the book, note the measurement of the narrowest leaf. Mark a point at both top and bottom on the top endpaper, the same measurement from the back as the narrowest leaf *minus* 3mm ($\frac{1}{8}$in). Join the two points in pencil to make a trim line.
Place the ruler up to the trim line. Put a cutting board under the book and then, pressing firmly or with the book clamped to the lower pressing board, draw the knife gently towards you along the trim line, cutting through one or two leaves at a time. Measure the length of the shortest leaf and, subtracting 3mm ($\frac{1}{8}$in) at each end from the measurement, mark a trim line at the top and bottom edges. Use a set square or carpenter's square to measure and mark the trim lines. Trim both edges, drawing the knife towards you from the back to the foredge. (This prevents the paper from tearing at the glued edge.)

Hollow lining. First check the grain of the lightweight cardboard in the same way as for the boards, then cut a piece the width of the back and the same length as the book.

Making the case
Two types of case are described here. Quarter binding, as shown in the photographs, uses two materials—in this case bookcloth for the spine and paper for the sides. One material only is used for full binding.

Quarter-bound case. Place the bookcloth on a cutting board, wrong side up. Using the cardboard strip previously cut for the hollow lining as a guide, mark up the cloth with a turn-in allowance of 1.75cm ($\frac{5}{8}$in) at both head and tail and about 4cm ($1\frac{1}{2}$in) on either side (fig.8). Using one of the boards as a guide, mark two parallel lines down the length of the cloth to give from 3mm–0.5cm ($\frac{1}{8}$–$\frac{1}{4}$in) for a joint space between the hollow lining and the boards. Cut the cloth.
Check the grain of the marbled or similar paper to be used for the sides, then cut two pieces the same length as the cloth and about 1.5cm ($\frac{1}{2}$in) less than the width of the board. Place one piece of paper, wrong side up on a cutting board, then position one board on top with a 1.75cm ($\frac{5}{8}$in) turn-in allowance on three sides. Trim the 2 corners at an angle of 45° to the board and 3mm ($\frac{1}{8}$in) away from the points as shown in fig.9. Repeat with the second board for the remaining two corners.

Quarter-bound case: turning in the cloth.

Casing in
Experimenting
with designs

Casing in: pasting the endpaper.

Place the cloth strip on a sheet of newspaper and apply adhesive, then place the boards up to the marked lines and position the cardboard strip between them. Place a sheet of wax paper on top and rub down. Turn in the cloth at head and tail and rub gently with a bone folder.
Turn the case over so that the right side is uppermost. Apply paste or adhesive to one sheet of paper, then position it over the board, so that it overlaps the cloth spine by 3mm ($\frac{1}{8}$in). Turn in at the edges, paying particular attention to the mitered corners. Use your thumbnail or the small pointed bone folder to make a neat finish. Repeat for the second side.
Run the flat side of the bone folder against the edge of the case to make it neat and also to ensure adhesion, and then across the boards and spine to eliminate any air bubbles. Run the folder along the crease at the joint space through wax paper. Place the case between two sheets of wax paper

and press between boards with a weight on top for at least an hour. Substitute two sheets of ordinary paper for the wax paper and press for a further 12 hours.
Full-bound case. Place the covering material on a cutting board, wrong side up. Mark up the positions for the boards and cardboard strip, allowing 1.75cm ($\frac{5}{8}$in) turn-in all around and 3mm ($\frac{1}{8}$in) at joint spaces as before. Trim the corners as described for the quarter-bound case. Apply adhesive to the paper, reposition both the boards and the cardboard strip and turn in. Rub down and press as before.

Casing in
Position the book on the opened case, allowing for a 3mm ($\frac{1}{8}$in) projection of the boards at the head, tail and foredge. Place a sheet of waste paper under the top of the first endpaper leaf. Paste and lay down the tape slips and mull lining. Remove the waste paper. Bring over the case board and press lightly onto the endpaper. Lift and adjust to the correct position if necessary by sliding the paper. Rub down.
Turn the book over and repeat for the second board.
Pressing and drying. Insert sheets of wax paper between the pressing boards and the book. Place sheets of aluminum between the wax paper and the book and clean paper between the pressing boards and wax paper. Press under a weight for at least 12 hours.
Make a title label for the spine, using hand lettering or transfers and glue to the spine when the case is dry.
Opening the book. All newly bound books must first be opened carefully. If a book is forced open the back can break and the book will then always open at the same place. Remove the book from the press, then crease each free endpaper lightly at the glued edge. Open the book alternately from either side, working towards the center and easing the back.

Experimenting with designs
Paper. Instead of buying decorative paper for covering you can create your own designs by using linoleum cutting, screen printing, potato printing or photographic techniques. Always remember that paper

An Italian goatskin binding with handpainted decoration for George Mawe's *The Genus Crocus*.

needs careful handling, especially when pasting. Do not wet it too much, always rub down through wax paper, and take care not to dig into the surface. However, the fact that paper marks easily can be a positive advantage if you want to create embossed designs. Use pattern-making tools such as those designed for leatherwork, dampen them and then press onto the surface of the paper. Allow the paper to dry under light pressure.
You can also create a decorative covering with collage or make one from papier mâché and then paint and lacquer the surface.
Fabric. Many different fabrics are suitable for coverings and offer a wide choice of colors and textures. Use fabrics as they are or decorate them with embroidered or appliquéd designs. Try to link the cover design with the content and purpose of the book.

A raised appliqué technique was used for this modern
binding by Faith Shannon to create a marvellous
three-dimensional effect for Lewis Carroll's famous
and much-loved classic *Through the Looking Glass.*

Recycling

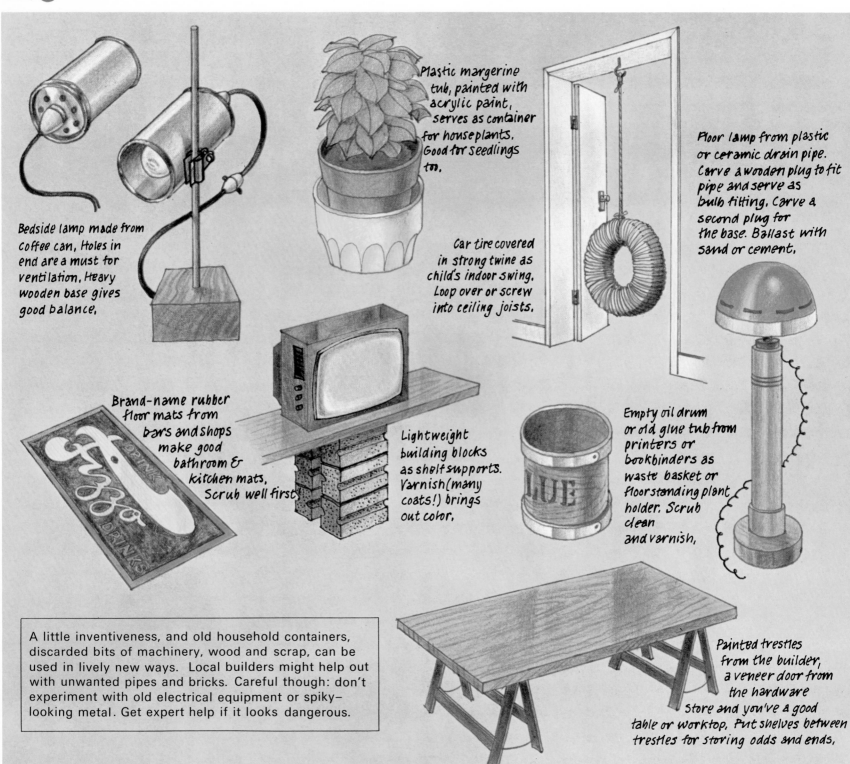

Bedside lamp made from coffee can. Holes in end are a must for ventilation. Heavy wooden base gives good balance.

Plastic margerine tub, painted with acrylic paint, serves as container for house plants. Good for seedlings too.

Floor lamp from plastic or ceramic drain pipe. Carve a wooden plug to fit pipe and serve as bulb fitting. Carve a second plug for the base. Ballast with sand or cement.

Car tire covered in strong twine as child's indoor swing. Loop over or screw into ceiling joists.

Brand-name rubber floor mats from bars and shops make good bathroom & kitchen mats. Scrub well first.

Lightweight building blocks as shelf supports. Varnish (many coats!) brings out color.

Empty oil drum or old glue tub from printers or bookbinders as waste basket or floor standing plant holder. Scrub clean and varnish.

A little inventiveness, and old household containers, discarded bits of machinery, wood and scrap, can be used in lively new ways. Local builders might help out with unwanted pipes and bricks. Careful though: don't experiment with old electrical equipment or spiky-looking metal. Get expert help if it looks dangerous.

Painted trestles from the builder, a veneer door from the hardware store and you've a good table or worktop. Put shelves between trestles for storing odds and ends.

Tickets—train, theater, movies—in a decorative pattern make a good picture. Complete by framing with rope.

Unusual beach pebble, when varnished to preserve color makes a neat candle holder. (Even better when colors match!)

Old farm machinery seat makes good "dog basket" grate for country fireplace. Use old cover from manhole as "fire back."

Take lids off small jars and containers, screw them underneath a shelf. Attach jars to make handy storage space in kitchen or workshop.

Pins, paperclips, staples, needles, buttons—anything small will be easy to find in this "chest of drawers" made from match boxes covered in shiny paper. Handles are brass paper studs.

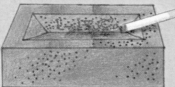

Housebrick—a ready made ash tray. Cover base with self-adhesive green felt.

Handy, modern looking table lamp is easily made from plastic container. Take cord through base, weigh down with sand. Fit bulb to suit.

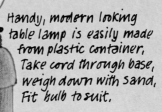

Take a balloon, fill it with air; wrap around and around with string dipped first in fiberglass resin or wood glue. Burst with pin, take out remains of balloon and you have one lampshade.

Not only bed coverings but curtains too look good made from those scraps of material you've collected.

Metalwork

One of the oldest known metalwork crafts is still being practiced by this coppersmith at Trabzon, Turkey.

The word "metal" comes from the Greek *metallan* which means "to search after" and was applied to some of the earliest known metals—gold, silver, copper, iron, tin and lead. Archaeologists have established the existence of copper objects in Egypt and of copper mines in Sinai dating back to 4700 BC. By about 3000 BC there had begun the first workings of copper mines on the island of Cyprus. Copper soon replaced the use of stone in the making of weapons, tools and artifacts for decoration. This was possible because, while stone had to be painstakingly carved, metal could be easily converted into intricate shapes and polished to a high luster. Bronze was the first alloy to be discovered. The art of fusing copper and tin to obtain bronze was first developed in Asia Minor in about 3500 BC and was extensively developed in the Ancient Egyptian and Assyrian civilizations. The making of bronze soon spread to the Mediterranean region. The Phoenicians obtained tin in Spain and later in Britain and greatly developed the

production of bronze and the bronze trade. By 1000 BC iron was replacing bronze. Due to its extreme strength, iron was preferred for making tools while bronze was limited to decorative and domestic purposes.

According to the Odyssey, the Greeks had a knowledge of steel: they also knew mercury, which they called quicksilver. By early Roman times, brass, an alloy of copper and zinc, was developed and brass-making was established as an industry. Many other metals were not discovered until much later. Bismuth and antimony were not known until the Middle Ages, nickel, manganese and platinum were first used in the 18th century and aluminum in the 19th century. By the end of the 19th century most metals were known. The production of metals on a commercial scale as well as nuclear metallurgy are developments of the 20th century.

Most techniques used in metalwork were known to ancient civilizations. The Egyptians were the first to join sheets of copper by using rivets, but it was the Greeks who perfected many of the metalwork techniques used today such as embossing, chasing and enameling. They were also familiar with soft soldering with silver and tin, and hard soldering with various copper alloys.

The only metals which are found in a pure state are gold, platinum, some silver and copper. Most metals exist in the form of ore—a mixture of soil and rock where they are chemically combined with other substances such as oxygen, carbon and sulphur. Some metals, such as tin, can be extracted from the ore by crushing, stamping and washing, followed by refining. Refining is a process of melting so that the metal content can be run off, leaving behind the non-metallic residue or slag. Other metals are much harder to refine and call for complicated metallurgical techniques.

Precious metals are usually defined as those which are used in the manufacture of jewelry. They include gold, silver and platinum, although these are by no means the most costly metals: californium, for example, being a very rare metal, is worth far more.

These decorative doorknockers made from bronze (*above*) and brass (*below*) capture the beauty and artistic possibilities of metal alloys.

The delicacy of wrought-iron work is beautifully expressed in these villa gates silhouetted against Lake Como.

Characteristics of metal

All metals can be subdivided into two categories depending on the quantity of iron they contain. *Ferrous* metals are iron-based and include cast iron and steel. *Nonferrous* metals contain no iron. Brass, lead and aluminum fall into this category. Most metals expand when heated and contract when cooled.

Metals can be changed into fluids by the application of heat, but melting points vary: mercury melts at well below freezing point, caesium melts at about the same temperature as butter, while tungsten only melts at about 3400°C (6150°F).

The strength and hardness of metals can be altered by alloying (mixing with another metal). A metal is usually softer and weaker when pure than if it is alloyed. Pure copper and tin are both soft and weak, but mixed together they make a strong alloy, bronze. **Annealing.** A metal can be returned to its former, softer state by heating to a dull red color. This process is called annealing. For example, if you are stretching and forming copper into a dish or bowl shape, it is necessary to anneal the metal frequently to return it to a malleable condition. The object must be heated evenly using a blowtorch of the butane type and then cooled slowly in the air. Do not quench in water as this hardens some metals.

Corrosion

Many metals are subject to a physical and

The malleability of a metal refers to its ability to be beaten or stretched; ductility, to its ability to be easily shaped without springing back to its former shape and cracking. If a metal is said to work-harden, this means that the metal becomes stiffer with hammering and bending.

chemical alteration due to contact with the environment and especially with oxygen. This chemical alteration is termed "natural corrosion," and can be brought about by, among other factors, exposure of the metal to air and water. The corrosion process on iron is referred to as rusting. Some alloys, such as magnesium alloys, corrode very quickly in air alone. Gold, on the other hand, has always been revered for its ability to resist all forms of corrosion or tarnishing. Electrolytic corrosion is another form of corrosion which occurs through the contact of two dissimilar metals. Electrolytic corrosion is due to the flow of minute quantities of electricity from one metal to the other in the presence of water. Metals

Ferrous

Metal	Properties	Useful qualities	Melting point (approx.)	Comments
Cast iron	Brittle, weak, fairly soft	Wears well, easy to cut or drill	1204°C (2200°F)	Can be polished
Wrought iron	Ductile and malleable	Easily welded	1427°C (2600°F)	Readily worked by hand tools
Mild steel	Strong and ductile	Easily cut, bent and shaped	1482°C (2700°F)	Readily worked by hand tools
Carbon steel	Very strong, less ductile	Used for making cutting tools	1538°C (2800°F)	Hard to work

Nonferrous

Metal	Properties	Useful qualities	Melting point	Comments
Copper	Ductile and malleable	Easily worked by hand tools. Easy to shape	1082°C (1980°F)	Work-hardens but can be softened. Polishes well
Tin	Malleable, tough	Non-rusting	228°C (442°F)	Seldom used "as is" but normally as a rust-proof plating on steel
Zinc	Soft and ductile	Corrosion resistant	412°C (773°F)	Low strength
Lead	Very soft	Easily worked	325°C (617°F)	No great strength
Aluminum	Malleable and ductile	Soft and easily worked	660°C (1220°F)	Readily worked by hand tools. Polishes well
Duralumin	Very strong	Almost as strong as steel	660°C (1220°F)	Not easily shaped. Work-hardens
Brass	Easily worked	Wears well	1082°C (1980°F)	Strong. Polishes well

Weather-resistant treatments
Basic materials

are less likely to corrode if they are given some kind of protective treatment. These vary depending on whether the metal is to be kept indoors or exposed to the weather. Indoor protective treatments for most metals consists of an easily applied coat of paint, which also provides a decorative finish. External weather-resistant treatments depend on whether the metal is ferrous or nonferrous.

Weather-resistant treatments

Ferrous metals. Many techniques such as applying an anti-corrosive pigment paint, galvanizing, cadmium plating and chromium plating, have been perfected for protecting the surface of ferrous metals against natural corrosion.

Painting requires careful surface preparation beforehand in order to remove all traces of old rust. Remove the rust with a wire brush and file. Then paint on a coat of zinc-rich primer paint. If you cannot obtain a zinc primer paint, then use a red oxide primer.

Note: follow the manufacturer's instructions carefully as some brands require washing the metal in cold water after painting, in which case, let the metal dry thoroughly before working it.

Galvanizing, cadmium plating and chromium plating must all be done commercially. Galvanizing consists of coating iron or steel with zinc to give an electrochemical protection to the metal. Cadmium plating is used for plating steel and chromium plating is used on iron, steel and nickel.

Nonferrous metals. If untreated copper is exposed to the weather, it acquires a fine green patina which in itself can be very attractive. Alternatively, protect the surface with a transparent lacquer for metal use. Indoors, copper is best left alone, but can be polished with metal polish.

Brass is mainly used for its lustrous color when polished, so it is best not to paint or otherwise obscure the surface. However, brass does tarnish with time, and fingermarks show up as brown stains. A thorough polishing followed by a coat of spray-on lacquer is ample protective treatment.

Light alloys. Light alloys such as mag-

nesium alloys need a special primer—a chromate-based etching paint—before painting. Then spray on the subsequent undercoat and finish paint in thin coats. Allow plenty of time for the metal to dry between coats as the solvents in the paint may otherwise attack the primer and cause it to bubble.

Aluminum alloys. Anodizing, which is done commercially, is required on aluminum alloys. Anodizing imparts a dull silvery finish to the metal. The anodic film can be dyed during processing and some very attractive colors are available which add a lustrous sheen to the metal. Color anodizing is especially appropriate for aluminum fire screens, decorative plaques and ashtrays.

Basic materials

Intricate metalwork can be done with basic tools, which are easy to use.

Measuring ruler. You will need a 30cm (12in) steel ruler to use as a straightedge or guide for the scriber.

Scriber. For the purpose of marking out metal, use a scriber. This looks like a pencil with a sharpened, pointed end, and leaves a fine clear scratch mark when held firmly and drawn over metal.

Flat try-square. An engineer's flat try-square is also useful for marking the metal.

Metal dividers. Use metal dividers for transferring dimensions from a drawing, a ruler or another object and for drawing circles and curves.

Tinsnips. For cutting thin metal use a pair of special hand shears, known as tinsnips. These cut fairly thin mild (malleable) steel, but will cut thicker gauges of softer metals as well. Tinsnips are either straight or curved. The advantage of curved snips is that they enable you to keep the handles of the snips, as well as your hand, above the line you are cutting. This facilitates cutting and prevents you from skinning your knuckles on the sharp edge of the metal. Curved snips are made for left and right-handed use in order to cut curves in either direction.

Metal "nibbling" shears. This tool "nibbles" out a thin strip of metal so that you do not have to distort or bend the metal as you cut. Nibbling shears are suitable for cutting

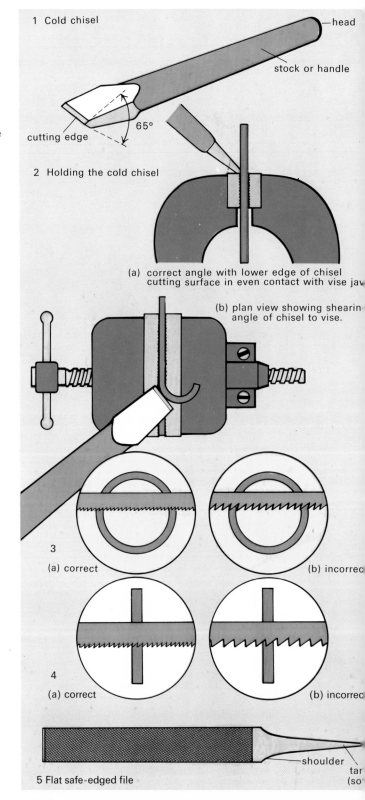

1 Cold chisel — head

stock or handle

cutting edge 65°

2 Holding the cold chisel

(a) correct angle with lower edge of chisel cutting surface in even contact with vise jaw

(b) plan view showing shearing angle of chisel to vise.

3
(a) correct

(b) incorrect

4
(a) correct

(b) incorrect

5 Flat safe-edged file

shoulder

tang

thin metal such as thin copper and aluminum. The shears cut a flat sheet as well as circles and curves.

Vise. Use a large metalworking vise with jaws which are more than 10cm (4in) wide. Most vises have serrated metal jaws so that objects clamped into them do not slip. Although the serrated edges are suitable for general purpose work, they leave ugly marks on the surface of soft metals. However, some vises have reversible jaws which can be unscrewed, turned around and refitted.

Vise clamps. If the vise is not reversible, you will need a pair of vise clamps which are pieces of metal used for padding the jaws. These are available ready made from a tool shop. However you can make your own by folding up some pieces of scrap steel, lead, copper or brass and keeping them in place in the jaws of the vise at all times.

Hammers. You will need a ball pein or engineer's hammer weighing 0.5kg (1lb). A ball pein hammer has the usual sort of hammer shape on one side but the other face is spherical or ball-shaped. You will need a cross pein hammer weighing 0.5kg (1lb) for intricate metalwork involving flanging (bending) thin metal. The cross pein has a normal or claw face but is wedge-shaped at the other end. Use a planishing hammer which has a large, usually round face for dressing and shaping metal without bruising the surface. The planishing hammer is intended for metal finishing only, and if it is used for anything other than this—such as driving nails or striking iron—the face will become bruised so that any uneven surfaces on the hammer will eventually be stamped into the metal.

Cold chisel. This is another type of shearing tool and is always used in conjunction with a bench vise and a heavy hammer. Use a cold chisel to remove strips or sections of metal from a narrow bar or plate which is thick enough to be held securely in the vise. In order to function properly, the tip of the cold chisel must be kept sharpened to an angle of 65° (fig.1). The steel is not hardened so it can be filed to shape without difficulty. Hold the cold chisel at the angle to the vise as shown in fig.2a and b.

Hacksaw. Hacksaws are available in a variety of different shapes and sizes and are fitted with replaceable blades. Choose a hacksaw with a comfortable handle to suit your hand—a totally enclosing hand grip prevents bruised fingers if the blade should break during use. Select a hacksaw with a rigid, preferably tubular frame which can be adjusted to take both 25cm (10in) and 30cm (12in) standard length hacksaw blades. Most hacksaw frames incorporate a useful feature which enables you to turn the blade to a 90° angle to the frame. This means that you can cut long, thin strips from a piece of metal by holding the saw sideways with the frame clear of the cutting line.

Hacksaw blades. There are two types of blade—low tungsten steel for general work and high-speed steel for quality precision work. High-speed steel blades last longer, stay sharper and are less likely to break during use. Low tungsten blades are usually self-colored, that is, more or less black, while high-speed blades are colored blue or green.

The blades are defined by the number of teeth per centimeter (inch). The greater the number of teeth, the more slowly but smoothly the saw will cut. Widely spaced teeth are unsuitable for cutting thin metal since they will straddle the metal and probably snap (see fig.3a and b). A good rule to follow is that there should be no fewer than three teeth in contact with the metal at any one time (see fig.4a and b). For thick metal use the coarsest blade you have to accelerate the work.

Files. You will need a small assortment of files for shaping edges and removing sharp corners after sawing or chiseling. There are three main shapes for a file—flat, half-round and round.

Flat or hand files include bellied flat files, which have teeth cut along the narrow edges as well as on the wide flat faces. A parallel safe-edge flat file (fig. 5) has one edge left smooth to enable you to file accurate corners and angles.

Half-round files have one surface flat and the other convex. In plane view, the file is slightly bellied, that is, the sides are not parallel. Use half-round files on interior curves.

Round files are, as the name suggests, round in section and usually tapered. The largest is about 1.5cm (½in) in diameter. Smaller round files with a diameter of less than 0.5cm (¼in) are known as "rat-tail" files.

The coarseness of the cutting teeth on a file varies from smooth, second-cut (also known as medium) and bastard which is the roughest. Use a rough file on heavy work to remove a lot of metal quickly, a second-cut flat file for accurate work and filing to size and a smooth file for imparting a smooth neat edge. Other files which are useful for specialized work are triangular or three square files for saw sharpening, jeweler's files for very delicate work and warding files for modelmaking.

Drills. An electric drill is easy and quick to use. Choose an electric drill with a chuck which will take a 7.5mm ($\frac{5}{16}$in) drill. If you do not have an electric drill, use a set of hand drills ranging from 1.5mm ($\frac{1}{16}$in), 3mm ($\frac{1}{8}$in), 4.5mm ($\frac{3}{16}$in) to 0.5cm ($\frac{1}{4}$in) in diameter. This assortment is adequate for general purpose work.

Grindstones. Grindstones available for craftwork are only suitable for use on ferrous metals. Any attempt at grinding aluminum or copper, for example, will ruin the grindstone. When buying a grindstone for use with an electric drill make sure that it is suitable for the rotational speed of the drill. You can also use grinding disks, which are made of thin metal into which are embedded hard abrasive particles.

Warning: a grindstone is a potentially lethal weapon as the centrifugal forces exerted within a grindstone are very high. Always wear goggles when using the grindstone or grinding disks to protect the eyes from splinters of hot metal.

Caring for tools

Keep your tools in order by hanging them on a workshop tool rack. This is especially necessary for tools with a cutting edge, such as saws, chisels and sharp pointed scribers.

Files are brittle and easily damaged. Hang them on the tool rack or alternatively, wrap them in newspaper or cloth and store them in a drawer. After some use, your files may become clogged with particles of metal, glue, plastic or wood. Clean the files with a scratch card which is a flexible brush-like

Metalwork techniques

pad made of wire. Obstinate clogging will come free by first soaking the file in hot water and then cleaning with a scratch card.

Using a file on light alloys will inevitably clog the teeth of your file. To minimize clogging before filing, rub a piece of chalk across the file so that a thin coat of chalk is deposited in the recesses between the teeth. Corrosion or rusting also affects tools: keep them dry and, when not in use, wipe them with a little light oil or petroleum jelly.

Metalwork techniques

Using the file. Check that the file is fitted with a wooden handle (fig.6) otherwise the sharp end called the tang may gash your hand. Support the workpiece securely in the bench vise so that it will not slip. Clamp the piece close to the part you want to file otherwise the metal will vibrate. Now hold the file at an angle to the metal, with the body of the file in one hand and the end of the file with the thumb and forefinger of the other hand. This position steadies the

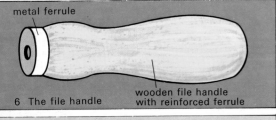

metal ferrule

wooden file handle with reinforced ferrule

6 The file handle

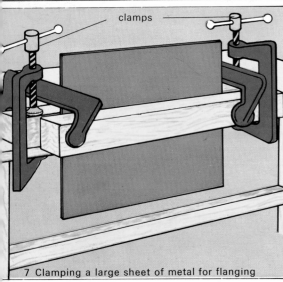

clamps

7 Clamping a large sheet of metal for flanging

file and makes it easier to file in a straight line. Put your weight behind the "push" stroke, and then draw the file back lightly for the next cutting stroke. (A file only cuts in one direction; the teeth cut as you push the file forwards.)

The file cuts best when you can feel the teeth biting into the metal—with a little experience you will recognize this movement. Avoid filing in short strokes. Use the whole length of the file in a slow even manner while maintaining constant contact and pressure. If you file in the same direction continually with a coarse file, you may produce a slightly serrated edge on the metal which matches the pattern of teeth on the file. Rectify this by periodically shifting the direction of stroke.

Draw-filing. This is a finishing process used after filing and consists of filing along the length of the metal edge rather than at an angle to it.

Use a smooth file and hold it almost parallel to the edge you wish to draw-file. Place the forefinger of your free hand under the tip of the file as a guide. File with long slow strokes along the edge. Work slowly and carefully to prevent cutting your hand—there is no need for your fingers to touch the edge of the metal. Draw-filing is always more effective in one direction than in the other since the teeth of the file are angled towards the edges of the file. Experiment until you find the direction that suits you.

Using the vise. Bolt the vise firmly to the workbench so that the front edge of the fixed rear jaw projects about 1.5cm ($\frac{1}{2}$in) over the edge of the bench. With this position you can clamp long objects into the jaws so that they do not foul the edge of the bench.

Cutting. Support the metal in the vise as close to the point of sawing as possible. Unclamp and reposition the metal frequently as the cut progresses. The saw must be fully engaged in cutting the metal without making the metal vibrate. Make sure that the scribed line on the metal is toward you. Until you gain proficiency in the manipulation of saw and metal, keep about 1.5mm ($\frac{1}{16}$in) away from the scribed line so that if you make any errors in sawing you can file them out afterwards.

For very thin metal, use nibbling shears.

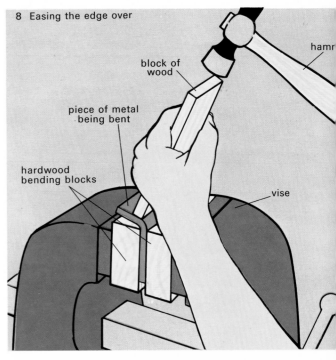

8 Easing the edge over

hamr

block of wood

piece of metal being bent

hardwood bending blocks

vise

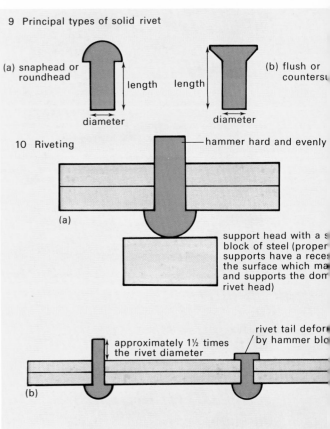

9 Principal types of solid rivet

(a) snaphead or roundhead

length

diameter

(b) flush or countersu

length

diameter

10 Riveting

hammer hard and evenly

(a)

support head with a s block of steel (proper supports have a reces the surface which ma and supports the dom rivet head)

approximately 1½ times the rivet diameter

rivet tail defor by hammer blo

(b)

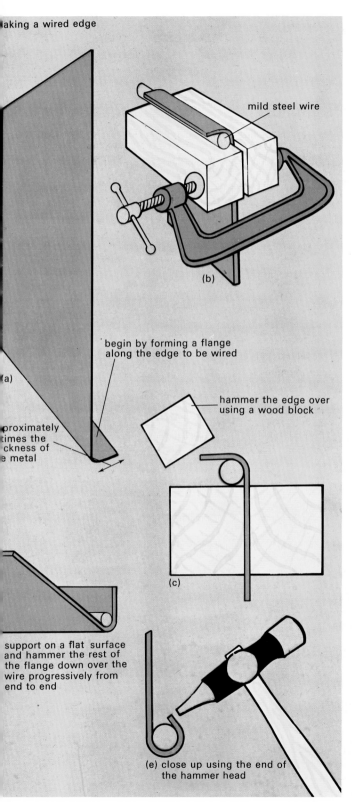

Making a wired edge

mild steel wire

(b)

begin by forming a flange along the edge to be wired

(a)

approximately times the thickness of the metal

hammer the edge over using a wood block

(c)

support on a flat surface and hammer the rest of the flange down over the wire progressively from end to end

(e) close up using the end of the hammer head

Flanging. Flanging or bending the metal provides either a neat edge or produces a three-dimensional shape from a flat surface. Place the metal in a C (G) clamp between two blocks of hardwood (fig.7). Then position another piece of hardwood against the edge of the metal, and with a heavy hammer ease the edge over (fig.8). The block of wood between the metal and hammer prevents the metal surface from becoming damaged.

Riveting. Riveting is used to join pieces of metal together. For metalwork purposes use rivets made from copper or brass. A solid rivet has a head at one end and the other end is plain (fig.9a and b). Fasten the rivet in position by hammering down the plain end (fig.10a and b). Use a pop rivet to create a decorative effect. Pop rivets are made from monel, a nickel alloy, which is silvery in appearance. Fasten the pop rivet into place with special pop rivet pliers.

Wiring (fig.11a–e). Wiring consists of folding the edge of the metal sheet over a length of mild steel wire to provide a neat finish. First flange the edge to be wired (a). Then insert the wire in the vise (b) and hammer the edge of the flange over the wire with a wooden block (c). Place the metal on a flat surface so that the flange and wire lie flat (d). Hammer down the edge completely (e).

Soldering. This is a method of joining two metals with a metal alloy. The solder or alloy is a compound of tin and lead of varying proportions, sometimes mixed with smaller amounts of other metals such as copper. The proportion of tin and lead depends on the type of metal you are soldering. For example, tin requires a solder of 60% tin and 40% lead (see fig.13). The solder must always have a melting point which is lower than the metals being joined. Soft solder melts below a temperature of 450°C (842°F) and is suitable for general purpose metalwork. Hard solder melts above 450°C (842°F) and is used mainly for joins that need to be particularly strong. If you use a soldering iron (fig.12a) or a blowtorch with a copper bit (fig.12b) make sure that the bit is clean before use. Remove dirt with a metal file.

Flux. This is a paste or liquid that ensures the cleanness of the metal—by preventing oxidation—so that if the metal is not clean, the solder will "take." Although the metal may look clean, it will naturally have a certain amount of oxide on it which increases with heating. Flux also helps the molten solder to flow smoothly onto the metal. Mild flux is noncorrosive and must be used with a copper soldering iron as it is inflammable and cannot be used with a naked flame such as a blowtorch. Acid flux is corrosive. Avoid all contact with the skin. It can be used with a soldering iron as well as with a blowtorch. Fig.13 shows the type of solder and flux suitable for different metals.

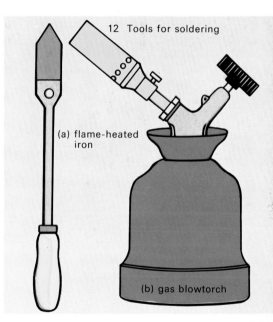

12 Tools for soldering

(a) flame-heated iron

(b) gas blowtorch

Soft solder and flux selection guide 13

Metal to be joined	Solder %Tin	%Lead	Flux
Brass or Copper	50	50	Acid or Mild
Tin	60	40	Mild
Lead	50	50	Mild
Iron or Steel	50	50	Acid
Gold or Silver	70	30	Acid
Nickel	50	50	Acid

Geometric
candlestick

Geometric candlestick

Here is an attractive and unusual table can-
delabrum for the dining room table or
sidetable. The most suitable metals to use
are aluminum as used here or copper and
brass since they can be highly polished.
However, steel sheet and iron are also suitable although iron requires plating and an
attractive finish.

Although precise measurements are given
here, the candlestick can be adapted to
another size—provided the proportions of
the parts remain the same.

The upperwork sections are cut from sheets
of metal, 3mm ($\frac{1}{8}$in) thick. A thicker metal
such as 0.5cm ($\frac{1}{4}$in) will make no difference to the structure of the candlestick
although more effort is required to cut out
the pieces. As the base needs flanging, do
not use metal thicker than 1.5mm ($\frac{1}{16}$in)
thick.

You will need:

2 sheets of aluminum 30 × 37.5cm
(12 × 15in) and 3mm ($\frac{1}{8}$in) thick for the
upperwork □ 1 sheet of aluminum
24 × 16.5cm ($9\frac{1}{2}$ × $6\frac{1}{2}$in) for the base □ vise
□ hacksaw □ bastard file □ smooth flat
file □ 3mm ($\frac{1}{8}$in) drill □ 2 thick blocks of
wood 22.5 × 15cm (9 × 6in) □ piece of
softwood the same dimensions as the base
□ block of wood for flanging □ electric or
gas jet soldering iron or blowtorch □ solder (50% tin and 50% lead) □ flux (acid)

compass □ wax (chinagraph) pencil □
steel ruler □ fine steel wool □ metal polish
□ linen cloth □ emery cloth □ 5 headless
2.5cm (1in) wire nails or metal tubing
2.5cm (1in) diameter □ green baize or
velvet □ resin adhesive □ suitable spray-
on varnish for metal.

Making the upperwork

Scribing. Draw the shapes X and Y from the
graph (fig.14a and b) in which 1 square
equals 2.5cm (1in). Mark these shapes
onto the metal with a wax (chinagraph)
pencil. Place the steel ruler on the metal
and holding the scriber firmly like a pencil,
make a deep score along the edge of the
ruler following the penciled outline. Make
sure the scriber does not scratch beyond
the saw cut you will be making, otherwise the scratch will remain visible.

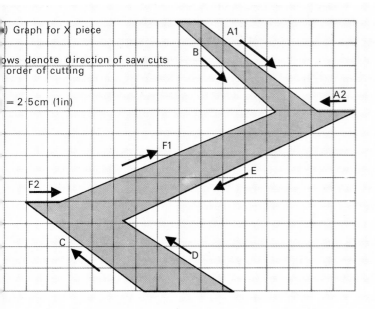

(a) Graph for X piece

ows denote direction of saw cuts
order of cutting

= 2·5cm (1in)

A1

B

A2

F1

E

F2

C

D

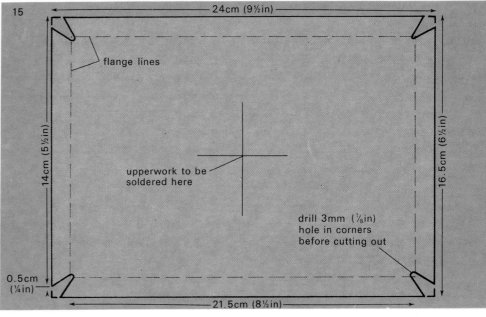

15

24cm (9½in)

flange lines

14cm (5½in)

16.5cm (6½in)

upperwork to be
soldered here

drill 3mm (⅛in)
hole in corners
before cutting out

0.5cm
(¼in)

21.5cm (8½in)

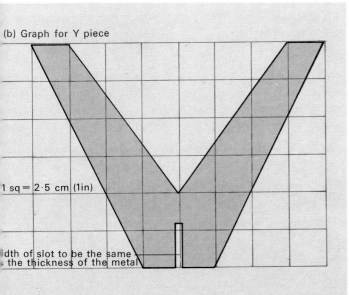

(b) Graph for Y piece

1 sq = 2·5 cm (1in)

dth of slot to be the same
the thickness of the metal

Cutting. Support X in the vise as close to the point of sawing as possible. Unclamp and reposition the metal frequently as the cut progresses. Follow the line of cut in the sequence shown in fig.14a.

When starting to cut at an angle to the edge of the metal as in cut A1, begin by cutting a notch with the saw (or file) so that the saw will not slip when angled to align with the scribed mark. At the end of cut A1, there is a discontinuity in the line to provide a ledge for the pricket or socket disk (A2). Stop sawing just short of this, reposition the metal and then cut A2, from the side of the metal sheet.

With cut F1, allow 3mm (⅛in) clearance from the scribed line. At the end of the ledge part (F2) reduce cutting pressure on the hacksaw and gradually, while still moving the saw in the usual manner, twist it. This has the effect of opening the saw slot into a slightly wider channel. Gradually, re-apply sawing pressure and, in this way, make a slight curved cut to align with the scribed mark again.

File down the edges to the scribed line, starting with a coarse file and finishing off with a smooth file.

Now clamp Y in the vise. Cut the V-shape and then the 2 remaining corners. File down the edges to the scribed line, starting with a coarse file and finishing off with a smooth file. Cut a slot in Y, at the base of the V intersection with a saw (fig.14b). Saw to the same depth as the metal, so that X fits neatly into Y to form one completed structure. Draw file the edges and polish with fine steel wool and metal polish. Finally, rub with metal polish and a linen cloth to remove all traces of roughness.

Making the base

Using a 3mm (⅛in) drill, drill a hole in each corner of the metal base, 0.5cm (¼in) from the edge as shown in fig.15. The holes make it easier to saw cut the corners neatly as well as preventing the metal from cracking with flanging. Saw out each corner to a V-shape ending at the hole.

Flanging. Clamp the metal base firmly between 2 blocks of wood in the vise. Using a heavy hammer and a block of wood, hammer the edges down.

Soldering the corners. Heat up the inside corners of the base. Then dip the stick of solder into the flux. Do not melt the solder in the flame of the gas torch or on the end of the soldering iron, but place it on the metal and allow the heat from the metal to do the melting. In this way you can be sure that the metal has reached the proper temperature for the solder to take. Let the solder flow into each corner at a time. Remove surplus solder which seeps through to the other (top) side later with an emery cloth, prior to polishing the base.

Joining the upperwork and base. To ensure a good soldered join, check that the bottom of the upperwork is perfectly flat and level. Take the scriber and mark out exactly where the intersecting sections of the upperwork will touch the base. Dip the end of

Scandinavian-style cocktail server

the solder into the flux. Then "tin" the bottom of the upperwork by coating the edges with molten solder. Joining the upperwork to the base needs a lot of heat so, unless you have a large heavy soldering iron use a gas blowtorch. Melt a little flux on the tinned surface of the bottom edges of the upperwork and stand the upperwork onto the base. Apply heat to the upperwork and base so that the solder gradually heats to melting point.

Use enough solder to allow a thin line of it to seep around the bottom edges of the upperwork. It is not necessary to solder the intersection where the two sections join to make up the upperwork.

Candle supports
Use the surplus metal left over from cutting the upperwork and base. Make a firm center into one piece with a small pointed punch called a centerpunch, or a nail that you hammer into the metal to make an indentation. Draw a circle with the point of the compass in the dent just made (fig.16). Alternatively, use a pair of dividers to make the circle. Mark out 5 circular pieces in this way.

Cut out the pieces by progressively cutting off the corners with a hacksaw. Finish off with a smooth file to give a polished edge. Drill a hole 3mm ($\frac{1}{8}$in) through the center of each disk. Then solder a disk to each end of the upperwork sections (fig.17). As you solder, insert a short length of plain iron

wire or a headless 2.5cm (1in) wire nail into the center hole so that it becomes soldered into place with the disk. This is the support or pricket for the candle. Alternatively, use sockets instead of prickets by soldering equal lengths of metal tubing 2.5cm (1in) in diameter to the disks (fig.18) and as shown in the photograph.

Finishing off
Glue a piece of softwood inside the base with resin adhesive. Then glue a piece of green baize or velvet to the bottom of the wood to prevent it from scratching a polished surface. Finally polish the completed candlestick with metal polish and to prevent discoloration from atmospheric pollution, lacquer with a spray-on varnish.

Scandinavian-style cocktail server
Use this elegant cocktail server to pass around light snacks or even playing cards. Although stainless steel is used here you can also choose aluminum, brass or copper. Copper keeps a warm glowing surface and does not require any finish. Aluminum is attractive if you have it color-anodized before fitting the handle, and brass can be polished to a high finish.

You will need:
15 × 25cm (6 × 10in) stainless steel sheet □ 12.5–15cm (5–6in) long ready-made wooden handle.□ wax (chinagraph) pencil □ hacksaw □ file □ 3mm ($\frac{1}{8}$in) drill □ 2 × 2.5cm (1in) roundhead wood screws.

Cutting the metal. Using a wax (chinagraph) pencil, mark the metal sheet as shown in fig.19, then follow fig.20 for cutting out the basic shape and flanging. With a hacksaw and file, curve the lines DA

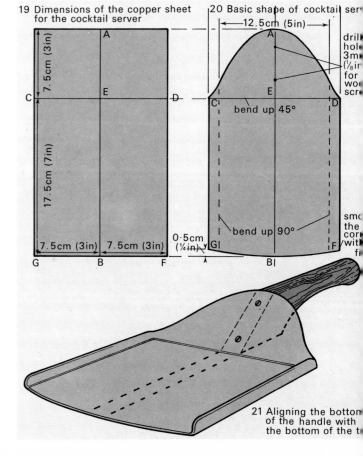

19 Dimensions of the copper sheet for the cocktail server

20 Basic shape of cocktail ser

12.5cm (5in)

7.5cm (3in)

17.5cm (7in)

7.5cm (3in)   7.5cm (3in)

0·5cm ($\frac{1}{4}$in)

bend up 45°

bend up 90°

drill hole 3mm ($\frac{1}{8}$in) for woo scr

smo the cor wit f

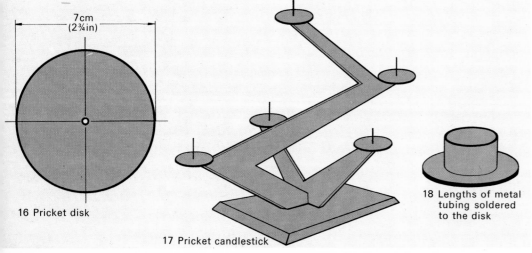

16 Pricket disk

7cm (2¾in)

17 Pricket candlestick

18 Lengths of metal tubing soldered to the disk

21 Aligning the bottom of the handle with the bottom of the t

and CA. Then slightly curve the lines FB and GB. (F and G are set in 0.5cm ($\frac{1}{4}$in) from the edge.) Flange each side piece FD and GC by 1.5cm ($\frac{1}{2}$in) and to an angle of 90°. Then flange the edge DC to an angle of 45°.

Attaching the handle. Drill 2 holes in the tray as indicated in fig.20. To find the correct position for the holes between E and A, place the handle against the flanged edge of the tray, making sure that the bottom of the handle is in line with the bottom of the tray (fig.21). Fix the wood screws in position.

For extra decoration, drill a pattern of holes in the tray or trace out your initials in a sequence of small holes.

Wrought-iron bracket

This bracket can be made in mild steel or wrought iron and is intended for use with a hanging basket or with an exterior porch light. The finished bracket measures 42.5 × 26.5cm (17 × 14$\frac{1}{2}$in).

You will need:

1m (3ft) mild steel bar, 2.5cm (1in) wide and 0.5cm ($\frac{1}{4}$in) thick ☐ 2.25m (7ft) mild steel bar, 1.5cm ($\frac{1}{2}$in) wide and 3mm ($\frac{1}{8}$in) thick ☐ 7 soft iron or copper rivets 3mm ($\frac{1}{8}$in) in diameter and 1.5cm ($\frac{1}{2}$in) long ☐

gas blowtorch ☐ old pair of pliers ☐ 0.5cm ($\frac{1}{4}$in) drill ☐ hacksaw ☐ 32.5 × 32.5cm (13 × 13in) piece of plywood or hardboard.

Making the L-shaped bracket. Using a vise and heavy hammer bend the shorter mild steel bar to form the main L-shape for the bracket, each "arm" being the same length.

Fish-mouth shape (fig.22). Make the fish-mouth shape at the end of the vertical side of the bracket by sawing down the center of the steel bar for about 4cm (1$\frac{1}{2}$in). Heat the 2 strips just formed with a gas blowtorch until the metal is red hot. Bend the strips outwards with an old pair of pliers. (Do not use a good pair of pliers as the heat may take the temper (hardness) out of the tool.) Leave the bracket to cool and file the rough edges with a smooth file.

Making scrolls. Scroll work is done with a special instrument called a scroll bar, which has a slot into which the steel bar fits. Make a scroll bar from a piece of iron or steel about 12mm ($\frac{1}{2}$in) thick. Cut a slot which is long enough and wide enough for the width and depth of the steel bar to fit into by using a drill with a diameter equal to the width of the slot you wish to cut in the scroll bar. Then make 2 cuts down from the point with a hacksaw so that the narrow piece can be removed leaving a slot. Now clamp the scroll bar into the vise (fig.23). Using the gas blowtorch, heat the end of the steel bar where you wish to make a scroll. Then quickly put it into the scroll bar and bend it around. Remove the metal from the scroll bar and allow to cool.

To make the scrolls for the lamp bracket, first make a scroll bar to the measurements of the steel bar. The graph (fig.24) in which 1 square equals 2.5cm (1in), gives the basic shapes for the 2 pairs of scrolls. Draw the shapes full size onto the piece of plywood or hardboard so that you have a guide to the proportions. Match the scrolls with this outline as you work. Heat the metal and as it bends, ease the strips around the scroll bar to the diameter you require. Aim to make each one of the pair of scrolls identical otherwise the appearance of the finished work will be spoiled. The symmetry of the individual pairs is more important than the overall design.

As the metal will be exposed to the weather, you will need to paint it. Use a

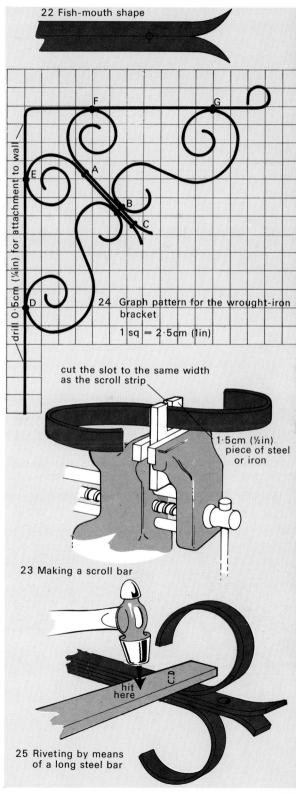

22 Fish-mouth shape

drill 0·5cm (¼in) for attachment to wall

24 Graph pattern for the wrought-iron bracket

1 sq = 2·5cm (1in)

cut the slot to the same width as the scroll strip

1·5cm (½in) piece of steel or iron

23 Making a scroll bar

25 Riveting by means of a long steel bar

Copper fireplace hood

primer and then an undercoat before applying the top coat. Alternatively, have the pieces plated commercially.

Riveting. Join the 4 scrolls to the L-shaped bracket with iron or copper rivets. To find the exact position for riveting arrange the pieces flat on the workbench as shown in fig.24 and loosely assemble the scrolls within the bracket piece. Make sure that the center scrolls are positioned accurately within the angle of the L-shaped bracket. Drill holes to join the scrolls at A, B and C. Place a rivet in the holes marked A. Rest the rivet head on a solid steel block (such as an anvil or top of the bench vise) and hammer the protruding end hard and evenly but without hammering the end flat. Rivet at C. Because of the proximity of the scroll work at B you will not be able to strike the rivet end directly. Fig.25 shows the correct way of resting a long steel bar on the rivet end so that it can be struck with a hammer. Drill holes to attach the scrollwork to the L-shaped bracket at D, E, F and G. Rivet the pieces together using the hammer and steel bar.

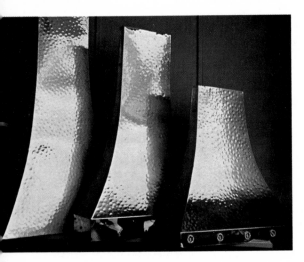

Brass and copper fireplace hoods.

Copper fireplace hood

A fireplace can be greatly enhanced with a hood, especially one made of copper, which will reflect the glow from the flames. The hood is made from three basic pieces, but the dimensions will depend entirely on the shape of the fireplace and the opening for which it is intended.

You will need:
3 sheets of copper 1.5mm ($\frac{1}{16}$in) thick (gauge 15 B & S) □ wax (chinagraph) pencil □ sheets of brown paper □ adhesive tape □ tinsnips or nibble shears □ smooth file □ wooden boards for flanging □ hammer □ wood block □ C (G) clamps □ pop or solid rivets □ pop pliers (if pop rivets are used) □ 3mm ($\frac{1}{8}$in) drill □ 3mm ($\frac{1}{8}$in) mild steel wire □ several grades of steel wool □ metal polish □ spray-on varnish (optional) □ self-adhesive foam weather strip.

Planning the design. The illustration (fig.26) will give you some idea for a suitable design for the hood. Decide on the shape and size required and work out the measurements carefully.

Cutting the metal

Front piece. If you wish to make a curved or fan-shaped hood, make sure that the 2 edges of the front piece are symmetrical. To do this, mark the center line down the sheet of metal with a wax (chinagraph) pencil. Cut a piece of brown paper to the required size. Fold the paper in half lengthwise and then mark out and cut the curve required for the edge. Open out the sheet of paper and place the center fold on the center line marked on the metal. Fix with adhesive tape. Cut the metal with tinsnips or metal shears. Then file with a smooth file at an angle of 45° to the metal edge.

Side pieces. Mark out 1 side piece from the metal sheet with a scriber. Cut the piece out with tinsnips or metal shears. Use this piece as a template to scribe around the metal for the second side piece. Cut the second side piece and then file down the edges of both pieces with a smooth file.

Flanging

Front piece. The front piece has a flange along each vertical side and this fits over the edge of each side piece (fig.27). Place the metal sideways between 2 wooden boards so that the edge to be flanged is uppermost. Secure the metal in the vise. Bend the flange over gradually to prevent any distortion to the metal, using a hammer and wood block.

If you are making a curved hood, cut the exact profile in plywood or hardboard to

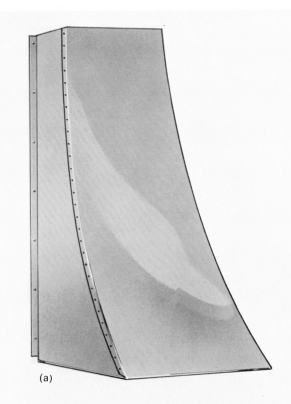

(a)

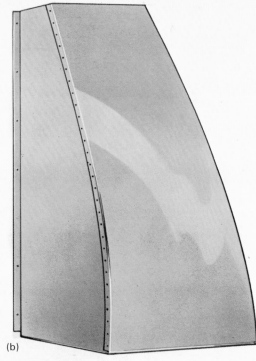

(b)

26 Designs for a fireplace hood

Copper fireplace hood

mark out the curve you want. Clamp the metal to the wood and bend the flanges over the edges of the wood. For a slight curve on the front panel make a flange no wider than 2cm ($\frac{3}{4}$in). If your design calls for sharp curves, make the flanges a little narrower.

Side pieces. The straight vertical edges of the side pieces must be flanged so that they can be screwed to the wall fireplace opening (fig.28). Flange as for the front piece.

Assembling the hood

Preparing to rivet. Drill 3mm ($\frac{1}{8}$in) holes in the flanges of the front piece, spacing each hole centrally and at intervals of 7.5cm (3in). Remove any sharp burrs (edges) on the inside of the flanges using the flat face of a smooth file. File until smooth. This is very important as it is difficult to rivet each flange to the side pieces without unsightly bumps showing, as the burrs will prevent the pieces from coming together neatly. Using small C (G) clamps, clamp the 2 side pieces to the front piece. Interpose a small block of wood between the pad of the clamp and the surface of the copper to avoid marking the metal.

Using pop rivets. To find the position for the hole in the side piece, place the end of the drill in one of the holes of the front flange. The position for the hole in the side piece will now be the same. Start drilling, making sure that the pieces are always in the correct position. The edge of the side piece, for example, must fit firmly into the inside corner of the flange.

Put in a pop rivet, squeezing it in place with pliers. Repeat for every other hole in the flange. Rivet the other flange and side piece in the same way.

Using solid rivets. Find the position for the holes in the side piece as described for pop rivets. Secure the side piece to the front piece by placing a small nut and bolt or a self-tapping screw into every third hole. The piece is now properly aligned. Remove the work from the clamp.

Solid riveting needs to be done by 2 people. Stand the assembled hood on the workbench. Put the rivet through from the outside of the hole so that the head remains on the outside. One person should hold a heavy smooth block of steel against the

rivet head while a second person hammers the end of the rivet into shape. Use a light-weight hammer—copper rivets are quite soft.

Continue in the same way until all the rivet holes are filled. Remove the locating bolts and screws and then rivet these holes together.

Preparing to wire. Trim the metal straight along the bottom edge and cut away the flanges in the front corners and the side flanges to a depth of 9mm ($\frac{3}{8}$in). Now flange along the bottom edge of the side and front pieces, also to a depth of 9mm ($\frac{3}{8}$in). Cutting away the original front corner flanges will facilitate flanging the whole front edge since the metal is now of a single thickness all around. Cutting the side flanges brings them to the same level as the other edges after they have been flanged (fig.29).

Wiring. Use 3mm ($\frac{1}{8}$in) mild steel wire. If the hood is particularly wide, use 0.5cm ($\frac{1}{4}$in) wire. With the metal still in the vise, insert the steel wire. Bend the wire carefully in the vise so that it fits tightly and neatly inside the bottom edge flange. Hammer the wire to form 2 right angles to fit into the flanged corners. Hammer until you have sharp precise right angles otherwise you will find it difficult to close the copper flange around it. Now hammer the edge of the flange over the wire with a wooden block.

Remove the work from the vise and position the metal so that the flange and wire are on a flat surface. Hammer the flange

down progressively from one end to the other with a wooden block. Finally, close up the edge using a ball pein hammer. Do not extend the wire around the attachment flanges of the sides or you will not be able to fix the hood securely against the chimney opening. (fig.30). Depending on the design and shape of the chimney, either wire the top of the hood in the same way, or bend up the top flanges so that they can be screwed to the ceiling as well as to the walls.

Polishing. If the copper is at all scratched after completion of the hood, polish all over with progressively finer grades of steel wool until all unsightly blemishes are removed. Use metal polish to complete the shine.

Note: you can get a really high gloss very quickly if you have a polishing mop attachment for an electric drill.

Finally, spray on a clear protective polyurethane varnish if desired.

Positioning the hood. Drill holes along the side flanges and, if you intend to attach the hood to the ceiling, along the top flange. Find the equivalent position for holes in the wall or chimney opening by placing the drill end through each hole you have just made in the flange and then drill.

Stick a narrow strip of self-adhesive weather strip around the inside edges of all the attachment flanges. This will prevent warm air from carrying dust through the inevitable gaps between the wall and the hood and so prevents the walls and ceiling from getting dirty.

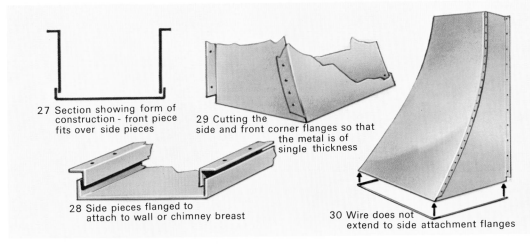

27 Section showing form of construction - front piece fits over side pieces

28 Side pieces flanged to attach to wall or chimney breast

29 Cutting the side and front corner flanges so that the metal is of single thickness

30 Wire does not extend to side attachment flanges

Adapting a design

A composition is made up of lines, shape and texture plus color, and a pleasing design incorporates all these basic elements. The positive shapes and negative spaces between must always be carefully considered, the area of interest or focal point chosen and a well-balanced but not necessarily symmetrical effect achieved. Try to introduce variety through shapes, groupings and uneven spacing. For example a shape on one side can often be balanced by two smaller ones on the other. To develop a simple design, take a piece of colored paper about 10cm (4in) square, and draw a line on it to create an interesting shape. Cut along the line, then re-arrange the two shapes on an oblong, a circle or a larger square. Add other lines quite freely to develop the design. Use tracing paper and re-arrange the design elements to suit the article for which it is intended.

1 Cut along a single line drawn on a 10cm (4in) square of paper. Add more lines and adapt for use.

2 Embroidered panel of dark brown textured tweed, medium brown corduroy and off-white tweed—appliqué and stitchery in three colors.

3 Beaten pewter firescreen.

4 Pottery vase.

5 Appliquéd border for skirt—appliqué, embroidery and beads.

6 Evening bag in gold with kid—appliqué and gold couching, beads and sequins.

7 Bedspread—patchwork and machine embroidery.

8 Needlepoint belt with dark shapes in leather—Gobelin and Florentine stitch.

9 Copper buckle or brooch.

Ounces to Grams

oz	g
$\frac{1}{2}$	14
$\frac{3}{4}$	21
1	28
$1\frac{1}{2}$	42
$1\frac{3}{4}$	50
2	56
3	85
4	113
5	141
6	170
7	198
8	226
9	255
10	283
11	311
12	340
13	368
14	396
15	425
16	453
17	481
18	510
19	538
20	566

1 gram = 0.035 ounces

Pounds to Kilograms

lb	kg
1	0.5
2	0.9
3	1.4
4	1.8
5	2.3
6	2.7
7	3.2
8	3.6
9	4.0
10	4.5

1 kilogram = 2.205 lb

Inches to Millimeters

in	mm
$\frac{1}{8}$	3
$\frac{1}{4}$	6
$\frac{3}{8}$	10
$\frac{1}{2}$	13
$\frac{5}{8}$	16
$\frac{3}{4}$	19
$\frac{7}{8}$	22
1	25

1 millimeter = 0.039 in

Inches to Centimeters

in	cm
1	2.5
2	5.0
3	7.5
4	10.0
5	12.5
6	15.0
7	18.0
8	20.5
9	23.0
10	25.5
11	28.0
12	30.5
13	33.0
14	35.5
15	38.0
16	40.5
17	43.0
18	46.0
19	48.5
20	51.0
24	61.0
36	91.5

1 centimeter = 0.394 inches

Yards to Meters

yd	m
$\frac{1}{8}$	0.15
$\frac{1}{4}$	0.25
$\frac{3}{8}$	0.35
$\frac{1}{2}$	0.50
$\frac{5}{8}$	0.60
$\frac{3}{4}$	0.70
$\frac{7}{8}$	0.80
1	0.95
2	1.85
3	2.75

1 meter = 1.094 yards

U.K. Fluid Ounces to Milliliters

fl oz	ml
1	28
2	57
3	85
4	114
5	142
6	171
7	200
8	227
9	256
10	284
20	568
30	852
40	1137
50	1421
60	1705
70	1989
80	2273
90	2557
100	2841

1 U.K. pint = 20 U.K. fluid ounces
1 milliliter = 0.035 U.K. fluid ounces

U.S. Fluid Ounces to Milliliters

fl oz	ml
1	30
2	59
3	89
4	118
5	148
6	177
7	207
8	237
9	266
10	296
11	325
12	355
13	384
14	414
15	444
16	473
17	503
18	532
19	562
20	591
30	887
40	1183
50	1479
60	1774
70	2070
80	2366
90	2662
100	2957

1 U.S. pint = 16 U.S. fluid ounces
1 milliliter = 0.030 U.S. fluid ounces

Degrees Fahrenheit to Degrees Centigrade

To convert Fahrenheit to Centigrade, subtract 32, multiply by 5 and divide by 9

e.g. 1472°C
$$1472 - 32 = 1440$$
$$1440 \times 5 = 7200$$
$$7200 \div 9 = 800°F$$

Freezing point of water
32°F   0.0°C

Boiling point of water
212°   100.0°C

Note: All figures in the chart have been rounded off to simplify the tables. Please remember when working that it is important to stick consistently to one system of measurements.

Suppliers

Basketry

The Bamboo People*, Godmanston,
Dorchester, Dorset. Cerne Abbas 393

Bookbinding

H.Band and Company Limited*, Brent Way,
High St., Brentford, Middx. 01 560 2025
(suppliers of vellum only).
J.Hewit & Sons Ltd.*, 89/97 St. John St.,
London E.C.1. 01 253 1431

Brass Rubbing

Studio 69*, 40 Elm Hill, Norwich, Norfolk.
0603 22827

Candlemaking

The Candles Shop*, 89 Parkway, London
N.W.1. 01 485 3232
Candle Makers Supplies*, 28 Blythe Road,
London W.14. 01 602 1812

Dyes (chemical)

Mathesons Dyes*, 8 Marcon Place, London E.8.
01 254 9684

Embroidery

Arts & Crafts Studio*, 14/16 St. Michael's Row,
Chester, Cheshire. 0244 24900
The Woolshop and the Home Artistic Ltd.*,
89/90 Darlington St., Wolverhampton, Staffs.
0902 21898

Jewelry

Leyborn-Naedham Ltd.*, 12 Market St.,
Altrincham, Cheshire. 061 928 4220

Goulds*, 68 Berwick St., London W.1.
01 437 4191

Knitting and crochet

Kiwi Wool Co.*, 32 Rebecca St., Bradford,
Yorks. 0274 732498

Lacemaking

E.Braggins*, 26/36 Silver St., Bedford, Beds.
0234 53292

Marquetry

Arts & Crafts Studio*, 14/16 St. Michael's Row,
Chester, Cheshire. 0244 24900
The Handicraft Shop*, 5 Oxford Rd.,
Altrincham, Cheshire. 061 928 3834

Metalwork

Hopkins of Cowley, 117–125 Hollow Way,
Cowley, Oxford. 0865 778127
Bristol Handicrafts*, 20 Park Row, Bristol 1.
0272 25729
J.Smith & Sons Ltd.*, St. John's Sq.,
Clerkenwell, London E.C.1 01 253 1277
(Suppliers of metals only).

Mosaic

Art & Crafts Shop, 21 Abington Square,
Northampton, Northants. 0604 36521
Berol Ltd.*, Oldmeadow Rd., King's Lynn,
Norfolk. 0553 61221

Needlepoint

The Campden Needlecraft Centre*, High St.,
Chipping Campden, Glos. 0386 840583

Papercraft

Paperchase*, 216 Tottenham Court Rd.,
London W.1. 01 637 1121

Plastics and resins

Trylon Ltd.*, Thrift St., Wollaston, Northants.
Wollaston 275

Pottery

Alec Tiranti Ltd.*, 70 High St., Theale, Reading,
Berks. 0734 312775

Rugmaking

Bristol Handicrafts*, 20 Park Row, Bristol 1.
0272 25729

Sculpture and modeling

Alec Tiranti Ltd.*, 70 High St., Theale, Reading,
Berks. 0734 302775

Shellcraft

Eaton's Shell Shop*, 16 Manette St., London
W.1. 01 437 9391

Smocking

Bedford Wool Shop, The Old Arcade, Bedford,
Beds. 0234 55385

Surface Decoration

Alanden Printing Supplies Ltd.*, 32 Edmonton Rd.,
Woodsmoor, Stockport, Cheshire.
061 483 2503

Selectasine*, 22 Bulstrode St., London W.1.
01 935 0768

Toymaking

Bristol Handicrafts*, 20 Park Row, Bristol 1.
0272 25729

Weaving and spinning

The Handweavers Studio and Gallery Ltd.*, 29
Haroldstone Rd., Walthamstow, London E.17.
01 521 2281

Woodwork

Arts & Crafts Studio*, 14/16 St. Michael's Row,
Chester, Cheshire. 0244 24900

Appliqué *Creative Appliqué* Beryl Dean (Studio Vista)

Basketry *Country Baskets* Evelyn Legg (Mills & Boon) ; *Straw Work and Corn Dollies* Sandford and Davies (B.T.Batsford)

Beadwork *Beadwork ; From American Indian Design* Marjorie Murphy (B.T.Batsford) ; *Beadwork ; Sewing and Weaving with Beads* Ida-Merete Erlandson and Hetty Moo (Van Nostrand Reinhold Company)

Bookbinding *Bookbinding and the Care of Books* Douglas Cockerell (Sir Isaac Pitman & Sons) ; *Bookbinding—Then and Now* Lionel Darley (Faber and Faber)

Brass Rubbing *Macklin's Monumental Brasses* John Page-Phillips (George Allen & Unwin)

Candlemaking *Modern Art of Candle Creating* Don Olsen (Thomas Yoseloff)

Collage *Fabric Pictures* Eugenie Alexander (Mills & Boon)

Crochet *Guide to Crochet* Joan Fisher (Ward Lock) ; *Complete Book of Crochet* (Octopus Books)

Découpage *Contemporary Découpage* Thelma Newman (George Allen & Unwin) ; *The Complete Book of Découpage* Francis Wing (Sir Isaac Pitman & Sons)

Design *Decorative Design* Brod (Sir Isaac Pitman & Sons)

Embroidery and Smocking *Craft of Florentine Embroidery* Barbara Snook (B.T.Batsford) ; *Florentine Embroidery* Barbara Snook (Mills & Boon) ; *Bargello* Geraldine Consentino (Pan Books) ; *Golden Hands Creative Tapestry and Canvaswork* (Marshall Cavendish) ; *The Needleworker's Dictionary* Pamela Clabburn (Macmillan Publishers) ; *Imaginative Canvas Embroidery* Nancy Hobbs (Sir Isaac Pitman & Sons) ; *Joan Fisher's Guide to Embroidery* (Ward Lock)

Enamelwork *Enamelling : Principles and Practice* Kenneth Bates (Constable & Co) ; *Enamelling on Metal* Millenet and de Koningh (The Technical Press) ; *The Craft of Enamelling* Kenneth Neville (Jarrold Publishers)

Flowercraft *Flower Decorations* Roberts & Patricia Easterbrook (Merlin Press)

Glasswork *Engraving and Decorating Glass* Barbara Norman (David & Charles) ; *Making Stained Glass* R. Metcalf & G. Metcalf (David & Charles)

Jewelry *Handmade Jewellery* A.Emerson (Dryad) ; *Design and Creation* Robert Von Neumann (Sir Isaac Pitman & Sons) ; *Art of Jewelry* Graham Hughes (Studio Vista)

Knitting *Book of Knitting Patterns* Mary Thomas (Hodder and Stoughton)

Lacemaking *Bobbin Lacemaking* Doreen Wright (G.Bell & Sons) ; *Traditional Lacemaking* Sally Johanson (Van Nostrand Reinhold Company)

Lampshades *Lampshades : Technique and Design* Angela Fishburn (B.T.Batsford)

Leatherwork *Leather* Donald Willcox and James Scott Manning (Sir Isaac Pitman & Sons) ; *Leathercraft* W.Attwater (B.T.Batsford)

Macramé *Practical Macramé* Eugene Andes (Studio Vista) ; *Macramé, the Art of Creative Knotting* Virginia Harvey (Van Nostrand Reinhold Company) ; *Macramé* Mary Walker Phillips (Pan Books)

Metalwork *Metalwork and Enamelling* Herbert Maryon (Dover Publications) ; *Constructive Art Metalwork* H.Stoddard (J.M.Dent & Sons) ; *Metalwork Designs of Today* Ed. Larkham (John Murray)

Mobiles *Mobiles* Peter Mytton-Davies (Ward Lock) ; *Making Mobiles* Anne and Christopher Moorey (Studio Vista)

Mosaic *Mosaics* Robert Williamson (Crosby Lockwood and Son)

Natural Dyes *The Use of Vegetable Dyes* Violetta Thurstan (Dryad) ; *Vegetable Dyes* Douglas Leechman (Oxford University Press)

Needlepoint *"Vogue" Guide to Needlepoint Tapestry* (William Collins Sons & Co)

Papercraft *All Kinds of Papercraft* John Portchmouth (Studio Vista)

Patchwork *"Vogue" Guide to Patchwork and Quilting* (William Collins Sons & Co) ; *One Hundred and One Patchwork Patterns* McKim (Dover Publications)

Pin Art *Thread : An Art Form* Waller (Studio Vista) ; *Pin and Thread* (Search Press)

Plastics and Resins *Creative Plastics* David Rees (Studio Vista)

Pottery and Ceramics *Potter's Book* Leach (Faber & Faber) ; *Potter's Companion* Birks (William Collins Sons & Co)

Quilting *Quilting* Cutbush (The Hamlyn Group)

Rugmaking *Techniques of Rug Weaving* Collingwood (Faber & Faber) ; *Rugmaking* Droop (G.Bell & Sons)

Sculpture and Modeling *Material and Methods of Sculpture* Rich (Oxford University Press) ; *Modelling and Sculpture* (3 vols) E.Lanteri (Dover Publications)

Shellcraft *Sea Shells* F.Dance (The Hamlyn Group)

Spinning *Handspinning : Art and Technique* Allen Fannin (Van Nostrand Reinhold Company)

Stripping and Decorating Furniture *Furniture Repairs* Hayward (Evans Brothers)

Surface Decoration *Tie-and-Dye as a Present Day Craft* Anne Maile (Mills & Boon) ; *Tie-Dyeing and Batik* F. Anderson (Octopus Books) ; *Contemporary Batik and Tie Dye* Dona Meilach (George Allen and Unwin) ; *Batik Unlimited* J.Gibbs (Sir Isaac Pitman & Sons) ; *Ideas for Fabric Printing and Dyeing* Peter Gooch (B.T.Batsford)

Tatting *Tatting Patterns and Designs* G.Blomquist and E.Persson (Van Nostrand Reinhold Company)

Toymaking *Wooden Spoon Marionettes* Audrey Vincente Dean (Faber & Faber) ; *Marionettes : How to Make and Work Them* Helen Fling (Dover Publications) ; *Doll Making, a Creative Approach* Jean Ray Laury (Van Nostrand Reinhold Company) ; *Colourful Kites from Japan* Tadao Saito (Ward Lock) ; *Making Masks* Barbara Snook (B.T.Batsford)

Upholstery *Practical Upholstery* C.Howes (Evans Brothers) ; *Mending and Restoring Upholstery and Soft Furnishings* Nellie Richardson and Will Morton (Garnstone Press)

Using Color *Basic Design ; The Dynamics of Visual Form* Maurice de Sausmarez (Studio Vista)

Weaving *Off-loom Weaving Book* Rose Naumann and Raymond Hull (Sir Isaac Pitman & Sons) ; *Weaving and Needlecraft Colour Course* Justema and Justema (Van Nostrand Reinhold Company)

Woodwork *Woodworking* Albert Gregory (Dryad) ; *Woodworking for Everybody* Ed. Shea (Van Nostrand Reinhold Company)

Acknowledgments

Contributors

Farida Abidi	Barbara Pegg
Conrad Bailey	Pat Phillpott
José Barretto	Rob-Ann Phoenix
Bernard Berthan	Susan Pinkus
Germaine Brotherton	Linda Proud
Jane Bruce	Kit Pyman
Patrick Carpenter	Gabrielle de Quay
David Constable	M.F.E. Read
Paula Critchley	Ena Ritson-Hall
Robert Dawson	Sue Rowlands
Audrey Vincente Dean	Angela Salmon
Erroll Downman	Sonia Scott
Trata Maria Drescha	Faith Shannon
Jane Everson	Jacqueline Short
Angela Fishburn	Anita Skjold
Kelly Flynn	Erika Speel
Maggie Franklin	Harry Horlock Stringer
John Goodall	Caroline Sullivan
Elizabeth Goodman	Fleur Tookey
Anna Griffiths	Pamela Tubby
Dorothea Hall	Lindsay Vernon
Norelle Hardie	Sheila Volpe
Pat Hardy	Jo Wale
Eleanor Harvey	Mary Young
Val Jackson	
Angela Jeffs	
Irene Jones	
Louis Jordan	
Eric Kenneway	**Artists**
Nancy Kimmins	
Michael King	Dick Barnard
Elizabeth Knolles	Stephen Cocking
Mary Konior	Paul Davies
Mary Labanowska	Judy Dunkley
Judith Lanyi	Barbara Firth
Gytha Lewis	Richard Geiger
Kate Lewis	Roger Gorringe
Edward Little	Bryon Harvey
Margaret Maino	John Hofer
Alf Martensson	Trevor Lawrence
Frances Newell	Yvonne McLean
Patsy North	Tony Morris
Arthur WJG Ord-Hume	Deborah Price
Tony Pearce	Graham Smith
	John Way
	Paul Williams

Credits

Page

16–17, 25, 28 Pattern and instructions for crewel work family tree, Hardanger window shade, drawn thread and drawn fabric overblouse, by J & P Coats Ltd., Glasgow, Scotland.

50 Pattern and instructions for baby's quilt by J & P Coats Ltd. Wooden crib from The John Lewis Partnership, Oxford Street, London, W.1.

58 Photographed at The Holiday Inn Hotel, Swiss Cottage, London, N.W.3. Suit from Hardy Amies at Way In, Knightsbridge, London, S.W.1. Scarf from Liberty & Co., Ltd., Regent Street, London, W.1.

69–70, 72 Stencils, canvas and yarns for the stitched rug and hooked rug designs supplied by Sirdar Ltd., Alverthorpe, Wakefield, Yorkshire.

73 Rya cushion by Ryagarn, T. Forfell & Son, Wigston, Leicester.

115 Hat and skirt from Laura Ashley, Harriet Street, London, S.W.1.

124 Denim dress from Tigermoth, Portobello Road, London, W.11.

125–6 Pattern and instructions for filet crochet bluebird by J & P Coats Ltd.

125 Skirt and shirt from Laura Ashley.

133 Blouse from Laura Ashley. Skirt from Fenwick of Bond Street, New Bond Street, London, W.1.

135 Hat and bag from Way In, Boots from Lillywhites Ltd., Piccadilly Circus, London, S.W.1.

211 Dresses from Laura Ashley.

244 Shirt from Way In, London.

287 Dress from Janice Wainwright, Poland Street, London, W.1.

308–313 Dylon Multi-Purpose Dyes and Dylon Cold Dyes for tie and dye and batik by Dylon International Ltd., Worsley Bridge Road, Lower Sydenham, London S.E.26.

314 Photographed at the gymnasium, The Michael Sobell Sports Centre, Hornsey Road, London, N.7.

328 Sweater from Way In. Skirt from Fiorucci, Knightsbridge, London S.W.1.

331–9 Candles designed by David Constable of Candle Makers Supplies, 28 Blythe Road, London, W.14.

417 Table of solder and flux supplied by Ronson Products Ltd., Leatherhead, Surrey.

Yarns for knitting and crochet by Patons & Baldwins, Darlington, Co. Durham.

Photographs

Farida Abidi, Winslow, Bucks. 32 left

Fratelli Alinari, Florence. 77 bottom left, 394.

American Museum, Bath (photo Derek Balmer) 9, 159 right, 299.

Mike Andrews, Bristol. 163.

Ardea Photographics, London. 68 bottom.

Lesley Astaire, London. 168 bottom.

R. Baymen, Herts. 251 right.

Bethnal Green Museum, London. 217 right, 242 left (photos John Freeman), 240 bottom.

Bibliothèque Nationale, Paris. 368 right.

Bodleian Library, Oxford. 222 bottom.

British Library, London. 77 top.

British Museum, London. 217 left, 222 top (photo Michael Holford) 240 top left, 254, 356 left and right, 383 bottom.

Di Brooke, London. 186

The Candles Shop, Parkway, London. 339 right.

Doreen Cavanagh, London. 275

Cooper Bridgeman Library, London. 168 top, 349.

Crafts Advisory Committee, London. 160 bottom, 165 bottom, 304, 323.

Robert Dawson, London. 393.

Mark Edwards, London. 356 top.

Elsevier Archives, Amsterdam. 383 top

Mary Evans Picture Library, London. 19, 40 bottom, 331.

Tony Evans, London. 408 bottom right, 409 (by kind permission of Faith Shannon).

Kelly Flynn, London. 157.

Werner Forman Archives, London. 98 left.

Myriam Gilby, Essex, 77 bottom right.

John Goodall, London. 320, 321.

Mrs Gore-Brown, Chichester. 401.

Sonia Haliday, Bucks. 364, 368 left, 412 left.

Ham House, Richmond (photo John Freeman) 322.

Norelle Hardie, London. 344.

Robert Harding Associates, London. 311.

Michael Holford Library, London. 172 left and right, 201 bottom, 234, 235.

Holte Photos Ltd., Stratford-on-Avon. 148 bottom.

Angelo Hornak, London. 182, 183.

Graham Hughes, Art Director, Goldsmiths Hall 177 top and bottom.

Alan Hutchinson, London. 129.

Irene Jones, Bude, Cornwall, 171.

Michael King, London, 367.

Elizabeth Knolles, Dundee. 140 top and bottom right, 144.

Kunsthistorisches Museum, Vienna (photo Meyer) 181 right, 212.

Mary Labanowska, London. 303.

Andrew Lawson, London. 68 top (by kind permission of Christopher and Nicola Legge, Witney, Oxon), 167 top and bottom right (collage by kind permission of Mrs. Hilda Robinson, Tewkesbury, Glos.), 382 top, 412 top and bottom right.

Lucinda Lambton, Oxford. 94.

Giles Lewis, Oxford. 209.

Liverpool Museum. 119, 255.

City of Manchester Art Gallery. 21.

Mansell Collection, London. 291 left.

Penelope Marcus, Oxford (photo Hills Harris) 237.

Metropolitan Museum of Art, New York. 54.

National Gallery, London. 136 top.

National Portrait Gallery, London. 181 left.

J.S. Newton Claire (photo Tripp Studios, Bristol). 98 right. (© B.T. Batsford Ltd., London).

Norsk Folksmuseum, Oslo. 24.

Patsy North, London. 153.

Parham Park, Sussex. 60.

Barbara Pegg, London. 316.

Picturepoint Library, London. 317.

Susan Pinkus, London. 278 top.

Vicky Potton, London. 91 right.

Royal College of Surgeons, London. 148 top.

Peter Sande, London. 422.

Mrs. Lettice Sandford. Leominster. 251 left.

Photo Scala, Florence. 48 left, 277, 382 bottom, 395 top, 395 bottom left.

Spectrum Colour Library, London. 106 left, 413.

Erika Speel, London. 204.

Dr. Y.S. Sahota, Westfield College, London. 106 right.

Harry Horlock Stringer, Taggs Yard International School of Ceramics, London S.W.13. 256, 257, 271.

Caroline Sullivan, London. 93.

Sungravure, London. 46, 108 right, 170, 240 top right, 290.

Kenneth Swain, London. Title page.

Tate Gallery, London (photo John Webb) 146, 165 top. (© S.P.A.D.E.M. Paris, 1977 and 1976).

Diane Taylor, London. 274.

David Thomas, London. 187 top and bottom.

Transworld Feature Syndicate, London. 13, 59, 151, 156, 238.

Trinity College, Dublin (photo Green Studio) 109.

H.P. Twilley, London. 355 bottom.

Lindsay Vernon, London 91 left.

Victoria and Albert Museum, London. 8, 16 top, 26, 30, 34 left and right, 40 top, 55, 67 left and right, 87, 128, 140 left, 149, 155, 159 left, 176, 177 top left and right, 201 (photo Michael Holford), 248, 254, 285 top, 291 right, 314, 359, 375, 402, 403.

Wallace Collection, London. 48 right, 136 bottom.

Jo Webster, London. 178 top.

Welsh Folk Museum, Cardiff. 158.

Index

Italics indicate projects of things to make.

Index